DESEGREGATING DIXIE

DESEGREGATING DIXIE

THE CATHOLIC CHURCH IN THE SOUTH AND DESEGREGATION, 1945–1992

MARK NEWMAN

UNIVERSITY PRESS OF MISSISSIPPI / JACKSON

www.upress.state.ms.us

The University Press of Mississippi is a member
of the Association of University Presses.

Copyright © 2018 by University Press of Mississippi
All rights reserved

First printing 2018

∞

Library of Congress Cataloging-in-Publication Data

Names: Newman, Mark (Historian), author.
Title: Desegregating dixie: the Catholic church in the South and
desegregation, 1945-1992 / Mark Newman.
Description: Jackson: University Press of Mississippi, [2018] | Includes
bibliographical references and index. |
Identifiers: LCCN 2018011383 (print) | LCCN 2018016597 (ebook) | ISBN
9781496818874 (epub single) | ISBN 9781496818881 (epub institutional) |
ISBN 9781496818898 (pdf single) | ISBN 9781496818904 (pdf institutional)
| ISBN 9781496818867 (cloth) | ISBN 9781496818966 (pbk.)
Subjects: LCSH: African Americans—Segregation—United States—Religious
aspects. | Catholics—Southern States—History—20th century. | Catholic
Church—Southern States—History—20th century. | Southern
States—History—20th century.
Classification: LCC E185.615 (ebook) | LCC E185.615 .N387 2018 (print) | DDC
975/.04—dc23
LC record available at https://lccn.loc.gov/2018011383

British Library Cataloging-in-Publication Data available

For my mother

CONTENTS

ix | Preface

xv | Acknowledgments

xvii | Abbreviations

3 | **INTRODUCTION**
The Catholic Church and African Americans in the South and Nation to 1944

19 | **CHAPTER ONE**
An Overview: Catholics in the South and Desegregation, 1945–1970

43 | **CHAPTER TWO**
The Sociology of Religion and Catholic Desegregation in the South

65 | **CHAPTER THREE**
Catholic Segregationist Thought in the South

83 | **CHAPTER FOUR**
Progressive White Catholics in the South and Civil Rights

111 | **CHAPTER FIVE**
White Catholics in the South and Secular Desegregation, 1954–1970

139 | **CHAPTER SIX**
Desegregation of Southern Catholic Institutions, 1945–1970

169 | **CHAPTER SEVEN**
African American Catholics in the South and Desegregation, 1945–1970

201 | **CHAPTER EIGHT**
Southern Catholics and Desegregation in Denominational Perspective, 1945–1971

237 | **CHAPTER NINE**
An Overview: Catholics in the South and Desegregation, 1971–1992

269 | **CONCLUSION**

277 | **APPENDIX 1**
Catholic Archdioceses and Dioceses in the South, 1945–1992

281 | **APPENDIX 2**
Ordinaries of Catholic Dioceses in the South, 1945–1992

285 | **APPENDIX 3**
Major Catholic Diocesan Newspapers in the South, 1945–1992

287 | **APPENDIX 4**
The Catholic Population in the South, 1945–1980

289 | **APPENDIX 5**
The African American Catholic Population in the South, 1945–1975

291 | Notes

403 | Selected Bibliography

425 | Index

PREFACE

Until the Second Vatican Council's reforms in the first half of the 1960s, its adherents widely regarded the Catholic Church as a hierarchical body that comprised the pope, prelates, clergy, and nuns, and the structures they controlled and operated. The Church's universality lay in the uniformity of its teachings, adherence to the canon law that governed its conduct, and administration of the sacraments. The "Church," in this conception, was a "perfect society" without fault or blemish, charged with inculcating the laity and secular society with moral teachings and values. Catholics found comfort and security in the seemingly unchanging nature of the Church across time and geography. Most laity regarded their religious duty as following Church practices and ritual, raising their children in the faith, and avoiding individual sin as delineated in the Bible's Ten Commandments. Efforts to desegregate southern Catholicism challenged and weakened conceptions of the Church's perfection, divided Catholics, and revealed the limited conception of Catholic social teaching held by many clergy and laity and even some prelates. Even before the Second Vatican Council sanctioned liturgical change and redefined the laity as part of a Church engaged in renewing itself and the temporal order, growing lay, and to a lesser extent, clergy assertiveness on both sides of the segregation issue posed challenges to the authority of prelates and clergy. Catholic desegregation proved to be a long, bitter, factious, and incomplete process.[1]

The Vatican had sanctioned the establishment of separate parishes and schools for African Americans by many southern and some nonsouthern American dioceses in the late nineteenth and early twentieth centuries. Created ostensibly as a means of evangelism and service to African Americans, separate Catholic institutions for blacks were also a pragmatic response to white American racism, exemplified in the segregation laws of the South and the de facto segregation of the North and West. Many of the overwhelmingly white clergy in the United States and their superiors, whether native born or immigrants, shared the racism and racial assumptions of the wider, white American society.

Like whites elsewhere in the country, most white Catholic laity in the South, defined in this study as the eleven states of the old Confederacy, accepted segregation in church and society. In the nineteenth, and much of the twentieth, century, the American Catholic hierarchy regarded African Americans paternalistically, as people in need of missionaries to convert them to Catholicism and uplift them spiritually, morally, and educationally. Catholic prelates in the

South encouraged and accepted religious orders of clergy and nuns to staff missions, churches, schools, and medical services for African Americans, both Catholic and non-Catholic. The orders were often northern based and, except for three orders of black nuns, mostly or entirely white. Beginning in the late nineteenth and early twentieth centuries, African American Catholics increasingly attended separate institutions from white Catholics. When permitted to attend largely white churches, blacks found themselves confined to segregated seating and communion after whites. While some black Catholics objected to the adoption of segregation by the Church and some left in protest, others gradually resigned themselves to the imposition of Jim Crow Catholicism.

In the 1930s and 1940s, the papacy endorsed and propagated the doctrine of the Mystical Body of Christ. Focused on the importance of every human being as a member of Christ's Mystical Body on earth, the doctrine overrode distinctions based on race and nationality to create one people united in Christ. The small number of Catholic integrationists in the United States drew inspiration from and embraced the language of the Mystical Body in articulating their message. By the late 1940s, the Vatican also excluded the racially prejudiced from consideration for episcopal office in the United States.

The doctrine of the Mystical Body, episcopal appointments, revulsion at Nazi racism, and the emerging civil rights movement and federal government measures in its support encouraged Catholic integrationists, clerical and lay, white and African American, to support desegregation of church and society in the decades that followed World War Two. While the sociology of religion suggests that, as a hierarchical body, the Catholic Church had considerable freedom of maneuver to desegregate its institutions, in practice prelates and their clergy often moved slowly, cautiously and, sometimes, reluctantly.

Most southern white Catholics in the civil rights era, like most other southern whites, were segregationists. Many of them found it difficult to accept, and some actively opposed, Church leaders and members who endorsed desegregation, especially in view of segregation's longevity and continued existence in many southern Catholic institutions. How could segregation, many southern white Catholic segregationists asked, be sinful and the Church a perfect society if segregation had been and remained commonplace within the Church's institutions? Often vocal and organized in their opposition, militant segregationists were a minority, albeit a significant one, among southern white Catholics. The majority of southern white Catholics, including some prelates, clergy, and nuns, were moderate segregationists, who considered segregation an acceptable and, for many a desirable, part of the prevailing order in Church and secular society.

A minority of white Catholics in the region were progressives who believed that segregation violated the Mystical Body of Christ and should be ended in Church and society. Progressives promoted desegregation and urged white

Catholics to accept it. They often acted cautiously and most conceived of Catholic desegregation in terms of closing black Catholic institutions and admitting their members to hitherto white Catholic facilities, rather than developing reciprocity in race relations and integration based on mutual appreciation, respect, and understanding between the races.

The marked tendency of many, although not all, white Catholic prelates, clergy, and religious orders, who worked among them, to regard African Americans as a missionary field, often resulted in little effort to discover black views and aspirations. Both active African American and white Catholic integrationists sometimes complained about what they regarded as black Catholic docility, although, at times, also recognizing that such timidity was often rooted in realistic fears of white retribution. African American voices were often absent from diocesan and religious orders archives because of the disinterest of many white clergy in ascertaining black perspectives and the reluctance of some black Catholics to express their views or to do so only guardedly. Until the second half of the 1960s, only a few of the southern dioceses that published newspapers included letters pages in which the voices of the laity could be heard, including, on occasion, those of African American laity. Black Catholics' response to desegregation, like that of prelates, clergy, and white laity, was diverse and depended in large part on the manner of its implementation by ordinaries and their subordinates.

The Vatican permitted archbishops and bishops substantial autonomy in running their dioceses, which produced considerable variation in their response to desegregation. Consequently, historian R. Bentley Anderson has argued that to "present a general account of the [Catholic] church and race in the South, one must examine each and every diocese and archdiocese." While this study does not present individual accounts of every southern diocese, it draws its evidence from them and from the relevant religious orders that operated within them to examine trends in Catholic response to both Catholic and secular desegregation in the region. In so doing, it provides the first overview of the response of Catholics in the South to desegregation during the civil rights movement and its aftermath. While in part an institutional history, the book also explores the diverse response of both African American and white Catholic laity to desegregation in the religious and secular realms.[2]

Like many works of history, this study both builds on, and seeks to address omissions in, the work of others, aided in part by the availability of new sources. Sociologist William A. Osborne's *The Segregated Covenant* provides a snapshot of the Catholic Church and (de)segregation in the United States of the mid-1960s. However, Osborne's account, published in 1967, when Catholic desegregation was ongoing is impressionistic and mostly descriptive. Osborne devotes only one chapter to the South, which focuses on Mississippi, the city of New

Orleans, and the Diocese of Lafayette in Louisiana. He also pays little attention to African American Catholic perspectives. Nearly thirty years later, Stephen J. Ochs's *Desegregating the Altar* chronicled the slow, tortuous history of the Society of St. Joseph of the Sacred Heart, a missionary order that staffed African American churches mostly in the South, in training and admitting black priests before the 1960s. In the past ten years, historians have produced several book-length treatments that address some aspects of the story of Catholics and desegregation in the South. They include Andrew S. Moore's study of Catholic desegregation in Alabama and the Archdiocese of Atlanta up to 1970, R. Bentley Anderson's work on the unsuccessful efforts of progressive African American and white Catholics in the city of New Orleans to achieve desegregation between 1947 and 1956, and Amy L. Koehlinger's account of white nuns who strove to alleviate America's racial problems in the 1960s.[3]

This study augments the more specifically focused contributions made by these earlier works to offer a detailed overview and interpretation of Catholics and desegregation in the South from the end of World War Two through the civil rights era and its aftermath. It ends with Father George A. Stallings Jr.'s unsuccessful attempt to draw a significant number of African American Catholics into a new independent black Catholic Church.

The introduction examines the Catholic Church in the South and African Americans from the colonial era until 1944. It discusses the development of racially segregated Catholicism in the region and the beginnings of Catholic progressivism on the issue. Chapter 1 provides an overview of Catholics in the South and desegregation between the end of World War Two and 1970 and places it within the context of the American Catholic hierarchy's response to southern segregation. Chapter 2 examines how the sociology of religion aids our understanding of the context in which Catholic prelates and clergy operated and of the constraints they faced. Chapter 3 addresses how southern white Catholic segregationists developed and articulated a religious and secular defense of segregation as Jim Crow came under increasing challenge from within and outside the Church. Chapter 4 explores the efforts of progressive Catholics in the South to counter segregationist arguments and pressure Catholic authorities to desegregate their institutions in the region.

The remaining chapters focus primarily on Catholic efforts to achieve desegregation in the South and their results. Chapter 5 investigates how white Catholics in the region responded to secular desegregation and the civil rights movement. Chapter 6 examines the pattern of Catholic institutional desegregation in the South between 1945 and 1970. Chapter 7 discusses African American Catholics in the South and Catholic and secular desegregation between 1945 and 1970. It argues that black Catholics were more involved in the civil rights movement than contemporaries and scholars appreciated. Chapter 8 compares Catholic response in the South to desegregation with that of Catholics in the

North and with other major denominations in the South and the nation. Chapter 9 discusses the impact and results of Catholic desegregation in the South after the 1960s. Chapter 10, the conclusion, notes distinctions between the peripheral and Deep South, and emphasizes the complexity and diversity of the Catholic experience of desegregation.

ACKNOWLEDGMENTS

Research and writing for the book was made possible by support from the following for which I am most grateful: the University of Edinburgh's Development Trust Research Fund and Moray Endowment Fund, Carnegie Trust research grants, a British Academy Larger Research Grant, a Leverhulme Research Fellowship, research leave funded by the Arts and Humanities Research Council, a Scouloudi Historical Award from the Institute of Historical Research, Founders' Awards from the British Association for American Studies, and sabbatical leave from the University of Edinburgh.

At the university, the research received the vital endorsement of the late Jim McMillan, Jay Brown, and Douglas Cairns, and the book's completion the welcome support and encouragement of Martin Chick. Beyond my university, many other scholars also supported my work, with Tony Badger, Robert Cook, Peter J. Ling, Richard H. King, and my friend, mentor, and former supervisor Michael Simpson especially prominent among them. I would also like to thank the many archivists who assisted me and so often went far beyond the call of duty.

I am very appreciative of the interest that Craig W. Gill of the University Press of Mississippi expressed in the manuscript and the support he subsequently gave to ensure its publication. Some of the material has appeared elsewhere in earlier versions: "The Catholic Church and Desegregation in the Diocese of Baton Rouge, 1961–1976," *Louisiana History* 51, no. 3 (Summer 2010): 306–32; "The Catholic Church in Arkansas and Desegregation, 1946–1988," *Arkansas Historical Quarterly* 66, no. 3 (Autumn 2007): 293–319; "The Catholic Church in Mississippi and Desegregation, 1963–1973," *Journal of Mississippi History* 67, no. 4 (Winter 2005): 331–55; "The Catholic Church in Tennessee and Desegregation, 1954–1973," *Tennessee Historical Quarterly* 66, no. 2 (Summer 2007): 144–65; "The Catholic Diocese of Miami and African American Desegregation, 1958–1977," *Florida Historical Quarterly* 90, no. 1 (Summer 2011): 61–84; "The Catholic Diocese of Alexandria and Desegregation, 1946–1973," *Louisiana History* 52, no. 3 (Summer 2011): 261–99; "Desegregation of the Catholic Diocese of Charleston, 1950–1974," *South Carolina Historical Magazine* 112, nos. 1–2 (January–April 2011): 26–49; "Desegregation in the Catholic Diocese of Richmond, 1945–1973," *Virginia Magazine of History and Biography* 117, no. 4 (2009): 356–87; "Progressive White Catholics in the South and Civil Rights, 1945–1970," in *Unsteadily Marching On: The U.S. in Motion*, edited by Constante Gonzalez Groba (Valencia: Universitat de Valencia, 2013); and "Toward 'Blessings of Liberty and Justice': The Catholic Church in North Carolina and Desegregation, 1945–1974," *North Carolina Historical Review* 85, no. 3 (July 2008): 317–51. I thank these publishers and copyright holders, including Constante Gonzalez Groba, the Florida Historical Association, and the Louisiana Historical Association, for permission to include parts of the articles here.

For their hospitality and help during research trips, I am grateful to Bart and Sharon Bartleson, the late Charles Boyle, Emily Clark, Steve and Barbara Landregan, Gary L. McDowell, Darla H. Rushing, the Marianist Brothers at Central Catholic High School, San Antonio, and the Sisters of St. Joseph, Rochester, New York.

ABBREVIATIONS

AACC	African-American Catholic Congregation
AIC	Academy of the Immaculate Conception
BEDC	National Black Economic Development Council
CCCO	Coordinating Council of Community Organizations
CCHR	Catholic Council on Human Relations
CCS	Catholic Committee of the South
CCUM	Catholic Committee on Urban Ministry
CHR	Commission on Human Rights
CICNV	Catholic Interracial Council of Northern Virginia
CORE	Congress of Racial Equality
FCC	Federation of Colored Catholics
F.S.C.	Brothers of the Christian Schools
F.S.P.A.	Congregation of the Sisters of the Third Order of St. Francis of Perpetual Adoration
GCSP	General Convention Special Program
HEW	Department of Health, Education and Welfare
KPC	Knights of Peter Claver
LCHR	Louisiana Council on Human Relations
NAACP	National Association for the Advancement of Colored People
NBC	Negro Betterment Council
NBSC	National Black Sisters' Conference
NCC	National Council of Churches
NCCB	National Conference of Catholic Bishops
NCCIJ	National Catholic Conference for Interracial Justice
NCCLA	North Carolina Catholic Laymen's Association
NCCW	National Council of Catholic Women
NCRR	National Conference on Race and Religion
NCWC	National Catholic Welfare Conference
NOBC	National Office for Black Catholics
OASIS	Organizations Assisting Schools in September
OCR	Office of Civil Rights
OEO	Office of Economic Opportunity
O.F.M.	Franciscan Friars
O.P.	Dominican Sisters (Adrian, Mich.)
O.P.	Order of Preachers (Dominicans)

O.S.B.	Benedictine Monks
PCUS	Presbyterian Church in the United States
PCUSA	Presbyterian Church in the United States of America
RDCCW	Richmond Diocesan Council of Catholic Women
SBC	Southern Baptist Convention
S.B.S.	Sisters of the Blessed Sacrament
SCLC	Southern Christian Leadership Conference
S.D.S.	Society of the Divine Savior
SERINCO	Southeastern Regional Interracial Commission
S.J.	Jesuit Fathers and Brothers
S.M.	Society of Mary (Marianists)
S.M.A.	Society of African Missions
SNCC	Student Nonviolent Coordinating Committee
SOS	Save Our Schools
SRC	Southern Regional Council
S.S.	Society of the Priests of Saint Sulpice
S.S.E.	Society of Saint Edmund
S.S.J.	Society of St. Joseph of the Sacred Heart (Josephites)
S.S.J.	Sisters of St. Joseph of St. Augustine, Florida
S.S.N.D.	School Sisters of Notre Dame
S.V.D.	Society of the Divine Word
TCC	Texas Catholic Conference

DESEGREGATING DIXIE

INTRODUCTION

The Catholic Church and African Americans in the South and Nation to 1944

As an institution, the Catholic Church in the South did not challenge prevailing race relations in the United States until the second half of the twentieth century. In the colonial era, and until the twentieth century, Catholic teaching generally accepted slavery, conditional upon slave owners attending to their slaves' physical and religious welfare. While the first decades of the new republic of the United States saw the beginning of gradual emancipation of slaves in northern states, slavery remained widely accepted among white Catholics, the vast majority of whom, like all Catholics, lived in the South and bordering areas. Religious orders of clergy and nuns and seminaries were slaveholders in Kentucky, Maryland, Missouri, Washington, DC, and "throughout the South."[1]

The ranks of free black Catholics grew in the 1790s and early 1800s with the arrival in Baltimore and New Orleans of refugees from the Haitian revolution. In 1829, women in Baltimore's Haitian community began the first African American religious order, the Oblate Sisters of Providence. Two years later, Pope Gregory XVI approved the order, which had begun teaching black children.[2]

In 1839, Pope Gregory condemned the slave trade. The United States had itself barred slave importation since 1807, although it had continued illegally in the South. Bishop John England of Charleston claimed that the pope had not condemned slavery itself, which, England declared, violated neither state law nor God's will. In keeping with Catholic tradition, the Catholic Church in the United States focused on personal sin and salvation achieved through the sacramental system. The Church did not regard slavery as inherently sinful and held aloof from social and political issues or reforms. Fear of arousing nativist Protestant opposition reinforced the Church's tendency to eschew involvement in what it deemed secular matters, especially as Catholics were vastly outnumbered in all parts of the nation beyond southern Louisiana. However, Catholic leaders and priests in the South engaged with political issues, such as slavery, when their positions were in accord with prevailing white opinion.[3]

Consequently, the Catholic Church in the South not only participated in slavery, it defended the practice while, in the Catholic tradition, urging masters to manage their slaves with compassion. "Like the dominant Protestant churches of the Old South," writes historian Randall M. Miller, "the Catholic church endorsed the racial and social values of its white parishioners by supplying biblical justifications for slavery and a conservative social order."[4]

Many antebellum southern Catholic churches practiced segregation. Free blacks received communion after whites, and slaves took communion after free blacks. However, in areas with many free blacks, such as Washington, DC, Catholic churches had mixed seating. In New Orleans, French-speaking Creoles of color, who prospered despite being denied the franchise, bought church pews and, in some parishes, constituted a majority of churchgoers and the wellspring of financial support. However, other Catholic institutions in New Orleans were segregated. State law reinforced the distinctiveness of Creoles of color by forbidding them to intermarry with slaves, as well as with whites. In 1842, two Creoles of color and a Haitian mulatto refugee established a new religious community, subsequently known as the Sisters of the Holy Family. The order, which throughout the antebellum period only accepted Creoles of color, tended to the medical and other needs of slaves and impoverished free blacks in New Orleans. The nuns also taught religion to both slave and free people of color.[5]

But the Catholic Church in the South, especially in rural areas, largely neglected the religious needs of slaves. Instead it concentrated its inadequate supply of priests, all of them white, on the white population. At the same time, the Catholic Church outside the South focused on serving the waves of Catholic migrants from Europe, especially Ireland and Germany, who brought a significant Catholic presence to the antebellum North. By 1850, European migration had made the Catholic Church the largest single denomination in the United States. Catholics formed a little under 5 percent (469,000) of the southern, border state, and Washington, DC, population and 9.5 percent (1,273,000) of the rest of the American population. In 1860, about 100,000 African Americans were Catholic, most of them located in the South. Although spread across many denominations, Protestants remained a large majority of the American population. Consequently, the Catholic Church in both halves of the United States continued to be acutely conscious of its minority condition and reluctant to address social and political issues that might provoke Protestant enmity.[6]

Widespread Catholic antipathy for abolitionism prevented the Catholic Church from dividing over slavery unlike the Presbyterians, Methodists, and Baptists. During the Civil War (1861–1865), Catholics, lay and clergy, were largely patriotic toward the section in which they lived, with Catholics serving in both the Union and Confederate armies.[7]

The Catholic Church did not fracture during the war, despite tensions during the conflict. In 1866, its prelates met under the leadership of Archbishop Martin J. Spalding of Baltimore in the Second Plenary Council of the Church in the United States to discuss their ministry in the reunited nation, which now had four million emancipated slaves. The Vatican's Congregation of the Propaganda, which held jurisdiction over the United States because of its mission status, supported the convening of the council and Spalding's plan for the evangelization of African Americans. However, the council rejected his proposals.[8]

With most bishops indifferent to evangelizing blacks, many priests reluctant to minister to African Americans, and a shortage of priests in the United States, the council decided bishops should invite European missionaries to conduct the black apostolate. The council issued a pastoral letter that regretted the absence of "a more gradual system of emancipation," and appealed for "Christian charity and zeal" in view of "the evils which must necessarily attend the sudden liberation of so large a multitude, with their peculiar dispositions and habits" and need of "Christian education and moral restraint."[9]

Unwilling to tolerate segregated seating and racism in church and often desirous of having African American clergy who would provide services in keeping with black culture, many emancipated slaves abandoned Catholicism. Many southern black Catholics joined African American Protestants in black-pastored Baptist, Methodist, and Presbyterian churches formed as African Americans withdrew from white churches during Reconstruction. Some black Catholics sought to establish their own Catholic churches. However, opposition from most of the American Catholic hierarchy thwarted the emergence of more than a handful of black priests, and most prelates had neither the funds, manpower, nor desire to initiate African American churches.[10]

When the Second Plenary Council met in October 1866, there were three African American Catholic priests and at least four Catholic churches and chapels serving African Americans. The priests were sons of Michael Morris Healy, an Irish immigrant farmer in Georgia, and Mary Eliza, one of his slaves. Educated in the North, Healy's sons had needed to leave the United States for seminary training. The eldest son, and the first black Catholic clergyman to serve in the United States, James Augustine Healy became a priest in the Diocese of Boston. Alexander Sherwood Healy taught in a provincial seminary in Troy, New York. According to historian Cyprian Davis, O.S.B., "the brothers were known to be Black" by many, but Patrick Francis Healy, who became president of Georgetown University in Washington, DC, had "to keep his racial origins secret" as the institution did not admit blacks. As Bishop of Portland, Maine, between 1875 and 1900, James Augustine Healy "never really hid his identity," but he did not work on behalf of African American Catholics or identify with them. Most of the Catholic hierarchy did not favor African American priests, despite the Vatican's preference for indigenous clergy.[11]

The first black Catholic churches developed outside the old Confederate states, in Baltimore, Maryland; Pittsburgh, Pennsylvania; Washington, DC; and Cleveland, Ohio, sometimes at the request of African Americans. In the aftermath of the Second Plenary Council, other black churches opened, including in the South, but their establishment was dependent upon the disposition of individual bishops, the availability of funds and priests, and the presence of enough black and white Catholics to justify a separate black church.[12]

In 1871, four members of the Mill Hill Fathers, an English missionary group, arrived in Baltimore to serve African Americans, but their early efforts were hampered by administrative and leadership problems and a lack of personnel and resources. In 1872, the Holy Ghost Fathers (Congregation of the Holy Ghost or Spiritans), a German order, committed themselves to work among African Americans but experienced several false starts before beginning a mission in Arkansas in 1878.[13]

Disappointed by the paucity of efforts to evangelize African Americans and discerning a need to regulate the Church, the Vatican initiated a Third Plenary Council. Held in Baltimore in 1884, the council sanctioned an annual Lenten collection in each diocese for African and Native American evangelism and created the Commission for the Catholic Missions Among the Colored People and the Indians to receive the collection and allocate it to prelates according to need. Heeding the Vatican's call for a consistent approach, the council advocated separate African American churches and schools, and it urged seminarians and religious orders to engage in African American missions.[14]

The Third Plenary Council had a greater impact than its predecessor. By 1893, there were twenty black Catholic churches in the United States. Apart from the council, enactment of segregation or Jim Crow legislation in the South in the late 1880s and subsequent decades that affected every secular public facility encouraged the growth of separate black Catholic institutions as the Catholic Church and its leaders accepted prevailing social and political norms. But in spite of Jim Crow, New Orleans continued to operate mixed parishes, which historian James B. Bennett attributes to "long-standing patterns of neglect," rather than "racial liberalism." Some white Catholic laity, he notes, opposed separate parishes believing that they would imply racial equality and, in any case, New Orleans's archbishops and clergy did not want to provide for them. Archbishops also lacked priests for new churches, and many clergy did not want to lose financial contributions from prosperous Creoles of color. Elsewhere in the South, prelates established separate institutions for African Americans as financial and manpower resources permitted, although the small numbers of Catholics of either race often made separate churches unrealistic. Racially mixed churches remained segregated, although some white churches, as in the past, excluded blacks.[15]

During slavery, white opposition and the small number of free African American Catholics had largely precluded the founding of black Catholic schools and those started had not endured. However, the Third Plenary Council led to the creation of black elementary parochial schools, designed to keep African American Catholics within the faith and also, in those beyond southern Louisiana, to convert the many Protestant children, who attended them in preference to inadequate segregated public schools, and their parents. The growth of black Catholic schools both contributed to and reflected increasing segregation in the South.[16]

In the North, prelates created national parishes for European immigrants based on their ethnicity and language that were designed to serve their religious needs and ease their transition to American life. A new wave of emigration to the northern United States that began in the 1890s brought millions of Catholics from eastern and southern Europe and greatly accelerated the establishment of national parishes. When African American Catholic numbers warranted it and resources allowed, northern prelates also sanctioned separate churches for blacks. Archbishop John Ireland of St. Paul, Minnesota, opposed separate black parochial schools and called for racial equality and integration in both the Catholic and secular realms, but he was atypical among Catholic leaders, north and south, most of whom assumed black inferiority and unsuitability for the priesthood.[17]

Prelates did not adopt the Third Plenary Council's recommendation for African American catechists, and the council had not discussed ordination of black priests. Yet, two years later, the United States gained its first self-identified African American clergyman. Born in slavery in Missouri but raised in Illinois by the mother with whom he had escaped from bondage, Augustine Tolton was trained and ordained in Rome in 1886 and, at the Vatican's urging, assigned to a parish in the Diocese of Alton in Illinois. He spent his last years as the priest of St. Monica's, a black church in Chicago where he died in 1897, aged forty-three.[18]

Despite racist reservations about the character of African Americans, the Mill Hill Fathers supported seminary training and ordination of black priests. In 1891, Charles Randolph Uncles became a Mill Hill Father and the first African American priest ordained in the United States. However, Uncles, the fifth African American priest, was also the last ordained that century. In 1893, the American branch of the Mill Hill Fathers broke away and formed the Society of St. Joseph of the Sacred Heart or Josephites. In a largely unsuccessful attempt to mollify their own misplaced concerns, and those of many prelates and clergy, about the moral fitness and suitability of blacks for the priesthood, the Josephites took a cautious and over-regulated approach that did not produce another African American priest, John Henry Dorsey, until 1902.[19]

African Americans had little representation among the Catholic clergy, and, with Bishop Healy unwilling to represent or address black concerns, none among the hierarchy. Consequently, African American Catholic laity defended their interests by holding five black Catholic lay congresses. The first congress held in Washington, DC, in 1889 called for more Catholic schools and deplored racial discrimination in housing, unions, and employment. Subsequent congresses in Cincinnati (1890), Philadelphia (1892), Chicago (1893), and Baltimore (1894) insisted on the need for more Catholic schools, equal access to religious education, and vocational training. The third congress also called for "co-education of the races," while the fourth condemned "the racist practices of some members of the Church," including clergy, as contrary to "the teaching of the Church," and welcomed the ordinations of Tolton and Uncles.[20]

The fifth congress was the final one of the century. The American Catholic hierarchy and clergy were dissatisfied by the congress's militancy and, more generally, by growing lay assertiveness. An ongoing struggle between liberals, who were sympathetic toward social action and African Americans, and conservatives for leadership in the Church ended with the latter's victory.[21]

Although the congresses had expressed opposition to racial discrimination in the Church, they were unable to overturn it. Discrimination against, and widespread neglect of, African Americans and their religious needs by the postbellum Catholic Church limited black Catholic numbers. However, in 1891, Katharine Drexel, an heiress to the Drexel banking fortune in Philadelphia, Pennsylvania, who had become a nun, founded the Sisters of the Blessed Sacrament (S.B.S.) to serve both Native Americans and African Americans. From its convent near Philadelphia, the S.B.S. trained and sent nuns to teach in schools in many parts of the nation, most of which the order founded, as well as supported, and it also funded some churches. The Sisters established most of their schools in the first half of the twentieth century and many of them during its second decade. Many of their African American schools were located in the South, especially in southern Louisiana. Although the S.B.S. fulfilled an educational need by providing a better education than the segregated public school system and, like the Josephites, did not advocate segregation, the order's schools and support for African American churches contributed to the growth of Catholic segregation.[22]

Segregation became increasingly common in New Orleans, not only in the secular realm but also with a twofold increase in black Catholic school enrollment in the city between 1888 and 1893 and Archbishop Francis Janssens's creation of a specifically African American Catholic church, St. Katherine's, in 1895. Janssens, a Dutchman, acted not because he was racist or supported segregation in principle, but because he believed that a designated black church would help stem a loss of African Americans from Catholicism that he had overestimated. The archbishop favored the ordination of black priests and directed two prospects north for seminary training, although neither became clergymen.[23]

During the 1890s, whites in many New Orleans's Catholic churches increasingly restricted and controlled the seating of blacks and, in others, dissuaded them from attendance by excluding them from full and equal participation. Inevitably, some black Catholics ceased going to church. Janssens's proposed solution was to create a parallel network of black churches in which blacks could participate unrestricted, supplemented by a network of black Catholic schools. He hoped to strengthen Catholicism among African Americans and their sense of self-worth, while placating white Catholics.[24]

Janssens's pragmatic solution fit with the Catholic tradition of accepting social and political norms. Even Archbishop Ireland, the Catholic hierarchy's foremost critic of segregation and racial inequality, had accepted the establishment of an African American Church, St. Peter Claver, in St. Paul, Minnesota, in 1892 as a necessary expedient to serve blacks given white racism, although his archdiocese's schools were integrated. The decision of the Josephites and Holy Ghost Fathers to focus solely on African Americans had been conditioned by encounters with white Catholic lay hostility toward mixed parishes and blacks.[25]

Religious orders staffed most of the growing number of African American Catholic churches in the South at the turn of the century. By 1903, the Josephites had thirty-one priests serving twelve churches and missions from Delaware to Texas. In 1905, the Society of the Divine Word (S.V.D.) or Divine Word Missionaries, a Dutch-based but mostly German order, initiated its first mission to African Americans, in Merigold, Mississippi. Additional black churches in Mississippi and Arkansas soon followed. In 1907, the Society of African Missions (S.M.A.), founded in France, began work with African Americans in the Diocese of Savannah, Georgia. While they were sincerely dedicated to blacks, these orders, together with the Spiritans and the S.B.S., made prelates' entrenchment of racial separatism in Catholicism possible and their members sometimes shared the racist assumptions of other whites. Furthermore, as ministries to African Americans became almost the sole preserve of a few religious orders, diocesan priests and other orders of clergy and nuns felt little need to concern themselves with blacks and their needs.[26]

In 1904, the Congregation of the Propaganda in the Vatican informed Archbishop Diomede Falconio, the apostolic delegate to the United States (the pope's legate or representative), that the American Catholic hierarchy should reduce and, ultimately, eliminate discrimination against African American Catholics. Pope Pius X made public his wish for "all Catholics to be friendly to Negroes, who are called no less than other men to share in all the great benefits of the Redemption." However, the nation's prelates did no more than set up an evangelism body, the Catholic Board for Mission Work Among the Colored People, in 1907 under Father John E. Burke, a New York priest. Concerned by the negative affects of white Catholic racism on black Catholicism and evangelism, Burke advocated separate parishes and schools, and the creation of a black priesthood and a separate black jurisdiction, to be headed by a black bishop. Yet, with few exceptions, the American Catholic hierarchy remained skeptical about black suitability for the clergy. The new commission lacked funds and influence, and the trickle of black ordinations virtually dried up. Most of the few blacks ordained suffered isolation, rejection, and poor treatment that reinforced many prelates' opposition to black ordinations.[27]

Although their concern was to evangelize and aid African Americans, the Josephites helped further institutionalize segregation by initiating a black men's fraternal and benevolent organization, the Knights of Peter Claver (KPC), in 1909. Begun in Mobile, Alabama, by four Josephite priests, including Father John Dorsey, and local black Catholics, the KPC was an African American equivalent of the Knights of Columbus, a white lay group that excluded blacks. Like the Knights of Columbus, the KPC provided members with insurance benefits and solicited their support for philanthropic and diocesan projects. By the mid-1940s, the KPC had become a national organization, with headquarters in New Orleans, and, after years of conservatism, it also began to challenge racial discrimination. The KPC was complemented by the Junior Knights begun in 1917, followed by the Ladies Auxiliary of Peter Claver in 1922 and the Junior Daughters in 1930.[28]

Despite protesting the treatment of African Americans within and outside the Church, in 1904 the Vatican, which allowed prelates a great deal of latitude in running their dioceses, accepted the creation of separate black parishes. Archbishop Giovanni Bonzano, the apostolic delegate to the United States, reported to the Vatican in 1914 that African Americans preferred white priests and that blacks had poor morals and lesser intelligence. A Vatican official tacitly accepted segregation by replying that American prelates should aid black evangelization through more schools, hospitals, and catechists, and the creation of black economic associations.[29]

Increased exclusion accompanied the creation of separate Catholic institutions for African Americans within and outside the South. Formerly mixed parishes often excluded blacks when black churches opened, and most seminaries in the United States would not admit them. Even the Catholic University of America in Washington, DC, one of the few Catholic higher education institutions that admitted blacks, began to prohibit their entry in 1914, although some were still admitted during the next seven years and the last of them graduated in the mid-1920s.[30]

During World War One, the Knights of Columbus provided aid for white Catholic troops but none for African American Catholic servicemen. In 1917, Thomas Wyatt Turner, a Howard University biology professor from Maryland, and a group of fellow laymen at St. Augustine's, a black church in Washington, DC, complained to Cardinal James Gibbons of Baltimore about the Church's neglect of black Catholic soldiers. Following Gibbons's advice, the group met with Colonel P. H. Callahan, the Knights of Columbus official on the National Catholic War Council, who decided to hire black Catholic workers to serve black Catholic soldiers in camp. The group, under a succession of names, also began protesting other forms of discrimination in the Catholic Church, and, by 1924, had developed into a national organization the Federation of Colored Catholics (FCC).[31]

In 1919, the United States experienced a resurgence of lynching of African Americans and numerous race riots. The Vatican pressed the American Catholic hierarchy to address racial violence when its members met at the Catholic University of America for their first annual meeting. In response, the meeting issued a pastoral letter that referred to racial problems but did not specifically denounce lynching as the Vatican wanted. The letter stated that "we deprecate most earnestly all attempts at stirring up racial hatred" since they hindered missions to blacks and undermined national unity. African Americans, the prelates claimed, needed education, "moral and religious training," and to learn from "their teachers the lesson of Christian virtue." The American Catholic hierarchy did not address what steps should be taken against violent white racists or racism within the Catholic Church.[32]

In November 1919, Pope Benedict XV's encyclical *Maximum Illud* supported indigenous clergy and seminaries in mission territory. Encouraged by the encyclical, the Divine Word Missionaries revived an earlier plan for a black seminary, abandoned after opposition from other missionaries. With financial support from the Catholic Board for Mission Work Among the Colored People and from Katharine Drexel, in 1920 the S.V.D. opened the Sacred Heart College in Greenville, Mississippi, to prepare African Americans for the priesthood and admitted two students. Some black Catholics criticized the seminary for perpetuating Jim Crow.[33]

The S.M.A. also fostered the creation of African American religious. The Reverend Ignatius Lissner, the society's mission superior in the Diocese of Savannah, worked with Elizabeth Williams, an African American, to form a third black order of nuns, the Handmaids of Mary. The order moved to Harlem, New York City, in 1922 to serve its black community. Lissner obtained agreement from Bishop John J. O'Connor of Newark for an integrated seminary, St. Anthony's Mission House, that opened in Highwood, New Jersey, in 1921. The seminary soon produced a black priest, Joseph Alexander John, from the island of Carriacou in the West Indies, ordained in 1923. But for several years, no southern bishop would take John, fearing white opposition. His difficulties and the continued opposition of many prelates, especially in the South, to black clergy led the S.M.A. to abandon training them, just as the Josephites and Spiritans had done.[34]

The seminary's failure and the unfortunate experiences of many black priests only reinforced the Josephites' belief that training black priests was unwise and also futile since southern ordinaries would not accept them either because of doubts about African Americans' abilities and rectitude, or because of white opposition from within and outside the Church. Local white, including Ku Klux Klan, hostility persuaded the S.V.D. to relocate its seminary from Greenville to the more Catholic environment of Mississippi's Gulf Coast. In 1923, St. Augustine's Seminary opened in Bay St. Louis, fifty miles from New Orleans, with a supportive letter from Pope Pius XI, who affirmed his preference for indigenous clergy in the encyclical *Rerum Ecclesiae* three years later. Assured that its students would be ordained as S.V.D., and not diocesan, priests, Bishop John E. Gunn of Natchez, a diocese that encompassed Mississippi, had dropped his opposition to the seminary. Its establishment seemed to vindicate white opinion about the impracticality of integrated seminaries and enabled the Josephites to refer black aspirants for the priesthood to St. Augustine's.[35]

Segregation grew ever more entrenched in Catholicism during the 1920s. Besides St. Augustine's, few seminaries, even in the North, admitted African Americans. New Orleans gained additional black parishes, and, by 1925, the archdiocese had established others across much of southern Louisiana. In 1925, the S.B.S. augmented an African American high school it had established in New Orleans ten years before with a college. Seven years later, the college became Xavier University, the only black Catholic university in the nation and a pragmatic response to the exclusion of African Americans from Catholic higher education institutions. The university had a biracial faculty.[36]

Exclusion had also seen the founding of the FCC. To its critics, the federation, which held its first convention in Washington, DC, in December 1925 practiced segregation, albeit self-segregation by African Americans, who led and comprised its affiliates, chiefly parish organizations and Catholic societies, and the vast majority of its membership. With Turner as president, the FCC sought to represent black Catholics, increase their status in the Church and involvement in secular matters, and widen black access to Catholic education. By 1932, the FCC claimed to represent 100,000 of an estimated 200,000 to 250,000 African American Catholics. However, the federation failed to organize in the Deep South and its claims that the Josephites excluded blacks from the order's seminaries ensured little cooperation from the region's many Josephite parishes, where black laity joined Josephite-supported groups, such as the KPC. Like the black lay congress movement, its nineteenth-century predecessor, the federation addressed racial discrimination in both the Church and society, and its meetings, held in northern and border south cities, witnessed disagreements between the mainly African American delegates and white clergy.[37]

In 1932, the FCC splintered between Turner's adherents and those of two white Jesuit priests, William M. Markoe, a Minnesotan based in St. Louis, and John LaFarge of New York. Markoe and LaFarge were dedicated to working among and on behalf of African Americans. But they found it difficult to accept that blacks could lead themselves, and the two priests believed that the FCC should practice and promote interracialism as a means of tackling racial discrimination. LaFarge, who wanted the FCC to be clergy controlled, emphasized education and moral suasion. By contrast, Turner believed that African American laity should lead the FCC and focus its objectives on publicizing and demanding an end to the Church's discriminatory practices. Turner was a former local organizer for the National Association for the Advancement of Colored People (NAACP), founded by African Americans and whites in 1909 to contest racial discrimination. Like the NAACP, he believed in challenging discrimination directly. However, Turner lost the presidency at the FCC's 1932 convention in New York City. The Federation split in two. Those associated with LaFarge and Markoe transformed the FCC into the National Catholic Interracial Federation under white clergy control. Turner's contingent operated a much-diminished new FCC that continued under his leadership, although without influence in the Church, until 1952.[38]

When the FCC divided, there were only two black priests in the United States. However, in 1934, St. Augustine's Seminary produced its first priests: Anthony Bourges of Lafayette, Louisiana; Maurice Rousseve of New Orleans; Vincent Smith of Lebanon, Kentucky; and Francis Wade of Washington, DC. After protracted discussions, which included Archbishop Amleto Giovanni Cicognani, the apostolic delegate, Bishop Jules B. Jeanmard of Lafayette, who headed a diocese with fifty thousand black Catholics in southwest Louisiana, abandoned his initial opposition and accepted the four priests. Jeanmard, a native Louisianan, assigned them to a specially created black parish, Immaculate Heart of Mary, in north Lafayette. African American Catholics in Lafayette, and throughout the nation, welcomed the four clergymen's ordination and placement, and their pastoral success contributed to a more favorable environment for black Catholic ordinations and missions.[39]

The mass migration of African Americans, including Catholics, from the South to many of the nation's major cities during World War One and the 1920s in search of better economic opportunity and in hope of escaping discrimination increasingly made black Catholic missions a national concern. Separate black parishes developed in areas of northern cities that gained large African American populations, although racial separation in northern Catholicism was less marked than in the South. Some northern prelates, such as Archbishop George W. Mundelein of Chicago, specifically established separate parishes for African Americans. In some cases, whites moved to another area rather than live in proximity to black migrants, thereby creating de facto black parishes. A desire to escape white Catholic racism, foster ties among black Catholics, and enable unfettered participation in church activities led some blacks to request separate parishes, but other African Americans objected to black parishes as stigmatizing them. In 1928, 23 percent of African American Catholics in the North belonged to black parishes, compared with 81 percent in the border states and 59 percent in the South.[40]

In 1934, John LaFarge founded the Catholic Interracial Council of New York. The council sought to remove racial discrimination from Catholic institutions and educate white Catholics about racism. It endorsed ordinations of blacks and cooperated with the NAACP's unsuccessful campaign for federal antilynching legislation. The New York council promoted the establishment of similar groups and became de facto leader of the Catholic interracial council movement. With the exception of San Antonio, Texas, councils were confined to urban areas outside the South.[41]

In the 1930s, the Vatican exerted growing pressure on the southern Catholic hierarchy to address racial discrimination and foster black evangelism. In May 1935, Archbishop Cicognani asked Joseph F. Rummel, the newly appointed Archbishop of New Orleans, for the southern bishops' response to recommendations made by the Vatican's Consistorial Congregation, which oversaw dioceses and named bishops, for desegregated schools and seminaries. Mistakenly, Rummel replied that integrated parochial schools would be illegal under Louisiana state law. Southern bishops, he claimed, opposed desegregation of diocesan seminaries, and they preferred to leave African American missions to the religious orders already engaged in them, although willing to accept involvement by other suitable orders. The prelates thought that the region's racial problems should be left to resolve themselves, warned that drawing public attention to them would be counterproductive, and claimed that much progress had occurred. In September 1936, the Consistory, with the pope's approval, issued an instruction to the American Catholic hierarchy calling for more schools, churches, and priests, including black vocations in diocesan seminaries, to serve African Americans.[42]

In the early 1920s, the papacy had unsuccessfully urged the Catholic University of America to restore African American admissions. In 1936, the university, having admitted some Oblate Sisters of Providence three years before, quietly dropped discriminatory admission practices. The capital's other white universities continued to bar blacks. While the change of policy seems to have been unrelated to the Consistorial Congregation's letter to the American Catholic hierarchy, that letter and the emergence of the Catholic Interracial Council of New York were indicative of a new atmosphere that also saw some, although not all, northern Catholic higher education institutions begin to permit African American admissions in the late 1930s and, especially, the early 1940s.[43]

The Consistorial Congregation's letter led to an increase in the ranks of clergy and nuns devoted to black evangelism, while antiracist Catholics took encouragement from, and made use of, papal condemnations of racism prompted by Nazi and Fascist racial policies and practices. In his 1937 encyclical to the German people *Mit brennender Sorge*, Pope Pius XI condemned the "myth of race and blood." In 1938, he denounced Fascist racism in Italy, declaring that "The human race, the whole human race, is but a single and universal race of man. There is no room for special races." In April that year, a decree, issued with the pope's approval, by the Vatican's Sacred Congregation for Seminaries and Universities ordered theology professors to rebut Nazi racist doctrine. In October 1939, Pope Pius XII issued an encyclical *Summi Pontificatus* on the "Unity of Human Society." In November, *Sertum Laetitiae*, his first encyclical letter to the American Catholic hierarchy, declared his "special paternal affection for . . . the Negro people" and their need for "special care and comfort."[44]

Many southern Catholic prelates became more attentive to their region's economic, social, and political problems, including race relations. Consequently, they agreed to the establishment of the Catholic Committee of the South (CCS). Paul D. Williams, a Catholic layman and sociology graduate from Richmond, Virginia, suggested to Monsignor John A. Ryan and Father Raymond McGowan, the director and assistant director of the National Catholic Welfare Conference (NCWC) Social Action Department respectively, the need for a meeting of southern Catholics. Prompted by Ryan, Williams agreed to develop a program for the South for inclusion at the Second National Catholic Social Action Congress held in Cleveland, Ohio, in June 1939.[45]

In developing and generating southern Catholic interest in the program, Williams worked with Peter L. Ireton, Coadjutor Bishop of Richmond and a native of Baltimore, and with Bishop Gerald P. O'Hara of Savannah-Atlanta, a Pennsylvanian, and his diocesan superintendent of schools, Father T. James McNamara, a Georgian. Many southern bishops attended, and some addressed, the Cleveland panels on the South from which emerged a proposal for a coordinating agency to apply Catholic principles to regional issues, including race relations. In April 1940, O'Hara called a meeting of interested people in Atlanta, which established the Catholic Conference of the South, renamed the CCS in January 1941. Over four hundred people, including some African Americans, attended the Atlanta meeting. The CCS did not seek a large membership. Although it underwent organizational changes over time, the CCS and its clergy and lay membership were under the control of the southern bishops who comprised the committee's governing board.[46]

In its early years, the CCS, which focused on ten of the former Confederate states and, at times, also on Texas and Kentucky, struggled financially and organizationally. It never gained unequivocal support from southern prelates. Nevertheless, the committee managed to hold annual, nonsegregated conventions in major southern cities, using hotels, Church property, or other amenable facilities. The CCS and its conventions concentrated on education, rural life, industrial relations, race relations, and youth. During its first few years, the committee relied on Williams, its first executive secretary, to run its operations from Richmond. The CCS depended on southern bishops for financial support, but it was perennially short of funds as some prelates balked at its requests. The CCS annual conventions called for greater efforts to evangelize African Americans, recognition of their worth and achievements, and efforts to address discrimination.[47]

In November 1942, the American Catholic hierarchy addressed race relations in the annual statement issued on its behalf by the NCWC Administrative Board, with Rummel the only southern-based representative on the ten-man board. United States entry into World War Two in December 1941, revulsion at Nazi treatment of Jews and subject peoples in Europe, and *Sertum Laetitiae* led the nation's Catholic archbishops and bishops to call for "acknowledgement and respect" of the rights of "our colored citizens" and to declare that they "should enjoy the full measure of economic opportunities and advantages."[48]

A year later, the American Catholic hierarchy called for African Americans to be accorded their constitutional rights, meaning "not only political equality, but also fair economic and educational opportunities, a just share in public welfare projects, good housing without exploitation, and a full chance for the social advancement of their race." The hierarchy made only indirect reference to race riots and attacks on African Americans that peaked in the summer of 1943, many of them in the industrial North and West to which southern blacks, including many Catholics, had migrated to fill a wartime labor shortage. The prelates noted that "In many of our great industrial centers acute racial tensions exist," and they affirmed "the duty of every good citizen to do everything in his power to relieve them."[49]

Some Catholic advocates of racial equality drew on the doctrine of the Mystical Body of Christ, derived from St. Paul's words in 1 Corinthians 12:12–13. The doctrine argued that all Catholics were members, and all non-Catholics potential members, of the Mystical Body since the Catholic Church was universal and humans were created in the image of God. Any injustice committed against a member or potential member of the Mystical Body was an injustice against Christ, the head of the Mystical Body that united its members through supernatural bonds to one another and to Christ. Pope Pius XI endorsed the doctrine of the Mystical Body and his successor, Pius XII, devoted a lengthy encyclical to it.[50]

Catholic integrationists argued that the Mystical Body rejected racial discrimination, segregation, and exclusion. Although it took some years for Mystical Body thought and teaching to permeate the southern Catholic leadership and Catholic education, even in the early 1940s some Catholics applied it to American race relations. In his 1942 CCS convention address "The Church and the Negro," Father Edward Murphy urged Catholics to "remember that the Mystical Body of Christ is not something to talk about so much as to live by."[51]

Even southern white Catholics who were in sympathy with African American aspirations for equality were divided about the approach to take, given popular southern white support for Jim Crow. The CCS forged links with the Southern Regional Council (SRC), a biracial organization founded in 1944, with headquarters in Atlanta. Like the committee, the SRC advocated equal opportunity within segregation. However, Monsignor T. James McNamara's address to the CCS convention in Memphis in 1944 indicated that some southern white Catholics, albeit a small minority, wanted segregation overturned. McNamara called segregation immoral and urged Catholics "to be militantly sympathetic with the Negro in his struggle." Although CCS conventions drew attention to racial problems, the bishops who governed the committee were unwilling to challenge segregation in southern Catholic institutions. The Catholic Church in the South, for the most part, would only desegregate in the postwar era when segregation crumbled in secular establishments under pressure from the civil rights movement and the federal government.[52]

CHAPTER ONE

An Overview: Catholics in the South and Desegregation, 1945–1970

Catholics increased to 10 percent of the South's population during the civil rights era, aided in part by Sunbelt migration from the North and West. With some exceptions, notably in southern Louisiana, their area of greatest concentration, they lived mostly in urban areas. Although segregation laws did not apply to private institutions in most southern states, most prelates were unwilling to defy segregationist white majority opinion, both Protestant and Catholic, and risk opposition that might undermine their primary duty of preserving and spreading the faith. While some ordinaries and many priests supported or accepted segregation, other Catholic prelates, and some clergy and white laity, were troubled by discrimination inherent in southern segregation and by a growing appreciation that Jim Crow conflicted with Vatican condemnations of racism and support for the doctrine of the Mystical Body of Christ. Nevertheless, whatever their personal feelings, and with few exceptions, prelates ordered desegregation in the postwar decades only in anticipation of, or to correlate with, secular desegregation in their dioceses.[1]

Until at least the mid-1960s, most southern white Catholics, like other southern whites, favored overt segregation. According to a 1956 survey, 80 percent of white southerners disapproved of the *Brown* decision in May 1954 that declared public school segregation unconstitutional and 16 percent favored the ruling. Another poll that year found that 76 percent of southern white Catholics endorsed segregation, 19 percent opposed it, and 5 percent had no opinion.[2]

Catholic segregationists, like Jim Crow's other supporters, varied in their commitment to maintaining racial separation. A minority of Catholic segregationists were militants, unwilling to countenance any change. Some militants defended segregation as God's will, and they included a small number who cited selected biblical verses and texts, invariably drawn from the Old Testament, in justification. A majority of white Catholics were moderate segregationists, who supported segregation as an accepted custom in Catholic and secular institutions. They did not advance a religious defense for Jim Crow, but neither did they regard desegregation as a religious or moral issue. Like many militants, they claimed that secular segregation was a political matter, and they could not understand why the Church was abandoning a practice, they believed, it had long observed. Many moderate segregationists sought to evade the consequences of desegregation, especially when it exceeded tokenism, but, as loyal Catholics, most accepted the authority of the Church to teach and act against segregation, even when they disagreed with its stance.[3]

A minority of southern white Catholics, laity and clergy, were progressives who favored integration and criticized racial discrimination. Even before the *Brown* ruling, some progressives condemned Jim Crow, and a few progressive ordinaries ordered desegregation of Catholic institutions ahead of secular change. Progressive clergy and laypeople disseminated their views in the Catholic press and in organizations they founded, which often produced newsletters and other literature and arranged interracial activities. Some progressives supported, joined, or worked with the National Association for the Advancement of Colored People (NAACP) and, in the 1960s, some also cooperated with other civil rights groups, including in a few cases joining civil rights demonstrations.[4]

Although the Vatican expressed disapproval of racial discrimination through the apostolic delegate to the United States and its newspaper *L'Osservatore Romano*, Rome allowed prelates to administer their dioceses as they thought appropriate to local circumstances, thereby allowing for gradualism in reaching the ideal of inclusiveness without racial barriers. The 1963 papal encyclical *Pacem in Terris* (Peace on Earth) and the Second Vatican Council, held in Rome between 1962 and 1965, condemned racial discrimination and, alongside growing dissemination of the doctrine of the Mystical Body of Christ, encouraged ordinaries to act against segregation.[5]

The postwar migration of Catholics to some parts of the South, especially the Sunbelt, from nonsouthern states seemed to offer a more favorable atmosphere for prelates to act. Although white Catholics living outside the South included supporters as well as opponents of racial separation, some of those who went South were shocked by Jim Crow and urged their new prelates to support its removal. However, some Catholic migrants either adjusted to Jim Crow or took segregationist preferences with them to the South.[6]

The efforts of the Church to convince Catholics of the injustice of discrimination and segregation, together with secular and diocesan desegregation, led some Catholic segregationists to relinquish their views, while others accepted desegregation as a fait accompli. However, many militant Catholic segregationists tried to mobilize Catholic opinion against desegregation and to exert pressure on their ordinaries. Even when desegregation occurred, some militants remained committed to segregation.[7]

Those prelates who were reluctant to desegregate often felt compelled to act when secular desegregation became inevitable in order to satisfy the Vatican, implement Church teachings, protect the Church's image, and widen Catholicism's appeal to African Americans. Even when state segregation laws had not applied to Catholic schools, ordinaries had felt obliged, either from conviction or pragmatism, to apply Jim Crow in their dioceses. Equally, when the civil rights movement and the federal government overturned secular segregation in their dioceses, Catholic prelates followed suit. Ordinaries believed in the rule of law as a religious, democratic, and patriotic duty, and, consequently, they called on Catholics to accept *Brown*, the Civil Rights Act of 1964 that outlawed segregation in public accommodations, and the Voting Rights Act in 1965 that enfranchised African Americans in the South. Despite operating a parochial school system, ordinaries believed that public education was vital for an individual's development and financial security, and for the nation's democracy and economic well-being. Consequently, many prelates supported public education when it came under threat from massive resistance by state governments, or from parents who removed, or contemplated removing, their children from public schools subject to desegregation.[8]

Dioceses sometimes came under direct pressure to desegregate from African American Catholics and, in the second half of the 1960s, from the federal government for noncompliance with civil rights legislation that brought the withdrawal, or the threat of withdrawal, of federal financial support from Catholic schools and hospitals. Some religious orders, which staffed most of the Catholic schools and churches for African Americans, also exerted pressure for desegregation, while, at the same time, the rising costs of Catholic education and a decline in Catholic vocations exerted an additional pressure for desegregation. From conviction about the necessity to move from token desegregation to integration, practical needs, or a combination of the two, in the 1960s and early 1970s prelates merged many black and white schools, discontinued many black schools, and closed black churches or changed them from special racially defined parishes to territorial parishes that covered a geographical area. While many African Americans reluctantly accepted closure of black institutions as the price of integration, others protested these decisions or left the Church altogether as they felt unwelcome in previously white churches and schools, and regretted the loss of institutions that had been at the center of family and community life.[9]

In the quarter century after World War Two, Catholics in the South passed through three stages regarding desegregation. In the first stage between 1945 and the *Brown* ruling in 1954, a few dioceses, mostly in the peripheral South, began limited, piecemeal desegregation. In the second stage, between 1954 and 1965, every southern diocese began parochial school desegregation, with those in the Deep South usually only acting in tandem with, or after, the beginning of public school desegregation. In the third stage, beginning in 1966, dioceses attempted to achieve desegregation in all their institutions, sometimes closing black Catholic churches and schools in the process, or pairing black with white schools.

During the first stage, in the late 1940s and early 1950s, a few Catholic prelates in the South publicly criticized segregation and began the first tentative steps toward removing it from their dioceses. And increasingly, southern ordinaries, albeit sometimes with significant reservations, expressed themselves in favor of black priests, marking a significant shift in policy that, in most dioceses, was not to be realized for many years.

In 1944 and 1945, Archbishop Joseph F. Rummel of New Orleans informed both the Society of the Divine Word (S.V.D.) and the Society of St. Joseph of the Sacred Heart that he would accept black priests from religious orders for service in his archdiocese should their orders wish to send them and that he also favored dioceses ordaining black clergy as secular priests; that is, diocesan clergy directly under diocesan authority. According to Monsignor Charles J. Plauche, the archdiocesan chancellor Rummel had preferred integration at the time of his appointment in 1935 but, aware of the depth of white segregationist sentiment, he had expected a long, gradual, and difficult transition and so acted with caution. Plauche said of Rummel, a childhood German immigrant raised in Pennsylvania and New York, "When he first came here, he didn't move fast to do away with segregation. He did visitations, and any time he saw such things as signs saying, 'This room is for colored only,' he would say take them out." Nevertheless, even in the 1940s, Rummel continued a policy of sanctioning and building black churches and schools inherited from his predecessors.[10]

Whatever Rummel's disposition, there were formidable barriers to creating a black diocesan clergy in the South. Southern seminaries, except St. Augustine's, did not admit African Americans. Although in the 1940s more northern seminaries decided to abandon racial discrimination in admissions policies, many southern black aspirants lacked the necessary funds to attend them. Consequently, the S.V.D. proposed to Rummel that it provide black candidates for the secular priesthood in southern dioceses with initial high school training at St. Augustine's Seminary in Bay St. Louis, Mississippi, after which southern prelates would either fund the completion of candidates' training in northern seminaries or open southern seminaries to them for that purpose.[11]

In February 1946, Rummel sounded out southern bishops and Archbishop John A. Floersh of Louisville, Kentucky, about the proposal, informing them that "Personally, I believe that a way must eventually be found for giving to worthy Colored prospects the opportunity to become diocesan or secular priests." Rummel's letter exposed divisions among the bishops. Floersh, Bishop-elect Charles P. Greco of Alexandria, in Louisiana's northern half, and Bishops William L. Adrian of Nashville and Gerald P. O'Hara of Savannah-Atlanta, whose dioceses covered Tennessee and Georgia respectively, welcomed the S.V.D's proposal, with Greco declaring himself "heartily in favor."[12]

However, Bishops Emmet M. Walsh of Charleston and John B. Morris of Little Rock, whose dioceses encompassed South Carolina and Arkansas, argued that the time was not yet right for black secular priests, who would, they believed, face prejudice and social and geographical isolation as pioneering figures among an otherwise white diocesan clergy. Instead, the two bishops argued that African Americans should be encouraged to become priests of religious orders, which would provide them with support and companionship. In a similar vein, Bishop Thomas T. Toolen of Mobile, a diocese that covered Alabama and the Florida Panhandle, replied, "Personally I feel that we ought to make a start to see if colored priests will work out among the colored people. I feel that it will be better if they were members of a [religious] community rather than seculars."[13]

Bishop Jules B. Jeanmard of Lafayette, whose diocese had a large African American Catholic population, agreed in principle that blacks should be permitted to train for the secular priesthood. However, he argued that his diocese would be unlikely to have vacancies for black secular priests since all of its black parishes were run by religious priests. And he asked, "Even if small parishes were available at that time, how will these priests stand up against temptations to which, living singly, they will be much more exposed, for various reasons, than our white priests?" He worried too that the S.V.D. would absorb the best students, that whites would donate less to collections if their dioceses disproportionately funded impoverished black students, and that "the training of these young men in major seminaries above the Mason and Dixon Line is not likely to fit them very well for the service of poor parishes and for the segregation that exists in the South."[14]

By contrast, Bishop Richard O. Gerow of Natchez, Mississippi's diocese, sided with the S.V.D.'s proposal and held out the prospect that after applicants had completed their lengthy training race relations might have improved, making conditions more amenable for them. Nevertheless, he warned that black secular priests would face isolation and racial prejudice from white diocesan priests, and that blacks trained partly in the North might be unable to readjust to the segregated South. Gerow also feared that local whites would not accept black priests having authority over white nuns who taught in many black Catholic schools.[15]

Whatever the divisions and anxieties among Catholic bishops in the South, successive popes had called for the training of indigenous clergy, and Archbishop Amleto Giovanni Cicognani, the apostolic delegate to the United States, asked Cardinal Samuel A. Stritch of Chicago, the chairman of the American Board of Catholic Missions, to move the southern bishops toward acceptance of black priests. Acting through Rummel, Stritch secured a meeting with the South's prelates after the Catholic Committee of the South (CCS) convention in New Orleans in September 1946. He told them that the Vatican expected them to increase outreach to African Americans, whereupon they agreed to accept suitable black candidates for the diocesan clergy and discussed increasing black parochial school provision.[16]

In November 1946, Rummel called another meeting of southern prelates at the Catholic University of America in Washington, DC, where they were gathered for the American Catholic hierarchy's annual meeting. The southern ordinaries unanimously approved a resolution, proposed by Toolen, that declared their support for diocesan "negro priests" and "pledged mutual cooperation in the training of, and, in the adjustment of, such priests in the various Southern dioceses."[17]

Months earlier, Rummel had offered a practical lead by accepting Aubrey Osborn, a black prospect raised in a Josephite parish near New Orleans, for training for the archdiocese's clergy. After finishing his initial studies at St. John's Abbey Seminary in Collegeville, Minnesota, Osborn and another African American, Bernard Dunn, entered Notre Dame Seminary, the archdiocese's major seminary in 1948, following a seminary poll indicating general student acceptance of African American admissions. In September 1951, Rummel desegregated St. Joseph's College, its preparatory seminary at St. Benedict, and, in May 1953, he personally ordained Osborn, the first African American archdiocesan priest, at St. Louis Cathedral.[18]

In 1947, Bishop Jeanmard accepted a black prospect, Vernon Dauphin, for training for the diocesan priesthood. Dauphin dropped out of St. John's Abbey Seminary in 1948, but another African American, Louis V. LeDoux, ordained by Jeanmard in December 1952, became the first black diocesan priest ordained for a southern diocese.[19]

Vincent S. Waters, who became Bishop of Raleigh in March 1945, a diocese that encompassed most of North Carolina, accepted three African American seminarians for the diocesan priesthood in 1947, and, in 1951, he borrowed a black priest from a northern diocese for work among African Americans in North Carolina. However, the Diocese of Raleigh did not gain its first black diocesan clergy until the late 1950s: Thomas P. Hadden ordained in Rome in 1958 and Joseph L. Howze ordained in Raleigh in 1959.[20]

Ten years earlier, Bishop Gerow, who, as the local prelate for St. Augustine's Seminary, had ordained the majority of African American S.V.D. priests, began a mission in the all-black town of Mound Bayou in the Yazoo-Mississippi Delta under Father John W. Bowman, an African American S.V.D. he had ordained in 1939. But the Diocese of Natchez-Jackson did not ordain its first black diocesan priest until 1974, and some other southern dioceses gained theirs even later.[21]

In the late 1940s and early 1950s, the Church's teachings, especially the doctrine of the Mystical Body of Christ, and personal conviction, combined with an assessment of the feasibility of change in their dioceses, led a few prelates to take some other steps against segregation. The apostolic delegate's concern about both racial discrimination and Catholic neglect of the problem also encouraged ordinaries to act.[22]

Bishop Waters chipped away at segregation. Born in Roanoke, Virginia, in 1904 to a Catholic family, Waters first questioned segregation while studying at St. Mary's Seminary in Baltimore after he had exited a streetcar because an

African American man had sat by him. After seminary, Waters studied at the North American College in Rome, where he was impressed by the devoutness and frustrated desire of its black cook to become a priest. As a consequence, Waters became convinced that race should not be a bar to the priesthood or to Catholicism.[23]

He returned to Virginia from Rome in 1932, serving first as a priest and from 1936 as chancellor of the Diocese of Richmond and personal secretary to its bishop, Andrew J. Brennan. As chancellor, Waters helped orchestrate Catholic involvement in the Virginia Commission on Interracial Cooperation in 1941 and the subsequent establishment of a committee on Catholic Interracial Cooperation. He also promoted interracial discussion meetings between African American leaders and white lay Catholics.[24]

In the Diocese of Raleigh, Waters acted without attracting publicity that might arouse opposition from segregationist Catholics and the white Protestant majority. In 1946, the diocese began gradual desegregation of citywide Catholic societies and diocesan societies, and Waters launched the North Carolina Catholic Laymen's Association (NCCLA) on a desegregated basis. In 1948, the NCCLA and another Catholic society, the Legion of Mary, elected African American officers and held integrated conventions. The diocese also held integrated "spiritual retreats and exercises." A year later, black and white Catholic churches exchanged pastors on one Sunday, and the diocese invited "outstanding Negroes" to address Catholic conventions and priests.[25]

Despite his personal opposition to segregation, Waters made compromises. During 1948, he noted that three black churches were "built on old locations; one new school on a new location; and two on old locations." In 1949, the diocese built new churches for blacks in Salisbury and Sanford. But Waters made his aspirations clear by writing in January 1950 that "It will be some time in North Carolina before we can open our schools to both colored and whites but that time is not as distant as it seemed five years ago." Waters added that the NCCLA had "done good work in gradually harmonizing the races."[26]

He was troubled by racial discrimination and segregation in some Catholic churches. In January 1951, Waters issued a pastoral letter, read at every Catholic church in the diocese, that declared racism "heresy." He argued that the "various nations and races are in one communion in the Church . . . as they form, with their head, the one Mystical Body of Christ in the world." Consequently, pastors were responsible for eliminating segregation in Catholic churches and discrimination in the administration of Holy Communion.[27]

Waters's pastoral letter relied on pastors to enforce nondiscrimination, leaving considerable scope for evasion because he instituted no mechanism to ensure compliance. He recognized that many white Catholic churches continued to practice racial discrimination and so, in February 1953, he issued another pastoral letter. The letter declared:

Every human being [in the Catholic Church] has a right to worship God together with every other member of the human family in the one unbloody sacrifice which God Himself instituted to perpetuate His death on the Cross.

A Church not uniting all races and peoples in one body could not be Christ's Mystical Body.

In affirmation of his position, Waters quoted St. Paul's statement that "There is neither Jew nor Greek, bond nor free, male nor female . . . for you are all one in Christ Jesus."[28]

On June 12, 1953, Waters issued another pastoral letter condemning racism and forbidding segregation in Catholic churches, but in much stronger terms and with greater theological emphasis, linking racism with "the wiles of Satan." The bishop quoted Jesus's teachings regarding the necessity of loving one another. Waters reminded Catholics that in the worldwide Catholic Church, whites were a minority. He also cited Nazi Germany as an example of the consequences of racism: "May the example of our American soldiers, who died to stamp out a philosophy of 'the Master Race' in a war with Hitler in Germany, prevent us from following a similar course." The bishop declared that, if his orders against segregation and racial discrimination in Catholic churches were not followed, he would immediately abolish "all special churches for Negroes." Once again, though, he left pastors with the responsibility of implementing his instructions without offering any special training, preparation, or guidance for them or their parishioners. The *Raleigh News and Observer* reported accurately that "Catholic Directive Brings Few Congregation Changes" since whites and blacks who had worshipped in the same church, or in different churches, continued to do so.[29]

In New Orleans, Archbishop Rummel also tried to steer Catholics toward desegregation. In June 1949, the Seventh Synod of the Archdiocese of New Orleans decreed that "The designation of a section of the church or of pews for the use of either race is forbidden, as is their segregation when they receive Holy Communion." The synod instructed priests to encourage Catholic societies "*to establish committees* [emphasis in the original] devising ways and means for removing disharmony between the races," and it informed clergymen that they "may not deny to Negro Catholics the ministration of the sacraments or sacramentals." Although the synod stressed the need for Catholics to "cast aside" regional customs that conflicted with "divine precepts and Church doctrines," it compromised its bold language by stating that priests "may with charity and prudence suggest" African Americans "frequent the churches specially built for them, *if there are any nearby* [emphasis in the original]."[30]

A month later, Rummel, under pressure from the archdiocese's recently formed biracial Commission on Human Rights and leaders of the black and white Holy Name societies, agreed that the annual Holy Hour parade scheduled for October in City Park would be integrated by having parish societies march in alphabetical order, rather than black parish societies marching after their white counterparts. When the park's board of commissioners refused to accept an integrated parade, the archdiocese twice urged the board to reconsider. When it refused and Holy Name African Americans voted to participate in the procession in defiance, Rummel canceled the Holy Hour observance and released a statement contending that "Certain forms of segregation, and we dislike the term, may be justifiable, but frankly we can see no necessity for the ruling when there is a question of a purely religious observance under circumstances which offer every guarantee of orderliness and disciplinary control." While the *Louisiana Weekly*, an African American newspaper, cautiously welcomed Rummel's action, editor C. C. Dejoie Jr. wrote that Rummel's sincerity would be tested by the action he took to discontinue segregation in the Church "immediately."[31]

In May 1950, Father Joseph H. Fichter, S.J., of Loyola University of the South in New Orleans informed archdiocesan chancellor Plauche that at least seven churches in the city had signs, such as "reserved," or a movable screen designed to maintain segregation during services, and he noted that two of these churches had not used signs in 1949. Furthermore, there were "numerous churches which *enforce segregation* [emphasis in the original] by means of the ushers, but display no signs." Although the archdiocesan synod of 1950 repeated its instructions of the year before regarding segregation, many priests continued to ignore them.[32]

However, Loyola University began partial desegregation. Fichter and another Jesuit priest Louis J. Twomey, who headed the university's Institute of Industrial Relations, which provided noncredit adult education, urged Loyola to admit African Americans. The university rebuffed black applicants, but Father Thomas J. Shields, S.J., its president, changed his mind in 1950, convinced by African American participation in the Korean War that blacks deserved the democratic rights for which they were risking their lives in Korea and by a federal court ruling in September ordering desegregation of Louisiana State University's School of Law. Anxious to avoid publicity that might arouse protest, Shields quietly permitted selective desegregation in the fall when three Sisters of the Holy Family nuns registered for credit-bearing Saturday classes. Twenty African American men also enrolled in Twomey's institute, studying for certificates, and another joined an evening class at the university. By this time, Ursuline College, a female college in New Orleans, had admitted a nun from the Sisters of the Holy Family.[33]

In August 1952, thirty-six Jesuits belonging to the New Orleans Province of the Society of Jesus met at Saint Charles College in Grand Coteau, Louisiana, to devise a common approach to race relations. Although the "the group attending the meeting had no prerogative to determine policy," the meeting accepted that racial segregation was "morally evil" because it "implicitly denies the unity of the human family and the equal rights of all men." The majority of the participants urged the province to desegregate its priesthood, retreat houses, white high schools in areas where there was no black Catholic high school, programs at Loyola University that did not duplicate those offered by Xavier University, and Spring Hill College in Mobile, Alabama. The meeting sanctioned gradualism, with local superiors determining desegregation's implementation. In October 1952, Loyola University's Law School admitted two African Americans, but the university's undergraduate programs continued to bar them, as did the province's retreat houses and high schools.[34]

Segregation and racial discrimination also remained commonplace in the Archdiocese of New Orleans's white churches. In a February 1951 pastoral letter, read in the archdiocese's churches and published in the diocesan newspaper, *Catholic Action of the South*, Rummel informed Catholics that "The principles of Christian charity and justice should prompt us to recognize the Negro as the creature of God, made like ourselves after the divine image and likeness." These "principles," he continued, "should prompt us to cooperate in breaking down painful lines of segregation in the ordinary relations of human life and in the fields of education, industry and opportunity." Rummel called for "equal educational opportunities" and wages that enabled African Americans to enjoy the same living standards as the white majority. Citing the Mystical Body of Christ, the archbishop declared that "The lines of segregation must disappear in our churches, not only physically but in the true spirit of Christian brotherhood, in the seating accommodations, at the confessional, at the Communion rail and in general in the reception of the sacraments and sacramentals of the Church."[35]

In November 1952, at Rummel's instigation, delegates from the Archdiocesan Union of Holy Name Societies, which had separate "colored" and white organizations, voted to form one archdiocesan group. In presenting the resolution for their approval, the archbishop said a merger was "consistent with the teachings of the Catholic Church, of Our Lord and Savior, Jesus Christ, that all men are equal in the sight of God since all are created in the likeness of God."[36]

In March 1953, Rummel issued a lengthy pastoral letter, "Blessed are the Peacemakers," that focused entirely on "making segregation disappear in our Catholic church life." The letter acknowledged that "there still persists in some churches the practice of expecting the Colored to occupy a certain section of pews and to wait at the end of the line for Holy Communion." In calling for these practices to cease, Rummel cited the "Mystical Body of Christ" and observed that "there will be no segregation in the kingdom of heaven."[37]

However, faced with widespread support from white parishioners for segregation and many diocesan priests who were either segregationists or, as Fichter noted, "at best lukewarm to the whole program of desegregation within the church," Rummel was unwilling to attempt to enforce racial equality in parishes, or to institute a widespread educational program to prepare white Catholics for change. Consequently, some churches continued to designate areas for African Americans.[38]

Whereas Rummel was cautious, Archbishop Robert E. Lucey of San Antonio adopted a more direct approach. Born in Los Angeles in 1891, Lucey had grown up in and attended seminary in California. He finished his theological training in Rome, where he was ordained in 1916. After serving several parishes in Los Angeles, Lucey reluctantly accepted appointment in 1921 as director of the Bureau of Catholic Charities for the Monterey–Los Angeles diocese. Exposed to the poverty, deprivation, and wretched working conditions of Mexican immigrants, he developed a commitment to social justice and to Pope Leo XIII's 1891 encyclical *Rerum Novarum* that endorsed unions and state intervention to ensure just wages and humane working hours and conditions. Lucey was also influenced by Pope Pius XI's encyclical *Quadragesimo Anno* (1931) that reaffirmed Pope Leo's teachings but added that workers should be paid enough for them to accumulate savings and warned against untrammeled property rights. Lucey championed organized labor both in California and during his appointment as Bishop of Amarillo, Texas (1934–1941), and as archbishop of San Antonio (1941–1969).[39]

Lucey's commitment to social justice led him to establish the Archdiocesan Committee on Interracial Relations, comprising whites, African Americans, and Hispanics, which produced a pamphlet, *Interracial Justice*, in 1945 that condemned segregation. He also attacked Jim Crow in speeches. In October 1947, addressing the Southwest Regional Conference of the Council of Catholic Women in El Paso, Texas, Lucey denounced "lynching and sins of segregation," and he focused on "the doctrine of the Mystical Body of Christ—new to us but very old in our ancient faith." In 1948, he endorsed a pamphlet, *Race Riddles*, which he sent to his pastors, reminding them that "all men are created equal . . . all of us are brothers in Christ and . . . discriminations against minority groups are a denial of democracy." When the States' Rights Party, or Dixiecrats, organized in the South in opposition to President Harry S. Truman and the national Democratic Party's support for civil rights in the 1948 presidential election, Lucey publicly condemned states' rights for protecting lynchers from justice, allowing discrimination in employment and perpetuating disenfranchisement.[40]

Archdiocesan Vicar General J. L. Manning recalled that Lucey instigated desegregation gradually. Manning explained:

> We learned sometimes to our sorrow that large and/or public meetings on interracial justice were very ill-advised. Thus while still taking advantage of every opportunity that offered itself to give expression to Christian principles we did our real work in small groups of solidly Catholic men. We were soon able to open the doors of the local Council of the Knights of Columbus, our parochial Holy Name Society, St. Vincent de Paul, etc., to Colored men. The next step was in the inter-parochial athletic organizations where the small teams of baseball, volley ball, softball, both

boys and girls, were pitted against each other. This last caused a few raised eyebrows and wagging tongues but it soon died down.[41]

While the Marianists chose to admit an African American to Central Catholic High School in the city of San Antonio in 1952, in other cases, Lucey wrote to Catholic orders that operated elementary and high schools for whites and asked them to begin token desegregation "Because of our larger understanding of the Mystical Body of Christ." In July 1953, Lucey noted that "of thirteen privately owned and operated Catholic high schools in this archdiocese twelve have consented in a spirit of Christian charity and justice to accept one or two Colored students at the opening of the fall term."[42]

By this time, the parish school in New Braunfels—that is, a school belonging to the archdiocese—had admitted seven African Americans, and, Lucey noted, "Several of our Pastors, at our urging, have arranged to accept Colored children in their parish schools next fall." By January 1954, all three of the city's three Catholic higher education institutions had admitted African American undergraduates. Although Texas public schools remained segregated, in April 1954 Lucey ordered all archdiocesan schools "henceforth" to ignore race in admitting Catholic students, and he urged all private Catholic schools to do likewise. While Lucey was undoubtedly aware that the United States Supreme Court was about to rule on the constitutionality of public school segregation, his decision was the culmination of a gradual policy for which the diocese had long instituted a preparatory educational program.[43]

Lucey, Rummel, and Waters all took well-publicized positions against segregation prior to *Brown*, with Lucey achieving most in terms of implementation. However, Lucey led an archdiocese in which the comparatively small African American population meant that desegregation involved only a small number of blacks and therefore appeared less threatening to white Catholics even though most of them, like other whites, preferred segregation. Historian Saul E. Bronder notes that when Lucey ordered parochial school desegregation in April 1954 "only 101 black students were enrolled in the elementary, secondary, collegiate, and graduate schools of the archdiocese."[44]

Other southern prelates avoided issuing pastoral letters about segregation in the pre-*Brown* era, either because they felt no discomfiture or moral qualms about Jim Crow, or they feared that to raise the issue would alienate or divide their laity and clergy, and also expose the Church and Catholics in their dioceses to reprisals from segregationists within or outside their ranks. Many prelates remembered the resurgence of the anti-Catholic and antiblack Ku Klux Klan that began in 1915 and peaked in the 1920s, and some were concerned by the reemergence of Klan and other white supremacist organizations after World War Two. In February 1950, signs reading "The K.K.K. [Ku Klux Klan] Is Looking At You" appeared at St. Elizabeth's, an African American Catholic church in

Selma, Alabama, pastored by Father Norman Lambert of the Society of Saint Edmund, a religious order with headquarters in Winooski, Vermont.[45]

Before *Brown*, many southern prelates continued to attend CCS conventions, which issued statements and resolutions on major issues confronting the South that permitted participating bishops to express their views collectively and thereby lessen the possibility of opposition being directed at them individually. At the CCS convention in Columbia, South Carolina, in January 1951, eleven prelates approved a resolution that called for "the ultimate integration of all members of our Church in accordance with the ideas set forth by Our Holy Father" Pius XII. The presence of apostolic delegate Archbishop Amleto Giovanni Cicognani provided assurance of Vatican approval.[46]

However, the resolution lacked specifics and was much weaker than recommendations made by the convention's race relations workshop, which had called for the abolition of segregation in Catholic churches, diocesan organizations, and hospitals; nondiscriminatory admissions policies in Catholic colleges; race relations education in parochial schools and pastoral letters denouncing racism; establishment of Catholic interracial councils; and liaison with non-Catholic groups committed to racial justice. The workshop had also suggested that the CCS adopt a March 1950 statement by the Vatican's Sacred Congregation of the Propagation of the Faith that asserted: "The major obstacle to the conversion of the American Negro is the attitude of white Catholics themselves." By issuing a general resolution that supported integration without a timetable or method of achievement, the prelates made a gesture in response to Vatican pressure that entailed no firm commitments.[47]

Wary of generating opposition, a few ordinaries took quiet and often unpublicized action against aspects of racial discrimination, while otherwise leaving segregation intact. As far back as 1944, Bishop Toolen, a native of Baltimore, Maryland, had permitted the Dominican Nuns of Perpetual Rosary and Adoration, a cloistered order, to open an integrated convent in Marbury, Alabama. In March 1950, *Look* magazine reported that "The white laity of Alabama is never forced to accept Negroes into Catholic organizations; but the congregations sometimes mingle at mass and colored altar boys serve in many white churches."[48]

In 1945, Bishop William L. Adrian of Nashville, an Iowan, who, like Toolen, seemed untroubled by Catholic segregation, agreed to allow a student from Immaculate Mother Academy, a black Catholic girls' school, to compete with white teenagers in an oratorical contest in Nashville. The event happened without incident, despite anonymous telephone call threats and opposition from some white parents.[49]

Another innately cautious man, who was also acutely conscious of Catholics' minority status, Bishop Gerow of Natchez, a Mobile native, nevertheless responded to appeals from Gulf Coast S.V.D. and Josephite clergy by informing his diocesan priests in June 1951 that "the colored people are not to be discriminated against in any way as regards seating in our churches." Some parishioners at St. Clare's Parish, a white church in Waveland three miles from St. Augustine's Seminary, complained that the seminary had sent Father Carlos Lewis, a black S.V.D. priest, to say Mass in place of their regular pastor, Father M. J. Costello. In February 1954, Gerow wrote to Father Robert E. Pung, the seminary's rector, "If any of the people don't like it, then that is their responsibility and not ours." When Costello became alarmed by further parishioner opposition, Gerow held firm, unwilling to accept any challenge to his authority or disrespect toward the clergy.[50]

Bishop Jeanmard, who had accepted the first black S.V.D. priests in the South, oversaw segregation in his diocese, but, in a November 1951 pastoral letter, he condemned "the official who has recourse to subterfuge in order to rob a citizen, otherwise qualified, of his right to register and vote, because of the color of his skin."[51]

By early 1954, there were further inroads against parochial school segregation, such as high school desegregation in the Diocese of Amarillo, Texas, an area with a relatively small African American population. And Bishop Peter L. Ireton of Richmond, whose diocese encompassed Virginia, declared ten days before the *Brown* ruling in May 1954 that, regardless of the Supreme Court's decision, white Catholic high schools in the city of Richmond would accept African American students in September.[52]

Catholics in the South entered their second stage after *Brown*. The Catholic Church had traditionally called for obedience to the law and respect for authority. Accordingly, no prelate or diocesan newspaper condemned *Brown*, and some in the peripheral South and in the Archdiocese of New Orleans called for its acceptance. Bishop Adrian declared: "This is the law of the land, and it must be obeyed." In July 1954, Archbishop Rummel objected to bills passed by the Louisiana legislature that sought to circumvent *Brown*. He complained that they placed public "education under the state police power, were conceived in an atmosphere of haste, prejudice and controversy and conflict with the federal constitution as interpreted by the supreme court."[53]

With the exception of New Orleans, the ordinaries of dioceses in the Deep South avoided public comment on *Brown*. Wary of the strength of white segregationist sentiment in the region, where African Americans formed a higher ratio of the population than elsewhere in the South, the leaders of the Catholic Church there opted for silence.

Nevertheless, some Catholic orders that worked with African Americans addressed segregation. In July 1954, delegates to the Josephites' general chapter unanimously agreed to create a commission on integration with regional sections "to work with the bishop in order to accomplish integration in the best possible way." The delegates welcomed *Brown*, condemned segregation as an "immoral and a vicious sin," and urged Josephites to strive for integration of "the Negro into Catholic life." The Sisters of the Blessed Sacrament (S.B.S.), which provided many teachers in black Catholic schools, correctly anticipated that implementation of *Brown* would take many years. Accordingly, the S.B.S. regarded its function as unchanged by the ruling, but it altered Xavier University's charter to permit enrollment of white students. In September, Father A. William Crandell, Provincial of the New Orleans Province of the Society of Jesus, issued a statement of policy, based on the province's discussions at Grand Coteau two years before, that declared "segregation, based solely on race, is seriously immoral and therefore, may not be approved by a Catholic" and provided guidelines for the gradual desegregation of the province's institutions.[54]

Before *Brown*, most of the South's Catholic prelates had felt bound by school segregation laws, even though, in most southern states, they applied only to public institutions. After *Brown* changed the Supreme Court's interpretation of federal law, many southern bishops in the peripheral South, who had not acted previously, began some parochial school desegregation, despite, in most cases, acting in states that maintained public school segregation in the hope of delaying and obstructing *Brown*'s implementation.[55]

During the summer of 1954, Bishop Waters instructed the Diocese of Raleigh's high schools to desegregate in September. In August, Bishop Albert L. Fletcher of Little Rock announced that in Arkansas African American Catholic children would be admitted to Catholic schools in places without a black Catholic school. A month later, Bishop Adrian desegregated two white high schools in the city of Nashville, but he left parochial school segregation untouched elsewhere in Tennessee. By September 1954, a small number of African Americans had been admitted to some formerly white diocesan schools in every southern state beyond the Deep South, except Florida. Spring Hill College in Mobile and Belmont Abbey College in North Carolina also desegregated their undergraduate programs. But only one Catholic school in the Deep South, St. Anne School in Rock Hill, South Carolina, run by a religious order, the Oratorian Fathers, was desegregated in 1954. As white southern opposition to public school desegregation intensified and southern state governments adopted a series of instructive measures in the mid-1950s, the CCS ceased its annual meetings and the Archdiocese of New Orleans shelved plans for parochial school desegregation.[56]

In September 1957, Governor Orval Faubus of Arkansas defied federal court-ordered desegregation at Central High School in Little Rock, leading President Dwight D. Eisenhower to dispatch federal troops to ensure implementation. In response to the crisis, Father John F. Cronin, a Sulpician Father from upstate New York who served as an assistant director of the Social Action Department of the National Catholic Welfare Conference (NCWC) in Washington, DC, drafted a statement condemning racial discrimination for consideration by the administrative board that represented the nation's Catholic hierarchy.

Archbishop Patrick A. O'Boyle of Washington, DC, who had persuaded Cronin to include an explicit condemnation of segregation in a revised draft, asked his fellow prelates on the board for their response and found "they didn't want it brought up."[57]

In the summer of 1958, the NCWC sounded out Catholic prelates in the South about a proposal from the Rockefeller Foundation to fund meetings across the region of Catholic clergy to discuss desegregation methods. None of the replies on record supported the idea. Diocese of Raleigh chancellor George F. Lynch explained that Bishop Waters "does not think that such discussions would accomplish any more than the methods already being used by the Bishops of the South in dealing with this problem," neglecting the fact that many prelates were doing little or nothing. Writing on behalf of Bishop Toolen, Diocese of Mobile-Birmingham chancellor Philip Cullen replied, "I will assure you that His Excellency will have nothing to do with the project. The matter here is too delicate for anything like public meetings."[58]

Bishop Fletcher, who had experienced the tensions and passions aroused by the Little Rock school desegregation crisis, believed that the Rockefeller proposals would not "produce any good," and he doubted that desegregation itself was worth the cost involved. He explained: "I am not in principle opposed to desegregation. I think it is a mighty big price to pay for it by sacrificing mutual understanding and charity as well as the justice which the Negro has a right to expect. I don't think we can legislate this matter by desegregation any more than we could temperance by the Prohibition Amendment." Fletcher did not consider that many African Americans favored desegregation as a means of achieving equal treatment and opportunity, and that many southern whites had little understanding of black aspirations and frustrations under a Jim Crow system that imposed inequality and injustice.[59]

Nevertheless, in 1958, Cronin resurrected his proposed bishops' statement on race, despite opposition from a conflicted Cardinal Edward F. Mooney of Detroit. Mooney, who headed the NCWC, feared, as Cronin recalled, that "The statement would split the bishops apart." However, Cronin persevered. A fervent anticommunist, he wrote to Archbishop O'Boyle that if the United States and "the entire world" did not address racial tensions at a time when the United States competed with the Communist Soviet Union for the allegiance of Asian and African nations that were gaining their independence from colonial rule, "the end result will certainly be strife and possibly war and a practical invitation for communism to take over the vast non-white areas of the world." O'Boyle endorsed the statement, arguing that it provided essential "moral guidance to our people" and "the American public will feel that silence on our part would mean acquiescence." Archbishop Joseph E. Ritter of St. Louis also offered Cronin his support, writing, "This is a moral question which demands leadership which only the Bishops can give."[60]

Cronin received a favorable reply from Bishop Thomas K. Gorman of Dallas–Fort Worth and conditional support from Bishop John J. Russell of Richmond. Gorman welcomed the draft's "moderate approach" and added, "Personally, I think some such statement by the bishops might help, but we do have some extremists among us on both sides of the controversy who might not think so." Russell was more circumspect and suggested some relatively minor modifications, explaining that "I can understand why many thoughtful persons feel the need of a statement and can agree to having one if it will be such as not to harm the Church in the South where conditions are hard enough."[61]

Russell explained that the bishops of some southern dioceses had not desegregated any diocesan Catholic schools "lest whites be lost to the Church and non-Catholics . . . be embittered toward the Church." These prelates, Russell argued, believed that "the salvation or loss of souls" was paramount. He quoted an unnamed southern ordinary who asserted that "The principal and primary mission of the Church, as of Christ, is to save souls and not to better the material lot of minorities. This latter the Church should promote, as it is in her competence and missions, but only in a secondary way and not to the detriment of the principal objectives, the spiritual welfare and salvation of her people." While such sentiments should not simply be dismissed as a convenient rationale for inaction, they ignored the fact that segregation and discrimination in many southern Catholic institutions dissuaded some African Americans from joining the Catholic Church and led some to leave it.[62]

Bishop Paul F. Tanner, the NCWC general secretary, sent Cronin's draft statement to apostolic delegate Archbishop Cicognani. After forwarding it to the Vatican, Cicognani received a cable from Pope Pius XII in October declaring, "Statement approved. Let Bishops issue it at once." But the pontiff died a day later. When Cicognani called a meeting to discuss the statement with American cardinals about to leave for the conclave in Rome to elect a new pope, Cronin recalled, "They decided to suppress the cablegram as unofficial, since it lacked the papal seal." The decision infuriated O'Boyle, who asked Cronin to write to Mooney in Rome asking for the statement to be submitted to the NCWC Administrative Board. Mooney did not reply, but Cardinal Francis J. McIntyre of Los Angeles sent a cablegram refusing the request. Mooney died a day later. After the election of Pope John XXIII, O'Boyle invited McIntyre and the sympathetic Cardinal Francis Spellman of New York to Washington, DC, in November 1958. With McIntyre outnumbered at the meeting, O'Boyle prevailed.[63]

When the American Catholic hierarchy gathered at the Catholic University of America two days later for its annual meeting, O'Boyle proposed adoption of Cronin's statement "Racial Discrimination and the Christian Conscience." According to the minutes, eighteen bishops, many of them from the South, "thoroughly considered" the proposal "with particular attention to harm that might be done to work of the Church in some areas" by its publication. Nevertheless, "Despite the difficulty it might cause them, all the Bishops agreed to support the statement if the majority of the Bishops were in favor of making it." Consequently, with Bishop Russell as seconder, the hierarchy, with four dissenters, approved the statement, which was then issued in the name of the American Catholic hierarchy by the NCWC Administrative Board, and widely and favorably reported by the national press and southern diocesan newspapers.[64]

The statement began by quoting from the hierarchy's 1943 statement calling for African Americans to be accorded equal opportunities and their constitutional rights, and expressed the hope that "the overwhelmingly majority of our white citizens" supported blacks' struggle for "their full rights as given to them by God . . . and guaranteed by the democratic traditions of our nation." The bishops cited biblical and papal statements about the universality of the Christian faith and "the great Christian law of love of neighbor and respect for his rights." Appropriating the language of the Declaration of Independence and of the *Brown* decision, they asserted "all men are equal in the sight of God" and argued that segregation "by its very nature imposes a stigma of inferiority upon the segregated people." The statement maintained that "segregation in our country has led to oppressive conditions and the denial of basic human rights for the Negro" and noted that, just two months before, Pope Pius XII had claimed that "The Church has always been energetically opposed to attempts of genocide or practices arising from what is called the 'color bar.'"[65]

However, the bishops cautioned that "Changes in deep-rooted attitudes are not made overnight." Consequently, they advocated a middle ground between "a gradualism that is merely a cloak for inaction" and "rash impetuosity that would sacrifice the achievements of decades in ill-timed and ill-considered ventures." But they did not discuss segregation and racial discrimination in Catholic institutions or suggest a timetable for ending these practices. The statement implied parity between civil rights activists, who were seeking their constitutional rights, and their opponents by asserting the need to "seize the mantle of leadership from the agitator and the racist." Despite its shortcomings, the statement put the Catholic Church in the United States on record against segregation for the first time. Progressive Catholics often cited the declaration when they urged action against segregation and discrimination, and many southern Catholic prelates referenced it when taking or endorsing such action.[66]

Gradualism, largely tied to secular change, became the policy of Catholic prelates in the South who had yet to initiate parochial school desegregation. In July 1959, Archbishop Rummel indicated through a spokesman that it would occur "at the earliest possible opportunity and definitely not later than when the public schools are integrated." When the Citizens' Council enforced a white boycott of two New Orleans public schools that desegregated in November 1960 and segregationists ran riot downtown, the archdiocese postponed Catholic school desegregation indefinitely. Although New Orleans began its second year of public school desegregation peacefully in 1961, Rummel waited a further year before desegregating parochial schools in September 1962.[67]

Other Catholic prelates in the South who began parochial school desegregation in the 1960s generally acted in line with public school desegregation, although some ordinaries desegregated more grades than the public system and most limited African American admissions to white schools to Catholics. As public school desegregation, mandated by federal court orders, often occurred in only a section of their dioceses, prelates sometimes desegregated parochial schools only in those sections, although other ordinaries adopted more widespread action.

Parochial school desegregation commenced in the city of Miami in 1960, a year after beginning in the public system, and in the cities of Galveston and Houston in 1961, along with or after public schools. Although parochial school desegregation did not begin in Atlanta until 1962, two years after the public system, and in Pensacola, Florida, in 1963, a year after public schools, elsewhere it mostly began alongside public school desegregation that was also token. The dioceses of Alexandria and Lafayette in Louisiana were the last in the South to begin parochial school desegregation, acting as public schools desegregated under federal court order in September 1965.[68]

Southern ordinaries came under pressure to desegregate Catholic institutions from the apostolic delegate, Catholic interracial councils, and some African American Catholics. In May 1961, Archbishop Egidio Vagnozzi, the apostolic delegate, declared that "it is essential to progress in the line of integration without ever going back," and he welcomed the fact the United States had 112 African American priests, compared with 7 twenty years earlier.[69]

In 1961, the National Catholic Conference for Interracial Justice (NCCIJ), an unofficial independent Catholic group established in 1960 with the support of many American bishops, began a Southern Field Service under businessman Henry A. Cabirac Jr. in New Orleans. Cabirac, and his successor John P. "Jack" Sisson, worked with and encouraged the formation of Catholic interracial councils, and, with some success, they urged the councils and black Catholics to pressure bishops to desegregate, while at the same offering prelates encouragement and practical advice regarding desegregation and race relations.[70]

Southern prelates also came under pressure from the papacy, the federal government, the wider American Catholic hierarchy, and the civil rights movement. In April 1963, Pope John XXIII's encyclical *Pacem in Terris* declared that "racial discrimination can in no way be justified" and asserted the duty of the oppressed to claim their rights. Civil rights protests, which peaked in the summer of 1963, and concerns about racial violence led President John F. Kennedy to propose a civil rights bill in June to outlaw segregated public accommodations. Thirty-seven Catholic leaders, including bishops from ten southern dioceses, were among 250 of the nation's religious leaders who gathered at the White

House in late June and heard Kennedy urge them to work locally to address the race crisis. As spokesman for the Catholic prelates present, Archbishop O'Boyle stated that civil rights was "now widely recognized as a moral problem and a crusade for basic human rights."[71]

In August 1963, the American Catholic hierarchy issued a widely publicized joint pastoral letter "On Racial Harmony," drafted initially by Father Cronin, that reaffirmed its 1958 statement against segregation and quoted from *Pacem in Terris*. The letter urged Catholics "to make the quest for racial harmony a matter of personal involvement" and affirmed that "We should do our part to see that voting, jobs, housing, education and public facilities are freely available to every American." A week later, Archbishop O'Boyle gave the invocation at the civil rights movement's March on Washington, which 200,000–300,000 people attended, an estimated 10,000 of them or more Catholic clergy and laity who had responded to invitations mostly from nonsouthern prelates and the NCCIJ, one of the march's organizers.[72]

Some S.B.S. nuns were active in the civil rights movement. In 1963, seven nuns joined a march to Atlanta's federal courthouse alongside Martin Luther King Sr. The order's Superior General Mother Mary David (Virginia Young), a Philadelphian, permitted nuns to participate in nonviolent civil rights marches and demonstrations but only by invitation of the local ordinary.[73]

During the summer of 1963, several Catholic prelates in the South issued pastoral letters, or made addresses, urging Catholics to work for racial harmony or accept desegregation. Laypeople also formed several more interracial councils in southern cities. Some ordinaries condemned segregationist violence in their dioceses, among them Bishop Gerow and Archbishop Toolen. However, most prelates were ambivalent toward or opposed to local civil rights demonstrations and clerical participation in them, regarding such protests as endangering law and order and those involved.[74]

In October, the American Catholic hierarchy supported Bishop Robert E. Tracy of Baton Rouge when he successfully urged the Second Vatican Council to adopt a condemnation of racial discrimination. A month later, America's Catholic prelates called for full recognition of African American rights in a statement, "Bonds of Union," issued by the NCWC, in which they lamented "racial injustice in schools, jobs, housing, communal facilities, even in the most obvious area of democratic suffrage."[75]

Some peripheral South bishops, their clergy, and members of Catholic interracial councils urged passage of the civil rights bill, notably in the Archdiocese of San Antonio and the dioceses of Richmond and Galveston-Houston. When the bill became law in July 1964, many Catholic prelates in the South and their diocesan newspapers called for compliance and some, such as Louisiana's prelates, declared that the bill was necessary to "remove and even expunge the causes of past injustices and discriminatory practices." However, lay letters to diocesan newspapers revealed sharp divisions among Catholics about the legislation.[76]

The Knights of Columbus were indicative of divided white lay opinion. The overwhelmingly majority of local councils of the Knights in the South, and across America, were entirely white. In some instances, white members denied African American applicants membership by anonymously blackballing them. In November 1964, at their annual national convention in New Orleans, the Knights changed the rules so that applicants could only be refused membership by a third of those voting, rather than by five blackballs. A very small number of southern councils had African American members, but no southern states were included among the eight state councils (and two Canadian provinces) that called for the change. Despite pressure from several prelates, such as Bishop Russell of Richmond and Bishop Vincent M. Harris of Beaumont, Texas, few councils in the South admitted blacks during the remainder of the decade.[77]

A significant number of white Catholic women in the South were also segregationists. The Catholic Daughters of America, founded in 1903 by members of the Knights of Columbus as a "charitable, benevolent and patriotic sorority for Catholic ladies," had many courts in the South that did not admit African Americans until the civil rights era. Courts in North Carolina did not do so until 1958. In 1962, some white women refused to serve as officers of the Archdiocese of New Orleans Catholic Schools Cooperative Club when Archbishop John P. Cody announced that some African American women would also be officers. The State Court of the Catholic Daughters of America did not agree to end discrimination in its courts in the Diocese of Baton Rouge until 1965.[78]

In 1965, hundreds of priests and nuns from at least fifty dioceses, but only a handful from the South, responded to Martin Luther King Jr.'s call for clergy and religious of all faiths to come to Selma, Alabama, to support protests against African American disenfranchisement that had seen demonstrators beaten and tear-gassed while attempting to cross the Edmund Pettus Bridge. Archbishop Toolen condemned the protests, but a few of the South's prelates allowed priests to participate. To Catholic clergy and lay protesters, their participation was in accord with the Second Vatican Council's call for the Church to be involved in addressing the problems of the world. The Selma protests helped produce the Voting Rights Act of August 1965, which many Catholic prelates in the South and their diocesan newspapers endorsed.[79]

Catholics in the South entered their third stage in 1966, when their dioceses sought to accelerate and complete desegregation. Catholic schools and hospitals came under increasing federal pressure to desegregate because the Civil Rights Act of 1964 and the Medicare Act of 1965 denied federal funds for use in institutions judged not to be in civil rights compliance. Often run by religious orders, some Catholic hospitals in the Deep South initially resisted full desegregation of wards and staff, while others, there and in the rest of the South, worked toward compliance.[80]

Combined with federal pressure, a shortage of vocations to staff schools and escalating running costs encouraged prelates to further desegregation by taking steps to eliminate dual school systems. Federal regulations required dioceses to file desegregation reports or lose federal funds. In the late 1960s, Catholic prelates across the South closed or paired African American schools with white schools in an effort to produce a unitary system. In almost all cases, they retained formerly white schools that were invariably better equipped and better built.[81]

At the same time, many prelates closed black churches to promote desegregation of white churches and to accommodate the withdrawal of many religious orders that had staffed black churches but now suffered from the general decline in Catholic vocations. While some African American Catholics reluctantly accepted the closure of many black churches and schools as a necessary but regrettable price for integration, others protested in vain to their bishops, unwilling to lose valued community institutions which had nurtured them and their families. Some African Americans, especially among the young, left Catholicism. Despite successful examples of integration, many whites were unwilling to accept any more than token desegregation of churches and schools, and they often made African Americans feel uncomfortable and unwelcome. Whites sometimes withdrew from desegregated Catholic schools that had a sizable black enrollment, and many white Catholics joined white flight to the suburbs, where dioceses built new Catholic churches and sometimes schools.[82]

Apart from desegregation, southern dioceses participated in efforts to address the economic consequences of racial discrimination. The archdiocese of San Antonio and the dioceses of Nashville and Galveston-Houston joined Project Equality, an ecumenical program, originally proposed by Father Cronin and initiated by the NCCIJ, in which religious bodies undertook to buy from businesses with equal opportunity policies. Many southern dioceses participated in federal antipoverty programs, such as Head Start for deprived preschool children, and federally financed low-income house building projects. Such actions fitted thinking among mainstream Catholic leaders, and in November 1966 the American Catholic hierarchy issued a statement, "Race Relations and Poverty," drafted by Cronin, that supported "strong governmental intervention at appropriate levels" and called for improved provision for the poor in education, welfare, employment, and housing.[83]

Annual summer riots in African American sections of mostly northern and western cities in the mid-1960s, culminating in further riots in many black urban areas in the country after the murder of Martin Luther King in Memphis, Tennessee, in April 1968, drew national attention to the economic problems of the inner city. The nation's prelates condemned King's assassination when they attended the National Conference of Catholic Bishops in St. Louis, Missouri, later that month and adopted a statement on the "National Race Crisis." The document called for the "total eradication" of racial discrimination from all Catholic institutions and "enactment of critically needed legislation in the fields of employment, housing, health and welfare." It created an "Urban Task Force to coordinate all Catholic activities ... for the common goal of one society." Although strong on rhetoric, the statement lacked measurable targets, and the task force it inaugurated had no enforcement powers and only $25,000 funding.[84]

Southern Catholic prelates continued to close African American churches and schools, convinced such action was essential to achieve integration, rather than token desegregation. When the federal courts ordered completion of public school desegregation in the Deep South by early 1970, the region's Catholic prelates appealed for lawful obedience and support for public education. They also ordered Catholic schools not to accept whites withdrawn from the public system to escape segregation. Some ordinaries temporarily closed schools to new admissions. However, some white parents, sometimes with the connivance of their pastors, managed to relocate their children to parochial schools from the public system or place them in private schools created to evade desegregation.[85]

Even so, by 1970 few southern white Catholics identified themselves as segregationists, and southern Catholic institutions had abandoned overt exclusionary or segregationist practices. Yet, in many cases desegregation of Catholic institutions did not exceed tokenism, and the closure of many black schools and churches had upset and alienated many African American Catholics, leading many of those who had not left the Church to seek recognition, representation, and respect for their distinctiveness within it. Separated in many cases by residence, many black and white Catholics attended churches and schools with people mostly of the same race as themselves. Catholic churches were more likely than their Protestant counterparts to have biracial attendance given the long and distinctive history of many white and black Protestant denominations. Yet, many white Catholic laity, and some of their priests, had not internalized the doctrine of the Mystical Body of Christ and its rejection of race-based distinctions, despite efforts by many prelates and a progressive minority of Catholics. Subject to pressure from the Vatican, the American Catholic hierarchy, African American Catholics, the civil rights movement, and the federal government on the one hand, and southern white culture and southern state segregation laws and practices on the other, Catholic prelates had found significant limitations to the exercise of their hierarchical powers, whatever their personal dispositions.

CHAPTER TWO

The Sociology of Religion and Catholic Desegregation in the South

Sociologists and some historians have attributed the reluctance of predominantly southern white evangelical Protestant denominations to address race relations and desegregation, or to do so effectively, in the civil rights era to the privatization of religion and an emphasis on personal regeneration, bureaucratic concerns, and decentralized polities. By contrast, American Catholic prelates condemned racism and belonged to an episcopal organization that could exercise significant sanctions against those who contravened church discipline. Yet, in practice, the Catholic Church's episcopal polity often did not ensure that statements issued by the hierarchy against racial discrimination and segregation were implemented, or implemented effectually, at the diocesan or parish level. Many of the factors that inhibited evangelical southern white Protestant denominations from taking action, or stronger action, against segregation also influenced Catholic prelates and clergy in the South, sometimes considerably.[1]

Sociologists have often maintained that hierarchical denominations possessed and exercised greater freedom to address controversial issues, including racial segregation, than denominations endowed with less formal authority in a congregational or presbyterian system. In 1972, James R. Wood argued that "The implementation of racial integration values within a denomination depended less on personal commitment of officials than on the freedom from constraint afforded by the structure of their denomination." Subsequently, Meredith B. McGuire contended that "The American Roman Catholic church was able to racially integrate its congregations and schools long before most Protestant denominations or public schools because it used an authority that superseded local authorities and opinion."[2]

In fact, many Catholic prelates in the South, especially the Deep South, tied Catholic school desegregation to public school desegregation, even though they possessed the authority to act against segregation and the papacy, the apostolic delegate to the United States and the American Catholic hierarchy condemned racial discrimination. The approach of Catholic prelates to racial matters was influenced, to a considerable degree, by local secular and Catholic opinion and pressure, and by bureaucratic and organizational imperatives, as well as by their own personalities and views on race. Appointed by and subject to the authority of their prelates, priests might have been expected to accept and implement their ordinaries' wishes, regardless of personal opinion and the sentiments of their parishioners, but this was not always, or necessarily, the case.

The Vatican appoints and exercises authority over cardinals, archbishops, and bishops, but as historian R. Bentley Anderson explains, "Rome did not meddle in local affairs, as the papacy concerned itself with matters of faith and doctrine." The apostolic delegate to the United States served as "an intermediary between the hierarchy of the country and the Holy See" and held "precedence over all members of the [American] hierarchy, except Cardinals." Responsible to the pope, ordinaries—that is, bishops who headed dioceses—exercised "his delegated authority in their dioceses" as they believed appropriate, which brought disparity in their approaches to segregation and its removal. In 1961, apostolic delegate Archbishop Egidio Vagnozzi explained that, although there should be continued progress in integration, "The Holy See has full confidence in the American Bishops, and each Bishop in his own diocese will have to decide what measures to take and what changes to be adopted." Dioceses were grouped together in provinces headed by the senior prelate among them, but ordinaries retained the right to independent action in their dioceses, although they sometimes acted together or issued joint declarations.[3]

Prelates appoint and direct secular—that is, diocesan—priests, with the power to transfer them to other parishes or duties, and to punish them for disobedience by means such as suspension and, in extreme cases, excommunication from the Church. Congregations have no formal authority over their priests. Religious priests, meaning priests who belong to religious orders, and nuns serve in a diocese with the agreement of the prelate. Ordinaries invite orders of priests and nuns from different parts of the United States and, sometimes, from abroad into dioceses to serve designated churches, schools, hospitals, and other institutions. A prelate cannot prevent an order withdrawing from his diocese, but he can compel its withdrawal and request the removal of any of its priests and nuns that displease him. Prelates exercise control over all diocesan institutions but have no direct authority over any hospitals and schools that are owned and administered, rather than merely staffed and serviced, by religious orders.[4]

Appointed by and serving at the ordinary's discretion, a board of consultors, comprising a group of senior priests, performed an advisory function and served renewable three-year terms. There was no requirement for ordinaries to follow their consultors' counsel, and they did not have to seek their advice. In the late 1960s, as part of the Second Vatican Council's reforms, dioceses created senates of priests to provide all clergy with a forum and to serve ordinaries in an advisory capacity. Although not bound by the senates' recommendations, many prelates treated the senates as consultative bodies, while a few, such as Bishop Vincent S. Waters of Raleigh, clashed with them and dismissed their views.[5]

Canon law governs the operations of the Catholic Church and applies to clergy and laity alike. Lay Catholics have a duty to attend Mass and confession and observe Holy Days and Catholic teachings. They must marry in the Catholic faith and baptize and raise their children as Catholics. Traditionally, parents were required to send their children to Catholic schools, except in exceptional circumstances specifically agreed by their prelate, or, in the absence of a Catholic school, ensure that their offspring received "Christian training and instruction." When available, children were to attend a Catholic school in the parish where they lived. In segregated Catholic school systems, African American Catholic children were required to attend a designated black Catholic school. In the absence of such a school, black students could attend a public school, providing their parents, like other Catholic parents, ensured their children received appropriate "religious and moral training." Unless they belonged to a national parish, designated for a particular ethnic group, or to a personal or special parish, catering to African Americans, Catholics were traditionally obliged to attend the church of the parish in which they resided, called a territorial parish. In theory, and often in practice, African American Catholics could attend a territorial church, although, in the segregation era, they were often denied membership in white churches and, sometimes, forced to sit at the back of a white church or in designated pews, and frequently given communion after white parishioners.[6]

The papacy conveys its thoughts or positions to the Catholic world through encyclicals and other pronouncements. However, in 1955, Henry C. Bezou, superintendent of schools for the Archdiocese of New Orleans, explained that "The Holy Father does not address an Encyclical Letter to a city, state, region, or country nor does he settle a local problem or treat a regionally circumscribed issue through an Encyclical," because it is "intended for the whole Catholic world." Hence, although the pope might discuss racism in an encyclical, he would not, Bezou implied, address a regional matter, such as segregation in the southern United States.[7]

The papacy could convene synods and councils to discuss and decide church governance, doctrine, and teachings. Catholics are obliged to follow papal (and bishops') "instructions and propositions." Historian Richard D. Cross explains that "According to canon law, the Church, and ultimately the Pope, exercised final authority over Catholics in all religious matters" and, "through clerical instruction of individual Catholics," it "also possessed an 'indirect' power over the faithful in all secular matters when they affected spiritual interests." Although not carrying the same weight as papal pronouncements, reports and editorials on Vatican radio or in the Vatican newspaper, *L'Osservatore Romano*, indicate Vatican thinking and have "semi-official" status. Cardinals, archbishops, bishops, and the editors of diocesan newspapers often echoed or cited papal or Vatican condemnations of racism, when they denounced segregation or justified desegregation.[8]

Most prelates exercised tight control over diocesan newspapers. Their editors served at the prelates' behest and generally reflected their views. In February 1964, for example, the Reverend Francis R. Moeslein, editor of the *North Carolina Catholic*, declined to publish a letter critical of integrationist Father Louis J. Twomey, S.J., director of Loyola University of the South's Institute of Industrial Relations in New Orleans, because "I am sure Bishop Waters would not like to see a controversy in this field."[9]

Until 1966, the administrative board of the National Catholic Welfare Conference, comprising bishops elected by, and from among, the nation's Catholic prelates and cardinals, issued annual statements in the name of the American hierarchy. These expressions of Catholic principles and teaching were widely reported in Catholic, and sometimes secular, newspapers, and often cited in prelates' pastoral letters. Individually or collectively, Catholic prelates issued pastoral letters that were read at Mass in Catholic churches and published in diocesan newspapers. Such letters were educative and informative about the Church's teachings and doctrine, and, often, they also announced diocesan policy, such as desegregation of Catholic schools or other institutions.[10]

Statements by the papacy, Vatican sources, and American prelates staked out positions on race and segregation that were more progressive than those held by most of the southern white Catholic laity. They substantiate sociologists Charles Y. Glock and Rodney Stark's argument that "The church does not merely support the *status quo* [emphasis in the original], nor merely follow the lead of its parishioners in the formulation of its social and economic policy. [T]he church is in fact ahead of (more liberal than) its laity on most issues. It is more receptive to social change than its parishioners."[11]

Canon law obliged Catholics to follow the teachings of their local prelate. A Catholic school syllabus explained that "Although the Bishop is not personally infallible, he shares in the infallibility of the 'teaching' Church when he teaches what is taught throughout the world by his fellow Bishops, in union with the Holy Father." Citing Pope Pius XII and canon law in support, in 1956 the *American Ecclesiastical Review* maintained that except in the unlikely circumstance that a prelate(s)'s teaching was at variance with papal teaching, Catholics were "obliged to accept the doctrines officially proposed by their respective local Ordinaries." In 1964, Catholic columnist Dick Meskill asserted that "The Archbishop, as the Apostolic Successor with whom, as Brothers of Christ we are most associated, has powers in this diocese commensurate with those of the Pope in the Universal Church." Although Catholics might follow their conscience, they also had an obligation to recognize the virtue of prudence, "meaning obedience to authority and church doctrine."[12]

Just as prelates had sanctions available against recalcitrant priests, they also had disciplinary measures they could apply to disobedient laity. An ordinary could issue a warning, and he could deny a Catholic the right to hold office or otherwise participate in diocesan societies. He could declare individuals guilty of a reserved sin that could "be absolved (forgiven) only by the Bishop of the diocese after those involved have shown sufficient proof of change of disposition." Having first warned them, a bishop could interdict disobedient Catholics, barring them from the sacraments while still regarding them as within the Catholic fold. Excommunication, a higher sanction, expelled those affected from the Church altogether, until they did penance deemed satisfactory by the prelate who had excommunicated them or by a priest authorized by the prelate to remove the penalty. Excommunicates were not only denied the sacraments, they could not act as a sponsor at a baptism or confirmation and, if "under a special condemnatory or declaratory sentence," a severe type of excommunication, receive a Catholic burial. Catholic polity, then, gave bishops great power to run their dioceses as they saw fit and, if necessary, to discipline priests and laity.[13]

However, the Catholic Church in the South was shaped to a significant degree by many of the same pressures as the mainstream white Protestant denominations to which most southern whites in the region belonged. Glock and Stark note that the Church is "an adaptive institution in society, an institution which is prone to compromise with the dominant secular point of view." Beginning in the late nineteenth century and extending, in some cases, to the 1960s, Catholic prelates in the South built separate missions, churches, schools, and other diocesan institutions for African American Catholics that mirrored secular Jim Crow, even though most southern states did not mandate segregation of private educational institutions.[14]

Although some Catholics in the civil rights era attempted to justify the Church's initial adoption of segregation on the basis that its variance with Christianity had not at that time been evident, revealed, or clarified, or even claimed that the Church had never adopted segregation, others conceded that the Church had practiced segregation as a pragmatic way to minister to whites and African Americans in a segregated society. Bishop Charles P. Greco of Alexandria, Louisiana, claimed in a 1963 pastoral that the Church had not approved of segregation "as a matter of principle" but had "worked within the framework of an existing segregated society because, true to her nature, she considered the care of individual souls, the administration of the sacraments and Christian education her primary and essential task." In 1964, two Charleston priests, Leo Croghan and Eugene Kelly, argued that "It must be always kept in mind that the Church's intention was not the segregation of the Negro but rather the service of the Negro in the only place in which he could be reached. Because of the pressures of society it would have been impossible in many instances to reach the Negro in any other way."[15]

Many prelates also regarded separate Catholic institutions for African Americans as necessary to keep black Catholics in the faith and as a means to evangelize black Protestants. When available, African American Protestants often sent their children to black Catholic schools because they provided a better education than the black public school system and, sometimes, parents and children became Catholic. Frequently, Protestants formed the majority of enrollees in black Catholic schools. Medical care in black Catholic hospitals was a religious act of charity that also served an evangelistic function.[16]

By practicing segregation, the Catholic Church helped bolster it in the South. Glock and Stark argue that "the church seldom acts to foster social change but rather functions to preserve the *status quo*." Fathers Croghan and Kelly claimed that "Since the Church, especially in the South, developed within a slave and segregated society, the institutions of the Church (e.g. parishes, schools, hospitals, religious communities) reflected the influence of that society."[17]

Catholic churches began to observe segregation in heavily Catholic southern Louisiana as the races became subject to secular segregation laws in the 1890s. In other areas of the South, the very fact that Catholics were a minority, and one that many Protestants were suspicious of, or openly hostile to, encouraged the Catholic Church to emulate secular segregation in its institutions, rather than risk incurring the animosity of Protestant segregationist whites. The Ku Klux Klan was anti-Catholic as well as antiblack, and many southern white Protestants harbored hostility toward and suspicion of the Catholic Church. Many southern white Catholics, especially among the laity, supported segregation as a desirable social norm, and some of them believed that God favored segregation. In 1956, a white Catholic mother in Virginia admitted that "I'm more Southern than Catholic when it comes to colored children in our schools." Although he ignored a diversity of opinion among them that went beyond region, in 1968, Auxiliary Bishop Harold R. Perry of New Orleans, the first African American Catholic bishop in the South, commented, with some justification, that among whites "We have a Southern attitude or a Northern attitude no matter what our religious beliefs are."[18]

Catholic prelates and clergy in the South did not defend segregation as biblical or as sanctioned by God, but the Church's practice of segregation not only met the wishes of many southern white Catholics, it provided de facto justification for, and even encouraged, segregationist sentiment. Furthermore, until the civil rights era, the region's Catholic bishops, for the most part, did not condemn segregation as unchristian, or as being at odds with Church doctrine. Consequently, as Bishop Greco explained, "From what they saw, our Southern [white] Catholics formed their conscience as to the moral lawfulness of segregation. They concluded that if the Church practiced it, it must be right and therefore had the approval of God."[19]

There were some common themes in the southern Catholic and evangelical Protestant denominations' experience that affected their approach to racial issues. In 1967, historian Samuel S. Hill Jr. argued that southern white evangelical Protestantism's primary emphasis was converting "the lost from a state of guilt before God the Righteous Judge in a datable experience of salvation." Evangelicals focused on individual sin and "the purity of private morality" and did not develop a social ethic. "The white Christian's duty toward the Negro, as seen by the southern church," Hill contended, "is to convert him and befriend him (in a paternal framework), not to consider altering the social traditions and arrangements which govern his (and everyone else's) life to so significant a degree." Evangelical southern white Protestantism, Hill believed, "restricted its concerns largely to the conversion of individuals, the cultivation of piety, and institutional expansion." Although subsequent historians noted that Hill neglected social Christianity among mainstream Protestant denominations in the South, his observations have some congruence with southern white Catholicism.[20]

The Catholic Church did not advocate born-again Christianity, and its members, clergy and laity, were generally much less aggressive about evangelism than evangelical Protestants. Catholic prelates in the South, like their counterparts elsewhere in the nation, supported hospitals and orphanages in a form of social Christianity. Although the papacy began to develop social doctrines in the late nineteenth century, it seldom condemned racism until the late 1930s when it attacked racist Nazi and Fascist practices and doctrines. Until, and in some cases even during, the civil rights era, Catholic prelates in the South regarded their duties to African Americans much as Hill described those of evangelical Protestants: that is, to minister to blacks and help them with paternalistic concern in a segregationist framework. Bishop Greco explained:

> The initiation of social reforms could not be allowed to take precedence over the all important work of sanctifying souls. Had the Church undertaken to remove segregation from the Southern scene, her effectiveness in carrying out her fundamental spiritual mission would have been seriously hampered, and many souls would have gone without the supernatural graces that could come to them only from having the Church active in their midst.[21]

In 1965, sociologist William A. Osborne offered an interpretation of American Catholicism that was similar, in some ways, to Hill's view of southern white evangelical Protestantism. Osborne wrote:

> In interviews with bishops and priests it appeared that their central concern was for what we might call the "salvational process." Their responsibility to the Negro meant a responsibility to provide churches, priests, novenas, retreats and a Catholic education (elementary, usually), and this invariably transcended their concern for the socio-economic welfare of the Negro.

Although some southern prelates, drawing on papal teachings, began, in the 1940s and subsequently, to emphasize the immorality of racism and segregation and the doctrine of the Mystical Body of Christ, many Catholics, especially among the laity, remained wedded to a traditional Catholic theology that "promises salvation to him who avoids mortal sin and frequents the sacraments." Such Catholics did not regard segregation as sinful, especially as the Church had long practiced it and, in many dioceses, continued to do so. The many Catholics who conceived of their religious duty as avoiding personal sin and receiving the sacraments developed little sense of social responsibility.[22]

Sociologists have stressed the importance of the social location of religion in influencing a denomination's response to social change. Like other major Christian faiths in the United States, the Catholic Church was subject to privatization "by which," Meredith B. McGuire explains, "certain differentiated institutional spheres (e.g., religion, family, leisure, the arts) are segregated from the dominant institutions of the public sphere (e.g., economic, political, legal) and relegated to the private sphere." Father Joseph B. Gremillion, pastor of Shreveport, Louisiana's St. Joseph Church, argued in the mid-1950s that "Bringing God into the private life of the person is *sine qua non*, but some short circuit has obstructed the expected overflow of godliness into the public life of society. Private morality is insulated from public morality." In 1959, Father Louis J. Twomey lamented:

> One of the most disturbing features of the current controversy is the refusal of countless Catholics, many priests included, to accept the racial doctrine of the Church. Through one rationalizing route or another they somehow arrive at the conclusion that the race problem is purely political and social and hence beyond the competency of the Church.[23]

Although Catholic prelates could order desegregation of diocesan institutions, privatization significantly limited their ability to influence their laity's social, economic, and political outlook. Many parishioners objected when a prelate or priest opposed massive resistance to public school desegregation, supported civil rights legislation, or endorsed or participated in the civil rights movement. Such parishioners argued that the Church should not involve itself in politics and should instead keep to religion. In November 1955, a layman complained to Bishop Jules B. Jeanmard of Lafayette that "The problem you are trying to deal with is social and political and not religious. Besides, the church's power in that regard is nil, to say the least." Sociologist Peter L. Berger noted that privatization explains "why the churches have had relatively little influence on the economic and political views of even their own members, while continuing to be cherished by the latter in their existence as private individuals." In 1967, a national survey for *Newsweek* reported that only 21 percent of Catholics felt "bound to respect a priest's exhortation to integrate their neighborhoods," and, a year later, a Gallup poll found that 57 percent of Catholics believed that "churches should avoid involvement in political and social issues."[24]

Many Catholics rejected the Church's social teachings. In 1951, Bishop William T. Mulloy of Covington, Kentucky, told the Catholic Committee of the South's convention that "It is due time that Catholics come to realize that they cannot excuse themselves from grave sin if they deliberately disregard or deride the contents of the social Papal Encyclicals." Some Catholics lacked interest in the Church's social teachings and were largely ignorant of them. Referring to Louisiana members of the Knights of Columbus, Father Gremillion questioned "How many Knights really grasp what those social encyclicals are all about? that socio-economics must be subject to the moral law of Christ's justice and love?" In 1963, Archbishop Robert E. Lucey of San Antonio lamented that "For many years I have tried to organize study clubs on that doctrine [the social doctrine of the Church] and my success has not been spectacular. Our men seem to shy away from Catholic social teaching." In 1966, the *Catholic Virginian* editorialized that "Statements from popes and bishops . . . may frequently go unread."[25]

Some Catholics lacked familiarity with the Church's social teachings because the Church had made insufficient efforts to instill such knowledge. Father Gremillion believed that among Catholic lay organizations "The critical problems daily headlined are barely touched by group awareness or action, nor by the individual Catholic conscience. In their programming our organizations seem quite insulated from 'outside' realities like industry-labor tensions, race relations, plantation tenancy." In 1961, Father Louis J. Twomey told an interviewer:

> For too long, we priests and we nuns and we lay people in the classroom have given the idea that being a good individual is confined to certain compartments of human living; it is not taught as a way of life. Most of the Catholic college graduates that I have met have little or no knowledge of the papal social encyclicals.

In correspondence, Twomey often lamented the prevalence of "compartmentalized Catholics," meaning "Catholics who are well trained in private and family morality, but hardly trained at all in social morality."[26]

The bureaucratic nature of the Catholic Church tended to limit prelates' engagement with social issues or relegate them to secondary importance. Peter L. Berger noted "the progressive bureaucratization of the religious institutions," which selected staff from, and shaped, personalities who were "activist, pragmatically oriented, not given to administratively irrelevant reflection, skilled in interpersonal relations, 'dynamic' and conservative at the same time." Administrative ability was an essential prerequisite for appointment to bishop, archbishop, or cardinal. "Bishops and other ecclesiastical officials hold their posts," William A. Osborne observed, "not usually because of their prophetic or spiritual qualities, but generally because of desirable and necessary abilities for the effective command of a complex organization." Once in office, the everyday demands of running their dioceses often took precedence for prelates and chancery officials over tackling segregation or other social issues.[27]

In 1964, an unnamed New Orleans priest commented that "Archbishop [John P.] Cody is preoccupied with perfecting the administrative machinery of his diocese. Consequently he is reluctant to 'rock the boat' of the existing social structure." A year later, Osborne observed that "Building more schools, financing or seeking the manpower to operate them, and reforming their curricula all add up to a first priority on most diocesan agendas." Prelates often prided themselves on increasing the number of Catholic schools, churches, missions, medical facilities, and coreligionists in their dioceses, and success in these activities was an important factor in promotion to a larger or more prestigious diocese or to an archdiocese, or to receiving other recognition, such as the personal title of archbishop.[28]

Furthermore, for decades, there was no bureaucratic imperative to abolish segregated Catholic institutions since there was no papal pronouncement that specifically condemned racial segregation and canon law did not address the subject. However, in the second half of the 1960s, the threatened loss of federal funds to Catholic schools and hospitals for noncompliance with civil rights legislation, and the need to merge Catholic schools and churches as declining vocations forced the withdrawal of many of the religious orders who staffed them, provided an administrative rationale for desegregation of Catholic institutions, in addition to moral justifications and pressure advanced from within and outside the Church. Consequently, in the mid-1960s and early 1970s, Deep South dioceses that had largely maintained segregation began to desegregate, or, along with most other southern dioceses, accelerated desegregation, usually by amalgamating black and white churches and schools.[29]

Prelates who wished to desegregate their dioceses faced formidable practical difficulties. Although in theory, the Catholic Church's episcopal polity gave them great authority to act, in practice their exercise of that authority was often shaped and limited by pressures emanating from within and outside the Catholic Church. Ordinaries made different assessments of their powers, and these calculations often influenced their willingness to act, or the manner in which they acted, on behalf of desegregation. In 1971, after the Second Vatican Council and the social reform movements of the 1960s had helped foster clergy and lay assertiveness, Bishop Ernest L. Unterkoefler of Charleston, an advocate of desegregation, said that "We have parish lines but no one observes them. One word and the people do what they please, if it comes from me." Asked two years earlier to comment on priests who had taken part in demonstrations supporting African American hospital workers striking for union recognition and increased pay in Charleston, Unterkoefler replied, "I can't coerce them one way or another. We don't run a gestapo state in the church. They have rights as American citizens and this has to be recognized whether they are priests or laymen."[30]

Understandably, many bishops were reluctant to act against, or without, majority clergy support in their dioceses. In 1967, Tom Gibbons of Project Equality, a projected nationwide church program that would require churches to do business with equal opportunity employers, reported that Bishop John L. Morkovsky of Galveston-Houston favored the program's adoption, but "he wants the priests in the diocese along with him if at all possible."[31]

Some prelates consulted with or sought approval from their priests regarding desegregation. In 1954, Bishop William L. Adrian of Nashville allowed priests in the deaneries of Memphis and Nashville to vote on parochial school desegregation. Adrian accepted the outcome by initiating Catholic school desegregation in the city of Nashville but leaving segregation intact in Memphis's Catholic schools, since priests in the Memphis deanery believed that many white Catholics, including some of the clergy, were not ready for school desegregation.[32]

In 1961, when Bishop Wendelin J. Nold of Galveston-Houston ordered desegregation of parochial schools in Galveston and Harris counties, he informed pastors there that "This step was not taken without long and mature deliberation, nor without first advising with the Diocesan Consultors and with a representative number of Pastors, both secular and religious, and carefully weighing their recommendations and suggestions."[33]

In June 1963, when Bishop Francis F. Reh of Charleston announced, after only a year in office, that Catholic schools in the diocese would desegregate the following year he indicated that he had acted only after consulting his priests at an annual retreat. A New Yorker, conscious of his status as an outsider, Reh emphasized the predominantly indigenous origins of his priests. He declared: "It was by no means a decision by me alone—by a man adopted by the South only a short time—but rather by me and the majority of the state's Catholic clergy who are more than 50 percent South Carolinians themselves, and many of them Charlestonians."[34]

Opposition from powerful figures within a diocese could inhibit a prelate from acting. In May 1966, the National Catholic Conference for Interracial Justice (NCCIJ) organized a private consultation on race relations in Jackson, Mississippi, attended by twenty-five priests from several southern dioceses. A participant observed: "The point was made that in most dioceses the existing power structure, those who are consultors or pastors of large parishes, are not interested and sometimes even opposed to interracial justice. Some felt that some ordinaries were reluctant to push the Negro question too strongly."[35]

Nevertheless, prelates had powerful means available to them to ensure obedience with desegregation orders, chiefly the prestige of their office and their disciplinary authority. Although segregationist opposition from within and outside Catholic ranks led Archbishop Rummel to postpone parochial school desegregation repeatedly until the fall of 1962, when the order came the vast majority of Catholics acquiesced. Loyalty to the Catholic Church, rather than commitment to desegregation, accounted, in many cases, for their response. Father John Reedy, editor and publisher of the national Catholic magazine *Ave Maria*, observed: "We have the impression that Catholic faithful may be complying with the school integration edict, but many white parents are sincerely distressed. We feel that all too many are obeying their religious leaders *only* [emphasis in the original] out of a sense of obedience."[36]

Obedience was not confined to New Orleans. In March 1964, a few months after Catholic school desegregation had begun in the city of Charleston, Joseph L. Bernardin, the Diocese of Charleston's chancellor, reported that "Many Catholics have told me and a number of our priests that, although they may not like it, they will go along with the Church's teaching and policies regarding racial justice." Their obedience may also have been influenced, at least in part, by their bishop's earlier firm response to Catholic segregationist opposition in the city.[37]

In February 1961, Bishop Paul J. Hallinan of Charleston had issued a pastoral letter stating that he would desegregate parochial schools not later than the public system. The Organization of Catholic Parents, a group of Catholic segregationists in the city of Charleston, responded by proposing to open a private Catholic school. Hallinan squelched the plan by threatening to inform parents that the school was "not approved to teach the Catholic religion" and would not "satisfy the moral obligation of providing a Catholic education" for their children. The bishop also warned that he would, in the first instance, deny members of the Organization of Catholic Parents "participation in the privileges or activities of Catholic life beyond those of a strictly sacramental or moral nature." Members would thereby be ineligible "to hold office or committee assignments in Catholic societies." If they continued to defy the bishop's wishes, he would excommunicate them.[38]

However, prelates' use of their disciplinary authority often produced mixed results as Bishop Waters found in Newton Grove, North Carolina. Waters was a blunt autocrat, not given to consultation, who expected his orders to be obeyed by clergy and laity alike. Without prior consultation and with only a month's notice, he ordered the merger in 1953 of an African American and a white church that lay two hundred yards apart in Newton Grove. Father Timothy O'Sullivan, a Redemptorist Father (that is, a religious priest), who pastored both churches, privately urged Waters to reconsider, but the bishop refused. He also declined to meet with parishioners who had written to him protesting the merger decision. Waters replied that "The Catholic Church does not get its teaching from the laity but from Christ. It teaches the laity in the Name of Christ. The Catholic Church does not obey the mandate of the laity but of the Pope, the Bishop, the Priest and the people obey the mandate of Christ through them. I shall see you only after you have obeyed this command."[39]

Unannounced, Waters appeared at the church on the day of the merger to lead services and ensure enforcement of his order, despite protests from an intimidating mob that gathered outside. Most of the parishioners, African American and white, stayed away either because they had anticipated trouble or because they feared the mob that jeered Waters and those entering the church. The merged church at Newton Grove lost many of its parishioners and, even five years later, African Americans and whites sat on opposite sides of the church during Mass.[40]

Archbishop Rummel's attempt to use his authority against segregationists in Jesuit Bend, sixteen miles from New Orleans, was largely ineffective. In October 1955, Father Gerald Lewis, a black Panamanian priest from the Society of the Divine Word (S.V.D.), went to St. Cecilia's Chapel in Jesuit Bend to say Sunday Mass. When Lewis arrived, he found two armed policemen standing in front of the chapel. Three white parishioners told the priest he could not celebrate Mass or go into the church. Reluctantly, Lewis left without giving a service. In response, Rummel suspended services at the chapel using an interdict, and said he would permit only one Mass at churches in neighboring Myrtle Grove and Belle Chasse until the area's Catholics indicated "their willingness to accept for service in these churches whatever priest or priests we find it possible to send them." The archbishop kept this instruction in force as white residents formed a Citizens' Council to defend segregation and supposedly 250 Catholics signed a petition to Rummel affirming their opposition to the sending of the black priest. Praised by *L'Osservatore Romano* for his "prompt [and] admirable" action, Rummel kept the interdict in place until April 1958 when a few families signed a letter of repentance. St. Cecilia's Chapel reopened with segregated services. The chapel's destruction in a hurricane during the summer removed the immediate problem and it was not rebuilt.[41]

In the neighboring Diocese of Lafayette, Bishop Jeanmard used excommunication against segregationist opposition in Erath, which emerged two months after segregationists had turned Lewis away from Jesuit Bend. With Jeanmard's approval, Our Lady of Lourdes Church, the only Catholic church in Erath, had long held catechism classes for children who attended public schools. Black children sat at the back of the church and white children at the front. However, in 1954, the classes moved to a smaller location in a new church school building with the children still segregated but seated much closer together. Unfounded rumors began to circulate that the classes would integrate by seating students alphabetically and serve as a test case for integration of other church schools. Alarmed by the rumors, two segregationist Catholics, Etta B. Romero and her sister Lota B. Menard, assaulted a white catechism teacher, Lula B. Ortemond, in November 1955.[42]

One week later, Jeanmard excommunicated the two assailants "until such time when they shall have repaired the scandal they have caused to the Church." The bishop warned that he would automatically excommunicate anyone "who, by threatening violence, or by spreading malicious gossip, dares to interfere" with

Our Lady of Lourdes's priest or catechism teaching, or who removed the decree, which he ordered "attached to the doors of the Church" after it was read at Mass. Jeanmard added that "Any further act of violence that may occur within the parish of Our Lady of Lourdes in connection with the work of the Church will result in the closing of the Church." Within days, the two women repented. Jeanmard removed their excommunication and the catechetical classes restarted. A month later, apostolic delegate Archbishop Amleto Giovanni Cicognani wrote to Jeanmard praising his "prompt and wise action."[43]

Had Rummel excommunicated recalcitrant Catholics at Jesuit Bend, he might also perhaps have induced repentance and brought the matter to a swift conclusion. But Jeanmard's action did not silence opposition in Erath. On December 1, 1955, more than two hundred people, including many Catholics, gathered in Erath to organize a branch of the Southern Gentlemen's Organization of Louisiana, a segregationist organization affiliated with the Citizens' Councils. Romero attended the meeting, where speakers lambasted Jeanmard for supporting integration. Jeanmard took no action against the group's Catholic members, perhaps fearing that he would drive them from the Church.[44]

In 1956, Archbishop Rummel ran into more difficulties with segregationist laity. In March, encouraged by mounting segregationist opposition to the *Brown* decision, diehard Catholic segregationists in metropolitan New Orleans organized the Association of Catholic Laymen after Rummel had condemned segregation a month earlier and indicated his intention to desegregate Catholic schools. Although the association's members obeyed Rummel's order in May to disband or suffer excommunication, they unsuccessfully appealed the ban to the pope. Asked by newsmen why the association had discontinued, Emile A. Wagner Jr., its president, declared: "Purely and simply, it was the dire threat of excommunication. As good Catholics, we bow to His Excellency's authority, but we question the propriety of the decision." Segregationist Catholics, including association members, continued to oppose parochial school desegregation by working through the Citizens' Council of New Orleans and a splinter group, the South Louisiana Citizens' Council.[45] Even when Rummel excommunicated three outspoken segregationists in April 1962, they continued to be active, vocal opponents of desegregation, demonstrating the limitations of a prelate's disciplinary powers against those determined to defy him.[46]

Among Catholic prelates in the South, only Rummel and Jeanmard excommunicated Catholics for opposing desegregation during the civil rights era and then only on two occasions. Aware that most southern white Catholics favored segregation, prelates were reluctant to adopt the potentially divisive use of excommunication. Prelates may also have feared that excommunication would create martyrs and alienate the moderate segregationist Catholic majority the Church hoped to win over or at least neutralize, or drive some of the moderates into the diehard camp. Conceivably, excommunication might have brought many segregationists to heel, but it might also have led some to leave the Church. Prelates proved unwilling to take the risk of splitting, perhaps irreparably, the Church in their dioceses. That was probably the answer to Wagner's rhetorical question, "If the dread threat of excommunication could have been made against the Association of Catholic Laymen, then why was it not made against the Catholic members of the citizens' councils?"[47]

Many prelates weighed financial and institutional considerations in deciding their policy toward segregationists and segregation since segregationists might withhold financial support for the Church and diocesan projects, withdraw their children from Catholic schools subject to desegregation, or leave the Church. In 1961, Louisiana state senator J. D. DeBlieux reported to the Catholic Council on Human Relations of the Archdiocese of New Orleans that Father Abadie of Baton Rouge's St. Gerard Church "has just conducted a drive up there and many have told him that if the [parochial] school was integrated that they would not pay the balance of their pledge. Most of them want to avoid all discussion of the subject matter." The next year, Archbishop Thomas J. Toolen of Mobile-Birmingham informed an African American Catholic parent, who appealed for parochial school desegregation: "In regard to the schools we have hesitated because of the fact that we know that if we accepted colored children for our schools that we will lose a great number of the white children."[48]

Fears that white Catholics might boycott desegregated schools, and thereby deprive their children of a Catholic education, while often not realized in practice, were not altogether unfounded. In Buras, sixty miles from New Orleans, most white parents withdraw their children from Our Lady of Good Harbor School when it admitted five African American children in September 1962. The black children did not attend the next day after their parents received harassing telephone calls. As a result of segregationist pressure and harassment, the number of children in attendance gradually trickled to zero, although the school remained open for the rest of the year.[49]

Henry A. Cabirac Jr., director of the Southern Field Service of the NCCIJ, observed that "Most Southern Bishops to some degree or other fear the loss of white Catholics and/or revenue whenever they desegregate any of their facilities. Frequently those who have the ear of the Bishop will caution him to go slow because of a fear of loss of the above mentioned items." In early 1965, Father Harold R. Perry, then S.V.D. provincial of the Divine Word Fathers United States Southern province, claimed that the Catholic Church was inhibited from acting in race relations by the fear of the damage that such action might cause to its institutions, image, and membership numbers.[50]

Some bishops nevertheless pressed ahead with racial equality policies, despite the risks involved. In March 1967, Bishop Joseph A. Durick of Nashville implemented Project Equality in Tennessee despite "getting all kinds of letters and protests over P.E." Even some of Durick's advisers cautioned him against acting when he did, only a month before the start of the Diocesan Development Program, expected to raise $3,500,000. After the fundraising campaign secured pledges totaling only $2,700,000, Durick acknowledged that the shortfall occurred because, as a diocesan agency reported, "'Project Equality' whether warranted or unwarranted was used as a reason for not giving by a sizeable segment of the population." Even so, Durick committed the diocese to underwriting Project Equality's costs. He wrote to the NCCIJ that opposition from Tennessee Catholics to the program only illustrated "the tremendous educational responsibility we have to our own people.... [A] challenge that must be met in the most dramatic fashion."[51]

Financial pressure sometimes emanated from state assemblies. In the 1950s, the Louisiana legislature considered bills that would have removed state support for Catholic schools if they desegregated, and Mississippi legislators unsuccessfully proposed a bill that would have withdrawn tax exemption from any religious organization that desegregated any of its facilities. In 1961, Henry C. Bezou opposed parochial school desegregation fearing passage of punitive state legislation against the Church, such as ending free textbook provision or taxing church property and parochial schools. Reassured by state legislator Maurice "Moon" Landrieu of New Orleans that punitive sanctions were unlikely, Bezou backed desegregation, and, in November, Archbishop Rummel indicated his willingness to initiate school desegregation in the fall of 1962.[52]

Even when bishops chose to address desegregation, they could not always ensure that recalcitrant or segregationist priests would toe the line. In February 1956, Archbishop Rummel issued a pastoral letter, designed "as a guide not only for the laity and the religious but also for the Clergy of the Archdiocese," that described racial segregation as "morally wrong and sinful." Although priests were obliged to read the letter to their congregations, some refused to do so.[53]

Even priests who did not defy the archbishop outright could dissent in other ways. When Father Carl M. Schutten of St. James Major Church in New Orleans read Rummel's pastoral letter at Mass to his mostly white congregation, he made his dissent clear. According to Clarence A. Laws, an African American Catholic, Schutten began by sarcastically saying that he had a "long" letter from Rummel to read out, before offering a negative commentary as he did so. The priest told his congregation, "The Archbishop says this is a moral issue, I still think it is social," denigrated the morality, behavior, and abilities of African Americans, and concluded by saying, "I know what is on your minds and I am in sympathy with you." Although Laws made a written complaint to Rummel, the archbishop took no action and appears not to have replied.[54]

Father Louis J. Twomey believed that opposition from a substantial number of priests contributed significantly to their archbishop's reluctance to desegregate archdiocesan schools and inhibited Rummel from taking "any disciplinary action" against them. Even when Rummel ordered parochial school desegregation, some pastors refused to register African American Catholics in white schools. Inaction and indifference could also undermine bishops' initiatives. In 1962, Bishop Maurice Schexnayder of Lafayette called on every deanery in his diocese to create human relations councils. Two years later, half of the deaneries had not responded.[55]

Besides their own clergy's views, prelates also had to consider whether the adoption of desegregation might produce significant, or even violent, opposition from within or outside Catholic ranks. In 1956, Bishop Adrian explained that "Integration at three parochial schools in Nashville is going very well, but we want to see what the public reaction is before we go ahead in Memphis."[56]

Older prelates remembered the ingrained hostility and suspicion that many Protestants harbored toward Catholics, manifested most strikingly in support for the Ku Klux Klan during the 1920s, and they did not wish to reignite it. In 1956, journalist Wilson Minor observed that Bishop Richard O. Gerow of Natchez-Jackson had "avoided public statements which would toss the Church into the heat of the state's segregation controversy." Minor explained that "Cast in a minority role, the Catholic Church in Mississippi has always felt the opposition and suspicion, however subtle, of the predominantly Protestant community. The feeling is now stronger than ever."[57]

The problem was even greater and more immediate in Alabama, where, in January 1958, Archbishop Toolen reported that "Great difficulties have been encountered this year from the K.K.K. [Ku Klux Klan]. They are growing stronger in Alabama and make things most disagreeable for the priests and our people." Joseph A. Durick, Toolen's auxiliary bishop, recalled Toolen refusing to desegregate parochial schools because "He was sincerely convinced that our churches might be bombed . . . if we were too strong or if we went forward too fast or too progressively."[58]

According to historian Andrew S. Moore, anti-Catholicism in Alabama and Georgia "united southern white Protestants and gave them common cause with non-southern Protestants" and continued into the 1960s. In 1959, journalist Charles Harbutt claimed that "Besides immediate social ostracism, Catholic integrationists have been beaten, shot at and raped." Although Harbutt offered no examples and may have exaggerated, ostracism, intimidation, and violence occurred.[59]

In the 1950s, segregationists in heavily Protestant Shreveport, Louisiana, launched an economic boycott of a family business, the Red Ball Battery and Oxygen Supply Company, because its Catholic owners, Mr. and Mrs. Joseph R. Daniell, supported Catholic interracial activities. The Ku Klux Klan also burnt a cross on the couple's lawn. Crippled by the boycott, the Daniells sold their business for a fraction of its true worth and relocated to California. In May 1956, segregationists set fire to a cross in front of desegregated Notre Dame Seminary, New Orleans, where Archbishop Rummel had a residence, and, in January 1957, the Klan burnt a cross outside Spring Hill College, a desegregated Jesuit-run institution in Mobile, Alabama.[60]

Sometimes segregationist opposition went beyond intimidation to violence. In April 1963, Father Frank Ecimovich, S.V.D., the white pastor of Our Lady of Perpetual Help in Belle Chasse, Louisiana, was assaulted by a white parent, upset that his child had received First Communion instruction with African Americans. In August, a week before it was due to reopen for the new school year, segregationists bombed Our Lady of Good Harbor School in Buras, the subject of a white boycott the previous year for admitting black students. Following the explosion, Archbishop Cody, acting "with the greatest reluctance," temporarily closed the school to "protect the lives of the priests, Sisters and children" in the parish. When school repairs were complete, the local authorities refused to permit its reopening, claiming several building code violations. In March 1965, a parishioner discovered a bomb outside Our Lady Queen of the Universe, an African American Catholic church in Birmingham, Alabama.[61]

Conscious of their responsibility to clergy and laity alike, prelates had to consider whether the adoption of desegregation, or even speaking publicly against racial discrimination, might endanger Catholics, or lead segregationists to abandon the Church, thereby placing their souls at risk. Consequently, many prelates considered it irresponsible to impose desegregation without first preparing Catholics and educating them about its necessity. In April 1961, Bishop Francis E. Hyland of Atlanta explained to Father Twomey:

> It is much easier for you, my dear Father, to speak freely in the South on the subject of race relations than it is for me who carries on his soul the onerous responsibilities of the episcopal office. It is true that a Bishop is a ruler of the Church; but it is also true that a Bishop must strive to be a Father in Christ to *all* [emphasis in the original] the people committed to his charge. I am gravely torn between the two above-mentioned aspects of the episcopal office.

In a letter read on April 16 at the city of Atlanta's two African American churches, the bishop pleaded for patience. Hyland explained that he needed time to prepare white Catholics for change because he did not "want to harm spiritually any of our white Catholic people, however wrong some of them may be objectively in respect to proper race relations."[62]

Less than two months before, Hyland had issued a pastoral letter about desegregation, in tandem with identical letters released by Bishops Thomas J. McDonough of Savannah and Paul J. Hallinan of Charleston. The letter declared that diocesan schools would desegregate when it could be "done with safety to the children and the schools," and after implementation of a preparatory program explaining Catholic teachings on racial justice. In the event, Atlanta's parochial school desegregation fell to Hyland's successor, Hallinan, as Hyland retired in October 1961, aged only sixty, having suffered a "nervous breakdown," brought on by anxiety over "the racial issue."[63]

Understandably some prelates opted to be silent about desegregation when they believed that to act might bring danger and division. In June 1963, Henry A. Cabirac Jr. visited Bishop Greco and reported that the bishop "would like to do something but is fearful of the harm that he thinks might be done the Church." In August, after seventeen years of public silence on the issue, Greco issued a pastoral letter, prompted by what he now regarded as its inevitability and called for adjustment to and acceptance of desegregation, but he did not mention desegregation of diocesan schools. In January 1964, Cabirac visited Bishop Gerow in Jackson, Mississippi. The bishop, Cabirac concluded, had two objections to desegregating diocesan parochial schools: "One is that he wants more time to prepare the white Catholics and the other is the possibility of violence because Catholics are in such a minority group."[64]

In practice, the hierarchical polity of the Catholic Church did not endow Catholic prelates with as much freedom to desegregate as might first appear. And prelates could not compel institutions owned and operated by Catholic orders to desegregate, or end discriminatory practices. In October 1969, two hundred black workers at Memphis's St. Joseph Hospital struck for union recognition. Operated by the Sisters of St. Francis of Perpetual Adoration and beyond Bishop Joseph A. Durick of Nashville's direct control, the hospital resisted the strikers' demands. As the situation intensified, Durick called for an "equitable solution" and declared his intention to intervene if necessary, but the hospital's board of administrators stood firm. After twelve weeks, the strikers called off their action and accepted Durick's proposal that the hospital reinstate them in return for a settlement of the dispute through mediation, but the hospital refused to rehire all the strikers or resume negotiations. The strike had divided Memphis's Catholic priests, with a third of them strongly in support of the strikers and a third strongly opposed.[65]

A minority of Catholic priests in the South, diocesan and religious, were committed integrationists, who urged their leaders and fellow Catholics to support, initiate, and accelerate desegregation. Some integrationist activists eagerly participated in the civil rights movement. But the Catholic clergy, like their prelates, evinced a range of responses to desegregation that included opposition, apprehension, and fear, apathy and indifference and lukewarm support, as well as enthusiasm, dedication, and commitment. In January 1960, Father Twomey assessed clergy opinion in the Archdiocese of New Orleans regarding potential desegregation of parochial schools. He wrote: "Possibly three-fourths of the priests would like to forget the whole thing and to allow the race problem to work itself out as best it could. Of the remaining one-fourth, I would say that maybe ten per cent are really anxious for forthright action."[66]

Whatever their disposition, secular priests and to some extent religious priests were circumscribed by the approach to segregation taken by the ordinary of the diocese in which they served. Prompted by his apostolic administrator Archbishop Cody, Archbishop Rummel forbade his priests from participating in civil rights demonstrations or writing to newspapers without his permission. Until 1968, Archbishop Toolen of Mobile-Birmingham barred secular and religious priests in his diocese from participating in demonstrations.[67]

Yet, despite his vocal objections, Toolen had been unable to stop more than two hundred and fifty priests and nuns from at least fifty other Catholic dioceses, mainly in the North and West, from participating in the Selma, Alabama, voting rights demonstrations in March 1965. Archbishop Paul J. Hallinan of Atlanta at first barred his priests from participation in the Selma protests for fear they would place themselves in danger, but he soon relented and permitted voluntary participation, deciding the cause justified the risk.[68]

A prelate's support for integrationist activity could be withdrawn, as well as proffered. Bishop Greco agreed enthusiastically to the opening of Friendship House in Shreveport, Louisiana, in February 1954, and appointed Father Joseph B. Gremillion as its chaplain. However, white segregationist opposition to Friendship House, which maintained a biracial lay Catholic staff and held biracial public meetings to promote racial equality, grew increasingly vociferous. Consequently, in 1955, Greco ordered its closure after only eighteen months in operation.[69]

Although Gremillion and Greco remained on good terms, prelates could undermine priests they regarded as too vociferous or active on behalf of integration and civil rights. In 1963, Bishop Albert L. Fletcher of Little Rock appointed Father David A. Boileau as chaplain of the Catholic Interracial Council of Little Rock. But Fletcher soon found Boileau too outspoken and too involved in interfaith activities. In February 1964, the bishop transferred Boileau away from Little Rock and removed him as chaplain. In October, an unnamed Louisiana priest complained to *Look* magazine: "Would that we Southern white priests who want to stand up and be counted could do so, but our bishops effectively silence us with certain removal, probable suspension and possibly worse."[70]

Priests had to consider the disposition of their prelates before deciding whether and in what ways to support desegregation. Although Catholic polity protected clergymen from dismissal by their congregations, Catholic priests needed support or at least an absence of opposition, from their ordinaries and, if applicable, their religious orders to engage in integrationist or civil rights activity. Otherwise, priests would have to operate furtively. After Toolen had forced his removal from Selma in 1965 for working with the civil rights movement, Father Maurice F. Ouellet of the Society of Saint Edmund observed that "A lot of other priests in Alabama are working quietly for integration. They have gone underground to escape the Bishop's notice and they keep silent, but they are doing their best."[71]

But many priests did not align themselves with the civil rights movement. They declined to do so not necessarily because they were segregationists, although some were, but because they feared opposition from within their churches and dividing their congregations. William A. Osborne observed that in Louisiana, "Even when a priest might himself be somewhat more enlightened on the race question than his parishioners, it would take more than the common allotment of courage to risk the inevitable hostility, ridicule or ostracism that would follow the expression of untraditional views." Priests, especially in areas where Catholics were a minority and often already regarded by Protestants with latent or manifest suspicion and hostility, also had reason to fear that endorsing desegregation might endanger not only themselves but their parishioners and church property. In June 1964, segregationists in Hattiesburg, Mississippi, burned down the Rosary Catholic Mission Hall, which served African Americans, and damaged the Catholic Church nearby.[72]

Aside from fear of segregationist resistance or retribution, many priests had a narrow conception of reform that prevented them from understanding that good race relations entailed more than expecting their parishioners to treat others with courtesy in a segregated society. Father Joseph B. Gremillion observed that "Most pastors think in terms only of the spiritual motivation and reform of *individual persons* [emphasis in the original]. They do not understand the institutional pattern of society and the necessity of reforming these institutions."[73]

Just as they were affected by the privatization of religion, many priests were also subject to the demands of its bureaucratization. Often priests judged themselves, and were appraised by superiors and parishioners, according to their administrative ability. Osborne explains that "Promotion to the pastorate in most dioceses is geared to what might be called organizational welfare. Seniority plays a major role, as does ability to 'run a parish'—that is, to administer an organization." Father Harold L. Cooper, S.J., of Loyola University of the South in New Orleans, believed that most priests were fully absorbed by a "confused hubbub of practical duties—running bazaars, heading-up drives, pushing the eternal building programs, the ladies sodality, etc." In white Catholic churches, pastors who championed integration, especially if their advocacy outstripped that of their prelates, ran the risk of alienating their parishioners, some of whom might withdraw or scale back financial support for parish projects and even leave the Church. In 1961, Rudolph Ehrensing argued that "Many of the [New Orleans Catholic] clergy fear that integration will cause many white Catholics to leave the Church." Three years later, Jennings, Louisiana-based Josephite pastor Father Leo Farragher, wrote that "Some pastors fear that their 'little kingdoms' will crash financially if Negroes are welcomed [in their churches]." Furthermore, Benjamin B. Ringer and Charles Y. Glock observed that the most active parishioners and often the largest financial donors tended to be the Church's most conservative adherents. Among white Catholics, they were frequently the main opponents of church and parochial school desegregation.[74]

Ehrensing observed that priests who "were educated on integration from a religious aspect were often afraid to preach integration due to social pressure that would result and because they were unable to answer the objections to integration requiring knowledge in such fields as genetics, anthropology and medicine." He also found that "many priests were ignorant on the meaning of Christianity in the racial situation."[75]

Even priests who sought to address racial injustice were often ineffective, despite their good intentions. Ehrensing explained, "The sermon is the only effective means of reaching all Catholics but, as is generally true of sermons, they only contain at best vague generalities concerning social justice and charity. The layman is expected to see the relevance and meaning of these general principles in complex twentieth century life and to apply them to his own situation in the world." Laypeople were "seldom able to accomplish this adequately," and those who were racially prejudiced thought "of the sermon's justice and charity in relation to other white men."[76]

While Catholic prelates and priests who favored desegregation knew that the weight of Catholic teachings was on their side, they faced considerable difficulties regarding when and how to advance racial justice within Catholic ranks. Cognizant of what the Church proclaimed nationally and internationally, they also had to contend with constraints imposed by local and regional circumstances and by their desire not to harm or fracture the Church. Consequently, many Catholic integrationists recognized a need to strike a balance between what the American Catholic hierarchy described in 1958 as "prudence and rashness." They would also need to address the contentions of committed Catholic segregationists who advanced an array of arguments intended to justify segregation and its maintenance.[77]

CHAPTER THREE

Catholic Segregationist Thought in the South

It might be supposed that as a minority in the South who had long faced suspicion and even hostility from the Protestant majority, southern white Catholics might have sympathized with African Americans as victims of discrimination. While some southern white Catholics exhibited empathy during the civil rights struggle, most of the region's white Catholics, like other southern whites, favored segregation. The shared preference of most lay white Protestants and Catholics for Jim Crow, during a period when it came under sustained challenge from the civil rights movement, lessened or neutralized a good deal of lingering anti-Catholicism among Protestant segregationists. White Catholic preference for segregation was not a strategic ploy to deflect white segregationist Protestant hostility. While only a minority of southern white Catholics declared God's approval for segregation, many Catholic segregationists criticized the Church for condemning segregation and offered a range of secular arguments in its defense. However, it is possible that more white Catholics believed that segregation had religious sanction than were prepared to say to their priests or in public forums.[1]

Only a very few of the Catholics who claimed that God approved of segregation offered, what they believed to be, scriptural justification. Even then, despite some duplication, they did not always invoke the same verses, indicative of the weakness and lack of coherence of the biblical defense. Biblical segregationists did not mount a widespread coordinated campaign in the South, although housewife Una M. Gaillot sought to organize sympathizers with her beliefs in her native New Orleans.

Gaillot, who founded a small group in 1960 called Save Our Nation, Inc., was the most vocal Catholic proponent of the biblical defense of segregation and employed it in outspoken condemnation of public and parochial school desegregation in the city. However, she was sometimes inconsistent in her exposition. Gaillot, a sixth-generation Catholic, asserted that Adam and Eve, the first humans according to the Old Testament book of Genesis, were white. In a newspaper advertisement, Gaillot adhered to a view commonly held by Catholic and Protestant biblical segregationists that Noe (Noah) had cursed Cham (Ham) and Cham's son Chanaan (Canaan) with black skin and that Chanaan's descendants formed "the Negro race" who inhabited the land of Chanaan.[2]

However, in a privately printed explication of her views, Gaillot argued that God had marked Cain and turned his skin from white to black. Cham had married Cain's black daughter and their offspring, including Chanaan, had been black. Gaillot argued that when God gave Moses the Ten Commandments and made his covenant with the Israelites, who in her view were white, he promised them the land of Chanaan, providing they "did not mix with the inhabitants." According to Gaillot, this law of racial segregation remained in force among Christians, who had become God's "chosen by adopting Christ," and Jesus, who she claimed was "pure white," had promised to observe the laws of the Old Testament, not change them. Gaillot also cited other biblical verses, mostly drawn from the Old Testament, which she claimed proved that God had mandated racial separation and punished those who had defied him and integrated. She predicted that God would likewise punish integrationists in the United States.[3]

Although she frequently insisted that she was not a biblical scholar, Gaillot claimed support from an unnamed biblical expert and asserted that no scholar had refuted her contentions. However, Gaillot's assumptions about the whiteness of Adam and Eve and Jesus lacked any biblical support. The curse on Cham supposedly outlined in Genesis 9:21–27 made no mention of race or color, and Noe placed a curse on Chanaan and his descendants, not Cham. Likewise, instances in which God ordered Jews to separate themselves referred to religious, not racial, separation, and there was no biblical support for Gaillot's assertion that the Israelites were white.[4]

Less well known than Gaillot, Patrick Warren Mernagh and Deane Settoon Mernagh, a husband and wife team of segregationist propagandists, also from New Orleans, produced a pamphlet, *The Pope on Segregation*, in 1955 that claimed God had originated segregation, although their arguments were much briefer than Gaillot's and mostly misconstrued from other biblical verses taken from Genesis. The Mernaghs argued that equalitarianism was Satanic because "Lucifer was the first apostle of equality" and had sought equality with God. They interpreted the Genesis account of the Fall to mean that Lucifer had "used Eve as his instrument to convert Adam to the doctrine of equalitarianism, thus bringing the world into turmoil, dissension, and strife." The Mernaghs also alluded to the Tower of Babel incident from Genesis 11:1–9 in which God punished an attempt to build a tower to heaven by scattering the people across the world and giving them different languages. The Mernaghs claimed that God put "different languages on the tongues of his followers, thus segregating them into groups of different nations or races that developed different attitudes, customs, and traditions."[5]

Jackson G. Ricau, a founder of the Association of Catholic Laymen and a Citizens' Council leader in New Orleans, also claimed biblical support for segregation in a privately printed booklet in 1957, although the organizations in which he was involved did not invoke the Bible in their defense of Jim Crow.

Ricau cited the Curse on Cham and the Tower of Babel from the Old Testament. He also quoted the Apostle Paul's admonition in the New Testament (I Corinthians 7:20): "Let every man remain in the calling in which he was called," although this and surrounding verses referred to slavery, not racial segregation. Ricau's other biblical references (I Timothy 6:1–2; I Peter 2:17–19, 3:1–7) concerned slaves, servants, or women, and made no mention of race.[6]

Some of Gaillot, the Mernaghs, and Ricau's arguments were shared by Protestant segregationists, but biblical justifications of segregation were rare among Catholics and, even then, often vague when asserted. For example, layman Herman P. Folse of Arabi, near New Orleans, wrote in defense of Jim Crow, but without biblical citation, "Who was this guy, Noah, that his curse should be permitted to carry on through the pages of history, even down to our present day?" In another letter, Folse claimed that racial segregation was "the continuance of a practice dating back to the Jewish tribes from which Our Lord and Savior Jesus Christ descended." Dr. Urban E. Mathieu of New Orleans claimed: "There are many passages proving the Lord does not want integration," but he cited only one example, Genesis 21:9–12. However, these verses concerned the desire of Abraham's wife, Sara, to protect the inheritance of her son Isaac, not racial segregation. Joyce Carmouche of Baton Rouge provided no biblical citations in support of her contention that "In our Gospels, we have read where God separated man in tongue and color so that people would be different from one another."[7]

Some Catholics who claimed biblical justification for segregation, such as Deane Settoon Mernagh, were converts from Protestantism. Their familiarity with supposedly segregationist biblical verses may have reflected a Protestant background in which the laity interpreted the Bible for themselves, rather than the Catholic tradition in which the Vatican determined doctrine and prelates and priests disseminated the Church's teachings.[8]

Catholics who claimed religious, if not biblical, support for segregation usually asserted that God had created different races and so his creation should be maintained. An unnamed Catholic mother in New Orleans complained, "Why mix the whites with the negros [sic], God forbade the mixing of white and black." Religious segregationists often asserted that God had an unknown purpose in creating separate races. Alfred J. Kronlage of Chalmette, Louisiana, wrote to integrationist Jesuit priest Louis J. Twomey, S.J., of Loyola University of the South's Institute of Industrial Relations that God "is the one who segregated the negro, not you, nor I or anyone else. It is my belief that God had a good reason for creating the negro different from the white."[9]

Some religious segregationists also made analogies to the animal kingdom in their defense of Jim Crow. A Covington, Louisiana, laywoman wrote to Reverend Emery Labbe of Erath's Our Lady of Lourdes Church: "GOD ONLY made all races EQUAL SPIRITUALLY for when he created races different colors,

White, Red, Yellow and Black he meant for them to remain so. Who are you and others to go against his discrimination of humans, animals, birds, etc., who practice carrying out his wishes?"[10]

The vast majority of Catholic segregationists did not make a biblical or religious case for segregation, but many questioned why their prelates and the Church condemned segregation after many years of silence on the issue, during which time southern Catholic institutions and societies had themselves become segregated. In 1965, layman H. G. Odenthal of Fairfax, Virginia, asked Bishop John J. Russell of Richmond, "Why has the Church participated and accepted segregation and discrimination in the past if it was morally wrong[?] I find it hard to believe that she would allow participation in segregation and discrimination if she felt they were morally wrong."[11]

A variation on this theme was to argue that if the Church had decided segregation was sinful, surely all prelates should abandon it. After Archbishop Joseph F. Rummel of New Orleans denounced segregation in a February 1956 pastoral letter, layman Emile A. Wagner Jr. wrote to Rummel that if segregation was wrong, why did the archbishop not desegregate Catholic schools peremptorily. Aware that the prelates of neighboring dioceses had not condemned segregation, Wagner added: "The Catholic layman is placed in the impossible position of sinning in New Orleans if he practices segregation, and being virtuous in the same practice in Mobile, Alexandria, Lafayette, or in many other dioceses throughout the world."[12]

Some Catholic segregationists argued that the papacy had either endorsed segregation in the past or, at least, had never condemned it, and they disputed the authority of prelates to do so. In 1958, Archbishop Robert E. Lucey of San Antonio, who had long championed desegregation, wrote to John LaFarge, chaplain of the Catholic Interracial Council of New York:

> Down in Louisiana the faithful say that they are confused. Segregated schools were constitutional until 1954 and both segregated schools and churches had the approval of the Holy See because a Bishop couldn't even establish a segregated parish without the approval of the Holy See. Now the people say that all this has changed and a segregated school is no longer constitutional and the Church calls segregation a sin.[13]

The Mernaghs argued that Pope Gregory XV and Pope Benedict XIV had recognized segregation in seventeenth- and eighteenth-century south India so that missionaries could minister to different castes. The couple also reprinted an editorial defense of segregation from *Leaves*, a magazine published in Detroit by the Mariannhill Fathers who sent missionaries to apartheid South Africa. In an implicit acknowledgment that segregation denied African Americans equal rights, the editorial cited in its defense of racial separation and exclusion Pope Pius XI's 1937 encyclical *Divini Redemptoris* that stated, "It is not true that all have equal rights in civil society." Ignoring the fact that segregation was itself arbitrary, *Leaves* also quoted Pope Pius XII's 1944 Christmas message, which declared:

> Those inequalities among men which are not imposed by arbitrary will but arise from the very nature of things, inequalities of culture, fortune, social position—without prejudice, of course, to justice and mutual charity—oppose no obstacle whatever to the existence and prevalence of a genuine spirit of common fellowship and brotherhood.[14]

The Mernaghs challenged integrationist claims that the doctrine of the Mystical Body of Christ rejected race-based distinctions among Catholics. They wrote that "the oneness of His fold or Mystical Body, does not demand, by any intrinsic necessity, the destruction of segregated parts. Desegregation is not at all an essential, while the diverse nations or races pay Him homage and obedience."[15]

Emile A. Wagner Jr. made a negative case for the maintenance of Catholic segregation by arguing that Pius XII and the Vatican had not condemned it, and historically the clergy had contributed to racial separation. Wagner wrote: "I . . . can find no dogmatic pronouncement by the Pope, nothing in the encyclicals . . . and nothing in canon law that denounces segregation. On the contrary, I have discovered a considerable number of instances in history where segregation has not only been tolerated, but actively fostered and sponsored by the clergy." He denied Rummel had the authority "to declare that racial segregation is unnatural, when the Pope himself has not seen fit so to do." Wagner did not understand that the pope, concerned with the doctrine of the entire faith, and canon law with the governance and organization of the Catholic Church, did not ordinarily make pronouncements on matters in a single region in the worldwide Catholic Church and left such matters to local ordinaries.[16]

In 1956, he, along with Ricau and twenty-eight others, formed the segregationist Association of Catholic Laymen in New Orleans. In July 1957, more than a year after Rummel had forced the association officially to cease operations, Wagner cowrote its appeal to Pope Pius XII. In a covering letter, Wagner objected to Rummel's "strange new doctrine . . . that the segregation of the white and Negro races is 'morally wrong and sinful,'" noting that "the Clergy and the Church itself have participated and are participating in the perpetuation of this type of segregation by . . . sanctioning the establishment and maintenance of separate churches and schools." The appeal asked the pope to provide instruction "on the morality of racial segregation, and on the authority of bishops to define matters of morals," to rescind Rummel's ban on the association, and to force the archbishop to retire.[17]

An unnamed Vatican official criticized the association, stating that "It is utterly disquieting that there should be Catholics so ignorant of Christian doctrine and fundamentals. The only charitable view one can place on the request is that those who uttered it have some difficulty in mentally understanding the doctrine of the Church—or else ignore it altogether." An editorial in *L'Osservatore Romano* expressed "painful amazement," and the paper declared that "racial exclusion is a sin against the nature of Catholicism." But the appeal itself went unanswered. In vain, Father Twomey urged the Vatican to respond directly as its silence encouraged segregationists to believe that "the archbishop has been secretly instructed by the Holy See" to abandon desegregation.[18]

Some segregationists interpreted papal silence as confirmation that racial separation was not a religious or moral but a secular issue beyond the Church's purview. Wagner maintained that "The South, including its Catholic citizens, does not accept the validity of the immorality of racial segregation," and, ignoring the American Catholic hierarchy's recent condemnation of segregation in 1958, he added, "the Bishops and the clergy do not agree among themselves on the matter of the morality of segregation." Viola Johnson of Marion Junction, Alabama, wrote to Archbishop Thomas J. Toolen of Mobile: "As a catholic I do not approve of the church mixing in politics. I learned in my catholic school that we in America had 'Separation of Church and State[.]' I do not believe in force[d] integration."[19]

Segregationist Catholics also complained that desegregation of Catholic institutions ignored the wishes of many Catholics and would, as Herman P. Folse wrote to Father Twomey "drive them from the Church." Folse insisted that missions could be conducted "on a separate but equal basis, and still remain within the teachings of the Bible," and he objected to parochial school desegregation as "in complete disregard for the feelings of thousands of devout Catholics whose only crime is to want to choose with whom they will associate." Most Catholic segregationists either did not consider the wishes of African American Catholics or assumed that they preferred Jim Crow. Dr. Frank J. O'Conner, a member of the Knights of Columbus in Norfolk, Virginia, asserted that "The colored man seeks his own kind. He wants his own church and his own lodge [a reference to the Knights of Peter Claver]."[20]

The vast majority of southern Catholic segregationists, including many who used biblical and religious defenses, advanced secular reasons to justify segregation and to condemn both integration and its supporters. Many southern white Catholics argued that desegregation, especially the Civil Rights Act of 1964, was an unconstitutional infringement of states' rights, property rights, and the individual's freedom of association, and a violation of democracy. Jackson G. Ricau wrote that "We should make a bold determination to win, not only against forced integration and civil 'rights,' but for the larger issues of states' rights involving the precious right of private ownership and the right of retail businesses to select their own clientele or patrons." In September 1963, J. M. Boggan, a layman from Birmingham, Alabama, praised

Governor George C. Wallace's defense of segregation. Boggan wrote of the Methodist Wallace: "Governor Wallace, by his stand and actions, is attempting to show the people of this State and Country how far we have gone down the road to anarchy: how close we are to a central government controlling every facet of our daily lives."[21]

As Catholic clergy and nuns participated in the civil rights movement's Selma, Alabama, demonstrations in 1965, layman A. N. Manucy of Charleston, South Carolina, wrote to Archbishop Toolen:

> I believe the white man is committing suicide, and I am afraid we have already gone beyond the point of 'no return.' As we gradually destroy States['] Rights we lose a proportionate part of our freedom. States['] Rights is the foundation of our Constitution, and our forefathers must have realized that to preserve freedom it was necessary to divide it into so many parts under the protection and discretion of the individual states, rather than have it concentrated in one place in the form of a strong and over-powerful central government.

Esma Champagne of New Iberia, Louisiana, argued that the voting rights bill, proposed by President Lyndon B. Johnson in the wake of the Selma protests, was designed for Johnson's political benefit, rather than civil rights. She warned that the Johnson administration was "slowly eating away into our freedoms and constitutional rights."[22]

Many self-identified segregationists regarded Catholic desegregation as unlawful. In 1953, layman Frank Gawrych of St. Petersburg, Florida, complained to Bishop Vincent S. Waters of Raleigh, after he had called for an end to church segregation in his diocese, that "You are acting in direct violation of state laws," seemingly unaware that North Carolina's segregation laws did not apply to churches. Segregationists claimed that civil rights demonstrations were disorderly and violent, ignoring the fact that nonviolent demonstrators in such cases were victims of segregationist violence. Sidney L. Villeré of New Orleans asserted that "The leaders of integration will have to answer one day for acts of violence and bloodshed."[23]

Segregationist Catholics charged that Catholic clergy and nuns who participated in civil rights demonstrations neglected their duties and defied lawful authority. Layman Francis O. Leach of Falls Church, Virginia, asked Cardinal Francis Spellman of New York "why so many priests and nuns went to Washington, D.C. [for the March on Washington in 1963] and Selma, Alabama, to demonstrate when each had enough problems in their own parish." Houston oilman Arthur Leman wrote to Bishop Russell of Richmond to complain about clergy and nuns who went to Selma with their prelates' permission but against the wishes of Toolen, the local ordinary. Leman wrote: "If these prelates have respect, neither for the Divine Right of an Archbishop to govern the church in his diocese, nor for the civil laws of a state, how do they expect to merit obedience from the clergy and laity of their own jurisdiction?"[24]

Accusations that communism was either behind or manipulating the civil rights movement frequently appeared in segregationist Catholic letters and in those of other Catholics who criticized the movement. In 1963, Ella DeMattie of Warrington, Florida, wrote to the *Catholic Week,* the Diocese of Mobile-Birmingham's newspaper, that "This NAACP [National Association for the Advancement of Colored People] is communist controlled. I would hate to believe that our good Catholics as well as Negroes were being blind folded to communism. It is undermining the U.S.A. in every way it can." Philip R. Viviani of Macon, Georgia, erroneously claimed that "Martin Luther King, Jr., . . . had schooling under Communist principles" and that the civil rights movement was "riddled with Communist elements."[25]

Some Catholic clergy shared the belief that communism was involved in the civil rights movement and their concerns helped to legitimize such fears among the laity. Jesuit Father Sam Hill Ray Jr., of Loyola University of the South, claimed that "This Supreme Court segregation decision [*Brown*] was a victory for Communism—a victory long sought through Communistic activities. . . . The Court listened to the Communists through the NAACP."[26]

Even some Catholic leaders who cautiously called for acceptance of desegregation believed that communism was either involved in or seeking to influence integration and the civil rights movement, and thereby helped to justify segregationist claims of Communist infiltration. According to the *Mobile Register,* Archbishop Toolen "conceded that Communists may be using racial unrest in an effort to 'tear up our laws,'" although he also called for recognition of human rights. In a private letter, Toolen told Cardinal Lawrence J. Shehan of Baltimore that "Martin Luther King didn't spend fifteen months in Moscow for nothing," although King had never been to the Soviet Union.[27]

Some lay Catholics accused outspoken integrationist prelates and clergy of using Communist tactics. Upset by Bishop Waters's church merger order in Newton Grove and his refusal to meet with malcontents until they had obeyed, Mrs. Leo Tart of Four Oaks, North Carolina, wrote to the bishop: "To deny people the right to speak out in their own behalf is leaning strongly toward Communism, and I definitely do not have any sympathy with communist tactics." Deane Settoon Mernagh complained to Father Joseph H. Fichter, S.J., of Loyola University of the South that by applauding students who opposed the segregationist views of their parents he was taking "a leaf out of the Communist book which instructs children to spy on and report the 'delinquencies' of their parents."[28]

Many Catholic segregationists contended that communism had infiltrated the Church. Kathleen B. Marston of Aiken, South Carolina, complained to Bishop Francis F. Reh of Charleston that "Since the Communists have begun playing the tunes, the Catholic Church has abandoned all self-respect and the respect of its followers and jostles to be the first on the Red wagon." Convinced that communism lay behind the civil rights movement, Catholic segregationists accused Catholic leaders who supported the movement of guilt by association. Although the National Urban League did not engage in demonstrations and focused on equal employment opportunity for African Americans, segregationists tarred the organization and its supporters as Communist. A Committee for Catholic Truth, an anonymous segregationist lay group, lamented that "Archbishop Rummel has been an honorary chairman of the Urban League [of New Orleans], an organization wherein some of its leaders are also members of Communist-front organizations. The Jesuit, Father Louis J. Twomey of Loyola University, is a very active member of the Urban League." A Louisiana layman directly accused Rummel of having "Communistic ideas."[29]

Segregationists argued that Communists supported, infiltrated, or instigated the civil rights movement to create racial strife and disorder that would weaken America and its institutions, and make the nation ripe for a Communist takeover. Emile A. Wagner Jr. asserted that "Marxism urges integration in the United States because of the strife it will engender." After it had donated $25,000 to provide shelter and food for participants in the March on Washington in 1963, Dr. Urban E. Mathieu, like Wagner a New Orleans resident, complained to the Knights of Columbus Supreme Council in New Haven, Connecticut, "You have aided and abetted the Communist movement to destroy our constitutional rights and way of life."[30]

Segregationists sought to exploit fears of internal subversion that were widely shared by Catholics and non-Catholics alike in Cold War America. Many Americans supported United States senator, and Catholic, Joseph R. McCarthy's anticommunist witch hunts in the early 1950s. Even after McCarthy's downfall in 1954, the United States House Committee on Unamerican Activities continued to make charges of Communist infiltration in American life. Often drawing on the committee's material, southern segregationist politicians, Citizens' Council leaders, and Catholic segregationist groups and laity made frequent accusations of communism in the civil rights movement and among its supporters. Catholic segregationists also expressed fears that communism had infiltrated the government. Deane Settoon Mernagh claimed that "In both the Government and the Church the Satanic wielders of the Hammer and sickle have made frightful inroads."[31]

Like other southern Citizens' Councils, the Greater New Orleans Citizens' Council and the South Louisiana Citizens' Council, both of which had significant Catholic memberships, put communism at the centerpiece of their attack on integration. The Louisiana councils argued that communism was directing the civil rights movement and influencing and penetrating the federal government. The councils also claimed that Communist integrationists had infiltrated the clergy and influenced archdiocesan desegregation policy.[32]

Although many Catholic segregationists believed that communism lay behind the civil rights movement, they were divided in their attitudes to African Americans. Some segregationists took an overtly white supremacist view. Mrs. Richard of New Orleans wrote to Father Fichter that God had created the races. She continued: "What is false about the White man being Superior to the negro? Jesus was White: none of His 12 Apostles were black—men are not created equal! If the Aid of the White man was taken from the negro in 20 yrs he would be back in the jungles."[33]

However, other segregationists denied that they were racists, and many claimed that they favored equality within segregation and felt no ill will toward blacks. Catherine M. West of Mobile wrote to Archbishop Toolen: "I am a segregationist, not a racist. I believe in equal rights but separate facilities. I believe a negro can make his mark in the world, but he must earn it."[34]

Some Catholic segregationists acknowledged that discrimination had played a role in limiting African American educational and economic achievement. Mrs. Leo Tart wrote:

> There is no hatred in my heart for the colored race nor any other race for that matter. I do truly believe in justice and equal rights for all human beings, but so far, I have not been able to bring myself to believe that the different races should intermingle. God, Himself, drew a line by the very fact of creating people with different colored skin and different languages. This does not mean that I think the colored race is not loved as much by God as is the white race. Nor do I think the colored people should be the "underdog." I know there have been, and are still, many instances of injustice toward colored people.[35]

Emile A. Wagner Jr. stressed that he favored separate but equal facilities, which he conceded had been absent, and he maintained that "segregation in itself is not discrimination nor racism."[36] Wagner explained that "I have no hatred of the Negro; I will and do work arduously for the general improvement of his condition; I recognize that we have great amends to make for the treatment accorded him in the last century, although admittedly the Negro has done little for himself."[37]

While Catholic segregationists sometimes argued that they favored improved facilities and opportunities for African Americans within segregation, they drew the line at what they called social equality. G. C. Boucvalt of Lutcher, Louisiana, wrote to Archbishop Toolen: "I am for segregation, but I treat and respect the Colored people in my community, I am trying to help as much as possible, but it doesn't mean that I have to entertain them socially." Segregationists saw no contradiction in demanding freedom of association for themselves but denying it to others through enforced segregation. Herman P. Folse wrote to Father Twomey: "I have no desire to ever subject myself or my family to their [African American] social companionship." Folse argued that segregationists' "only crime is to want to choose with whom they will associate," and, he affirmed, "We do not want to see the negro downtrodden."³⁸

Many segregationists denied, like Folse, that "because a man believes in segregation, he is an advocate of White Supremacy." Rather, they claimed, "What the Negro is and the way he lives his life is the cause of his being segregated." Such segregationists argued that while African Americans were not inherently inferior, most were culturally inferior in terms of their educational and economic achievements, behavior, and moral standards, and these alleged differences justified segregation. Emile A. Wagner Jr. claimed that African Americans had much higher rates of illegitimacy and venereal disease than whites, significantly lower educational achievement, much lower living standards, paid much less attention to "sanitation and cleanliness," and lacked "social, civic, and moral responsibility." Consequently, Wagner argued, the protection and well-being of white children necessitated segregation "so long as the great disparity between the races exists." Betty Tecklenburg Long, a South Carolina native now resident in Atlanta, wrote to Bishop Francis E. Hyland:

We fear inter-marriage, and justly so.

I believe that instead of trying to force the races together which are at present so far apart morally, economically, intellectually, and especially from a health standpoint, it would be far better to have separate schools even if we white people have to help in maintaining them. Teach the negro to accept responsibility.³⁹

Such contentions, although articulated less starkly, were not just the preserve of disgruntled Catholics voicing their criticism of diocesan authorities and progressive Catholics. With the permission of Bishop Albert L. Fletcher of Little Rock, William W. O'Donnell, managing editor of diocesan newspaper the *Guardian*, wrote and published a series of six weekly editorials in the summer of 1959 that offered an analysis of "America's race problem" and proposed "a simple first step toward a solution." Unlike Fletcher, a native of Little Rock, O'Donnell was not a southerner. Born in East Orange, New Jersey, in 1914 and raised in New England, he had spent his life in the northeast before joining the *Guardian* in August 1954.⁴⁰

In his editorials, O'Donnell condemned race-based segregation as immoral and contrary to Catholic teachings, but he distinguished between race-based unjust discrimination and just discrimination based on cultural differences. He maintained that only a "cultured Negro minority" could and should be integrated and that white southerners were justified in opposing integration of "'black trash' [who] constitute a majority among southern Negroes" because of "the prevalence of physical filth among the mass of Negroes; the general lack of ambition and civic interest they display" and their "obvious primitiveness." O'Donnell provided no evidence to support such racist caricatures.⁴¹

He conceded that "token integration ... is possible in some southern areas. But before even token integration can be realized generally, the South must be guaranteed protection against destruction or diminution of its white culture." Beyond that, integration should only occur when the "mass of Negroes" had raised their "moral standards," created "a sense of personal pride ... a genuine sense of ambition, civic pride, abhorrence of dirt and immorality ... [and] a general yearning ... for education," and "a willingness to carry their full share of tax and other civil burdens." O'Donnell speculated that this "may even take generations," while suggesting parenthetically that the adoption of a sex-segregated public education system might ease white anxieties and thereby shorten "the time needed for the aforementioned civic effort to raise Negro standards."[42]

He claimed that "the Caucasian is blamed for the cultural inferiority of the mass of Negroes" but maintained that the race problem was that of black "cultural inferiority," rather than of white attitudes and behavior, denial of equal opportunity, segregationist laws, and disenfranchisement. Until blacks became worthy of integration, O'Donnell maintained, white southerners' "Delaying tactics are entirely justified, so long as those exercising or supporting them are acting in accordance with their consciences." The *Guardian* published the series in pamphlet form for wider distribution.[43]

Some segregationists who emphasized alleged cultural, behavorial, and attainment differences between African Americans and whites but denied any belief in racial superiority, nevertheless sometimes indicated such beliefs explicitly or implicitly, especially when they articulated fears of miscegenation. Herman P. Folse asserted that:

> The Negro, having no history of his own worth mentioning, must amalgamate himself with other races, so that eventually he will have some history to be proud of. The surest way for him to do this is to begin on the lowest level possible, the elementary school. Thus having established a foothold, he may proceed to lower other races to his levels as he has done in all other instances where he has suc[c]eeded in amalgamating himself.[44]

Emile A. Wagner Jr. argued that African Americans would have to qualify for "first class citizenship," but he was skeptical about their capacity for doing so. Woefully ignorant, like Folse of African and African American history, he claimed that "The Negro on the whole has done little to help himself over the centuries and throughout the world. How swiftly, if ever, he achieves equality in all phases of life is in direct proportion to his innate capacity and the intensity of his desire to qualify." Wagner added that southern white Catholics "would literally do anything, go to any extreme, to save their offspring from the miscegenous degeneracy that would follow unrestricted racial intermingling as the dark night must follow the brilliant day."[45]

Fear of miscegenation, like fear of communism, was a recurrent theme in white Catholic segregationist thought, and articulated by many who defended segregation on religious and secular grounds. Indeed, some segregationists explicitly linked these fears. In 1956, a Slidell, Louisiana, layman warned Bishop Jules B. Jeanmard of Lafayette that America had to be protected from being "sold into the Communist camp with the aid of their Satanic mongelization scheme."[46]

Many segregationists worried that parochial school and church desegregation would lead to interracial marriage, usually between black males and white females. Donald J. Plaisance wrote to the Commission on Human Rights in New Orleans: "Who is going to draw the line when your's [sic] or my daughters ask for permission to marry a member of the colored race?" Many segregationists also feared that black boys in desegregated schools would corrupt, seduce, or even rape white females, and some also expressed anxiety about supposed black female lasciviousness. Jackson G. Ricau and Joseph E. Viguerie, president of the South Louisiana Citizens' Council, seized on a congressional subcommittee's report on public school desegregation in Washington, DC, which claimed that "attempted rape, assaults, chasing girls, and even teachers, Negro girls soliciting boys at school, sex talk, and suggestive talking and attempted foundling of white girls, and innumerable sex affronts were reported by the school personnel that was interviewed."[47]

Segregationists who took a white supremacist stance were especially vehement not only in expressing fears of miscegenation but also in accusing African Americans of lacking hygiene and moral restraint and of possessing ingrained licentiousness and criminality. M. Basilico of New Orleans claimed that of every five hundred African American children born, "400 will be potential customers for our jails as soon as they reach the tender age of ten. In over a century of associating with them we have failed to find out where they keep their goodness." A group of New Orleans Catholic parents wrote to Father Twomey that they would not let their children "be innocent victims of rape, assaults, sex talks, etc." and claimed, "If you could see the southern negger [sic] living in a world of filth and sin, I feel sure that you will be intellectually convinced that segregation is not sinful." Laywoman Joan B. Thyson of Sawyerville, Alabama, complained: "Negroes are not especially IMmoral; they are practically ALL UNmoral! More than 80 per cent of the children born to Negro women are illegitimate."[48]

Some segregationists argued that priests were neither trained nor suited to comment on the "management of our social affairs" and on "political and business affairs." Parents and Friends of Catholic Children, a New Orleans segregationist group, declared its "opposition to the clergy intruding into the management of family affairs, including the selection of friends, school mates and environmental circumstances for those of tender years, as by training and by virtue of the state of celibacy they are singularly unsuited to undertake such a responsibility, which must be discharged by the head of each Catholic family." Priests, the group insisted, should restrict themselves to "their proper and appointed sphere, the strict practice of the sacerdotal and ecclesiastical profession," meaning "to preach the word of God, to baptise babies, to marry persons, to bury the dead, administer the Sacraments, and to keep prescribed records normally maintained in connection therewith."[49]

A handbill produced in New Orleans objected to what it called "the push-button morality of this Archdiocese." Its anonymous author(s) claimed that the archdiocesan hierarchy and priesthood had no understanding of the practical implications of desegregation. The notice continued:

> Their wealth and luxury hardly fits them to speak out on a social issue which they neither appreciate nor live with. It is easy for a bishop or a priest, who seldom use a public facility and who is not faced with the problem of integration in his practical everyday life, to wax eloquent with righteous indignation and then retire to a nice segregated rectory. The clergy is ill suited to dealing with problems in the world. Too many clergymen are arrogant and ignorant men without any larger motivation for integration beyond the fact that the Archbishop wants it.[50]

Although Catholic segregationists often fiercely complained when their prelates supported or announced desegregation and some organized against it, when it became clear that opposition could, at most, delay desegregation, they had to consider their response to what became the inevitability of change. Some segregationists tried to insulate themselves from desegregation. Layman Alfred J. Kronlage wrote that "If integration is ordered by Archbishop Rummel and it comes to my parish, then I will not have any choice but to remove my children from school and deprive them of a Catholic education. My wife and I will abandon all school and church organizations and activities."[51]

Some segregationists either left or threatened to leave the Church because of integration. A Richmond, Virginia, native wrote to Bishop Waters in the aftermath of the Newton Grove crisis, "This is to inform you and your Catholic Church of which I have been a member with five of my immediate family, that we are pulling out of the church we loved but for which we now have a supreme contempt." After Bishop Jeanmard excommunicated two segregationists in Erath in 1955, a Louisiana laywoman asserted that "Many of we parents will continue to fight and if we are excommunicated there are other churches, many roads lead to Heaven."[52]

Some of those who withdrew from, or threatened to abandon, Catholicism were converts. Deane Settoon Mernagh wrote to Father Fichter: "If you are permitted to keep on spewing your poison, refuting Biblical teachings, etc., some of us might get the notion that we can't go to heaven if we belong to the Catholic Church. We might think it's time to turn back to the 'Old Time Religion.'" Contemplating leaving Catholicism was probably less wrenching for those who had not been raised as Catholics and had not had their family, forebears, community, and social lives so significantly shaped by the Church and its institutions.[53]

Many Catholic segregationists did not need to take the drastic step of leaving the Church because they were able either to avoid, or to minimize, the impact of desegregation upon themselves and their families. While remaining Catholics, some segregationists avoided desegregated parochial schools and churches by relocating to white suburbs away from downtown and inner-city areas that had become increasingly African American in the postwar era as a result of black rural to urban migration in search of employment and opportunity.

While many segregationists probably retained their views in private, a few remained publicly unrepentant. In 1959, Emile A. Wagner Jr. still forlornly hoped that the pope would answer the Association of Catholic Laymen's appeal against its ban by Archbishop Rummel three years before, and Wagner claimed that he remained president of the association. His was a lone voice on the New Orleans public school board in 1960 arguing for defiance of federal court-ordered public school desegregation. Unable to prevent the beginning of token public school desegregation in November 1960 and discouraged in 1962 by the defeat in the legislature of a bill to withdraw tax exemption from the Catholic Church's institutions in Louisiana if parochial schools desegregated, Wagner resigned from the board.[54]

In April 1962, Rummel excommunicated three outspoken segregationists: Leander Perez, president of the Plaquemines Parish Commission Council and a leader in the Greater New Orleans Citizens' Council; Jackson G. Ricau; and Una M. Gaillot, for trying to "provoke" Catholics to "disobedience or rebellion" regarding parochial school desegregation, scheduled for the fall. Perez remained outspoken. Gaillot faded into obscurity, but she remained a biblical segregationist, who because of her excommunication, could not attend her son's wedding. Ricau still denounced segregation as executive director and later president of the South Louisiana Citizens' Council, although the council, like the Greater New Orleans Citizens' Council, had run out of momentum by 1964 after failing to prevent New Orleans from abandoning de jure segregation under pressure from the federal government and the civil rights movement.[55]

The three excommunicates argued that they had remained true to authentic Catholicism and that it was the archdiocese's leaders who had departed from Catholic truth by embracing desegregation. Perez explained to a Citizens' Council meeting, "I am a Catholic, although not an archbishop Catholic." Gaillot declared that "The Church has definitely made a serious mistake" and, in vain, appealed her excommunication to the pope. Ricau protested to Rummel that he was "a loyal American Catholic" and added that "The forced mixing program lacks scriptural approbation." In July 1962, Ricau assured a meeting of Parents and Friends of Catholic Children that "I am not in any way opposing the Catholic religion" but instead, what he regarded as, Rummel's error.[56]

A few segregationists continued to voice their views in the Catholic press. In 1968, Peter J. Samkovitch of Cape Coral, Florida, complained to the *Voice*, the Archdiocese of Miami's newspaper, "The Voice and other Catholic publications seem to indict the whole white community for the plight of the ill-bred, ill-mannered, lazy, immoral, free-sexed, irresponsible, inconsiderate, brazenly defiant, inhuman, dishonest booze and drug crazed Negroes who are being used by the Communist agents working all over the world to loot, burn and destroy the white man and all democracies of the world."[57]

Nevertheless, by the late 1960s, segregationist letters to diocesan leaders, agencies and newspapers, and priests had fallen sharply, and, by the 1970s, they had virtually disappeared. In part, the decline reflected a sense of futility in protesting against desegregation once it became the officially proclaimed policy of every southern diocese, albeit with variations in implementation, and a belief that desegregation either could not be reversed or had become inevitable.

In 1971, graduate student Dolores Egger Labbé surveyed white Catholic opinion in south Louisiana. Although she did not find "many respondents whose attitudes favored integration. Most white Catholics . . . indicated their willingness to obey the instructions of the bishop," including parish integration. One layman stated: "I believe in segregation and have always practiced segregation. I believe it will prevent mongrelization of the races," but he conceded that if churches were integrated, "I would abide by the bishop's decision even if I would not approve of it." A laywoman similarly believed that "mixing the races can do no good and will probably do harm," although she would "accept the ruling of the bishop."[58]

Acceptance of Church-ordered desegregation did not necessarily induce any commitment to integration among parishioners. Another woman informed Labbé that she would continue to attend her church if African Americans came but "would make it my business not to sit near one if possible." Many segregationists did not articulate segregationist views publicly, aware that such views violated Church teachings and official policy in churches and schools, and might prevent their children from being admitted to parochial schools in areas subject to public school desegregation. Secular desegregation mandated by law also made public expressions of segregationist sentiment increasingly unacceptable.[59]

However, other segregationists, both priests and laity, gradually reexamined and repudiated their views, influenced by the Church's teachings, diocesan desegregation, and secular desegregation. Father T. R. Sehlinger, O.P., of Dallas, who had been reared in New Orleans, recalled, "I had to relearn, to be retaught, often by myself. Race prejudice is not a congenital disease. It must be contracted from parents, relatives and friends who take great care to transmit it." Layman Oscar B. Hofstetter Jr., of Nashville, explained, "I grew up in an atmosphere of legally mandated segregation. As the law changed, I have tried to accept the change and to realize that the early condition was morally wrong."[60]

Opinion polls of southern whites found growing acceptance of desegregation. The percentage of southern whites who objected to token school desegregation fell from 72 percent in 1959 to 16 percent in 1970. However, many Catholics, like other white southerners, balked at desegregation when it exceeded tokenism, suggesting that progressive Catholic priests and laity who had worked hard to persuade their white coreligionists to accept desegregation still had more work to do.[61]

CHAPTER FOUR

Progressive White Catholics in the South and Civil Rights

A progressive minority of Catholics in the South strove to counter segregationist arguments and, when necessary, to persuade and pressure southern prelates to inaugurate and enforce desegregation in their dioceses. The progressive minority included some ordinaries, religious and diocesan priests, nuns, editors of diocesan newspapers, faculty and students at seminaries and Catholic and secular higher educational institutions, and laity. Progressives disseminated their message through pastoral letters, sermons, classes, editorials, articles and letters in the diocesan press, pamphlets, and newsletters. With the approval of their ordinaries, progressives often formed Catholic organizations, most commonly interracial councils, to disseminate their message. Sometimes progressives cooperated with or joined civil rights organizations. A few progressives also participated in civil rights protests.

Although often constrained by segregationist opposition and by bureaucratic and administrative imperatives, at times progressive prelates used their authority against segregation in their dioceses. However, most progressives did not hold episcopal office and could only seek to persuade and influence their coreligionists, and, if they were members of Catholic organizations or holding diocesan positions, they needed the support, or at least tolerance, of their ordinaries for their activities. Progressives who were members of religious orders, likewise, needed the approval or forbearance of their superiors that could, when afforded, provide some protection from the criticisms of local prelates, clergy, or laity.

Most progressive white Catholics in the South were southern born and raised. Progressive Catholics, although often small in number, were located in virtually every part of the South where there was a Catholic presence. They were found in both the Deep South, the area of deepest segregationist sentiment and strength, and in the peripheral South. Some progressives, whether prelates, clergy, or laity, were not southerners and a few were immigrants.

Regardless of their geographical origins, progressives argued that Catholicism rejected race-based discrimination and prejudice. Many progressives, especially those most familiar with Catholic theology, such as prelates and clergy, seminary and Catholic college professors, and editors of Catholic newspapers, claimed that segregation was incompatible with the doctrine of the

Mystical Body of Christ. Monsignor Josiah G. Chatham, a white Mississippian who pastored St. Richard Church in Jackson, explained:

> Through baptism we are so incorporated into Christ and united with all the baptized, that we become one body of which Christ is the head and all the baptized are the members. Negroes and Whites are co-members of Christ's Mystical Body. There is no distinction of race in Christ's Body and Christ's Body is the Church. Saint Paul pounded racism to dust on the doctrine of Christ's Mystical Body.[1]

Some progressive lay Catholics cited the Mystical Body of Christ when they advocated interracialism. In 1950, a group of white students from the Southeastern Regional Interracial Commission (SERINCO) of the National Federation of Catholic Students, which consisted of Louisiana's five Catholic colleges, including Xavier University, issued a statement calling for college integration. They declared: "We think that it is a progressive step toward the integration of Catholics in the Mystical Body of Christ."[2]

A corollary to the doctrine of the Mystical Body of Christ was a belief in the universality of the Church. In 1964, Auxiliary Bishop Joseph B. Brunini of Natchez-Jackson, a Mississippian, explained to the Knights of Columbus annual convention, held in New Orleans, that the universality of the Church left no place for segregation. Furthermore, Brunini declared that "members of the great universal Church, with the clear understanding of the universal brotherhood of man, should be the leaders in breaking down any walls of separation between the peoples of the many races that live within our borders."[3]

Progressives argued that segregation violated the unity of mankind whom God, according to Genesis 1:26–27, had created "in his own image." In calling for the abolition of segregation and discrimination in churches, Archbishop Joseph F. Rummel of New Orleans reminded Catholics in a 1953 pastoral letter that "We are all created to the image and likeness of God, endowed with a spiritual nature, and called to participate in the eternal happiness of heaven."[4]

Jesus's ministry recorded in the New Testament provided progressives with most of their biblical justifications for integration. Both charity and justice, progressives insisted, demanded the end of segregation and other forms of racial discrimination. In 1949, Archbishop Robert E. Lucey of San Antonio informed the Southwest Regional Conference of the National Council of Catholic Women that "Segregation is a sin against charity[,] but it is also a sin against justice."[5]

The themes of charity and justice often appeared in the sermons progressives gave on racial segregation and discrimination. Monsignor Hugh A. Dolan told his parishioners in St. Benedict Church, Greensboro, North Carolina: "Moved by the charity of Christ, Who died for all men, we shall resolutely set ourselves to the task of abolishing the myth of racial superiority by prudent constructive action, based on justice and tempered by charity."[6]

Progressives cited many biblical verses from the gospels regarding love, as well as charity and justice. Most often they quoted Jesus's admonitions that "Thou shalt love thy neighbor as thyself" (St. Matthew 22:39; St. Mark 12:31); "A new commandment I give you that you love one another: that as I have loved you, you also love one another" (St. John 13:34); "By this will all men know that you are my disciples, if you have love for one another" (St. John 13:35); "If anyone says, 'I love God,' and hates his brother, he is a liar" (I St. John 4:20); and "Amen I say to you, as long as you did it for one of these, the least of my brethren, you did it for me" (St. Matthew 25:40). Progressives also cited Jesus's parable of the Good Samaritan (St. Luke 10:25–37), in which the Samaritan, a figure hated and discriminated against by Jews, came to the aid of a man who had been beaten and robbed, and then ignored by passers-by. A few progressives, including Archbishop Rummel, cited Jesus's admonition to the Apostles to "Go . . . and make disciples of all nations" (St. Matthew 28:19) to argue that racism was incompatible with Catholicism.[7]

Occasionally, progressives argued that domestic racism retarded Catholic missions in nonwhite countries. In 1955, Shreveport, Louisiana, pastor Joseph B. Gremillion told the Diocese of Lafayette's Annual Teachers' Institute that "We must receive the Negro, on a status fully equal and without reserve, into our Church and School and Society for the advance of the world-wide mission of Christ. Surely we still hear the command of Christ: Go and teach all nations."[8]

However, the foreign missions theme was seldom raised by progressives. To some degree, this reflected an understanding that southern white Catholics felt no great responsibility for the success of the Catholic missionary endeavor abroad as they were but a small part of a worldwide Catholic faith directed from Rome. American Catholics had a relatively small foreign missionary presence, with only about 160 missionaries in Africa in 1950. It did not seem credible to argue that the health, vitality, and expansion of the worldwide Catholic movement was dependent on the removal of segregation from southern Catholicism, a minority religion in most of the South.[9]

Progressive Catholics were not always themselves persuaded by reports from American Catholic missionaries abroad. While acutely conscious that American racism harmed the United States in its Cold War competition with the Soviet Union for influence in the developing world, Father Louis J. Twomey, S.J., of New Orleans's Loyola University of the South sometimes bristled at foreign criticism of the United States. In February 1964, Father Richard H. Brown, an American Jesuit missionary in Mexico, wrote to Twomey that racism gave America a poor image. Twomey replied:

> Granted that our treatment of the Negro is no better than the treatment of the little people in Latin America, the fact is that most of our Negroes, for all their sufferings under racial discrimination, are better off than the average campesino

in Latin America. Of course, this doesn't excuse us in the least. But I would be inclined to take criticism from the Latin Americans much more readily if they were willing to admit the terrible crimes of social injustice they have committed against their own people.

Progressives were more concerned by the damage that segregation did to domestic missions among African Americans. Father Alexander O. Sigur, chaplain of Our Lady of Wisdom Catholic Center at the University of Southwestern Louisiana Catholic Center in Lafayette, explained in a sermon:

> Our colored "mission" is here. Formerly we always thought of going way out to the mission. The mission is at home. There are over 15,000,000 Negroes outside the Catholic faith in this country. Our sincere service of them in a just cause of humane, Christian race relations will show more than anything startling or stupendous the reality of our Catholicism.[10]

Like foreign missions, domestic missions to African Americans did not occupy a prominent place in progressives' appeals. Before the 1970s, and in many cases the 1980s, southern dioceses did not operate offices or agencies for African American evangelism, which was usually conducted not by diocesan priests but by members of religious orders of nuns and clergy, especially orders devoted solely to black missions. As black evangelism was not a central diocesan concern or function but one largely left to religious orders, which often had little or limited contact with diocesan officials and clergy, domestic missions featured little in the arguments advanced by progressives to try to persuade prelates and white Catholics to abandon segregation.

The existence of a black apostolate conducted by religious orders, many of them northern staffed and based, and the fact that African Americans were often admitted to otherwise white churches, albeit segregated in seating and communion, also made it difficult for progressives to argue persuasively that segregation prevented Catholic evangelism among blacks and hard to convince segregationists of its harmful effects on missions work. Nevertheless, some religious clergy and nuns assigned to southern black Catholic churches and schools called for and worked on behalf of integration and racial justice in southern communities, although many of their converts left the region.[11]

In the decades after World War II, many African American Catholics, whether cradle Catholics or converts, joined black migration from the South to northern and western cities in search of better opportunities and to escape Jim Crow. As a consequence, in many southern dioceses the total number of black Catholics, always small outside of southern Louisiana, rose slowly. Missions work among African Americans in the South seemed less productive and successful than it actually was and to many white Catholics, including some diocesan clergy as well as white laity, a relatively minor aspect of the Church's work. In 1963, the Diocese of Baton Rouge observed that "There is the very real danger in a segregated area that the Church be presented as a 'church for whites' with the few Negro (and segregated) members as a curious but unimportant appendage."[12]

The missions theme also lacked potency among many Catholics because the laity were less inclined than evangelical Protestants, such as Southern Baptists, to try to convert others. Furthermore, as the New York–based Catholic magazine *Jubilee* observed in 1959, "The average white Catholic in the South has never shown much interest in converting the Negro."[13]

Although progressive religious clergy and nuns, who worked among African Americans, were often supportive of integration and civil rights, particularly in the 1960s and early 1970s, and sometimes tried to persuade southern prelates to desegregate, they often had little contact with, or opportunity to influence, local white Catholic communities. White religious and diocesan priests who worked among African Americans were, as Father Bernardin J. Patterson, a black Benedictine, observed, "ostracized by priests working in white parishes, by white Catholics and sometimes even by the chancery office." Some white diocesan priests in New Orleans, including those with whom he had been in seminary at St. Mary's in Baltimore, would not even talk with white Josephite priest Father McNamara of Corpus Christi parish because he was a "nigger priest."[14]

A few progressives used printed material to address predominantly white audiences about the effects of racism on missions to African Americans. In October 1954, a few months after the United States Supreme Court's *Brown* ruling outlawed public school segregation, an editorial in the Diocese of Charleston's *Catholic Banner* affirmed that "The recent Supreme Court decision provides an opportunity to show the Negro that the Catholic Church cares for his welfare." In a "Syllabus for Racial Justice" produced in 1963 for use in grades seven through twelve of its parochial schools, the Diocese of Baton Rouge observed that "Racial segregation with its accompanying attitudes and influences is harmful to the Church's present-day mission to the Negro."[15]

When progressives looked to the Bible for guidance on race, they concentrated on its inclusive message. It followed that those who rejected that message, as progressives interpreted it, by supporting segregation were guilty of sin. Leading progressive Catholic prelates in the South, such as Lucey, Rummel, and Bishop Vincent S. Waters of Raleigh, forthrightly condemned segregation as sinful.[16]

Aside from the Bible, southern white Catholic progressives cited parental influence, childhood familiarity with African Americans, sensitivity to racism produced by exposure to anti-Catholicism, revulsion at white treatment of or violence toward blacks, college and seminary classes that critiqued racism, and exposure to African Americans under conditions of equality as crucial factors in shaping their views. However, progressives did not recall hearing segregation addressed from a moral perspective as children in Catholic churches, or in the segregated parochial or public schools they had attended.[17]

Some progressives were reared by unprejudiced parents and had recognized racial injustice since childhood. Born in Vicksburg, Mississippi, in 1909, Joseph B. Brunini, Auxiliary Bishop and later Bishop of Natchez-Jackson, recollected that the influence of his parents and his childhood horror at the lynching of an African American man in Vicksburg led him to oppose racial discrimination.[18]

Born in Houston, Texas, in 1930, Father John E. McCarthy (later Bishop of Austin) was raised by his mother, a New Yorker, who, "When we were little[,] would never let us say any derogatory things about colored people or black people" and believed that because of their difficult lives "we should be very kind to them." Like McCarthy a cofounder of the Diocese of Galveston-Houston's Catholic Council on Community Relations, Father Joseph A. Fiorenza (later Archbishop of Galveston-Houston) understood racial discrimination from childhood. Born in Beaumont, Texas, in 1931, Fiorenza was reared in the city only a street away from an African American neighborhood and played with local black children. His mother often attended Mass in an African American Catholic church. As he grew up with black people, Fiorenza recalled that he "felt great ease with them" and always "had a sense that there was something not right about the laws of segregation."[19]

Many progressives were influenced by observing the conditions in which African Americans lived. Born in 1919, Father Joseph B. Gremillion of St. Joseph Church in Shreveport, Louisiana, grew up on his father's cane and cotton farm in southern Louisiana. Despite his background, which included a grandfather who had fought for the Confederacy, Gremillion denounced segregation. He observed to some parishioners that "My dad had Negro sharecroppers—maybe that's what opened my eyes," referring to the poverty, meager education, and second-class status that the sharecroppers and their families experienced.[20]

M. F. Everett's sensitivity to racial discrimination developed in response to the deprived conditions in which many African Americans lived and his experience of anti-Catholicism. In 1954, he wrote in an editorial in *Catholic Action of the South*, the New Orleans archdiocesan newspaper:

> I lived as a youth in a semi-Southern community [on a farm near Belton, Missouri]. Negroes in the town, hard working and respectable, had no school. They were barred from the public school and there were too few Negro children for a separate school to be set up as provided by law.
>
> We were one of two Catholic families in a large district, Ku Klux Klan meetings were held and fiery crosses burned not far from our home. If you think we were considered the "equals" of others in the community of the Klan mentality, you don't know prejudice.

Anti-Catholicism also influenced the racial views of other progressive laity. In 1963, Mrs. N. C. Brunson wrote from Birmingham, Alabama, to her diocesan newspaper the *Catholic Week*, that "Southern Catholics certainly know to what lengths religious persecution can go. Racial persecution is but a step away."[21]

Some progressive southern white Catholics grew up sharing the racial prejudices of other whites but changed their views in response to exposure to societies that did not have Jim Crow laws, and college education. In 1955, a Lake Charles, Louisiana, laywoman wrote to Bishop Jules B. Jeanmard of Lafayette:

> In the past, because of my southern background, I frequently felt that the south was justified in her stand on the colored question. However, with the study of history, travel to other parts of our country, and finally, five years abroad where I worked for the armed forces in Europe, I came to realize that our particular situation was unique, and only an accident of a strange tradition, or an accident of history. For some years now I have, in the face of family, friends and others, openly expressed my views that we were all God's children, and as Americans, all created free and equal.
>
> I have seen integration work. In Federal agencies, in the army, and in other parts of the country.[22]

Layman John P. "Jack" Nelson, a lawyer who worked for desegregation in New Orleans and was involved in many Catholic interracial activities, was born in Gulfport, Mississippi, in 1921. Nelson, who grew up in New Orleans and on a Louisiana sugar plantation, shared the segregationist views of many other white southerners into adulthood. A decorated veteran of World War Two, Nelson's views on race changed not through military service but partly under the influence of Father Louis J. Twomey when Nelson, a student at Loyola University's Law School, took Twomey's compulsory course on natural law in the late 1940s. Nelson explained that "My only education in race relations, until I met Father Twomey, was to observe how my family acted toward our Negro maid."[23]

When he met Nelson, Twomey, a lifelong Catholic, was himself only a recent convert to integration. Born in Tampa, Florida, in 1905, Twomey had, according to novelist and friend Walker Percy, "as late as 1943 still wondered whether the difficulties of Negroes might be traced to the curse of Ham." Twomey was proud of his southern heritage, which included a great-grandfather and five great-uncles killed fighting for the Confederacy. He recalled:

> I was raised in a rigidly segregated community. In the Catholic elementary and high schools in the South that I attended, there was never a word about how I could prepare in a Catholic or democratic way to face the most serious social problem we had. And there was no help from the pulpit. As a Southern boy, I absorbed that pattern of segregation around me as the very air I breathed.

Twomey attributed his change of views to "the grace of God." In 1963, he told a radio audience that "I began to be less and less complacent with the community's and my own callous acceptance of the sufferings inflicted on the Negro through compulsory segregation." Although no particular incident brought about Twomey's rejection of segregation, by 1948 he was writing and speaking out against racial discrimination.[24]

Twomey's fellow Jesuit Father Albert S. Foley had similarly been reared as a segregationist and had a grandfather who had fought for the Confederacy. Born in New Orleans in 1912, Foley had grown up proud of the city's Confederate history and memorials, and he had regarded the Confederates who formed the first Ku Klux Klan as "boyhood heroes." Foley accepted segregation as "normal" and during his childhood never heard it questioned in church or parochial school. He recalled that "These early convictions and prejudices were not even affected very deeply by my theological studies [at St. Mary's College in Kansas] during the war years, 1939–1943." Foley "stayed away from courses in race relations," but after joining Spring Hill College, a Jesuit institution in Mobile, Alabama, was assigned to teach a course on "Migration, Immigration and Race." His preparatory reading convinced him of the injustice and irrationality of segregation. Consequently, Foley became involved in interracial organizing and encouraged students to question racial inequality.[25]

Several progressive priests were shaped by their seminary experiences. Born in 1931, Father Gerald M. LeFebvre grew up in Port Allan, near Baton Rouge, and attended Notre Dame Seminary in New Orleans. He first became conscious of civil rights issues as a seminarian when Archbishop Rummel ordered an end to segregated seating and communion in the archdiocese's churches. LeFebvre belonged to the Summer School of Catholic Action, which included seminarians and young people from Alabama, Louisiana, Mississippi, and Texas. The group met for one week annually and included race among the topics addressed by its speakers. Participants included African Americans from St. Augustine's Seminary, Mississippi. LeFebvre also took a seminary ethics class under Father Vincent J. O'Connell, a Marian from Philadelphia, Pennsylvania. An outspoken critic of segregation, O'Connell was the archdiocese's director of action and became general chairman of the Catholic Committee of the South (CCS).[26]

Like O'Connell, some white Catholic migrants from outside the region expressed disapproval and discomfort when they moved South and encountered de jure segregation for the first time. In 1953, Norfolk, Virginia, residents Janet and Harlan Hall explained:

> A few years ago we moved from California to New Orleans, and it was quite a shock to see Nuns and Priests of the negro race experiencing the ignominious position of being forced to sit at the rear of the buses.

It is our deepest desire to see this evil of segregation and intolerance be eliminated and if your example is followed perhaps we shall see it in our life time.

Some migrants expressed relief when they traveled outside the Jim Crow South. Louise Schaiell of Asheville, North Carolina, wrote in the same year: "Just recently we spent our vacation back home in Chicago and it was good to be back where there is no segregation—publicly at least." However, she acknowledged that it was "very sad" that in Chicago "They still draw the color line in hotels, places of the more exclusive forms of amusement, etc."²⁷

Father Bernard F. Law, editor of the *Mississippi Register*, the diocesan newspaper of Natchez-Jackson, had also been raised outside the South. Law was born in 1931 in Mexico where his Pennsylvanian father, a pilot, and his mother, originally from Washington State, had met and married. He spent his early childhood in several states before attending high school in St. Thomas in the Virgin Islands. Law later recalled that his "positive experience of racial harmony" in predominantly black St. Thomas became "a tremendous sign of hope to me."²⁸

Progressive white Catholics in the South who, like Law, occupied leadership positions in the Church, sought to exert leadership on desegregation as their offices and their sense of possibility and circumstances allowed. Progressive members of the laity sometimes wrote to the secular and diocesan press and to prelates in support of desegregation, but they also sought to exert influence through diocesan lay organizations and groups they organized with the approval of their prelates.

Three main stages marked the development of progressive Catholics in the post–World War Two South. In the first stage between 1945 and 1953, progressives increasingly criticized segregation publicly, and some created or participated in Catholic organizations that called for desegregation of Catholic and, in some cases, secular institutions. During their second stage between 1954 and 1960, concerned by mounting segregationist opposition to the *Brown* decision, progressives sought to counter segregationist arguments and prepare Catholics for Church and secular desegregation. However, massive resistance by the white South to *Brown*'s implementation and Catholic segregationist resistance to change undermined progressives and often halted or blocked their efforts. During their third stage, which began in 1961, progressives challenged segregation anew and in greater numbers, and some established Catholic interracial councils with the permission of their ordinaries and in partnership with African American Catholics. Some nuns and some clergy, both diocesan and religious, participated in civil rights activity, and some religious orders pressured prelates to desegregate churches and schools.

Most of the South's progressive white Catholics did not criticize segregation publicly until their first stage began after World War Two. In a pamphlet, *Interracial Justice*, issued in 1945, Archbishop Lucey wrote that "in our country some men have lifted up the master race idea almost to the level of a religion." The pamphlet declared:

> Segregation, as now practiced, involves discrimination; discrimination in educational opportunity, in economic life, in housing and in scores of other areas. It arises from a sense of racial superiority, and results in injustice—a constant grinding down of the aspirations of individuals for no other reason than racial origin.

Lucey addressed the CCS when it met in New Orleans for its sixth annual convention in September 1946 after a hiatus of two years. He cited papal condemnations of racism and urged the committee to work for its elimination by organizing lay discussion clubs, ensuring Catholic schools taught racial justice and working with union leaders to remove "race discrimination in our economic life."[29]

In 1946, Paul D. Williams, the CCS's cofounder and first executive secretary, became president of the biracial Southern Regional Council (SRC). Although the SRC, formed in 1944, focused in its early years on making separate but equal truly equal and fostering economic growth, Williams was committed to desegregation. He declared: "If we can't do everything, that's no excuse for doing nothing. If we can't remove all the fences that separate the races all over the South let us remove as many fences as we can wherever we can."[30]

Civil rights was a national political issue. In 1947, the President's Committee on Civil Rights, which included Catholic bishop Francis J. Haas of Grand Rapids, Michigan, called for federal antilynching legislation, establishment of a Civil Rights Division in the United States Justice Department, abolition of the poll tax, a permanent fair employment practices committee, and desegregation of federal employment, interstate transportation, and the armed forces. In February 1948, President Harry S. Truman addressed a joint session of Congress and in vain requested passage of many of the committee's recommendations.[31]

Catholic progressives in the South responded. In April 1948, the Reverend Frederick A. Koch editorialized in the *North Carolina Catholic* that "Catholics must understand that any failure to respect the rights of the individual is unChristian, unAmerican and a civil wrong in our Christian democracy. Unequal opportunity, exploitation and segregation to disease ridden slums are among the civil wrongs that we must fight to right."[32]

The national Democratic Party agreed and adopted a stronger civil rights platform than Truman now wanted, which drew, ironically, on his presidential committee's recommendations. In response, some white southerners bolted the party and formed the rival States' Rights Party, or Dixiecrats, that opposed civil rights and nominated a separate ticket under Governor Strom Thurmond of South Carolina for the presidency.[33]

Without naming the Dixiecrats, the CCS issued a statement condemning their viewpoint. The committee declared that "'States Rights' cannot be invoked to suppress inalienable rights guaranteed by the Constitution of the United States" including "the right to vote, the right of personal safety, the right to adequate educational advantages and the right to organize freely for economic, social and cultural improvements." It added that "The term 'Southern Tradition' is misused and dishonored when it is employed to justify a continued state of unjust discrimination against the Negro."[34]

Father Vincent J. O'Connell, CCS general chairman between 1946 and 1951, condemned the Dixiecrats for their anti–civil rights and antiunion policies and called for "fair labor standards and fair employment practices." In 1948, he told the Louisiana convention of the Congress of Industrial Organizations that the "Dixiecrat movement is based on concepts of white supremacy and company unionism." As fears of internal Communist subversion mounted in the ongoing Cold War between the United States and the Soviet Union, O'Connell compared the Dixiecrats to the Communists and thereby turned the tables on segregationists who argued that communism lay behind the civil rights movement and labor unions. He claimed that "Communists try to hide Red supremacy behind the sacred name of 'democracy' while Dixiecrats hide white supremacy behind the sacred name of 'States' Rights.' While the communists establish political dictatorship, the Dixiecrats support economic dictatorship." Many white Louisianans, including many Catholics, evidently did not share O'Connell's views. The Dixiecrats won the state in the presidential election, along with Alabama, Mississippi, and South Carolina, although they were unable to prevent Truman's election.[35]

Days after the Dixiecrats' convention in July 1948, a group of African American and white students from SERINCO presented Archbishop Rummel with a resolution urging him to desegregate archdiocesan schools and support desegregation of Catholic graduate schools in the archdiocese. Father Joseph H. Fichter, a Jesuit sociologist at Loyola University and New Jersey native, who had stimulated SERINCO's formation that year and become its chaplain, attended the meeting, held in the office of university president Thomas J. Shields, S.J. After noting widespread white Catholic support for segregation, Rummel advocated gradualism. He encouraged the group but took no action.[36]

Subsequently, Shields sought to ban African American speakers from addressing students on campus and prevent publication of *Christian Conscience*, SERINCO's monthly newsletter, at Loyola University of the South and SERINCO meetings on its campus. He also urged Fichter to be cautious. Nevertheless, SERINCO survived and continued its newsletter. With Rummel's support, in March 1949 SERINCO organized an Interracial Sunday at Ursuline College, attended by over five hundred people. The event featured a Mass, breakfast, and an invited speaker from both races, followed by discussion. Interracial Sunday became an annual observation held at one of SERINCO members' colleges. However, SERINCO was a small group. Its monthly meetings, which featured guest speakers, averaged only thirty attendees.[37]

SERINCO's Interracial Sundays were supported by the Commission on Human Rights (CHR) that Fichter founded in February 1949 with the support of Father O'Connell. Twenty-two people, African American and white, attended the commission's organizational meeting at Loyola University. The commission sought "the removal of prejudice, intolerance, segregation, jim-crowism and kindred evils from within the framework of Catholic life in New Orleans." It insisted that the universality of the Catholic Church and the Mystical Body of Christ rendered all Catholics, regardless of race, equal and "brothers in Christ."[38]

The commission's membership grew to around one hundred, including approximately sixty whites, 75 percent of them southern born. All Catholic adults in the city were eligible for membership, except students because they could join SERINCO. A significant segment of the commission's members were schoolteachers and Xavier University professors, black and white, although fewer than 10 percent of its members had Xavier connections. A. P. Tureaud, a Creole of color from New Orleans who was a civil rights attorney and a leading figure in the state National Association for the Advancement of Colored People (NAACP), was also a CHR leader.[39]

The commission's members envisioned attending Mass together once a month, alternating between African American and white churches. But initially only two white parishes, St. Raphael's and St. Louis Cathedral, accepted them, although they were welcomed "at the convent chapels of the Madames of the Sacred Heart, the Ursuline Sisters, and the Missionary Servants of the Most Holy Eucharist." Fichter recalled that "The [religious] priests in Negro parishes were always cooperative, but this could be said of only a few [diocesan] priests serving in white parishes." CHR members attended and helped raise financial support for SERINCO's annual Interracial Sundays, and the two organizations had similar programs. Each group met monthly, organized social events, published a monthly newsletter, and had an invited speakers program. However, their literature had small print runs.[40]

In January 1951, SERINCO member Norman C. Francis, a student at Xavier University, spoke at the CCS convention, held in Columbia, South Carolina, which adopted an integration resolution. Citing Pope Pius XII's 1939 encyclical *Summi Pontificatus* on the unity of human society, the resolution supported "ultimate integration . . . in the religious, economic, and cultural life of the nation, so that, in the justice and charity of Christ, all, regardless of race, color, or language, may enjoy their rights and privileges as creatures made to the image and likeness of God." The CCS's ordinaries who approved the resolution covered all of the South, except Arkansas, Texas, and Tennessee, indicative of the committee's fluctuating membership. In the resolution's wake, Bishop Waters and Bishop Richard O. Gerow of Natchez-Jackson ordered their priests not to allow segregation in church seating or communion, and Rummel reiterated an earlier call for these practices to end. However, these efforts had only partial success.[41]

Supported by Twomey and Fichter, SERINCO members tried to desegregate Loyola University's Law School. Their efforts helped push the New Orleans Province of the Society of Jesus to sanction desegregation of Jesuit institutions and Loyola University to admit Xavier University graduates Norman C. Francis and Benjamin Johnson in 1952. In the winter of 1952–1953, SERINCO organized intermural basketball games at Xavier University between its member colleges, with the result that the color bar was broken.[42]

Despite enjoying some success, neither the numbers nor the influence of lay and clergy Catholic progressives in the South were substantial. The region's few progressive ordinaries acted gradually and, except for Archbishop Lucey, they faced significant lay and clergy opposition or foot dragging that inhibited the limited desegregation of Catholic institutions they ordered. Of the South's Catholic diocesan newspapers, only the *North Carolina Catholic*, editorialized in favor of desegregation, although most reported some news about desegregation in the religious and secular world. There were few active interracial Catholic lay groups. They included those of the archdioceses of San Antonio and New Orleans, and Catholic interracial councils in Greensboro and Rock Hill, North Carolina, and Richmond, Virginia.[43]

Progressives sometimes expressed frustration at their lack of influence and the apathy of their own membership. When Patricia Ryan, the CHR's executive secretary, addressed the CCS convention in 1951 to inform it of CHR activities, she noted "The general unwillingness on the part of so many white people to hear what we have to say." Despite having over ninety members, attendance at the CHR's monthly meetings in the early 1950s was usually between twenty-eight and thirty-eight, comparable to that of SERINCO meetings, and "the membership committee expressed concern over the failure of so many new members to attend meetings regularly." CHR leaders were often exasperated by Rummel's caution and by the continuation of many separate black and white archdiocesan societies. Fichter recalled that "Archbishop Rummel was ineffectual in race relations because of an excess of prudence and a failure of nerve. He did not lead the campaign for racial desegregation, but he did cooperate with the laity in a benign and interested way."[44]

Archbishop Gerald P. O'Hara of Savannah-Atlanta, who succeeded Rummel as CCS episcopal chairman in January 1951, was acutely conscious of the committee's shortcomings. In June, O'Hara wrote to Bishop Peter L. Ireton of Richmond: "[T]he Catholic Committee of the South has been largely ineffective, not only on the diocesan but also on the regional level because our priests are not well acquainted with the nature and objectives of the C.C.S." To address the problem, the CCS sponsored institutes that explained regional problems to several hundred priests and suggested remedial action.[45]

In April 1953, the CCS met in Richmond for what became its final convention. The convention's interracial workshop reported that "The great need is for actual present racial integration at all levels and in all of the activities and programs of the Church in the South." Although the nine bishops present, six of them from five southern dioceses and the remaining three from Washington, DC, and Covington, Kentucky, praised the work of the CCS department of race relations and encouraged it "not to lose heart despite the difficulties," southern prelates withdrew their remaining, and often tenuous, support from the CCS in the next few years.[46]

Progressives entered their second stage after the *Brown* decision in May 1954. Shortly before the ruling, Father Maurice V. Shean of the CCS, an Oratorian based at Rock Hill, South Carolina, but raised in New Jersey and New York City, invited prelates or representatives from southeastern dioceses and other interested parties, including Paul D. Williams, Father Albert S. Foley, and George S. Mitchell of the SRC, to meet in Atlanta. Shean hoped the meeting would "determine a united front," but representatives from only seven dioceses attended. They asked him to prepare a detailed analysis of the racial demographics of southern dioceses and economic factors affecting segregation. Speaking on behalf of the CCS, Shean, subsequently, welcomed *Brown*.[47]

Delivered in June, Shean's seventy-four-page report called on southern prelates to meet and devise a common policy, which, the report strongly implied, should be a moral justification of integration based on church teachings. Shean drew on papal and prelates' statements for support. He also included pastoral letters, issued by Rummel and Waters in March and June 1953 respectively, that ordered an end to racial segregation and discrimination in Catholic churches, and an April 1954 instruction from Bishop Ireton to begin desegregation of Catholic high schools in the city of Richmond in September. Shean included a section refuting the arguments made by opponents of desegregation. He ended the report by suggesting that after formulating a shared approach, prelates desegregate schools and other Catholic institutions with minimal publicity, acting gradually as local circumstances permitted and after instituting a preparatory education campaign that emphasized church teachings rejecting racism.[48]

Southern prelates did not adopt a collective approach to advance desegregation. According to John J. Russell, then Bishop of Charleston, "half a dozen" ordinaries prevailed on their fellow southern prelates to prevent the CCS from meeting in convention after 1953 because racial "conditions differ so much in the various dioceses, and none wanted outsiders coming in and making statements which might cause trouble and do no good." Consequently, the bishops decided "to let the Catholic Committee of the South be quiet, since it was not possible to hold regional conventions, meetings, or institutes, and to ignore the race problem, and also impossible or at least imprudent to issue statements that might do harm in some dioceses." Some prelates feared that segregationist opposition from within and outside the Church would endanger its well-being, strength, and unity. Nevertheless, the CCS continued some activity at its headquarters, transferred from New Orleans to Rock Hill, South Carolina, in 1951, and through the CHR in New Orleans.[49]

Despite the CCS's troubles, the *Brown* decision gave progressives encouragement. For the first time, *Catholic Action of the South*, which had a circulation of over forty thousand, criticized Jim Crow. M. F. Everett editorialized that "The [*Brown*] decree should be respected as the law of God, from which it arises, and as the just law of man." He quoted "all men are created equal" from the Declaration of Independence and contended that "All its citizens must be granted equal opportunity, or America is not a democracy." Everett stated that segregation was incompatible with Jesus's admonition "Love thy neighbor as thyself." He argued that southern political leaders committed to evading *Brown* were "flouting democracy and Americanism," and he claimed that "Their appeal to 'states' rights' is political piffle."[50]

While Everett condemned segregation, attendance at CHR meetings in 1954 and early 1955 varied from the low teens to seventy but often numbered between fourteen and twenty-six. Fichter saw an opportunity to reinvigorate the commission when Archbishop Rummel appointed a committee in June 1955 to study parochial school desegregation and, in the summer, accepted its recommendation to begin with the first grade in September 1956. Rummel wrote to the archdiocese's priests and school officials that school desegregation would commence no earlier in order to prepare Catholics to accept the change. With Rummel's support, Fichter secured a $10,000 grant from the Fund for the Republic of the Ford Foundation, disbursed to the CHR by Loyola University of the South, to launch a six-month program in January 1956. Aimed at "Catholic parents, teachers and priests in New Orleans," the program was "meant to give them basic preparation and motivation for the desegregation of the parochial elementary schools in September 1956."[51]

Between January and May 1956, a total of eight speakers, half of them Catholic and two of them African American Catholics, spoke at the CHR's invitation on their areas of expertise. Only three speakers were southern. Collectively, the speakers refuted segregationist claims that desegregation would spread venereal disease in elementary schools, children's intelligence depended on their race, and segregation was God's will. Speakers also discussed "racial differences in delinquency," "the constitutional and legal angles of Catholic school desegregation," and "the religious, ethical and moral advantages of school integration."[52]

To attract the largest possible audience, the lectures took place on Sunday afternoons. Nevertheless, "only about a half-dozen priests and an equal number of Sisters" attended, and "a general lack of cooperation on the part of pastors and principals of elementary schools" forced the commission to hold the meetings at Xavier and Loyola universities, Dominican College, a parish hall, and three high schools run by religious orders. Overall attendance "ranged from about a hundred at the smallest meeting to almost a thousand at the largest."

The city's three daily newspapers "gave full and excellent coverage," ensuring that the lectures and discussions reached a wider audience. WDSU television and radio also covered the lecture forums, although Loyola University's own radio station WWL did not because, as the university's president Father Patrick Donnelly told Fichter, they were "too controversial."[53]

When the program was only in its second month, controversy erupted when SERINCO invited Hulan E. Jack, president of New York City's Borough of Manhattan, to address its eighth Interracial Sunday on February 26, supported by the CHR's Fund for the Republic grant. Emile A. Wagner Jr., a Loyola University alumnus, pressured Loyola University and Rummel, who was due as usual to participate in Interracial Sunday, to withdraw Jack's invitation, claiming that Jack had been associated with organizations deemed subversive by the United States attorney general. When Rummel and Loyola University stood firm, Wagner made his accusations, based on information received from the United States House of Representatives UnAmerican Activities Committee, public. Jack denied the charges, which received extensive coverage in secular newspapers. Ironically, the publicity may have swelled attendance because the event, held at the Holy Name of Jesus School, attracted between 850 and nearly 1,000 people, the best attendance for any Interracial Sunday. A quarter of the audience was white.[54]

Progressives and segregationists competed to win or keep white Catholics, lay and clergy, on their side, but, significantly outnumbered by segregationists, progressives had the harder task. Writing to Fichter about the CHR, Rummel conceded that "When we compare the numbers that attend our gatherings with those who attend the meetings of the Citizens Councils we are certainly not reaching the masses," but the archbishop believed that "those who are doing the calm thinking still outnumber those that are doing so much of the shouting."[55]

To reach its target audience of those "who would be most immediately involved in the desegregation of the parochial school system," the CHR compiled a mailing list of four thousand people in New Orleans and began a seven-month mailing program in mid-January 1956 that sent 201,200 pieces of literature. The materials included the *Christian Impact*, which summarized the lecture series, every other issue of the *Christian Conscience*, and articles and news stories about school desegregation. The commission also published eight thousand copies of a forty-page *Handbook on Catholic School Integration* based on the lecture program and discussions, with half sent to its city mailing list in August and most of the remainder to the Catholic school systems of other southern dioceses. An essay contest for parents of parochial schoolchildren in New Orleans, entitled "Why an Integrated School Is Better than a Segregated School," produced thirty-seven entries, some of them from segregationists refuting the claim. The commission published the nine prize-winning essays in a pamphlet *Southern Catholic Parents Speak Up for Integrated Schools*, mailed to 10,500 people. It sent another pamphlet, *Southern Catholic Teachers Favor Integration*, to over 6,000 recipients.[56]

The apparent imminence of Catholic school desegregation and the CHR's supportive campaign stimulated a great deal of white opposition. Fichter and the commission received many hostile letters from segregationists. Some parents on the CHR's mailing list demanded that their names be removed. Many Catholic segregationists joined the Greater New Orleans Citizens' Council, which at a rally in May booed Rummel's name on learning that he was a board member of the New Orleans branch of the National Urban League. In response, the CHR branded council members as "anti-American, anti-Southern, anti-Catholic, and irreligious people."[57]

That same month, the state assembly passed a raft of segregationist measures, including dismissal for public schoolteachers who advocated integration. In June, the CHR advised members endangered by the legislation to resign from the commission. Thirty members, all African American public schoolteachers, did so. The commission's membership fell to seventy.[58]

In June, Fichter left New Orleans to take up a visiting professorship at the University of Notre Dame in Indiana. Without his dynamic presence, the CHR stopped releasing press statements. It lapsed into inactivity when the Citizens' Council called for disclosure of its membership list and, discovering the source of its grant, erroneously accused the Fund for the Republic of Communist sympathies. On July 31, Rummel announced that he would postpone Catholic school desegregation and began a lengthy public silence on the issue. Urged by Fichter, the CHR planned to apply for a second grant from the fund but Loyola University, alarmed by adverse publicity, refused to administer another grant. Rummel was unenthusiastic about a further information campaign by the commission. By October, the commission had withered. Fichter's periodic efforts to revive it from Notre Dame, and later on his return to New Orleans, failed and lacked Rummel's support.[59]

SERINCO folded after Loyola University forced the organization off campus by withdrawing the university's membership of the National Federation of Catholic College Students in September 1956. Loyola officials had long been uncomfortable with SERINCO's outspoken antisegregationist message, and the Hulan Jack affair had further alienated university officials.[60]

In early 1957, Fichter learned that the CCS was "in the process of dissolving itself." Despite losing the support of southern bishops who feared that it would only inflame segregationist opposition, the committee had produced a series of pamphlets in the mid-1950s that supported *Brown* and desegregation, and condemned massive resistance. In 1957, Father Shean, who had kept the CCS afloat from his base at the Oratory in Rock Hill, South Carolina, resigned as the committee's executive secretary.[61]

In the late 1950s, southern progressive Catholics had few outlets as many of the region's prelates wanted to avoid discussion of desegregation for fear of antagonizing segregationists within and outside the Catholic fold. With the exception of San Antonio, the small number of southern Catholic interracial councils had become paper organizations. Father Louis J. Twomey lamented that "the lack of exchange among us [progressives] is a very serious handicap."[62]

However, in August 1958, over four hundred delegates from thirty-six interracial councils, mostly from the North and West, met in Chicago at the initiative of the city's Catholic interracial council. They received an encouraging letter from Acting Papal Secretary of State Monsignor Angelo Dell'Acqua, who wrote that "Holy Father again expresses warm commendation for the praiseworthy work of the Catholic Interracial Councils of the United States." Archbishop Lucey sent a message of support, as well as two priests, to the meeting, which Father Fichter attended. The assembled delegates passed resolutions that condemned segregation and discrimination in the Catholic Church and secular society. They also established an interim committee, with Elmer S. Powell, a black S.V.D. Father at Mississippi's St. Augustine's Seminary, as its only southern member, to "study the possibility of some form of closer association of the various Catholic Interracial Councils."[63]

In 1960, these efforts led to the National Catholic Conference for Interracial Justice (NCCIJ)'s formation. In 1961, Matt Ahmann, its executive director, established the organization's headquarters in Chicago. Affiliated with the Social Action Department of the National Catholic Welfare Conference (NCWC), the NCCIJ operated with the approval of the American bishops, but, in practice, it was autonomous and reliant on funding from charitable foundations and dues from member councils. The conference, which held annual conventions, sought to foster Catholic interracial councils and "represent these organizations in the national civil rights movement."[64]

In 1960, the southern civil rights movement began a period of sustained direct action when sit-ins at segregated lunch counters spread from Greensboro, North Carolina, to many other southern cities. The NCCIJ approved the sit-ins at its first convention that year. While most southern Catholic newspapers ignored the protests, the *North Carolina Catholic*, often a progressive voice, declared: "What they want, and rightly, is to dramatize the meaning of personal and racial degradation." The direct-action phase of the civil rights movement and violent responses to it by some southern segregationists dramatized the issues of racial discrimination. Anxious to organize Catholic interracial councils in the South and to support desegregation, in 1961 the NCCIJ established a Southern Field Service with a $30,000 grant from the Taconic Foundation, as southern white Catholic progressives entered their third stage.[65]

The fledgling NCCIJ encouraged the formation and growth of Catholic interracial councils in Little Rock, New Orleans, and other southern cities.

Established in March 1961, the Catholic Council on Human Relations (CCHR), as the New Orleans council was known, included M. F. Everett among its charter members and Jack Nelson as secretary. Like all Catholic interracial councils, the CCHR was established with the support of the local ordinary. Archbishop Rummel appointed Monsignor Charles J. Plauche, the archdiocese's chancellor, as its chaplain.[66]

Like its predecessor the CHR, the CCHR did not disclose its membership list, but, unlike the CHR, it sought mass membership. Three hundred laymen and women attended the council's organizational meeting, but it struggled to recruit more members, ending the year with 376 applications. Initially, it relied on Twomey's Institute of Industrial Relations for both funds and office space.[67]

Henry A. Cabirac Jr., the council's executive director, was a white New Orleans businessman and NAACP member. On Father Twomey's recommendation, he also headed the NCCIJ's Southern Field Service, which established its headquarters in New Orleans in September 1961. Cabirac and the CCHR focused on encouraging Rummel and diocesan officials to begin desegregation of parochial schools, with Cabirac also traveling the South to support and promote the establishment of Catholic interracial councils.[68]

With few exceptions, in the early 1960s white progressives' links with the civil rights movement were confined to the NAACP and state advisory civil rights committees. Jack Nelson joined the NAACP, successfully defended sit-in protesters in New Orleans, and won several desegregation suits in Louisiana. In May 1961, Twomey told an NAACP membership rally in New Orleans that "The NAACP in working for its objectives is aiding not only the Negro people but the entire world." Twomey also worked with the Louisiana State Advisory Committee to the United States Commission on Civil Rights. Father Albert S. Foley of Spring Hill College chaired its Alabama counterpart, which in a 1961 report detailed police brutality against African Americans, based on replies to a questionnaire Foley had circulated. At the urging of Joseph Langan, Mobile's Catholic mayor, Foley convened a biracial meeting that resulted in peaceful desegregation of the city's lunch counters in 1961.[69]

At the start of the decade, very few white Catholics participated in southern civil rights direct-action protests. But, in 1961, Father Sherrill Smith, a Chicagoan who was assistant moderator of San Antonio's Catholic Interracial Council, joined local college students in weekly Sunday stand-ins at the Majestic, a segregated San Antonio theater. The black, white, and Hispanic protesters tried to buy tickets in pairs. When refused, they returned to the back of the line and repeatedly tried again. After a year of the protests, the theater desegregated and others followed suit.[70]

Although Smith's archbishop, Robert E. Lucey, supported the priest's involvement in the protests, Lucey, like many Catholic progressives in the South, was wary of the more militant civil rights groups, such as the Congress of

Racial Equality (CORE) and the Student Nonviolent Coordinating Committee (SNCC), and limited his public support of the civil rights movement to the NAACP. Consequently, Lucey prevented Smith from accepting Matt Ahmann's invitation to join CORE's National Advisory Committee. Lucey told Smith that "CORE has done a very good job and deserves our support," but he feared that CORE might adopt "some rather imprudent line of action" that would harm the Church by association if Smith joined the committee. Father Twomey was similarly wary about SNCC. Asked by a Baltimore Catholic for his assessment of the organization, he wrote:

> In one place it does undoubtedly good work, in another its activity is at time[s] quite irresponsible. Maybe some communists have been active in certain demonstrations but I am not at all convinced that it is in any way fair to say that SNCC is communist infiltrated or communist dominated. I certainly do not feel that I can honestly condemn SNCC. I would advise, however, that you proceed with caution in cooperating with SNCC.[71]

Like Twomey, Henry A. Cabirac Jr. worked with the NAACP. In 1963, Cabirac supported an NAACP membership drive in southwest Louisiana, and he was the main speaker at an NAACP rally in Opelousas, twenty miles north of Lafayette. Cabirac visited southern ordinaries, encouraging them to desegregate and offering advice. Some prelates, such as Archbishop Paul J. Hallinan of Atlanta, an Ohioan, were enthusiastic and responsive. However, many prelates were cautious about desegregation and Cabirac's advocacy, and a few, such as Archbishop Joseph P. Hurley of St. Augustine, Florida, Archbishop Thomas J. Toolen of Mobile, and Bishop Robert Tracy of Baton Rouge, rejected the Southern Field Service's approaches altogether. Cabirac helped Catholic progressives form interracial councils in most southern states and revive dormant councils. With some success, he urged African American Catholics to write letters to their bishops pressing for parochial school desegregation. Catholic interracial councils also urged their often-cautious ordinaries to desegregate diocesan institutions, but the councils' dependence on the support, or at least the tolerance, of prelates for their existence induced a degree of caution in their members' approach. A small membership also hampered many councils.[72]

In August 1963, Matt Ahmann coordinated Catholic participation in the civil rights movement's March on Washington, attended by many thousands, and served as one of its ten chairman. The 150 guests on the platform included Bishop John J. Russell of Richmond, his auxiliary bishop Ernest L. Unterkoefler, Jack Nelson, and Father Harold R. Perry of St. Augustine's Seminary in Mississippi, along with seven Catholic clergy and laity from outside the South. The Catholic interracial councils of Richmond and Northern Virginia sent delegations of 132 and 76 respectively. Their combined total comprised seven priests, six brothers, two seminarians, and 193 laypeople, including a few Protestants.[73]

Although reassured by the careful organization of the March on Washington, until 1964 Russell opposed clergy and lay participation in civil rights protests. Concerned for their safety, Bishop Waters also barred any priest in his diocese, secular or religious, from joining civil rights demonstrations. However, Archbishop Lucey permitted his clergy to demonstrate. In August 1963, four San Antonio priests, including Sherrill Smith and Lawrence Murtagh, an Irishman, joined an interracial march and rally of six hundred people in Austin in protest at Governor John Connally's opposition to the federal civil rights bill proposed by President John F. Kennedy.[74]

In March 1965, Smith and Murtagh joined the Selma, Alabama, protests. The NCCIJ, including John P. "Jack" Sisson, Cabirac's successor as Southern Field Service director, coordinated Catholic participation. Most of the Catholic clergy who joined the protests came from the North and West, but they also included Fiorenza, McCarthy, and several other priests from Houston, present with the permission of Bishop John L. Morkovsky of Galveston-Houston, a Texan. Six priests from Atlanta went to Selma with the approval of Archbishop Hallinan, who had cosponsored a reception in Atlanta for Nobel Peace Prize winner Martin Luther King Jr. in January. Although Bishop Russell would permit nuns and priests to go to Selma, he would not finance their trips. Only one Virginia priest, William Stickle, O.P., of Charlottesville's St. Thomas Church, participated.[75]

On the same day the Selma to Montgomery march began, the NCCIJ ended a long-planned three-day conference of southern Catholics in Memphis, Tennessee, to discuss race relations and offer practical guidance through a program of workshops. Attended by 250 people, including fifty priests, fifty nuns, Bishop Joseph A. Durick of Nashville, Catholic laity, Protestants, and Jews, the conference reflected the Southern Field Service's success in assisting or establishing Catholic interracial councils in every one of the eleven southern states, except Alabama and Mississippi. However, the councils varied considerably in their active membership, vibrancy, and impact.[76]

In July, the NCCIJ followed the Memphis meeting with a three-day conference on "Social Change and Christian Response," intended for southern diocesan officials and Catholic leaders, lay and religious. Only five prelates, including host Archbishop Hallinan, attended the conference in Atlanta, which included addresses by three civil rights leaders: African American Protestant ministers Andrew J. Young and C. T. Vivian of King's Southern Christian Leadership Conference (SCLC) and Rudolph Lombard, CORE's national vice president.[77]

Although a few southern-based, white Catholic clergymen participated in civil rights organizations, most of them were nonsoutherners who belonged to religious orders that served African Americans. Often reared without racial prejudice, these clergymen were committed to helping southern blacks in their struggle for equality. Responsible to superiors of orders located outside the South, religious priests had considerably more freedom in some dioceses to participate in civil rights activity than secular priests, who were subject directly to the authority of their prelates.

In 1965, Josephite pastors Richard J. Swift, a Boston, Massachusetts, native born in 1915, and William J. Morrissey, a New Yorker born in 1918, were delegates at the NAACP's convention in Denver, Colorado. Pastor of St. Peter Claver Church in New Orleans, Swift represented NAACP branches in Louisiana and was the organization's only white member in the Pelican state. Morrissey was vice president of the board of directors of the Natchez, Mississippi, branch. Pastor of Holy Family Church in Natchez between 1961 and 1969, Morrissey housed the NAACP office in the church hall from 1965 to 1970 and endured harassment from the police and threats. In 1965, he participated, along with fellow Josephite Father Paul Klutke, in an NAACP test of restaurant desegregation in Natchez. Another religious priest in Mississippi, Father Nathaniel Machesky, a Franciscan from Detroit, was one of the Greenwood movement's three leaders when it organized a largely successful boycott in the late 1960s that brought African American employment in local stores and the police force.[78]

Some nuns based in the South also worked for racial justice. Benedictine Sisters who ran St. Scholastica's Academy in Fort Smith, Arkansas, played a major role in the city's Catholic interracial council, which they helped organize. By the mid-1960s, several southern and nonsouthern white diocesan Catholic clergy, nuns, and laity were members of state or local human relations committees and state civil rights committees. Diocesan priest Father Walter B. Clancy, a native of Helena, Arkansas, and chaplain of the Little Rock Catholic Interracial Council, was state president of the Arkansas Council on Human Relations. Father David A. Boileau, originally from Kalamazoo, Michigan, served on the Arkansas State Advisory Committee to the United States Commission on Civil Rights. George Barrett, a Nashville native, headed the Tennessee Council on Human Relations. Father Vincent M. Rizzotto, who chaired the Race Relations Committee of the Diocese of Galveston-Houston's Catholic Council on Community Relations, served on the triracial Houston Council on Human Relations, which had a membership of 650 Catholics, Protestants, and Jews. Sister de la Croix, president of Marymount Junior College in Boca Raton, Florida, was a member of the Florida State Advisory Committee to the United States Commission on Civil Rights.[79]

In June 1963, Bishop Coleman F. Carroll of Miami, a Pennsylvanian, played a major role in initiating the Dade County [Metro] Community Relations Board and served as its first chairman. The board included George A. Simpson, the vice president of the Miami NAACP branch; Dr. John O. Brown, vice chairman of the Miami CORE chapter; and leaders from business, industry, religion, and media. In early 1964, Carroll established a Diocesan Council on Human Rights, chaired by Father John F. Kieran, the Josephite pastor of Miami's Holy

Redeemer Church. In April, the council urged public officials and other leaders to work "toward the total elimination of discrimination and segregation in our communities." Designed to tackle prejudice through education, the council held seminars and workshops on human relations and worked with diocesan and parish groups.[80]

Some clergy in the Deep South were also active. Monsignor John D. Toomey, pastor of St. James Church, Savannah, who was born and raised in Augusta, Georgia, sat on the Georgia State Advisory Committee to the United States Commission on Civil Rights. Gerard E. Sherry, a naturalized British immigrant who edited the *Georgia Bulletin*, Atlanta's archdiocesan newspaper, and was president of the archdiocese's St. Martin's Human Relations Council, served on the Georgia Council on Human Relations' board of directors.[81]

Auxiliary Bishop Brunini participated in the Mississippi Council on Human Relations, and Father Bernard F. Law served as vice president of the council's Jackson chapter. In March 1964, Law published an editorial, "Legal Segregation Is Dying," that urged Paul B. Johnson Jr., the segregationist governor of Mississippi, to accept the end of Jim Crow and appoint a Commission on Human Relations to assist "all levels of state leadership for smooth and peaceful desegregation." Mississippi, Law insisted, had to "move off dead center on this issue of segregation and move on to other business." Although Governor Johnson did not accept the editor's advice, the Catholic Press Association later recognized the editorial as the best that year.[82]

African American and white Catholics, including Henry A. Cabirac Jr. and Jack Sisson, predominated among those who met in February and May 1964 to organize the Louisiana Council on Human Relations (LCHR), launched in July. The LCHR's board of directors included Monsignor Alexander O. Sigur, who had served as the council's chairman during its organizational phase, and Jack Nelson. Dr. James R. Oliver, a Catholic layman and dean of the University of Southwestern Louisiana's Graduate School, served as the LCHR president. In 1965, Oliver, a native of Egan, Louisiana, published a series of articles in Louisiana's diocesan newspapers, in support of integration, equal opportunity, and racial equality. Many Catholics served on the LCHR's Advisory Board, including Bishop Charles P. Greco of Alexandria. Catholics were also prominent in the Louisiana State Advisory Committee to the United States Commission on Civil Rights. They included Sisson, Jack Nelson, state senator J. D. DeBlieux, who chaired the committee, and Bernard Raynal "Ray" Ariatti, who worked with Twomey at the Institute of Human Relations.[83]

In July 1964, President Lyndon B. Johnson appointed Twomey and Bishop Carroll to the National Citizens Committee for Community Relations, established to promote acceptance of the Civil Rights Act. Catholic progressives in the South supported that act, the Voting Rights Act of 1965, and racial equality in statements, letters to the diocesan press, and diocesan newspaper editorials.

During the Selma protests, layman John Catullus of Houston wrote to the *Texas Catholic Herald*: "As the Negro struggles to achieve some measure of social justice in our country and some standing in our community, surely no Christian can afford to be apathetic, or to close his eyes or his heart to the struggle."[84]

Inspired by the President's Committee on Equal Employment Opportunity and by Father John F. Cronin, S.S., assistant director of the Social Action Department of the NCWC, the NCCIJ initiated Project Equality in 1965. Open to all religious bodies regardless of denomination, the program required participants to eliminate employment discrimination in their institutions, adopt affirmative action to hire nonwhite staff, and confine their purchase of goods and services to approved companies that operated fair employment practices and affirmative action. To establish regional Project Equality programs, the NCCIJ provided participating judicatories with guidance and a contribution to start-up funding. Individual programs were responsible for meeting administrative costs and hiring a local program director. The NCCIJ planned to establish programs in every major city with a substantial minority population.[85]

In August 1965, the Archdiocese of San Antonio began the first southern Project Equality program and the third in the nation after Detroit and St. Louis. However, the program encountered significant employer resistance in the archdiocese, and some pastors refused to cooperate. Appointed to oversee the program as director of the archdiocese's newly established Social Action Department, Father Sherrill Smith struggled with its administrative demands, at least in part because of his pastoral duties and other commitments, and his reputation as a labor and civil rights activist alienated some companies. Although Lucey replaced Smith in 1967, the archdiocese's Project Equality program remained ineffective.[86]

In the second half of the 1960s, the Southern Field Service devoted much of its time, energy, and resources to attempts to persuade southern dioceses to adopt Project Equality, but many prelates balked at its administrative costs and requirements, and some refused to participate without the involvement of other denominations. The Diocese of Nashville, led by Coadjutor Bishop Joseph A. Durick, adopted Project Equality in 1967, and the dioceses of Beaumont and Galveston-Houston agreed to launch the Southeast Texas regional conference of Project Equality in January 1969. However, these programs had little effect on employers, and most Catholic dioceses in the South did not participate.[87]

Besides making presentations to diocesan bodies on Project Equality, the Southern Field Service continued to service Catholic interracial councils and to urge dioceses to desegregate, providing them with advice and support. In June 1966, Sisson joined Martin Luther King, the SCLC, CORE, and SNCC as they completed the Meredith March from Memphis, Tennessee, to Jackson, Mississippi, after James Meredith, an African American who had desegregated the University of Mississippi in 1962, had been shot and hospitalized on the second day of his solo march against fear. Sisson liaised with the Diocese of Natchez-Jackson and some Catholic priests on the route. After Mississippi state troopers clubbed and gassed the marchers at Canton in a dispute over their camping arrangements, a three-man team assembled by the Southern Field Service that included Father Sherrill Smith helped negotiate a settlement. Some members of the Little Rock and Memphis Catholic interracial councils participated in the march, as well as at least nine priests from outside the Diocese of Natchez-Jackson, including Father Edwin J. Wallin, chaplain at Memphis State University's Newman Center and pastor of St. Patrick's Church. One nun, Sister Mary Peter (Margaret Ellen) Traxler, S.S.N.D., a Minnesotan who was the NCCIJ's director of educational services, joined the march near its finish. Bishop Gerow permitted clergy and religious from outside, but not inside, his diocese to march. Nevertheless, Sisson reported that "several Catholic churches and many priests and nuns offered hospitality and sanctuary to marchers" en route, and four priests and eight nuns from the Diocese of Natchez-Jackson attended a rally at the march's end in Jackson.[88]

Although some southern Catholic interracial councils continued active programs in the second half of the 1960s, many lost impetus or folded altogether. Ignored and starved of funds by Archbishop John P. Cody, who became Coadjutor Archbishop of New Orleans in August 1961 and archbishop after Rummel's death in November 1964, the CCHR ceased meeting. The Richmond council was defunct by February 1966 and the Northern Virginia council by August. Some councils had never been very strong or had been overly dependent on a few or even one individual. They atrophied when key persons left the area. Growing desegregation of diocesan institutions addressed the main driving force behind many councils. Councils no longer seemed necessary when dioceses, influenced by the Second Vatican Council's call for the Church to be involved in the world, established social action agencies and priests councils, and invited greater lay participation in the Church. At the same time, the fragmentation of the civil rights movement, the emergence of Black Power organizations, and riots by African Americans in some northern and western cities alienated some council members from the struggle for racial equality.[89]

With many commitments and struggling for funds, the Southern Field Service decided in March 1967 that "We will continue to service existing councils, with small effort toward establishing new groups." In February 1969, Sisson observed that in the fourteen southern, southwestern, and border states that the Southern Field Service covered, "Many of the CIC's [Catholic interracial councils] have been very quiet.... The councils in Charleston, Atlanta, West Virginia, Memphis, Nashville, Little Rock, Oklahoma City, and Lafayette, La. have been inactive for the most part for the past year."[90]

Discouragement led some councils to collapse. By 1969, the Little Rock council was in decline, and the Fort Smith council had disbanded. They were casualties of members' dejection at their lack of influence, widespread Catholic indifference, and lack of cooperation from Bishop Albert L. Fletcher, priests, and laity. Soon, the South's remaining councils could no longer look to the Southern Field Service for support and guidance. At the end of September 1969, the service closed "due to lack of funds" as the NCCIJ struggled to obtain support from the charitable foundations and Catholic sources that had sustained it through the 1960s.[91]

Despite the decline of the Southern Field Service and Catholic interracial councils, in the late 1960s at least two bishops in the South joined civil rights demonstrations. Bishop Durick of Nashville, and some priests, participated in demonstrations in his native state: a memorial march for Martin Luther King Jr. in Memphis after his murder there in April 1968, and another march in the city on the first anniversary of King's death.[92]

In May 1968, Bishop Ernest L. Unterkoefler of Charleston, a Philadelphia, Pennsylvania, native, and some white priests and nuns walked with the SCLC's Poor People's March on Washington when it passed through Charleston and Greenville, South Carolina. Catholic churches in Danville, Norfolk, Richmond, and northern Virginia supplied Poor People's marchers with food, shelter, and transportation. In vain, the SCLC's campaign urged the federal government to create full employment, fund a guaranteed annual minimum income, and spend more on low-income housing.[93]

By the end of the decade, every southern diocese had, at least, begun desegregating its institutions. A few progressive prelates had led the way, although they had recognized practical constraints on the exercise of their theoretically inviolable authority by acting gradually. Despite the opposition of militant Catholic adherents of Jim Crow, progressive prelates positively influenced the views of some Catholic segregationists. After Archbishop Rummel denounced segregation as sinful and announced his intention to desegregate parochial schools, Mrs. J. C. Campbell of Baton Rouge wrote: "I believe that our schools should be integrated because segregation is not in compliance with the teachings of our Church. I cannot, in good conscience, question the decisions of our Archbishop." Campbell's commitment to her religion triumphed over her commitment to segregation. She explained:

> I was brought up in a home where beliefs regarding segregation were typical of all Southern homes. I grew up with and retained these racial prejudices long after I became a Catholic. When the Church's stand on segregation came to the front a few years ago, I knew in my heart that the Church was right and that I had been wrong again. It took a while for me to really accept the idea, but now I am ready to plea[d] with the "cradle Catholics" of the South to swallow that bitter pill. They will feel better for it; I promise.[94]

Although progressive priests and laity lacked the authority of prelates, they also changed the views of some Catholic segregationists. Born in Shreveport, Louisiana, Mrs. Albert Davis grew up sharing the segregationist beliefs of her family and peers. However, she rejected Jim Crow segregation as a student at Loyola University of the South, influenced by Father Twomey, who taught her that all men were brothers. Davis later joined the Little Rock Catholic Interracial Council and, as part of a biracial women's panel, related her experience to parent-teacher associations in the city's Catholic schools. After attending a Summer School of Catholic Action, a week-long youth training program, in Houston, Texas, one participant commented that "Only one thing was wrong with this week. We Southerners should not have been allowed an elective at the time of Father Twomey's interracial talk. Most of us went to it. All of us should have gone. Some of us were racists last Monday. Thank God we are not now."[95]

However, many Catholic segregationists accepted Catholic desegregation unwillingly under the instruction of their prelates. Secular desegregation, endorsed by progressive Catholics and implemented under pressure from the civil rights movement and a sometimes reluctant federal government, also contributed significantly to the reluctant acceptance of desegregation in Church and society by many white Catholics.

CHAPTER FIVE

White Catholics in the South and Secular Desegregation, 1954–1970

The Catholic Church in the South, as in the rest of the United States, taught its members to respect legitimate authority and obey the law, unless doing so contravened their duty to God and the Church. The Church proudly celebrated American democracy and the rule of law, enshrined in the Declaration of Independence and the United States Constitution and, while patriotically supporting the United States in the Cold War, condemned communism for its denial of God and for its ruthless, arbitrary authoritarianism. Although the Church required Catholics to educate their children in parochial schools, except when impractical, prelates regarded the maintenance of public education as vital, not only for the many Catholics who attended public schools but also to ensure an educated, informed, and productive citizenry, regardless of denominational affiliation, that would preserve American and, hence, Catholic freedom.[1]

For decades prior to the civil rights movement, most Catholic prelates, clergy, and white laity in the South did not perceive or acknowledge any conflict between their commitment to law and order and democracy, and the existence of public segregation and the denial of voting rights to most African Americans in the region. However, by outlawing public school segregation in May 1954, the United States Supreme Court's *Brown* ruling brought southern state and federal law into conflict and bore directly on Catholic leaders' concerns about public education, law and order, democracy, and the Cold War. When southern state governments took measures designed to thwart *Brown*'s implementation, or when public school desegregation under federal court order became imminent, diocesan leaders and some lay groups in the areas affected often spoke out in defense of public education and obedience to federal law, and called for acceptance of desegregation.[2]

Some southern politicians, such as Mississippi's United States senator James O. Eastland, vigorously condemned the *Brown* ruling, but many outside the Deep South waited to see how and when the Supreme Court would implement its decision. Initially, most southern Catholic leaders did not comment on *Brown*. Conscious that most white southerners, including Catholics, supported segregation, many Catholic leaders feared they might generate hostility against Catholics who formed a small minority in most southern states, as well as divide the Church. Catholic leaders also waited for the court's implementation ruling and to gauge the white South's reaction.[3]

However, there were exceptions to Catholic silence in both the peripheral South and the Deep South. Catholic educators led the way. In May 1954, Monsignor J. Louis Flaherty, the Diocese of Richmond's superintendent of schools and a native of Norfolk, Virginia, declared that *Brown* "is in accord with Christian principles." The Very Reverend Andrew C. Smith, a native of Natchez, Mississippi, and president of Spring Hill College in Mobile, Alabama, which had three blacks enrolled in its downtown evening classes, welcomed *Brown* as "a historic stand for equal justice and equal opportunities for all our citizens" and "a forward step toward bringing our Constitution, its interpretation and practice of it, into line with the Declaration of Independence." Monsignor Henry C. Bezou, the Archdiocese of New Orleans's superintendent of schools, observed that "the decision is in accordance with what has been expected on the basis of natural justice and with the clear intent and purpose of the Constitution of the United States."[4]

Although Bishop William L. Adrian of Nashville called for lawful obedience to *Brown*, other southern prelates said nothing publicly about the ruling. However, the rise of massive resistance to public school desegregation led some diocesan leaders to defend public education. Monsignor Charles J. Plauche, chancellor of the Archdiocese of New Orleans, appealed to "all responsible members of the community not to rebel against constituted authority or to waste time in useless gestures of defiance" after Louisiana state legislators, about one-third of them Catholic, adopted a series of bills in the summer of 1954 drafted by the newly formed Joint Legislative Committee to Maintain Segregation.[5]

M. F. Everett, editor of the archdiocesan newspaper *Catholic Action of the South*, vigorously condemned segregationist bills approved by seventy-eight votes to eleven in the Louisiana house on June 28, 1954. The bills, which applied to all public and private schools, including Catholic schools, stipulated that schools must be segregated to "protect public health, morals, better education, and the peace and good order in the state"; limited free books, lunches, and other state support to segregated schools; allowed local school boards to determine each child's school; and made it illegal for those other than parents or guardians to file school desegregate suits.[6]

Everett argued that the bills "would in effect deny free speech, freedom of the press, and the basic right of parents to send their children to a school of their choice; would penalize parents, children, and others for obeying the supreme law of the land; and would set up a police state rivaling those of Hitler and Stalin." If Catholic schools desegregated, Everett pointed out, their students would lose free state-supplied textbooks and lunches, and the state could also prevent enrollment in Catholic schools. Rummel endorsed the editorial in a private letter to Governor Robert F. Kennon, telling him that the bills "should have no place on the Statute Books of a democratic State or in the government of a free people."⁷

Pressure from six Catholic senators from New Orleans brought amendments that excluded private schools from the bills before they passed the Senate with overwhelming support. Catholic segregationist and district attorney for St. Bernard and Plaquemines parishes (counties), Leander Perez, claimed that the six senators had acted under Bezou's instructions and engaged "in a traitorous action . . . to sell down the river the inherent rights of the majority of White children in this state." Rummel and other archdiocesan leaders were not appeased by the exclusion of Catholic schools from the legislation. Everett wrote that "The measures, despite modification, still strike at fundamental human rights. They are an incentive to antagonism and strife. . . . They set an evil pattern of law evasion."⁸

The bill that required segregated schools by virtue of the "inherent police power of the state," and permitted the state assembly to propose constitutional amendments when it chose, rather than in alternate years, was subject to approval by the voters in Constitution Amendment 16. Everett responded by writing articles, published in the eight weeks before the vote, that supported desegregation and refuted segregationist arguments. Each article ended with a plea to voters to reject the constitutional amendment on November 2.⁹

Everett's efforts had limited effect as voters overwhelmingly approved Amendment 16, which garnered strongest support from white voters in heavily black parishes. However, only 30 percent of the state's registered electorate voted, suggesting substantial disinterest and perhaps some misgivings among voters. Furthermore, despite massive support in Perez's Plaquemines Parish, almost a third of voters in Lake Charles and Lafayette, also heavily Catholic like Plaquemines, voted against the amendment. Nevertheless, segregated public school education remained intact in Louisiana, as it did in almost every southern school district.¹⁰

In May 1955, the United States Supreme Court issued a second *Brown* ruling, which determined that public schools should desegregate "with all deliberate speed" but at a pace decided by federal district courts. As African Americans petitioned sixty school boards to desegregate, white Citizens' Councils, first formed in Mississippi after the first *Brown* ruling, spread across much of the South. The councils, and other like-minded groups that emerged, sought to protect segregation by using propaganda and economic pressure and intimidation against integrationists.¹¹

State senator William M. Rainach, who chaired the Joint Legislative Committee to Maintain Segregation, helped organize the council movement in Louisiana from his base in the state's northern half. Close ties existed between the committee and Louisiana's burgeoning Citizens' Councils. In July 1955, the

Southwest Louisiana Register, the Diocese of Lafayette's newspaper, responded by condemning *Brown*'s opponents. The paper asked:

> How can we teach respect for legitimate government . . . when those who govern us rebel against legitimate authority?
> This is beyond prejudice. This is principle; profound, basic, democratic principle. It is beyond mere dissatisfaction with changing social patterns when we reject, rebel against, and openly attack the highest authority of the land.[12]

When Catholics in Erath attended a meeting in December 1955 of the Southern Gentlemen's Organization of Louisiana, a secretive segregationist group affiliated with the Citizens' Councils, the Reverend A. J. Vincent, vice chancellor of the Diocese of Lafayette and secretary to Bishop Jules B. Jeanmard, attacked the organization for encouraging lawlessness. Vincent wrote to the *Daily Advertiser* of Lafayette: "They are undermining the very foundations of the United States of America, who urgently appeal to their fellow citizens to take the law into their own hands, and to ignore spitefully the decisions of our courts and the clear meaning of the Declaration of Independence as well as the Constitution and the Bill of Rights." He also turned on their head segregationist claims that communism lay behind the civil rights movement or would benefit from the strife and miscegenation that integration would supposedly bring. Vincent argued that "They render a distinct service to the cause of Communism, who proclaim to the world in public meetings that they are bigots and that they will openly fight against the equality of men in democratic society."[13]

In February 1956, Archbishop Rummel also challenged segregation when he addressed the eighth annual Interracial Sunday, held at Loyola University of the South in New Orleans. He warned that "the controversy over segregation has . . . lessened the respect of a great many abroad for the sincerity and the honesty of our dedication to the democratic way of life." Like Vincent, Rummel tackled segregationist accusations that "integration is being fostered and promoted by Communism." The archbishop pointedly asked:

> Sometimes I wonder who is doing the work of the Communists: whether we are doing the work of the Communists when we speak for honesty and sincerity in the interpretation of the democratic way of life and the assertion of human rights for all our American citizens, or whether those are doing the work of the Communists who are striving to keep up, just because of the difference of color, certain inhibitions and restrictions and privations of the Negro race.[14]

Southern white Catholic attacks on massive resistance and its proponents were not confined to Louisiana, or only to diocesan officials and spokesmen. In February 1956, the annual convention of San Antonio's Archdiocesan Council of Catholic Men adopted a resolution addressed to the "colored people," without a dissenting vote from the five hundred delegates who represented some twelve thousand men. The brief resolution declared: "[W]e wish you to know that you have our confidence, our understanding, our sympathy and our best wishes." Sam V. Snell, the council's corresponding secretary, proposed the resolution, because, as he told the convention, "In the last few months, in some Southern cities, we have seen this clash of Races fester and come to a head like an ugly boil, demagogues shouting their bigotry. All this in rebuke of and contrary to our laws of State, our laws of Morality, and most important, our laws of God and Church."[15]

That same month Virginia's General Assembly adopted an interposition resolution, and, in the fall, it discussed legislative proposals to prevent public school desegregation. The Richmond Diocesan Council of Catholic Women (RDCCW) responded to a bill under consideration by a special session of the General Assembly that would withdraw funds from local school systems that desegregated public schools. Adele Clark presented a RDCCW resolution to a joint committee of the General Assembly that called for preservation of "a state-wide system of public schools according to basic Christian principles."[16]

Clark explained why the issue mattered to Catholics. She told legislators:

> Although most Catholic children attend parochial schools, privately supported, we as citizens are concerned with the welfare and education of our neighbors, as citizens, under our American system of government. And under that system the taxes of all citizens are applied to the support of the public schools. In a democracy it is essential that there be an educated electorate.

Clark complained that the General Assembly had done "very little" to comply with *Brown*, although "obedience to the law of the land" was "a basic Christian principle." She argued that African American views had been ignored and called for an interracial conference of educators. However, the General Assembly ignored the suggestion and adopted a package of massive resistance bills.[17]

Bishop Vincent S. Waters of Raleigh spoke out against massive resistance and in support of public education in North Carolina, where 3,379 Catholics attended public schools and 4,957 Catholic children were enrolled in parochial schools. In July 1956, the North Carolina General Assembly condemned the *Brown* decision as a "tyrannical usurpation of power." State legislators approved recommendations for a state constitutional amendment that would allow local school boards to close schools if racial conditions became unacceptable to a majority of local voters. The amendment also sanctioned state-funded tuition grants for parents who sent their children to private segregated schools. North Carolina's electorate would vote on the proposed constitutional amendment on September 8.[18]

On August 16, 1956, Waters responded to these developments by issuing a hard-hitting pastoral letter in which he called for "Obedience to both National and State Law," with any conflict between them "settled constitutionally on a National basis and not by evasion or fiction." The bishop noted that Catholics paid taxes toward a public school system they wished to see preserved, and "we are also interested in seeing equality of opportunity and justice for every American no matter what his race." Waters appealed to patriotism and obedience to law and authority. He wrote:

> The real enemies of America are those who teach by word or example disrespect for lawful authority and who advocate lawlessness either by positive contrary attitudes or by neglect of obedience.
>
> Every good American whether in high or in low station should be expected to be outstanding for his respect for lawful authority and obedience to law and order, under God, with freedom and justice for all.
>
> The Law of the Land should not be prejudicial to minorities, whether on account of race, nationality or religion.[19]

Waters criticized the provisions of the proposed constitutional amendment as preserving prejudice against African Americans and called it constitutionally questionable. He urged Catholics to vote on the amendment as a "conscientious civic duty." While he did not specifically instruct them how to vote, the entire thrust of his message was unmistakably in favor of the amendment's rejection. Waters well knew that Catholics were a small minority in the state. How many of them heeded his words is unknown, but, in any case, Catholics could not have determined the vote's outcome since the electorate approved the constitutional amendment by 471,657 votes to 101,767.[20]

Elsewhere in the peripheral South, in the fall of 1956, Governor Allan Shivers sent Texas Rangers to Mansfield, near Fort Worth, where a white local mob had gathered to prevent desegregation of Mansfield High School under federal court order. Shivers instructed the Rangers to ensure order, prevent violence, and preserve school segregation. He blamed the National Association for the Advancement of Colored People (NAACP) for creating the crisis at Mansfield High by pursuing desegregation. The *Alamo Register*, the Archdiocese of San Antonio's newspaper, defended the NAACP's conduct and condemned "the impulsive and wildly unsound move by Governor Shivers to disobey contemptuously a federal court order in Mansfield." When Attorney General John Ben Shepperd of Texas accused the Texas NAACP of falsely registering as a nonprofit agency, tax evasion, and illegal political engagement, the *Alamo Register* correctly claimed that "the attack is not so much an attack on the NAACP as upon eventual integration in Texas" and dismissed the charges as "poppycock."[21]

In 1957, the Texas legislature considered an interposition resolution condemning *Brown*, a pupil placement bill designed to preserve public school segregation by using ostensibly nonracial criteria in student assignment, and a local referendum provision preventing desegregation unless at least 20 percent of voters had petitioned for it and a majority had subsequently endorsed desegregation in a special vote. Invoking democracy, law and order, and the Cold War, Archbishop Robert E. Lucey of San Antonio condemned the bills. He declared:

> These bills offer resistance to the Constitution of the United States, attempt to persecute Texas citizens, give a frightful example of lawlessness to the youth of our State and oppose the foreign policy of our country at a time when our federal government is trying desperately to maintain friendly relations with the colored nations of the world.

Lucey insisted that "this hate legislation plays right into the hands of godless communists everywhere" and added, "There is nothing that destroys law and order so effectively as rebellion against the Constitution and tyranny against the people." However, his protests were largely in vain as the assignment and referendum measures became state law.[22]

Neighboring Arkansas, like Texas, witnessed overt defiance of federal court-ordered school desegregation. In September 1957, Governor Orval Faubus dispatched the National Guard to block desegregation of Little Rock's Central High School. An editorial in the *Guardian*, the Diocese of Little Rock's newspaper, argued that sensationalist press reporting—"'scare headlines' and slanted 'dope' stories"—had inflamed white public opinion and forced Faubus to act to forestall possible violence by dispatching the National Guard. Although the editorial passed over Faubus's role in creating the crisis, it maintained that "Integration is the law, and it is wrong to interfere with its peaceful inauguration."[23]

Under judicial order not to thwart desegregation, Faubus withdrew the National Guard on September 20, and a white segregationist mob surrounded the school when it desegregated on September 23. Police authorities managed to drive African American students who were inside the school to safety. After the incident, President Dwight D. Eisenhower, who had tried to persuade Faubus to allow desegregation to proceed, federalized the National Guard and sent United States troops to ensure implementation of desegregation.[24]

Encouraged by Eisenhower's dispatch of federal troops and a presidential appeal for clergy involvement, an interdenominational group of Little Rock ministers, Arkansas congressman and Southern Baptist Convention president Brooks Hays, and Robert R. Brown, the Episcopal Bishop of Arkansas, met to discuss how the churches might ease the crisis. They decided on a special citywide Day of Prayer to be held in participating churches and synagogues on Saturday,

October 12, Columbus Day. Albert L. Fletcher, the Catholic Bishop of Little Rock, who had been out of town when the group first met, embraced the idea.[25]

On the Sunday preceding Columbus Day, Fletcher issued a pastoral letter, read at all masses in Greater Little Rock, that appealed for attendance at the Day of Prayer. The bishop called on Catholics "to observe and support law and order" and warned that "These problems which face us today will not be solved justly and fairly in the traditional American way by representative legal processes, unless we all fulfill the obligation we have to take a personal, intelligent and patriotic interest in the affairs of our Government both state and national." The bishop ended his letter with an appeal for peace. "Violence breeds only hatred and injustice," he warned, "not peace and mutual understanding."[26]

At least 6,000 people, and perhaps as many as 10,000, participated in the Columbus Day prayers. Eighty-five Catholic and Protestant churches and synagogues had issued invitations, though fewer than half of them were white. While estimates varied as to how may churches participated, 2,053 Catholics attended the services, about one-third of the Catholic population in Little Rock and North Little Rock. Rather than ascribing their attendance to support for integration, an unnamed Catholic spokesman insisted that "The fact that 2,000 Catholics went to churches today to petition for guidance is powerful proof of their respect for authority." While a third of city Catholics may have attended in deference to their bishop, two-thirds did not, suggesting that even in so hierarchical institution as the Catholic Church bishops could not compel obedience. How many of the 2,000 Catholic participants were African American is not indicated in the sources.[27]

In September 1958, Governor Faubus used new legislative powers to close the city's public high schools. St. Bartholomew's, a black Catholic high school in Little Rock, responded by admitting thirty African American students whose black public school had closed but lacked the facilities to admit more.[28]

In August 1959, layman William W. O'Donnell, the managing editor of the *Guardian*, claimed "**There is at least some doubt about the** [*Brown*] **decision from a constitutional standpoint** [emphasis in the original]." While he conceded that "the Supreme Court has the right to pronounce on the racial question," O'Donnell condoned massive resistance to *Brown* by arguing that "States also have the right to use every legal device to forestall enforcement of the court's decision." Several readers wrote to complain, suggesting that a body of lay Catholics placed commitment to law above segregation. C. J. Westerer of Prairie View, Arkansas, reminded O'Donnell that "[T]he Supreme Court is the highest, and the final interpreter of our Constitution and Laws."[29]

As the Little Rock crisis receded, Georgia faced becoming the first state in the Deep South to commence public school desegregation when, in December 1959, a federal district court ordered the Atlanta board of education to desegregate its schools. Conscious that under Georgia's massive resistance laws every public school in the state would close if the Atlanta board complied and that the Georgia General Assembly was due to convene in January 1960, Bishop Francis E. Hyland of Atlanta declared that "The time to speak out . . . has come." Hyland admitted that he had hesitated to speak out before because most Catholic children in the state attended parochial schools, but he claimed that as citizens and taxpayers Catholics "desire ardently" the maintenance of public schools and called for the state to obey the law "with a keen Christian sense of justice to all her citizens without exception."[30]

In January 1960, the federal district court accepted the Atlanta board of education's desegregation plan. The Georgia General Assembly eventually repealed massive resistance legislation in January 1961, rather than close the University of Georgia that was subject to a federal district court order to admit two African Americans. After desegregation brought a campus riot, the *Bulletin of the Catholic Laymen's Association of Georgia*, the state's Catholic newspaper, editorialized, "Georgia's citizens will never agree with a rock-throwing mob of ruffians that 'Due Process of Law' is merely an archaic phrase found in an ancient and musty document, instead of an integral and essential safeguard of true democracy." The riot in Athens made Catholic and many other political and educational leaders in Atlanta even more anxious to achieve public school desegregation, scheduled for the city in September, peacefully.[31]

Consequently, Hyland consented to diocesan representation in Organizations Assisting Schools in September (OASIS), an Atlanta organization, comprising fifty-three civic and religious groups, that promoted acceptance of public school desegregation. The bishop also permitted Catholics to sign a "laymen's letter to his child," issued by OASIS for publication in Atlanta's newspapers as part of a "law and order week-end" the organization sponsored immediately prior to the beginning of the new school year. Signed by 850 white Catholic, Jewish, and Protestant laymen, the letter counseled Atlantans "to meet the unfamiliar with calmness, dignity and peace; to recognize that obedience to the rules of law, which bring order to our family society, is rooted in our spiritual faith and must be respected and revered."[32]

Hyland issued a pastoral letter read in all of Atlanta's Catholic churches on August 20, designating the following Sunday as a "Day of Prayer for Law and Order" in coordination with OASIS's "law and order week-end." The letter claimed that "The Catholic Church has always and will always condemn racial bias in all its various shapes and forms," although Hyland had yet to set a date for parochial school desegregation. Over 750 Atlanta churches and synagogues observed "law and order week-end," and Catholic churches recited a litany to mark the occasion. Atlanta's public schools desegregated peacefully.[33]

The situation was very different in New Orleans. Hoping to ensure a smooth and peaceful transition to desegregated public schools, a group of whites in the city, assisted by the Southern Regional Council, organized Save Our Schools

(SOS) in April 1960. Father Joseph F. Fichter, S.J., of Loyola University of the South, cochaired SOS alongside Rabbi Julian B. Feibelman and Bishop Girault M. Jones, the Episcopalian Bishop of Louisiana. John P. "Jack" Nelson, a Catholic lawyer, was vice chairman. Although integrationists predominated among SOS's leaders, officially SOS took no position on "the relative merits of segregation, or de-segregation." Instead, it called for preservation of law and order and "the continuation of a statewide system of free public education."[34]

While SOS hoped to win over community leaders, it also released media statements and, assisted by funding from the Stern Family Fund, distributed thirty thousand brochures in an effort to influence public opinion. SOS helped focus attention on preserving the public school system, but, dominated by figures known for their support for integration, for the most part it did not appeal to the most powerful and influential in the community.[35]

The Archdiocese of New Orleans had no official connection with SOS. However, in June 1960, Archbishop Rummel wrote to the Orleans Parish School Board, urging it to comply with a recent federal court order, issued by native New Orleans Catholic and alumnus of Loyola Law School Judge J. Skelly Wright, that mandated desegregation of the first grade of public schools in September. Nevertheless, Emile A. Wagner Jr., a Catholic and Citizens' Council founder, remained unwilling, unlike the board's other members, to accept token desegregation in order to keep the public schools open.[36]

The Louisiana legislature empowered Governor Jimmie Davis to close the entire public school system. In June, Rummel wrote to Davis that closing the schools would be "a retrogressive measure for which no comparative justification exists." In August, Rummel issued a pastoral letter that reiterated his commitment to eventual parochial school desegregation and stressed that he, and the American Catholic hierarchy, had affirmed the Church's opposition to racial segregation. Rummel warned Catholic parents with children in public school of "the danger of chaos and moral irresponsibility which is latent in the prevailing efforts to nullify or circumvent or even defy a ruling proclaimed by the supreme legal authority of our country." As closing the public schools would bring not only "financial and economic losses" but untold "social, moral and cultural damage," Rummel appealed to parents "to become concerned and vocal against such an unrealistic prospect." He designated August 21 as a "Day of Prayer" throughout the archdiocese and appealed to Catholics to pray for "an early solution of the race problem."[37]

At the end of August, the New Orleans public school board proposed to implement token desegregation under the state's pupil placement law. Judge Wright accepted the plan and postponed public school desegregation until November 14, hoping to secure United States Justice Department backing in the interim. In early November, Governor Davis called the legislature into special session, where its members passed a barrage of segregationist bills designed to avert public school desegregation. Representative Maurice "Moon" Landrieu, a twenty-nine-year-old Catholic from New Orleans, who had attended desegregated Loyola Law School with Norman C. Francis in the early 1950s, was one of the few legislators to vote against the bills. Wright invalidated the legislation as fast as it was passed and obtained the Eisenhower administration's backing. On November 14, Bezou instructed pastors and Catholic school principals not to "accept transfers of public school children into Catholic schools in the event that any public school is closed" because of desegregation. That same day, United States marshals escorted four African American girls to the two schools, McDonough No. 19 and William J. Frantz, subject to token desegregation, which passed off peacefully the first day, despite the jeers of segregationist bystanders assembled in front of the schools.[38]

However, at a Citizens' Council rally the following evening attended by six thousand people, Leander Perez urged segregationists to protest at the city's public school board offices. He exclaimed, "Are you going to wait until these Congolese rape your daughters? Are you going to let these burrheads into your schools? Do something about it now!" The next day, hundreds of white teenage students ran riot downtown and massed outside City Hall and the Public School Office, sometimes rushing into public buildings. The Citizens' Council threatened economic retaliation against white parents who kept their children enrolled in the two desegregated schools, while a mob of shouting white women, sometimes including Catholic biblical segregationist Una M. Gaillot, confronted the few white parents who continued to bring their children to school. By the end of November, white enrollment had ceased at McDonough 19 and fallen to two at Frantz. On one occasion, Father Jerome A. Drolet, the Kankakee, Illinois, born pastor of Our Lady of Perpetual Help Church in Kenner, located just outside New Orleans, went to Frantz school to act as a decoy to distract attention away from the Reverend Lloyd A. Foreman as the white Methodist minister picked up his child from the school.[39]

SOS members organized car pools to transport parents and children to the schools that increased white enrollment at Frantz to twenty-three. Segregationists responded by targeting the homes and property of white parents, and both they and SOS members suffered harassment. Consequently, white enrollment at Frantz plummeted again. Although Rummel had spoken out in August for compliance with public school desegregation, he was silent about the issue thereafter and, alarmed by the violence, abandoned plans to desegregate parochial schools.[40]

Elsewhere in the South, in the early 1960s a few white Catholics assisted or publicly supported desegregation of public accommodations. John P. "Jack" Sisson, who was born in Milwaukee but spent much of his childhood in Pensacola, Florida, and returned there in 1960, helped negotiate lunch counter desegregation in Pensacola as a member of the Escambia County Community Council.[41]

Segregationist hoodlums sometimes abused or attacked sit-in protesters, which appalled some militant Catholic segregationists. Catholic convert James Jackson Kilpatrick, editor of the Richmond *News Leader* in Virginia, wrote:

> Many a Virginian must have felt a tinge of wry regret at the state of things as they are, in reading of Saturday's "sit-downs" by Negro students in Richmond stores. Here were the colored students, in coats, white shirts, ties, and one of them was reading Goethe.... And here on the sidewalk outside, was a gang of white boys come to heckle, a ragtail rabble, slack-jawed, black-jacketed, grinning fit to kill, and some of them, God save the mark, were waving the proud and honored flag of the Southern States in the last war fought by gentlemen. Eheu! It gives one pause.[42]

In May 1961, a biracial Freedom Ride to test desegregation of terminals serving interstate buses began in Washington, DC. The two buses carrying the Freedom Riders passed through Virginia and North Carolina without incident. A Freedom Rider was beaten in Rock Hill, South Carolina, and in Anniston and Birmingham, Alabama, groups of whites brutally attacked the Freedom Riders. Father Robert L. Wilken, editor of the *North Carolina Catholic*, vigorously defended the riders. He wrote:

> Christ said boldly: "Blessed are they who suffer persecution for justice' sake, for theirs is the Kingdom of Heaven." To the Freedom Riders we say the same.
> Christ came to redeem not only private, individual souls, but also mankind and all its artificial and unnatural institutions and folkways, prominent among them discrimination and segregation.

Wilken rejected claims that Communists had organized the Freedom Rides. He argued, rather, that Communists exploited "our glaring hypocrisy" in maintaining "a caste system which denies both Christianity and Democracy."[43]

Even when they disagreed with, or had reservations about, direct action, Catholic leaders and some laity condemned segregationist violence. The *Catholic Week*, the Diocese of Mobile-Birmingham's newspaper, editorialized that during the Freedom Ride in Alabama state authorities had "by culpable default, allowed unauthorized persons blinded by fury [to] take the law into their own hands." Concerned primarily with order, the newspaper ignored the fact that the Freedom Riders had been exercising their constitutional right to use desegregated interstate transport and argued that the Riders "must examine their own consciences before God and the welfare of their country." The *Catholic Week* regarded both the protesters and their attackers as extremists and denounced "the silence and apathy and indifference of the people of our State who have left all the talking and planning to the extremists on both sides of our racial problem and have allowed local and state authorities to mouth irresponsible and non-representative utterances calculated to condone mob rule, if not incite it."[44]

Some Catholic laity also expressed abhorrence at the violence. Laywoman Mrs. Frank Dominick of Birmingham wrote to the *Catholic Week* that "We have suffered a grievous loss in the eyes of the nation and of the world." The state Knights of Columbus was holding its convention in Montgomery when a segregationist mob beat the Freedom Riders on their arrival in the city. In response, the convention adopted a resolution that accused state and local officials of being "derelict" and called on them to prevent any continuation or reoccurrence of the violence. Although the resolution stated that Alabama had been entered by "an element which we feel may be subversive," the Knights asserted that "It is the patriotic duty of all officials to use their authority to safeguard the name and reputation of the State and its citizenry."[45]

In Alabama, as in most other southern states, Catholic leaders spoke out against defiance of public school desegregation. In January 1963, Governor George C. Wallace of Alabama, a Methodist, declared in his inaugural address that he would disobey any federal court order to desegregate public schools. Wallace vowed "segregation today, segregation tomorrow and segregation forever." With the permission of Archbishop Thomas J. Toolen of Mobile, Auxiliary Bishop Joseph A. Durick signed an interdenominational statement, "An Appeal for Law and Order and Common Sense," released by eleven white Catholic, Jewish, and Protestant leaders in Alabama, directed at Wallace. The statement argued "That laws may be tested in courts or changed by legislatures, but not ignored by whims of individuals." The clergymen insisted that "our American way of life depends upon obedience to the decisions of courts." The *Catholic Week* published the statement and a column by Ed Clark, who argued that Wallace's "defiant promise of 'segregation forever' is an impossible one to keep and can only bring shame and chaos to our state."[46]

Catholic officials' support for law and order sometimes led them to criticize civil rights protests. Such was the case in Birmingham, Alabama, where in spring 1963 Martin Luther King Jr. and the Southern Christian Leadership Conference (SCLC), invited to the city by a local affiliate the Alabama Christian Movement for Human Rights, engaged in an economic boycott and demonstrations to protest against segregation and employment discrimination. Many of the protesters were arrested. In response, Durick and seven of the other white Alabama religious leaders who had signed the January appeal issued a second statement on Good Friday, April 12, 1963. They argued that the demonstrations were "unwise and untimely," "extreme," and incited "hated and violence." The eight religious leaders urged African Americans to stop demonstrating and, in a criticism of King and the SCLC, "unite locally in working peacefully for a better Birmingham." Local blacks and whites, the clergymen maintained, should negotiate a settlement and "observe the principles of law and order and common sense." King rejected the ministers' criticisms in a "Letter from a Birmingham Jail" that justified the concept of nonviolent civil disobedience and the right to confront injustice whenever it existed.[47]

Father Albert S. Foley, S.J., who chaired the Alabama State Advisory Committee to the United States Commission on Civil Rights, also criticized King. In lengthy telephone calls, Foley tried to persuade King to relinquish demonstrations and seek negotiations after Birmingham's new moderate segregationist mayor Albert Boutwell took office. King rejected Foley's advice in favor of continuing demonstrations that he deemed necessary to exert pressure on the incoming administration. Foley's incautious repetition to a *Birmingham News* journalist of a local businessman's claim that the SCLC adopted demonstrations to boost its coffers with sympathizers' donations further exacerbated tensions between him and King.[48]

After the SCLC had enlisted children to demonstrate and go to jail, and Birmingham's commissioner of public safety Eugene "Bull" Connor had permitted the use of fire hoses and police dogs against African American protesters and onlookers, Durick issued a statement that gently called the protesters' techniques into question and appealed for "respect for law and order." Durick wrote that "Even though those who are staging these demonstrations may be convinced of the sense of urgency attending them, it does not mean that one can ignore the question of seeking the best and most peaceful techniques." Whereas Durick ignored Connor's methods, Foley condemned "police violence against the non-violent demonstrators" and defended the right to protest.[49]

Although downtown merchants reached a settlement that conceded some of the SCLC's demands, segregationist and police violence resumed and in response African Americans in Birmingham's ghetto rioted. Hitherto silent on the city's racial crisis, Archbishop Toolen issued a statement that deplored violence and declared that "We are glad that Negroes are obtaining some rights, but do not approve of some of their methods." He urged civil rights leaders to "remind the Negro race of their obligation to their fellowmen."[50]

Toolen's belated lukewarm endorsement of equal rights contrasted with that of Bishop Coleman F. Carroll of Miami. In April 1963, the bishop convened a meeting of Miami's lay and religious leaders, African American and white, at his chancery, where they agreed to form a committee to study the issue. In June, the committee, presided over by Coleman, issued a statement, which declared that "racial prejudice, discrimination and segregation are a violation of justice and an affront to the dignity of man" and called for "equality without discrimination of any kind in employment, education, housing, hospitals, public accommodations, labor unions, job training, political organizations, recreation and worship." The signatories included the Reverend Theodore R. Gibson, head of the Miami NAACP.[51]

In Mississippi, the murder of Medgar Evers, the Mississippi NAACP's field secretary, by a white segregationist led Richard O. Gerow, the state's Catholic bishop since 1924, to condemn racism publicly for the first time. Although Evers was a Methodist, his two children attended Christ the King Catholic school in Jackson. Gerow knew the family and attended Evers's funeral. Afterward, the bishop, a native of Mobile, Alabama, issued a strongly worded press statement that went beyond condemnation of the murder to an indictment of the society in which it had occurred. The bishop declared:

> As a loyal son of Mississippi and a man of God, I feel in conscience compelled to speak out in the face of the grave racial situation in which we now find ourselves.
>
> This problem is unmistakably a moral one. We need frankly to admit that the murder of Mr. Evers and the other instances of violence in our community tragically must be shared by all of us. Responsible leadership in some instances has been singularly lacking.

No other prominent white Mississippian issued such a strong denunciation of the murder. Gerow also argued that "Our conscience should compel us all to acknowledge the deep moral implications of this problem and to take positive steps toward recognizing the legitimate grievances of the Negro population."[52]

Only hours before Evers's murder, President John F. Kennedy had announced in a televised speech that he would ask the US Congress to pass a civil rights bill, outlawing segregation in public accommodations. Some lay Catholics responded positively to Kennedy's address. Layman A. J. Frederic Jr., of Lutcher, Louisiana, wrote to the *Catholic Commentator*, the Diocese of Baton Rouge's newspaper, that "good Americans should begin immediately to take action in backing our President, the constitution and the laws of their great democracy. The Negro . . . has to be recognized as a complete citizen of this country."[53]

In June 1963, Bishop John J. Russell of Richmond was one of thirty-seven Catholic leaders who attended a meeting of 250 religious leaders with Kennedy at the White House. The president asked them to make efforts to diminish the racial crisis at the local level as civil rights protests reached their zenith. In July, Russell wrote in a pastoral letter:

> [T]he Negroes, as any minority group seeking its lawful rights has the obligation of respecting the lawful rights of others. That being understood, a Catholic cannot fail to recognize the right of the Negro people to secure proper housing, equal opportunity for work, full participation in educational facilities, both public and private, and the right to equal accommodation both on public property and within those enterprises licensed and protected by the State for the service of the general public.[54]

In the same month, civil rights demonstrations in Savannah intensified, amid fears that the situation would escalate from sporadic to widespread violence. In response, an interdenominational group of thirty-one white clergymen, including Bishop Thomas J. McDonough of the Catholic Diocese of Savannah, his chancellor Monsignor Andrew J. McDonald, and three local Catholic priests, Monsignor John D. Toomey, Father Raymond Bane, and Monsignor T. James McNamara, issued a statement calling for talks to resume and offering to help negotiate a settlement. They implored "all persons [to] restrain themselves from violence and seek to restore peace and order" and urged "that recognition and guarantees be given to the rights of all citizens." The *Southern Cross*, the diocesan newspaper, also appealed for a peaceful resolution. With McDonough's permission, Toomey helped broker an agreement in which white businessmen agreed to desegregate hotels, motels, and bowling alleys.[55]

Escalating civil rights protests in the South and white segregationist violence led Bishop Charles P. Greco of Alexandria to issue a pastoral letter on race relations in August 1963, his first public statement on race in seventeen years as the diocese's bishop. Fear of violence and disorder coupled with appeals for calm acceptance of change pervaded the letter that was read in all of the diocese's churches and given front-page coverage by local secular newspapers. Greco wrote that "A social revolution, underscored by agitation, turmoil, violence and even bloodshed, is sweeping the country and striking at our Southland. It has moved into our own diocese. Varying in aspect and intensity according to region, it has reached alarming proportions." Nevertheless, change had to be accepted. Greco explained:

> [D]esegregation is inevitable. The Supreme Court has declared it to be the law of the land and has reaffirmed this decision at every challenge. It will gradually be enforced in every part of our country.
>
> We earnestly appeal to our people to accept the inevitable with understanding and restraint, with true Christian charity and an awakened sense of justice, with good grace and characteristic American fairness.

He called for "an end to discrimination based merely on race, color, creed or national background" and referred to the "just aspirations of the Negro race."[56]

Public schools in Greco's diocese remained segregated but token public school desegregation increasingly penetrated other areas of the Deep South. In the neighboring Diocese of Baton Rouge, the twelfth grade of public schools in East Baton Rouge Parish desegregated under federal court order in September 1963. In response, Bishop Robert E. Tracy of Baton Rouge issued a pastoral letter appealing to Catholics "to provide right-minded leadership in the community" and exercise "the judgment to be faithful to our religious principles, our concept of human dignity and our respect for the law and order of the land."[57]

After Charleston, South Carolina, peacefully desegregated four public schools under federal court order that same month, Bishop Francis F. Reh of Charleston praised "The sound policy of quiet official acceptance by our civic leaders of the legal order for our public schools." Father Gregory F. Wyse, O.F.M., chaplain of the University of South Carolina Thomas More Center, praised the university for desegregating in September "with good order."[58]

By contrast, violence and disorder accompanied the beginning of public school desegregation in Alabama, which commenced under federal court order in three Birmingham schools in September 1963. Nearly two hundred whites protested outside one of the schools. In the evening, the bombing of the home of NAACP attorney Arthur Shores led to a riot in which one person died and twenty more suffered injury. Prompted by Governor Wallace, who had opposed school desegregation, the school board temporarily closed the schools.[59]

Auxiliary Bishop Durick, and most of the seven other white church leaders who had spoken out in April, condemned the bombing in a joint statement. They also called for "law and order," "obedience to the orders of the courts of our land," and the maintenance of public education. When the schools reopened, Wallace deployed the National Guard to prevent African Americans from entering schools subject to desegregation. President Kennedy quickly ensured desegregation by federalizing the National Guard. The eight church leaders sent the board of education a letter of encouragement. However, the following Sunday, a bomb exploded at Birmingham's black Sixteenth Street Baptist Church, killing four African American girls.[60]

Archbishop Toolen issued a pastoral letter that denounced the bombing as a "dastardly act." He declared that "We are much ashamed before our fellow countrymen and before the world because of the lawlessness of our State and its people as seen in the recent events in Birmingham and elsewhere." Toolen appealed to everyone to "remain calm and reasonable" so that "Violence should not beget violence." Durick issued a statement denouncing the murders as "satanic hoodlumism" that displayed a "callous disregard for life and law and religion." The *Catholic Week* published the pronouncements on its front page, along with those of *L'Osservatore Romano* that decried the bombing "by the racist insanity of some fanatical adherents of segregation" and endorsed "the just battle for integration." Durick and twenty Catholic priests attended the funeral of three of the murdered girls.[61]

Catholic Week columnist Ed Clark argued that Wallace bore "the greater share of responsibility for the despicable and cowardly bombing" by "leading his people down the road to racial chaos and anarchy" and acting on his pledge to defy federal court orders mandating public school desegregation. Clark also claimed that "The guilt must be shared by the thousands of Alabamians who have stood quietly and meekly by and allowed Wallace and the other fire brands to speak for them." Strikingly, he argued that "the church, has failed miserably" to influence "the public conscience." Clergymen and lay leaders of all faiths, he wrote, had failed "to concern themselves with the great racial problems of their time."[62]

However, fear of segregationist violence made bishops who called for passage of the civil rights bill wary of civil rights demonstrations and Catholic participation in them. In January 1964, Bishop Waters declared in a pastoral letter that "It is necessary . . . to remove the last vestige of every unjust law and custom and to frame laws which will guarantee every citizen impartial treatment," a tacit endorsement of the civil rights bill. Waters argued that racial segregation violated democracy and the United States Constitution and, adopting the slogan of the civil rights movement, announced, "We Shall Overcome." He recognized "the right of citizens to protest unjust laws or customs" as in the tradition of the American Revolution and noted that the movement's nonviolent demonstrations have "corrected some of [the] . . . injustices involving the freedom of American citizens." Yet Waters still felt some ambivalence toward demonstrations, claiming that "many" had begun nonviolently but ended in violence. He did not specify who perpetrated such violence but warned that without the adoption of just laws properly obeyed "civil disobedience practiced by large numbers will increase the lawlessness of our people."[63]

Bishop Russell was also ambivalent about protests. In March 1964, he replied to a query from the Sisters of Mercy that it was not "necessary or advisable" for its members "to participate in demonstrations." Yet in the same month, Henry A. Cabirac Jr., director of the National Catholic Conference for Interracial Justice's Southern Field Service, reported, after visiting the bishop, that Russell had "agreed to let the Catholic laity and priests participate in peaceful demonstrations." Subsequently, some priests joined protests against segregated restaurants in Richmond.[64]

At Russell's suggestion, in April 1964 members of the Catholic Interracial Council of Northern Virginia (CICNV) wrote supportive letters to United States senators who favored the civil rights bill that had just passed the House of Representatives. Eight priests also wrote to Republican Senate Minority Leader Everett M. Dirksen urging the bill's passage. Russell called on priests and laity, especially in northern Virginia, to join him at an Interreligious Convocation held in April at Georgetown University, Washington, DC, to support the bill. Seven thousand people attended the event, including many CICNV members, several Catholic priests, and hundreds of lay Catholics.[65]

Some Catholic leaders in Texas also publicly supported the civil rights bill. In late April 1964, Monsignor Roy Ribn represented the Archdiocese of San Antonio at an Interfaith Convocation on Civil Rights held in Austin. In May, Archbishop Lucey endorsed the civil rights bill in a pastoral letter "as a legitimate means to a necessary end: interracial—that is, human—justice" that was in accord with the nation's Constitution. Lucey directed his priests to preach sermons explaining the bill's necessity, and he ordered handbills to be distributed at the doors of churches calling on Catholics to write to their United States senators in support of the bill's passage. *Alamo Messenger* columnist Dick Meskill reported that "a few people in various parishes got up and walked out of church when the priests preached on the subject," but "the dissent was minuscule" and "The assent was overwhelming."66

In May, John L. Morkovsky, the Coadjutor Bishop and Apostolic Administrator of Galveston-Houston, wrote to Texas United States senators John G. Tower and Ralph Yarborough in support of the civil rights bill. Morkovsky explained that "Where the local units of government . . . fail to guarantee . . . [the] basic principles upon which our Republic is founded, it certainly devolves upon the Federal government to pass necessary legislation." Morkovsky, Bishop Wendelin J. Nold of Galveston-Houston, another native Texan, and two hundred priests of the diocese signed a statement in May calling for passage of the civil rights bill and urging "letters be written to our U.S. Senators asking their support of the Civil Rights Bill . . . without weakening its present form."67

In Florida, the *Voice*, the Diocese of Miami's newspaper, gave civil rights legislation editorial support, despite encountering opposition from some Floridians, and it urged Americans to support the civil rights movement's "program of non-violence in the quest for justice." The Miami Diocesan Council on Human Relations, which included Dr. George A. Simpson, vice president of the Miami NAACP on its board, exhorted "all Catholics to support the passage on national and community levels of adequate and just civil rights legislation to guarantee equal protection for the rights of all men under the sanction of laws." However, Archbishop Joseph P. Hurley of St. Augustine, Florida's other diocese, was silent about the civil rights bill, and when Martin Luther King Jr. asked him in June 1964 to support protests against segregation in the city of St. Augustine, Hurley refused. The archbishop believed that communism permeated the movement, and he opposed the demonstrations as disruptive of law and order, writing in his diary, "Those who dislike the law should go to the courts."68

Deep South prelates also avoided public comment on the civil rights bill, but a few diocesan newspapers in the region endorsed the proposal. The *Southern Cross* argued that, as they considered the bill, United States senators "ought to stop letting themselves be bullied by racists in the Senate and out." A supporter of nonviolent civil rights demonstrations, Gerard E. Sherry, editor of the *Georgia Bulletin*, Atlanta's archdiocesan newspaper, welcomed the bill as "an encouraging step in the quest for racial justice." Columnist Paul H. Hallett wrote in the *Southwest Louisiana Register*, the Diocese of Lafayette's newspaper, that the bill's purpose "is to guarantee to the Negro, or any other minority group that may suffer from discrimination, rights of citizenship that should have been his all along."69

After the bill passed in July, a large majority of southern prelates and diocesan newspapers called for its acceptance, and many ordinaries and clergy enthusiastically endorsed the act. Bishop Fletcher reminded Catholic Arkansans that the act was "a law of the land" and urged Catholics to regard it "as an effort to require all of us as citizens to give every man at least that which he can expect of us as his brother in Christ." At Bishop Russell's invitation forty-one priests in the city of Richmond and its environs issued a statement calling for obedience to the legislation. Bishop Waters signed a statement by the interdenominational North Carolina Council on Religion and Race that supported the act and urged North Carolinians "to practice the biblical command to love our neighbors as ourselves." The Catholic Interracial Council of San Antonio hailed the bill's passage as "the end of a long, moral ordeal for the American people." Every diocesan head in the five Deep South states, except Archbishop Toolen in Alabama, called for obedience to the Civil Rights Act and many also welcomed its passage.[70]

While many Catholic leaders and opinion makers in the South favored the Civil Rights Act, some of them also exhibited paternalism and condescension toward African Americans. Father M. C. Deason, editor of the *Lone Star Register*, the Diocese of Austin's newspaper, welcomed the act, condemned the "immorality of discrimination," and called for an attitude of "color blindness." Yet, Deason also wrote, "Give them equal job opportunities, and they will bring up their standards, and they will do it in a way that will be most agreeable to us."[71]

Some Catholic lay groups in Texas urged compliance with the Civil Rights Act or endorsed it. They included the Catholic State League of Texas, the Archdiocese of San Antonio's Council of Catholic Men, and the Area 11 Christian Family Movement convention held in Lubbock, Texas. Beyond Texas, very few, if any lay groups, besides Catholic interracial councils, took a position on the legislation, indicative both of its divisiveness and the strong opposition it aroused from many white Catholics.[72]

Even in Texas, white Catholic lay opinion was divided, with many Catholics opposed. Several laypeople wrote to the *Alamo Messenger* that the bill would unnecessarily expand the powers of the federal government, infringe on states' rights, and endanger constitutional freedoms and individual liberty. Some readers associated the bill with socialism or communism. Retired brigadier general Richard B. Moran of Kerrville complained to Archbishop Lucey that the legislation was "designed as a major step in the satanic plan to destroy this Republic, make it a socialist dictatorship, and eventually cause it to become a province in an atheistic, terroristic one-world government." However, Robert Wilson of San Antonio rejected such claims as belonging to "the hate-mongering type with a touch of the lunatic fringe." Henry L. Stille, another San Antonio layman, cited Catholic teachings against segregation and condemned "systematic efforts to circumvent the law, sabotage the national interest and the American image throughout the world."[73]

Bishop Russell told his priests that "It is up to us to make our people aware of what the Church teaches regarding segregation," when the Diocese of Richmond, the Protestant Council of Churches of Greater Washington, and the

Jewish Community Council of Greater Washington sponsored an interdenominational fair housing campaign in northern Virginia. The campaign addressed a growing problem of block-busting by realtors and panic selling by white home owners as African Americans moved into formerly white areas. Russell endorsed a statement that parishioners were asked to sign on February 14, 1965, designated Fair Housing Sunday. The statement supported everyone's "moral right to purchase or rent a home anywhere." Catholics comprised nine thousand of the fifteen thousand signatories. In March, more than two thousand people, half of them Catholic, canvassed door-to-door for more signatures. Altogether forty thousand people, about one-third of northern Virginia's population, signed the statement. Despite this noteworthy effort, white flight, which included Catholics, continued.[74]

The Selma, Alabama, voting rights protests in 1965 also produced a sharp division among southern white Catholics. After Alabama state troopers attacked several hundred civil rights marchers with clubs and tear gas on the Edmund Pettus Bridge on March 7 when they refused an order to return to Selma, Archbishop Toolen's commitment to law and order and the nation's Constitution impelled him to speak out. While he denounced the attack and expressed sympathy for the civil rights cause, Toolen disapproved of the movement's tactics when they included defying state authority and seeking to evoke public sympathy by eliciting violence from segregationist opponents. He wrote in the *Catholic Week*:

> Justice, human decency and Christian brotherhood demand recognition of the real needs of our Negro people and every legitimate effort in their struggle to exercise fully all their constitutional rights has our complete support. We condemn without reservation a harsh and brutal exercise of the police power vested in the hands of our public officials as beyond the requirements of present difficulties and unable to effect their solution. At the same time we cannot condone a complete disregard on the part of citizens for statutes legally enacted in the interest of the common good and public safety.

Toolen staked out a middle position between the protesters and the troopers by condemning violence whether "used to perpetuate existing injustice or deliberately provoked for the sake of influencing public opinion, especially where other means exist," although he did not indicate these means.[75]

Toolen banned clergy and nuns resident in Selma from demonstrating. He complained that the priests and nuns who joined the Selma protests from other dioceses, mostly outside the South, had not observed the custom of asking his permission to enter the diocese, knew little about southern conditions, and should remain "at home doing God's work." He dismissed clerical protesters as "eager-beavers who feel this is a holy cause." Toolen was equally scathing toward

King, claiming that he was "taking children out of school to demonstrate on the streets," "hurting the cause of the Negro rather than helping it," and "trying to divide the people."[76]

The archbishop regarded the demonstrations as inimical to law and order. He declared: "All citizens are entitled to equal rights and privileges under the constitution. But these problems must be solved in a lawful way." Toolen did not comment directly on the denial of voting rights to African Americans in Selma and much of the South, nor did he acknowledge that the protests had contributed substantially to President Lyndon B. Johnson proposing a voting rights act just two days earlier. Instead, Toolen insisted that "The demonstrations are not helping, and I do not believe that priests are equipped to lead groups in disobedience to the laws of this state." He also appealed to patriotism in defending the state from criticism. Toolen wrote: "There are no more loyal citizens in this country than the people of Alabama. They have led in the defense of their country in war." The Alabama legislature adopted a resolution praising Toolen's words and "wise guidance."[77]

However, Archbishops Lucey and Hallinan argued that Alabama officials had failed to uphold the law and thereby precipitated the crisis. Hallinan wrote in the *Georgia Bulletin* that "The tragedy there is caused by state and local officials who refuse to live up to their office, and by the voters who let them get away with it." He approved of priests and nuns participating in the Selma marches "Because non-violent protest is a virtue and demonstrations of this kind are Christian acts of charity."[78]

In a front-page article in the *Alamo Messenger*, Lucey cited Pope John XXIII's assertions in his 1963 encyclical *Pacem in Terris* that people should claim their rights and that unjust laws or commands "opposed to the moral order" were not binding. Lucey added that Jesus had forcibly driven animal sellers and money changers from the temple using "a whip of cords," a method "much more vigorous than a peaceful march." In an appeal to patriotism very different from Toolen's, Lucey concluded that "If it is wrong to defy an unjust law the leaders of the American Revolution were traitors to the crown and Benedict Arnold was a saint."[79]

Toolen received considerably more letters from southern white Catholics praising than opposing his stand, and most letters on the subject in the *Catholic Week* and other southern diocesan newspapers also supported the archbishop or criticized the protests. Toolen's supporters and opponents of the protests argued that by demonstrating in Selma, clergy and nuns had disrespected authority, supported lawless protests that aided communism or promoted anarchy, and neglected their responsibilities to their home dioceses and the problems therein. Laywoman Caroline Krackenberger of Montgomery, Alabama, wrote to Toolen:

> Catholics have been taught that constituted authority is from God, and when we see products of that teaching—especially our religious—join in this ridiculous political

and publicity-seeking parade, see them defy and break our laws and set themselves up as law makers, thereby encouraging anarchy, we need to know where our spiritual leader stands. I am glad that you did not wait longer to let us know.

Many Catholics claimed they felt ashamed of the clergy and nuns who marched in Selma and that their participation was undignified. Mrs. Charles J. Van Trier of Bay St. Louis, Mississippi, wrote to Toolen: "I think it is beneath the dignity of a man or woman in holy robes to participate in any public march, or in any disregard of law and human safety."[80]

Catholics who criticized the Selma demonstrations and Catholic participation in them were not necessarily overt or covert segregationists. When Ann M. Lloyd of Jacksonville, Florida, wrote to Pope Paul VI inquiring why priests were "permitted to take part in something as distasteful, as unlawful, as the mobs who form these integration marches," she approvingly acknowledged that Catholic teachings rejected segregation. Lloyd explained that "I am not saying that I feel it is *wrong* [emphasis in the original] for our priests and nuns to abhor the injustices under which the negroes labor in parts of the world, but I simply feel that their methods of expressing their abhorrence are misguided."[81]

Some southern white Catholics, including Alabamians, criticized Toolen and supported the Selma protests. James R. Jackson of Mobile wrote to him: "I don't see why the[y] [clergy and nuns] should have to get your permission to participate in a march for freedom. I believe if Jesus Christ himself was here on earth he would be in Alabama or in the south helping oppressed people. The local negro can not accomplish his goal without help from the outside." Eileen B. James of Arlington, Virginia, was scornful. She told Toolen:

> I was and am extremely proud of both our Sisters and Priests. However, I feel it is a disgrace that in the cause of human dignity they were our only representation.
>
> [Y]ou were soothing your vanity because a group of Nuns and Priests dared to march without first obtaining your permission.
>
> Have you no moral conscience?
>
> You are a disgrace to the Catholic Church.[82]

In August 1965, Johnson signed the Voting Rights Act, which suspended literacy tests in states and counties in which a majority of the voting-age population had either not registered to vote, or voted, in the 1964 presidential election and allowed the attorney general to dispatch federal registrars to enroll voters in those areas. A *Catholic Week* editorial defended the legislation as necessary since Alabama had often used literacy tests specifically to disenfranchise African Americans and thereby applied states' rights irresponsibly. The newspaper also reminded Catholics that "The voting rights bill is now the law of the land. As a result, a largely increased number of Negroes will enjoy the right to vote which is the source of identity in a democratic society."[83]

Toolen denied that he was a segregationist, but, at the same time, he remained unwilling to champion secular desegregation. Consequently, he did not join thirteen southern and three border state ordinaries, headed by Bishop Russell, in signing an amicus curiae brief prepared for the United States Supreme Court by the NCCIJ to support a legal challenge by an interracial Protestant couple against Virginia's antimiscegenation law. Submitted in February 1967, the brief argued that the Virginia statute restricted the free exercise of religion and the right to have children. In June, the Supreme Court unanimously overturned antimiscegenation laws in *Loving v. Virginia*.[84]

In late 1967, the NCCIJ and twenty-four Catholics bishops, including six in the South, filed an amicus curiae brief asking the United States Supreme Court to make racial nondiscrimination in housing a constitutional right. Some Catholic leaders also endorsed an open housing bill under consideration by Congress. In March, Archbishop Hallinan declared that "we, the white majority, must open up our neighborhoods" in order that "Negroes can exercise the right of every American to live where he wishes." In the same month, Auxiliary Bishop J. Louis Flaherty of Richmond unsuccessfully asked a Virginia legislative committee to approve a bill that would enable local communities to adopt open housing ordinances. Flaherty argued that housing discrimination was "diametrically opposed to the central teaching of Jesus: 'Thou shalt love thy neighbor.'" Mrs. George Bartek, the Diocesan Council of Catholic Women's housing chairman, also pleaded on behalf of the bill. A *Catholic Virginian* editorial supported the federal open housing bill as necessary to help "curb panic-selling and contribute to the stability of neighborhoods." But some white lay Catholics openly disagreed with their clerical leaders. James M. Ober of Alexandria called the editorial "pure garbage" and open housing a Marxist violation of property rights.[85]

In April 1968, while Congress considered open housing legislation as part of a civil rights bill, Martin Luther King was assassinated in Memphis, Tennessee. Southern prelates and diocesan newspapers condemned King's murder and called for racial reconciliation. Many ordinaries attended or held memorial services for King. In many cities, some African Americans rioted in response to King's death, repeating on a wider scale riots that had occurred in recent years in some northern and western cities. Influenced perhaps by these developments, which made King's nonviolent protests seem relatively moderate, Archbishop Toolen, who had been highly critical of King during his lifetime, praised him as "not only a great leader to his people, but a true apostle of Christian charity and human brotherhood." Toolen directed that Masses or memorial services be held throughout his diocese "in tribute to the memory of Dr. King and as a reminder that the unfinished work for which he gave his life is the responsibility of all of us."[86]

A week after King's death, Congress passed the Civil Rights Act, including a provision banning racial discrimination in the sale or rental of housing, and, in

June, the Supreme Court upheld open housing in *Jones v. Alfred H. Mayer Co.* After the bill's passage, Bishop Louis J. Reicher of Austin told Catholics in a pastoral letter that "This is a law that is rooted in a Christian concept—the brotherhood of all men" and reminded them that collectively the American Catholic bishops had called for the act's "strict implementation, nationally and locally."[87]

Despite exhortations by their prelates, some southern white Catholics, like some other white southerners, sought to evade the impact of desegregation. When Bishop Russell urged parishes to observe a Fair Housing Sunday organized by the Richmond Diocesan Council of Catholic Men in June 1968, reports indicated lay objection to the event at some white churches in northern and southwest Virginia, with some parishioners refusing to accept window stickers that declared "Open Housing is Morally Right" and, in one case, distributing pamphlets that opposed the idea. White flight, including that of Catholics, to the suburbs from increasingly African American southern cities accelerated in the late 1960s.[88]

Public school desegregation also increased suburban white flight. Federal courts ordered public school districts in the Deep South and Miami, Florida, to replace token with full desegregation in 1970. Across the Deep South, and in some other parts of the South, dioceses declared their support for integrated public education and some announced that they would not allow white students to transfer to parochial schools when their intention was to evade public school desegregation.[89]

While some dioceses, such as Savannah and Baton Rouge, relied on pastors and school administrators to sift out segregationist applicants to parochial schools, others, such as the Archdioceses of Atlanta and Miami and the Diocese of Mobile, either temporarily closed parochial school enrollments or refused to accept transfers from local public schools. Bishop John L. May of Mobile declared that "Catholic schools must never be used to undercut the public schools in their strenuous efforts to implement the law of the land requiring full racial integration and equal educational opportunity for all children. We must do all we can to help our public schools."[90]

Nevertheless, some Catholic schools admitted children of parents trying to evade public school desegregation. Bishop Gerald L. Frey of Savannah conceded that in considering applications to parochial schools "motivation is difficult to determine in some instances." Bishop Tracy maintained that the Diocese of Baton Rouge's parochial schools had not "become havens for students fleeing desegregated public schools," but he conceded that "it may well be that a few students may have slipped by our guard." Although he announced that "deviation from diocesan policy ... will not be tolerated," the bishop admitted that the policy's implementation relied upon "self-enforcement." Despite the diocese's public stand against segregation, many white Catholics were not receptive and some priests allowed white Catholic children whose parents had withdrawn them from parochial schools when they desegregated to reenter them now that the public schools in which they had been enrolled were subject to full integration.[91]

In Mississippi, the Catholic response to public school desegregation became a matter of public controversy. In response to an initiative from Bishop Joseph B. Brunini of Natchez-Jackson, the state's religious leaders formed the biracial Mississippi Religious Leadership Conference in January 1970, with Brunini as chairman. In its first act, the conference issued a statement that praised the public education system and appealed to Mississippians to make their state "a model of racial harmony in her schools as well as in other areas of life."[92]

The day before the public schools reopened on a desegregated basis, priests throughout Mississippi read a pastoral letter from Brunini during Mass. The letter condemned segregation as "an affront to the informed conscience." Brunini affirmed "that our future in large measure depends upon a public system of education committed to excellence," and he stressed that only a public system was "capable of adequately serving the vast majority of Mississippi's younger citizens." Mindful that some whites might try to transfer their children to parochial schools in order to evade desegregation, Brunini warned them that "every Catholic school in Mississippi is obliged to admit Catholic applicants without regard to race."[93]

A few days later, Father James D. Gilbert, the diocese's superintendent of education resigned, because, he said, Mississippi's parochial schools were becoming "havens for segregationists" as many whites withdrew their children from the public system. He pointed to increased second semester enrollment at "four or five" Catholic schools, where school boards had voted to accept new students not enrolled in the first semester. Brunini denied Gilbert's charges. The bishop asserted that second semester enrollment had increased by about only one hundred students and that "most of the schools are not accepting anybody." However, Frank Soleevila, president of the St. Elizabeth School Board in Clarksdale, claimed that Brunini had given permission for the school to reopen grades seven and eight, closed in 1967, to accommodate Catholic children who had left public schools. The bishop, Soleevila continued, had only reversed his decision under pressure from priests, nuns, and the NAACP. Fear of controversy had led to Brunini's change of mind, but Gilbert overstated the case against the parochial school system. Nevertheless, by ignoring Gilbert's advice not to accept any transfer students in the second semester and letting schools decide admittance individually, the diocesan school board had opened the way for some schools to accept whites fleeing from desegregation.[94]

In February 1970, Monsignor Paul V. Canonici, Gilbert's successor as superintendent, announced that the diocesan school board had adopted strict new guidelines against segregation. Non-Catholic children were prohibited from joining parochial schools in which their race formed a majority.[95]

As a result of federal court orders, by early 1970 desegregation in southern public schools far outstripped that found in Catholic schools. Given the public support that most Catholic prelates in the South had given to law and order and compliance with secular desegregation in the 1950s and 1960s, it was ironic that many segregationists increasingly found enrolling their children into, what for the most part, were still lightly desegregated Catholic schools preferential to keeping them in public schools. In January 1970, F. N. Boney, a University of Georgia history professor, explained that "For segregationists, especially but not exclusively Catholic segregationists, the status quo in the parochial schools is becoming more and more attractive, for tokenism is about the best deal racists can hope for today." The next chapter examines the widespread failure of southern Catholic schools and other institutions to achieve more than token desegregation.[96]

CHAPTER SIX

Desegregation of Southern Catholic Institutions, 1945–1970

Many of the values that led southern Catholic leaders to support secular desegregation and oppose massive resistance also led them to desegregate Catholic institutions. In some cases, particularly in parts of the peripheral South, prelates desegregated Catholic schools, hospitals, and churches ahead of secular change. In other instances, especially in the Deep South, ordinaries acted largely in tandem with secular desegregation, although occasionally more extensively, and sometimes in the case of schools and hospitals partly or substantially in response to federal regulatory and financial pressure. Some prelates worked together on desegregation initiatives, while others operated independently, although cognizant of the segregation situation in secular society and neighboring dioceses. Some ordinaries eschewed publicity, while others publicly announced desegregation. In deciding policy, all prelates considered the extent or absence of secular desegregation and the nature of public and Catholic lay and clergy opinion in their dioceses, as well as the views of their consultors. Most prelates confined school desegregation to Catholic admissions, thereby restricting its impact because of large African American Protestant enrollment in black Catholic schools and limiting opposition to a change that brought only token desegregation.

Southern prelates claimed that Catholic churches were open to all regardless of race. However, some white churches refused blacks admittance, and when whites attended black churches they usually sat separately from African Americans. In many white churches, blacks sat at the back in pews to which signs or ushers directed them, or to which they went in customary recognition of segregation. African American and white Catholics typically received communion separately, with blacks following whites. When prelates had sufficient financial resources and a parish had a sufficient number of African American Catholics, dioceses established a personal or special parish for blacks to attend.[1]

In the late 1940s and early 1950s, a few progressive prelates took the first steps toward breaking down segregation in Catholic institutions. The Synod of the Archdiocese of New Orleans ordered an end to segregation in churches in 1949 and 1950. Archbishop Joseph F. Rummel repeated this instruction in 1951 and 1953. However, the archdiocese's churches remained largely segregated. In 1951 and 1953, Bishop Vincent S. Waters of Raleigh ordered an end to segregation in churches. However, except in Newton Grove, where he merged the black and white Catholic churches in 1953, he continued special parishes for blacks and African Americans could attend, but not join, white churches.[2]

Influenced perhaps by Rummel and Waters's actions, in August 1953 Bishop Wendelin J. Nold of Galveston-Houston ordered his pastors to ensure that African American churchgoers were not allocated segregated seating. However, unlike Waters and Rummel, Nold insisted that his pastors keep his directive "confidential," ordering that "The ushers are to be instructed without naming the bishop." Perhaps Nold hoped that by avoiding publicity, he might prevent opposition from coalescing, but his secrecy also meant that he did not try to educate his laity in the need for change. Furthermore, Nold did not create any means of enforcing his decision or monitoring its implementation. Consequently, it was ineffective.[3]

In the same year, the Diocese of Lafayette's synod banned racial discrimination in churches but failed to enforce its decision. Elsewhere in the South, prelates made little or no effort to end segregation in churches in the 1940s and 1950s, although the Diocese of Charleston made a gesture toward equal treatment in 1953 by adopting a policy of confirming "all of the adult converts of the City of Charleston—including the Negroes— . . . together on Passion Sunday."[4]

All of the region's ordinaries maintained, renovated, or increased the number of personal and special parishes and missions for African Americans, intended to evangelize and retain them in the Church. In 1948, the Diocese of Lafayette established two new African American parishes and added more into the 1960s. In 1954, the Passionist Fathers, a religious order, founded St. Paul of the Cross parish in Atlanta, Georgia, for African Americans, and, three years later, Archbishop Amleto Giovanni Cicognani, the apostolic delegate to the United States, dedicated Our Lady of Consolation Church, in an African American section of Charlotte, North Carolina.[5]

Most southern black Catholic churches were served by priests from religious orders, rather than by diocesan priests, usually from orders devoted to African American missions, such as the Society of the Divine Word (S.V.D.) or Divine Word Missionaries, the Society of St. Joseph of the Sacred Heart, and the Holy Ghost Fathers. Although most of the religious priests assigned to black churches were white, the S.V.D. led the way in ordaining African American clergymen, many of whom subsequently pastored southern black churches. By 1945, there were twenty-one black priests in the entire United States, twelve of them Divine Word Missionaries. The S.V.D. continued to train more black clergymen and by 1957 had twenty-four. In the 1950s, the dioceses of New Orleans, Lafayette, and Alexandria in Louisiana and Raleigh ordained a very small number of African American diocesan priests and assigned them to black churches or missions. The Josephites ordained only two black priests during the decade: in 1955 Joseph C. Verrett from New Orleans, who returned to the city to teach at St.

Augustine High School run by the order, and in 1959 Rawlin B. Enette from Port Arthur, Texas, who later became Catholic chaplain of Southern University, a state-supported black institution in Baton Rouge. The Society of Saint Edmund, headquartered in Vermont, ordained two black Alabamians from its Selma mission: James P. Robinson in 1957, who became an assistant in the Diocese of Raleigh's Missionary Apostolate, and Moses B. Anderson in 1958, who was appointed associate pastor of Our Lady of Consolation Church in Charlotte, North Carolina. By 1958, there were seventy African American priests serving in the United States and twelve more in foreign missions.[6]

With the exception of three African American orders that taught in black Catholic schools in several southern dioceses, white orders of nuns, mostly headquartered outside the South, taught in black schools or assisted in black Catholic hospitals. Their membership was largely nonsouthern, but an increasing number of novitiates across the nation, including the Deep South, indicated their willingness in the early postwar years to accept black applicants. However, there was only one integrated convent in the South, located in Marbury, Alabama, and very few elsewhere.[7]

In the late 1940s and early 1950s, segregation was the norm in southern Catholic institutions. A few dioceses operated or built hospitals for African Americans both as an act of charity and as a means of evangelism, but most white Catholic hospitals did not admit blacks, although some, such as St. Joseph of the Pines in Southern Pines, North Carolina, allocated a floor to black patients. Apart from churches and missions, African American Catholic schools served as important agents of evangelism, both of parents and children. In 1948, Bishop Emmet M. Walsh of Charleston observed that "The school is the most fruitful missionary agency and gives the most enduring results."[8]

Nevertheless, several dioceses desegregated a few lay organizations. In the late 1940s, the Diocese of Richmond desegregated its Diocesan Holy Name Union. In 1961, Monsignor Joseph L. Bernardin, chancellor of the Diocese of Charleston, reported that "On the deanery and diocesan levels, the Councils of Catholic Men, Women and Youth and the Confraternity of Christian Doctrine have been integrated for nearly ten years." In 1953, the Diocesan Council of Catholic Men appointed a black vice president, Paul M. King. However, many blacks felt unwelcome at deanery and diocesan meetings.[9]

The late 1940s and early 1950s saw the first inroads against segregation in Catholic education in the South. St. John's Seminary (later renamed Assumption) in San Antonio desegregated. Rummel desegregated Notre Dame Seminary, his archdiocese's major seminary, in 1948 and St. Joseph's College, its preparatory seminary, in 1951. The first breach of segregation in a southern Catholic college occurred in Jesuit-controlled Spring Hill College in Mobile, Alabama, which admitted African Americans to campus summer classes in 1949 and blacks to evening classes at McGill Institute, a Catholic high school for boys, in 1952. In

1950, Loyola University of the South in New Orleans, also Jesuit run, admitted three nuns from the Sisters of the Holy Family to Saturday morning classes, an African American man to a biology evening class, and twenty black men to the university's Institute of Industrial Relations. Ursuline College for women also located in New Orleans enrolled a black nun.[10]

The first Catholic colleges in the South to admit African Americans to regular classes were located in the city of San Antonio, Texas, where by August 1952 Incarnate Word College and Our Lady of the Lake College had desegregated graduate education and St. Mary's University undergraduate and graduate classes. In Louisiana, Loyola University desegregated its Law School in September 1952. One year later, the Diocese of Lafayette's only Catholic college, the College of the Sacred Heart for women located in Grand Coteau, operated by the Religious of the Sacred Heart, admitted a black undergraduate and became, according to diocesan newspaper the *Southwest Louisiana Register*, "the first college in the deep South to integrate effectively."[11] By January 1954, a few African American undergraduates attended Incarnate Word College and Our Lady of the Lake College, completing desegregation of the Archdiocese of San Antonio's three Catholic colleges.[12]

Catholic school desegregation first began in the South in the city of San Antonio. In 1952, Central Catholic, a boys' high school run by the Marianists, which had white and Hispanic students, admitted an African American. Brother Henry C. Ringkamp, S.M., Central Catholic's principal, acted on his own initiative, with the "encouragement and approval" of Archbishop Lucey and of "Our house council and the larger portion of our faculty," but over the objections of Father Peter Resch, the Provincial of the St. Louis Province of the Society of Mary. Ringkamp, a native of St. Louis, Missouri, wrote to Resch that the school's decision did not require the Provincial's permission, and he argued that, in any case, desegregation was in "close accord with the [American Catholic] hierarchy on their social doctrine pronouncements." Aware that state law mandating segregated public schools was under challenge, Ringkamp wanted to act immediately. He believed that it would be "a sad historical commentary on Catholic educators who preach the Mystical Body of Christ doctrine, to have it said of them that they only admitted negroes to their schools when the discriminatory laws of the State of Texas affecting education were abrogated."[13]

While Ringkamp acted with Lucey's support, Bishop Albert L. Fletcher of Little Rock, and a native of the city, said nothing publicly about segregation and maintained segregated diocesan institutions. However, he raised no objections when St. Scholastica's Academy, a girls' high school in Fort Smith run by the Benedictine Sisters, admitted two African Americans in 1952.[14]

Lucey urged all the orders operating high schools in the Archdiocese of San Antonio to desegregate them, and by the summer of 1953, all but one had agreed to do so in the fall. In April 1954, a month before the United States Supreme Court declared segregated public schools unconstitutional in the *Brown* decision and with the case pending, the archbishop ordered diocesan schools to admit all Catholic children without regard to race, keen to act before the court ruled, and he urged all private Catholic schools to desegregate. He explained that "In the field of morality and particularly in the field of social justice and social charity Catholics should lead, not follow. If secular government, military leaders and private organizations can eliminate the sins of segregation and discrimination we can do so too."[15]

Most white Catholic parents calmly accepted Lucey's announcement. Vicar General J. L. Manning recalled that desegregation in the archdiocese was "far less of a problem because our percentage of Colored Catholics is so very small." There were little more than eight hundred African American Catholics in the archdiocese in 1954, part of a total Catholic population of 300,187 that included whites and Hispanics, and Lucey's desegregation order applied only to the admission of Catholic children.[16]

Manning also observed that "Fortunately, we have no large co-educational high schools, hence the high schools followed [desegregation] without incident." Fear of miscegenation was a major theme in southern white segregationist rhetoric and the fact that many Catholic schools and especially Catholic high schools, educated boys and girls separately, unlike public schools, made Catholic desegregation less unpalatable to many white southerners, Catholic and Protestant alike.[17]

Like Lucey, Bishop Peter L. Ireton of Richmond announced desegregation of diocesan schools before the *Brown* ruling but only on a limited basis. The court's deliberations emboldened Ireton, a native of Baltimore, Maryland, to declare ten days before the ruling that, regardless of the court's decision, white Catholic high schools in the city of Richmond would accept African American students in September 1954. Ostensibly, Ireton acted because there was no Catholic high school for blacks in Richmond, the Church had an obligation to provide education for all Catholic children and, as he told a Catholic men's group, "Before God, all men are equal, whether they are red or yellow or white or black." But since Van de Vyver School, the city's only black Catholic school, had ended high school classes in 1951 because of insufficient enrollment, Ireton's decision seems to have been strongly influenced by the segregation case before the Supreme Court. Shortly after the ruling, Monsignor J. Louis Flaherty, diocesan superintendent of schools, told reporters, "Most certainly Catholic schools will not remain segregated when the public schools are integrated."[18]

The diocese expected black enrollment in Richmond's four white Catholic high schools to be small. Ireton left school segregation intact elsewhere in the diocese, although he endorsed a decision by the Norfolk Catholic High School Board to accept African American students if local authorities condemned St. Joseph's, the city's black Catholic high school, to make way for a housing development.[19]

In September 1954, eleven African Americans (six boys and five girls) enrolled in three of Richmond's previously all-white high schools. The continuation of St. Joseph School left Catholic segregation in place in Norfolk, but African Americans were quietly enrolled in formerly white schools in Arlington and Annandale in northern Virginia and in Roanoke as desegregation extended beyond the limits that Ireton had indicated in May. Apart from high school desegregation, a few African Americans were also admitted to formerly white Catholic elementary schools that lacked black Catholic counterparts. In all, sixty African Americans joined fourteen formerly white Catholic schools which had 5,228 white students. Although desegregation had been token, parochial schools had moved ahead of the public school system, which remained entirely segregated as Governor Thomas B. Stanley appointed the Gray Commission to devise ways to limit desegregation. After the school year ended, Monsignor Flaherty reported that "Everything has been most satisfactory. Opposition came from about six mothers, all Army people. I offered them transfers. They refused. Several of these people have changed since the original opposition."[20]

Parochial school desegregation also began in some other peripheral South dioceses in September 1954. After the Diocese of Amarillo, Texas, desegregated its high schools, Monsignor Francis A. Smyer, the diocese's chancellor, recalled that there were "very few problems," because, he implied, "Our numbers . . . are small." In 1954, there were only 57,031 Catholics, including about 530 African American Catholics, in the diocese's total population of 700,000. At least partial Catholic school desegregation also occurred in 1954 in the dioceses of Dallas-Fort Worth and Corpus Christi, where the black Catholic populations of approximately 920 and 245 were part of a wider Catholic population of 86,340 and 500,000 respectively.[21]

The African American Catholic population in the Diocese of Nashville was also small, approximately 2,006 people among a Catholic population of 53,303. Bishop William L. Adrian of Nashville took a cautious approach to desegregation of Catholic schools by asking priests in his diocese's deaneries to vote on the issue. In Memphis, which had an African American population of nearly 40 percent, Catholic priests concluded that white Catholics were not ready for parochial school desegregation, and many of the priests were themselves opposed to it. By contrast, in Nashville, where blacks formed approximately 30 percent of the total population, the deanery voted for desegregation.[22]

According to Monsignor Owen F. Campion, the *Brown* ruling allowed "Bishop Adrian to do what he long had wished to do," by closing two black parochial schools in south Nashville (Immaculate Mother Academy and Holy Family) and the Holy Family Parish, one of the city's two black parishes, in which they stood. However, Adrian was motivated not by a desire to promote integration but by the need to find alternative Catholic education for their students because the schools were expensive to run and had a combined enrollment of 172 students, only 60 of them Catholic. Adrian felt obliged to offer the students the opportunity to continue Catholic education, even if it meant admitting them to white Catholic high schools. A day after the announcement of the diocese's decision, St. Cecilia Academy and Overbrook School, two girls' schools owned and run by the Dominican Sisters and therefore outside diocesan control, announced that they would allow the admission of "qualified" African American students beginning in the fall of 1954.[23]

With the agreement of the Sisters of the Blessed Sacrament (S.B.S.), the majority landholders, the diocese sold the land occupied by the two closed black schools in Nashville. The Sisters directed some of the proceeds to the city's remaining black parish, St. Vincent de Paul, in north Nashville, which had an elementary school that Adrian hoped would absorb many of the displaced children. The diocese used its share of the sale for the construction of Father Bertrand High School in Memphis, a new African American parochial school that replaced another black school, St. Augustine High School.[24]

By desegregating its schools in Nashville, the diocese acted three years before the city desegregated the first grade of public elementary schools in what became the initial step of a grade-a-year federal court-ordered desegregation plan. Desegregation of the diocesan school system helped ease the way for public school desegregation, but Catholic school desegregation was in practice also token, incomplete, and conditioned by white opposition.[25]

"Many Nashville Catholics," Campion argues, "felt Bishop Adrian had exposed themselves, their children, and the church, not only to possible violence, but to hatred in the community." Long-standing Protestant hostility to Catholicism had encouraged Catholics to maintain a low profile, which now seemed under threat. However, Campion recalled that "the Catholic community over the years had developed such a sense of respect for the clergy ... they had the feeling that, 'We don't like it, but we'll go along.'" Adrian also tried to soothe white Catholic opposition. Under diocesan rules, Catholic parents were required to send their children to Catholic schools on pain of excommunication, unless granted an exemption by their ordinary. With desegregation imminent and Adrian's popularity among white Catholics disappearing, the diocese "relaxed its ruling."[26]

Despite concerns among leading Catholic officials, white Nashville parents only withdrew a few children from Catholic school. Some of them later returned. The diocese's low-key approach, the small numbers involved, the single-sex nature of the two Catholic high schools affected, and the fact that many Protestant whites dismissed Catholics as a peripheral second-class minority helped prevent significant opposition from the white non-Catholic majority. However, the two Catholic high schools scheduled for desegregation, Father Ryan for boys and Cathedral for girls, endured threats during the summer. Desegregation passed off peacefully in September 1954 when fifteen African American boys entered Father Ryan, named after Father Abram J. Ryan the unofficial poet laureate of the Confederacy, and black girls registered at Cathedral, making the two schools the first to desegregate in Tennessee. Despite a peaceful start, during the first year of desegregation Father Ryan regularly had windows broken by bricks thrown from passing cars.[27]

According to historian Reavis L. Mitchell, a former student at Father Ryan, Father Ryan and Cathedral remained the only desegregated Catholic schools in Nashville until 1963. He claims that the two schools operated by the Dominican Sisters in the city only considered black girls for admission who had scored close to or the maximum on high school qualifying tests, and, even then, they screened out those who were not from families in the professions.[28]

The *Brown* ruling convinced Bishop Waters that the time was right to take further action against segregation in North Carolina. He wrote to the superintendents of his diocese's four Catholic hospitals asking them by September 8, 1954, to "Open all facilities . . . to Catholic Negroes in any places where this has not been done already, and to non-Catholic Negroes as far as extra room may permit," and to "Permit qualified Negro physicians and surgeons to take care of these patients whenever possible." Desegregation, though, would be limited because African American medical staff would only be allowed to treat black patients.[29]

Waters also employed a gradualist approach in desegregating parochial schools. In August 1954, he ordered the diocese's five Catholic high schools (three white and two black) to admit all educationally qualified Catholics regardless of race in September. Although exempt from the desegregation mandate, white elementary schools and Catholic colleges could also admit black Catholics "by special arrangements." For schools, this meant that pastors of the black and white parishes affected had to agree on how Waters's order would be implemented. In September 1954, three African American girls enrolled in Raleigh's Cathedral Latin Catholic High School. Charlotte's two Catholic high schools also enrolled some blacks. Two white elementary schools admitted black students. There were no incidents accompanying desegregation, partly because Waters had not informed the newspapers and had asked those involved—principals, pastors, teachers, new students, and their parents—to keep the school desegregation order confidential until its implementation. Diocesan chancellor George F. Lynch estimated that "about one to three percent of the children were taken out of the schools when integration began, but many of them were later returned to the parochial schools."[30]

However, merger of the two Catholic schools in Newton Grove left an enrollment of only six students, all white. Most white parents had not registered their children, fearing the school would be mixed, and black parents were concerned that their children would be made unwelcome. Consequently, the school closed.[31]

The *Brown* decision prompted Bishop Fletcher to address parochial school desegregation in the Diocese of Little Rock, which had approximately 945 African Americans in a Catholic population of 40,335. In August 1954, Fletcher issued a pastoral letter stating that although "not subject to the Supreme Court decision," Catholic schools would desegregate. Fletcher claimed that the Catholic Church had hitherto observed segregation in the South because "In places where segregation is enforced by law or custom, the Church simply does the best she can by trying to provide separate Churches and schools for the different races." Despite his earlier assertion that *Brown* was not binding on Catholic schools, he declared that "This decision clears the way legally for the Church to act more freely in giving to all races the same benefits she is able to provide for the practice of their holy religion."[32]

Even so, Fletcher argued that "Everybody realizes that it is practically impossible" to effect desegregation "immediately in all places." Such an action "would be the height of folly" and against the wishes of "the vast majority of the members of either race." Nevertheless, the bishop insisted "Catholic Negro children be admitted to any Catholic school available in places where there is no Catholic school especially for them," and he announced that he would personally review all such cases. Although there was less "spiritual urgency" for desegregation in places with separate Catholic schools for blacks and whites, diocesan policy, he announced, would be to end racial barriers for Catholic children in school admissions. Fletcher considered his policy "consistent with our faith as Catholics and with our patriotic duty as Americans." In a tacit admission that segregation and exclusion of African Americans occurred, he also stated that "persons of every race, creed and nation should be made to feel at home in every Catholic Church."[33]

Fletcher's statement had little immediate impact on segregation in the diocese, although in September 1954 two African American children enrolled in the formerly all-white Catholic elementary school in Paris and black enrollment at St. Scholastica's Academy had risen to eight. Otherwise, segregation remained virtually intact in Arkansas's Catholic schools and churches. Fletcher suggested that the Church was simply honoring black people's wishes, writing that "it will be a long time before the majority of our Negro Catholics in the South will prefer to send their children to other than a Catholic colored school."[34]

By September 1954, Catholic school desegregation had begun in every peripheral southern state, except in the Diocese of St. Augustine in Florida led by the cautious conservative, Archbishop Joseph P. Hurley, a native of Cleveland, Ohio. Prone to racial stereotyping, Hurley was not discomforted by the preference of most white Catholics in his diocese for segregation, and he was also reluctant to desegregate schools because of state segregation law that included private schools. Apart from Florida and diocesan schools in Arkansas, parochial schools in the peripheral South began desegregation ahead of the public schools, many of which would not begin token desegregation for several years.[35]

The *Brown* ruling and its anticipation were key factors in the timing of Catholic school desegregation in the peripheral South. While some prelates were anxious not to trail or to be seen to lag behind secular change, *Brown* emboldened others to act. Given the small black Catholic populations in most peripheral South dioceses and the limiting of desegregation, in most cases, to black Catholics, ordinaries did not expect parochial school desegregation would exceed tokenism, or generate serious opposition among white Catholics. And as the Catholic population was itself also a small minority in most of the peripheral South, most prelates believed correctly that limited desegregation in a few parochial schools would also not produce significant hostility from the white Protestant and largely segregationist majority.

Conversely, the Diocese of Galveston, Texas, which had a sizable African American Catholic population of approximately 20,277 in 1954, maintained parochial school segregation. East Texas, the area encompassed by the diocese in 1954, had a significant total black population, and the white population largely shared the entrenched segregationist attitudes commonly found in the Deep South. Anti-Catholicism, significant in east Texas, also induced caution among diocesan leaders.[36]

Anti-Catholicism, although much less overt than in the first decades of the twentieth century, also remained potent in the northern half of Louisiana and in the other four Deep South states. Its existence contributed to the reluctance of prelates in these areas to dissent from or challenge segregation. Outside of southern Louisiana and the Gulf Coast of Mississippi and Alabama, Catholics formed a small, potentially vulnerable, minority of the population in the Deep South and, in any case, many white Catholics across the region shared the same commitment to segregation as white Protestants. No prelate in the Deep South began parochial school desegregation in 1954.[37]

Operated by the Oratorian Fathers, who were semiautonomous and nominally under the control of Bishop John J. Russell of Charleston, St. Anne School in Rock Hill, South Carolina, became the only desegregated Catholic school in the Deep South when it admitted five African American children in September 1954.[38] There was a further breach in segregation in the Deep South when Spring Hill College desegregated its undergraduate program in September 1954, a decision reached ten days before the *Brown* ruling but several years in the making, and admitted eight African Americans. Loyola University of the South also desegregated its graduate school of education and evening division. Beyond the Deep South, in Belmont, North Carolina, Belmont Abbey College desegregated and Sacred Heart Junior College for girls admitted three African Americans.[39]

The prospect of significant Catholic school desegregation in the Deep South arose after Archbishop Rummel established a committee in June 1955 to consider desegregation of archdiocesan schools. In August, he and his consultors, an advisory board of priests, unanimously accepted its proposal to begin first grade desegregation in September 1956. Rummel then publicly announced that parochial school desegregation would not begin before then.[40]

During 1955, Catholic school desegregation slowly moved ahead in parts of the peripheral South. In September, Jesuit High School for boys in Dallas, Texas, operated by the New Orleans Province of the Society of Jesus whose provincial had gone on record a year earlier in favor of desegregation, admitted two African Americans. In a joint statement, school president Thomas J. Shields, S.J., and principal Michael P. Kammer, S.J., justified the school's desegregation as a matter of lawful obedience and patriotism. They declared: "Jesuit High School, although not a public but a private educational institution of the Catholic Church, is thoroughly American and is committed to thorough adherence to the government of the United States and its Supreme Court." Shields told diocesan newspaper the *Texas Catholic* that he received one complaint, from the white mother of a newly enrolled boy.[41]

Encouraged by the success of parochial school desegregation in some Virginia cities, the board of Norfolk Catholic High School, which comprised local pastors, announced that the school would admit African American Catholics in September 1955. In making its decision, the board argued it was acting "in the spirit" of the *Brown* decision and Bishop Ireton's directives. The board reassured whites that desegregation would be token, with an expectation that twelve African Americans would enroll, and referred to "the immense difficulty of changing long-established customs and usage." The board added that the "success or failure" of black students would "largely depend upon them." It warned white students that "any violation of the virtues of Charity and Justice is a serious breach of Christian morality" and reminded Catholics that African Americans had endured a "sometimes unspeakably hard lot." Desegregation occurred without incident.[42]

In neigboring North Carolina, Bishop Waters took further action against segregation. In 1955, he ordered white Catholic grammar schools located in towns without a black Catholic grammar school to admit black Catholic applicants in the new school year. Waters also acted to tackle bias in another aspect of grammar and high school admission. He wrote to all pastors and Catholic school principals that "if we are taking Protestant students who are white and refusing equally qualified colored students, we can be accused of prejudice towards the colored." Consequently, the only criteria for admitting Protestant students would be educational qualifications as determined by pastors and principals. Such a decentralized enforcement mechanism could not guarantee observance, although all Catholic high schools had already admitted some black students.[43]

Waters made advances in other areas. In January 1957, he reported that "In our Catholic camp of Our Lady of the Hills at Hendersonville, there was integration both during the boys' period and the girls' period during the past summer. Some four hundred children were registered in all." Interracial groups in the diocese also met to discuss racial problems. Although committed to school desegregation, Waters allowed three schools for Catholics to be opened in African American areas of Greenville, Fayetteville, and Charlotte between 1956 and 1957, regarding them as a necessary part of the Church's outreach.[44]

By 1956, many southern state governments had adopted a policy of massive resistance to public school desegregation, and the white Citizens' Councils and their equivalents mushroomed across the region in an attempt to enforce conformity in the white community and intimidate both African Americans and whites from challenging segregation. White opposition to desegregation was most rigid in the Deep South. Consequently, Catholic leaders, who wanted to desegregate their institutions, retreated or acted quietly without publicity.

Mounting state, lay, and even some clerical opposition led Rummel to decide in July 1956 that Catholic schools in the Archdiocese of New Orleans would not desegregate before September 1957. However, the New Orleans Province of the Society of Jesus continued its policy of gradual desegregation by accepting its first African American candidate for the priesthood in July 1956, when Numa J. Rousseve Jr., from New Orleans, entered the novitiate at Grand Coteau. The move was made without publicity or advance notice for fear of generating opposition from within and outside the order. In the same month, *Sign*, a Catholic magazine published in New York, reported that in the Diocese of Alexandria "Bishop Charles P. Greco has made no official statement on integration, but he encourages positive work toward it. Sodality activities are integrated; colored priests attend monthly clergy conferences; there are no segregation signs in churches."[45]

Although he did not offer any public explanation, Rummel did not desegregate parochial schools in September 1957, concerned by threats of punitive sanctions from the state legislature, substantial lay resistance, and many clergy who either opposed desegregation or feared its divisiveness. Rummel was not alone in stepping back from desegregating parochial schools. In October 1957, Bishop Francis E. Hyland of Atlanta asked his consultors for their views on desegregating a new white high school as there were eighty-seven African American Catholics of high school age. He found that "the majority agreed that integration at this time because of the political climate would be imprudent and leave us open to punitive measures by the State, such as taxes and loss of teaching licenses." Although not bound by the consultors' advice, Hyland accepted it and left segregation intact.[46]

Progress toward desegregation continued to be largely confined to the peripheral South in the late 1950s. In 1957, the personnel of the Chancery of the Diocese of Raleigh were desegregated. In 1959, Waters told a University of Notre Dame Law School symposium that "We insist on the biracial aspect in all

Church sponsored sports events." He also explained that "All sodalities, confraternities, societies, are encouraged to have a bi-racial membership and to work towards this Catholic goal." African American enrollment in formerly white parochial schools increased. By 1959, Catholic high schools in North Carolina had more than eighty-two African American students. Afraid of a hostile public reaction, Waters banned dances at the diocese's desegregated high schools. The ban aggrieved some white Catholics who focused their resentment on African Americans.[47]

Neighboring South Carolina also saw some progress toward desegregation. In May 1958, the Synod of the Diocese of Charleston, the first held for more than thirty years, decreed that "No person shall be refused admittance to any church or the Sacraments because of race or color." According to Chancellor Bernardin, this was "only an official affirmation of a tradition that has been observed for a number of years." Nevertheless, Paul J. Hallinan, who replaced Bishop Russell as Bishop of Charleston in 1958, informed his priests two years later that "The steady *opening up of all our churches to everybody* [emphasis in the original] should continue," suggesting that some churches still barred African Americans.[48]

In the second half of the 1950s, Catholic desegregation began in Florida. According to historian Father Michael J. McNally, Archbishop Hurley ordered Mercy Hospital in Miami "to allow African Americans treatment and accessibility to private rooms," three years before the Diocese of Miami was carved out of the Diocese of St. Augustine in 1958. In September 1959, public school desegregation began in Florida when Orchard Villa school in Miami desegregated voluntarily. Coleman F. Carroll, a Pennsylvanian installed as bishop of the Diocese of Miami in October 1958, "introduced a course of instruction throughout the Diocese in 1959 on the subject of racial justice" to prepare Catholics for school desegregation, which began in September 1960 when Archbishop Curley High School in the city of Miami admitted three African Americans with, a diocesan official wrote, "as little publicity as possible," and Notre Dame Academy admitted a black girl. The diocese limited desegregation in admissions to Catholic students.[49]

Some other dioceses also shunned publicity when they desegregated schools. Bishop Louis J. Reicher of Austin, Texas, did not issue a statement on desegregation, but, in June 1962, the Reverend D. C. McLeaish of the diocese's Chancery Office noted that "all of the Catholic schools in Austin have been integrated for some years now. Catholic schools in other parishes of the Diocese have admitted Negro Catholic children, I know of no refusals." In 1960, the Diocese of Nashville quietly permitted Knoxville's Immaculate Conception Church to admit an African American student to its school when the city's public schools began a grade-a-year desegregation plan under federal court order.[50]

In neighboring Arkansas, Bishop Fletcher issued a catechism on segregation for discussion during Lent 1960. Fletcher wrote that "Segregation as we know it in Arkansas is immoral . . . because it discriminates unjustly and uncharitably against human beings on the basis of race alone." Racism, he affirmed, was contrary to the Church's teachings. Fletcher reminded Catholics that they were all members of the Mystical Body of Christ, which obligated them "to show fraternal charity to Catholics of every race." Catholics, he declared, could not join organizations seeking to perpetuate segregation, and those who opposed the admission of black Catholic students to a Catholic school when it was the only one serving that area committed "a grave sin."[51]

Consistent with his commitment to gradual desegregation, in September 1960 Fletcher sanctioned the admission of two African American boys to St. Anne's Academy, a formerly all-white coeducational high school in Fort Smith. To preserve peace and forestall any possible opposition, the bishop adopted a low-key approach, eschewing public statements. He reported that desegregation had occurred at the school "without fanfare, publicity, or serious incident."[52]

In September 1960, federal court-ordered, grade-a-year public school desegregation began in Houston. At the same time, the Diocese of Galveston-Houston quietly desegregated a few grades of St. Mary's parochial school, located in a white parish in Houston that was "rapidly becoming colored," due largely to the presence of employees from nearby Texas Southern University, a black institution. Diocesan Chancellor Vincent M. Harris reported that "Only a handful of colored children enrolled, and there was no difficulty," not only because of the small numbers involved but also because those whites most opposed to desegregation had already moved away from the area.[53]

Except for St. Anne School in Rock Hill, South Carolina, where many white parishioners continued to object to the school's desegregation, Catholic schools in the Deep South remained segregated. Prelates there were unwilling to desegregate them ahead of public schools.[54] In July 1959, the Archdiocese of New Orleans announced that parochial schools would desegregate as soon as possible and no later than public schools in the archdiocese. In August 1960, federal district judge J. Skelly Wright, a Catholic, accepted the Orleans Parish School Board's plan to desegregate the first grade of public schools in the city of New Orleans in mid-November to fulfill his court's desegregation order. In private, Wright urged the Archdiocese of New Orleans to desegregate its schools in September before the public schools. The next day, Rummel chaired a meeting of the Archdiocesan School Board and rejected Wright's request as impractical. Monsignor Henry C. Bezou, superintendent of archdiocesan schools, told the meeting that white Catholic parents remained as opposed to parochial school desegregation as they had been five years earlier. The board recommended that Rummel order first grade desegregation in Orleans Parish, the parish slated for first grade public school desegregation, no later than public school desegregation and only in schools, many of which were already fully subscribed, that had class space. The next day, the Archdiocesan School Board announced the policy, which meant that parochial schools would remained segregated when the school year began.⁵⁵

On October 9, the archbishop, who was nearly eighty-four, fell and broke an arm and a leg in Baton Rouge, leading to his hospitalization there. Contraction of pneumonia lengthened his stay. On October 19, the Archdiocesan School Board and diocesan consultors met in New Orleans and decided that if public schools desegregated as planned by November 14, parochial schools in Orleans Parish would also do so at that time. Monsignor Lucien J. Caillouet, who presided over the meeting, traveled to Rummel's bedside in Our Lady of the Lake Hospital on October 20 to discuss its outcome. However, Rummel's health seriously deteriorated that day, making policy discussions impossible. With Rummel on the critical list until October 30, archdiocesan policy remained to desegregate Orleans Parish schools no later than the public schools.⁵⁶

On November 11, a recovering Rummel met with Bezou and other diocesan officials. The next day, the archbishop issued a telegram informing his clergy and the principals of nonparochial elementary schools that Catholic schools in Orleans Parish would "be integrated as originally planned if and when public schools are actually integrated" but only after "public school integration has been effectively carried out."⁵⁷

On November 14, desegregation began at two public schools. Their locations had been kept secret, and there was no disorder. Authorized by Rummel, Bezou issued a confidential letter in the afternoon to clergy and all Catholic elementary school principals, stating that Catholic school desegregation would be effected on November 21 "if at that time the public schools are integrated and operating." The next day, jeering demonstrators gathered outside the two desegregated schools, where attendance had dwindled. That night, a leaked copy of Bezou's letter was read at a mass meeting of the Citizens' Council in the city and became national news. On the morning of November 16, a highly placed state official warned the Chancery Office by telephone that the legislature would most likely approve punitive measures against the Church, including taxing its property, if parochial schools desegregated. As archdiocesan leaders convened for a meeting that day, rowdy, and sometimes violent, white teenage students surged downtown and descended on City Hall and the Public School Office. The Mayor's Office telephoned the chancery and requested postponement of parochial school desegregation, claiming that the already overstretched police department would be unable to ensure law and order.⁵⁸

Buffeted by the pressures from the legislature and the mayor's office and concerned by reports from pastors that desegregation was impractical in their schools, the archdiocese issued a statement on November 16 declaring that it had never set a "definite date" for parochial school desegregation and none would be set or a desegregation order given "until the Archbishop and his Counsellors deem it prudent and advisable."⁵⁹

At a meeting two weeks later, the Archdiocesan School Board expressed fears that mounting white Catholic parental opposition to parochial school desegregation would lead to demonstrations at every Catholic school that desegregated, necessitating police protection. At the same time, the board believed that the threat of a school boycott and of punitive state legislation remained. Consequently, the archdiocese's schools remained segregated.[60]

The success of segregationists in preventing parochial school desegregation in New Orleans seemingly doomed its prospects in the rest of the Deep South, especially as the ecclesiastical Province of New Orleans that Rummel headed included, apart from the Diocese of Little Rock, the Deep South dioceses of Alexandria, Baton Rouge, and Lafayette, Mobile-Birmingham and Natchez-Jackson. Although ordinaries ran their own dioceses, parochial school desegregation in the Archdiocese of New Orleans would have provided an example for them to emulate and one that they could have cited in justification of desegregation. Nevertheless, some Deep South ordinaries indicated their intentions regarding parochial school desegregation. In November 1960, Bishop Maurice Schexnayder of Lafayette announced that he would desegregate schools in his diocese when the public schools desegregated, although not before.[61]

In early January 1961, Bishop Thomas J. McDonough of Savannah invited Bishop Hyland of Atlanta and Bishop Paul J. Hallinan of Charleston to meet with him to discuss making a joint statement on racial problems. Although Hyland had deferred to his consultors in 1957 and maintained parochial school segregation, he had since publicly called for acceptance of federal court-ordered public school desegregation, and, in January 1960, Hallinan had told South Carolina governor Ernest F. Hollings that he would desegregate Catholic schools as soon as he believed this could be done with safety for those involved. After receiving McDonough's invitation, Hallinan drafted a statement to this effect and added that diocesan schools would desegregate no later than public schools. Although his consultors were divided on the matter, Hallinan maintained his position and took the statement to the bishops' meeting in Savannah on January 12, a day after a campus riot against federal court-ordered desegregation at the University of Georgia in Athens. McDonough explained at the meeting that he had formulated a similar communiqué to Hallinan's, until dissuaded by the misgivings of his superintendent of schools, Father John Cuddy. After discussions, however, the three bishops resolved to publish an identical pastoral letter individually.[62]

Drafted by Hallinan, with only minor revisions from the three bishops thereafter, the letter was read in the Catholic churches of each diocese on February 19, 1961, and appealed to Catholics' faith and patriotism. It argued that racial "hatred is neither Christian nor American" and cited Jesus's admonition "A new commandment I give you, that you love one another" (St. John 13:34) and the Declaration of Independence. The letter also quoted from the American Catholic hierarchy's condemnation of segregation in November 1958. The three bishops did not set a timetable for parochial school desegregation, indicating only that it would occur no later than public school desegregation, be limited to all "Catholic pupils, regardless of color," and occur "as soon as this can be done with safety to the children and the schools." During 1961, the letter continued, the dioceses would undertake a preparatory program to "explain the full Catholic teaching on racial justice." The bishops did not apologize for or even acknowledge the Church's complicity in segregation, recognizing only that "changing times have called for fresh application of the eternal God-given principles." African American Catholic schools, the bishops stated, would continue as long as they were needed as their purpose was "to reach and teach the Negro, not to segregate him."[63]

The letter was published in diocesan newspapers and widely reported in the secular press. Father John Cuddy remained unenthusiastic, telling the *Savannah Morning News* that the letter seemed to indicate that Catholic schools would not desegregate before Savannah's public schools and, even then, parochial schools might not desegregate in areas where there was racial strife. Cuddy also considered it "very possible that no Negro will ever apply to enter a white Catholic school here" because of what he believed was the adequacy of black Catholic schools. Cuddy claimed that his parishioners at St. Michael's Church, Savannah Beach, had responded to the bishop's announcement with "mixed emotions." McDonough received letters of support and opposition, but, a cautious man, he dwelt on the negative, writing to a non-Catholic supporter on February 21, "I have already received much abuse because of the statement I made."[64]

A month after the pastoral letter, Hallinan thanked his priests for their support and reflected that "The over-all reaction was somewhat milder than was expected." He had received only ten letters in opposition and forced Catholic opponents to cancel a protest meeting in Charleston by threatening them with punitive sanctions for opposing church teachings. The organizers were also deterred by the efforts of the local Citizens' Council and New Orleans biblical segregationist Una M. Gaillot to take over the proposed meeting. The bishop told his pastors that he had no plans to desegregate the parochial schools in 1961 and would introduce a syllabus on racial justice in the fall for their use. A year later, Hallinan observed that he had received a roughly equal number of letters approving and disapproving the pastoral letter, but donors had canceled $35,000 worth of subscriptions to a $300,000 hospital fund.[65]

Hyland also received a mix of favorable and unfavorable correspondence, with some of his detractors writing from northern states or anonymously. He considered that "the reaction does not seem to have been too unfavorable. This gives me courage and hope, although I fully realize how difficult it is going to be to implement the pastoral letter." In fact, implementation proved more difficult for Hyland than he had imagined. In September, Atlanta's public schools began token desegregation peacefully under federal court order. Hyland's pastoral letter obliged him to desegregate parochial schools, but he did not act and became ill under the strain. He retired prematurely in October 1961, aged sixty. For several months the diocese lacked a successor, making action on desegregation impossible.[66]

Outside of Rock Hill, South Carolina, Catholic schools remained segregated throughout the Deep South in 1961. The Archdiocese of New Orleans continued parochial school segregation, even after the city of New Orleans desegregated four more elementary schools in September without incident. However, even then, only twelve African Americans attended formerly white public schools in the city and a continued white boycott of McDonough No. 19, one of the two schools desegregated in November 1960, limited its attendance to four white and five black children.[67]

Neither McDonough nor Hallinan took any action to desegregate Catholic schools in their dioceses where public schools remained segregated. In October 1961, Hallinan distributed copies of *A Syllabus on Racial Justice*, for use in grades seven through twelve of the Diocese of Charleston's schools. Written by a teacher-priest and a nun and edited by the diocesan superintendent of schools, the lessons outlined in the syllabus based their condemnation of racial discrimination and segregation on the universality of the Church, the Mystical Body of Christ, and the virtue of justice. In the introduction, Hallinan argued that teachers should explain that "this is a *development, not a reversal,* of traditional Catholic doctrine," conscious of segregationist claims that the Church had long practiced segregation.[68]

Unlike the February 1961 pastoral letter, the syllabus excoriated segregation, describing it as supporting "a theory of Racism" and "unjust and immoral *wherever it is found* [emphasis in the original]." Racial segregation, the syllabus noted, had been declared unconstitutional by the United States Supreme Court and condemned by the nation's Catholic bishops. The syllabus rejected segregationist arguments, stating that "There is no section of the Bible, Old or New Testament, which can be used to defend racial segregation today," and claiming that "The issue of States's Rights cannot be invoked here to defend Racial Segregation since the State has no power to uphold a law or custom that is unconstitutional and unjust." The syllabus acknowledged that "*de facto* segregation in churches and parishes," and segregation in Catholic education, hospitals, and organizations "severely hindered" the Church's "universal mission," and listed steps the diocese had "taken to do away with the evil effects of Racial Segregation."[69]

While the Diocese of Charleston undertook an educational program, parochial school desegregation continued incrementally in the peripheral South. In April 1961, Bishop Nold ordered elementary Catholic schools in Harris and Galveston counties, which contained the cities of Houston and Galveston, to desegregate in September by admitting "all qualified Catholic children regardless of color" because of a federal court order to implement a grade-a-year public school desegregation plan in the city of Galveston that month and a similar federal court order that had taken effect in Houston in September 1960. In deciding to desegregate all grades of elementary Catholic schools in Harris and Galveston counties, the bishop had been bolder than the courts, although he had acted after they had issued their decisions, and he had removed racially discriminatory admissions only for Catholic students.[70]

In April 1961, Nold explained in a pastoral letter that he had acted because the diocese's public schools had begun to desegregate, and he appealed to Catholics to accept desegregation "as loyal Americans and true Christians." In May, Chancellor Harris reported that "to our surprise there have been absolutely no complaints—only a couple of letters praising the Bishop for taking such action." Parochial school desegregation occurred peacefully in September 1961 and, Harris noted, "did not bring on a flood of Negro children to the previously all-white schools." Although black children entered previously white Catholic schools that were near them, the numbers involved were small because of de facto residential segregation.[71]

Like the Diocese of Galveston-Houston, school desegregation in the Diocese of St. Augustine proceeded intermittently and was usually tied to public school desegregation. When five public high schools and junior colleges in St. Petersburg desegregated in September 1961, Bishop Barry High School, a Catholic institution in the city, admitted three African Americans. In September 1962, Jacksonville's only Catholic high school, Bishop Kenny, desegregated, followed a year later by Tallahassee's Blessed Sacrament elementary school. In September 1963, St. Francis Xavier School in Fort Myers desegregated, but the last of the diocese's schools, including those in the city of St. Augustine, did not desegregate until 1964, a year after local public schools. By contrast, all of the Diocese of Miami's schools were desegregated by September 1961, and Barry College in Miami Shores, which had enrolled part-time African American graduate students in education in the 1950s, admitted a black undergraduate, Cassandra Gray, in 1962.[72]

Significant parochial school desegregation began in the Deep South in 1962, after the Vatican appointed John P. Cody, a St. Louis, Missouri, native, as coadjutor archbishop, with the right of succession, to run the Archdiocese of New Orleans because of Rummel's poor health and, most likely, also to ensure desegregation. Acting in Rummel's name, Cody insisted that it encompass all grades of all of the archdiocese's schools. Cody explained that "Archbishop Rummel's desire was to take this action, but the good man, in his aging condition, needed some support and encouragement."[73]

In March 1962, Rummel announced that all of the archdiocese's parochial schools would desegregate in September by accepting all Catholic applicants who met educational standards. The archdiocese acted after assurances that the threat of punitive state action had receded and under pressure from progressive Catholics. With Cody's support, in April, Rummel excommunicated three vocal lay Catholics who publicly opposed his desegregation order, one of whom, Leander Perez, organized an effective white boycott when Our Lady of Good Harbor elementary school in Buras, Plaquemines Parish (county), became the first archdiocesan school to desegregate in late August. Segregationists also managed a partial boycott of a desegregated white school in Westwego. Parochial school enrollment dropped by about two thousand in the first year, or nearly 3 percent, after an initial fall of five thousand, but donations to the archdiocese's Easter Sunday collection increased from $75,000 in 1962 to $215,224 in 1963. During the 1962–1963 school year, nearly two hundred African Americans attended over thirty formerly white schools, but some schools had no black students, although open to all Catholics regardless of race. In 1962, Jesuit High School in Orleans desegregated, and Loyola University of the South desegregated its undergraduate programs.[74]

In 1962, the Archdiocese of New Orleans ended special parishes for African Americans in metropolitan New Orleans by establishing new boundary lines for all parishes in the city. Yet, according to Catholic lay magazine *Ramparts*, black parishes still overlapped with white parishes two years later. Furthermore, in the mid-1960s, the archdiocese accelerated its building of new schools and churches in New Orleans's largely white middle-class suburbs to serve whites who had moved to them from the city and other parts of Louisiana and the nation. The archdiocese thereby helped perpetuate racial separation among Catholics and make anything more than token integration among them unachievable, although it seems inconceivable that the archdiocese could have prevented or reversed increasing de facto residential segregation.[75]

Atlanta, to the north, had far fewer Catholics, but it experienced a similar pattern of white migration to the suburbs and black migration to the city. Installed as the first archbishop of the newly created Archdiocese of Atlanta in March 1962, Paul J. Hallinan announced in June that the archdiocese's twenty-one white and two black schools that taught 8,000 students, including 735 African Americans, would desegregate all grades in September by admitting Catholics regardless of race. Although concerned that the state might take punitive action against the Church, Hallinan told reporters that "I believe it is less likely than it would have been a year ago." Within two weeks, Hallinan received "more than a hundred letters, telephone calls, telegrams and messages—the vast majority from within the Archdiocese" in support, while unfavorable responses totaled "six erratic letters, only one from Georgia, plus one anonymous telephone call." Catholic schools desegregated as scheduled without incident or state intervention and their overall enrollment increased. Seventeen African Americans joined six previously white schools. By desegregating all grades, the diocese surpassed the gradual desegregation of Atlanta's public schools, and whereas public schools in Marietta and Athens remained segregated Catholic schools in those areas desegregated. Hallinan also introduced *A Syllabus on Racial Justice* for use in grades seven through twelve, modeled on that he had instituted in the Diocese of Charleston.[76]

In March 1963, Hallinan announced that the archdiocese's hospitals, all operated by religious orders, had agreed to immediate and complete desegregation, although other hospitals in north Georgia remained segregated. The Catholic institutions comprised St. Mary's Hospital in Athens and, in Atlanta, the Catholic Clinic, St. Joseph's Infirmary, and the soon-to-be-opened Holy Family Hospital, which would admit its first patients in September 1964. However, both St. Joseph's Infirmary and St. Mary's Hospital continued to segregate patients, despite rules to the contrary. St. Joseph's also continued discrimination against African American staff and hired only one black doctor during the next three years because of a dearth of qualified applicants.[77]

Desegregation began in some other southern Catholic hospitals with more success. By common agreement, all religious hospitals in Knoxville, Tennessee, including St. Mary's Memorial (Catholic) Hospital permitted African American patients beginning on August 1, 1963. Desegregation occurred without incident. In August 1963, Nashville's St. Thomas Hospital agreed to desegregate, after a group of African American and white Catholics, advised by the National Catholic Conference for Interracial Justice (NCCIJ) warned the hospital that it might be picketed if it did not. In the same year, St. Paul's, a new Catholic hospital in Dallas, Texas, opened without segregation.[78]

In April 1963, the Vatican appointed John L. Morkovsky, a Texan, as Coadjutor Bishop of the Diocese of Galveston-Houston to take over administrative control from Bishop Nold, whose health was failing. In August, Morkovsky quietly desegregated all of the diocese's hospitals without a formal order, and he did the same for all of the diocese's schools in September. By contrast, public schools in Houston and Galveston, and Beaumont, which began grade-a-year desegregation in September 1963, operated gradual desegregation policies. Few, if any, southern Catholic churches outside of St. Mary's in Houston could claim to be genuinely integrated in 1963, but migration patterns soon made St. Mary's a largely African American church.[79]

A few prelates in the Deep South continued to establish churches specifically for African Americans, but in 1963, Bishop Waters initiated the merger of the white parish of St. Agnes with the black parish Mother of Mercy in Washington, "despite a minor opposition at the outset." During the remainder of the decade, he pursued a piecemeal process of merging black and white churches in the Diocese of Raleigh, involving in nearly every case the closure of the black church affected.[80]

Although southern prelates insisted that Catholic churches did not bar anyone from worship on racial grounds, incidents of exclusion still occurred, notably in the Deep South, where white segregation sentiment was most engrained. In September 1963, some male parishioners prevented Eddie L. English and some other African Americans from Mobile from attending Mass at the Chapel of the Immaculate Conception, a white parish in Orrville, Alabama. English complained to Archbishop Thomas J. Toolen of the Diocese of Mobile-Birmingham, who responded by ordering parish priest Father Thomas Lorigan to "tell the people of the Orrville church that it is a Catholic Church and belongs to all our people and that if such a thing happens again I will close the church." However, Toolen did not take any action against segregation within the diocese's white parishes that still forced African Americans to take the rear pews and communion after whites.[81]

Toolen was responsive, albeit very reluctantly, to African American Catholic pressure in Pensacola, a part of the diocese in northwest Florida, for him to emulate federal court-ordered public school desegregation that began in the coastal city in August 1962. The archbishop ordered partial parochial school desegregation in Pensacola, which began in September 1963.[82]

African American pressure led Bishop Adrian to countenance desegregation of Christian Brothers High School in Memphis in September 1963, two years after the city had desegregated the first grade of public schools under federal court order. Run by the De La Salle Christian Brothers religious order, the school became the city's only desegregated high school. The bishop also desegregated the first four grades of parochial schools in Memphis and surrounding Shelby County that month, marking the first stage of a four-year gradual desegregation plan for the area's Catholic elementary schools.[83]

In the Deep South, dioceses invariably desegregated schools in response to federal court-ordered public school desegregation, but sometimes they opened all grades, unlike the public system, and, occasionally, they acted across their entire dioceses, rather than just in areas subject to court orders. However, as elsewhere in the South, Catholic school desegregation resulted in tokenism. It usually entailed only permitting the small number of African American Catholics to enter formerly white schools, whereas a significant number and often a majority of those who attended black Catholic schools were not Catholic.

When Chatham County public schools, including Savannah, came under federal court order to desegregate at least one grade in September 1963, the Diocese of Savannah desegregated all of its schools by opening them to all Catholics regardless of race. Consequently, Mount de Sales High School, operated by the Sisters of Mercy in Macon, desegregated while the city's public schools remained segregated. In all, about thirty-seven African Americans enrolled in formerly white schools across the diocese, including ten in the city of Savannah and fifteen in Albany's St. Theresa Grammar School. Desegregation, Bishop McDonough wrote, occurred "without any unpleasant incident," although a "very few" white Catholic parents withdrew their children. By contrast, the twelve African Americans who desegregated Savannah High School by entering the public school's twelfth grade were harassed and attacked by white students.[84]

Dioceses sometimes altered their plans in response to secular change. In June 1963, a day after Bishop McDonough announced his diocese's schools would desegregate in September, Bishop Frances F. Reh of Charleston revealed that his diocese's schools would desegregate all grades, by opening them to Catholics regardless of race, in September 1964. However, on August 22, 1963, a federal district court ordered the city of Charleston to begin public school desegregation in September. The diocese responded by ordering its elementary schools in Greater Charleston to desegregate at the same time to honor the commitment made by Bishop Hallinan in February 1961 to desegregate Catholic schools no later than public schools. Fifteen African American Catholics entered four formerly white Catholic schools in Charleston in September. Diocesan schools beyond the city desegregated a year later. In both cases, there were no incidents.[85]

The Diocese of Baton Rouge was unable to keep step with the judiciary. In July 1963, a federal judge ordered desegregation of the twelfth grade of East Baton Rouge Parish's public schools in the fall, as part of a grade-a-year desegregation plan. The next week, Bishop Robert E. Tracy issued a pastoral letter announcing that the eleventh and twelfth grades of four white Catholic high schools in East Baton Rouge Parish would desegregate in September 1964 by accepting all qualified Catholic students. Tracy explained that the federal ruling had come too late for the diocese to adopt the same plan, but he noted that both public and parochial schools in East Baton Rouge Parish would be pursuing the same policy by September 1964. East Baton Rouge was only one of twelve parishes within the Diocese of Baton Rouge and so Catholic school segregation remained largely intact. Tracy signaled his intention to desegregate all Catholic institutions in the diocese but did not give a timetable.[86]

Parochial school desegregation in the Diocese of Mobile-Birmingham was also piecemeal. In September 1963, public schools in Birmingham, Huntsville, Mobile, and Tuskegee, Alabama, desegregated despite Governor George C. Wallace's temporarily successful efforts to block the process by dispatching state troopers and then National Guardsmen. President John F. Kennedy federalized the Guard and the federal courts enjoined Wallace from obstructing desegregation. Although Archbishop Toolen had not issued a diocesan school desegregation order, two days before Wallace sent state troopers to Huntsville, St. Joseph's, a Catholic elementary school in the town, opened with 12 white students enrolled alongside 106 black students. White parents from Huntsville and a federal military installation nearby had initiated desegregation by approaching Father Mark Sturbenz, S.D.S., pastor of St. Joseph's Mission. Desegregation occurred without incident.[87]

In April 1964, Toolen issued a pastoral letter announcing that all of the diocese's schools, including those in northwest Florida, would desegregate in September by admitting all qualified Catholic students. He declared that "I know this will not meet with the approval of many of our people, but in justice and charity, this must be done" and appealed for acceptance of "this decision as best for God and country." Student applications to elementary schools would continue to require support from the parish priest, and other regulations established by the diocesan superintendent of education also ensured that enrollment was highly selective. The *New York Times* noted that "Presumably this would allow for some flexibility in the desegregation order in areas where passions might become aroused."[88]

The procedures produced token desegregation. Even so, Toolen received segregationist protest letters. He noted that "There have been many bitter and hard letters, but the strange part of it is that they came from all over the country and Canada and very few from Alabama. I don't know why those people in Canada or California or New York or Illinois should be so interested in what goes on down here." In September, parochial school desegregation began peacefully without difficulty and overall enrollment reached a record level.[89]

Neighboring Mississippi desegregated the first grade of public schools in Biloxi, Carthage, Clarksdale, and Jackson peacefully under federal court order in September 1964. Bishop Gerow responded by opening the first grade of the Diocese of Natchez-Jackson's schools to all Catholics at that time. Only three African American children enrolled in a formerly white Catholic school, which Gerow attributed to some schools' class lists already being full before his announcement and "the fear of the Negro children that though they might be admitted they would not be welcome." There were some incidents of minor harassment of black children who entered the formerly white school. Gerow commented that "I was surprised at the fine reaction I got from a number of our Catholic people. I can't say that the same reaction was found in all cases. I did get some pretty bad reaction. In fact, a few, not many, of our parents were withdrawing their children from the Catholic school."[90]

In August 1965, Gerow announced that Mississippi's seventy-five Catholic schools would admit "all qualified Catholic students in all grades" in September to "bring our practice into full conformity with the teachings of Christ." For the first time, the bishop moved ahead of secular change. Mississippi's public schools adopted a policy of freedom-of-choice which in practice severely restricted desegregation. With some relief, Gerow wrote in his diary: "The number of Negroes coming to our formerly white schools is small. Probably it is good that for this year in the beginning this is so." The small numbers involved allowed desegregation to occur without sustained opposition, although some white parents withdrew their children from parochial schools to evade desegregation.[91]

That summer, Bishop Tracy responded to a federal order to accelerate desegregation of public schools in East Baton Rouge Parish in September. In June 1965, Tracy issued a pastoral letter announcing that in September Catholic schools in the entire diocese would open at least their first and second grades in the case of elementary schools and the ninth through twelfth grades of high schools to all Catholic children. The move put Catholic school desegregation one grade ahead of federal court-ordered desegregation in the public schools of East Baton Rouge Parish and covered a wider area. Tracy's plan envisioned complete parochial school desegregation by the fall of 1967. A substantial number of whites withdrew from a Catholic school in New Roads after desegregation in 1965, and there were white withdrawals elsewhere, mostly to the still largely, segregated public school system.[92]

In 1965, the dioceses of Lafayette and Alexandria, also in Louisiana, became the last southern dioceses to begin parochial school desegregation. In May, the Diocese of Lafayette announced that Catholic schools in Lake Charles and the parishes (counties) of Calcasieu, Lafayette, and St. Landry would desegregate by accepting "all qualified students," which in practice meant Catholic, to align with court-ordered public school desegregation in these areas in the fall. When public schools in other areas of the diocese desegregated, the diocese declared it would follow suit. In September 1965, an estimated twelve to fifteen African American families enrolled children in formerly white Catholic schools. Desegregation occurred peacefully, and by May 1966 had been extended to all of the diocese Catholic schools.[93]

In June 1965, Bishop Greco issued a pastoral letter read in all the Diocese of Alexandria's churches that called on them "to discontinue discrimination," a reference to those churches that still segregated seating and Holy Communion, a continuing problem in parts of the Deep South. "If we hope to live as brothers of Christ," wrote Greco, "we must be willing to pray to Him as brothers of one another." The filing of several court suits to desegregate public schools in parts of the diocese spurred the bishop to address the issue of Catholic school segregation. Greco announced that "Because of the closely knit method of operation of our Catholic schools with the public schools, in most parts of our diocese, it will be our policy beginning with the 1965–1966 school year, to desegregate some of our Catholic schools as the public schools desegregate."[94]

Greco later set out a timetable for parochial school desegregation, which began in the fall with the first, second, and twelfth grades in the civil parishes of Bossier, Caddo, Natchitoches, and Rapides. As a result, nine African American students attended formerly white parochial schools during the school year 1965–1966. In September 1965, the bishop announced that "We propose to desegregate all the grades in all our diocesan schools next school year," beginning in September 1966, by admitting "all qualified students." The decision marked a departure from Greco's previous policy of following the timetable set by federal court-ordered public school desegregation and advanced desegregation of parochial schools beyond the freedom-of-choice plans applicable to public schools.[95]

By 1966, every diocese had begun school desegregation and most had officially desegregated every school, although many formerly white schools had few or no African American students. Several circumstances produced token desegregation. Tuition fees were often substantially higher in formerly white schools and beyond the reach of many black parents. A few parishes subsidized tuition rates for poor Catholic families (and on rare occasions for poor black children), but many African American children were not Catholic and their parents found increased tuition fees prohibitive. Residential segregation sometimes left African Americans outside the catchment area of a formerly white school, or created insurmountable transportation difficulties. Parish priests had to approve applicants to parochial schools, a sifting process that sometimes disadvantaged black applicants because inferior schooling had limited their academic achievement in comparison to white applicants, or because some pastors were racially prejudiced. Many dioceses permitted only African American Catholics to enter formerly white schools. Some Catholic schools were already full and unable to enroll more students.[96]

Some white Catholic parents withdrew their children when parochial schools admitted even a few African Americans and enrolled them in private schools or in still segregated public schools. However, many white Catholic parents reluctantly accepted token parochial school desegregation, either because they could tolerate their children attending school with a few blacks or because no blacks had actually enrolled, leaving schools desegregated officially but not in practice.[97]

By the mid-1960s, virtually every southern diocese had issued instructions to diocesan and parish societies to desegregate, and every diocese had outlawed discrimination within church seating and communion. But dioceses relied on parish priests, church ushers, and the officers of organizations and societies for enforcement of nondiscrimination policies, leading to wide variations in compliance, with resistance greatest at the local parish level and in parts of the Deep South. Despite the Archdiocese of New Orleans's long-standing prohibition of church segregation, in May 1965 Bogalusa's Annunciation Church still segregated seating, and nearly three years later, an usher prevented Xavier University professor Loretta Butler and her friend from attending Mass at New Orleans's St. James Major Church.[98]

In March 1966, Bishop Tracy claimed that "we have now completed our program of opening all our Catholic institutions, organizations and activities to all our Catholic people." However, he recognized that the absence of discriminatory policies did not in itself ensure integration. Consequently, in July, he directed that new employees in Catholic parishes, schools, institutions, and diocesan offices must be chosen according to ability, noting that the Catholic Church should at least follow federal practices in this regard. But the diocese encountered severe difficulties in recruiting qualified African Americans for supervisory and clerical jobs because of the legacy of the poorer education they had experienced in segregated public and Catholic schools. Other dioceses also adopted equal employment policies and some applied the principle to business contracts. The Diocese of Mobile-Alabama gave preference to firms that practiced fair employment. The dioceses of San Antonio, Nashville, Galveston-Houston, and Beaumont joined Project Equality, an interdenominational program that promoted fair employment practices in member judicatories and in the firms with which they did business.[99]

In the second half of the 1960s, federal pressure forced southern dioceses to address continued segregation and discrimination in schools and hospitals, including hiring and admissions. Title VI of the Civil Rights Act of 1964 prohibited federal funds from use in institutions that practiced racial discrimination. As many students in Catholic schools received federal aid and Catholic hospitals admitted patients under the Medicare Act of 1965, federal money could be withdrawn for noncompliance. In the fall of 1965, the National Association for the Advancement of Colored People (NAACP) Legal Defense and Education Fund filed suit under Title VI against discrimination in eleven Catholic hospitals in Florida, North Carolina, and four Deep South states. In June 1966, the federal Department of Health, Education and Welfare (HEW) threatened to terminate federal assistance to two Catholic hospitals not named in the NAACP's suit, St. Joseph's Infirmary and Holy Family Hospital in Atlanta, for noncompliance. Both hospitals took immediate remedial action. By August, fewer than twenty-four of the one hundred Catholic hospitals in the South had failed to comply with nondiscrimination requirements. By December, only St. Francis Hospital in Monroe, Louisiana, had not complied.[100]

Operated by the Franciscan Missionaries of Our Lady (Calais) and so outside the direct control of local prelate Bishop Greco, the hospital lost federal funds for segregating patients. Mother Marie Finbarr (Anne Marie Twohig), the hospital's administrator, admitted that the hospital did not integrate patients in the same room, although African American and white patients were not segregated by floor. Finbarr, a native of Ireland, declared: "I think it's up to the community and they do not want it right now. Monroe is not ready for it. I don't think it's up to me. If it were, I would start it tomorrow, but it's up to the doctors and the community." Greco exonerated the sisters from blame. In July 1968, he informed the NCCIJ that the hospital's staff had forced the sisters to maintain segregation but added that "total integration had been effected since last October."[101]

HEW pressure forced southern Catholic dioceses to satisfy its school desegregation guidelines, regarding both faculty and student intake or face withdrawal of federal assistance. At the same time, a decline in vocations, which saw the number of nuns in the United States fall from 181,421 in 1965 to 160,931 in 1970, brought a teacher shortage in Catholic schools, leaving dioceses with the option of raising tuition costs to employ more lay teachers or closing schools. Many prelates felt a moral obligation to move beyond token parochial school desegregation to genuine integration, but the immediacy of HEW pressure, augmented by the teacher shortage, played a major role in leading them to address that obligation in the second half of the 1960s. Some orders of nuns that staffed Catholic schools also exerted pressure on ordinaries to desegregate them.[102]

An HEW official who visited Baton Rouge in June 1966 expressed dissatisfaction with the tokenism of Catholic school desegregation in Louisiana. Bishop Tracy closed four of the Diocese of Baton Rouge's nine black Catholic schools as "a step toward the elimination of racial barriers" on the assumption that "the Negro children will now attend former white schools" and because "the Negro schools which were closed hardly deserved the name of school at all." In February 1967, he claimed that "our motive in adhering to the [HEW] guidelines is not simply that of receiving federal assistance for our school children but of achieving a full measure of Christlike brotherhood among all our Catholic people." The diocese's actions satisfied HEW in June 1967 and, in line with additional HEW demands, the Diocesan School Board instructed schools in November to increase efforts to recruit African American teachers, although few would accept Catholic school salaries, which lagged behind those in public schools.[103]

In 1966, the Office of Education, part of HEW, cut off federal funds to Catholic schools in the Louisiana dioceses of Lafayette and Alexandria for noncompliance with the Civil Rights Act based on the continuation of all-black enrollments in many traditionally African American schools, despite official desegregation, and insufficient faculty integration. Father Murray Clayton, director of the Diocese of Alexandria's Bureau of Information, responded that the diocese had already closed one black Catholic school, decided to close another at the end of the school year, and intended to "phase out at least one, possibly two, more schools in the near future." Clayton did not address the unwillingness of many white parents in his and other southern dioceses to send their children to traditionally black Catholic schools that reflected continued segregationist sentiment and sometimes an often-justifiable concern that black Catholic schools were less well equipped than traditionally white schools.[104]

Teacher integration was another one area of difficulty, partly because dioceses sometimes assigned nuns from African American orders to teach black students. However, federal officials came to accept that orders of nuns could not simply be relocated to teach with members of other orders in different schools, since orders had their own convents and systems of governance. Both the dioceses of Alexandria and Lafayette formulated plans for further student and faculty desegregation that HEW accepted in the summer of 1967.[105]

Many dioceses closed black churches, as well as schools, in the middle and late 1960s with the intention and expectation that their parishioners would join the white territorial parish in which they lived. In some cases, dioceses made a few black parishes into territorial parishes, open to all neighborhood Catholics. The Diocese of Nashville redrew its parish lines to eliminate nonterritorial parishes for African Americans and to ensure a more even population distribution and financial burden for parishes, although some African American Catholics complained that the redrawn lines deliberately created de facto black parishes. The Archdiocese of New Orleans closed some of its remaining African American parishes outside the city of New Orleans and assigned their members to formerly white territorial parishes. The Archdiocese of Atlanta suppressed the African American parish of Sacred Heart and incorporated its parishioners into St. Joseph's territorial parish.[106]

White Catholics often did not make blacks welcome in church, and some excluded them altogether. In July 1968, Bishop Schexnayder lamented that in the Diocese of Lafayette, "It is unfortunately true that Negroes are not allowed in a few of our churches." Black and white Catholic churches continued to exist in close proximity in some of the diocese's rural towns. In urban areas of the South, white flight from increasingly African American cities meant that many whites and blacks lived in different parishes, which limited the prospects for church integration. Residence patterns meant that several territorial parishes in the Diocese of Richmond were entirely black, among them Holy Rosary, Richmond, St. Mary's, Norfolk, and St. Gerard, Roanoke. In 1970, Father Frederick A. Heckel of Newport News's St. Vincent de Paul Church, which had absorbed African American parishioners from the closed St. Alphonsus Parish, noted that "We have one of the few totally integrated parishes on every level in the diocese. One of the few parishes also where the bulk of the black parishioners have continued to come to the white church." However, many southern white Catholics remained unreconciled to desegregation.[107]

When federal courts forced public schools in the Deep South to complete desegregation in 1969 and 1970, every diocese affected declared support for public education. Nevertheless, and despite diocesan policies to the contrary, some parochial schools, mostly in Louisiana's four dioceses, accepted whites fleeing public school desegregation. In south Louisiana, an estimated sixty-seven hundred students transferred into parochial schools from the public system, and, as early as September 1969, when pairing or consolidation of public schools for racial balance began in the Diocese of Lafayette, four hundred white students transferred into the diocese's schools to avoid desegregation. The S.B.S. noted, with disapproval, that in the diocese, "White public students were fleeing integration—being admitted to Catholic schools in this area in considerable numbers, even being bussed to Catholic schools at a distance, with the full knowledge, planning and consent of the pastors involved."[108]

For the most part, southern dioceses had achieved no more than token desegregation by 1970. Diocesan leaders had mostly formulated desegregation policy without consulting black Catholics, and ordinaries frequently made assumptions about black concerns. However, African American Catholic opinion was far from monolithic, and it became increasingly vocal about the nature and impact of Catholic desegregation.

CHAPTER SEVEN

African American Catholics in the South and Desegregation, 1945–1970

In 1945, there were an estimated 142,505 African Americans in southern black parishes and missions. An unspecified but small number attended predominantly white churches. Black Catholics were most numerous in the Diocese of Lafayette (53,610), the Archdiocese of New Orleans (40,982), and the dioceses of Galveston (11,869), which attracted black Catholic migrants from southern Louisiana, and Mobile (9,000). Apart from the cradle Catholics of southern Louisiana and the Gulf Coast, African American Catholics were often converts. Together, they formed a tiny minority of the South's small Catholic population.[1]

Like all Catholics, African American Catholics had a religious duty to send their children to Catholic schools when available to them, but non-Catholic blacks often made up a substantial part, or even a majority, of their enrollment. Enrollee's parents believed that Catholic schools delivered better education than the segregated public school system, and they welcomed the discipline and morality inculcated and demanded by parochial schoolteachers. Based in Pensacola, Florida, Father Arthur Butler, O.F.M, enthused:

> [M]any of the better Negro families, the real leaders of the people, tried so hard and so insistently to enter their children in our school. Some were even willing to enter the Church in order to have their children in our School. It makes us realize that they have great respect for the Church and for the ability of our Sisters to give the children an intellectual and a moral education.[2]

Historian Father Michael J. McNally criticizes African American Catholic schools in the southeast. He claims that "the black Catholic schools did not communicate to their students a very positive self-image or a strong sense of self worth, or a pride in one's ethnic heritage, all of which are so necessary in the fulfillment of one's human potential." However, testimonies from former students often present a positive appreciation of black Catholic schools primarily for their educational quality but also, in many cases, for their emphasis on self-worth and also, occasionally, on black culture and heritage.[3]

Most African Americans who attended black Catholic churches and schools in the middle third of the twentieth century did not recall that the white priests and nuns, who mostly staffed them, discussed race relations or criticized segregation and discrimination. However, there were exceptions. In the late 1950s, nuns from St. Benedict the Moor School in Savannah, Georgia, took some black children to a downtown department store. When store clerks refused to serve the group food, the nuns refused to leave until they relented. Many African Americans fondly remembered particular nuns and parish priests, and they valued the education given them by Catholic schools in a strict, disciplined environment. Although their teachers usually did not address race overtly, many told their students that they were as good as anyone else and all pushed their classes hard to achieve. Lester Johnson recalled nuns at St. Benedict's telling his class: "'I know you are smart, so don't come in here telling me you don't know the answer to that question. I know better.' That had to have a subconscious impact on how we felt about ourselves." Another former student at St. Benedict's, Joseph Williams, explained that "We knew that segregation and discrimination existed. But those nuns instilled in us that we were equal."[4]

Some black children in Catholic schools and churches so appreciated and accepted their white nuns and priests that they regarded them as part of their community rather than as "white." Geraldine Abernathy, an African American laywoman, remembered from her New Orleans childhood, "Little black boy would say, 'I hate white people,' so sister [a Franciscan] say, 'Don't you hate me; I'm white, I'm a nun.' 'No sister. You one of us, you not no white.'"[5]

However, students taught by African American nuns were more likely to be inculcated with a sense of black achievement and pride. Joseph A. Francis Jr., who was ordained a Society of the Divine Word (S.V.D.) priest in 1950 and Auxiliary Bishop of Newark, New Jersey, in 1976, fondly recalled his childhood education in Lafayette, Louisiana. Born in 1923, the eldest of five children, Francis, like his parents and siblings, attended a black Catholic school taught by the Sisters of the Holy Family. Francis remembered:

> These Sisters gave us a sense of pride in who we are. Long before Black became beautiful, they taught us Black History, introduced us to Black poets, musicians, educators, scientists and hosts of heroes and heroines from slavery, as well as great Black men and women who led their people in the difficult post-emancipation years.[6]

Most southern black Catholics resented segregation and discrimination in Catholicism and secular society, but they sought to make the best lives that they could under a system that denied African Americans power and authority. Francis remembered that "As early as 1937, several young blacks and I reacted strongly, but in frustration to the obvious and not so obvious segregation under which we were born, educated, churched and employed. Like our slave ancestors, some of us—not many—dreamed of freedom, talked among ourselves about racism and segregation and looked upon the outspoken blacks in the freedom movements as our heroes." Bishop Harold R. Perry, who was born into a Catholic family in Lake Charles, Louisiana, in 1916, also objected to the segregation and discrimination he observed as a child within and outside the Church. In 1944, Perry became an S.V.D. priest, and, in 1966, Auxiliary Bishop of New Orleans.[7]

However, deference was ingrained in some African American Catholics, especially the old. In the 1940s, Marian Lyman belonged to St. Nicholas Church in Houston, Texas, a black church pastored by white Josephite priests that was segregated when whites attended. Lyman explained that "The whites who came to St. Thomas Novena sat on the left side of the church, and we the parishioners sat on the right. The priest tried to stop it, but the elderly people would say we know our place."[8]

In parts of the South, and especially southern Louisiana, there were sometimes divisions within the African American Catholic community based on skin color. Some light-skinned Creoles of color looked down upon darker-skinned blacks. In 1940, the Society of Saint Edmund conducted a mission in Mon Luis in Mobile Bay, Alabama, and reported that "Mon Luis is an island inhabited entirely by Creoles, all of whom are Catholic" but despite having "some Negro blood" the Creoles "will not mingle with the Negro since they are Spanish and French enough to feel superior to the colored folks." More than twenty years later, Mon Luis Creoles still had a separate church.[9]

Madeline E. Johnson, who was born in Houston, Texas, in 1943, recalled that during her youth, she and a cousin went to Mass at Our Mother of Mercy, a Creole of color church in the city's Fifth Ward, where they had to sit in a black section and wait until Creoles had received communion. When Johnson and her cousin went to the altar rail, another Creole arrived and "The usher pushed us aside to let that last person come before they would let our little black selves kneel down to receive the body of Christ." Johnson never returned, instead preferring St. Nicholas where "we were all the same." She recalled Creoles "thought they were better than us. We had segregation within segregation, that hurt me so bad."[10]

Future US Supreme Court justice Clarence Thomas attended St. Benedict the Moor School in Savannah between 1955 and 1962, where according to social anthropologist Gary Wray McDonogh, "students paid attention to skin shades as marks of class."[11] In July 1962, *Commonweal*, a Catholic magazine, reported that along the lower Louisiana coast, "Most mulattoes are Catholic, and in the larger churches try to preempt the center Gospel section, while blacks are forced to occupy the narrow Gospel side section along the windows."[12]

Just as there were some separate or segregated churches for Creoles of color and darker-skinned blacks, there were sometimes also separate schools. In August 1962, whites boycotted Our Lady of Good Harbor School in Buras, when it admitted African American students. When Father Christopher Schneider, pastor of Our Lady of Good Harbor Church, closed the desegregated school because of threats of violence, two African Americans went to the Catholic school for Creoles of color, where, as a result, the *New York Times* reported, "the mulattoes protested."[13]

Despite divisions within the African American community, there were efforts to pursue shared interests, notably in the Knights of Peter Claver (KPC). A self-governing organization of Catholic men, rather than an institution of the Catholic Church, by 1941 the KPC had 3,663 male members in seventy-six councils in fourteen states, including Alabama, Louisiana, Mississippi, and Texas. Louisiana had more members than any other state, and the KPC maintained its headquarters in New Orleans. The KPC's Ladies Auxiliary had 2,713 members in sixty-one courts. Apart from providing its members with insurance benefits, the KPC, along with the Ladies Auxiliary, raised money for charitable causes and Catholic education for African American children.[14]

In the early 1940s, the KPC forthrightly began to address racial discrimination, influenced by the emerging civil rights movement. In December 1942, Grand Knight Edward LaSalle wrote in the *Claverite*, the KPC's monthly magazine, "We are in a period of change, war accelerates change. Why not change the traditional attitude on the race question."[15]

Several Knights were crucial in forming the Group in New Orleans, comprised of young African Americans who reinvigorated the local branch of the National Association for the Advancement of Colored People (NAACP) after gaining control in 1941. A. P. Tureaud, a Creole of color born in New Orleans in 1899, who held a law degree from Howard University in Washington, DC, was a key member of the Group. In 1927, Tureaud, who had returned to New Orleans to practice law, began taking NAACP cases. In 1940, he became the association's chief counsel, while continuing to serve private clients. The KPC's national advocate between 1932 and 1948 and then its national secretary, Tureaud used both the Knights and the NAACP to mount a postwar voting rights drive in Louisiana. Despite some refusals, many Catholic priests publicized voter registration dates. Between them, the Knights, the NAACP, and the Congress of Industrial Organizations significantly increased African American voter registration in Louisiana. Tureaud also filed a succession of salary equalization suits for black teachers that gradually chipped away at discrimination.[16]

In the 1940s, the Group's efforts helped generate a massive expansion in membership of the New Orleans NAACP branch. As elsewhere in the South during the war, the NAACP also increased its branches and membership in Louisiana. While historian Justin D. Poché emphasizes the links between the NAACP, the KPC, and some white Catholic priests in advancing African American voter registration in Louisiana, Adam Fairclough, a historian of the state's civil rights movement, is less sanguine. Fairclough writes:

The paucity of NAACP branches in southwestern Louisiana can be explained, in part, by its large population of black Catholics. The Catholic churches, in every case pastored by white ministers, provided the association with no direct assistance. The Knights of Peter Claver ... supported the NAACP financially, but it did not have the same close association with the NAACP that, for example, the Prince Hall Masons did.

Fairclough's analysis neglects black S.V.D. clergymen in the Diocese of Lafayette and the efforts of some white Catholic clergymen, such as Josephite priest Harry J. Maloney in Bertrandville, in support of black registration. While some individual Knights were prominent in the NAACP, outspoken for equal rights and active in the civil rights movement, the KPC, as Fairclough suggests, was not at the movement's center.[17]

Some Knights criticized the Catholic Church for observing segregation, and articles in the *Claverite* attacked both secular and Catholic racism and segregation. In February 1947, Peter Wellington Clarke's monthly column "Je Parle" condemned racial discrimination unflinchingly. Clarke wrote:

> Such social blights as segregation, discrimination of minority groups and the like have no place in the life-sphere of the real honest-to-goodness Christian. [T]here should be no room for Jim-Crow activities within the confines of the Catholic Church, or within its immediate environs.

He noted approvingly that an unnamed KPC member had condemned segregation at a Holy Name rally, arguing that there should not be separate white and African American Holy Name societies.[18]

Tureaud worked diligently against racism in both state and Church. He helped found and served a term as chairman of the Commission on Human Rights (CHR), formed in February 1949 by a biracial group of Catholic progressives. Dedicated to the elimination of segregation from Catholicism in New Orleans, the CHR had a sizable black membership and promoted interracial Catholic activities. African American members included Clarence A. Laws, who belonged to the Group and served as executive secretary of the New Orleans Urban League, and Oscar A. Bouise and Numa J. Rousseve, professors at Xavier University in New Orleans, the nation's only black Catholic university. Along with white students from Louisiana's four white Catholic colleges, Xavier students participated in the Southeast Regional Interracial Commission (SERINCO), an organization committed to integration. Some CHR meetings and some of SERINCO's annual Interracial Sundays took place at Xavier University, the South's only black Catholic university, with the agreement of the Sisters of the Blessed Sacrament (S.B.S.), which owned and operated the university.[19]

In 1949, Tureaud stood ready to file suit against the New Orleans City Park Improvement Association on behalf of one or more black members of the Archdiocesan Union of Holy Name Societies who were aggrieved that seating for October's Holy Name Parade in City Park would be segregated. The KPC agreed to pay the suit's legal costs. However, Archbishop Joseph F. Rummel of New Orleans, who had tried unsuccessfully to persuade officials to lift segregation for the event, canceled the parade.[20]

There were also other indications of African American Catholic opposition to forced segregation. In 1949, Father Joseph H. Fichter, S.J., the CHR's instigator and a sociology professor at Loyola University of the South in New Orleans, instructed some students to survey local African American opinion. Several respondents commented that racial discrimination in the Catholic Church was "particularly offensive." That same year, Father Clarence J. Howard, an African American from Norfolk, Virginia, who had been ordained by the S.V.D. in 1937, addressed SERINCO's Interracial Sunday event. Howard asked his audience: "How can a Catholic love Christ when he is not willing to receive Christ in his body at the Communion Rail next to his Negro brother? Or to sit in the same pew with him?"[21]

Catholics who challenged segregation in the Deep South sometimes suffered retribution. In 1950, Clarence A. Laws, chair of the CHR's Information Committee, relinquished the position when the army recalled him back to active service. Acting on charges made by Leander Perez, the segregationist Catholic political boss of Plaquemines Parish, Louisiana, that Laws had consorted and worked with Communists in civil rights activities, in June 1951 an army board of inquiry held hearings to consider discharging him. With Rummel's approval, John McCann, a member of the Catholic Committee of the South, testified in Laws's support at the hearing in Fort Hood, Texas. Although the board exonerated Laws, the army discharged him as a security risk in 1955, only to reverse the decision and give him an honorable discharge in 1957.[22]

Wary of retribution from white segregationists, many African American Catholics looked to the Church's prelates to provide a lead. However, a few black Catholics took the initiative themselves. As a child, J. Terry Steib, who later became an S.V.D. priest and, in 1984, Auxiliary Bishop of St. Louis, Missouri, attended Our Lady of Peace Church in Vacherie, Louisiana, with his Catholic family. Born in Vacherie in 1940, Steib recalled that segregation compelled blacks to sit in the church's last seven pews, even when they were overcrowded and empty pews lay ahead. Furthermore, the church's parishioners received Holy Communion only at the first Sunday Mass, with African Americans held back until last. In 1951, two nuns from the Sisters of Mercy of the Holy Cross, an order based in Merrill, Wisconsin, began an evangelism program that took them into the black public school Steib attended because the town had no black parochial school. One of the nuns, Sister Maria Theodosia Laufer, told Steib's class that they could seek Holy Communion at any Mass. The next Sunday, Steib went to a later

Mass and, alone, sought Communion, which a surprised priest then administered. Thereafter, African Americans arrived for Communion at different Masses as they chose. Consequently, black attendance rose, with African Americans occupying half the pews, although the church remained segregated.[23]

African American Catholics endorsed desegregation initiatives by Catholic ordinaries. In November 1952, they welcomed the vote by the five hundred delegates of the Archdiocesan Union of Holy Name in favor of Archbishop Rummel's resolution for the merger of the black and white Holy Name societies.[24]

When 1953 Bishop Vincent S. Waters of Raleigh ordered the merger of a black and a white church in Newton Grove in 1953, two female members of Our Lady of the Miraculous Medal Church, an African American parish in Greensboro, were among those who congratulated him. One lady expressed her "humble gratitude" and reminded the bishop that "prejudice on the part of Catholic laity is a barrier to the conversion of the Negro and a trial to the newfound faith of the Negro convert." Another laywoman, Doris B. Rice, condemned "this evil monster of segregation" and praised Waters's action. For Rice, and probably many other black Catholics, the issue was less integration than the removal of discrimination. She explained, "My personal opinion . . . is that Negro Catholics here are not anxious to move over into the white churches with our brethren there, but like to feel it is our right and privilege if we want to do so." Opposed to forced segregation and discrimination, some African American Catholics joined and helped form Catholic interracial councils in a few peripheral southern cities in the 1940s and 1950s, including Greensboro.[25]

The KPC, for its part, continued to oppose discrimination. In August 1954, fifteen hundred delegates from sixteen states gathered in New Orleans for the Knights and Ladies of Peter Claver's annual convention. The delegates approved a resolution that deplored efforts by some southern states to circumvent the United States Supreme Court's *Brown* ruling that declared public school segregation unconstitutional. The KPC voted to donate $1,000 and the Ladies Auxiliary $500 to the NAACP, which through its legal arm, the Defense and Educational Fund, Inc., had litigated *Brown*. The Knights and Ladies also asked their courts and councils to make further donations to the association. A year later, the KPC convention praised prelates and priests who had "taken positive steps to discontinue" segregated parochial schools and urged other dioceses to act.[26]

Although most African Americans objected to forced segregation, they often did not want to enroll their children in white parochial schools when the opportunity arose, and the children were themselves often reluctant to leave black Catholic schools. In 1954, Bishop William L. Adrian of Nashville closed two black parochial schools in south Nashville that enrolled 172 students, about 60 of them Catholic, and permitted African Americans to enter two white Catholic high schools in the city, Father Ryan for boys and Cathedral for girls. Charles Kinnard, a student at a black school, Immaculate Mother Academy, recalled,

"We were very sad when they said they would close the school. Most of us, we didn't want to go anyplace else."[27]

When African American parents enrolled their children in formerly white Catholic schools, they did so primarily for educational reasons. Barbara Davis Hatfield, who enrolled in Cathedral High School, explained that "My mother . . . told me we were over there to get an education. We weren't over there to socialize. She was more interested in my grades." Other parents wanted not only a quality education for their children but, as King Hollands, who transferred to Father Ryan High School from public school, explained, "an opportunity for some different experiences."[28]

African American children often faced considerable difficulties in majority white Catholic schools. While they attended desegregated classes, the fifteen black students who joined Father Ryan in September 1954 found themselves excluded from social activities, and, until 1966, they were not permitted to attend the junior-senior prom. Although some teaching staff wanted African American students included in extracurricular activities, white parents organized to prevent it. Black students also could not participate in interscholastic sports because the Tennessee Secondary School Athletic Association and the Nashville Interscholastic Athletic Association prohibited integrated sport.[29]

Interpersonal experiences varied in desegregated Catholic schools. Matthew Walker, who joined Father Ryan in 1955, recalled beating a white boy who picked a fight with him, but Kinnard did not encounter such problems. Although some interracial friendships developed, and the faculty encouraged white students to accept desegregation, many African American students experienced low-level hostility and resentment from white classmates. Overall, black students at Cathedral High School reported less hostility from white students than at Father Ryan. Jean Winchester Coleman recalled that "Some of them were stand-offish. There were some of them that welcomed us." In 1954, the school ended its prom, replacing it with a desegregated banquet at the Hermitage Hotel after city restaurants refused to host the banquet. To fulfill their social needs, African American students from both Father Ryan and Cathedral often formed friendships with students from the Pearl and Cameron black public high schools.[30]

In 1956, a poll of students at St. Augustine's, an African American school in Memphis, Tennessee, that had a majority Catholic enrollment, found that 84 percent wanted to remain at the school, although "some" children indicated a preference to attend "the better equipped white school." The poll did not ask why the majority preferred their current school, but a sense of comfort and familiarity, satisfaction with their education, friendships, and social networks, and concerns about proximity, transportation, and reception in white schools were likely factors.[31]

Another perspective on Catholic educational desegregation is provided by Spring Hill College, a Jesuit institution in Mobile, Alabama, that admitted its first black undergraduates in September 1954. Initially, eight African Americans entered the college, with another, Fannie Motley, joining in the spring semester and more in September 1955. Most of the black students at Spring Hill College were non-Catholic southerners, although three converted to Catholicism. The students enrolled for educational reasons, rather than to break the barrier of segregation and, in the case of Julia Ponquinette of Mobile, to return South after homesickness while studying at Loyola University Chicago.[32]

In 1955, Spring Hill sociology professor Father Albert S. Foley, S.J., wrote a private report on the college's progress in desegregation, based on interviews with African American and white students. Foley noted that black students did not feel completely integrated, although most felt welcome in class, despite some prejudice from one or two teachers. He wrote:

> They still did not attend dances and socials. But they were admitted to the co-eds club, the band, the glee club, the Sodality. They ate in the student cafeteria; however, they did not mingle freely with the other students there, keeping to themselves, and being consciously avoided by the [white] Southerners who had never eaten with Negroes before.

Four of the fourteen African American students interviewed had experienced "unpleasantness" from "some white students," but the problem "was not widespread," and most white students were as friendly off as on campus. However, whites had not invited any black students to any social events unconnected with college.[33]

By 1955, parochial school enrollment was under consideration by the Archdiocese of New Orleans. During the first five months of 1956, some black and white Catholics attended CHR public forums in New Orleans, intended to help prepare Catholics for the change. In May, Father Clarence J. Howard, now vice-provincial of the Southern Province of the S.V.D. after returning from four years service in New Guinea, addressed the last CHR forum. Howard, who was based at St. Augustine's Seminary, told his interracial audience that "At least you must resent it [segregation] and not agree with it," and he asserted that "any injustice is a sin against God."[34]

By the mid-1950s, the S.V.D. had changed its policy of admitting only African Americans for training at St. Augustine's Seminary and thereby produced an integrated, seminarian body, alongside an already integrated faculty. Black S.V.D. clergymen from the seminary occasionally substituted for the priests of white parishes in southeast Louisiana and the Mississippi Gulf Coast when they were absent through illness or holiday leave, but this brought white Catholic opposition at Waveland, Mississippi, in 1954 and Jesuit Bend, Louisiana, in 1955, and some white pastors specifically requested that the seminary send only white clergy as substitutes. Ordinaries generally assigned the few African American priests ordained by southern dioceses in the 1950s to black ministries believing that they were particularly suited for that work, and because prelates feared segregationist opposition if they assigned black priests to white parishes.[35]

Segregationist opposition among white laity and in the state legislature led Archbishop Rummel repeatedly to postpone parochial school desegregation in the Archdiocese of New Orleans. Clarence A. Laws, who had returned to New Orleans after military service and, in 1955, become the NAACP's field secretary, argued in August 1956 that African American Catholics should "express, in the clearest terms possible, their disappointment over this additional delay." Laws hoped that the KPC would provide a lead on the schools issue, but its convention ignored the matter. Addressing a Holy Name Society at Epiphany Church in August 1957, he expressed shame and disgust at minimal black Catholic participation in the southern civil rights struggle. Laws declared that "Negro Catholics as all citizens must speak out against human injustices or our silence might be construed as a satisfaction with the status quo."[36]

Contemporary sociologist Daniel C. Thompson attributed what he described as an "under-representation" of African American Catholics among black community leaders in New Orleans to the absence of any black Catholic pastors in the city, minimal black access to leadership training in the Catholic Church, and the "formal, ritualistic" style of Catholicism that, in comparison to black Protestant churches, allowed less opportunity to "create an atmosphere of race pride and a sense of racial responsibility." Nevertheless, Thompson conceded that "there have always been some outstanding Negro Catholic leaders in New Orleans," who belonged to a wide range of civic groups and professional associations, as well as to church organizations and fraternal groups. However, he claimed that a class division among African Americans was also a color divide and most marked among Catholics. Reared in middle-class homes with access to better educational opportunities, light-skinned Catholic Creoles of color, Thompson argued, often prospered in business and valued their light skin "above identification with the Negro masses."[37]

However, Adam Fairclough contends that the civil rights struggle largely overrode the divide between Creoles of color and darker-skinned African Americans in New Orleans and notes that Catholic Creole A. P. Tureaud was at the forefront of the civil rights struggle in New Orleans and the state. Yet, even after the civil rights movement, shades of color still reportedly divided African Americans in parts of rural south Louisiana and that divide did not altogether disappear from New Orleans.[38]

Opportunities for African Americans to develop and exercise leadership skills, while widely available in black Protestant churches, were very limited in southern Catholicism. In June 1957, there were only sixty-two black priests working in the entire United States. No Catholic equivalent of the Southern Christian Leadership Conference (SCLC), an association of affiliated Protestant church-based black organizations led by Martin Luther King Jr., developed among black Catholics. Yet, many southern black Protestant clergy, especially in rural areas, did not participate in the civil rights movement.[39]

African American Catholics struggled with white dominance within, as well as outside, the Catholic Church. The *St. Augustine's Messenger*, the S.V.D. seminary's monthly journal, gave extensive and supportive coverage to secular and Catholic desegregation, as well as to black ministries at home and Catholic evangelism in Africa. The magazine took particular exception to a series of articles published during the summer of 1959 in the *Guardian*, the Diocese of Little Rock's newspaper, in which managing editor William W. O'Donnell defended segregation by claiming that most blacks were culturally inferior to whites. Writing on behalf of the *St. Augustine's Messenger*, the Reverend Hubert D. Singleton vociferously denied that blacks had an inferior culture. Singleton also attacked O'Donnell's assertion that if their consciences dictated whites were justified in opposing desegregation.[40]

An African American Catholic from Little Rock, who requested that his name be withheld, wrote to the *Guardian* that the issue was the "Civil or Constitutional justice" that whites denied blacks. Insofar as African Americans lacked culture or morality, he argued, it was the result of poverty and discrimination imposed by whites. Unlike the poor, he noted, "The well-to-do of both races can use facilities and most acts or results of [their] immorality never become a matter of public record." Furthermore, he rejected O'Donnell's argument that whites possessed a superior culture, contending that "Perhaps the Negro is a little leery of a culture that practices divorce, birth control, abortion, mob violence, night riders and so called just discrimination." Integration, he maintained, had begun when "**the Negro . . . first saw the privacy of his bedroom invaded by his white master during slavery** [emphasis in the original]." It was incumbent upon whites to end discrimination and their expectation of black deference, and to provide equal educational and employment opportunities so that African Americans would have the "first class citizenship" to which they were entitled.[41]

The Catholic Church in the South continued to provide very limited opportunities for black aspirants to the priesthood. In 1959, Father Joseph C. Verrett, the only African American Josephite in the South, who taught at St. Augustine High School in his native New Orleans became the order's vocations enlister for the city. He persuaded several prospects to emulate him by attending Epiphany Apostolic College, the order's preparatory seminary in New Windsor, New York. In June, the Josephites assigned a second black pastor to the South by sending the very light-skinned Father Charles Chester L. E. Ball to serve as assistant at Our Mother of Mercy Church in Houston, Texas. Ball had been ordained in his native Washington, DC, in 1941.[42]

With few black Catholic priests and many white pastors acquiescing in or even supporting segregation, many black Catholics felt increasingly frustrated with the very slow erosion of discrimination in Catholic institutions. At the same time, many also felt unable to challenge such discrimination because of Catholic emphasis on reverence and respect for the clergy and obedience to their authority.

Laywoman Ora M. Lewis Martin of New Orleans argued in an address to a KPC Ladies Auxiliary council that while African American Catholics owed priests reverence, many priests wrongfully expected "blind respect" and for black Catholics to be "docile, meek, and patient with wrongs." Martin argued that while some African American Catholics had abandoned Catholicism in frustration, "more often" they had retreated, rather than oppose racist clergy. She contended that black Catholics often confused the reverence necessarily due a priest, with respect clergy deserved only if they conducted themselves properly and did not belittle or denigrate African Americans. In late 1959, the *Claverite* published the address, ensuring it received a wider audience. That year, the KPC convention urged African American Catholics to become more involved in social justice issues, both in and outside the Church.[43]

Even before Martin's address, some black Catholics had protested against the Church's practice of discrimination. In May 1959, Mrs. B. Hubbard of Hampton, Virginia, wrote a respectful letter to her bishop complaining that Monsignor Gill of St. Vincent's School operated a policy of rejecting black Catholic applicants on the grounds that they had attended another school, while, at the same time, he admitted whites from other Catholic schools and even a few white non-Catholics. Hubbard's concern was "the inability of Negro children in the Hampton-Newport News area to continue in Catholic school after the 9 grade" since their parents could not afford to send them to Catholics schools outside the area and the "very real dangers that exist in public schools to our children's faith and morals." No reply is extant, but the letter demonstrates that the religious duty to educate children in Catholic schools, whenever possible, could lead black Catholic parents to challenge white pastors who maintained segregation. Hubbard's decision to complain was most likely encouraged by the diocese's five-year-old policy of gradual school desegregation.[44]

Although churches in the Archdiocese of New Orleans had been instructed to desegregate by the Archdiocesan Synod of 1949, some, especially in more rural areas, continued to seat blacks separately. In 1959, two black teenagers, Carroll Pierre and John Mitchell, defied segregation at St. Joseph the Worker Church in Marrero by sitting in the church's front pew and ignoring threats from white ushers. When parish priest Father Anthony Rousso ordered the ushers to desist, fifty whites walked out in protest. Archbishop Rummel denounced white resistance, and many whites found new parishes, either to escape the turmoil or in protest at Rummel's intervention. After *Jet* magazine reported the story against the wishes of both Rummel and Rousso, a mob of fifteen white parishioners brutally beat two black teenagers when they left the church after

Mass and a black man who came to their aid. Despite the attack, the pews were desegregated, although segregation in local parish organizations continued. Ignoring black fears of segregationist retribution but cognizant of the impatience of black youth with segregation, Rousso claimed that "Ninety-five per cent of the Negroes in this congregation don't want integration; it's just a few young ones that do."[45]

Some young African American Catholics joined other black youths in challenging secular segregation. In February 1960, Joseph McNeil, a Catholic from Wilmington, was one of four black college students who sat in at a segregated lunch counter in Greensboro, North Carolina, an action that stimulated similar protests in other parts of the state and the South. In May, Savannah's Saint Pius X High School, a black Catholic high school in Savannah, Georgia, hosted a civil rights mass meeting of over twenty-five hundred people presided over by the NAACP. Dr. Carl Jordan, a member of St. Mary's black Catholic church, served as main speaker. Some of St. Pius X High School's students participated in the movement. Myers Anderson, a Catholic convert and St. Benedict the Moor parishioner, was a longtime member of the Savannah chapter of the NAACP and provided bail for demonstrators from his own resources. The Savannah NAACP chapter also had other African American Catholic members. Some Xavier University students joined the Freedom Rides in 1961 and were arrested in Jackson, Mississippi, for violating state segregation laws. African American Catholics also participated in civil rights marches and protests and voter registration programs in the South during the early 1960s.[46]

Some black Catholics pressed their ordinaries to desegregate. In December 1960, a group of seven African American Catholics from Atlanta, five men and two women, wrote to Bishop Francis E. Hyland informing him of black Catholic support and involvement in the city's civil rights movement. They also sought clarification of the Church's position regarding segregation, which still existed in parochial schools. They wrote:

> Many of your parishioners are in sympathy with, some actively support and participate in, the peaceful demonstrations which have transpired here in recent weeks.
>
> We respectfully request of Your Excellency . . . an interpretation of diocesan policy with regard to ethnic groups.

There is no record of a reply from Hyland, but in February 1961 he joined Bishops Paul J. Hallinan of Charleston and Thomas J. McDonough of Savannah in announcing that their dioceses' schools would desegregate no later than public schools.[47]

African American Catholic responses to the declaration demonstrated both frustration with the pace of change and fear of white segregationist hostility. James Sulton, a convert from Orangeburg, South Carolina, complained that

Hallinan had been too cautious in not immediately eliminating segregation from Catholic schools and hospitals when he had become bishop in 1958. Sulton wrote:

> Since when does the Church follow? I always thought it led on all moral issues. Some people will never accept anything that is good for the Negro unless it is forced upon them. I can't understand the prejudice that now exists in our Catholic hospitals, when all it would take is an order from the Bishop. It is always the Negro who has to wait until the white man is educated to enjoy a human right. The only way to solve this problem is directly from you. Those people who are real Catholics will obey any order from the Church. Those who do not are not real Catholics to begin with.

Hallinan replied that he feared that there might be violence if he desegregated parochial schools prematurely and added that "I will not risk the lives or the dignity of little Negro children (or white children) in this manner." The bishop feared a reoccurrence of the intimidation and violence that accompanied token public school desegregation in New Orleans in November 1960 and the admission of two African Americans, one of them Charlayne Hunter, a Catholic convert from Atlanta, to the University of Georgia in January 1961.[48]

Despite the risks both to their children and themselves, a few African American Catholic parents were prepared to send their children to white Catholic schools. In August 1962, Father Clarence J. Biggers, S.M., of St. Joseph School in Marietta, Georgia, wrote to Hallinan, now Archbishop of Atlanta, that two African American couples, the Robinsons and the Sadlers, were "willing to undertake any risks that may be involved" as they were determined that their daughters, about to enter the first grade, would have a Catholic education. Although parochial school desegregation in the archdiocese occurred without incident, elsewhere, problems sometimes occurred.[49]

In August 1962, Jesse H. Turner Sr., a non-Catholic who worked with the NAACP and his wife, Allegra W. Turner, a sixth-generation Catholic from Louisiana, applied for the admission of their eldest son, Jesse, to Christian Brothers High School in Memphis, a school operated by the De La Salle Christian Brothers and so outside diocesan control. In October, a school representative visited the Turners, and by the end of the month, the school had accepted their son for ninth-grade enrollment in August 1963.[50]

Unaware of Christian Brothers High School's pending desegregation, Bishop Adrian announced on March 31, 1963, that the first four grades of diocesan parochial schools in Memphis and surrounding Shelby County would desegregate in September, extend desegregation through the ninth grade by 1966, and then continue the process by a grade a year. When Allegra W. Turner learned of Adrian's decision, she contacted Brother I. Terence, F.S.C., the superior at Christian Brothers High School, concerned that Adrian's plan would jeopardize her son's enrollment. Although not bound by diocesan policy, Terence did not wish to undermine the diocese and asked Adrian for guidance. While Adrian regretted Turner's registration, he left Monsignor John A. Elliott, the diocese's superintendent of schools, to respond. Concerned that Turner's admission would undermine Adrian's plan and possibly lead to a disturbance, Elliott counseled against enrolling the boy, a recommendation subsequently endorsed by diocesan chancellor the Right Reverend Monsignor Charles M. Williams.[51]

When the school canceled the boy's registration and returned his registration fee, the Turners appealed the decision in July 1963, warning that Jesse H. Turner Sr., president of the Memphis NAACP, would take legal action if necessary. Rather than face a lawsuit for breach of contract, Adrian agreed that Jesse's admission could proceed, and his August enrollment made Christian Brothers High School the city's first desegregated high school. Although the school desegregated peacefully, students harassed Jesse, even spitting on him and overturning his dinner tray. During his enrollment, Turner made one friend but achieved academic success.[52]

Given the dangers to themselves and their children, and often difficulties transporting their children to white schools that could be quite some distance away in cities with de facto residential segregation, many African American parents chose not to send their children to desegregated white Catholic schools. In any case, many parents and children preferred black Catholic schools and churches, although they regretted that these institutions were often less well funded and equipped than their white counterparts because of lower school tuition rates and smaller church collections and funding drives that reflected African Americans' ability to pay and diocesan funding decisions.[53]

Nevertheless, black Catholics frequently took pride in their institutions and sought to maintain and bolster them. By 1962, the parishioners of Holy Rosary, an African American church in a black section of Richmond, Virginia, had raised much of the money needed to build a new church to replace the multipurpose hall they had been using, and they asked Bishop Russell's approval for its construction. Pragmatically, the bishop agreed and continued this special parish for African Americans. Russell explained that "Because they have shown goodwill, I have permitted the building of the church even though, because of the very nature of the neighborhood, it will be practically a segregated church."[54]

In the early 1960s, Bishop Coleman F. Carroll of Miami wanted to close Holy Redeemer, a black Josephite church in the city of Miami, and direct its parishioners to Corpus Christi, but Holy Redeemer's congregation successfully prevailed on him to maintain their church and parochial school. While African American Catholics objected to exclusion and discrimination, many valued black Catholic institutions and wanted them retained.[55]

More and more African American Catholics, like other black southerners, were drawn to the civil rights movement's struggle against de jure segregation and black voter disenfranchisement. Many black parents, regardless of religion, worried that their children's involvement in civil rights protests risked danger, arrest, and disruption of their education, but white efforts to repress protests often rallied parents and the adult black community behind the protesters.

In the early 1960s, both white and African American Catholic students joined marches and sit-ins at segregated facilities in downtown Nashville, Tennessee. After girls from Cathedral High School took part in the protests, the school called the black participants together and warned them that Catholic schools did not allow students to participate in public protests. There was a clear underlying threat that continued participation would mean expulsion.[56]

In this experience, St. Vincent de Paul Church emerged as the epicenter of African American activism. In March 1962, physician Noella Mitchell and other church members wrote to Sister Mary Bonaventure, the principal of Cathedral High School, with examples of Catholic teachings against racial discrimination. They also protested against the warning given to black students. When Bonaventure passed the letter to Bishop Adrian for reply, Adrian found it "uncalled for" and maintained that "there was nothing in the incident that was intended to be embarrassing or to offer discredit on the Negro students." Denying that a moral issue was at stake, Adrian responded: "All your words about tenets of the Catholic Church etc., are just words and having nothing to do with this matter. In my opinion the Catholic Church has been very good to the Negroes of Nashville. A little more charity will help a lot."[57]

After this reply, the Holy Name Society of St. Vincent de Paul Church sent Dr. G. J. Tarleton Jr., Robert Craighead, Paul King, and Dr. R. A. Wilson to meet with Adrian about desegregation. Adrian rejected their argument that segregation was a matter of faith and morals, a point he reiterated by letter in April 1962. In a mixture of paternalism and condescension, Adrian declared:

> I do not advocate insisting too much on complete desegregation at once. Take it gradually, strive by your proven actions that you are deserving of such. I shall do what I can to create harmony and goodwill. It took years and years before the Irish and the Italians and other races were freely accepted in the United States, but they finally proved themselves.[58]

Dissatisfied with Adrian's reply, St. Vincent de Paul parishioners enclosed it with a letter of complaint to the apostolic delegate to the United States, Archbishop Egidio Vagnozzi. In reply, Vagnozzi instructed Adrian to write to St. Vincent de Paul's members and concede that "the principle of racial segregation according to the mind of the Church is a matter of faith and morals." Further, the bishop admitted that "Negroes have God given rights, the same as white people" and stated that his objection to immediate and full desegregation reflected a concern that it "would do more harm than good to the community."

He insisted that "more time was needed to educate our people in these matters, especially in social integration."[59]

Josephite institutions and their priests, black and white, were often more receptive to racial change and the civil rights movement than local ordinaries and, sometimes, encouraged and facilitated parishioner involvement. In 1960, St. Augustine High School in New Orleans, staffed by an integrated Josephite faculty, became a center for teaching voter registration. A year later, a faculty member served on a committee working for equal job opportunities in downtown Canal Street stores. In 1962, the school allowed its facilities to be used by civil rights groups that desegregated the city's lunch counters. In 1964, school faculty organized New Orleans's first interracial home visit program, in which whites visited black homes as part of an effort to promote interracial contacts and dispel fear and ignorance.[60]

By 1965, over 250 students at New Orleans's St. Peter Claver School, operated by the S.B.S. in a Josephite parish, had become junior members of the NAACP. Fern G. Brady, president of the school's parent-teacher association, had taken out a life membership in the NAACP. In the 1960s, students from several black Catholic girls' and boys' high schools in the city formed the Negro Betterment Council (NBC), with Father William H. Barnes, S.S.J., of St. Augustine High School as moderator. The council surveyed inequality in segregated recreational facilities and, following their desegregation under court order, helped persuade the New Orleans Housing Authority to plan a new recreational center in a black neighborhood. NBC members distributed thousands of leaflets at Catholic and Protestant churches asking their parishioners to support a boycott organized by the NAACP, the Congress of Racial Equality (CORE), and the Consumers League of downtown stores that refused to hire African Americans. In September 1962, council members tested desegregation of lunch counters. Two years later, NBC members participated in a voter registration campaign organized by the Coordinating Committee of Greater New Orleans, a coalition of local black organizations, that had Josephite support. The students canvassed in African American neighborhoods, urged residents to vote, and showed them how to complete the complicated voter registration forms.[61]

Young black Catholic and Josephite involvement in the civil rights movement was not confined to Louisiana. In 1964, three black students at Cathedral High School in Richmond, Virginia, each of them members of St. Joseph's parish and the Virginia Council on Human Relations, participated in an NAACP voter registration drive, with support from Father Norbert Stein, their white Josephite priest, who was a native of Newton, Wisconsin.[62]

In the early 1960s, African American and white Catholic adults formed more interracial councils in many southern dioceses. The councils promoted Catholic integration, conducted information campaigns, and pressured ordinaries and Catholic hospital administrators to desegregate. The Catholic Council on

Human Relations in New Orleans was the largest southern council and included African American veterans of the CHR and SERINCO, such as Dr. Leonard L. Burns, Norman C. Francis, and Clarence A. Laws. The council helped persuade Archbishop Rummel to announce that he would desegregate parochial schools in 1962. Francis and Laws also served on the board of directors of the National Catholic Conference for Interracial Justice (NCCIJ) and Father Harold R. Perry, rector of St. Augustine's Seminary and the KPC's national chaplain, on the conference's executive committee.[63]

In 1962, Laws, the NAACP's southwest regional secretary since March 1961, addressed the KPC's convention. He urged the Knights to become involved in all facets of the civil rights struggle and claimed that African American Catholics "tend to remain aloof from the common struggle of Negroes." Laws expressed concern that "the percentage of Catholics engaged in the causes of freedom would suffer by comparison with Negroes belonging to other religious faiths."[64]

Henry A. Cabirac Jr., the white executive director of the Catholic Council on Human Relations and NCCIJ's Southern Field Service, often expressed frustration with what he saw as the apathy of African American Catholics, and he claimed that some bishops, such as Bishop Maurice Schexnayder of Lafayette, had told him they would welcome letters from African American Catholics as they could cite them to white Catholics as reasons to desegregate. However, Schexnayder was a very cautious bishop who was probably seeking to deflect attention away from his own inaction. Some prelates, such as Bishop Richard O. Gerow of Natchez-Jackson and Archbishop Thomas J. Toolen of Mobile, objected to the NCCIJ's efforts to encourage African American Catholics to ask their prelates for parochial school desegregation. However, such letters could be effective. As much as Toolen resented Pensacola, Florida, black Catholics sending him letters requesting parochial school desegregation, he acceded to their wishes in September 1963, a year before he desegregated the entire diocesan school system.[65]

While apathy and conservatism may have prevented some African American Catholics from taking the initiative, in order to act they had to be convinced of the desirability of integration, which was not always clear-cut in the case of parochial schools or even churches, and they needed to believe that exerting pressure would be effective. In many cases, disincentives in the form of indifferent, cautious, or segregationist clergy and hesitant or disinterested bishops were sufficiently commonplace to deter action. Members of a hierarchical denomination, black Catholics often hesitated to challenge their appointed priests and prelates in deference to ecclesiastical authority.

When priests were supportive, African American laity were more likely to act. Encouraged by Josephite Father John F. Quinn, his former pastor at San Antonio's St. Peter Claver Church, to "speak to the issue," James E. Taylor Jr. worked with other members of the Archdiocesan Inter-racial Council and KPC council no. 35 to draw up a proposal urging Archbishop Robert E. Lucey to eliminate race-based special parishes and designate them as missions of a territorial parish. Taylor submitted the proposal to Quinn for prior approval. In 1964, Lucey, a longtime supporter of integration, made St. Peter Claver a territorial mission parish under St. Joseph's Parish.[66]

Elsewhere, especially in the more militantly segregationist Deep South, an often-justified fear of white retaliation proved a powerful disincentive for African American Catholics to challenge segregation. In February 1963, Cabirac visited Dr. John I. Reddix, a KPC member and president of Monroe, Louisiana's NAACP chapter, and a group of black Catholics. Seven years earlier, the local Citizens' Council, formed to maintain white segregationist control and dominance primarily through economic intimidation, had purged many African American voters from the city's registration rolls. Since then, Reddix and the NAACP had tried unsuccessfully to reverse the purge. After the meeting, Cabirac wrote to Reddix, "I can well understand the group's fear about making themselves targets by trying to remove any of the barriers in the community." The group also feared the consequences of trying to address discrimination in Catholic institutions. Cabirac wrote to Matt Ahmann, the NCCIJ's executive director, "These are scared people. They are even reluctant to try to register their children in all white Catholic schools because of the fear of retaliation. I can't say that I blame them."[67]

Nevertheless, in the early 1960s, African American Catholic opposition to racial discrimination in both Church and society became increasingly apparent and vocal. In 1962, the KPC national convention issued a comprehensive indictment of segregation that, although more acute, drew substantially on a statement adopted at its 1961 convention. The Knights argued that Jim Crow undermined democracy, the Mystical Body of Christ, and the universality of the Church. Pope Pius XII, the delegates noted, had declared "That all men are brothered in Jesus Christ." Catholics, they believed, had a "moral duty to resist segregation and discrimination as a whole." The delegates urged President John F. Kennedy to fulfill a neglected campaign promise to issue an executive order to ban discrimination in federally funded housing and enforce nondiscrimination employment clauses of federal contracts. The *Brown* ruling, they declared, had to be "fully realized in our time with more deliberate speed" and federal judges had to uphold the United States Constitution. Labor unions, for their part, needed to eradicate all vestiges of discrimination. The delegates declared their support for lawful protests and litigation in the civil rights struggle and pledged "to continue the fight for the right to vote and for full and unhampered participation in the political democratic process."[68]

The statement praised Catholic bishops who had acted against segregation and discrimination in the South and urged other prelates "to emulate their example." Ordinaries, the convention declared, should consult African American Catholics, establish Catholic interracial societies on a diocesan level, issue pastoral letters supporting racial justice, and include nondiscrimination clauses in all contracts relating to "the construction, repair or maintenance of Church property." The convention voted to donate $490 to the NCCIJ's headquarters in Chicago and $600 to its Southern Field Service.[69]

Individual Knights and Ladies were active in the civil rights movement, but, despite making supportive statements, the KPC did not become involved to any significant degree and struggled to persuade member councils to make "Social Justice Contributions" for disbursement to civil rights and other social action groups. Although the bulk of its members lived in the South, the KPC's adult male and female southern membership was not large. It was concentrated in Louisiana (3,979 members) and Texas (1,064 members), with the remainder in Alabama (251), Mississippi (261), and South Carolina (21).[70]

Nevertheless, the civil rights movement, papal condemnations of racial discrimination, and Catholic desegregation in some southern and border state dioceses encouraged African American Catholics, including some KPC members, to challenge more conservative prelates to eliminate segregation. In May 1963, the annual meeting of the Gulf Coast Conference of the KPC adopted a resolution in Mobile, Alabama, urging Archbishop Toolen "to effect immediate desegregation of our Parochial Schools, Hospitals, Orphanages and Institutions for the Aging." Characterizing themselves as "obedient, prudent and loyal members of the laity," the delegates complained about "members of the Church, including the clergy, lagging behind instead of leading the breakdown of the color line" and displaying "apathy or hostility" that made the professed universality of the Church appear "hypocritical when it tolerates racial prejudice and segregation." With characteristic brusqueness, Toolen dismissed the resolution, declared that he would take no part in future KPC events, and informed the KPC, "You take care of the Knights of St. Peter Claver and I will take care of the Church."[71]

In 1963, the KPC, whose national membership comprised 6,180 men and 6,077 women, had representatives among the Catholic groups involved in the March on Washington. Eugene B. Perry, the KPC's Supreme Knight, wrote that "My experience as one of the rank and file marchers . . . will remain in my memory as long as I live." Some southern black Catholics participated in the march as members of the Catholic interracial councils of Richmond and Northern Virginia. Father Harold R. Perry also attended and had a place on the guest platform.[72]

However, Perry did not otherwise participate in civil rights protests and was not active in civil rights organizations. Nevertheless, some of the few black Catholic pastors in the South participated in the civil rights movement, although constrained in some cases, like white pastors, by ordinaries who prohibited or placed limitations on clerical involvement in demonstrations. Father Thomas P. Hadden, an African American diocesan priest who, in 1962 became pastor of St.

Joseph, a black parish in New Bern, North Carolina, worked with black Protestant ministers in the civil rights movement and served as youth adviser to the town's NAACP chapter to which some of his parishioners belonged. Hadden visited jailed protesters, served as secretary of the New Bern Civil Rights Committee, and mediated during protests by meeting with white leaders, including the mayor. Father Moses B. Anderson, a Selma, Alabama, born African American priest from the Society of Saint Edmund (S.S.E.) pastored St. Catherine's Church in Elizabeth City, North Carolina, and played a supportive role in that city's civil rights movement, which saw hundreds of demonstrators arrested in 1963. Both Hadden and Anderson obeyed Bishop Waters's order not to demonstrate.[73]

Some African American priests criticized the Catholic Church's toleration of segregation. Interviewed in 1963 by writer and white Catholic convert John Howard Griffin, Father August L. Thompson, a Louisianan who had become the Diocese of Alexandria's first black diocesan priest six years before, voiced his frustration with the persistence of segregation in many southern Catholic churches, black exclusion from many church societies, and a widespread expectation among many white Catholic clergy and laity that blacks should attend special parishes. Thompson, who pastored St. Charles, an African American church in Ferriday, complained that because of segregation, "I have people come to my church from as far as seventeen miles away, and some from towns ten or eight miles away." He lamented that African American Catholics, other than himself, were not permitted to march in the diocese's annual Christ the King parade.[74]

White priests, Thompson noted, seldom invited him to recreational activities, a difficulty caused in part by state and local segregation laws. He recalled that "In the early days of my priesthood, this isolation was very difficult for me. It is hard to be young and to be alone and to try to live the priestly life without the companionship of fellow priests." As for black Catholic laity, Thompson explained that "All they want is to be treated exactly the same as any other Catholic." His bishop, Charles P. Greco, tried unsuccessfully to prevent the interview's appearance in *Ramparts*, a lay Catholic magazine published in California.[75]

Thompson's claim that black Catholics resented forced segregation were echoed by the KPC council no. 110, St. Peter's Parish, Charleston, South Carolina. In December 1963, council officers wrote to Bishop Francis F. Reh complaining that they had received information that St. Francis Xavier Hospital, which was soon to be rededicated, would have a separate ward for African Americans. The council declared that "we would prefer not to be accepted in any manner whatsoever, if this acceptance must be on the basis of a segregated hospitalization."[76]

In February 1964, a group of African American Catholics in Mississippi wrote to Bishop Gerow that "[I]t is impossible to see your reasoning behind maintaining complete segregation of Catholics of color." They argued that "Holy Mother the Church has taught us, through your guidance, that all men are children of

God regardless of color and that segregation is evil and sinful in the sight of God regardless of how others may try to justify otherwise by their actions."[77]

Apart from challenging racial discrimination in the Church, African American Catholics became increasingly involved in the civil rights movement. Some black Catholics in south Louisiana worked with CORE, which conducted voter registration and direct-action campaigns. In September 1963, some students from black Catholic high schools in New Orleans participated in a civil rights march of over 10,000 people to City Hall which presented a petition, submitted by the Citizens Committee of Greater New Orleans, calling for desegregation of public accommodations and schools. The committee included black Catholics Oretha Castle, chairman of New Orleans CORE, Ernest N. Morial, president of New Orleans NAACP, Dr. Leonard L. Burns, and Norman C. Francis. Monsignor Charles J. Plauche, chancellor of the Archdiocese of New Orleans, delivered the march's invocation.[78]

In 1964, African American Catholics in St. Augustine, Florida, a largely Catholic city, participated in desegregation protests organized by local NAACP leader Robert B. Hayling and the SCLC. They acted even though Archbishop Joseph P. Hurley of St. Augustine refused to cooperate with the civil rights movement, and Monsignor John P. Burns of the Cathedral of St. Augustine read out a statement, written by Hurley, urging parishioners not to demonstrate or engage in any actions that "might occasion or increase disorder or strife or lawlessness in our city."[79]

In the same year, African American Catholics were among those who participated in a voter registration drive in Canton, Mississippi, and were jailed for their activities. In June, the Ku Klux Klan murdered James Chaney, a Mississippi Catholic and CORE activist, and two white non-Catholic civil rights workers, Michael Schwerner and Andrew Goodman, in Neshoba County.[80]

Regardless of whether they were directly involved in the civil rights movement, black Catholics welcomed any lifting of discrimination, Catholic and secular. When Archbishop Toolen announced in April 1964 that he would desegregate diocesan schools in September, he received a commendatory letter from the Drexel Court no. 1 KPC Ladies Auxiliary in Mobile. In August, a month after President Lyndon B. Johnson signed the Civil Rights Act outlawing segregation in public accommodations, the KPC's national convention in Beaumont, Texas, adopted a resolution urging members to "seek the unlimited and uninhibited use of all public facilities and accommodations" and to "request of the local officials, Catholic and public, that there be immediate desegregation of all schools within their jurisdiction." The resolution also called on local KPC units to work with civil rights groups in "fostering ways of registering effectively their demand of equal employment to all citizens."[81]

In Elizabeth City, North Carolina, Father James P. Robinson, an African American S.S.E. pastor from Selma, Alabama, became very active in community affairs when he replaced fellow Alabamian Father Anderson at St. Catherine's Church in 1964. Robinson explained to Father Eymard P. Galligan, the S.S.E. Superior General in Winooski, Vermont, that "my policy has been to infiltrate the local power structure, open avenues of communications, and thereby negotiate peaceably with various groups concerning problems." The mayor appointed Robinson to a Citizens Advisory Committee, which gave him access to the city's leading figures. However, Robinson chafed at Bishop Waters's ban on clergy participating in demonstrations. The priest feared that if he did not participate in direct action, he would lose the "confidence and respect" he enjoyed among local African Americans who regarded him as "one of their leaders."[82]

In 1965, at least two African American nuns, Sister Thea [Bertha] Bowman, a Yazoo City, Mississippi, born Franciscan Sister of Perpetual Adoration and Sister Mary Antona [Betty Ebo], a Sister of St. Mary raised in Bloomington, Indiana, joined the Selma protests. The two sisters flew from St. Louis with interdenominational groups of nuns, clergy, and rabbis.[83]

Archbishop Toolen severely criticized King and the Catholics who joined him in Selma, but many Catholic participants believed they were acting in the spirit of the Second Vatican Council. They were also aware that the council had urged laypeople to become more involved in the Church and prelates to be more responsive to their concerns. Although the thirty-nine members of Montgomery, Alabama's St. Jude and St. John the Baptist churches did not mention the council when they wrote a letter to Toolen, also published in the *Catholic Week*, the diocesan newspaper, rebuking him for his stance, they demonstrated a growing assertiveness among the laity that the council had encouraged. These African American parishioners condemned Toolen's criticisms as "unwarranted," castigated him for being "conspicuously silent" about racial discrimination and complained that "We have long looked for some leadership in our diocese to protest the degrading injustices perpetrated upon the Negroes of the State of Alabama." They praised the "noble and brave people" who had gone to Selma and informed Toolen "we will welcome the nuns and priests into our hearts and homes when the pilgrimage from Selma is over." The archbishop seems not to have replied.[84]

Many parishioners at St. Elizabeth Church, Selma's African American Catholic church, marched or housed demonstrators. In March, Sister Mary Christopher of the Sisters of St. Joseph, Rochester, New York, which staffed the church's school, wrote:

> Of the twelve members in our Holy Name Society—5 had been put in jail, one of whom was 80 years old, a daily communicant . . . of about 25 Sodalists at least a third have been in jail, some of them 4–5 times. Even 8 children from our grammar has time in. Usually one must be at least 12 years old to march in a deminstration [*sic*]. This list of jail birds has become some kind of an honor role at St. Elizabeth's.[85]

In June, Archbishop Toolen insisted on the departure of St. Albans, Vermont native, Father Maurice F. Ouellet, the white S.S.E. priest of St. Elizabeth's, who had assisted the civil rights movement in Selma while, ostensibly, obeying Toolen's instruction not to march. Ouellet's parishioners organized a campaign in which 853 members of the community wrote to Toolen asking him to reconsider. A committee from the church told Toolen by telegram: "We think that your removal of Father Ouellet is wrong and will diminish Catholic influence in this community." Ouellet and Archbishop Vagnozzi, the apostolic delegate, received over two thousand letters from African American Catholics and Protestants, and petitions signed by thousands more protesting Toolen's action. Three hundred parishioners and sympathizers in Selma signed an appeal to Pope Paul VI urging him to intervene, describing Ouellet's removal as a "personal insult." However, it was not Vatican policy to intercede in local matters, and Toolen stood by Ouellet's removal.[86]

Despite such examples of black Catholic assertiveness, in August 1965, Father Harold R. Perry, the KPC's chaplain, lamented at its national convention that the Church's paternalism toward African American Catholics and "slow acceptance" of them had "produced a strong conservatism, fear, and a distrust among Negro Catholics when faced with opportunities to promote better relations within the Church." Perry urged his fellow Knights to "join the Negro freedom movement" and "initiate planned efforts by Negro Catholics and the missionaries who serve them to end segregated churches." Apart from neglecting Catholic participation in the civil rights movement, Perry failed to recognize that although African Americans opposed discrimination, exclusion, and forced segregation, they did not necessarily want to leave black churches and schools to attend white equivalents.[87]

Nevertheless, with approximately 115 black priests in the entire United States, 34 of them in the South, and no African American bishops, it remained difficult for blacks to challenge discrimination in the Church and to do so effectively. Father Jerome LeDoux, S.V.D., a black Louisianan and professor of moral theology and canon law at St. Augustine's Seminary, complained to the Catholic magazine *Sign* that "there are alarmingly few places or institutions which go after Negro vocations with anything akin to real enthusiasm," and he blamed the Church's leaders for the failure of most white Catholics to accept African American priests.[88]

Some black Catholics also expressed frustration with the Church's paternalism and treatment of them as people without efficacy and initiative who needed white missionaries to guide and lead them. In 1965, Mrs. O. J. Cansler of Dallas explained that "I am especially concerned that missionaries STOP demanding that we be grateful for what they did a hundred years ago for the Negro." Clarence A. Laws of the NAACP condemned the "Negro Apostolate" as "discriminatory and divisive" and called on "the Church to discuss and devise ways and means for abolishing it."[89]

Despite their earlier history of paternalism and exclusion of African Americans beyond a token few of the light-skinned, and in growing recognition of African Americans' abilities and assertiveness, the Josephites made efforts to recruit blacks. In 1965, four of its five ordinands were African American southerners. Three of the four men had attended Josephite schools in Mobile, Alabama, Pascagoula, Mississippi, and Baton Rouge, Louisiana, and the fourth was from a Divine Word parish in St. Martinsville, Louisiana. In recognition of their origins, the Josephites broke with custom and ordained them in New Orleans, rather than Washington, DC.[90]

For many young southern African American Catholics, the pace of change remained too slow. In March 1965, at least ten Xavier University students picketed a reception for Catholic prelates of the Province of New Orleans, who were attending the investiture of the pallium for Archbishop John P. Cody of New Orleans. They demanded that the Church became more involved in civil rights and address discrimination within its own ranks. Nearly two hundred Xavier students signed a follow-up letter to the prelates which described civil rights as "a moral issue" and claimed that "We know that there are Catholic hospitals that are still segregated, [and] that [African American] Catholic schools are prohibited from participating in athletic competitions with Catholic white schools."[91]

As part of a drive, influenced by the Second Vatican Council's reforms, to bring greater lay involvement in its administration, Xavier University made Norman C. Francis, younger brother of Joseph A. Francis Jr., executive vice president. Francis, a native of Lafayette, Louisiana, was the first layperson and the first African American to hold that position. His appointment as president of the university, which had 10 percent white enrollment, followed in June 1968.[92]

In October 1965, the Vatican announced that Father Harold R. Perry would be installed as auxiliary bishop of New Orleans in January 1966. Although Perry had called for the elimination of segregated Catholic institutions and black Catholic involvement in the civil rights movement, he declared that "I've never taken part in any civil rights movements. I'm not the Catholic answer to Martin Luther King." Pressed by journalists for his opinion of King, Perry replied, "I think Mr. King is doing what would be considered a wonderful job following the path of his calling. However, I am not a civil rights leader and I have no intention of becoming a civil rights leader." As well as bishop, Perry also became pastor of St. Theresa, a traditionally white church in an integrated section of New Orleans. In a later interview, Perry reiterated that he would confine himself to his religious duties. He stated:

> My appointment is a religious one, not a civil rights appointment. My religious work comes first. I have no desire to work directly as a civil-rights leader. My past history shows that I have spoken out in favor of civil rights, that I am a foe of all social

injustices wherever met in my work. However, I feel that the greatest contribution I can make to raise the dignity of my people is being a good religious bishop and fulfilling my office to the utmost of my ability.[93]

The civil rights movement was itself undergoing change. In June 1966, some African American participants in the Meredith March in Mississippi called for Black Power. Although defined in various and sometimes contradictory ways by its advocates, Black Power signaled a rejection by its supporters of integration, an assertion of the right to armed self-defense and a celebration of black culture and distinctiveness. In August 1966, Perry told the KPC's national convention that African Americans should seek equality and integration, not Black Power. He declared that "We must become interested in integration not because it is something we can demand, which we can, but because it is God's plan for the human race that we may all be one. We want to become an integral part of this country. We want to have a voice in running this country."[94]

In the second half of the 1960s, southern Catholic dioceses increasingly took measures to eliminate personal or special parishes and to desegregate Catholic schools in order to move toward realization of Catholic teachings about the unity of mankind and the Mystical Body of Christ. More immediately, they acted in response to ongoing pressure from African American and white Catholic integrationists, a shortage in personnel caused by declining vocations and consequent withdrawal by religious orders from many of the South's black churches and schools, and pressure to comply with federal desegregation guidelines or face withdrawal of federal funds from Catholic schools and hospitals. With rare exceptions, prelates ordered the closure of black, rather than white, schools and churches to achieve desegregation and expected displaced African Americans to attend formerly white institutions.[95]

Many African American Catholics resented diocesan policies that required them to sacrifice treasured black institutions, and the failure, in many cases, of diocesan officials to consult with them or to respond positively to their concerns. White hostility, a widespread failure to welcome blacks, and indifference to black cultural needs also made many African American Catholics reluctant to attend formerly white churches and schools or apply for Knights of Columbus membership. Higher tuition rates, often charged by traditionally white parochial schools, and transportation issues frequently made it difficult or impossible for blacks to attend them. Although faced with a fait accompli, some African American Catholics tried to resist the one-sided nature of desegregation's implementation, and they also exposed the persistence of discrimination. However, some blacks, especially younger Catholics, left the Church, as they became increasingly frustrated and disillusioned. Other African American Catholics reluctantly accepted the loss of black institutions as the price of integration, a goal they supported.[96]

Between 1961 and 1967, the number of African American Catholic churches in the Diocese of Little Rock declined from eleven to six, and four black schools closed between 1964 and 1968 as orders withdrew from them. Many of those who had attended them did not transfer to formerly white Catholic schools and churches. In January 1967, Bishop Fletcher noted that in the five black parishes that had schools, "The majority of the members of these parishes wish to retain their own church and school. These parishes exist in areas which are centers of Catholic Negro population."[97]

In May 1967, a decline in vocations forced the S.B.S. to withdraw from Our Mother of Sorrows parish elementary school in Biloxi, Mississippi, and brought about its closure. Consequently, the Josephites decided to phase out the parish and sell its church and land. Both the order and the diocese expected neighboring white territorial churches to absorb nearly five hundred African American parishioners. Black Catholics reported being welcomed at St. Michael's Church, but at Nativity Church, one African American observed, "The ushers do not make much of an effort to assist them [black Catholics]. They feel they are not welcome." African Americans mostly sat at the back of the church. Another black Catholic observed, "If there are vacant seats up in the front, the ushers aren't going to bring you up there."[98]

Father Charles Hanks, S.S.J., Our Mother of Sorrows's white pastor, reported that many of his parishioners were unhappy about the church's planned closure. Hanks explained that "The older ones, while they want integration and do attend the other churches occasionally, still have parting pangs. They would like to keep the church open a little while longer." African Americans also wanted to retain their parish organizations, although that, he claimed, was undesirable as "it would lead to a division." Nevertheless, Hanks conceded that other churches had not welcomed blacks "en masse," notwithstanding a good reception from some whites. The *Josephite Harvest*, the order's magazine, concluded that "The Negro is accepted into the white parishes with neither gladness nor malice. He fits somewhere in between, in a twilight zone of permissiveness and tolerance, in a nowhere land between love and contempt. He is learning that indifference is the most unkind cut of all, and has become very sensitive to it."[99]

In September 1967, Father August L. Thompson complained to Archbishop John F. Dearden of Detroit, president of the National Conference of Catholic Bishops (NCCB), about the persistence of segregation and discrimination in the Church and its institutions, the absence of black clergy from leadership positions in the Church and the failure of the Church to consult African Americans and make them welcome in ostensibly desegregated Catholic churches, societies, and organizations. Thompson wrote:

> Right now it is most disgustingly appalling to see the Church hurrying and scurrying about doing a bit of token [school and hospital] integrating in order to obtain

some of the federal money. We have kept everything segregated all this time, twenty years after the first statements, saying we just could not open things to all who came even if they were Catholics, but of the wrong hue. Now we open, but only enough to get by, to get the money.

He argued that rescinding segregation policies had not and would not in themselves produce genuine integration. Thompson explained:

I]n every phase of life even in the Church the Negro has been and in many cases is still systematically excluded from a full Catholic life. It is not enough to say to him that he is now included. We must go out and really convince him that this time it is true love that prompts what is said and being done. His name must be on every list of invites.... What massive efforts have been made to recruit Negroes to be priests, Brothers and Sisters in every Order or diocese? What efforts have been made to open doors to Negroes in societies, organizations, in short to all of Catholic life[?][100]

Thompson's arguments anticipated those made by the Black Catholic Clergy Caucus. In April 1968, he attended the group's founding meeting in Detroit, along with 57 of the 166 black priests and monks active in the nation. In a statement that Bishop Perry helped prepare, the caucus characterized the Catholic Church in the United States as "primarily a white racist institution" and warned that if it did not immediately eradicate "all forms of racism within its ranks and institutions," it would "become unacceptable in the Black Community." The caucus demanded that black clergy and laity be consulted and trained for "leadership and advisory positions in the whole Church." It called for recruitment of more black priests, choice in priests' assignments, and black clergy appointments to "decision-making positions." Dioceses, the caucus declared, should provide training centers for white priests assigned to African American communities, and the Church should establish a black diaconate, which should be open to single and married men. The caucus also demanded the establishment of a "black-directed department" within the United States Catholic Conference to "deal with the Church's role in the struggle of Black people for freedom," and affirmed that black Catholics should "direct, for the most part, the mission of the Church in the Black Community." Like Black Power organizations, the caucus emphasized African American empowerment and control of institutions in the black community, and it recognized the right to "legitimate self-defense" and "militant protest."[101]

The statement did not address integration overtly but caucus chairman Father Rollins Lambert, a Chicago priest, observed that "Black priests are asking for a greater role within the Church" and "a degree of separatism may, of course, be necessary to enable black men to finally achieve true integration." Lambert conceded that "there was considerable conflict over the statement's militancy."

Historian and monk Cyprian Davis, O.S.B., who was at the caucus, recalled that its southern-based members, who comprised at least twelve of the fifty-eight present, were, for the most part, "less radical in their call, in their demands."[102]

The caucus delivered its statement to Archbishop Dearden. Although the NCCB ignored the document, the caucus persisted in making its demands. It also influenced the establishment of other black Catholic groups, such as the National Black Sisters' Conference, the National Black Catholic Seminarians Association, and the National Black Lay Catholic Caucus.[103]

While African American priests debated the future of blacks within the Catholic Church, black parents continued to voice their opposition to school desegregation plans that closed black schools or paired them with white schools in ways that usually placed the burden of desegregation on black students and their parents. Determined to end dualism in his diocese's schools and motivated by religious commitment and need to comply with federal guidelines, Bishop Ernest L. Unterkoefler of Charleston imposed desegregation plans when localities failed to devise satisfactory plans of their own. In June 1968, Unterkoefler announced that he would terminate grades four through eight of St. Anthony's, an African American school in Greenville, and permit displaced students to attend the white schools of Our Lady of the Rosary and St. Mary's. St. Anthony's would teach kindergarten through grades three, with enrollment open to the culturally deprived of both races, including poor white non-Catholics.[104]

Many parents of St. Anthony's students, Catholic and non-Catholic alike, wrote to Unterkoefler protesting against his decision. Non-Catholic parents Claude S. and Nettie M. Jones explained that "This decision concerns us for many reasons; first, our children would be attending two separate schools; secondly, the tuition would be far greater than it is presently; and thirdly, transportation would prove to be a tremendous problem." The couple also objected to the one-sided nature of parochial school desegregation that required blacks to transfer to white schools, while reducing or ending provision at black schools. They argued that "*All* [emphasis in the original] schools concerned should be involved, not just St. Anthony" and the burden shared equally. Mr. B. F. and Mrs. Martha Richardson objected that African Americans were being forced to pay the price, in terms of higher tuition rates and the reduction in St. Anthony's grades, for the refusal of whites to integrate. Pointedly, they noted that "Father the doors of St. Anthony's are open to all. It be no fault of ours if the people don't integrate. We the members of St. Anthony's can't make the whites come to St. Anthony's." Several other couples warned Unterkoefler that higher tuition rates would force them, and many other black parents, to send their children to public schools.[105]

Many parochial school desegregation plans in the South required African American schools to cater for the deprived or to become adult basic education and vocation centers, often with some funding provided by federal antipoverty programs. Black parents resented such plans as a slight against their schools. Mr. and Mrs. Thomas A. Mosley Sr. complained to Unterkoefler that "Being at Saint Anthony's such a long time and knowing how hard the priests and sisters have worked to make the people affiliated with Saint Anthony's independent and proud, to go out and recruit sorry whites and sorry Negroes, would be degrading to the people."[106]

African American children enrolled in black Catholic schools shared the views of their parents, with most unwilling, but a minority prepared, to accept closing black schools to further integration. In the late 1960s, a poll of 158 Catholic and non-Catholic students at St. Pius X High School in Savannah found that 25 agreed, 105 disagreed, 23 were not sure, and 5 did not respond to the statement "Predominantly Negro schools should be closed to aid integration." The school's Catholics and non-Catholics disagreed with the statement in almost equal proportion, 69 percent (66 students) and 68 percent (39 students) respectively, although 22 percent (21 students) of Catholics and 7 percent (4 students) of non-Catholics agreed.[107]

The late 1960s saw a growing feeling among African Americans, including many Catholics, of racial pride that contributed to a desire to retain black institutions and led many to question the desirability of integration. While some black Catholics favored separatism, many wanted autonomy and representation in the hierarchy of the Church and the offices of their dioceses. In January 1969, twenty-five priests attended the Southern Regional Black Clergy Conference in New Orleans, part of the Black Catholic Clergy Caucus that had subdivided into four regional groupings after its second meeting in November 1968. Afterward, conference chairman Father Rawlin B. Enette, S.S.J., Catholic chaplain at Southern University, a traditionally African American institution in Baton Rouge, claimed that all of the South's forty-five black priests:

> strongly endorse and encourage, and do positively labor for the continuation of the black territorial parish as a black unit not only for the spiritual formation of souls, but as a unit for self determination and black development socially, psychologically, economically, and politically.
>
> We reject the current practice and trend toward "integration" (solely according to white specifications) which is neither a present reality nor will be in the future until black Catholics have achieved self determination.

Father Elmer S. Powell added that black priests "want black people to be human beings, and want the black parish to serve as a source of pride and dignity to them." Before black parishes could be eliminated and genuinely integrated churches established, Powell argued "black people will have to do their own thing." Influenced by Black Power organizations, the priests adopted the term black in place of the traditional Negro. One priest wore buttons proclaiming, "Black and Beautiful" and "Say it loud, I'm Black and Proud." Another priest, the *New York Times* reported, supported the idea of "Afro-style vestments and love beads."[108]

In March 1969, after persistent pressure from the Black Catholic Clergy Caucus, the NCCB appointed Bishop Harold R. Perry and Auxiliary Bishop Joseph F. Donnelly of Hartford, Connecticut, to a committee chaired by Bishop Peter L. Gerety, apostolic administrator of Portland, Maine, to meet with the caucus's leaders, discuss their concerns, and make recommendations to the American Catholic hierarchy. In November, the committee persuaded the hierarchy at its annual meeting to support the creation of a National Office for Black Catholics (NOBC). Perry explained in February 1970, five months before NOBC opened its headquarters in Washington, DC, that it was not intended to create a separatist movement within the Catholic Church but to enable black people to forge a role within it. He commented:

> There has been a hesitancy to give black people a self-determining role, a decisional role in the education of their children and in the operation of their churches.
>
> In general there has been a paternal attitude. What the black community is asking now is that they be given a chance for self-determination.
>
> Perry rejected allegations of separatism and argued that integration, as practiced by the Church, had failed to give blacks leadership positions and achieved no more than tokenism. He explained that "So what we are really doing is stepping aside for a while to see how we can push ourselves, our leaders and the mass of people into the mainstream of Catholic life."[109]

The desire for self-determination within the Church and disillusionment with its method of implementing integration was shared by many African American laity in the South, as well as by many black priests. In 1970, the Shrine of the Holy Cross in Daphne, Alabama, a mostly black parish with over four hundred members, voted "with only one exception, to keep it open."[110]

Some African Americans turned to litigation in an attempt to combat discrimination by the Church. In May 1970, the Diocese of Lafayette school board mandated the ending by September 1972 of the diocese's dual school system. The diocese, which had twelve dual school situations involving twenty-six of the diocese's fifty-seven schools, would merge the relevant twenty-six black and white schools.[111]

After what he described as "intense white opposition," Bishop Maurice Schexnayder vetoed the merging of two Catholic schools in Opelousas. Although they shared the same church property, separated only by a Catholic cemetery, Holy Ghost School in Opelousas was all black and the Academy of the Immaculate Conception (AIC) all white, except for five African American students. In June 1970, black Catholic parents asked a federal district court to enjoin the Diocese of Lafayette from operating a dual school system in Opelousas in *Auzenne v.*

School Board of the Roman Catholic Diocese of Lafayette. In August, Schexnayder responded by announcing that the diocese's entire dual school system would be ended by September 1971 through pairing—that is, merging to achieve a racial balance—or consolidation, including Opelousas's two schools, which would begin faculty integration in September 1970. The *Auzenne* plaintiffs, then, asked for an injunction to implement student desegregation by September 1970. The diocese responded by successfully asking the court to stay further proceedings.[112]

The school merger went ahead in September 1971, but some former AIC parents organized a private school, Belmont Academy. The Opelousas Catholic High School that resulted from the merger was approximately 60 percent white and 40 percent black in its student body and faculty. In December 1971, Salvador L. Diesi, chairman of the new school's board, reported that "the racial situation in our school has resulted in expected problems which have not been major in nature and which have been largely solvent. A large majority of blacks and whites are committed to the success of the merger."[113]

Although the African American Catholic community had never been monolithic, desegregation of Catholic institutions by southern dioceses in the 1960s and the rise of black consciousness in the second half of the decade further divided black Catholics. Some African American Catholics continued to try to integrate Catholic institutions, while others, if they did not leave Catholicism, strove to preserve the black churches that had nurtured them. A comparison with other denominations places the Catholic experience of desegregation in a broader context.

CHAPTER EIGHT

Southern Catholics and Desegregation in Denominational Perspective, 1945–1971

Judged by the pronouncements of some of its prelates, the Catholic Church in the South was among the more racially progressive of the region's predominantly white denominations. Catholic churches, unlike most white Protestant churches, were supposedly open to all races, and white Catholic schools and colleges often desegregated no later, and sometimes earlier, than white Protestant institutions. However, like the major white Protestant denominations, Catholic prelates and clergy took a more progressive approach to desegregation in the peripheral than the Deep South, where they often were inhibited by, when they did not share, the segregationist preferences of the white majority, Catholic and Protestant alike. Even in the North and West, Catholic prelates and clergy often encountered strong opposition to desegregation of churches and schools from white laity, and some pastors, and, on occasion, some ordinaries, shared these parishioner sentiments.

This chapter compares the response of the Catholic Church in the South to desegregation with that of the larger white denominations in the region: the Southern Baptist Convention (SBC), the Methodist Church, the Presbyterian Church in the United States (PCUS), the Protestant Episcopal Church, and the Presbyterian Church in the United States of America (PCUSA). It also makes comparisons with Catholics outside the South and with southern Jews, a minority, like Catholics, subject to suspicion and even hostility from the Protestant majority, and with the Northern (later American) Baptist Convention and the Disciples of Christ, both of which had a substantial black membership. The comparison suggests that white lay sensibilities, more than polity or theology, influenced the implementation of desegregation in the South by the major white religious bodies.

In 1940, the Catholic Church in the United States claimed to have 296,988 African Americans among its 21,403,136 members. Despite continuing black migration to the North and West in search of economic opportunity and an escape from the most overt forms of racial discrimination in the nation, 197,481 black Catholics lived in southern and border south states.[1] In 1945, the SBC had few, if any, African Americans among its 5.9 million members. However, the other major white Protestant denominations with a southern presence had both

African American membership and black churches. National statistics for 1943–1944 indicate 330,600 of 8,046,129 Methodists were African American; 60,326 of 2,227,524 Episcopalians; 60,000 of 1,672,354 Disciples of Christ; and 3,132 of 565,853 Southern Presbyterians. The PCUSA had 40,581 African Americans among its 2,040,399 members, and the Northern Baptist Convention 45,000 among its 1,555,914 members. By the early 1950s, there were 265,000 Jews in a southern population of forty million.[2]

As leaders in a hierarchical institution, in theory Catholic bishops, like their Protestant Episcopal counterparts, could order desegregation in their jurisdictions. In the Methodist Church, another hierarchical denomination, the General Conference, which met quadrennially, established policy and regulations in *The Discipline*. Governed by congregational polities, the churches of the SBC and the Disciples of Christ possessed local autonomy, making them more subject to the views of their parishioners. Neither episcopal nor congregational, Presbyterian polity included a series of hierarchically constituted church courts from the session, or local court, to the presbytery and synod, and, above them, the General Assembly, the highest court, that met annually and formulated policy.[3]

Whatever their polity, in practice every largely white denomination was influenced, to some degree, by the disposition of its members when determining and applying policies on desegregation and race. Denominational organizations and leaders at the national, regional, and state or diocesan levels often advanced more progressive positions than those shared by the majority of their coreligionists. Nevertheless, church bodies and leaders usually considered the firmness of local segregationist commitment before making decisions and pronouncements about race relations and desegregation.

Ostensibly, Catholic, Episcopalian, Methodist, and Presbyterian clergymen were freer than pastors of congregational churches to address racial issues, but, in reality, they too were often constrained or influenced by segregationist sentiment among their parishioners. Regardless of polity, ministers shared a concern to demonstrate their worth and achieve upward mobility by efficiently managing and enlarging their churches, without alienating parishioners by advocating controversial or divisive views about desegregation and race relations.[4]

Among the laity, the position of Jews in southern society was analogous in some ways to that of southern white Catholics beyond southern Louisiana. Although Catholics were far more numerous than Jews, both groups were a minority in the region and both predominantly urban residents. Furthermore, Catholics and Jews faced suspicion and latent, and sometimes overt, hostility from the Protestant majority for their religious beliefs, and they had been habitual targets for the Ku Klux Klan, particularly during the 1920s. While Jews were members of a historically persecuted minority internationally, both they and Catholics had experienced discrimination in the South. Consequently, some Jews and white Catholics in the region sympathized with, and, in some cases, actively supported, the civil rights movement and its goals. However, fear of retribution inclined many of the South's Jews and white Catholics toward silence about segregation and a desire for their clergy and coreligionists, North and South, to avoid the issue for fear of stirring up anti-Semitism and anti-Catholicism. In the 1950s and early 1960s, attacks on some southern synagogues testified to the persistence of anti-Semitism.[5]

Some southern white Catholics felt vulnerable and exposed by their Church's endorsement of desegregation. Catholic laywoman Mary Bennett complained to Bishop Thomas J. McDonough of Savannah about her sense of "humiliation," after he had issued a pastoral letter in February 1961 declaring his intention to desegregate parochial schools no later than public schools in his diocese. Bennett explained that "I have never felt the need to lower my head until this morning. I am employed in a large office of non-catholics, I am the only catholic." Concerned that McDonough's letter would inflame anti-Catholicism, Bennett wrote of her co-workers, "They are not only bitter toward my faith, but also toward the negro." She added: "Bishop McDonough, you are not out in the world earning a small salary and taking the abuse that is often dealt with the job." Bennett argued that African Americans had not contributed to the building of white churches and parochial schools and should not go where they were unwelcome.[6]

Some Jews joined Citizens' Councils because they feared retribution or ostracism, but many of those who enlisted acted from conviction and supported segregation. On the other hand, among Jews, as among white Catholics, recent migrants to the South were more inclined to accept and support desegregation than their southern coreligionists who had been reared under segregation.[7]

Despite some similarities between southern Jews and southern white Catholics, historian Clive Webb claims that "Jews counted less ardent segregationists among their number than any other white group in the South," and he notes that no Jewish segregationist organization arose. When questioned, southern Jews were less favorable to segregation than southern white Christians. According to a 1956 poll in the *Catholic Digest*, 45 percent of southern Jews supported segregation compared with 75 percent of southern white Protestants and 76 percent of southern white Catholics. Conversely, 33 percent of southern Jews wanted to bring the races together, compared with only 17 percent of the region's white Protestants and 19 percent of its white Catholics.[8]

The South's major white denominations, Catholic and Protestant alike, largely segregated African Americans. The Methodist Church, which had split in 1844 over the issue of slaveholding clergy, reunited in 1939, but at the price of placing its African American members, mostly resident in the South, in an all-black Central Jurisdiction to placate southern whites. Historian Peter C. Murray explains that the Church "created the most rigid and segregated church structure of any national Protestant denomination." However, the Central Jurisdiction elected its own bishops and so not only continued a Methodist tradition of consecrating black bishops but created them in greater numbers. The Central Jurisdiction also assured African Americans of representation in the General Conference and on the Church's national boards and agencies.[9]

The PCUS, likewise a product of a nineteenth-century sectional divide, segregated most African Americans in the Snedecor Memorial Synod, established in 1917 after the failure of earlier efforts to create a black Presbyterian Church. Although the PCUS was entirely southern in membership, the PCUSA also had a southern presence and operated all-black synods and presbyteries in the region, whereas its African American churches elsewhere belonged to general synods and presbyteries.[10]

The Protestant Episcopal Church, like the Catholic Church, had not divided over sectional tensions in the nineteenth century, but, until the mid-twentieth century, several of its southern dioceses kept African Americans in separate conventions and deprived them of a place at diocesan meetings. The Disciples of Christ placed black churches in the ostensibly nonracial National Christian Missionary Convention, but, in practice, the Disciples organized their work with African American churches separately. While the Northern Baptist Convention had no African American churches in the South, in other parts of the country its black churches participated in local Baptist associations, state conventions, and the denomination's annual conventions.[11]

In theory, Catholic Churches were open to all regardless of race, but particularly in the South and border states, African Americans were largely confined to separate churches, or relegated to the back pews of predominantly white churches, when not excluded altogether, and given communion after whites. African American migration from the South to the North and West, which began on a large scale during World War One, led to a significant growth in black Catholic churches outside the South. Dioceses created some of these churches in response to requests by African Americans who wished to avoid racial discrimination in white parishes or because such parishes excluded them. Some bishops established separate parishes for African Americans against their wishes. However, most black parishes became so as whites moved away after first resisting, often violently, black migration into the neighborhood. Catholic parishes had a permanence rooted in geography and canon law that meant they remained to serve and convert black migrants after white parishioners left. By contrast, Protestant and Jewish houses of worship were more mobile and tended to move with their members.[12]

In some cases during the interwar period, predominantly white Catholic churches in the urban North consigned African Americans to rear pews, and white churches and parochial schools often refused blacks admission altogether. Although the Archdiocese of Philadelphia ordered parish schools to admit local black applicants in 1932, some pastors tried to defy or evade the order. As in the

South, prelates varied in their attitude to segregation, and change often came only after the appointment of a new ordinary. When he became Archbishop of New York in 1939, Francis Spellman ordered all parochial schools to accept African Americans. But, in 1945, Catholic schools were still segregated in the District of Columbia and border state dioceses, such as Baltimore and most of St. Louis, and racial discrimination persisted in some nonsouthern Catholic schools. De facto residential segregation in nonsouthern cities increasingly produced de facto parochial school and church segregation as black migrants replaced whites, who left for other city neighborhoods or the suburbs. Across the country, most Catholic hospitals segregated or did not admit African Americans and few employed black medical staff. Most of the nation's Catholic colleges and universities did not admit African Americans.[13]

Revulsion at Nazi racism, the emerging civil rights movement, and wartime race riots and disturbances encouraged America's major Christian denominations to reexamine racial problems and to reassess their approach to racial minorities in the United States. Increased efforts to evangelize African Americans and, in some cases, the world's nonwhite majority also spurred growing denominational concern with race relations at home. In the 1930s and 1940s, the papacy condemned Nazi racism, endorsed the doctrine of the Mystical Body of Christ, and expressed increasing interest in African Americans. The Vatican also became increasingly attentive to the racial attitudes of candidates in making appointments to the episcopacy.[14]

Among Protestants, northern white denominations far outstripped those in the South in their support for civil rights after the war. In 1946, the Federal Council of Churches, which consisted of twenty-five Protestant denominations with a total membership above twenty-five million people, issued a nonbinding statement that denounced segregation and urged its constituent denominations to "work for a non-segregated church and a non-segregated society." The PCUSA and the Disciples of Christ adopted the declaration, and the Northern Baptist Convention and the Protestant Episcopal Church condemned segregation. In 1948, the Methodists decried "racial discrimination" as "unchristian" and recommended that "every Methodist, and every Methodist church, conference, and institution accept the achievement of full fellowship in our churches as a vital responsibility." However, the PCUS did not condemn segregation, and neither did the SBC, which, unlike the Southern Presbyterians, did not belong to the Federal Council of Churches. The distance between northern and southern white religious bodies on race grew further when some northern Protestant denominations backed fair employment practices legislation and denounced segregated housing.[15]

Rather than antagonize segregationist parishioners by rejecting racial separation, southern white Protestant denominations decried inequities within Jim Crow, solicited studies on racial issues, and sought to inculcate their members with Christian attitudes toward other races. In 1945, the PCUS declared its opposition to racial discrimination in education, employment, health, housing, law enforcement, and the franchise. The denomination appointed an Ad Interim Committee on Negro Work, which, in 1946, advocated increased efforts to evangelize African Americans, the improvement of Stillman College (its institution for training black ministers), and greater responsibility for blacks in managing their own affairs. In 1946, the PCUS converted a poorly funded Permanent Committee on Social and Moral Welfare into a $20,000 Department of Christian Relations with a full-time secretariat, charged with producing educative literature and addressing and speaking for PCUS churches on social issues. The denomination encouraged the establishment of new black churches, and, in 1952, it inaugurated a $2 million appeal to upgrade Stillman College and support black evangelism.[16]

In a manner akin to the Southern Presbyterians, in 1946 the SBC appointed a Committee on Race Relations, and, a year later, gave its Social Service Commission a $10,000 budget. The convention, like the PCUS, decried discrimination in education, employment, housing, the courts, and the ballot, and advocated equal rights within segregation. In 1947, the SBC approved a program of education in race relations to be conducted by its agencies and colleges and a Charter of Principles in Race Relations that advocated equal opportunities and justice but did not address segregation. At its General Assembly in 1947, the PCUS, much like the SBC, urged Christians to support minorities' civil rights, but, in contrast to the convention, the meeting censured the Ku Klux Klan.[17]

However, in the late 1940s, predominantly white northern Protestant denominations continued to outdistance their southern equivalents by rejecting segregation. Although the SBC Social Service Commission endorsed the "major objectives" of President Harry S. Truman's Committee on Civil Rights, the commission did not discuss the presidential committee's far-reaching legislative recommendations. The PCUS, for its part, offered no more than recognition of the need for education and legislation in ensuring rights. By contrast, the Northern Baptist Convention welcomed Truman's civil rights program, called for "the ending of all racial segregation in employment, the armed forces and housing," and deplored segregation among its churches.[18]

Although segregation remained the norm in white Protestant churches and schools in the South, in 1947 John E. Hines, the Episcopal Coadjutor Bishop of Texas, condemned segregation in an address to the Texas diocesan convention in Beaumont. Between 1947 and 1949, several southern Episcopal dioceses abandoned discrimination in their conventions, among them Arkansas, Georgia, Southern Virginia, Upper South Carolina, and Virginia, but most southern parishes remained segregated.[19]

Unlike most of the major white Protestant denominations, the American Catholic hierarchy did not make any collective statements on race relations in the second half of the 1940s, although in 1943 it had called for African Americans to be accorded their constitutional rights and equal opportunities. However, in the immediate postwar period, a few bishops and Catholic colleges outside the South adopted desegregation.[20]

In 1945, the Archdiocese of Philadelphia announced that from January 1, 1946, African Americans could join the territorial parish in which they lived, meaning they would no longer be restricted to special black parishes. Pastors generally observed the order, despite their sometimes hostile personal feelings and opposition from many white parishioners. In 1946, the Diocese of Buffalo discontinued its two black Catholic churches and assigned African Americans to territorial parishes in order to end segregation. In 1949, ten years after his school desegregation directive, Cardinal Spellman proudly claimed that "In the archdiocese of New York, there are no schools for Negroes, there are no schools for whites. There are only schools for children." A few more nonsouthern Catholic colleges and universities admitted African Americans in the 1940s, including St. Louis University (1944), Loyola College, Baltimore (1946), Webster College, Missouri (1946), and Georgetown University, Washington, DC (1948).[21]

Despite such changes, some Catholic priests outside the South continued to exclude African Americans from parishes and schools or segregate them. Father George H. Clements, an African American, recalled that in 1947 he tried as a fifteen-year-old to enter a Chicago church, but its white pastor shouted at him from the altar, "Niggers don't go to church here." According to historian Timothy B. Neary, "Chicago's Roman Catholic parishes remained almost completely racially segregated during the 1930s, 1940s, and early 1950s."[22]

Despite some resistance, gradual change came to some border states in the early postwar years. In the months prior to Joseph E. Ritter's arrival as Archbishop of St. Louis in October 1946, token desegregation began in a few Catholic schools in the city of St. Louis, Missouri. In September 1947, Ritter ordered parochial school desegregation across the Archdiocese of St. Louis, although public schools remained segregated. Faced with opposition from seven hundred white parents in forty-three parishes that culminated in plans to seek a court injunction to block desegregation, Ritter threatened the malcontents with excommunication for defying his authority. The parents abandoned the planned suit and, after a failed appeal to apostolic delegate Amleto Giovanni Cicognani, who endorsed Ritter's action, disbanded their group. Although one hundred white families withdrew their children from Catholic schools, 90 percent of them subsequently returned.[23]

Elsewhere in Missouri, Catholic schools desegregated in the Diocese of St. Joseph in 1948 and in the Diocese of Kansas City in 1949. Installed as the first archbishop of the Archdiocese of Washington in January 1948, Patrick A. O'Boyle soon began gradual desegregation of Catholic schools in the District of Columbia and in two counties, Montgomery and Prince George's, in north

Maryland that lay within the archdiocese. In the early 1950s, the Archdiocese of Louisville, Kentucky, began parochial school desegregation.[24]

However, Catholic institutions in the South lagged behind their counterparts in the rest of the nation in beginning desegregation. Although the Synod of the Archdiocese of New Orleans ordered an end to segregation in churches in 1949 and 1950, the archdiocese's churches, like others in the Catholic South, remained largely segregated. In 1948, Notre Dame Seminary in New Orleans admitted two African Americans, but other southern Catholic seminaries continued to exclude blacks. Southern Catholic schools also remained segregated.[25]

Despite issuing some pronouncements and reports in support of equal opportunity in the 1940s and early 1950s, the major white Protestant denominations continued to observe segregation in the South, with the exception of a few seminaries. Located in Richmond, Virginia, the Southern Presbyterians' Union Theological Seminary had admitted African American graduate students as far back as 1935. By 1951, each of the four Southern Presbyterian seminaries had abandoned racially discriminatory admissions policies, and three of the SBC's four seminaries in the South had desegregated. Concerned that the black seminaries they supported were inadequate, both denominations desegregated white seminaries in the interest of improving black ministerial education. In 1951, the Protestant Episcopal Church's Virginia Theological seminary in Alexandria also desegregated. The Perkins School of Theology at Southern Methodist University in Dallas, Texas, desegregated a year later, but other theological schools at Methodist universities in the South remained segregated. Regardless of denomination, seminary desegregation resulted in token African American admissions.[26]

Similarly, other gestures toward desegregation by Protestant and Catholic bodies produced little practical change. In 1951, the PCUS General Assembly voted for the gradual elimination of the Snedecor Memorial Synod. Although white synods in the Deep South received its presbyteries, PCUS churches remained segregated, and African American churches continued to be regarded as a separate category, the Snedecor Region, in denominational programs. Despite adopting a policy in the 1940s of encouraging interracial churches, the PCUSA had not developed many by the early 1950s. In 1952, the Methodists announced that "there is no place in The Methodist Church for racial discrimination or racial segregation," yet the Central Jurisdiction continued, despite calls for its removal by some African American Methodists.[27]

At its 1952 gathering, the triennial meeting of the Protestant Episcopal Church's General Convention adopted a resolution declaring that Christianity was "incompatible with every form of discrimination based on color or race." Nevertheless, the trustees of the School of Theology at the University of the South, an Episcopalian institution in Sewanee, Tennessee, refused to desegregate. In 1953, after widespread criticism and the resignation of the dean and eight theology faculty members, the trustees relented. All Episcopalian seminaries had desegregated by 1954, and the Diocese of South Carolina became the denomination's last diocese to give African Americans full voting rights at diocesan meetings.[28]

Catholic action against desegregation was likewise limited and small scale. Founded in 1940 to promote social justice and backed by many southern bishops, the Catholic Committee of the South (CCS) adopted a resolution in 1951 endorsing "ultimate integration" of African Americans into all aspects of American life, but the bishops let the CCS, which never held another convention after 1953, wither as desegregation became an increasingly controversial and divisive issue. In the early 1950s, several southern dioceses, including Galveston-Houston, Lafayette, Raleigh and, once more, New Orleans, ordered an end to segregation and discrimination in their churches, but their directives had little impact.[29]

In 1953, a nationwide poll of Jesuit high school students found that younger Catholics were more amenable to change than their elders. Ninety-three percent of those polled, including 91 percent in the South, replied that they would not refuse communion from an African American priest. However, there was some regional differentiation with slightly more than two-thirds of southern white students and over 80 percent of white students in New England and the Far West opposed to segregation at Mass and in other parish activities. The differences became sharper when the focus turned from religious to social activities. Ninety-four percent of those in New England, 100 percent in the Far West, and 77 percent in the South said they would not refuse to participate in athletics with an African American.[30]

In the early 1950s, a few southern Catholic colleges admitted African American students to regular classes, including Incarnate Word College, Our Lady of the Lake College and St. Mary's University in San Antonio, and the College of the Sacred Heart in Grand Coteau, Louisiana. Before the *Brown v. Board of Education* public school desegregation ruling in May 1954, several more border state and some peripheral South Catholic dioceses initiated or announced full or partial school desegregation, among them Wheeling, West Virginia, San Antonio, and Richmond.[31]

In meetings held after the *Brown* ruling, the major white Protestant denominations supported desegregation, including those with an entirely or significantly southern constituency. The PCUS General Assembly adopted a report, initiated before *Brown*, affirming that "enforced segregation of the races" was "out of harmony with Christian theology and ethics." Approved by 239 votes to 169, the report urged all denominational institutions and bodies to desegregate. By approximately 9,000 votes to 50, the SBC endorsed the *Brown* decision as constitutional and Christian, but it neither condemned segregation explicitly nor asked its churches, agencies, colleges, and hospitals to desegregate, and it commended the court for allowing a transitional period for enforcement of its ruling.³²

The Council of Bishops of the Methodist Church found the Supreme Court ruling "in keeping with the attitude of The Methodist Church" but, conscious of "difficulties of enforcement," welcomed its gradual implementation. Although the Southeastern Jurisdiction's bishops conceded that *Brown* was in "harmony" with Church teachings, they forlornly pleaded for the Council of Bishops to be silent about the ruling, concerned that any statement would "make our task more difficult," given segregationist sentiment in the South.³³

Major white Protestant denominations that had considerably less or no southern membership made more potent declarations. The American Baptist Convention, as the Northern Baptist Convention became in 1950, praised the court's ruling and urged "American Baptists to increase their opposition to other areas of segregation—housing, employment, recreation, [and] church participation." The PCUSA General Assembly expressed "thanksgiving" for *Brown* and called on Presbyterians to assist in ensuring its successful application. The International Convention of Disciples of Christ commended the court's decision and urged its churches, agencies, and institutions to desegregate and promote compliance with *Brown*. In 1955, the General Convention of the Protestant Episcopal Church declared that "discrimination and segregation are contrary to the mind of Christ and the will of God" and called on Episcopalians to "accept and support" *Brown*.³⁴

Some state-level bodies, especially in the peripheral South, supported denominational statements regarding *Brown* or desegregation. They included Southern Baptist state conventions in North Carolina and Virginia; PCUS synods in Arkansas, Texas, and Virginia; the executive council of the Episcopal Diocese of North Carolina; and Methodist conferences in Florida, Little Rock, North Arkansas, North Carolina, North Texas, and Southwest Texas. In the Deep South, responses from major white Protestant denominations ranged from calls for calm and lawful obedience to silence and opposition. In December 1954, Girault M. Jones, the Episcopal Bishop of Louisiana, endorsed desegregation and equality of opportunity, but C. C. J. Carpenter, the Episcopal Bishop of Alabama, described *Brown* as a "set back" in race relations. Some Presbyterian groups openly opposed desegregation. In 1954, the Synod of Mississippi urged the PCUS to withdraw its support for *Brown* and desegregation of the church, the Synod of Alabama tabled a resolution that supported desegregation, and the Synod of South Carolina voted 125 to 80 to keep segregated institutions. On his return to Birmingham, Methodist Bishop Clare Purcell stated that the Southeastern Jurisdiction opposed the Methodist Council of Bishops' resolution on *Brown*. The Mississippi Conference of the Methodist Church, for its part, went on record in support of church segregation.³⁵

Unlike white Protestant denominations, the American Catholic hierarchy made no collective statements on *Brown*, either immediately or during the ruling's aftermath. A few bishops spoke about the decision in public. Archbishop Ritter declared that the ruling "timely reaffirms before the whole world those basic principles on which, under God, our nation was founded," and Bishop William L. Adrian of Nashville called for obedience to *Brown*. However, many prelates in the South and border states, the areas most affected by the ruling, did not comment.[36]

Opposition to desegregation, especially of housing and Catholic organizations, existed among elements of white Catholic laity and some clergy outside, as well as within, the South. According to a 1956 *Catholic Digest* poll, 30 percent of white Catholics in the North favored racial segregation. In the 1940s and 1950s, white working-class Catholic opposition to housing and, to a lesser extent, church desegregation arose in northern cities, such as Buffalo, Chicago, Detroit, and Omaha, sometimes with active clergy support and participation. Whereas many southern white Catholics opposed desegregation in any form, historian John T. McGreevy argues that in the white Catholic urban North "the same individuals accepting of an African American presence in the workplace violently resisted neighborhood integration." Encouraged by their priests, white working-class Catholics in northern cities had bought homes in and closely identified with their local parish, which occupied a place at the center of community and family life. The laity had worked hard to buy their homes and gave generously to their churches. Consequently, white Catholic opposition, lay and clergy, to desegregation, McGreevy explains, "evoked the sacred character of parish neighborhoods, the social ties established through the parish community, and the financial and religious investment in the physical plant."[37]

In 1953, a white Catholic home owner wrote to the *Michigan Catholic*:

> I am sure that most Catholics don't feel that colored people are inferior to them, but it is a undisputed fact that, as they move into a neighborhood, property values go down. The investment most of us have in our homes represents our whole fortune. Few people can afford to take a loss and then start over again. Their chief resentment against the Negro is the way his inroad affect[s] their pocketbook.

White home owners' fears that property prices would decline as African Americans moved into the neighborhood became a self-fulfilling prophecy as whites, often encouraged by realtors, sold their homes when the presence of blacks increased or following racial clashes. McGreevy also notes that in the context of the Cold War between the United States and the Soviet Union, some northern Catholic segregationists claimed that Communists were promoting housing desegregation as a means of fomenting strife.[38]

Northern Catholic priests sometimes shared these fears of Communist agitation, and some participated and encouraged parishioner involvement in neighborhood associations and other efforts designed to preserve a community's white ethnic character. White mobs sometimes took matters into their own hands by attacking African Americans and the homes they had bought in previously white areas. Opposition to housing integration was shared by white Catholics of both sexes. Both men and women heckled blacks who moved into substantially Catholic Trumbull Park, Chicago, in the first half of the 1950s. African Americans who attended the local Catholic church were jeered at, insulted, and assaulted. On one occasion, a sixty-four-year-old female parishioner punched a member of the Chicago Catholic Interracial Council who was accompanying blacks to the church.[39]

Adult white male lay opposition to desegregation was manifested in the all-white composition of most Knights of Columbus councils in the United States. After Cleveland Council no. 733 refused three African American applicants membership in 1953, Floyd L. Begin, Auxiliary Bishop of Cleveland, Ohio, told a Cleveland Knights Fourth Degree initiation meeting in 1954: "Either I have to say that Negroes are second-rate Catholics or I must say the Knights are not acting as Catholics." Begin appealed for, and received, a unanimous standing vote to petition the Knights' Supreme Board of Directors in New Haven, Connecticut, to grant a charter to a recently formed interracial council in Cleveland to which he planned to transfer his membership. However, the Supreme Board refused. Supreme Knight Luke E. Hart argued that the proposed council, initiated by sympathetic whites who favored black admissions, was organized "on a racial basis" in an attempt to "evade the ballot box," the blackball system that enabled as few as five members of a council to deny an applicant membership. Although the proposed council would have been interracial, albeit largely African American, Supreme Treasurer Francis J. Heazel, based in Asheville, North Carolina, claimed that granting it a charter "would have been countenancing a principle of segregation, and I have always understood that the Catholic Church is opposed to the principle of segregation."[40]

Hart and Heazel were being disingenuous since the Knights had long granted and continued to grant charters to all-white councils, many of which blackballed African Americans, or made clear that black applications were unwelcome. However, there were exceptions. In March 1954, an editorial in *America*, a New York-based Jesuit weekly, observed that "A number of K. of C. Councils have for some time admitted and welcomed their colored Catholic brethren." In San Antonio, Texas, Our Lady of the Holy Rosary Council no. 3345, formed in 1950, had five black members. Emanuel A. Romero, a Jamaican immigrant, had been a member of the Knights in New York City since 1923. By 1954, St. Columba Council no. 1119, in Brooklyn, which had desegregated in 1950, had forty-three African American members, but Columbus Council no. 126, also in Brooklyn, refused an African American, John T. Yancey, membership. *America* observed that "the racialist pattern is sufficiently widespread among the Knights to cause anxious questioning among Negro Catholics, and among prospective Negro converts to the Catholic faith about the real attitude of the Church itself."[41]

As the Brooklyn example suggests, segregationist views were not confined to southern white Knights. In the wake of the Cleveland, Ohio, controversy, William J. Gaffney, a Knight from Moses Lake, Washington, wrote to Hart, "I believe that these advocates of non-segregation are supporting measures that will go far to destroy racial purity in this country. I say that nature has provided five races. Let us not disturb nature's balance." Maurice J. McAuliffe, past state deputy for the District of Columbia Knights, informed Hart, "The fear of many of us is that the primary purpose of the negro is not merely to secure equality before the law but to obtain equality with the white man in social relations, leading ultimately to marriage between the races."[42]

Influenced by widespread white lay support for racial separation, desegregation of Catholic institutions moved slowly in both halves of the country. In the fall of 1954 Bishop Vincent S. Waters of Raleigh ordered diocesan high schools in North Carolina to admit African American Catholics. Two Nashville Catholic schools admitted black students at that time, and Bishop Albert L. Fletcher of Little Rock announced that black Catholics would be admitted to white schools in areas without black Catholic schools. St. Anne Catholic school in Rock Hill, South Carolina, operated by the Oratorian Fathers, became the only desegregated parochial school in the Deep South. Almost completing the desegregation of Catholic schools in border south states, the Diocese of Oklahoma City and Tulsa ended segregation in all its schools in September. In more northerly cities, such as Chicago and Philadelphia, Catholic schools were often segregated in practice, partly because of residential separation of African Americans and whites but also because of the preference of some local priests.[43]

Across the South, Catholic hospitals, like those of the other major white denominations in the region, continued to segregate patients or operate separate hospitals for blacks and whites, but racial discrimination in Catholic hospitals was, with some exceptions, a national problem. In May 1955, Archbishop Ritter informed the Catholic Hospital Association's annual convention that "Catholic hospitals, along with the whole Church, have a most serious obligation to carry out courageously the teachings of Christ and the Church and to put aside in their policies and practices, if they exist, any and all discrimination because of race, color or religion."[44]

Nonsouthern Catholic dioceses were also not much ahead of their southern counterparts in desegregating seminaries or ordaining African American priests. In both halves of the country, African American vocations tended when possible to join the religious orders that had trained them, but few seminaries admitted blacks prior to 1945. Consequently, black diocesan priests remained rare in the United States during the 1950s. Between 1945 and 1960, nonsouthern dioceses ordained approximately fifteen black priests and southern dioceses six. In 1949, the Diocese of Brooklyn ordained its first African American priest, William J. Rodgers. After training at the Archdiocese of Chicago's major seminary, African American Rollins Lambert also received ordination that year, but the archdiocese's next black priest, George H. Clements, was not ordained until 1957, following twelve years in minor and major seminary. As late as 1967, the Archdiocese of Philadelphia's seminaries had not had an African American finish his studies and become an archdiocesan priest. In the South, the Diocese of Lafayette ordained a black priest in 1952 and 1958, the Archdiocese of New Orleans in 1953, the Diocese of Alexandria in 1957, and the Diocese of Raleigh in 1958 and 1959.[45]

In the mid-1950s, the American Catholic hierarchy maintained a collective silence about desegregation. Influenced by growing southern white opposition to *Brown*, after 1954 the SBC issued no recommendations or resolutions regarding race relations until the 1960s. However, other leading predominantly white denominations addressed race relations anew and more trenchantly. The American Baptist Convention, the Disciples of Christ, and the PCUSA urged their churches to disregard race in choosing staff and to back attempts to eliminate discrimination in education, housing, and public accommodations. In 1956, the Methodists' General Conference recommended that "discrimination and segregation by any method or practice, whether by Conference structure or otherwise in The Methodist Church be abolished with reasonable speed." However, a constitutional amendment stipulated that African American churches and conferences in the Central Jurisdiction could only transfer into other jurisdictions after a two-thirds majority vote of the conferences, black and white, concerned. Segregation largely continued as its removal required agreement from a large white majority, which explains the absence of opposition to the proposal at the General Conference and its endorsement by the bishops of the Southeastern Jurisdiction and by the South Central Jurisdiction.[46]

In 1957, the Southern Presbyterian General Assembly condemned racial bias in education, employment, politics, and the church, and it denounced the Ku Klux Klan and the Citizens' Councils. The American Baptist Convention called for "racial nondiscrimination" in church membership, clergy appointments, and "each Baptist organization, school, home, and hospital." The convention also counseled Baptists not to support "any organized group or movement that works to retain segregation . . . the Ku Klux Klan, White Citizens Councils, and all exclusive groups that deny membership to others on the basis of race."[47]

Despite the American Catholic hierarchy's collective silence, a few Catholic prelates in the South, border states, and North spoke out against racial discrimination. In February 1956, Archbishop Rummel condemned segregation in a pastoral letter, and Archbishop O'Boyle asked in an address that year, "Do we segregate, condemn and degrade people on the basis of race? Or do we acknowledge that all men are our brothers in Christ?" In 1957, Cardinal Spellman expressed support for fair housing legislation affecting New York City.[48]

Belatedly, the American Catholic hierarchy joined the major white Protestant denominations, except the SBC, in issuing a statement opposing segregation. In November 1958, the Administrative Board of the National Catholic Welfare Conference (NCWC) issued a statement in the name of the American hierarchy that condemned segregation laws and called for equal economic and educational opportunity. The twelve signatories included Spellman, Ritter, and O'Boyle, all outspoken opponents of segregation. No southern prelates served on the board that year.[49]

Nevertheless, many Catholic churches in the South and the vast majority of white Protestant churches in the region continued to segregate African Americans when they did not exclude them altogether. Many of the state-level white Protestant organizations in the peripheral South that had endorsed desegregation of their institutions or the public school system lapsed into silence as state resistance to school desegregation increased. In the Deep South, white Protestant conventions either rejected desegregation, made uncontroversial appeals for peace and calm, or disregarded the matter. Southern Baptist state conventions in Louisiana and Alabama supported segregation but, like most other mainstream white denominations in the Deep South that took this position, did not claim religious justification. However, in 1956, the Episcopal Diocese of South Carolina's annual convention adopted a resolution that affirmed "that there is nothing morally wrong in a voluntary recognition of racial differences and ... voluntary alignments can be both natural and Christian."[50]

In an effort to gain influence, some clergymen and laypeople, especially in the Deep South, formed groups designed to prevent their state denominational bodies from addressing desegregation and adopting it in their institutions. Formed in December 1954 to preserve segregation in the church, the Association of Methodist Ministers and Laymen was strongest in Alabama and Mississippi, while its successor, the Laymen's Union, organized in 1959, also drew support from adjacent states. Other segregationist laymen organizations formed in the Deep South during the second half of the 1950s included the New Orleans–based Association of Catholic Laymen, the Baptist Laymen of Alabama, the Baptist Laymen of Mississippi, and the Presbyterian Laymen for Sound Doctrine and Responsible Leadership, Inc. Some Protestant congregations sent resolutions to their denominations condemning statements and reports on race made by denominational social action agencies.[51]

Although generally unable to stop their denomination's regional and national meetings from addressing race relations, southern white Protestant segregationists were largely successful in averting, or limiting, desegregation of denominational institutions in the region during the remainder of the decade. The

Methodist Church's Central Jurisdiction remained in place. Although the 1954 PCUSA General Assembly had ordered synods and presbyteries to commence desegregation, little change occurred, and a policy of promoting desegregated churches that dated back to the 1940s remained mostly a paper commitment. By 1957, only 13 percent of the denomination's mostly white churches had at least one African American participant and, in the South, just three white churches had any black involvement. The Protestant Episcopal Church and the American Baptist Convention were much the same in this regard as the PCUSA, and, according to historian David M. Reimers, the Methodist Church "had proportionately fewer racially inclusive congregations" than the PCUSA. Although more successful in desegregating churches than most other white Protestant denominations, in 1956 only 464 Disciples of Christ churches of 7,000 surveyed across forty states were desegregated in some degree.[52]

No statistics are available for Catholic Church desegregation, but it seems likely that the denomination's southern churches were more often desegregated, if not by any great margin, than white Protestant churches in the region. And the Catholic Church enjoyed a marked advantage over white Protestant denominations in southern college desegregation. By 1957, 35 of the 45 Catholic higher education institutions in the South had desegregated, compared with only 55 of the region's 188 Protestant colleges and universities.[53]

Although Bishop Waters and Archbishop Lucey publicly opposed state government efforts to protect segregation in North Carolina and Texas, the adoption of massive resistance policies by many southern state governments in the second half of the 1950s and segregationist parishioner sentiment encouraged caution among Catholic prelates in the South. Confined to the peripheral South, Catholic school desegregation came almost to a standstill in the decade's second half.[54]

White Catholics in southern Louisiana were no less likely than white Protestants elsewhere in the South to join Citizens' Councils, but their prelates' authority and disapproval prevented Catholic clergy from officiating at council meetings. By contrast, Protestant clergy were among the councils' leaders. The editorial board of the *Citizens' Council* newspaper, included the Reverend James P. Dees, rector of Statesville, North Carolina's Trinity Episcopal Church and president of the statewide Defender of States' Rights, and the Reverend L. B. McCord, an ordained Southern Presbyterian clergyman and executive secretary of the South Carolina Association of Citizens' Councils. Protestant clergy served as council chaplains. Whether council participants or not, according to historian Howard Dorgan, "a majority of 1958 white Protestant clergymen in at least South Carolina, Alabama, Arkansas, and Mississippi were not in favor of compliance" with *Brown*.[55]

A minority of Catholic clergy aligned themselves with desegregation, but, whatever their views, most priests were silent about the topic. Although Catholic priests could only be removed by their prelates and not by their parishioners, ordinaries varied in their approach to desegregation issues and their willingness to permit clergy to address or champion them. Segregationist parishioner, or community, sentiment also intimidated some integrationist clergy into silence, whatever the disposition of their bishop. Likewise members of a hierarchical denomination, integrationist Episcopalian ministers in the South had similar concerns to progressive Catholic clergy and, with reason, most trod cautiously. Disgruntled by his endorsement of racial change from the pulpit, in 1958 the parishioners of Montgomery, Alabama's Church of the Ascension successfully prevailed on Bishop C. C. J. Carpenter of Alabama to remove their pastor, the Reverend Thomas P. Thrasher.[56]

The pressures were even greater for Southern Baptist clergy, who served at the discretion of the congregations that hired them. Most Southern Baptist pastors, like Catholic clergy, were silent about race relations and segregation. Nevertheless, some spoke out for integration at the risk of their pulpits and, inevitably, some lost them. In October 1955, the Reverend G. Jackson Stafford of Batesburg, South Carolina's First Baptist Church resigned under segregationist pressure. Some other white Protestant ministers also lost their southern pastorates for addressing race, including Robert McNeil, pastor of Columbus, Georgia's First Presbyterian Church (PCUS), dismissed by the Southwest Georgia Presbytery in 1959.[57]

A few white clergymen, Protestant and Catholic, risked physical attack by taking an active part in public school desegregation. In December 1956, four whites assaulted the Reverend Paul Turner of Clinton, Tennessee's First Baptist Church when he returned alone from escorting African American children to their first day at a formerly white public school accompanied by a deacon from his church and a Methodist layman. In September 1957, Dunbar H. Ogden Jr., pastor of Little Rock's Central Presbyterian Church (PCUS) and president of the Greater Little Rock Interracial Ministerial Alliance, his son David, Will D. Campbell, an ordained Southern Baptist minister working for the National Council of Churches (NCC) Department of Racial and Cultural Relations, and two African American ministers, Z. Z. Driver and Harry Bass, led Central High School's first African American students to school in defiance of a mob, but the National Guard turned them away. In 1960, Father Jerome A. Drolet, the Catholic pastor of Kenner, Louisiana's Our Lady of Perpetual Help Church acted as a decoy when a mob surrounded Frantz school in New Orleans when it desegregated.[58]

Despite the traditional separation of Catholic, Protestant, and Jewish clergy before the Second Vatican Council's reforms supported ecumenical cooperation, concern for the preservation of public education and law and order saw Catholic clergymen join Protestant, and sometimes Jewish clergy, in signing interdenominational statements calling for peaceful acceptance of federal court-ordered public school desegregation in the late 1950s and early 1960s.

Such statements were confined to major cities or large urban areas, where segregationist commitment was less strong and contacts between clergy of different faiths closer than in rural locations. In 1958, 173 Catholic, Protestant, and Jewish clergymen, including Wendelin J. Nold, the Catholic Bishop of Galveston-Houston, Episcopal Bishop John E. Hines, and Methodist Bishop A. Frank Smith signed a statement in Houston calling for obedience to *Brown*. In August, forty-eight Catholic and Protestant clergymen from Falls Church and Fairfax County in northern Virginia signed a statement that declared that "segregation not only defies the basic law of the land but more importantly contradicts that very gospel which we are called upon to preach." In December 1960, Bishop Francis E. Hyland of Atlanta was among thirty African American and white religious leaders who signed a statement appealing for continued "give and take" discussions between the races. Interdenominational statements gave their signatories, Catholic, Protestant, and Jewish alike, a sense of strength in numbers and, except for bishops, relative anonymity.[59]

Public school desegregation encouraged Protestant denominations to begin a slow resumption of college desegregation in the peripheral South during the early 1960s. In 1962, Wake Forest and Meredith colleges (both Southern Baptist), Davidson College (PCUS) and Duke University (with Methodist links) in North Carolina, and Southern Methodist University in Dallas desegregated undergraduate programs. Largely in response to public school desegregation, several Catholic dioceses in the South began parochial school desegregation in 1961 or 1962, including Atlanta, New Orleans, and in Galveston-Houston in Galveston and Harris counties. Bordering the South, the Archdiocese of Baltimore desegregated all of its schools in 1962, and Catholic hospitals in the archdiocese also adopted desegregation policies regarding patients and staff, although some residual discrimination remained.[60]

In a reminder that racial segregation in Catholicism was not just a southern or border state phenomenon, McGreevy notes that two Chicago priests "quietly pressured the archdiocesan board into integrating a number of large, informally segregated Catholic high schools" in 1960, and the Diocese of Cleveland ended the last of its racially defined special parishes. Matt Ahmann, the National Catholic Conference for Interracial Justice's executive director, claimed that "There is . . . segregation in the Catholic school[s] of the North. I have seen parishes redefine their boundaries to exclude Negro children who have moved into the parish neighborhood. Parishes have made private deals with each other so that one becomes predominately Negro while the other nearby stays white. And sometimes Catholic schools have been closed as a neighborhood becomes largely Negro."[61]

The late 1950s and early 1960s also saw the growth of Catholic interracial councils in the urban North in response to racial problems and sympathy for the civil rights movement. Cardinal Albert G. Meyer, the Archbishop of Chicago, made diocesan clergy attendance at a conference on black Catholics in 1960 mandatory and called for the removal of "any possible taint of racial discrimination or racial segregation" in the Church. In the same year, Archbishop John F. Dearden of Detroit established the Archbishop's Commission on Human Relations and held a race relations conference for clergy. Much like southern Catholic interracial councils, which mostly developed in the early 1960s, the commission encountered opposition to desegregation from some pastors and white laity in racially changing parishes.[62]

Chicago was the headquarters of the NCCIJ, which endorsed the sit-ins and Freedom Rides at its conventions in 1960 and 1961, and urged both clergy and laity to join nonviolent direct action. Whether under the NCCIJ's influence or not, some Catholics participated. In 1960, Catholic students in New York City, Worcester, Massachusetts, and Jersey City picketed chain stores that discriminated against African Americans in the South. In Oklahoma City, Father Robert McDole was arrested twice for participating in sit-ins with African American students. Bishop Victor J. Reed of Oklahoma City and Tulsa responded: "I am inclined to think that the present situation justifies Father McDole's action." In 1961, Father Sherrill Smith joined stand-ins at the Majestic, a segregated San Antonio theater. However, collectively, the American Catholic hierarchy, like that of most of the other major white denominations, did not comment on civil rights protests.[63]

The two main white Baptist denominations were divided in their response to the protests. In 1961, the SBC adopted a resolution that condemned segregationist "mob violence" and, referring to civil rights protests, "unwarranted provocation." By contrast, the American Baptist Convention praised the civil rights movement for adopting "nonviolent methods to break the patterns and injustices of segregation and discrimination in public places and in public transportation."[64]

Although some northern Protestant ministers and rabbis participated in Freedom Rides in the South during 1961, Catholic clergy did not. Catholic pastors who wished to join southern civil rights protests faced formidable obstacles. According to established Catholic custom, a priest could not enter another diocese without the permission of its ordinary, which proved an insuperable barrier in most cases until the mid-1960s as most southern, and indeed many prelates outside the region, opposed clerical participation in direct-action civil rights protests. In 1961, Josephite priests Philip Berrigan and Richard Wagner, both teachers at St. Augustine High School in New Orleans, planned to join a desegregation protest organized by the Congress of Racial Equality (CORE) in Jackson, Mississippi, but pressure from Bishop Richard O. Gerow of Natchez-Jackson on the Very Reverend George F. O'Dea, the Josephites' Superior General, forced their withdrawal. Gerow threatened to expel all Josephite clergy from Mississippi if the two priests joined the protest.[65]

A few northern African American and white laypeople joined southern civil rights protests. In 1961, Catholics Bill Hansen, Phil Havey, Terry Sullivan, and

Diane Nash of the Student Nonviolent Coordinating Committee (SNCC) participated in the Freedom Rides. In August 1962, a biracial and mixed sex group of nine Catholic laity from the Chicago area marched in Albany, Georgia, along with Protestant ministers and laity and rabbis, in response to Martin Luther King Jr.'s invitation. However, most white Catholic laity across the country were opposed to civil rights protests and to clerical involvement in them.[66]

Anna Holden, CORE's national secretary, attributed her fellow Catholics abstinence from civil rights protest to a belief that racial discrimination was in decline, a reluctance to work with non-Catholics "in secular organizations concerned with public issues," a suspicion that racial liberals were Communist, insecurity as second- or third-generation Americans about their own status, and an insularity produced by memberships limited largely to Catholic church and fraternal organizations. She might also have added that many white Catholics did not favor racial integration.[67]

Despite, and partly because of, widespread white Catholic indifference and opposition to the civil rights movement, Matt Ahmann organized an interdenominational National Conference on Race and Religion (NCRR) in January 1963, the one hundredth anniversary of the Emancipation Proclamation. The NCC, the Synagogue Council of America, and the NCWC Social Action Department sponsored the event, which attracted 657 delegates from sixty-nine national religious groups. Twenty-four Catholic bishops, including Archbishop Paul J. Hallinan of Atlanta, Archbishop John P. Cody of New Orleans, and Cardinal Meyer of Chicago, attended the conference, which reflected an ecumenical spirit in accord with the new direction charted by the Second Vatican Council, then in its second year of deliberations in Rome. In his keynote address to the conference, Martin Luther King chided America's denominations for failing "to take a forthright stand on the question of racial justice." Before departing, the delegates issued "An Appeal to the Conscience of the American People" that described racism as the country's "most serious domestic evil" and endorsed civil rights protests. The NCRR established a basis for further cooperation across denominational lines, including ten regional conferences, and marked the beginning of an alignment of the Catholic Church's national leaders behind the civil rights movement.[68]

Civil rights protests peaked in 1963 and included some Catholic religious. In July, seven nuns and a priest joined the Chicago Catholic Interracial Council and students in a picket line to protest the refusal of the Illinois Club for Catholic Women, housed at Loyola University Chicago, to admit African Americans. The club changed its rules after what McGreevy describes as "perhaps the first demonstration by women religious in American church history." In the same month, fifty white priests and seminarians and nearly twenty-five hundred Catholic laity, most of them black, participated in a civil rights march of twenty thousand people in the city, organized by the National Association for the Advancement of Colored People (NAACP).[69]

In a reflection of the NCRR's ecumenicalism and call to action, on July 4, 26 Protestant, Catholic, and Jewish clergymen, were among 283 black and white demonstrators arrested in a CORE-sponsored protest against black exclusion from Gwynn Oak Amusement Park, near Baltimore. Those arrested included Eugene Carson Blake, the highest official in the United Presbyterian Church U.S.A.; Bishop Daniel Corrigan of the National Council of the Protestant Episcopal Church; Monsignor Austin J. Healy, representing Archbishop Lawrence J. Shehan of Baltimore; Father Joseph Connolly, a local Catholic and cochairman of the Baltimore Clergymen's Interfaith Committee on Human Rights; and Rabbi Morris Lieberman of the Baltimore Hebrew Congregation. Local white Catholic laity were hostile to the action. Their letters denounced the priests for breaking the law and acting in an undignified manner. Three days later, seven priests participated in another protest. The park desegregated in August.[70]

In 1963, virtually all of the nation's major Protestant denominations, except the SBC, expressed support for civil rights. Arthur Lichtenberger, Presiding Bishop of the Protestant Episcopal Church, called on Episcopalians to work for improved race relations and assist the civil rights movement. He declared that "We must support and strengthen their protest in every way possible, rather than give support to the forces of resistance by our silence." The United Presbyterian Church in the United States of America's General Assembly established a Commission on Religion and Race with a $500,000 allocation. The American Baptist Convention reaffirmed its commitment to open churches and praised "Martin Luther King, Jr., Ralph B. Abernathy and others who are in the forefront of the non-violent struggle for justice and peace and assure[d] them of our support." The General Assembly of the PCUS called on every level of the denomination's institutions to "abolish all racial barriers and references."[71]

Catholic leaders also addressed civil rights. In June 1963, the nation's Catholic president, John F. Kennedy, proposed a civil rights bill to outlaw segregation in public accommodations. Shortly after, Kennedy met with 250 of the nation's religious leaders, including 37 Catholics, who agreed to create an interfaith committee to promote local desegregation efforts. A month later, Mrs. Joseph McCarthy, president of the National Council of Catholic Women, joined three hundred leaders of at least one hundred women's groups at a White House conference on civil rights. Afterward, McCarthy declared that "As Catholic women, we express our urgent moral concern for the racial crisis in our country and pledge to support the President's civil rights program and to continue to cooperate and work with all women of good to secure justice for all Americans."[72] In late July, the NCWC Social Action Department, the NCC, and the Synagogue Council of America presented a joint statement in support of Kennedy's civil rights proposals to three House and Senate committees that were considering them.[73]

In August, the American Catholic hierarchy issued its first collective condemnation of segregation for five years in the pastoral letter "On Racial Harmony," which endorsed the civil rights movement's goals. Archbishop O'Boyle, chairman of the NCWC Administrative Board, explained to his fellow prelates that the board would release the statement three days prior to the civil rights movement's March on Washington for Jobs and Freedom because "A timely word to our people should help to set a proper and peaceful tone to this and other demonstrations taking place in the country."[74]

The NCC, the NCCIJ, and the American Jewish Congress joined civil rights groups on the committee that organized the march, which brought between 200,000 and 300,000 people to the capital, including at least 10,000 Catholics among the more than 40,000 clergy and laity present. Although O'Boyle gave the invocation, he did so only after successfully insisting that march organizers make SNCC chairman John Lewis tone down his speech by softening his criticism of Kennedy's civil rights bill. Most Catholic bishops endorsed the march and clergy participation. Platform guests included John LaFarge, NCCIJ representatives, and bishops and auxiliaries from the South and border states.[75] Many Catholic prelates, among them Pennsylvania and New Mexico's bishops, Archbishop Karl J. Alter of Cincinnati, Archbishop Dearden of Detroit, Archbishop Lucey of San Antonio, Bishop Nold of Galveston-Houston, Cardinal Ritter of St. Louis, and Cardinal Spellman of New York, endorsed the civil rights bill in messages to their dioceses.[76]

Although most of the nation's major religious bodies, with the exception of the SBC, endorsed the civil rights bill, they also, like Southern Baptists, had far to go before eradicating segregation from their institutions. Catholic schools remained segregated in Mississippi, in most of Alabama and South Carolina, and in three of Louisiana's four dioceses. Tokenism and de facto segregation occurred elsewhere in the South's Catholic schools and largely formed the pattern in Catholic schools outside the region. While segregation and racial discrimination prevailed in staffing and admissions of most Catholic hospitals in the South, some dioceses, including Atlanta, Nashville, and Galveston-Houston took action to eliminate such practices, which were largely in retreat, if not entirely eradicated, in Catholic hospitals elsewhere in the nation, with the exception of some border states.[77]

White lay Catholic opposition to desegregation remained widespread in the United States. Many Knights of Columbus councils continued an informal policy of excluding African Americans and blackballed membership applications when necessary. In July 1963, the Chicago Catholic Interracial Council claimed that there were no African American Knights in the Chicago area, and, in August, a group of black Catholics complained that there were only two African Americans among the fifty-five hundred Knights in the St. Louis area. The *Criterion*, the Indianapolis archdiocesan newspaper, editorialized that "Granted there have been minor breakthroughs in the Deep South and the Far West, but by and large, the Knights are still operating, in practice at least, under a banner emblazoned 'For Whites Only.'" In November, Eugene R. Liner, Grand Knight of Chicago Council No. 182, and five other council officers resigned their positions when five votes blackballed the application of an African American, Joseph Bertrand. The ensuing negative publicity led even Supreme Knight Luke E. Hart, a longtime defender of the blackball system who routinely claimed, without supporting evidence, that the Knights welcomed African American applicants and had ten thousand black members, to concede that the Supreme Council's next convention should review membership application procedures.[78]

Racial exclusion and segregation largely characterized the major white Protestant denominations in the South. In 1963, surveys revealed that nearly 90 percent of SBC churches in the nation, most of which were located in the South and border states, would not allow African Americans membership. Of 1,178 Southern Presbyterian churches canvassed, 623 stated that blacks were welcome at services and 295 that they were not. Only twenty-eight PCUS churches had African American members.[79]

Nevertheless, in 1964, Catholic, Protestant, and Jewish religious groups contributed to the passage of the civil rights bill. Twenty-five hundred seminarians from each of the major faiths mounted a round-the-clock vigil at the Lincoln Memorial from late April until Congress passed the bill in July. In April, seven thousand people, including Catholic archbishops O'Boyle and Shehan, attended an Interreligious Convocation on Civil Rights held in support of the bill at Georgetown University, a Jesuit institution in Washington, DC. The NCC, the NCWC, and the Synagogue Council of America jointly sponsored the gathering. Church groups also lobbied congressmen for the bill's passage, and midwestern church organizations mounted an influential letter-writing campaign to their political representatives in Washington, leading Vice President Hubert Humphrey to claim that "[w]ithout the clergy, we could never have passed the bill." However, the SBC's annual meeting refused to endorse civil rights legislation, and the PCUS, like the SBC, did not participate in the Lincoln Memorial prayer vigil.[80]

Nevertheless, at its General Assembly in 1964, the PCUS "instructed" three synods in the Deep South to abolish all-black presbyteries and incorporate their churches into all-white presbyteries. It also barred segregation in churches, dependent upon the agreement of a majority of the denomination's presbyteries, and asked denominational agencies to assist clergy and congregations regarding "how we can effectively contribute to the elimination of segregation and racial discrimination."[81]

In 1964, the General Conference of the Methodist Church endorsed the civil rights bill and voted in favor of abolishing the all-black Central Jurisdiction within four years by voluntary methods. Jurisdictional and annual conferences, both African American and white, were to decide how to incorporate the Central Jurisdiction's seventeen black conferences. Integration of African American churches from the Central Jurisdiction into northern white annual conferences began immediately. However, Peter C. Murray notes that in the Northeastern and North Central Jurisdictions "Interracial congregations were ... still rare and largely characterized as token integration," and white churches either followed their congregations in suburban white flight from increasing black inner cities or drew white congregants from a larger area, neglecting African Americans. White conferences in the southern states took no steps to incorporate black Methodist churches.[82]

Largely white northern denominations also addressed segregation. In 1964, the General Assembly of the United Presbyterian Church in the U.S.A. elected its first African American moderator, Dr. Edler G. Hawkins, and set a timetable to desegregate southern presbyteries by 1967. At its annual meeting in 1964, the American Baptist Convention advised withholding loans from segregated Baptist churches, affirmed that racial discrimination should play no part in the "membership, leadership, ministry and staff" of the convention and its churches, and encouraged churches to include fair-employment practice clauses in construction contracts.[83]

Like its mostly white Protestant counterparts, the Catholic Church took action against segregation, largely prompted by secular change, and many Catholic prelates across the nation welcomed and endorsed the Civil Rights Act. In the summer of 1964, five of the nine Catholic bishops of California appealed in vain for voters to reject repeal of state fair housing legislation under Proposition 14. Under Hart's successor, John W. McDevitt, the Knights of Columbus national convention approved a rules change in August whereby councils could reject membership applications only by a vote of at least one-third of the members present.[84]

According to McGreevy's study of the urban North, "Catholic parishes were ... more likely to be integrated than Protestant congregations," but this mostly reflected the fact that Catholic parishes, unlike Protestant churches and synagogues, did not move with their parishioners to the suburbs. McGreevy also notes that national polls reported that white Catholics were at least as likely as other whites to support open housing and school integration. However, such commitments often foundered as Catholics perceived encroaching integration as threatening to their communities. In 1963, local people threw stones and vandalized the home of an African American family, the Bakers, who moved into the largely Catholic community of Folcroft, Pennsylvania. Aside from housing, McGreevy argues, "Surveys of Catholics ... found little enthusiasm for integrated congregations as an ideal." Campaigning for the presidency on a program of states' rights and opposition to the civil rights bill, George C. Wallace, the segregationist governor of Alabama, won support from a majority of white Catholics in Maryland's Democratic primary in 1964, and he also ran well among them in the Wisconsin primary, despite condemnation of his candidacy by the *Catholic Herald Citizen*, the Archdiocese of Milwaukee's newspaper, and the state's Catholic bishops.[85]

Across the country, many white Catholic laity were against their clergy participating in civil rights demonstrations, and many white laypeople also opposed diocesan interracial efforts. However, a few white Catholics, mostly from outside the South, participated in the civil rights movement. In the summer of 1964, laity and clergy participated in a CORE voter registration drive in Cincinnati, Ohio. The Grail, a laywomen's group, conducted a voter registration in Lafayette, Louisiana, in November 1963 and June 1964. Concerned about their priests' safety and encroaching on the prerogatives of local bishops or opposed to public protests and clergy participation, most Catholic prelates would not grant permission to the relatively few clergy who wished to join civil rights protests in the South.[86]

By contrast, in 1964, the NCC coordinated Protestant and Jewish clergy and laity participation as volunteers and minister-counselors in the civil rights movement's Mississippi Summer Project. Fearful that it would result in disorder and violence, Bishop Gerow publicly opposed the project. Gerow told interested University of Notre Dame seminarians not to come that summer, and, prior to the summer project, he sent six priests back to Oklahoma City and another back to Chandler, Oklahoma, for participating in voter registration work in Mississippi. Nevertheless, Father James Groppi, a diocesan priest who pastored a black Catholic Milwaukee church, spent a two-week vacation working in the summer project, and at least three lay Catholics also served as volunteers.[87]

In 1964, the PCUS General Assembly criticized civil rights direct action, but the General Conference of the Methodist Church endorsed orderly, nonviolent civil rights demonstrations. At its triennial convention that year, the Protestant Episcopal Church gave "unwavering material and moral support" to Episcopalian participants in the civil rights struggle, although, under lay pressure, it declined to endorse civil disobedience. The convention also adopted a resolution implicitly approving interracial marriage. The American Baptist Convention expressed support for nonviolent civil rights demonstrations, presented an award to Martin Luther King, and urged its members to join direct-action protests.[88]

In 1965, hundreds of Protestant and Jewish clergy and laity, the vast majority of them from outside the South, joined the Selma voting rights protests. Participants included the Episcopalians' Presiding Bishop John E. Hines, a native South Carolinian, and about 10 percent of the nation's Episcopal clergy. John Wesley Lord, the Methodist bishop of Washington, DC, and Archbishop Iakovos of the Greek Orthodox Church also marched. Southern Baptist clergy did not participate, but some Southern Presbyterians marched, including such prominent figures as Ernest Trice Thompson and James L. Mays of Union Theological Seminary, and Malcolm Calhoun of the denomination's Board of Christian Education. At its General Assembly that year the PCUS endorsed civil disobedience, providing participants accepted responsibility and any resulting court judgments.[89]

More than nine hundred Catholics, including clergy from fifty dioceses, fifty-six nuns, and laity, joined the Selma demonstrations and march to Montgomery with the NCCIJ encouraging and assisting Catholic participation. Although most of these Catholics were white, their number included a few African Americans. O'Boyle was the first Catholic prelate to give approval for priests to go to Selma, but he stipulated that they first seek permission from the local ordinary, Archbishop Thomas J. Toolen of Mobile. Expecting Toolen to oppose the priests' participation, chancery official Floyd H. Agostinelli had his secretary try to contact Toolen in Mobile, aware that Toolen was in Washington. Although O'Boyle's aide Auxiliary Bishop John S. Spence contacted Toolen, who refused his permission, Spence was unable to reach Agostinelli, who made himself unavailable in order to see the priests off at the airport before he or they could be stopped. Matt Ahmann used O'Boyle's initial permission to encourage priests in other dioceses to seek their prelates' approval to go. While some Catholic ordinaries, all but a few from outside the South, gave their priests full support to go to Selma, most gave permission implicitly, rather than risk a direct confrontation with Toolen. Both the dioceses of Portland in Oregon and Charleston refused their priests permission. Many priests, all of them from beyond the South, headed to Selma without seeking anyone's permission. James P. Shannon, Auxiliary Bishop-designate of St. Paul, Minnesota, was the highest-ranking Catholic participant.[90]

After President Lyndon B. Johnson submitted a voting rights bill to Congress, Father John F. Cronin of the NCWC Social Action Department, the Synagogue Council of America, and the NCC issued a statement calling on Congress to strengthen and support the bill. Cronin declared that it was "imperative that the Congress respond to the moral indignation of the nation by the enactment of the Voting Rights Act of 1965." The bill became law in August.[91]

According to a Gallup poll, 56 percent of white Americans disapproved of clergy participation in the Selma demonstrations, 32 percent approved, and 12 percent had no opinion. While Jews were most supportive, 60 percent of Protestants disapproved. Among Catholics, 44 percent disapproved and 40 percent approved, indicative of how clerical participation split Catholics almost down the middle. Civil rights organizers recognized the potency of Catholic participation, especially that of nuns who attracted a great deal of media attention. Organizers often put nuns, whom they urged to wear traditional habits despite the Second Vatican Council's reforms, in or near the front line of marches in the justified belief that their highly visible presence would help prevent violence as even segregationist Protestants shrank from attacking them. However, in March 1965, Viola Liuzzo of Detroit, a nominal Catholic, was murdered in Lowndes County ferrying civil rights workers in her car. In August, Catholic priest Richard F. Morrisroe of Chicago was critically wounded in a shotgun attack in Haynesville, Alabama, that left Episcopal seminarian Jonathan Daniels of Keene, New Hampshire, dead. The two men had been working with the civil rights movement.[92]

The movement, the Selma demonstrations, and the Second Vatican Council reforms stimulated further clergy and nun participation in civil rights activity and inner-city ministries, mostly outside the South. More than two hundred Catholic nuns and priests were among fifteen thousand people who marched through Harlem in a civil rights protest against racial violence and discrimination in Selma that Cardinal Spellman had condemned in a pastoral letter. Catholic clergy also joined sympathy marches or rallies in several cities, including Houston; Joliet, Illinois; Syracuse; Providence, Rhode Island; and Wichita, Kansas. After returning from Selma, Father James Groppi became the Milwaukee NAACP youth chapter's adviser. Groppi and nearly forty other Catholic priests and nuns helped teach freedom schools for African American students boycotting the de facto segregated Milwaukee public school system. The involvement of the clergy and nuns divided Catholics and drew significant criticism from some laity.[93]

Civil rights remained a fractious issue for the SBC. In 1965, the convention adopted a resolution that deplored "the open and premeditated violation of civil laws, the destruction of property, the shedding of human blood, or the taking of life as a means of influencing legislation or changing the social and cultural patterns" but also urged Baptists to work for "peaceful compliance with laws assuring equal rights for all" and "to go beyond these laws in the practice of Christian love."[94]

Some other major religious bodies began to address the economic consequences of racial inequality. In May 1965, the NCCIJ announced that the archdioceses of St. Louis and Detroit had become the first in the nation to adopt Project Equality under which religious institutions agreed to contract with companies that had equal employment opportunity policies. The Archdiocese of San Antonio followed in August.[95] In January 1966, forty-five leaders from the NCWC, NCC, the Synagogue Council of America, and other Jewish bodies formed the Inter-Religious Committee Against Poverty, designed to stimulate and coordinate antipoverty efforts by religious groups. Its cochairmen included Catholics Archbishop Robert E. Lucey and Bishop Raymond J. Gallagher of Lafayette, Indiana.[96]

Some dioceses still practiced segregation. However, in 1965, the dioceses of Baton Rouge, Lafayette, and Alexandria began gradual parochial school desegregation to align with federal court-ordered public school desegregation, and the nondiscriminatory provisions of Medicare encouraged all but one of the region's remaining segregated Catholic hospitals in the South to change policy. By 1966, only one southern Catholic college did not have any African American students since most of the Catholic colleges in the region had lifted racially discriminatory admissions policies some years earlier.[97]

Federal pressure helped bring change to major white Protestant denominations. To comply with the Civil Rights Act and thereby ensure institutional and student eligibility for federal monies, many Presbyterian, Methodist, and Southern Baptist colleges desegregated. In 1966, Belhaven College in Jackson, Mississippi, was the last Southern Presbyterian college to abandon segregation, and, by 1970, all Southern Baptist colleges had ended racially discriminatory admissions.[98]

By the mid-1960s, a few southern Catholic dioceses had begun to eliminate personal or special parishes for African Americans, mostly by closing them but occasionally by making them into nonracial territorial parishes. Often, the result was token church desegregation or the continuance, in practice, of racially distinct churches. Feeling unwelcome in formerly white churches, black Catholics left the Church in significant numbers in the second half of the 1960s and early 1970s as dioceses closed more and more black churches. Growing residential segregation also played an increasing role in separating black and white Catholics inside the South as it had done outside the region for many years.[99]

Despite measures they had adopted in 1964, the PCUS and the Methodist Church made little progress toward desegregation in the Deep South. By 1966, twenty-two black churches had yet to be received by seven presbyteries in the Deep South, and the Methodists had not agreed any transfers from the Central Jurisdiction into the South Central and Southeastern jurisdictions. Although the Disciples of Christ had often condemned segregation, it had separate African American and white conventions in six states. Episcopalian lay opposition to desegregation remained in the Deep South. In 1965, the parishioners of Savannah, Georgia's St. John's Episcopal Church voted overwhelmingly to leave the Protestant Episcopal Church, rather than allow African Americans entry.[100]

Race relations continued to be a national, and not just a southern, problem. During the mid-1960s, race riots broke out in several nonsouthern cities, and the call for Black Power, first popularized by Stokely Carmichael in 1966, gained growing support from elements of the African American population. In 1966 and 1967, the major white Protestant denominations, except the SBC, took further action that supported integration and racial equality. In 1966, the American Baptist Convention adopted resolutions endorsing open housing legislation and federal rent subsidies. Later that year, the convention's General Council supported Black Power, which it defined as the need for African Americans "to organize and unite with others" to achieve inclusion "in the decision making or power structures of our society." In 1966, the Southern Presbyterian Assembly urged the Church to "continue to support and regard with compassion those who practice civil disobedience when no legal recourse has been left open to them and who act in Christian conscience and allegiance to Almighty God."[101]

Many denominations also engaged in activities designed to address racial problems. In May 1966, the General Assembly of the United Presbyterian Church in the United States of America empowered church officials to participate in a Wilcox County, Alabama, school desegregation case. In September, the Methodist Board of Missions allocated $130,000 to the NCC's Delta Ministry, a program launched in 1964 to assist impoverished African Americans in parts of Mississippi. Every major white Protestant denomination, except the SBC, gave the Delta Ministry some financial support, albeit often in small amounts and with considerable internal opposition from those with a sizable southern white constituency. Aside from supporting the Delta Ministry, despite the hostility of Episcopal Coadjutor Bishop John M. Allin of Mississippi, the Protestant Episcopal Church launched the General Convention Special Program (GCSP) in 1967 with an initial outlay of $3.9 million, the largest race relations program of any denomination. Intended to assist racial minorities, the poor, and antiracist church and community organizations, the GSCP disbursed over $1 million in grants during its first year.[102]

Unlike the Protestant Episcopal Church, the American Catholic hierarchy did not forge a collective approach to racial problems, other than issuing a statement in 1966 calling for the strengthening of government antipoverty measures. However, an increasing number of dioceses, mostly but not exclusively outside the South, joined Project Equality, albeit with varying degrees of success, or, if they did not join the project, chose to do business only with firms that operated fair employment policies. Several southern, like some nonsouthern, dioceses participated in federal Office of Economic Opportunity (OEO) programs, among them Natchez-Jackson, which in 1965 sponsored an educational and training program, Systematic Training and Redevelopment, Inc., aimed at Mississippi's largely African American poor.[103]

While several Catholic dioceses in the Deep South grappled with parochial school desegregation in the second half of the 1960s, open housing often pitted Catholic prelates against significant numbers of white laity and some priests in some of the larger cities outside the South with significant Catholic populations. Cardinal John P. Cody of Chicago, formerly the Archbishop of New Orleans, supported the Coordinating Council of Community Organizations (CCCO) in its protests against segregated, inferior housing and schools that many African Americans experienced in the Windy city. In 1966, many Catholic priests, nuns, and laity participated in CCCO marches attacked by white mobs in some heavily Catholic areas. Appalled by the violence, Cody called for a moratorium on marches, helped negotiate what proved to be an ineffectual open housing agreement, and instituted an educational program on race relations. Some Catholics vehemently criticized Cody for supporting open housing, and some who opposed his call for a moratorium picketed the chancery.[104]

In Maryland, Cardinal Shehan was met with "hisses, boos and catcalls" when he testified in vain in favor of an open housing ordinance at a public meeting of the Baltimore City Council in 1966. A year later, Father Groppi led NAACP youth council open housing marches into Milwaukee's largely Polish South Side. The marches generated significant local white opposition and divided the city's Catholic population, but they contributed to the passage of an antidiscrimination city housing ordinance in April 1968 after two hundred nights of marching.[105]

In northern cities with large Catholic populations, residential segregation was concomitant with de facto parochial school segregation and often undermined, or at least limited the impact of, diocesan efforts to desegregate parochial schools. Furthermore, John J. Meng, executive vice president of Fordham University, a Catholic institution in New York, claimed that in racially changing districts "Catholic schools are being used by Catholic parents, not because of religious conviction, but as a handy escape for the avoidance of racial integration."[106] However, Monsignor George A. Kelly, secretary of education for the Archdiocese of New York, argued that "The very existence of a parochial school has helped to make or to keep many neighborhoods integrated." McGreevy observes that because Catholic schools kept white Catholics longer in the city than other whites, they "were often more integrated than already resegregated public schools."[107]

Nevertheless, many northern white Catholic laity opposed public school desegregation and busing on its behalf. In the mid-1960s, white lay Catholics opposed busing in Malverne, Nassau County, New York, and, in the 1960s and early 1970s, Louise Day Hicks, chair of the Boston School Committee, led largely Irish American Catholic opposition to public school desegregation and busing in Boston.[108]

In response to a growing African American population in northern cities, ghetto riots, and the Second Vatican Council, some prelates, clergy, and nuns focused on inner-city ministries and problems. Archbishop Dearden of Detroit organized Project Commitment to educate parish leaders in race relations and the Archdiocesan Opportunity Program, part-funded by the OEO and targeted at parochial school children in poor areas, exceeded $3 million in 1967. Fifteen Sisters of Saint Francis of Rochester, Minnesota, staffed OEO-funded Project Cabrini that provided summertime day and evening classes for black children and adults in a Chicago public housing project. Its success led the NCCIJ's Department of Educational Services, which cosponsored Project Cabrini with the Catholic Interracial Council of Chicago, to organize similar programs elsewhere, including Project SAIL in Charleston, South Carolina, in 1966.[109]

Annual urban riots and disturbances, the assassination of Martin Luther King in April 1968, and passage that month of a Civil Rights Act with a fair housing provision led the nation's major white Protestant denominations and the American Catholic hierarchy to give racial problems greater attention. At its annual meeting in May, the SBC declared its support for open churches and "equality of human and legal rights." Between 1968 and 1971, the convention's Home Mission Board established a $1 million church loan fund for ethnic groups and dispensed some small grants. The Southern Presbyterians endorsed open housing and donated to the Southern Christian Leadership Conference (SCLC) and striking Memphis refuse workers, who, with SCLC support, sought increased pay and union recognition. In 1969, the PCUS allocated $15,000 toward the set-up costs of the Black Presbyterian Leadership Conference. The conference, in turn, used some of its subsequent denominational funding to support African American economic development.[110]

African Americans also asserted themselves in some other predominantly white denominations. The Black Churchmen of the American Baptist Convention persuaded the denomination's General Council to accept many of the group's demands aimed at increasing blacks' presence in denominational agencies and boards and eliminating lingering racism in its communications. However, the convention balked at establishing a million-dollar fund for African Americans.[111]

Some major largely white Protestant denominations made financial commitments. In 1968, the Disciples of Christ adopted a two-year plan to raise $2 million for urban problems, while the United Presbyterian General Assembly asked Presbyterians to double the annual fund for freedom, targeted at African Americans, to $200,000, with half of this amount earmarked for the SCLC. The assembly instructed Presbyterian boards and agencies to favor equal opportunity employers and ensure investment of 30 percent of available monies in central city low-income housing and minority businesses. In addition, it advocated the eventual replacement of welfare with "an adequate income for all."[112]

In February 1968, three hundred African Americans formed Black Methodists for Church Renewal and exerted pressure on their denomination to achieve genuine inclusiveness and support inner-city regeneration. The recently created United Methodist Church budgeted $680,000 for Methodist, ecumenical, and community groups focused on poverty and racial problems, and endorsed Project Equality. The denomination's mission board inaugurated a $3 million fund for loans to ghetto businesses. Between 1968 and 1971, the Methodists set aside $35 million for "minority group empowerment and self-determination."[113]

Like most of the white Protestant bodies, the American Catholic hierarchy's response to racial issues was rhetorically robust but, unlike some of the other large denominations, weak in financial commitment. In April 1968, the National Conference of Catholic Bishops (NCCB), the NCWC's successor, unanimously approved a strong statement that called for the "total eradication of any elements of discrimination in our parishes, schools, hospitals, homes for the aged and similar institutions" and wide-ranging legislation in "employment, housing, health and welfare." The hierarchy also created an urban task force to coordinate

Catholic responses to urban problems, but, with no teeth and funding of less than $30,000, the task force paled beside the efforts of the Disciples of Christ, the Methodists, and the United Presbyterians. However, some urban Catholic dioceses, notably Detroit, and some orders of nuns continued antipoverty work in the inner city and some also made efforts to counter white suburban racism.[114]

Desegregation of Catholic schools in the South had produced no more than tokenism by the late 1960s, and, as McGreevy observes, "many residents of white, heavily Catholic neighborhoods were still quite willing to resist attempts to integrate particular areas of the northern cities." Like many of their southern counterparts, Catholic prelates in cities such as Boston, Buffalo, and Detroit issued letters and statements supporting public school desegregation in their dioceses, including busing in some cases. Bishops also tried to prevent whites enrolling their children in Catholic schools in an effort to escape public school desegregation but, just as in the South, such efforts were sometimes disregarded by local priests. Parochial school enrollment increased significantly in Boston after court-ordered busing for public school desegregation commenced in the 1970s.[115]

The major white Protestant denominations also struggled to overcome racism among their members and token desegregation in their institutions. In 1968, 11 percent of Southern Baptist churches nationally were willing to admit African Americans, a proportion virtually unchanged from five years earlier, despite some increase in black membership. The PCUS abolished segregated presbyteries in 1968, but church segregation was mostly unaffected. Although the Central Jurisdiction held its final meeting in 1967, mergers of African American and white annual conferences produced little integration in Methodist churches nationally, and, at the beginning of 1972, racial conferences remained in Alabama, Mississippi, and sections of Arkansas and Oklahoma.[116]

Many African American Episcopalians in the North and southern black Catholics otherwise sympathetic to church integration became disillusioned, when its implementation in their regions typically involved closing African American churches and absorbing them into white parishes. Many black Episcopalian and black Catholic clergy also resented their marginal status and lack of denominational representation and influence. Consequently, African American Episcopalian and Catholic clergy and laity, like blacks in several other predominantly white denominations, formed organizations to represent their interests and seek inclusion in decision making. In February 1968, seventeen black Episcopalian priests established the Union of Black Clergy and Laymen, and, in April, fifty-eight African Americans attended a meeting of the Black Catholic Clergy Caucus, the forerunner of the National Office for Black Catholics (NOBC) that opened in 1970. Both black Catholic and Episcopalian organizations called for self-determination within their denominations.[117]

The Protestant Episcopal Church and the American Catholic hierarchy responded differently to veteran civil rights activist James Forman's Black Manifesto. Adopted in April 1969 by the National Black Economic Development Conference (BEDC), the manifesto demanded reparations of $500 million (later increased to $3 billion) from the nation's white denominations for the historic injustices suffered by African Americans. According to a Gallup poll, 94 percent of white Americans opposed the proposal and only 2 percent approved of it, whereas 52 percent of African Americans were in favor, 21 percent against, and 27 percent had no opinion. Disavowing the manifesto's Marxist terminology, the NCC's General Board asked member denominations to donate $500,000 to black organizations outside the BEDC. A year after its launch, the manifesto had brought the BEDC only $300,000, with $200,000 of that amount channeled by the Protestant Episcopal Church through the National Committee of Black Churchmen, an ecumenical organization.[118]

Angered by the action, many white Episcopal parishes decreased their financial support to the Church. Faced with a budget deficit and opposition, particularly from the South and Southwest, to GSCP grants to some controversial organizations, including advocates of violence, the General Convention reduced the program's budget to $1 million for 1971 and gave diocesan bishops veto power over its grants in their areas. Two years later, the convention ended the GSCP.[119]

In May 1969, Forman presented a demand for $200 million from the Catholic Church to the headquarters of the Archdiocese of New York, which rejected both his Marxist rhetoric and call for reparations. However, at its November meeting, the American Catholic hierarchy pledged to raise $50 million to fight poverty and, as part of this effort, a year later it launched the Campaign for Human Development, which raised $8.6 million in its first annual collection. The campaign, which funded "educational, vocational training, and employment programs" to assist the poor, became an established program. Several southern dioceses, including the Diocese of Natchez-Jackson, also acted as sponsoring agencies to handle federal housing grants.[120]

Citing financial shortages and growing demands, in November 1970, the American Catholic hierarchy decided to provide the newly formed NOBC with just $150,000 of the $659,000 the office requested. After at first refusing the offer, the office accepted it six months later. In 1971, Harold R. Perry, one of the NOBC's founders, remained the sole black bishop among 280 Catholic prelates in the nation, and no African American headed a diocese. Nationally, there were an estimated 800,000 blacks among America's 48.2 million Catholics and 170 of the nation's 59,000 priests were African American. In September, the Josephites ordained their first class of permanent black deacons, some sixteen men, but the need for deacons, produced by a lack of black priests, far outstripped enrollment because diocesan programs to train black deacons were in their infancy. While far short of that called for by the NOBC and other African American Catholic organizations, such as the National Black Lay Catholic Caucus, Catholic progress in black representation among the episcopacy and clergy was comparable to and, in some cases, better than that of the nation's predominantly white Protestant denominations.[121]

In 1969, the American Baptist Convention elected its first black president, Thomas Kilgore Jr., and, a year later, John M. Burgess became the first African American to be elected diocesan bishop in the Protestant Episcopal Church for a mostly white diocese, Massachusetts. While neither the SBC nor its southern state conventions had black officials, in 1969, African Americans Irene James and Ira Martin were elected as second vice president of the (Southern) Baptist Convention of Oregon-Washington and to the executive board of the Utah-Idaho (Southern) Baptist Convention respectively.[122]

When federal court decisions mandated an end to public school desegregation in the Deep South in 1970, some white segregationist parents tried to enroll their children in Catholic and Protestant schools, or to send them to hastily created private schools in local Protestant churches. Many Catholic prelates in the region declared their support for the public school system, and, like the SBC's annual convention in 1970 and 1971, some agencies and leaders of Southern Baptist state conventions expressed support for public schools, sometimes in interdenominational statements. Many Catholic, and some Protestant, bishops and their diocesan educational offices issued instructions that their schools were not to admit the children of parents seeking to escape public school desegregation. Nonetheless, some segregationists succeeded in transferring their children to Catholic and Protestant schools.[123]

As northern cities had done for several decades, southern cities experienced growing white suburban relocation, and inner-city populations became increasingly African American. Nationally, white suburban growth affected all of the major predominantly white denominations and helped perpetuate de facto church segregation at the same time as denominational bodies endorsed integration. While Protestant and Jewish bodies often relocated from the city and built new churches and synagogues in the suburbs, Catholic dioceses created new suburban parishes and sought to maintain existing city parishes. However, by the late 1960s and early 1970s, a combination of budgetary problems, and declining vocations and overall enrollment made it increasingly difficult for northern Catholic dioceses to maintain parochial schools. Financial pressures were particularly acute for inner-city schools, now largely black and substantially non-Catholic in enrollment and situated in parishes with declining membership following the suburban migration of their white parishioners.[124]

Consequently, northern dioceses closed many schools they deemed too expensive to maintain, among them many inner-city schools. African American parents, who valued parochial schools for their educational and disciplinary standards, campaigned for them to remain open. In 1971, black parents succeeded in keeping St. Martin De Porres High School in Detroit open after a sit-in at the chancery and raising funds themselves. Black parents also kept St. Charles Borromeo School in Newark, New Jersey, open after a sit-in at Archbishop Thomas A. Boland's home and raising $115,000. Nevertheless, dioceses increasingly closed or consolidated inner-city schools, a trend that continued as the decade wore on, although a core of them endured. Instances of overt racial discrimination still occurred. In 1971, all-white Annunciata Elementary School in the southeast side of Chicago refused to admit two black applicants.[125]

After 1971, meetings of the American Catholic hierarchy and the major predominantly white Protestant denominations paid decreasing attention to racial matters. Increasingly, the NCCB focused on other issues and insofar as it considered inner cities largely sought to correct its neglect of their white ethnic inhabitants. Monsignor Geno Baroni of Washington, DC, who had championed civil rights in the 1960s and joined the Selma protests in 1965, established the independent, but United States Catholic Conference sponsored, National Center for Urban Ethnic Affairs in 1970, arguing that the Church needed to reconnect with the urban white ethnics that Catholic liberals and intellectuals had criticized and slighted as racist in the 1960s.[126]

Several factors contributed to a growing neglect of racial issues by both Catholic and the major white Protestant denominations. They included apathy, hostility toward, and alienation from the self-determination and separatist agendas of some African Americans, a conviction that racial problems had been tackled, and disillusionment and fatigue, arising from a belief that efforts to solve racial issues had failed. There was also a focus on other concerns, such as the elderly and the position of women. Such developments suggested that African American Catholics would struggle to have their concerns addressed by their denomination as the new decade unfolded.[127]

CHAPTER NINE

An Overview: Catholics in the South and Desegregation, 1971–1992

In the early 1970s, many southern, and some nonsouthern, dioceses continued to close African American churches to facilitate desegregation. They also closed or paired many black schools with white schools. The dioceses acted not only from commitment to desegregation but also in response to desegregation requirements attached to federal funding, increased withdrawals of orders of nuns from parochial schools as vocations declined, and rising costs, caused in part by employment of lay teachers to replace departing nuns. The cumulative effects of long-term African American, including Catholic, migration from southern to northern and western states in search of better opportunities also played a role. In January 1972, the Commission for the Catholic Missions Among the Colored People and the Indians reported that in the South "Few new missions have been established and last year alone nineteen churches and eleven schools were closed."[1]

Prelates in the Deep South generally faced the greatest challenges in trying to desegregate their institutions because of often entrenched white opposition. Furthermore, many African Americans were emotionally attached to and felt comfortable in black Catholic churches and schools, and they had often justified concerns that whites would not welcome them in their institutions and include them in decision making. A committed integrationist, Chicago native Bishop John L. May of Mobile, encountered such problems in Selma. In April 1971, May presided over an integrated meeting of Selma's Catholics to present his plans to merge Assumption, the white church pastored by diocesan priest Charles F. Aucoin, with St. Elizabeth's, a black church staffed by the Society of Saint Edmund (S.S.E.), and the two churches' schools. In an effort to forge a compromise between African American and white interests, May planned to make a renamed Assumption school the town's only Catholic school and have an Edmundite pastor serve the two churches until they merged as one church to be built near Assumption School. A show of hands indicated overwhelming approval for school amalgamation but also that most blacks supported and most whites opposed the church merger.[2]

Three weeks later, Father Paul Morin, the Edmundite mission director in Selma, wrote to Eymard P. Galligan, the order's Superior General, that Selma's black

Catholics were "having second thoughts" about the loss of their parish. Morin reported "expression of thoughts [such] as 'I don't want to push myself on them'" and "Why do we have to give up our church." The town's white Catholics, for their part, objected to May's plan to have an Edmundite pastor the proposed merged church. In an effort to placate white opposition, May decided that Father Edward A. Leary, the pastor of St. Elizabeth's, would be replaced by another Edmundite, Father Nelson B. Ziter, a Fort Kent, Maine, native currently serving a Swanton, Vermont, parish. Well known in Selma as a former pastor of St. Elizabeth's, Ziter had also formerly worked successfully as a supply pastor at Assumption.[3]

Upset by the loss of separate institutions they regarded as their own, some African American and white Catholics in Selma left the church. The diocese did not achieve its goal of building a new church. Instead, African Americans attended the former white church, now renamed Our Lady Queen of Peace. In September 1971, school desegregation saw the first four grades taught at Assumption School and higher grades at St. Elizabeth's. Enrollment at both locations immediately fell and continued to do so, with the result that Queen of Peace School, based entirely at Assumption from 1972, closed in May 1976. Catholic convert John Crear, president of St. Elizabeth's parish council, expressed the conflicted feelings of many African American parishioners:

> I love Father Ziter. He's the man who brought me into the Church. But when Father Ziter closed our old chapel and school, and told us blacks to start coming to the white church and sending our kids to the white school, it was almost more than I could take. Selma used to have two Catholic schools, and now we have none.[4]

In the early 1970s, prelates in other southern dioceses also merged many of the remaining African American and white churches and schools that were located in close proximity to each other, or in small towns, and, like May, ordinaries generally closed black institutions. However, prelates largely maintained churches situated in predominantly African American areas, although they sometimes made them territorial parishes in what amounted to a symbolic gesture toward integration since, for the most part, few, and sometimes no, whites attended them. After the Pastoral Council of the Diocese of Baton Rouge voted in 1971 to give black parishes territorial boundaries, Bishop Robert E. Tracy of Baton Rouge explained that "the black churches cannot be closed because they still serve a considerable number of black people."[5]

While emphasizing their commitment to integration, prelates often recognized that many African Americans valued retaining their own institutions, which provided them with a sense of community, identity, and belonging. Bishop Charles B. McLaughlin of St. Petersburg, Florida, noted that "While we have given every effort to the full integration of our Catholic people, we have in our diocese two parishes, special inner-city apostolates, used by predominantly

Negro congregations, who honestly want and love their own neighborhood parish facilities."[6]

Parochial school desegregation often required blacks to attend formerly white schools, but, by the early 1970s, there were indications that a few whites were willing to attend Catholic institutions in which they constituted a racial minority. Reflecting on developments during 1971, Bishop Albert L. Fletcher of Little Rock observed:

> This year, a number of Catholic white children are attending previously Negro schools. The reasons for this are lack of space in some of our white parochial schools and the realization of Catholic parents that there is better discipline and a more conducive atmosphere to learning in our Catholic schools than in the public schools.

Some Deep South prelates also found that white Catholics, albeit in small numbers, were attending formerly black parochial schools. The phenomenon even extended to Mississippi. Bishop Joseph B. Brunini of Natchez-Jackson reported that "A few white children are now attending predominantly black schools; this is a helpful sign, although involving only a few whites."[7]

More commonly, in the early 1970s, southern prelates were faced with the problem of some whites seeking to enroll their children in parochial schools in order to escape the impact of accelerated public school desegregation under federal court order. In April 1971, the United States Supreme Court ordered a new busing plan to desegregate the Mobile public school system. In response, Bishop May declared that the law had to be obeyed and Catholics "must uphold our public schools" since "we pay our taxes for them like all other citizens and many of our children attend these schools." Restating a rule adopted a year earlier, May announced that "Transfers from public schools will not be accepted unless the pupil has moved here from out of town." The bishop told his diocesan newspaper, the *Catholic Week*, that his office had been "besieged with calls from [white] parents who want our schools to accept their children."[8]

After the announcement in July 1971 of a public school pupil assignment plan to advance desegregation in the Mobile metropolitan area, May issued a supportive pastoral letter he ordered read in church by pastors in Mobile and Baldwin, the counties affected. Despite Governor George C. Wallace's publicly stated opposition to busing and his call for parents to disobey court orders for its implementation, busing proceeded quietly in Mobile as several thousand African American children took the buses from downtown to suburban schools. City leaders eased the way by endorsing the busing plan. Militant segregationists withdrew their children from the public schools and sent them to private segregationist academies.[9]

Southern Catholic dioceses faced pressure from the federal Department of Health, Education and Welfare (HEW)'s Office of Civil Rights (OCR) to desegregate their schools, or lose eligibility for federal funds. Father John M. Bond, the Diocese of Charleston's superintendent of schools, admitted that a January 1971 OCR review of desegregation in diocesan schools "prodded the Diocese to wake up again to a moral commitment it has long supported." Informed that the OCR intended to make an on-site review to see if diocesan schools were in compliance with Title VI of the Civil Rights Act of 1964, Bishop Ernest L. Unterkoefler appointed task forces to eliminate dual parochial school situations in Aiken, Charleston, Columbia, and Greenville, places in which African American and white Catholic schools existed in close proximity and had little or no racial mixing in their enrollments.[10]

Although progress occurred in Columbia, "the other three Task Forces met [an] impasse," leading the diocese to insist on solutions that involved pairing and consolidation of schools. The new arrangements required affected schools to provide specific, but complementary, grades so that all students, whatever their race, would be compelled to go to schools teaching their particular grade. The plans met opposition from among both African American and white parents, who were reluctant to send their children to another school amid concerns about uprooting their offspring and exposing them to a different and possibly uncomfortable or unwelcoming environment. Parents also objected to having their children divided between different schools according to grade. Some whites complained that their children would be in a racial minority in school.[11]

Consolidation of three Catholic schools in the Charleston peninsula illustrated problems involved in parochial school desegregation. Scheduled for the fall of 1971, the diocese's desegregation plan required Sacred Heart School, which had 30 percent black enrollment, and predominantly white Cathedral School to teach grades K–6, while Immaculate Conception, an entirely black school, would be reduced to teaching grades seven and eight. Ninety-six students enrolled at Sacred Heart and Cathedral would transfer to Immaculate Conception, which, in turn, would lose 125 of its students to the other two schools, and see its enrollment fall from 291 students to 167. Upset by the plan, members of the Immaculate Conception Parent Teacher Organization, the school board, and the Alumni Association placed a full-page advertisement in the *Charleston News and Courier* that claimed that their school was "being phased-out under the 'Disguise' of Integration'" and that Unterkoefler and Bond had ignored their objections.[12]

Some white parents and teachers were also dissatisfied with the plan. During the summer of 1971, some white parents at Sacred Heart registered their children in schools outside the peninsula in what John E. Ferrara, chairman of the school's board, told Bond was "clearly a move to avoid integration." Furthermore, none of Sacred Heart's teachers were willing to transfer to Immaculate Conception. Bond responded by asking the principals in the receiving schools to cancel registrations he believed were racially motivated. In the fall of 1971, the three schools began classes with significant desegregation in their student enrollment, although there was, Bond reported, "the one difficulty of racial balance at Sacred Heart" where 119 African Americans and 53 whites were enrolled.[13]

However, continuing white flight from the peninsula and a falling birthrate reduced downtown Catholic school enrollment. The decline, combined with rising educational costs, persuaded the diocese to close Immaculate Conception and transfer its students to Cathedral and Sacred Heart schools in the fall of 1973. According to Bond, in a tacit acknowledgment of past mistakes, the action did not produce African American protests because the protesters of two years before were now included in planning. However, many white parents withdrew their children from Cathedral School upset, they claimed, by a further splitting of grades under the new plan. Seventy-five percent black in 1973, Cathedral School's enrollment became 90 percent African American in 1974. Although Unterkoefler may have needed some prodding from the OCR, he was sincerely committed to desegregation. Like many of the nation's Catholic prelates whose dioceses included increasingly black urban areas, his attempts to desegregate Catholic institutions were undermined by white suburban flight.[14]

Opposition from some southern white lay Catholics also hampered efforts to desegregate Knights of Columbus councils. In August 1971, layman Ted Watson claimed that Council no. 704 in Charleston, South Carolina, would not allow African American membership. Despite strong opposition from its chaplain, Father T. W. Kappe, Galveston Council no. 787 in Texas eliminated Roy L. Calhoun, an African American applicant, from an initiation class that summer. Kappe informed Bishop John L. Morkovsky, apostolic administrator of the Diocese of Galveston-Houston, that "We have quite a few red necks." At the same time, Catholic laywoman Gladys Haak complained to the *Galveston Daily News* that Dickinson's Father Roach Council no. 3217 refused to permit integrated groups on its grounds. After receiving no response from the council, Haak forwarded her letter to Morkovsky, explaining that "I wanted to shame the K.C.s into doing something about it." Morkovsky raised both cases with Lino Perez Jr., the incoming state deputy of the Texas Knights of Columbus, reminding him that "racial segregation is not only unchristian and sinful, it is now, also, illegal." Perez promised to "take whatever remedial action is necessary."[15]

In his annual report to the Knights of Columbus Supreme Council in August 1972, Supreme Knight John W. McDevitt noted that the rejection of minority candidates by "a few councils ... have caused us to question the commitment of some members to the fulness of Christian charity." McDevitt reminded Knights that "The measure of Christian love today is the acceptance of all men in true human brotherhood without discrimination because of race, color, religion or condition of life," and he cited the Second Vatican Council's condemnation of "any discrimination against men or harassment of them because of their race, color, condition of life or religion." The meeting accepted McDevitt's recommendation to revise the Knights' membership admission procedures so that local councils would admit all qualified Catholic applicants who received a favorable vote from more than half, rather than more than two-thirds, of members present.[16]

There are no statistics to indicate the effect of the rules change on African American applications and membership. Histories of the Knights in Louisiana and Texas suggest a very limited increase in black membership that was conditioned less by white racial prejudice than other factors. Barbara Babin Lacour's study claimed that "Despite the fact that many black Catholics chose the [Knights of Peter] Claver organization over the Knights of Columbus, black membership grew in the Louisiana KCs." In 1978, William H. Dunn, observed that "The progress of local KC councils of Texas in building up their black membership in the 1970's has . . . been modest." Dunn believed racial prejudice was probably not a major reason, arguing instead that "the relatively small number of black Catholics in Texas and a lack of appreciation for the value of KC membership may be more important."[17]

African Americans remained even more underrepresented among Catholic clergy, but some progressive white Catholic clergy continued to oppose racial discrimination. Father John E. McCarthy remained a board member of the Houston Council on Human Relations. In 1971, Father William J. Morrissey, the white Josephite pastor of St. Anne's in Fayette, Mississippi, and vice president of the Natchez Branch of the National Association for the Advancement of Colored People (NAACP), ran unsuccessfully for the Mississippi senate.[18]

In the early 1970s, the mostly white Josephite order underwent a crisis. In March 1971, members of the National Black Lay Catholic Caucus held a sit-in protest at the society's Baltimore headquarters. They demanded that the Josephites "make black priests and brothers more visible in black communities," formulate a diaconate program "relevant to Black people," support programs for "the development of real Black leadership," and implement, under the leadership of the National Office for Black Catholics (NOBC), a black awareness training program for all Josephites. That summer, the Josephites completed a three-year chapter of renewal, required for religious orders as part of the Second Vatican Council's reforms, and affirmed their commitment to fostering African American lay and clerical development and leadership. Father Matthew J. O'Rourke, newly elected as the society's eighth Superior General, chose Father Eugene A. Marino, born in Biloxi, Mississippi, to hold the new post of Vicar General, effectively second in command. The society approved O'Rourke's choice of Marino, the first African American to hold a leadership post in its history, by a majority vote.[19]

Yet, the Josephite crisis was not over. Splits developed at St. Joseph's Seminary in Washington, DC, between older faculty, both black and white who were committed to integration, and young black seminarians who, as historian Stephen J. Ochs explains, "regarded much of the faculty as insensitive, irrelevant, white paternalists or as black Uncle Toms who did not understand the true black community and its need for autonomy and self-determination." Some African American seminarians also challenged the motivation of their white counterparts, some of whom also began to examine their own suitability. In 1972, some of St. Joseph's Seminary faculty were transferred and most black and many white seminarians left. Four African American Josephite priests resigned from the order, and during the 1970s it ordained only five black and twenty white priests.[20]

African American Catholic laity in the South also became more assertive, but many southern white Catholics, especially in the Deep South, continued to try to evade desegregation. In April 1972, the families of forty-three African American children in black Catholic schools in Marksville and Natchitoches, Louisiana, filed suit in federal court seeking to force the Diocese of Alexandria to desegregate and end discrimination in its school system by September, or lose tax exempt status and federal school aid. The parents charged in *Greenhouse v. Greco* that the diocesan school system had "served as a haven for white families fleeing public school desegregation orders." The black children had "either attended segregated parochial schools . . . , or within the past two years attended a segregated parochial school for black pupils which was closed without providing [them] . . . with an opportunity to attend a racially unitary parochial school." Thirty-nine of the forty-three children attended Marksville's Holy Ghost School, only five hundred yards from predominantly white Presentation School from which it was separated by an integrated cemetery.[21]

The diocese operated thirty-five schools in 1971–1972, with African Americans constituting about 20 percent of a total enrollment of 10,900. According to the plaintiffs, "25 of these schools have 90 percent or more white student enrollment, while 8 have 80 percent or more black student enrollment. Two schools have approximately 25 percent black enrollment and 75 percent white enrollment." The diocese, then, had failed to achieve substantial desegregation in its schools.[22]

In September 1972, the diocese paired Holy Ghost and Presentation schools. Indicative of substantial white opposition to school desegregation, only sixteen whites registered for the new school, renamed Marksville Catholic School. Eventually, thirteen white students withdrew in response to harassment from other whites. A federal district court dismissed the diocesan defendants and Natchitoches plaintiffs, a decision subsequently upheld by the Fifth Circuit of the United States Court of Appeals, which also declared that the pairing of the two Marksville schools had mooted the issue.[23]

Elsewhere in southern Louisiana and some other parts of the South, white parents sometimes thwarted desegregation plans by withdrawing their children from the schools affected. Awareness of that possibility sometimes made prelates reluctant to consolidate African American and white parochial schools. Although committed to a policy of pairing schools "in which formerly there were separate white and black schools in the same community," the Diocese of Baton Rouge hesitated in the case of St. Agnes, a desegregated formerly white school in the city of Baton Rouge, and St. Francis Xavier, a nearby black school. Bishop Tracy feared that if the schools were paired, whites would attend neither, so that, as he observed in January 1971, "we would wind up with two totally black schools."[24]

Nevertheless, under pressure from HEW to eliminate dualism and committed to the principle of desegregation, the diocese paired the schools in September 1971. Their combined white enrollment fell from 194 to 8 students. In response, Tracy indicated that he would close St. Francis Xavier and transfer its remaining grades to St. Agnes. African American parishioners, who had three years before supported closing St. Francis Xavier School in order to facilitate desegregation, reversed their position, unwilling to sacrifice their school in exchange for desegregation that was nominal and marked by white rejection and opposition. Black Power organizations' emphasis on black autonomy and identity, which was itself stimulated in part by disillusionment with the disappointments and failings of secular desegregation, also influenced the parishioners. Three hundred St. Francis Xavier parents registered their support for the school by assembling in front of Tracy's residence in a protest organized by Sisters of the Holy Family nuns, who taught at St. Francis Xavier, and Newman Club students from Southern University, a local black institution. Participants adopted the Black Power symbol of a raised fist. In observations that were equally applicable to African American Catholics elsewhere in the South, a study by Donald A. Erickson and John D. Donovan suggested:

> Many parishioners at St. Francis Xavier seem to have developed a new sense of identity.... Many blacks are disillusioned with what they find when transferring to white-dominated churches and schools, and as a consequence, are convinced that they must govern themselves, through their own institutions, at least for some time to come. Integration still seems to be the goal, but a goal to be achieved in such a way that the dignity and autonomy of black people is preserved. What is currently at issue, furthermore, is not only the future of the parish and its school, but the demand by black Catholics for self-determination. They are furious over the fact, as they see it, that whites continue to make vital decisions for them, no matter how well intentioned these decisions may be.[25]

Tracy also recognized these developments and agreed to subsidize the paired school during the school year before turning St. Agnes into a vocational rehabilitation center. Reflecting on the events of 1972, he noted that white withdrawals had increased financial pressure on the elementary school of St. Agnes–St. Francis Xavier that had resulted from pairing. The school, he wrote, "has become almost totally black in registration, and the situation requires that it be housed totally under the roof of the former all-black school of St. Francis Xavier." Tracy observed that "This is what the black community prefers, since the emphasis has shifted from integration by the elimination of dualism to black identity. The school has become a symbol of this identity."[26]

Affirmations of a distinctive black identity also occurred among Catholics in other southern states. Early in 1971, African Americans formed the Mississippi Black Catholic Caucus. Representatives from parishes in seven cities attended its first meeting. In October 1971, Nessa Johnson of Richmond, Virginia, attended a Mass with a large number of other African American Catholics at the city's cathedral. She recalled that "The Black Awakening Choir from Virginia Commonwealth University sang. The people dressed in black, red and green symbolizing the African nationalist colors . . . They gave the black power handshake at the sign of peace, signifying peace, love, and power for their people." After the Mass, black Catholics gathered to hear a delegate's report from the August 1971 convention of the National Black Lay Catholic Caucus and National Black Catholic Clergy Caucus, which sixteen hundred people had attended in Detroit. Organized on the theme of "black first, Catholic second," the convention had recommended investigating the possibility of establishing a black Catholic Church in the United States and included in its Mass a black liturgy, tributes to Martin Luther King and Malcolm X, and a clenched fist Black Power salute.[27]

Indicative of southern African American Catholic diversity, the Diocese of Richmond's black Catholics were not monolithic in their response to the recent convention. Johnson remembered that "Some said, 'We want no part of such a movement.' Some others said, 'We need this; let us begin a chapter here.' Others said, 'Let's watch and see what happens.'" Some of those present formed a Richmond chapter of the National Black Lay Catholic Caucus and subsequently received support from Bishop Walter F. Sullivan, the Apostolic Administrator and eventual Bishop of Richmond.[28]

The early 1970s saw growing disillusionment among southern African American Catholics with diocesan desegregation policies that had produced little desegregation, ignored blacks in the decision-making process, and deprived black communities of valued institutions, leaving their members often feeling unwelcome in formerly white schools and churches. Consequently, Erickson and Donovan reported that "Numerous black Catholics in Louisiana argue that racial integration in the schools should be delayed until it can be effectuated under conditions more favorable to the interests of black people." In March 1972, a clergy meeting in the Diocese of Lafayette recognized that "some blacks thought that they had given up their identity to obtain integration and that whites had done little." Although many priests still wanted churches integrated, an unnamed black priest told the meeting that separate parishes should continue.[29]

Southern dioceses did not create any new personal or special parishes for African Americans, but, as resources allowed, the vast majority of prelates continued, and some occasionally built new, de facto black churches, no longer viewing them as unacceptable signs of segregation but as a vital part of the Church's outreach to the African American community that many blacks themselves wanted. In 1972, the Diocese of Lafayette consolidated two black parishes with adjoining white parishes, but, at the same time, Bishop Maurice Schexnayder explained, the diocese aspired to build "two new churches for the colored in colored centers." In July 1972, a shortage of priests and a falling congregation led the Holy Ghost Fathers to withdraw from, and Bishop Albert L. Fletcher of Little Rock to close, St. Gabriel's Mission in Hot Springs, Arkansas. Nevertheless, Fletcher remained determined to maintain "Our present Negro parishes in Little Rock, North Little Rock, and Pine Bluff . . . as long as we can," arguing that they and their schools "are vitally necessary as the best means for keeping our Catholic Negroes faithful to their holy religion."[30]

Although, by 1972, almost all Catholic churches in the South had territorial boundaries, meaning they were open to all who wished to join them, in practice residential patterns and the personal preferences of many African Americans and whites, kept many former personal or special parishes largely, or entirely, black and made some formerly white churches likewise. In 1973, the Diocese of Charleston had sixteen de facto black parishes and the Diocese of Little Rock three. Some African Americans in the South attended predominantly white churches and vice versa, but, for the most part, black Catholics attended black churches. In 1974, Bishop Morkovsky of Galveston-Houston noted that "There are a number of predominantly black parishes, but there are also black families in the majority of our other parishes and schools."[31]

While African American attendance at black churches was in part a response to often justified perceptions of being unwelcome in many formerly white churches, their attendance was also conditioned by feelings of community and identity, and increasingly for some, a reflection of and attachment to a distinctive black Catholicism. In what historian Albert J. Raboteau explains as an "effort to define or reclaim Black Catholic identity" and encouraged by the Second Vatican Council's Constitution on the Sacred Liturgy, which permitted "adapting the liturgy to the culture and traditions of peoples," some black churches began to incorporate gospel and other forms of black music into the liturgy, along with hymns, hand clapping, and oral participation by worshippers in a manner traditionally associated with black Protestant churches.[32]

In 1972, Selma, Alabama, born Father Clarence J. Rivers of Cincinnati, who pioneered the development of a black liturgy and served as director of the NOBC's Department of Culture and Worship, was one of the leaders of a week-long liturgical workshop held at Xavier University, New Orleans. The participants, who were mostly from Louisiana, included black and white priests, nuns, and young African Americans.[33]

Although the workshop helped disseminate the idea of developing a black liturgy, a handful of southern African American churches had already incorporated black cultural elements into the Mass and black Catholic churches had, in any case, never been monolithic. In 1965, Father Maurice F. Ouellet, an Edmundite priest in Selma, wrote that "Our converts were used to singing together and praying together. They wanted participation so we gave it to them, long before the [Second Vatican] Council started talking about it." In 1991, Father Jerome LeDoux, an African American who had been ordained a S.V.D. priest in 1957, noted that "Even back in the days when we weren't allowed to sing gospel tunes and were relegated to singing Catholic hymns, we infected the songs with our style. We took them and made them ours, and the ways in which we did this varied from church to church."[34]

In 1968, St. Francis de Sales Church, which by the early 1960s had become a black church because of population change in New Orleans, began incorporating "Dixieland, rock and traditional black songs" into the Mass. However, for the most part, southern black churches did not initiate liturgical change until the 1970s and most did not act until the 1980s. There was no discernible or uniform pattern of change in the region, and African American Catholics were often divided in their openness to liturgical innovation.[35]

St. Francis de Sales lost a few of its older members when it began including black cultural music into services. Often it was younger and more militant black Catholics who favored change, with opposition more common among older Catholics who, Raboteau notes, "opposed changing the liturgy they had known for decades." Although its proponents hoped that incorporating black culture might aid in evangelizing African Americans from Protestant backgrounds, some existing converts, like some cradle Catholics, preferred the traditional Mass. Father Rivers observed that "The problem is not with whites, at least out loud, but with black Catholics who think black music is Protestant and therefore somewhat bad."[36]

Civil rights and Black Power organizations also influenced liturgical change in some black Catholic churches. By 1972, many parishioners at St. Francis de Sales wore dashikis in recognition of their African roots and the Mass climaxed with the singing of "We Shall Overcome," the anthem of the civil rights movement, sung during its final verse with fists raised in the Black Power salute. The church's white pastor, Father Joseph Putnam, wore "a long dashiki for vestments." Some other white pastors of African American Catholic churches also embraced black cultural adaptations in the liturgy. However, some white pastors either opposed or struggled to make such adaptations.[37]

Black Catholic organizations, such as the NOBC, not only promoted liturgical change, they also called for the development and training of more black deacons and vocations, greater sensitivity in the Church to black cultural needs, education to sensitize white priests of black churches to their parishioners' needs and culture, and the appointment of black laity and clergy to leadership roles. In 1971, a delegation comprising the leaders of the NOBC, the National Black Catholic Clergy Caucus, the National Black Sisters' Conference (NBSC), the National Black Lay Catholic Caucus, and the Baltimore Black Catholic Caucus went to Rome to "present the problems of the church in the black community and the problems of Black Catholics in the church." Although unable to secure a meeting with the pope, the delegation met with high Vatican officials and presented its demand that the Papal See appoint a black Archbishop of Washington to succeed Cardinal Patrick A. O'Boyle, who, in accordance with Vatican regulations, had submitted his resignation at the age of seventy-five. The delegation submitted a list of ten names for consideration, but Vatican leaders maintained that it was for the American Catholic hierarchy to nominate prelates for Rome's consideration.[38]

Nevertheless, the delegation's visit, which received widespread American Catholic and secular press coverage, probably contributed to the Vatican's appointment in November 1972 of a second black bishop in the United States, Father Joseph L. Howze. An Alabama-raised, North Carolina priest, Howze accepted appointment for the Diocese of Natchez-Jackson and joined his fellow African American Bishop Harold R. Perry of New Orleans in serving as an auxiliary bishop, rather than heading a diocese. Known as quiet and conciliatory, Howze had been pastor of St. Anthony's, a black church in Asheville, and, in 1970, he had presided over its merger with St. Lawrence, a white parish.[39]

While pleased with the appointment of an African American bishop, several of the Diocese of Raleigh's priests reportedly expressed concerns about Howze's selection since he had not been involved in the civil rights movement. One priest commented that Howze was "the kind of bishop whites would select" and another regarded the appointment as "tokenism." When questioned on these matters, Howze referred to his membership in the NAACP and the National Black Catholic Clergy Caucus, although he was not active in either and had not been among the nominees for the Archbishopric of Washington that black Catholic organizations had submitted to the Vatican a year earlier. Despite such criticisms, the appointment was significant not only for giving an African American a high-level position in the Church but one which also gave him some authority over whites, because only 10 percent of Mississippi's eighty-five thousand Catholics were African American. Before his installation, the National Black Catholic Clergy Caucus elected Howze as its president.[40]

Howze's installation ceremony in January 1973 sought to promote unity across racial lines, while also incorporating a black Catholic dimension. Howze adopted "Unity of God's People" as his motto and an integrated choir sang a soul-influenced special Mass, written and directed by Father Clarence J. Rivers. Interviewed a few months later, Howze observed that white Catholics in the United States were not willing to integrate African Americans fully into the Church, and he called for more dioceses and parishes to incorporate black culture into the liturgy. Although he rejected assertions that his appointment constituted "tokenism," Howze added, "it would be tokenism if no one else is named soon."[41]

Father Rivers promoted adoption of black liturgy in further trips to the South. In 1973, Nessa Johnson, who became president of the Richmond Black Lay Catholic Caucus, approvingly recalled his visit. She wrote:

> He came to teach the Catholics of Richmond his worship compositions. Voices came from everywhere, all sorts and ranges. They learned to sing the songs of the Mass... Spiritualized! They learned the centuries-old evangelized songs of their people, the somber ones, the hand-clapping ones. They were taught the Apostle's Creed and Come Holy Ghost... footstomping, the Hail Mary as had never fallen on their ears before... soft, mellow, haunting.

In 1974, Rivers issued a book *Soulfull Worship* under the NOBC imprint. Brother Joseph M. Davis, S.M., the NOBC's executive director, contended that African Americans felt most comfortable in churches that reflected their culture, adding that "In the U.S. until now, that has been in black Protestant churches, because these churches have been under the control of blacks."[42]

In the early 1970s, there was still a very limited number of African American deacons and clergymen, either religious or secular, in southern Catholic dioceses, and most black nuns in the region belonged to African American orders. Dioceses occasionally reported a little progress, but they also encountered setbacks. In 1972, the Diocese of Charleston had three African American students for the priesthood and six married black men preparing for the permanent diaconate, but, reflecting on withdrawals, Bishop Ernest L. Unterkoefler wrote a year later: "We continue to hope and pray that two black students for the priesthood, as well as four candidates for the permanent diaconate, will persevere."[43]

In 1973, Bishop Gerard L. Frey of Lafayette appointed an African American Father Mark Figaro, S.V.D., as the diocese's first Vicar for Black Catholics, charged with working "with people from the black community and with all others in the interest of the black community in the Bishop's name." In 1974, Bishop May of Mobile reported that "we have a black seminarian and a number of black applicants for the permanent diaconate," and Bishop Sullivan of Richmond reported, "We presently have a black deacon from Richmond who will be ordained next spring; we have three additional seminarians who will be ministering in the diocese during their summers and diaconate year." In 1974, the Diocese of Natchez-Jackson ordained an African American, Joseph Dyer, but many southern dioceses, such as Little Rock and Mobile, had no black diocesan priests. The Archdiocese of New Orleans and the Diocese of Lafayette had only four black priests between them, despite having the largest number of black Catholics in the South and the Diocese of Lafayette serving the highest percentage of African American Catholics in the nation.[44]

In 1974, Father Eugene A. Marino became auxiliary bishop of Washington, the nation's third African American bishop. However, blacks remained underrepresented among Catholic clergy and nuns, both nationally and in the South. There were 855,000 African Americans in a United States Catholic population that exceeded 48 million. Although one in every 57 American Catholics was black, there were only 175 African Americans among 57,000 American priests and 900 blacks among the nation's 140,000 nuns. Five hundred and ninety-five of the African American nuns belonged to the three orders founded for black women: the Sisters of the Holy Family (286); the Oblate Sisters of Providence (262); and the Franciscan Handmaids (47). Only four American dioceses had secretariats for black Catholics. No African Americans sat on the three executive committees of the National Catholic Education Association, or on other important committees, such as the Committee on Health Affairs of the United States Catholic Conference. However, in 1973, Wilhelmina P. Hall of Savannah, Georgia, became the first African American to be elected first vice president of the National Council of Catholic Women (NCCW). That year, Thelma P. Lombard became the first African American to serve as general chairman of the NCCW's convention, and she was elected to the board of the newly formed National Council of Catholic Laity. Progress was also made in creating a black diaconate to help offset the lack of African American priests; by 1974, 10 percent of the Church's deacons were black.[45]

The training, ordination, and retention of African American priests remained a key issue for many black Catholic organizations. Despite the Josephites' stated commitment to developing black leadership, in 1974, there were only nine blacks among the two hundred Josephite priests in the United States and the Bahamas. Josephite seminary enrollment had dwindled to thirty. Father Edward J. Gartmore, associate editor of the *Josephite Harvest*, commented that "There should be more black priests, and we wish we had the answer." Nationally, the Catholic Church was struggling to retain African American priests, nuns, and seminarians. In 1974, *Christianity Today* reported that across the country, "Since 1968, at least twenty [African American] priests have left the ministry, and 200 black sisters have withdrawn from congregations. And since 1973, twenty-five black seminarians have quit."[46]

African American withdrawals from vocations in part reflected a wider problem of disaffection with the religious life, which brought a decline of seventy-seven thousand in the total number of Catholic priests, brothers, seminarians, and nuns in the United States in the eight years since 1966. However, racial concerns were also factors in black dissatisfaction. In 1973, a survey of black college and theology students reported that most black respondents "are accepted around the white people they deal with and less than one-third feel oversensitive about their race," but "perceptions of difference causes over 60 per cent of the college students to state that a black seminary would better prepare them for the ministry." Black seminarians regarded "racial prejudice as a major problem," although "the majority would still encourage a black vocation."[47]

Southern Catholic dioceses, like many others in the nation, struggled to increase black vocations and deacons. Reflecting on developments during 1975, Bishop Sullivan of Richmond reported the ordination of the diocese's "first black priest," while Bishop James D. Niedergeses of Nashville observed that his diocese had only one black priest, an associate pastor at St. Vincent de Paul, a black church in Nashville. Bishop Morkovsky of Galveston-Houston stated that "Our need is more black priests. Last June we ordained one black priest for the diocese." Bishop Unterkoefler of Charleston wrote that "This year three lay men should be ordained as permanent deacons and a fourth is still in the program offered to candidates. Our candidates for the priesthood so far have not persevered."[48]

Southern prelates proudly reported instances of successful church and school desegregation in their dioceses. Unterkoefler claimed that "The continued growth of the schools in Georgetown and Orangeburg point to the 'new' day in South Carolina. These two schools once all black and still administered by black Sisters are now integrated and filled to capacity." However, Catholic bishops continued to maintain de facto black parishes in areas with large African American populations. Despite rising costs, they also tried to preserve black schools in these locations as a vital part of the Church's evangelistic program and a service to African Americans who, regardless of faith, often continued to value parochial schools for their quality and discipline. Bishop Sullivan wrote that "Subsidies continue to two black inner-city schools in Richmond and Norfolk," while Bishop May of Mobile declared that "It amazes me how much black people, many non-Catholic, will sacrifice to keep their children in Catholic schools."[49]

African American Catholics became increasingly vocal and assertive in expressing their aspirations and concerns, which extended beyond the issue of schooling. In November 1974, a group of black Catholic leaders, which included Perry, Howze, Marino, laity, and religious women, adopted a statement, "Black Perspectives on Evangelization," that called for "the promotion of black vocations," a permanent black diaconate in every diocese, "preparation of white priests who will serve in the black community," the appointment of blacks to leadership positions at the diocesan level, and the development of "authentic liturgical expressions" based on black "culture and heritage." The document cited the Second Vatican Council's Decree on the Apostolate of the Laity in support of its demand for the development of an indigenous church that included the laity in decision making. It voiced frustration at predominantly white orders that served in the black community, claiming that such "missionaries are reluctant to share responsibility with the laity, especially with black men" and "frequently confused the proclamation of the gospel with promulgation of their own culture."[50]

Bishop Sullivan was among the more perceptive and adaptable southern prelates who recognized the need for change. In 1974, Sullivan, who supported black lay Catholic caucus chapters in Richmond and Roanoke, told the *Catholic Virginian* that "The Church, by being white, is bound to be paternalistic and patronizing toward the black community. The white man speaking out for blacks is automatically paternal. What we need are blacks to speak out for blacks." In 1975, he gave three African American churches diocesan priests. His action removed white missionaries, regarded by their critics as obstacles to rather than facilitators of black development, who treated African Americans as people to be missioned to. In some dioceses, such as Little Rock and Raleigh, bishops appointed diocesan priests when orders withdrew because of a lack of vocations, but some prelates continued to use or solicit religious orders to staff black churches.[51]

Nessa Johnson recalled that African American laity in the Diocese of Richmond were divided in their response to the replacement of religious by secular diocesan priests, illustrating the diversity of black Catholic opinion. She remembered:

> Some of the people in the Josephite and Redemptorist parishes showed displeasure at the change. "You upstart ungrateful niggers," they lambasted, "You made the bishop send the missionary priest away after all they've done for us." Others were pleased. The move fitted into the order of things.[52]

In April 1975, a two-day workshop, held at Notre Dame Seminary in New Orleans to discuss "The Church's Ministry to Black People," illustrated growing ambivalence about integration, or, at least, the policies that southern dioceses had largely adopted on its behalf. Over one hundred African American and white Catholic clergy, seminarians, nuns, and laypeople from across the South attended. The workshop agreed that black Catholics wanted to keep their identity, and it opposed integration when it took the form of eliminating black parishes, schools, and institutions by assimilation or amalgamation. Participants welcomed what they saw as an emerging black Catholic identity, and they called for resistance to any further attempts to close black Catholic parishes and schools. Regarding genuine Catholic integration as a far-off ideal, they called for self-determination realized through black leadership development and black appointments to diocesan decision-making bodies and pastorates, and liturgical changes consonant with black culture. The workshop also called for Black Studies programs at all levels of Catholic education from elementary school to seminaries and universities, and for all clergy. Father Albert J. McKnight, C.S.Sp., an African American New Yorker based in Lafayette, gloomily declared that "There is very little hope for the Catholic Church among Black Americans. I would say that there is no hope, except that I am a man of faith."[53]

In November 1975, Archbishop Jean Jadot, the apostolic delegate to the United States, addressed the National Black Catholic Clergy Caucus at a Mass held at Bay St. Louis, Mississippi, to honor the nation's oldest black priests. Jadot endorsed many of the caucus's aspirations. His homily exclaimed: "[Y]our unique contribution and gifts of blackness.... must be recognized and incorporated in the mainstream of the church's life and structure." Jadot declared that black Catholics should be given and take "a greater role in the development and direction of the Catholic Church in the United States," and he endorsed "the development of strong black leadership and a strong sense of community among black Catholics," while cautioning blacks to avoid racism. Jadot's homily was both a recognition of, and a response to, growing black Catholic assertiveness.[54]

A month later, Brother Joseph M. Davis appeared before the American Catholic bishops' bicentennial hearing on justice. The hearing, held in Newark, New Jersey, formed part of a two-year grass-roots consultation process to recommend what action the Church should take in support of liberty and justice for all Americans when it organized a conference in 1976 entitled "A Call to Action." The hierarchy sponsored the conference in response both to the nation's bicentenary and the fifth anniversary of Pope Paul VI's encyclical letter *Octogesima Adveniens*, which had called on the Church to champion the cause of justice in the world. The Church, Davis told the hearing, treated blacks paternalistically and the black apostolate "as essentially a charitable endeavor." With some degree of hyperbole, given the almost entirely white character of the Southern Baptist Convention, he added that "Among the Christian institutions of this nation, the Roman Catholic Church has the poorest record of promoting indigenous leadership among blacks, or allowing the cultural adaptation which could produce the greatest harmony between the church and the people."[55]

Interviewed a few weeks later, Father Moses B. Anderson, S.S.E., the director of religious affairs at Xavier University, asserted that "For too long the Catholic missioners have been doing something *for* black folk, instead of *with* them [emphasis in the original]." Anderson argued that black Catholics had to evangelize African Americans and that "The church and America must be freed from their white racism and must be blackenized ... so that all may know that these bodies are multiracial."[56]

However, many Catholic interracial councils that had once exhorted their dioceses to address discrimination had withered. National Catholic Conference for Interracial Justice (NCCIJ) chairman Stanley P. Hebert observed that "In the mid-60s, many dioceses began to move on race and urban problems. Many of these efforts have been terminated or severely curtailed. The popular concern over injustice to minorities has decreased." In August 1975, lack of interest led the NCCIJ to cancel its national conference. In December, the Racial Attitudes Committee of the Diocese of Richmond's Social Ministry Commission noted that "many blacks and whites were simply tired of racial talk and racial actions which typified the 1960's." In the second half of the 1970s, the commission, like its counterpart in the Diocese of Mobile, increasingly focused on other issues, such as women in ministry and prison reform.[57]

Yet much remained to be done to ensure African American inclusiveness. According to a 1976 survey, the Archdiocese of Atlanta only had three African American priests and one black nun, and no black deacons or any blacks among decision-making administrative staff. By 1976, only 90 of the Catholic Church's 1,100 permanent deacons and approximately 225 of its priests were African American, and, with the appointment of Lafayette-born Joseph A. Francis as Auxiliary Bishop of Newark that year, there were only four black Catholic bishops in the entire United States, all of them auxiliaries. In February, Father Carl A. Fisher, an African American Josephite priest reared in Pascagoula, Mississippi, warned that "The failure of the Church to make full use of existing talent and leadership from among the ranks of its Black members can spell the doom of future and significant Black involvement."[58]

In October, the "A Call to Action" conference met in Detroit, attended by 2,840 bishops, clergy, religious, and laypeople. Of the 1,340 voting delegates, over 100 were bishops, 1,140 were "*ex officio* members or delegates appointed by bishops," and 92 represented national Catholic organizations, including the NOBC. All had an equal vote when the conference made recommendations for consideration by the National Catholic Conference of Bishops (NCCB). The working papers discussed in Detroit derived from hearings conducted in six cities, including Atlanta and San Antonio, and parish and diocesan consultations involving an estimated 350,000 Catholics.[59]

In its recommendations on ethnicity and race, the conference called on the Church to institute "proportional representation of racial, ethnic and cultural groups in the formulation and implementation of church policy"; ensure the adoption of affirmative action programs in every diocese; adopt equal opportunity policies in church employment and require businesses with which the Church contracted or invested to adopt affirmative action to achieve the same; and recognize, celebrate, and promote understanding of cultural diversity among Catholics. The conference also called for the preservation and formation of parishes and missions that "give emphasis to certain ethnic, racial and cultural groups but are open to providing services for all" and "the continued operation of parochial schools already existing in poor urban and rural areas." The Church's agencies for "social and legislative action," the conference recommended, should strive "to bring to an end all forms of racism and discrimination" in public policy, and each diocese should establish a black secretariat "to keep bishops informed on the needs and feelings" of African Americans. Furthermore, by April 1978, the NCCB should publish "a pastoral letter on the sin of racism in both its personal and social dimensions."[60]

"A Call to Action" foundered when many of the bishops and the Vatican opposed conference recommendations that rejected traditional Catholic teachings and practices. However, the bishops accepted the general thrust, if not all of the specifics, of the recommendations on ethnicity and race. But black Catholic leaders lacked the organizational strength necessary to exert telling pressure on the American Catholic hierarchy, and they could no longer rely on support from white allies. In February 1977, Auxiliary Bishop Francis, president of the National Black Catholic Clergy Caucus, conceded that the caucus was in a "holding pattern." It had not met for more than a year, had no plans, and lacked a full-time director. Furthermore, budget cuts had forced the NOBC to cut its staff to five from a peak of twelve. Nevertheless, Francis praised the NOBC, stating that "It's a major reason why we have some black bishops today. It has pushed successfully for liturgies that are culturally relevant to our people. It has encouraged black vocations. It has made the black church visible on a national level, and it has done all this without much encouragement and in the face of a lot of hostility."[61]

Whatever its merits, the NOBC's focus on blackness and its exclusively African American membership alienated interracialist Catholic organizations, such as the NCCIJ and the Catholic Committee on Urban Ministry (CCUM). Monsignor Joe Egan, the CCUM's founder, complained that "Joe Davis has antagonized everybody, the bishops, the priests, the nuns, the laity. The NOBC wanted to form the black agenda. Well, it's been seven years and we still don't know what it is." Noting that several NCCIJ officials had criticized Auxiliary Bishop Marino's proposal, at the "A Call to Action" conference, for a pastoral letter on racism, Davis responded, "Some of those old line liberals are still trying to run the show. Well, we're going to do our own thing, and they might as well get used to it." Anxious for African Americans to exercise leadership in the Church, Davis declared himself "very pleased" when the Vatican announced in March 1977 that Auxiliary Bishop Howze would head the new Diocese of Biloxi and become the first African American to head a see since the death of Bishop James A. Healy in 1900. Howze was installed in June.[62]

Black Catholics in other southern dioceses struggled to exert influence. In April 1977, ninety delegates attended the Texas Black Catholic Conference in Houston, instigated by the Texas Catholic Conference (TCC) with the support of the state's dioceses. In his address to the meeting, Father Elbert F. Harris, Josephite Consultor General and an African American Mississippian, forcefully articulated black Catholic discontent. He declared:

> [We] are responding to the unreasonable demands which would require us to give up much too much in the process of a white dominated "integration" movement.
>
> Black Catholics are telling the Church: we want to be Catholic and we want to be Black; we don't want to be uprooted from our parishes, our schools, our

hospitals—our security, in order to be thrust among those who deny our right to be what we are—persons who have heritage, a life-style, and unique experiences.[63]

The conference, the first of its kind in any state, adopted fifteen resolutions and sent them to the TCC. They included calls for the development of "meaningful liturgy that will express the Black culture," promotion of the permanent diaconate program in the black community because Texas had just four African American priests, and a reexamination of "the methods and approaches of recruiting Black men and women for all forms of ministry." However, procedural irregularities in the resolutions' submission led the TCC board to accept only a general umbrella resolution in support of black Catholic ministry. In subsequent years, African American delegates to the TCC complained, as delegate Tom R. Byrd explained, that "Black Catholics feel neglected and unfulfilled as individuals and as a group within the Church." Texas did not organize a second black Catholic conference.[64]

In 1977, the Diocese of Richmond held its second annual Black Catholic Eucharist Celebration, which used biblical readings in the liturgy that were in accord with the seven principles of Kwanzaa, a week-long celebration of African American life and culture devised by black nationalist and US leader Maulana Karenga in the 1960s. "The dancers," Nessa Johnson observed, "carried red feathers and danced at the altar."[65] In 1979, when the Diocese of Richmond conducted hearings on "Ethnicity and Race" for its own Call to Action program, some African American Catholic witnesses argued that blacks remained underrepresented among nuns, clergy, and teachers in diocesan schools, as well as in diocesan administrative and appointive posts.[66]

Bishop F. Joseph Gossman of Raleigh admitted that "As a diocese, we are not doing very much for black Catholics," and, in June 1979, he called a meeting of clergy and laity to discuss the Church's ministry to African Americans. The meeting revealed differing perspectives among black Catholics. One woman asked, "Why are we black people different? Do we always have to be a problem to be studied? There should be no black Catholics or white Catholics—just Catholics." However, a layman responded that "I don't mind being called a black Catholic. The reason black Catholics are different is their black culture. It's a lie to say there is no difference between blacks and whites. In order to get across to the black community the church will have to think black."[67]

A major complaint for many African Americans at the meeting, as among many other black Catholics in southern dioceses, was that integration had generally entailed the closing of black churches and, with it, a loss of community. One woman explained, "I'm for integration, but the black church is swallowed whole by the white church." Participants also urged the Church to ensure that white clergy assigned to black parishes were attuned to black culture. Gossman believed that the Diocese of Raleigh, which had only one black priest, Father

Thomas P. Hadden, needed black vocations and, in an interview with the *North Carolina Catholic*, said that he wanted, but had not seen much of, black liturgy in North Carolina.[68]

In November 1979, more than a year later than envisaged by "A Call to Action," the United States bishops issued a pastoral letter on racism, "Brothers and Sisters to Us." Written by a subcommittee chaired by Auxiliary Bishop Joseph A. Francis, the letter declared that "Racism is a sin." It noted a national "mood of indifference" toward racial discrimination engendered by a belief that the issue had been addressed effectively, and a focus on other, newer issues. Nevertheless, the bishops argued, a subtle but "unresolved racism" permeated "society's structures and resides in the hearts of many among the majority." Racial discrimination and its affects were manifest, they claimed, in the higher unemployment, lower incomes, inferior segregated education and housing, and crime experienced by minorities, and in growing opposition among the white majority to affirmative action programs. Arguing that racism and economic injustice were interlinked, the letter called for "authentic full employment" and "decent working conditions, adequate income, housing, education, and health care for all." The Catholic Church, the bishops declared, had to ensure that from the local parish to the hierarchy, minority representation exceeded "tokenism and involves authentic sharing in responsibility and decision making."[69]

The letter called for "the adoption of an effective affirmative action program in every diocese and religious institution," efforts to increase minority vocations and liturgies that incorporated minority cultures. "Training for the priesthood, the permanent diaconate, and religious life," the bishops declared, "should not entail an abandonment of culture and traditions or a loss of racial identity but should seek ways in which such culture and traditions might contribute to that training." Any "racist attitudes or behaviors among seminary staff and seminarians" had to be corrected, while "Seminary education ought to include an awareness of the history and the contributions of minorities as well as an appreciation of the enrichment of the liturgical expression, especially at the local parish level, which can be found in their respective cultures."[70]

All of the Catholic Church's institutions, the bishops stated, should be equal opportunities employers that directed their contracts and investments to businesses that took "affirmative action to achieve equal opportunity." Aware that dioceses were closing an increasing number of urban Catholic schools, particularly in large northern cities, because of declining income as white suburban migration accelerated and staff costs rose, the bishops recommended "the continuation and expansion of Catholic schools in the inner cities and other disadvantaged areas." The letter urged financial support for minority Catholic organizations and institutions, and recommended that "leadership training programs be established on the local level in order to encourage effective leadership among racial minorities on all levels of the Church, local as well as national."[71]

The letter addressed many of the major concerns expressed by the NOBC and other African American Catholic groups, but little effective action followed. In March 1980, the *National Catholic Reporter*, an unofficial Catholic weekly, reported that racism was a major cause of a high national drop-out rate among black seminarians. By 1981, the NCCIJ, which had once had one hundred local councils in the United States, had approximately fifteen, and Project Equality, initiated in 1965 by the NCCIJ to promote equality employment opportunity using the Church's purchasing power, had under ten offices in dioceses, down from a peak of fifty. Almost nine hundred Catholic schools in the nation, a majority of them situated in inner cities, closed between 1982 and 1991 because of insufficient enrollment or financial problems.[72]

In the South, the dioceses of Raleigh and Richmond both established an office for black Catholics in 1980. That year, Xavier University opened an Institute for Black Catholic Studies, "a summer graduate program . . . staffed by Black Catholic scholars and theologians" that was "open to all interested persons."[73]

Despite such efforts, racial discrimination often went unaddressed at the local level. In July 1980, Cyrus Jollivette, an African American who belonged to Miami's St. Rose of Lima parish, told the *Voice*, the Archdiocese of Miami's newspaper, two months after a city race riot:

> We need a series of sermons on race relations.
>
> Too many people think that blacks are not their equal, and that's the kind of thing that needs to be dealt with in the parishes.
>
> For example, at the kiss of peace during the Mass, some people will not shake hands with you because you are black.
>
> These are things that go on in the upper levels of the Archdiocese as well.[74]

In an article published in 1980, Father Cyprian Davis, a black Benedictine monk, noted that African Americans continued to be underrepresented among clergy and religious despite some increase in their number. There were approximately 250 African American priests, 700 black nuns, and 100 black brothers in the United States, but 1,000 churches and 550 schools were mostly African American or had a large black component. Davis claimed that African Americans were unwilling to accept white paternalism. He declared:

> Catholics in this country have not yet become accustomed to the idea that it does not have to missionize the Blacks or any other minority group.
>
> . . . the Black Catholic sees himself as an adult and no longer a child depending upon the largesse of others.[75]

In August 1980, two thousand delegates from across the nation met in Chicago for the first NOBC conference. They decided to petition the Vatican to allow older married African American men to become priests on the grounds that racism had excluded them when younger. The conference also called for the establishment of a national black seminary. Dr. Cyprian L. Rowe, Brother Joseph M. Davis's successor as NOBC executive director, claimed, "It's not separatism, quite the opposite. It's foolish to pretend the melting pot is working when it's not. We need a seminary where black Catholic culture and black theology can be developed and assimilated, not stuck on like some black-studies program." In another interview, Rowe declared: "I believe there is an authentic black experience which can enrich catholic worship. For example, I want to have gospel singing at my liturgy."[76]

However, African American Catholics, by now some one million people, remained diverse. Father Edward K. Braxton, a Chicago priest, theologian, and African American, observed that "Some black Catholics find their prayers enriched by elements of African and Baptist styles of worship and that is to the good! Others, however, feel no affinity for a gospel choir and are nostalgic for Gregorian Chant and Palestrina. Are the latter automatically less black?" African American Catholic leadership was also divided. The NBSC and the National Black Catholic Clergy Caucus disassociated themselves from the NOBC, claiming that its board was not representative of African American Catholic laity, clergy, and religious.[77]

In February 1982, a meeting of the Southeastern Lay Conference of the National Black Lay Catholic Caucus in Baton Rouge also indicated tensions within the African American Catholic community. Although the meeting discussed the need for the promotion of more black bishops, its discussion points also included a complaint that "Black bishops are not really intune to the needs of black lay ministry." In addition, the meeting reiterated long-standing demands that liturgy and preaching be adapted to black culture, asserted that there was "Too little black lay leadership," and argued that "Too few blacks [were] in the diocesan level for decision making policies."[78]

African American Catholics struggled to make the American Catholic Church attentive and responsive to their concerns. By 1982, the NCCIJ staff had shrunk to executive director Father Frederick M. Hinton, a black diocesan priest from Buffalo, and a secretary. Its $50,000 annual budget, the *National Catholic Reporter* lamented, was "just about enough to cover the quarterly publication, *Commitment*, and a couple of workshops." When the American bishops held their annual meeting in 1984, five years after their pastoral letter on racism, Auxiliary Bishop Joseph A. Francis told them:

> It would be comforting to millions of people of all races if I could relate that the pastoral on racism has made a significant difference in the racial attitudes and practices of sisters and brothers in the Catholic Church in the USA. I fear that it has not. In fact, I have often called it the "best kept secret in the U.S. church."[79]

In September 1984, the nation's African American Catholic bishops who now numbered ten, although still only two, Harold R. Perry of New Orleans and Howze, had southern dioceses, issued a pastoral letter on evangelization. The bishops argued that "racism, at once subtle and masked, still festers within our church as within our society" and remained "the major impediment to evangelization within our community." The United States bishops' 1979 pastoral letter on racism had "not had the full impact on the American church that was originally hoped." Consequently, the African American bishops asked the Church to take action to remedy their complaints that "Blacks and other minorities still remain absent from many aspects of Catholic life and are only meagerly represented on the decision-making level. Inner-city schools continue to disappear, and black vocational recruitment lacks sufficient support." The bishops also called for greater efforts to recruit black permanent deacons, culturally sensitive seminary training, and a more widespread introduction of "the African American cultural idiom into the expression of the Roman liturgy."[80]

The bishops celebrated their African heritage and claimed that black spirituality was "contemplative," "holistic," "joyful," and "communitarian." Although universal, the Catholic Church, they contended, was not uniform and "A people must safeguard their own cultural identity and their own cultural values." The bishops declared that "Our demand for recognition, our demand for leadership roles in the task of evangelization, is not a call for separatism but a pledge of our commitment to the church and to share in her witnessing to the love of Christ."[81]

A year later, the ten black bishops met for a one-day symposium in Harlem, held at the invitation of Cardinal John O'Connor of New York, to mark their letter's anniversary. O'Connor, who was white, argued that "very little" had been done in the intervening year to address the letter's concerns. Auxiliary Bishop Marino commented that "We cannot talked [sic] about the problems of reaching the unchurched and forget about the many who act with racism toward those already in the church."[82]

In November 1985, African American Catholic prelates issued a joint statement at the NCCB's annual meeting. They called for the appointment of more black ordinaries, the establishment of an office of black affairs at the NCCB's Washington, DC, headquarters, and greater efforts to evangelize non-Catholic African Americans. The group told their fellow bishops that many black Catholics believed that "the church is still European, the special home of the great ethnic and national groups from Europe." Earlier that day, in what Catholic officials described as a coincidence, the NCCB elected Auxiliary Bishop Marino as its secretary, the first African American to hold office in the organization.[83]

The Church's black bishops sought to influence a draft pastoral letter on the economy that was under discussion at the NCCB's meeting. A year later, the United States Catholic Bishops issued the letter as "Economic Justice for All," which reiterated their 1979 condemnation of "racism as a sin" and deplored racially "Discriminatory practices in labor markets, in educational systems, and in electoral politics."[84]

By 1986, most southern dioceses, like the Diocese of Birmingham, had established an office for black Catholics that sought "to provide training in intercultural and Black cultural awareness." In some African American parishes, such as Holy Ghost Church in Opelousas, Louisiana, black music permeated the Mass, church art depicted biblical figures with the same dark skin and hair found among parishioners and, as Sister Thea Bowman, F.S.P.A., director of the Diocese of Jackson's Office of Inter-Cultural Awareness, observed, "Red, black and green—Pan-African colors—adorn the altar and vestments to express black pride and solidarity with all African people."[85]

However, many African American parishioners remained divided by their churches' growing adoption of black liturgical forms that drew heavily on black Protestantism. In 1985, a study of the Edmundite missions of All Saints, Anniston, and St. Martin de Porres in Gadsden, Alabama, found that "attempts to introduce Black culture by a Black Edmundite pastor met with a wide range of both positive and negative responses." In 1986, Father Joe Cavallo, the white pastor of Our Lady of Lourdes, one of Atlanta, Georgia's six predominantly African American Catholic churches, noted that older parishioners "feel it's not the same without a lot of the old Latin and ritualism." Annabelle Jones, a parishioner since 1934, commented that "I think we need a little more discipline. Some of the parishioners have lost respect for the blessed sacraments."[86]

Nevertheless, Father Timothy Gollob, a white diocesan pastor at multiethnic Holy Cross Church, Dallas, Texas, successfully encouraged his parishioners to incorporate black and Hispanic culture into the liturgy. Delegates from his church, a leading exponent of liturgical innovation, brought their enthusiasm to the sixth National Black Catholic Congress, which met at Catholic University in Washington, DC, in May 1987.[87]

Sponsored by the nation's African American Catholic bishops, the National Black Catholic Clergy Caucus, the NBSC, the National Association of Black Catholic Administrators, and the Knights and Ladies of Peter Claver, the National Black Catholic Congress was the first to meet since 1894.[88] The sixteen hundred delegates, several of them white, and observers included the now eleven black bishops, black nuns and priests, and laity from 110 of the 184 United States dioceses. Over forty white prelates, among them Cardinal Bernard F. Law of Boston and Bishop Andrew J. McDonald of Little Rock, and the Apostolic Nuncio Archbishop Pio Laghi also attended.[89]

The congress adopted a National Black Pastoral Plan for presentation to the American Catholic hierarchy that, in restating concerns raised by black Catholic organizations throughout the 1970s and 1980s, indicated that much still remained to be done. The plan called for incorporation of black history and culture into Catholic institutions and religious education; continued development of black liturgy; the training, development, and empowerment of black Catholic leadership; black cultural awareness training for white Catholic leaders; greater efforts to recruit black vocations and permanent deacons; support for black Catholic schools and parishes; and efforts to support the black family and black youth and alleviate socioeconomic problems in poor black communities. The congress also adopted resolutions that called for the appointment of black ordinaries, in addition to Bishop Howze, and praised Xavier University for its "high quality of education, moral direction, and spiritual guidance."[90]

Enthusiastic in his praise of the event, Father Edward K. Braxton, a delegate for the Archdiocese of New York, wrote that "The liturgical expressions were rich in African-American music and symbols," and he maintained that "there was nothing separatist about the convocation which was unabashedly Catholic." However, Braxton noted that a small minority objected to the presence of whites. In an address to the congress, Sister Thea Bowman, an advocate of and contributor to black liturgy, observed that color remained a divisive issue among some African American Catholics. She declared: "We have to stop fussing and fighting about who's too yellow, and who's not Creole, who came from that Island, and how much money or education it takes to belong to this or that."[91]

Auxiliary Bishop Wilton D. Gregory of Chicago, an African American and liturgical scholar, observed that black Catholic diversity also influenced liturgy. Gregory told the congress:

> We are not a monolithic people, we are Haitian, urban, rural, life-long Catholics, recently initiated Catholics. This necessitates a diversity in styles. We do not all appreciate the same music, the same works of art, the same styles of preaching, the same manner of praying.[92]

Black diversity, Gregory explained, brought "a wide variety of liturgical styles in the Black Catholic Community." However, he argued that such variety was also partly conditioned by ignorance regarding the permissible limits of liturgical innovation "within the framework of the Roman Rite" and "a lack of awareness of the sources of our Black Religious heritage." Consequently, Gregory noted some parishes had a well-developed black liturgy, others were "lukewarm," and "There are still others who have not begun the important process of welcoming the cultural gifts of Black Americans." While these characterizations applied to black and largely black parishes across the nation, Gregory noted that "The development of an authentic Black Catholic liturgical style is made more complicated for some parish communities which are truly multi-cultural and multi-racial assemblies." The bishop's observations, like the issues raised by the National Black Pastoral Plan, applied as much to the South as to other parts of the nation.[93]

In September 1987, Pope John Paul II appeared before an audience of eighteen hundred African American clergy and laity in New Orleans. In an address to the pontiff on behalf of the nation's black Catholics, Bishop Howze drew attention to the pastoral plan which he said "proposes that the Church recognize shared responsibility for the development and empowerment of black Catholic leadership." Howze also made reference to the African American bishops' pastoral letter of 1984, which he noted "acknowledged that racism is a major hindrance to full development of black leadership within the Church."[94]

In reply, the pope emphasized "the universality of the Church and of her mission." Although he argued that the American Catholic hierarchy increasingly reflected "the cultural diversity of your nation" and claimed that there were "several hundred" black deacons, the pontiff appealed for more African American vocations. He urged black Catholics "to keep alive and active your rich cultural gifts" and approvingly clapped his hands during the singing of the hymn "Black Thankfulness." The pope praised the civil rights movement and Martin Luther King Jr.'s role within it, and expressed support for efforts to address economic and educational deprivation in the African American community. He also stated that Catholic schools "must continue to enrich the black communities of this nation."[95]

While the pontiff's message was supportive of African American Catholics, as the 1987 congress indicated black Catholics remained underrepresented among the Church's leaders, vocations, and deacons in proportion to their lay membership. African Americans constituted 2.5 percent or 1.3 million of the 52 million Catholics in the United States. Eleven out of the three hundred Catholic bishops were black, or 3.7 percent of the hierarchy, and so higher than the black percentage of the Catholic population. However, only one black bishop headed a diocese, and there were no black cardinals in the United States. African Americans remained substantially underrepresented among clergy and religious with only three hundred black priests among fifty-five thousand clergy and seven hundred black nuns.[96]

The problem was a southern, as well as a national, one. In 1987, Bishop Howze noted that the Diocese of Biloxi had no African American deacons, even though it had six black parishes, all but one of them served by religious orders. Although the Diocese of Lafayette had supplied several of the nation's African American Catholic bishops and many of its black clergy, the diocese had only two active black diocesan priests that year. While some Catholic churches in the South had African American and white parishioners, and, in parts of Texas, Hispanic parishioners as well, most black and white Catholics attended separate churches and lived in different neighborhoods from one another. Father Michael Aureli, pastor of St. Augustine's, an African American mission in North Little Rock, Arkansas, explained that "White and black folks still feel uncomfortable sitting with each other. When you're one black in a church of 700 white persons, it's natural to feel like you don't belong." In deference to the wishes of their members and to keep an evangelistic presence in the African American community, southern dioceses endeavored, when finances permitted, to preserve remaining black churches and schools, and, occasionally, they added a mission or church.[97]

In 1987, NCCIJ leaders tried to revive their organization, which had dwindled to a few, largely inactive chapters. The NCCIJ's decline symbolized the collapse of efforts by progressives to pursue integration based mostly on white Catholic institutions absorbing African Americans from black churches and schools after their dioceses had closed them. Desegregation had not eradicated racism among white Catholics, and it had not produced a church of integrated equals as the NCCIJ had hoped. Jerome Ernest, the NCCIJ's director, observed that "It's hard to find a black person in a responsible position in any chancery office."[98]

Ernest argued that many of the nation's white Catholics believed that the opening in many dioceses of offices for black Catholics and social justice demonstrated that the Church was tackling racial matters. He explained that "So many people feel the problem has been dealt with." Yet in practice, Ernest stated, black Catholic offices focused on evangelization and leadership development, and social action offices on "peace and justice," meaning that the issue of racism "largely falls between the cracks." Auxiliary Bishop Marino, cochair of the NCCIJ's senior advisory board, contended that "Racism's as big a problem as it's ever been. But it's more subtle. It's often unconscious. People don't perceive that the same attitudes are still there."[99]

In March 1988, the Vatican appointed Marino as the Archbishop of Atlanta, making him the nation's first black Catholic archbishop and bringing the number of serving black bishops to twelve, including the appointment in February of Curtis J. Guillory, a Louisiana native, as auxiliary bishop of Galveston-Houston. That year, the Vatican's Pontifical Commission on Justice and Peace issued *The Church and Racism: Towards a More Fraternal Society*, which declared that "Racism and racist acts must be condemned." The Vatican's statement prompted many American Catholic bishops, in both the South and other parts of the nation, to issue their own general condemnations of racism but only a few, such as Bishop Raymond W. Lessard of Savannah, addressed racism among Catholics. Lessard affirmed that "The whole question of racism is a reality, very much a reality across our country. And it affects the church as well, even locally. It is something that has to be addressed—the continuing cancer, the unhealed wound in our society of racism." To demonstrate its commitment to African American Catholics, the NCCB opened the Secretariat for Black Catholics in Washington, DC, which, unlike black Catholic organizations, was part of the Church's administrative machinery.[100]

The National Black Catholic Congress, the papal visit, attempts to revive the NCCIJ, Marino's appointment, and Vatican and prelates' statements suggested a renewed drive to address racial issues by the Church. Yet much remained to be done in the South, as well as the nation. For example, in May 1988 Lois Warren Harvey became only the first African American to be ordained in the Diocese of Little Rock and Robert Eugene Chaney only the second black priest ordained in the Diocese of Savannah and the first to be ordained as a diocesan priest. Only 15 of the nation's 151 Josephites were African American. The following years did not bring major advances for African American Catholics, although the Church managed to weather the threat of a race-related schism.[101]

In 1989, Cardinal James A. Hickey of Washington forbade Father George A. Stallings Jr., a forty-one-year-old African American originally from North Carolina, from establishing an African American congregation, Imani Temple, and celebrating Mass. Stallings had criticized what he regarded as the Archdiocese of Washington's white orientation and its lack of black priests, and had made liturgical changes unacceptable to the archdiocese. Days after Hickey suspended him for holding Imani Temple's first service at Howard University Law School, Stallings announced his goal of thousands of independent black Catholic churches. NCCB president Archbishop John L. May of St. Louis, the former head of the Diocese of Mobile, responded by issuing a statement to the nation's black Catholics. May conceded that racism still existed in the Church but appealed for them to stay within the fold. He argued that there needed to be more African American church leaders, greater attention to black concerns, and more African American "vibrancy" in the liturgy. May pledged "anew the energies and resources of the conference to give your vitality full voice."[102]

In a joint statement, the now thirteen African American bishops condemned Stallings's action as "ill-advised" and expressed their hope that his followers were not "comingling personal disappointment, individually felt frustrations and personal anger under the banner of racism," which the bishops acknowledged as a sin that the Church had to address. The bishops urged Stallings "to return to the unity of the Church" and work for its reform from the inside.[103]

However, many African American Catholics refused to condemn Stallings and some sympathized with him, even when they did not fully support his actions. Soon after Stallings's suspension, 350 clergy, nuns, and laity mostly from Texas and neighboring states met in Dallas, Texas, for a conference on black Catholic issues. Sister Eva Lumas of Oakland, California, urged participants to observe neutrality in the Stallings affair. Lumas declared that "Both sides are right. One side says it must be Black; one says it must be Catholic. The answer must be somewhere in the middle."[104]

In August, a national conference of African American lay Catholics met in Atlanta and revealed that converts were less receptive to Stallings's message than cradle Catholics. Dolores Grier, vice chancellor for black affairs for the Archdiocese of New York, explained that "Those of us who are converts left the black church and its emphasis on black culture by choice. But cradle Catholics have never experienced that and want to."[105]

The National Black Catholic Clergy Caucus released a statement arguing that the Church's long-standing neglect of black Catholics had brought about the establishment of Imani Temple. The caucus claimed that "We have been expendable to them—at least until an African American Catholic congregation disrupted the local church of Washington." In language reminiscent of the declaration issued by its founding meeting in 1968, the caucus urged the Church to "repent of her sin of racism and become a supporter of self-determination in the black community and a learner seeking to appreciate, understand and use the spiritual and cultural gifts of African Americans." The caucus accused the Church of continuing to exclude blacks from important decision-making roles. The statement was also dismissive of church agencies for black ministry, declaring:

> Too often, the entities serving black Catholics are poorly funded, out of touch with their own communities, excluded from decisions affecting black constituents or maintained for no other purpose than window-dressing.
>
> These offices exist in the same "bottom-line" climate that closes down inner-city parishes and schools.[106]

The response of black Catholics in the South (and elsewhere) to Stallings was complex, combining sympathy with his complaints mostly with rejection of his separatist founding of Imani Temple. Father Thomas P. Hadden, vicar for Afro-American Catholics in the Diocese of Raleigh, agreed that "there is racism in the church" and added, "But to leave, to put yourself outside of the church, means you can't have any effect on the inside." He declared that "Now I'm full of mixed emotions. I'm not understanding what he did. I sympathize with him, but I don't agree with him."[107]

Thomas St. Clair White, a permanent deacon at San Antonio's Holy Redeemer Church who had attended the National Black Catholic Clergy Caucus, noted that among his parishioners "Some think he's [Stallings] wrong, others think he's right but are too attached to the Catholic Church to break away, and still others say, 'Right on.'" White noted that Holy Redeemer, like many other southern black Catholic parishes, had addressed different preferences among its members by having one Mass on Sunday with gospel music and other Masses with Anglo-European liturgy. He favored more black cultural influence in the liturgy and concluded that "Stallings may be wrong to make it seem like he's acting outside the church, but I believe he is right in bringing out the issues."[108]

Several African American priests and laity, both within and outside the South, sided with Stallings and the several hundred followers of Imani Temple. Bishop Sullivan of Richmond fired Father Bruce Greening, S.D.S., as principal of St. Mary's Academy in Norfolk, after Greening asked for a leave of absence to establish a separate congregation for African Americans. Undeterred, Greening announced that he wanted "to challenge other black priests and other black sisters" to emulate Stallings's example.[109]

However, Stallings asked Greening to resign from Imani Temple after he refused to support his announcement in February 1990 that the temple would sever all ties with the Vatican; allow ordination of women, birth control, and abortion; sanction "optional celibacy" for priests; and give full communion to divorced and remarried Catholics without requiring them first to undergo annulment of a previous marriage. In response, the Archdiocese of Washington declared that Stallings and his followers had excommunicated themselves from the Church.[110]

Although Greening asked the Catholic Church to reinstate him, a few black Catholic priests joined the African-American Catholic Congregation (AACC), established by Stallings with himself as bishop and later archbishop. By 1991, AACC masses took place in Baltimore, New Orleans, Norfolk, and Philadelphia, as well as in Washington, DC, with the AACC claiming thirty-five hundred members. While Stallings found sympathy among many African American Catholics, the vast majority of them remained within the Catholic Church. Low attendance soon forced the closure of the AACC temple in Norfolk and two others, although the AACC also established a temple in Richmond and in Los Angeles, and a second temple in Philadelphia. However, the AACC became riven by internal disputes leading to the departure of some of its priests.[111]

While the AACC failed to live up to its founder's hopes of establishing a new home for African American Catholics, Stallings had drawn national attention to the persistence of racism in the Catholic Church, the continued underrepresentation of blacks among the Church's clergy, religious, and upper echelons, and the desire of many African American Catholics for a more culturally attuned liturgy, including, among some, an African American rite. By 1992, there were still only three hundred black priests in the United States as the Church remained unable to attract African Americans to the religious life in numbers commensurate with the African American share of the nation's Catholic population. Half of the three hundred black priests worked in parishes, including sixty who were pastors among eleven hundred mostly black parishes.[112]

Critics argued that not only had the Church failed to recruit sufficient African American priests for mostly black parishes, it had also failed to integrate black priests into the Church by according them roles unconnected with their race. Father Donald Sterling, president of the National Black Catholic Clergy Caucus, declared that "It seems strange to me that the Church can't put a black priest in a prominent place unless it has to do with black concerns." Father Raymond Kemp, the white pastor of Holy Comforter-St. Cyprian, a largely African American parish in Washington, DC, claimed that "The Church is still stuck using its talented black clergy to be symbolic presences in places where people expect to find a black person—so much so that there has been no thought given to blacks leading predominantly white parishes."[113]

Following Marino's resignation in 1990 after an affair with a female parishioner and the death of Auxiliary Bishop Harold R. Perry in 1991, there were only eleven black bishops, and some Catholics continued to disparage these officeholders. Father Lawrence E. Lucas, the black pastor of Harlem's Resurrection Church, asserted that "The black bishops are silent and useless," while Father Kemp claimed, "A number of the black bishops are symbols—spooks who sit by the door." Although the Catholic Church had avoided a potential schism led by Stallings, many African American Catholics remained dissatisfied with the Church's progress in race relations and ending discrimination, although they remained loyal to the institution. Bishop Guillory explained that "Black Catholics are committed to the church and to bringing the gifts of blackness into the church. They didn't leave 35 years ago when there were good reasons to leave because of segregation, and they aren't leaving now, especially not to follow one man."[114]

Although diminished, racial discrimination in southern Catholicism, as in the rest of the nation, persisted. Blacks remained underrepresented among southern Catholic clergy and religious and on the staff of diocesan agencies and newspapers. The Archdiocese of San Antonio, for example, did not have any black staff at its chancery. Southern, like national, Catholicism remained influenced by the wider culture. Father Jerome LeDoux, the African American pastor of St. Augustine Church in New Orleans, explained that "The church is made up of individual families and people from the United States, meaning that it is shot through with racism. But whatever sickness you find in the Roman Catholic Church, you'll find in any institution composed of individual Americans."[115]

Some southern Catholic churches were substantially integrated, and some had achieved integration based on reciprocity between cultures. Once the scene of racial strife, St. Joseph the Worker Church in Marrero, Louisiana, had a congregation 60 percent African American and 40 percent white, and a gospel choir, first introduced in the mid-1970s. However, for the most part, de facto residential segregation in the South went hand in hand with de facto Catholic church and school segregation, notwithstanding some limited desegregation that often did not exceed tokenism. Anthropologist Gary Wray McDonogh's observations about Savannah applied more widely across the South. "Blacks may be brought into previously white and dominant institutions," he wrote, "but whites will rarely venture into black neighborhoods, churches, or associations." Often feeling shunned or merely tolerated in white churches rather than welcome, many African American Catholics preferred to attend black Catholic churches where they felt at home and enjoyed a variety of liturgical styles. However, especially in Louisiana, color distinctions within the African American Catholic community, notably between Creoles of color and darker-skinned blacks, could still occasion discrimination in that community in the 1990s.[116]

CONCLUSION

In 1945, Catholic prelates in the South oversaw segregated Catholic institutions, and most did not criticize Jim Crow in secular society. In addition to their religious values, they held core commitments to the law, democracy, and, despite Catholic schools, public education that most did not regard as conflicting with legally imposed state segregation in the region. Providing their actions were not at variance with the tenets of the faith, the Vatican allowed prelates to manage their dioceses as they saw fit, including establishing further separate churches, missions, schools, and segregated hospitals for African Americans. Rome did not intervene directly in southern Catholic segregation, although it instructed the apostolic delegate to the United States to exclude the racially prejudiced from consideration for episcopal promotion. However, in 1943, the papacy had issued an encyclical on the Church as the Mystical Body of Christ that, alongside the civil rights movement, would help inspire Catholic integrationists in the South and elsewhere in the nation, to speak and organize against segregation. A few prelates, mostly but not exclusively outside the Deep South, took their first tentative steps toward Catholic desegregation in the late 1940s and early 1950s, encouraged by Mystical Body teachings and the American Catholic hierarchy's wartime collective condemnations of racial discrimination, but most took no action.

As a hierarchical body, the Catholic Church could in theory have ordered desegregation at any time, but in practice most Catholic prelates in the South felt as constrained by southern white segregationist sentiment, within and outside the Church, as other predominantly white denominations in the region. In most cases, prelates did not support desegregation publicly or begin Catholic institutional desegregation until, or in anticipation of, federal authorities acting against segregation under pressure from the civil rights movement.

When prelates endorsed desegregation, they often cited scriptural teachings and the Mystical Body, and they, frequently, also argued that Catholics should respect, obey, and act in the spirit of federal court desegregation rulings and federal legislation. When the federal courts and government outlawed segregation in public schools and accommodations, prelates often urged Catholic obedience as essential for the rule of law, democracy, and public education. Furthermore, in the second half of the 1960s, federal government threats and action to remove Catholic hospitals and schools from participation in federal assistance programs directly pressured Catholic prelates and institutions to desegregate, or accelerate desegregation.

Regardless of their geographical origins, prelates appointed before the second half of the 1940s tended to be more reluctant, or at least more cautious, than later episcopal appointments regarding desegregation and racial discrimination. Earlier appointees were more accustomed to, and generally more accepting of, segregation, the prevailing law and custom in the South until at least the mid-1960s, than later appointments, who were screened for their racial attitudes by the apostolic delegate, and also had more, and longer exposure, to Mystical Body teachings. Longer-established prelates, who remembered overt southern white anti-Catholicism in the 1920s, most vividly expressed in the Ku Klux Klan, feared that embracing desegregation would reignite such hostility and endanger clergy and laity. Prelates appointed when the civil rights movement achieved increasing success in prompting federal desegregation action, particularly in the 1960s, faced a more pressing issue than their predecessors that they could less easily avoid, down play, or slow peddle. Secular change, federal financial imperatives, the American Catholic hierarchy's endorsement of desegregation, and the efforts of progressive African American and white laity in the South, sometimes organized in Catholic interracial councils affiliated with the National Catholic Conference for Interracial Justice (NCCIJ), exerted a growing pressure on ordinaries to act.

Catholic prelates in the South were acutely aware that most southern white Catholics, like most other whites in the region, favored segregation. That realization and awareness of Catholics' small minority status outside of southern Louisiana, made many prelates, especially in the Deep South where segregationist sentiment was most pronounced among both white Protestants and Catholics, reluctant to act against segregation for fear of splitting the Church and endangering the Catholic minority. Even in southern Louisiana, Archbishop Joseph F. Rummel of New Orleans repeatedly postponed parochial school desegregation because of organized white Catholic resistance and concern that the state of Louisiana would withdraw aid from parochial schools.

Although they sometimes consulted, the South's Catholic prelates made their own judgments about desegregation and did not act as one body on the issue. Although in 1951 the Catholic Committee of the South passed a resolution against segregation, afraid of opposition from southern white Catholic and Protestant segregationists, some ordinaries abandoned the committee, which ceased to meet in convention after 1953 and gradually withered. The American Catholic hierarchy condemned segregation in 1958 and 1963, but Catholic polity left desegregation to the discretion of individual prelates.

There was a marked difference between the desegregation policies of Catholic bishops in the peripheral South, where token public school segregation generally commenced in the 1950s after the United States Supreme Court's *Brown v. Board of Education* public school desegregation ruling in 1954, and the Deep South, where it began in the first half of the 1960s after years of resistance. Peripheral

South prelates, except in Florida and east Texas, initiated or sanctioned Catholic school desegregation ahead of federal court-ordered local public school desegregation, whereas in the Deep South, ordinaries either desegregated Catholic schools to coincide with federal court-ordered public school desegregation, or after its initiation. Regardless of their locale in the South, when they acted prelates tended to desegregate all grades together, rather than adopt the gradualism of much of the public school system.

Personality also played a role in prelates' decision making. Bishop Joseph P. Hurley in Florida was politically conservative, personally untroubled by segregation's existence, and convinced that the civil rights movement was Communist infiltrated. By contrast, Archbishop Robert E. Lucey of San Antonio advocated desegregation long before *Brown* and began gradual school desegregation in the early 1950s. However, all prelates tailored desegregation to their perception of how much or how little resistance its adoption might bring from the local white population, Catholic and Protestant, and state authorities. As white resistance and opposition tended to be greater in areas with relatively high black populations, such as the Deep South, east Texas and west Tennessee and especially their rural areas, prelates there followed secular desegregation trends. Elsewhere ordinaries acted ahead of them.

Catholic desegregation occurred most effectively and with least resistance when it began quietly with no or little publicity, such as in the city of Nashville's diocesan schools. Long-term educational programs in the Church's teachings against racial discrimination could, as in the Archdiocese of San Antonio, help prepare the ground for diocesan desegregation, providing the prelate subsequently acted swiftly and decisively in announcing and implementing change. However, educational efforts accompanied by advance warning and discussion of intended Catholic school desegregation could allow opposition to coalesce and organize, and, as in the Archdiocese of New Orleans, stifle desegregation. In some places, such as Nashville, Catholics' status as a small minority eased desegregation as Catholic numbers seemed so insignificant to non-Catholic segregationists that they did not regard parochial school desegregation as a danger to the edifice of southern segregation. Furthermore, the desegregation of the many Catholic schools, especially high schools, that had sex segregated classes or single-sex enrollments seemed less threatening to many segregationists, Catholic and non-Catholic like, because they seemed less likely to result in interracial dating and eventual miscegenation than desegregated coeducational public schools.

Although Catholic schools, unlike the public school system, generally desegregated all grades simultaneously, they often experienced only token desegregation because dioceses usually limited desegregated admissions to Catholics, and many black Catholic schools had a substantial minority, or a majority, of Protestant students. Furthermore, white Catholic schools charged higher tuition fees than African American Catholic schools, which, in the frequent absence of tuition subsidies for transferring black children, limited black transfers. Consequently, in many cases, the announcement and implementation of parochial school desegregation occurred with little sustained opposition from within or outside local white Catholic communities. Opposition was even less likely when dioceses ordered parochial desegregation to coincide with federal court-ordered public school desegregation, even when Catholic school desegregation involved more grades. As public school desegregation increased, more African American parents of Protestant children in black Catholic schools sent their offspring to the desegregated public system, thereby further limiting the practical impact of desegregation on the parochial system.

Southern white lay Catholics shared the racial views of other southern whites. A large majority were moderate segregationists, with militant segregationists and integrationists constituting minorities. The Catholic Church's approach, since the late nineteenth century, of regarding African Americans as a domestic missionary field encouraged white and, to some degree, black Catholic acceptance of segregation and racial discrimination by adopting it within Church institutions. Relegating domestic missions largely to non-diocesan religious clergy and nuns reinforced white conceptions of blacks' second-class status, inferiority, and dependence. At the same time, domestic missions helped convince many southern white Catholics that the Church was serving blacks' spiritual needs by providing missions and churches specifically for them, and addressing their temporal needs in segregated schools and medical facilities. In most cases, religious orders of clergy and nuns, mostly white with headquarters in the North, staffed black Catholic institutions in the South. Religious clergy and nuns assigned to the black community were often shunned or ridiculed by the many diocesan clergy who had little or no interest in or involvement with African Americans. The Church's approach to African Americans was paternalistic and expected gratitude from people it treated as wards. While some clergy and nuns who worked among African Americans were paternalistic, condescending, or overtly racist, others opposed racial discrimination, and, increasingly, they sympathized with, and, in a few cases, participated in the civil rights movement. Some religious orders also pressured southern prelates to desegregate.

Pastors of white Catholic churches, whether southerners or migrants from abroad or elsewhere in the United States, often shared or came to share the racial perspectives of their flocks, although there was among the clergy, as among the white laity, a minority of integrationists, including in the Deep South. Most clergy, diocesan and religious alike, and most white nuns, avoided racial controversies. Some prelates, clergy, and nuns sincerely believed that the Church was helping African Americans through its missions program, although some undoubtedly adopted this view as a convenient rationale to justify or neglect segregation in

Church and society. Some ordinaries, clergy, and nuns focused on building and administering institutions, and took satisfaction from the prestige, and, in some cases, advancement and preferment, these activities brought them and their dioceses or orders. Operating directly in southern communities, prelates, clergy, and nuns also well knew the strength of white segregationist sentiment, which often made them cautious and circumscribed in matters of race.

Conditioned by Jim Crow practices in Church and secular society, some southern African American Catholics resigned themselves to their condition but others resented and chafed at their treatment, and, as the civil rights movement, NCCIJ and Catholic interracial councils developed, challenged racial discrimination within and outside the Church. Although the Knights of Peter Claver and the Sisters of the Holy Family to some degree gave African American Catholics a sense of racial pride, they did not participate as organizations in the civil rights movement to any significant extent. Younger African American Catholics, whether laity or part of the small number of emerging black clergy, were more likely than their elders to participate in the movement and challenge discrimination in the Church. However, some middle-aged and older black Catholics also wrote letters protesting against Catholic racial discrimination to their prelates and, on occasion, to the apostolic delegate, and some participated in civil rights organizations, primarily the National Association for the Advancement of Colored People.

Most African American Catholics wanted to see the removal of all racial barriers and practices in the Church that marked them with a badge of inferiority. However, when Catholic schools and churches desegregated, white Catholic officials generally expected blacks to enter formerly white institutions. In the second half of the 1960s and early 1970s, desegregation invariably saw the closure of African American, rather than white, Catholic institutions. While some black Catholics accepted the closure of black institutions as a regrettable but necessary step toward the goal of integration, others objected, and some, especially, younger black Catholics, left the Church altogether. Black Catholics became increasingly discontented, embittered, and/or disillusioned with the largely one-sided nature of Catholic desegregation that sacrificed treasured black institutions and expected blacks to integrate into white institutions and cultural practices in an often unwelcoming, hostile, or indifferent environment. Just as African Americans divided over the process and outcome of Catholic desegregation in the South, they differed in the post–Second Vatican Council era about developing a black liturgy that incorporated aspects of black culture and gospel singing, usually associated with black Protestantism. Some black Catholics, particularly younger elements, welcomed these innovations, but others preferred traditional Catholic worship.

African American Catholics were part of southern black migration to the urban North and West in the postwar decades in search of opportunity and an escape from southern racial discrimination. Although the North did not have de jure segregation, black migration to urban centers saw white flight and increasing de facto residential and school segregation. Urban white Catholic laity and some clergy in northern cities, such as Detroit and Chicago, opposed blacks moving into formerly all-white Catholic areas and attending white churches and schools. However, Catholic prelates in the North and West increasingly adopted positions against segregation in their dioceses, and many Catholic schools in northern and border south states desegregated in the late 1940s and early 1950s, ahead in most cases, of any in the South. Yet the desegregation efforts of Catholic dioceses outside the South, like those later in the South, often brought token desegregation. Nonsouthern dioceses were only a little ahead of those in the South in desegregating seminaries and ordaining African American priests, and, in both regions, such efforts brought token change.

While African Americans migrated away from the South, white Catholics were among those whites who joined northern white migration to the emerging Sunbelt of the South and West in the immediate postwar decades. Some of the white Catholic laity who migrated to the South favored desegregation and opposed both Catholic and secular segregation in their adopted region, but others accepted or adjusted to a de jure form of the more informal segregation they had been used to in the North.

Predominantly northern white Protestant denominations adopted earlier and more far-reaching statements on race relations and discrimination than their southern equivalents, and it was largely clergy and laity, whether Protestant, Catholic, or Jewish, from outside the South who joined the Selma demonstrations in 1965. Nevertheless, northern white denominations encountered opposition and resistance from some of their laity to their social activism that, in the second half of the 1960s, led some mainstream Protestant denominations to lose membership.

Occasional statements on race and desegregation by some Catholic prelates in the South, especially the peripheral South, were often as progressive as those of predominantly white northern denominations and as, when not more, progressive than those of major southern white denominations. White Catholic school and college desegregation in the South often outpaced, when it did not match desegregation of white Protestant counterparts in the region. However, southern white Catholic laity shared the racial views of their Protestant counterparts, and, despite being theoretically open to all, white Catholic churches in the South, often segregated African Americans or discouraged their attendance. Opinion poll evidence suggests that southern Jews were significantly more favorable to secular desegregation than southern white Catholic and Protestant laity, but many Jews, like some integrationist Catholics, were silent about Jim Crow, fearing segregationist retribution.

Before the 1960s, many Catholic prelates, diocesan newspaper editors and diocesan officials, and Protestant denominations in the South spoke publicly against segregation in anticipation of, or in response to, the *Brown* ruling. When massive resistance stymied public school desegregation in the South, Catholic school desegregation in the region also largely halted, only to resume in line with token public school desegregation under federal court order in the first half of the 1960s. Federal financial pressure was crucial in achieving desegregation of recalcitrant Catholic and white Protestant denominational hospitals in the decade's second half. Such pressure was also important in leading some resistant Protestant colleges and universities to desegregate in the Deep South at that time, and in making some Catholic school systems in the region, such as in the dioceses of Alexandria and Lafayette, address desegregation anew.

The early 1970s saw further closures of African American Catholic churches and schools in the South on behalf of desegregation and continuing white, including Catholic, flight to the suburbs from increasingly black inner cities. In response, southern prelates recognized a need to sustain remaining African American Catholic institutions, located in largely black areas, as a matter of service and evangelism to the black community. The late 1970s and thereafter brought the opening of diocesan offices for black Catholics, further efforts to support black churches, ordination of several more African American priests, and installation of the first black ordinaries in the South. However, most black Catholic churches, including those observing a black liturgy, remained staffed by white clergy, and, despite some token desegregation, most white and black Catholics inhabited different areas, attended different churches and sent their children to different schools. Although southern white Catholics, like most other southern whites, no longer publicly defended or supported segregation, and most had accepted the end of formal segregation within the Church and secular society, many had not embraced racial integration based on inclusiveness, reciprocity, and mutual understanding. The Catholic Church in the South had desegregated its institutions, but, for the most part, it had not truly integrated them.

After his retirement, Bishop John J. Russell, who had often been cautious regarding desegregation, regretfully observed that "We sort of went along with the general [white] populace." If "we had been more Christian," he argued, "there would be more Negro Catholics today." Twenty years later, disillusioned with continued tokenism and, what they regarded as, unresolved racism and a lack of substantive change in the Catholic Church, some African American Catholics followed Father George A. Stallings Jr. in forming an alternative church for black Catholics. However, while sympathizing with much of Stallings's criticisms of the Church, most African American Catholics, including most in the South, remained within it, determined to achieve change from within.[1]

APPENDIX 1

Catholic Archdioceses and Dioceses in the South, 1945–1992

Archdiocese of Atlanta (northern Georgia), elevated from the Diocese of Atlanta in 1962.

Archdiocese of Miami (southern Florida), elevated from the Diocese of Miami in 1968; territory lost to the Diocese of Palm Beach and the Diocese of Venice erected in 1984.

Archdiocese of Mobile (southern Alabama), elevated from the Diocese of Mobile in 1980.

Archdiocese of New Orleans (southeastern Louisiana), territory lost to the Diocese of Baton Rouge, erected in 1961, and to the Diocese of Houma-Thibodaux, erected in 1977.

Archdiocese of San Antonio (south-central Texas), territory lost to the Diocese of Austin, erected in 1947, and the Diocese of Victoria in Texas, erected in 1982.

Diocese of Alexandria (northern half of Louisiana); renamed the Diocese of Alexandria-Shreveport in 1976; divided into the Diocese of Alexandria (central Louisiana) and the Diocese of Shreveport (northern Louisiana) in 1986.

Diocese of Alexandria-Shreveport (northern half of Louisiana), created in 1976 from the renaming of the Diocese of Alexandria; divided into the Diocese of Alexandria and the Diocese of Shreveport in 1986.

Diocese of Amarillo (northwest Texas), territory lost to the Diocese of San Angelo, erected in 1961, and the Diocese of Lubbock, erected in 1983.

Diocese of Arlington (northern Virginia), erected in 1974 from territory taken from the Diocese of Richmond and the Archdiocese of Washington.

Diocese of Atlanta (northern Georgia), erected in 1956 with the division of the Diocese of Savannah-Atlanta; elevated to the Archdiocese of Atlanta in 1962.

Diocese of Austin (central Texas), erected in 1947 from territory taken from the Diocese of Dallas, the Diocese of Galveston, and the Archdiocese of San Antonio; territory lost to the Diocese of San Angelo, erected in 1961.

Diocese of Baton Rouge (southern Louisiana), erected in 1961 from territory taken from the Archdiocese of New Orleans.

Diocese of Beaumont (east Texas), erected in 1966 from territory taken from the Diocese of Galveston-Houston; territory lost with the erection of the Diocese of Tyler in 1986.

Diocese of Biloxi (southern Mississippi), erected in 1977 from territory taken from the Diocese of Natchez-Jackson.

Diocese of Birmingham (northern Alabama), created in 1969 from the division of the Diocese of Mobile-Birmingham.

Diocese of Brownsville (south Texas), erected in 1965 from territory taken from the Diocese of Corpus Christi.

Diocese of Charleston (all of South Carolina).

Diocese of Charlotte (western North Carolina), erected in 1971 from territory taken from the Diocese of Raleigh; territory added with the suppression of the Territorial Abbey of Belmont-Mary Help of Christians in 1977.

Diocese of Corpus Christi (south Texas), territory lost to the Diocese of Brownsville, erected in 1965 and to the Diocese of Victoria in Texas, erected in 1982.

Diocese of Dallas (north Texas), territory lost to the Diocese of Austin, erected in 1947; renamed the Diocese of Dallas-Fort Worth in 1953; redesignated the Diocese of Dallas in 1969 after the division of the Diocese of Dallas-Fort Worth; territory lost to the Diocese of Tyler, erected in 1986.

Diocese of Dallas-Fort Worth (north Texas), created in 1953 from the renaming of the Diocese of Dallas; territory lost to the Diocese of San Angelo, erected in 1961; redesignated the Diocese of Dallas in 1969 after the division of the Diocese of Dallas-Fort Worth.

Diocese of El Paso (west Texas), territory lost to the Diocese of San Angelo, erected in 1961 and the Diocese of Las Cruces, erected in 1982.

Diocese of Fort Worth (north Texas), created in 1969 from the division of the Diocese of Dallas-Fort Worth.

Diocese of Galveston (southeast Texas), lost territory with the erection of the Diocese of Austin 1947; renamed the Diocese of Galveston-Houston in 1959.

Diocese of Galveston-Houston (southeast Texas), lost territory with the erection of the Diocese of Beaumont in 1966, the Diocese of Victoria in Texas in 1986, and the Diocese of Tyler in 1986.

Diocese of Houma-Thibodaux (southern Louisiana), erected in 1977 from territory taken from the Archdiocese of New Orleans.

Diocese of Jackson (central and northern Mississippi), created in 1977 after the division of the Diocese of Natchez-Jackson.

Diocese of Knoxville (eastern Tennessee), erected in 1988 from territory taken from the Diocese of Nashville.

Diocese of Lafayette (southwestern Louisiana), territory lost to the Diocese of Lake Charles, erected in 1980.

Diocese of Lake Charles (southwestern Louisiana), erected in 1980 from territory taken from the Diocese of Lafayette.

Diocese of Little Rock (all of Arkansas).

Diocese of Lubbock (northwest Texas), erected in 1983 from territory taken from the Diocese of Amarillo and the Diocese of San Angelo.

Diocese of Memphis (western Tennessee), erected in 1970 from territory taken from the Diocese of Nashville.

Diocese of Miami (southern Florida), erected in 1958 from territory taken from the Diocese of St. Augustine; territory lost to the Diocese of Orlando and the Diocese of St. Petersburg, erected in 1968; elevated to the Archdiocese of Miami in 1968.

Diocese of Mobile (all of Alabama and the Florida Panhandle), renamed the Diocese of Mobile-Birmingham in 1954; redesignated the Diocese of Mobile (southern Alabama) in 1969 after the division of the Diocese of Mobile-Birmingham; lost territory to the Diocese of Pensacola-Tallahassee, erected in 1975.

Diocese of Mobile-Birmingham (all of Alabama and the Florida Panhandle], created in 1954 from the renaming of the Diocese of Mobile; divided into the Diocese of Birmingham and Diocese of Mobile in 1969.

Diocese of Nashville (all of Tennessee until territory lost to the Diocese of Memphis erected in 1970 and the Diocese of Knoxville erected in 1988).

Diocese of Natchez (all of Mississippi), renamed the Diocese of Natchez-Jackson in 1956.

Diocese of Natchez-Jackson (all of Mississippi), created in 1956 from the renaming of the Diocese of Natchez; territory lost to the Diocese of Biloxi, erected in 1977, when the remainder of the Diocese of Natchez-Jackson was renamed the Diocese of Jackson.

Diocese of Orlando (central Florida), erected in 1968 from territory taken from the Diocese of Miami and the Diocese of St. Augustine; territory lost to the Diocese of Palm Beach erected in 1984 and the Diocese of Venice, erected in 1984.

Diocese of Palm Beach (eastern Florida), erected in 1984 from territory taken from the Archdiocese of Miami and the Diocese of Orlando.

Diocese of Pensacola-Tallahassee (Florida Panhandle), erected in 1975 from territory taken from the Diocese of Mobile and the Diocese of St. Augustine.

Diocese of Raleigh (most of North Carolina and all of North Carolina after adding the Territorial Abbey of Belmont-Mary Help of Christians in 1960 [Gaston County]; territory lost to the Diocese of Charlotte, erected in 1971.

Diocese of Richmond (all of Virginia until territory lost to the Diocese of Arlington, erected in 1974).

Diocese of San Angelo (west Texas), erected in 1961 from territory taken from the Diocese of Amarillo, the Diocese of Austin, the Diocese of Dallas-Fort Worth, and the Diocese of El Paso; territory lost to the Diocese of Lubbock, erected in 1983.

Diocese of Savannah (southern half of Georgia), erected in 1956 with the division of the Diocese of Savannah-Atlanta.

Diocese of Savannah-Atlanta (all of Georgia), divided into the Diocese of Atlanta and the Diocese of Savannah in 1956.

Diocese of Shreveport (northern Louisiana), erected in 1986 with the division of the Diocese of Alexandria-Shreveport.

Diocese of St. Augustine (most of Florida until territory lost to the Diocese of Miami, erected in 1958); territory lost to the Diocese of Orlando and the Diocese of St. Petersburg, erected in 1968; territory lost to the Diocese of Pensacola-Tallahassee, erected in 1975.

Diocese of St. Petersburg (west Florida), erected in 1968 from territory taken from the Diocese of Miami and the Diocese of St. Augustine; territory lost to the Diocese of Venice, erected in 1984.

Diocese of Tyler (east Texas), erected in 1986 from territory taken from the Diocese of Beaumont, the Diocese of Dallas, and the Diocese of Galveston-Houston.

Diocese of Venice (west Florida), erected in 1984 from territory taken from the Archdiocese of Miami, the Diocese of Orlando, and the Diocese of St. Petersburg.

Diocese of Victoria in Texas (southeast Texas), erected in 1982 from territory taken from the Diocese of Corpus Christi, the Diocese of Galveston-Houston and the Archdiocese of San Antonio.

Source: http://www.catholic-hierarchy.org.

APPENDIX 2

Ordinaries of Catholic Dioceses in the South, 1945-1992

William L. Adrian, Bishop of Nashville, 1936–1969
Michael J. Begley, Bishop of Charlotte, 1971–1984
Raymond J. Boland, Bishop of Birmingham, 1988–1993
William D. Borders, Bishop of Orlando, 1968–1974
William Louis Boudreaux, Bishop of Beaumont, 1971–1977, Bishop of Houma-Thibodaux, 1977–1992
Andrew J. Brennan, Bishop of Richmond, 1926–1945
Joseph B. Brunini, Bishop of Natchez-Jackson (renamed Jackson in 1977), 1967–1984
Daniel M. Buechlein, Bishop of Memphis, 1987–1992
Christopher E. Byrne, Bishop of Galveston, 1918–1950
Edmond Carmody, Bishop of Tyler, 1982–2000
Coleman F. Carroll, Bishop of Miami, 1958–1968, Archbishop of Miami, 1968–1977
John Joseph Cassata, Bishop of Fort Worth, 1969–1980
John P. Cody, Apostolic Administrator of the Archdiocese of New Orleans, 1962–1964, Archbishop of New Orleans, 1964–1965
Thomas V. Daily, Bishop of Palm Beach, 1984–1990
Lawrence Michael DeFalco, Bishop of Amarillo, 1963–1979
Joseph P. Delaney, Bishop of Fort Worth, 1981–2005
Daniel F. Desmond, Bishop of Alexandria, 1932–1945
Thomas A. Donnellan, Archbishop of Atlanta, 1968–1987
John F. Donoghue, Bishop of Charlotte, 1984–1993
Norbert M. L. J. Dorsey, Bishop of Orlando, 1990–2004
Carroll T. Dozier, Bishop of Memphis, 1970–1982
Thomas J. Drury, Bishop of San Angelo, 1961–1965, Bishop of Corpus Christi, 1965–1983
Joseph A. Durick, Coadjutor Bishop of Nashville, 1963–1969, Bishop of Nashville, 1969–1975
John C. Favalora, Bishop of Alexandria, 1986–1989, Bishop of St. Petersburg, 1989–1994
David E. Fellhauer, Bishop of Victoria in Texas, 1990–2015
Joseph A. Fiorenza, Bishop of San Angelo, 1979–1984, Bishop of Galveston-Houston, 1984–2004, Archbishop of Galveston-Houston, 2004–2006
John J. Fitzpatrick, Bishop of Brownsville, 1971–1991
Laurence Julius FitzSimmon, Bishop of Amarillo, 1941–1958
Albert L. Fletcher, Bishop of Little Rock, 1946–1972
Patrick F. Flores, Bishop of El Paso, 1978–1979, Archbishop of San Antonio, 1979–2004
Harry J. Flynn, Bishop of Lafayette, 1989–1994
Gerard L. Frey, Bishop of Savannah, 1967–1972, Bishop of Lafayette, 1972–1989
William B. Friend, Bishop of Alexandria, 1982–1986, Bishop of Shreveport, 1986–2006

Francis J. Furey, Archbishop of San Antonio, 1969–1979

Sam J. Galip, Bishop of Alexandria, 1989–2003

Bernard J. Ganter, Bishop of Beaumont, 1977–1993

Mariano S. Garriga, Bishop of Corpus Christi, 1949–1965

Richard O. Gerow, Bishop of Natchez (renamed Natchez-Jackson in 1956), 1924–1967

Thomas K. Gorman, Bishop of Dallas-Fort Worth (renamed Dallas in 1969 after diocese divided), 1954–1969

Francis J. Gossman, Bishop of Raleigh, 1975–2006

Rene H. Gracida, Bishop of Pensacola-Tallahassee, 1975–1983, Bishop of Corpus Christi, 1983–1997

Thomas J. Grady, Bishop of Orlando, 1974–1989

Charles V. Grahmann, Bishop of Victoria in Texas, 1982–1989, Coadjutor Bishop of Dallas, 1989–1990, Bishop of Dallas, 1990–2007

Lawrence P. J. Graves, Bishop of Alexandria, 1973–1982

Charles P. Greco, Bishop of Alexandria, 1945–1973

Paul J. Hallinan, Bishop of Charleston, 1958–1962, Archbishop of Atlanta, 1962–1968

Philip M. Hannan, Archbishop of New Orleans, 1965–1988

Vincent M. Harris, Bishop of Beaumont, 1966–1971, Coadjutor Bishop of Austin, 1971, Bishop of Austin, 1971–1985

Charles E. Herzig, Bishop of Tyler, 1986–1991

William R. Houck, Bishop of Jackson, 1984–2003

Joseph L. Howze, Bishop of Biloxi, 1977–2001

Joseph P. Hurley, Bishop of St. Augustine, 1940–1949, Archbishop (Personal Title) of St. Augustine, 1949–1967

Francis E. Hyland, Bishop of Atlanta, 1956–1961

Peter L. Ireton, Bishop of Richmond, 1945–1958

Sam J. G. Jacobs, Bishop of Alexandria, 1989–2003

Charles M. Jarrell, Bishop of Houma-Thibodaux, 1992–2002

Jules B. Jeanmard, Bishop of Lafayette, 1918–1956

John R. Keating, Bishop of Arlington, 1983–1998

William T. Larkin, Bishop of St. Petersburg, 1979–1988

Emmanuel B. Ledvina, Bishop of Corpus Christi, 1921–1949

Raymond W. Lessard, Bishop of Savannah, 1973–1995

Stephen A. Leven, Bishop of San Angelo, 1969–1979

Oscar P. Lipscomb, Archbishop of Mobile, 1980–2008

Robert E. Lucey, Archbishop of San Antonio, 1941–1969

James P. Lyke, Archbishop of Atlanta, 1991–1992

Joseph P. Lynch, Bishop of Dallas (renamed Dallas-Fort Worth in 1953), 1911–1954

Eugene A. Marino, Archbishop of Atlanta, 1988–1990

Adolph Marx, Bishop of Brownsville, 1965

Leroy Theodore Matthiesen, Bishop of Amarillo, 1980–1997

John E. McCarthy, Bishop of Austin, 1985–2001

Charles B. McLaughlin, Bishop of St. Petersburg, 1968–1978

Andrew J. McDonald, Bishop of Little Rock, 1972–2000

Thomas J. McDonough, Bishop of Savannah, 1960–1967

John L. May, Bishop of Mobile, 1969–1980

Humberto S. Medeiros, Bishop of Brownsville, 1966–1970

Sidney M. Metzger, Bishop of El Paso, 1942–1978

John L. Morkovsky, Bishop of Amarillo, 1958–1963, Coadjutor Bishop of Galveston-Houston, 1963–1975, Bishop of Galveston-Houston, 1975–1984

John B. Morris, Bishop of Little Rock, 1907–1946

John J. Nevins, Bishop of Venice, 1984–2007

James D. Niedergeses, Bishop of Nashville, 1975–1992

Wendelin J. Nold, Bishop of Galveston (renamed Galveston-Houston in 1959), 1950–1975

Anthony J. O'Connell, Bishop of Knoxville, 1988–1998, Bishop of Palm Beach, 1998–2002

Gerald P. O'Hara, Bishop of Savannah, 1935–1959

Stanley J. Ott, Bishop of Baton Rouge, 1983–1992

Raymundo J. Pena, Bishop of El Paso, 1980–1994

Francis F. Reh, Bishop of Charleston, 1962–1964

Louis J. Reicher, Bishop of Austin, 1947–1971

Joseph F. Rummel, Archbishop of New Orleans, 1935–1964

John J. Russell, Bishop of Charleston, 1950–1958, Bishop of Richmond, 1958–1973

Enrique San Pedro, Bishop of Brownsville, 1991–1994

Maurice Schexnayder, Bishop of Lafayette, 1956–1972

Francis B. Schulte, Archbishop of New Orleans, 1988–2002

Michael J. Sheehan, Bishop of Lubbock, 1983–1993

John M. F. Smith, Bishop of Pensacola-Tallahassee, 1991–1995

John J. Snyder, Bishop of St. Augustine, 1979–2000

Jude Speyrer, Bishop of Lake Charles, 1980–2000

James F. Stafford, Bishop of Memphis, 1982–1986

Joseph V. Sullivan, Bishop of Baton Rouge, 1974–1982

Walter F. Sullivan, Bishop of Richmond, 1974–2003

Joseph K. Symons, Bishop of Pensacola-Tallahassee, 1983–1990, Bishop of Palm Beach, 1990–1998

Paul F. Tanner, Bishop of St. Augustine, 1968–1979

David B. Thompson, Bishop of Charleston, 1990–1999

Thomas J. Toolen, Bishop of Mobile, 1927–1954, Archbishop (Personal Title) of Mobile-Birmingham, 1954–1969

Robert E. Tracy, Bishop of Baton Rouge, 1961–1974

Thomas A. Tschoepe, Bishop of San Angelo, 1966–1969, Bishop of Dallas, 1969–1990

Ernest L. Unterkoefler, Bishop of Charleston, 1964–1990

Joseph G. Vath, Bishop of Birmingham, 1969–1987

Emmet M. Walsh, Bishop of Charleston, 1927–1949

Vincent S. Waters, Bishop of Raleigh, 1945–1974

Thomas J. Welsh, Bishop of Arlington, 1974–1983

Source: http://www.catholic-hierarchy.org.

APPENDIX 3

Major Catholic Diocesan Newspapers in the South, 1945-1992

Acadiana Catholic (Diocese of Lafayette, 1985–)
Alamo Messenger (Archdiocese of San Antonio, 1957–1972)
Alamo Register (Archdiocese of San Antonio, 1942–1957)
Amarillo Register (Diocese of Amarillo, 1948–1956)
Arkansas Catholic (Diocese of Little Rock, 1986–)
Bulletin of the Catholic Laymen's Association of Georgia (Diocese of Savannah/Diocese of
    Savannah-Atlanta, 1920–1963)
Catholic Action of the South (Archdiocese of New Orleans, 1932–1963)
Catholic Banner (Diocese of Charleston, 1951–1990, published for many years as a section of
    the national Catholic weekly, *Our Sunday Visitor*)
Catholic Commentator (Diocese of Baton Rouge, 1963–)
Catholic East Texas (Diocese of Tyler, 1987–)
Catholic Journal (Diocese of Austin, 1982–1983)
Catholic Lighthouse (Diocese of Victoria, 1986–)
Catholic Spirit (Diocese of Austin, 1983–)
Catholic Virginian (Diocese of Richmond, 1925–)
Catholic Week (Diocese of Mobile/Diocese of Mobile-Birmingham/Archdiocese of Mobile, 1934–)
Church Today (Diocese of Alexandria, c. 1970–)
Clarion Herald (Archdiocese of New Orleans, 1963–)
East Texas Catholic (Diocese of Beaumont, 1982–)
Florida Catholic (1939–, most Catholic dioceses in Florida, except the Diocese of Miami/
    Archdiocese of Miami, 1958–1990)
Georgia Bulletin (Archdiocese of Atlanta, 1964–)
(Southern) Guardian (Diocese of Little Rock, 1911–1986)
Lone Star Catholic (Diocese of Austin, 1957–1961)
Lone Star Register (Diocese of Austin, 1961–1968)
Mississippi Register (Diocese of Natchez/Diocese of Natchez-Jackson, 1953–1970)
Mississippi Today (Diocese of Natchez-Jackson/Diocese of Jackson/Diocese of Biloxi, 1970–1999)
Morning Star (Diocese of Lafayette, 1970–1985)
New Catholic Miscellany (Diocese of Charleston, 1991–2002)
North Carolina Catholic (Diocese of Raleigh/Diocese of Charlotte, 1946–2005)
North-Central Louisiana Register (Diocese of Alexandria, c. 1954–c. 1970)
North Texas Catholic (Diocese of Fort Worth, 1985–)
Rio Grande Catholic (Diocese of El Paso, 1991–)
Southern Cross (Diocese of Savannah, 1963–)
South Plains Catholic (Diocese of Lubbock, 1985–)

South Texas Catholic (Diocese of Corpus Christi, 1980–)
South West Catholic Register (Diocese of El Paso, 1922–1967)
Southwest Louisiana Register (Diocese of Lafayette, 1954–1970)
Tennessee Register (Diocese of Nashville, 1924–)
Texas Catholic (Diocese of Dallas, 1952–)
Texas Catholic, Fort Worth Edition (Diocese of Fort Worth, 1969–1984)
Texas Catholic Herald (Diocese of Austin edition, 1968–1980)
Texas Catholic Herald (Diocese of Beaumont edition, 1966–1982)
Texas Catholic Herald (Diocese of Galveston-Houston, 1964–)
Texas Concho Register (Diocese of San Angelo, 1964–1980)
Texas Gulf Coast Catholic (Diocese of Corpus Christi, 1970–1979)
Texas Gulf Coast Register (Diocese of Corpus Christi, 1964–1970)
Texas Panhandle Register (Diocese of Amarillo, 1936–1947)
Today's Catholic (Archdiocese of San Antonio, 1972–)
Valley Catholic Witness (Diocese of Brownsville, 1967–1972)
Voice (Diocese of Miami/Archdiocese of Miami, 1959–1990)
West Texas Angelus (Diocese of San Angelo, 1980–)
West Texas Catholic (Diocese of Amarillo, 1985–)
West Texas Register (Diocese of Amarillo, 1956–1984)

* The *Southern Guardian* became the *Guardian* on June 26, 1915.

Source: Diocesan newspapers; James F. Vanderholt, "Catholic Journalism," *Handbook of Texas Online*, accessed October 20, 2013, http://www.tshaonline.org/handbook/online/articles/emco1, Published by the Texas State Historical Association; Candy Brunet e-mail to author, October 28, 2013.

APPENDIX 4

The Catholic Population in the South, 1945–1980*

Year	Total population	Catholic population
1945	27,304,790	1,900,356 (6.96% of total population)
1954	36,226,637	2,971,241 (8.2%)
1964	41,248,795	4,452,015 (10.79%)
1980	57,281,432	6,006,203 (10.49%)

* The South is defined here as Alabama, Arkansas, Florida, Georgia, Louisiana, Mississippi, North Carolina, South Carolina, Tennessee, Texas, and Virginia. The figures are derived from the Catholic and total populations in those states' archdioceses and dioceses.

Source: *The Official Catholic Directory Anno Domini 1945* (New York: P. J. Kenedy and Sons, 1945), General Summary, 2; *The Official Catholic Directory Anno Domini 1954* (New York: P. J. Kenedy and Sons, 1954), General Summary, 2; *The Official Catholic Directory Anno Domini 1964* (New York: P. J. Kenedy and Sons, 1964), General Summary, 2; *The Official Catholic Directory Anno Domini 1980* (New York: P. J. Kenedy and Sons, 1980), General Summary, 2–3.

APPENDIX 5

The African American Catholic Population in the South, 1945-1975*

Year	African American Catholics
1945	142,505
1954	207,202
1965	281,593
1970	288,489
1975	290,450

* The South is defined here as Alabama, Arkansas, Florida, Georgia, Louisiana, Mississippi, North Carolina, South Carolina, Tennessee, Texas, and Virginia. The figures refer only to those African American Catholics who attended black churches and missions.

Source: *Our Negro and Indian Missions: Annual Report of the Secretary of the Commission for the Catholic Missions Among the Colored People and the Indians*, January 1946, 17–18, January 1955, 22–23, January 1966, 21–22, January 1971, 21–22, January 1976, 21–22, Archives of the Society of Saint Joseph of the Sacred Heart, Baltimore, Maryland.

NOTES

Preface

1. Marilyn Wenzke Nickels, *Black Catholic Protest and the Federated Colored Catholics, 1917-1933* (New York: Garland, 1988), 294-95; Mel Piehl, "American Catholics and Social Reform, 1789-1989," in *Perspectives on the American Catholic Church, 1789-1989*, ed. Stephen J. Vicchio and Virginia Geiger (Westminster, MD: Christian Classics, 1989), 335.

2. R. Bentley Anderson, *Black, White, and Catholic: New Orleans Interracialism, 1947-1956* (Nashville: Vanderbilt University Press, 2005), xvii.

3. William A. Osborne, *The Segregated Covenant: Race Relations and American Catholics* (New York: Herder and Herder, 1967); Stephen J. Ochs, *Desegregating the Altar: The Josephites and the Struggle for Black Priests, 1871-1960* (Baton Rouge: Louisiana State University Press, 1990); Anderson, *Black, White, and Catholic*; Andrew S. Moore, *The South's Tolerable Alien: Roman Catholics in Alabama and Georgia, 1945-1970* (Baton Rouge: Louisiana State University Press, 2007); Amy L. Koehlinger, *The New Nuns: Racial Justice and Religious Reform in the 1960s* (Cambridge, MA: Harvard University Press, 2007).

Introduction

1. Cyprian Davis, O.S.B., *The History of Black Catholics in the United States* (New York: Crossroad, 1990), 20, 35-237, 252-54, 274 n. 56; James Hennesey, S.J., *American Catholics: A History of the Roman Catholic Community in the United States*, with a Foreword by John Tracy Ellis (New York: Oxford University Press, 1981), 143-57 (quotation on p. 144); Dolores Egger Labbé, *Jim Crow Comes to Church: The Establishment of Segregated Catholic Parishes in South Louisiana*, 2d ed. (New York: Arno Press, 1978 [Lafayette: University of Southwestern Louisiana, 1971]), 8, 11-13; Ronald L. Sharps, "Black Catholics in the United States: A Historical Chronology," *U.S. Catholic Historian* 12 (Winter 1994): 119-21; R. Emmett Curran, S.J., "'Splendid Poverty': Jesuit Slaveholding in Maryland, 1805-1838," in *Catholics in the Old South: Essays on Church and Culture*, ed. Randall M. Miller and Jon L. Wakelyn (Macon, GA: Mercer University Press, 1983), 125-26, 129-46; Sr. Frances Jerome Woods, C.D.P., "Congregations of Religious Women in the Old South," in *Catholics in the Old South*, ed. Miller and Wakelyn, 112-15; James B. Bennett, *Religion and the Rise of Jim Crow in New Orleans* (Princeton, NJ: Princeton University Press, 2005), 138-40.

2. Davis, *History of Black Catholics in the United States*, 99-104; Diane Batts Morrow, "Outsiders Within: The Oblate Sisters of Providence in 1830s Church and Society," *U.S. Catholic Historian* 15 (Spring 1997): 35-54; Sr. M. Reginald Gerdes, O.S.P., "To Educate and Evangelize: Black Catholic Schools of the Oblate Sisters of Providence (1828-1880)," *U.S. Catholic Historian* 7 (Spring-Summer 1988): 183-99.

3. Davis, *History of Black Catholics in the United States*, 39–40, 46–48, 276 n. 82; John T. McGreevy, *Catholicism and American Freedom: A History* (New York: W. W. Norton, 2003), 49–50, 52; Randall M. Miller, "Slaves and Southern Catholicism," in *Masters and Slaves in the House of the Lord: Race and Religion in the American South, 1740–1870*, ed. John B. Boles (Lexington: University Press of Kentucky, 1988), 130; Madeleine Hooke Rice, *American Catholic Opinion in the Slavery Controversy* (New York: Columbia University Press, 1944), 62–69; Mel Piehl, "American Catholics and Social Reform, 1789–1989," in *Perspectives on the American Catholic Church, 1789–1989*, ed. Stephen J. Vicchio and Virginia Geiger (Westminster, MD: Christian Classics, 1989), 319–20; Randall M. Miller, "The Failed Mission: The Catholic Church and Black Catholics in the Old South," in *Catholics in the Old South*, ed. Miller and Wakelyn, 156, 170; Bennett, *Religion and the Rise of Jim Crow in New Orleans*, 148–49, 152.

4. Miller, "Slaves and Southern Catholicism," 128–33 (quotation on p. 130); Curran, "Splendid Poverty," 126, 129–46; Randall M. Miller, "A Church in Cultural Captivity: Some Speculations on Catholic Identity in the Old South," in *Catholics in the Old South*, ed. Miller and Wakelyn, 14–16.

5. Miller, "Slaves and Southern Catholicism," 135, 146–47; Miller, "A Church in Cultural Captivity," 41–42; John T. Gillard, *The Catholic Church and the American Negro* (Baltimore: St. Joseph Society's Press, 1929), 28–29; Bennett, *Religion and the Rise of Jim Crow in New Orleans*, 140–41, 143; Davis, *History of Black Catholics in the United States*, 90, 105–7; Tracy Fessenden, "The Sisters of the Holy Family and the Veil of Race," *Religion and American Culture* 10 (Summer 2000): 191, 195; Theresa A. Rector, "Black Nuns as Educators," *Journal of Negro Education* 51 (Summer 1982): 244, 246–47.

6. Miller, "Slaves and Southern Catholicism," 127, 132–33; Miller, "Failed Mission," 152–53; Bennett, *Religion and the Rise of Jim Crow in New Orleans*, 137; Dennis C. Rousey, "Catholics in the Old South: Their Population, Institutional Development, and Relations with Protestants," *U.S. Catholic Historian* 24 (Fall 2006): 3–5, 5 n. 9; Stephen J. Ochs, *Desegregating the Altar: The Josephites and the Struggle for Black Priests, 1871–1960* (Baton Rouge: Louisiana State University Press, 1990), 9–10, 17–18, 21.

7. H. Shelton Smith, *In His Image, but . . . Racism in Southern Religion, 1780–1910* (Durham, NC: Duke University Press, 1972), 74–128, 198–200; Aloysius F. Plaisance, O.S.B., "The Catholic Church and the Confederacy," *American Benedictine Review* 15 (June 1964): 159–67; Hennesey, *American Catholics*, 148–52, 154–55; Miller, "A Church in Cultural Captivity," 16; McGreevy, *Catholicism and American Freedom*, 71–72; Bennett, *Religion and the Rise of Jim Crow in New Orleans*, 152; James J. Thompson Jr., *The Church, the South and the Future* (Westminster, MD: Christian Classics, 1988), 35, 37–39.

8. Davis, *History of Black Catholics in the United States*, 116–20; Ochs, *Desegregating the Altar*, 39–41, 136; Hennesey, *American Catholics*, 161–62.

9. Joseph T. Leonard, S.S.J., *Theology and Race Relations*, with a Foreword by Most Rev. Patrick O'Boyle (Milwaukee: Bruce, 1963), 227; "From the Pastoral Letter of the Second Plenary Council of Baltimore on the Need to Evangelize Freed Slaves, 1866," in *American Catholics and Slavery, 1789–1866: An Anthology of Primary Documents*, ed. Kenneth J. Zanca (Lanham, MD: University Press of America, 1994), 255–57 (quotations on p. 256).

10. Miller, "Failed Mission," 167–69; Miller, "Slaves and Southern Catholicism," 149–50; Hennesey, *American Catholics*, 162–63; Ochs, *Desegregating the Altar*, 34–35, 38.

11. Cyprian Davis, O.S.B., "Black Catholics in Nineteenth-Century America," *U.S. Catholic Historian* 5 (1986): 11 (quotations); Davis, *History of Black Catholics in the United States*, 146–52; Beatrice H. Comas to the *New York Times*, June 21, 1988; Albert S. Foley, S.J., *God's Men of Color:*

The Colored Catholic Priests of the United States, 1854-1954 (New York: Farrar, Straus, 1955), 1-31; Albert S. Foley, S.J., "Adventures in Black Catholic History: Research and Writing," *U.S. Catholic Historian* 5 (1986): 106-11.

12. John T. Gillard, *Colored Catholics in the United States* (Baltimore: Josephite Press, 1941), 120-21; Edward D. Reynolds, S.J., *Jesuits for the Negro* (New York: America Press, 1949), 53-55; Sharps, "Black Catholics in the United States," 124; Bennett, *Religion and the Rise of Jim Crow in New Orleans*, 187; Davis, *History of Black Catholics in the United States*, 122-23, 130-31, 185; Gillard, *Catholic Church and the American Negro*, 38-39; *The Josephites: A Century of Evangelization in the African American Community* (Baltimore: St. Joseph's Society of the Sacred Heart, 1993), 10.

13. Ochs, *Desegregating the Altar*, 43-48; *Josephites*, 7, 9-10; Davis, *History of Black Catholics in the United States*, 125-32; Sharps, "Black Catholics in the United States," 124; Gillard, *Catholic Church and the American Negro*, 39-41.

14. Gillard, *Catholic Church and the American Negro*, 43; Gillard, *Colored Catholics in the United States*, 115-16; Davis, *History of Black Catholics in the United States*, 132-33; Ochs, *Desegregating the Altar*, 59-60, 62.

15. Gillard, *Catholic Church and the American Negro*, 42; Labbé, *Jim Crow Comes to Church*, 17-19; Bennett, *Religion and the Rise of Jim Crow in New Orleans*, 147-48, 150-51, 153, 163-64 (quotations on p. 164); Hennesey, *American Catholics*, 193.

16. Miller, "Slaves and Southern Catholicism," 145, 149; Bennett, *Religion and the Rise of Jim Crow in New Orleans*, 156-59; Labbé, *Jim Crow Comes to Church*, 19; William F. Powers, *Tar Heel Catholics: A History of Catholicism in North Carolina* (Lanham, MD: University Press of America, 2003), 383-84.

17. Labbé, *Jim Crow Comes to Church*, 38; Bennett, *Religion and the Rise of Jim Crow in New Orleans*, 160; Archbishop John Ireland, "No Barrier against Color," folder 9, box 48, Joseph H. Fichter Papers, Special Collections and Archives, Loyola University Library, Loyola University New Orleans, New Orleans, Louisiana; Leonard, *Theology and Race Relations*, 231, 285-86; Sr. Sharon M. Howell, CSJ, M.A., "'The Consecrated Blizzard of the Northwest': Archbishop John Ireland and His Relationship with the Black Catholic Community," in *Many Rains Ago: A Historical and Theological Reflection on the Role of the Episcopate in the Evangelization of African American Catholics* (Washington, DC: Secretariat for Black Catholics, National Conference of Catholic Bishops, 1990), 39-44.

18. Ochs, *Desegregating the Altar*, 62, 64; Davis, *History of Black Catholics in the United States*, 152-62; Foley, *God's Men of Color*, 32-41.

19. Ochs, *Desegregating the Altar*, 48-102, 111-14, 123-34; Foley, *God's Men of Color*, 42-62.

20. Davis, *History of Black Catholics in the United States*, 164-88 (second quotation on p. 187; third quotation on p. 188); David Spalding, C.F.X., "The Negro Catholic Congresses, 1889-1894," *Catholic Historical Review* 55 (October 1969): 337-42, 344-52 (first quotation on p. 347); Davis, "Black Catholics in Nineteenth-Century America," 14; Albert J. Raboteau, "Introductory Reflections," *U.S. Catholic Historian* 7 (Spring-Summer 1988): 299-300.

21. Spalding, "Negro Catholic Congresses," 353-55; Albert J. Raboteau, *A Fire in the Bones: Reflections on African-American Religious History* (Boston: Beacon Press, 1995), 128-29; Thomas W. Spalding, *The Premier See: A History of the Archdiocese of Baltimore, 1789-1994* (Baltimore: Johns Hopkins University Press, 1989), 288; Davis, "Black Catholics in Nineteenth-Century America," 15; Bennett, *Religion and the Rise of Jim Crow in New Orleans*, 148-49, 176.

22. Bennett, *Religion and the Rise of Jim Crow in New Orleans*, 147 193, 199-200; Ochs, *Desegregating the Altar*, 34-35; "Mother Katharine Is Dead," *Colored Harvest* 67 (April 1955):

10–11; *Century Book* (Bensalem, PA: Sisters of the Blessed Sacrament, 1991), 6–8, 17, 32–33, 38–55, 60–61, 63–64, 94–96, 98–101; Davis, *History of Black Catholics in the United States*, 135–36; "Sisters of the Blessed Sacrament," *Josephite Harvest* 78 (January–February 1966): 9; "Mother Katherine Drexel's Nuns in Macon and Atlanta," *Bulletin of the Catholic Laymen's Association of Georgia*, January 31, 1936; Sr. Patricia Lynch, S.B.S., *Sharing the Bread in Service: Sisters of the Blessed Sacrament, 1891–1991* (Bensalem, PA: Sisters of the Blessed Sacrament, 2001 [1998]), vol. 1, 96–109, 143–47, 182–88, 192–273, vol. 2, 9–11, 16–19, 35–51, 84–86, 99–103; Labbé, *Jim Crow Comes to Church*, 24.

23. "Dedication Ceremonies Conducted by Archbishop Janssens," attached to S. J. Iverson to Robert E. Tracy, July 2, 1963, box "School Integration Files, 1956–1965" AR/00166, folder "School Integration File Diocese of Baton Rouge Controversy September, 1961–February, 1964," Archives of the Archdiocese of New Orleans, New Orleans, Louisiana; Labbé, *Jim Crow Comes to Church*, 28, 30–31, 34, 37; Bennett, *Religion and the Rise of Jim Crow in New Orleans*, 157–58, 162–76; Leonard, *Theology and Race Relations*, 232; Ochs, *Desegregating the Altar*, 68.

24. "Dedication Ceremonies Conducted by Archbishop Janssens"; Labbé, *Jim Crow Comes to Church*, 33, 38–39; Bennett, *Religion and the Rise of Jim Crow in New Orleans*, 157–58, 188.

25. Bennett, *Religion and the Rise of Jim Crow in New Orleans*, 157–58, 165–66, 173, 178; Ochs, *Desegregating the Altar*, 68; Howell, "The Consecrated Blizzard of the Northwest," 39–40, 43; "Vatican City Daily Praises Archbishop's Action in Condemning Racial Prejudice," *Catholic Action of the South*, October 23, 1955; Spalding, *Premier See*, 285–86, 288.

26. *Josephites*, 26; *The Word in the World: Divine Word Missionaries '76 Black Apostolate* (N.p., n.d.), 66; Sharps, "Black Catholics in the United States," 127; Bennett, *Religion and the Rise of Jim Crow in New Orleans*, 199–200; "Franciscan Sisters Came Here in 1877," *Bulletin of the Catholic Laymen's Association of Georgia*, January 31, 1936; "Society of African Missions Nearly Thirty Years in Georgia," *Bulletin of the Catholic Laymen's Association of Georgia*, January 31, 1936; Gary Wray McDonogh, *Black and Catholic in Savannah, Georgia* (Knoxville: University of Tennessee Press, 1993), 90, 106–11; Davis, *History of Black Catholics in the United States*, 316 n. 131; Ochs, *Desegregating the Altar*, 179–80, 257.

27. Father G. Card. Gotti to "Your Excellency," January 18, 1904, RG13 Nicholas Gallagher Collection, Archives of the Archdiocese of Galveston-Houston, Houston, Texas; Davis, *History of Black Catholics in the United States*, 195–98, 200–204, 233–34; Richard A. Lamanna and Jay J. Coakley, "The Catholic Church and the Negro," in *Contemporary Catholicism in the United States*, ed. Philip Gleason (Notre Dame, IN: University of Notre Dame Press, 1969), 152; "The Catholic Board for Mission Work Among the Colored People," *Our Colored Missions* 28 (March 1942): 35; Ochs, *Desegregating the Altar*, 3–6, 135–75 (quotation on p. 141), 181–86, 219, 234–35, 276–77, 370, 440, 443; Labbé, *Jim Crow Comes to Church*, 64–65; Foley, *God's Men of Color*, 72–103; Bennett, *Religion and the Rise of Jim Crow in New Orleans*, 200–202.

28. Davis, *History of Black Catholics in the United States*, 236–37; Ochs, *Desegregating the Altar*, 182, 242; *New Catholic Encyclopedia*, 2d ed., vol. 8 (Detroit: Thomson Gale, 2003), s.v. "Knights of Peter Claver," by E. B. Perry and editors.

29. Davis, *History of Black Catholics in the United States*, 198, 206–8; Herbert J. May Jr., "A Canonical Investigation of Racial Parishes and Its Application to the Diocese of Lafayette, Louisiana, 1918–1978" (Degree of Licentiate in Canon Law diss., Catholic University of America, 1983), 66–68, 75–76, 78.

30. Bennett, *Religion and the Rise of Jim Crow in New Orleans*, 216; C. Joseph Nuesse, "Segregation and Desegregation at the Catholic University of America," *Washington History* 9 (Spring–Summer 1997): 56–60; William A. Osborne, *The Segregated Covenant: Race Relations and American Catholics* (New York: Herder and Herder, 1967), 29. Established in 1888, the Catholic University of America first admitted African American students in 1895. Albert S. Foley, S.J., "The Catholic University Story," *Interracial Review* 23 (September 1950): 134.

31. Davis, *History of Black Catholics in the United States*, 214–15, 220; Marilyn Wenzke Nickels, "Journey of a Black Catholic," *America* 135 (July 10, 1976): 6; Marilyn W. Nickels, "Thomas Wyatt Turner and the Federated Colored Catholics," *U.S. Catholic Historian* 7 (Spring–Summer 1988): 216–17, 220–26; Marilyn Wenzke Nickels, *Black Catholic Protest and the Federated Colored Catholics, 1917–1933* (New York: Garland, 1988), 2–4, 19–22, 31–32; Christopher J. Kauffman, *Faith and Fraternalism: The History of the Knights of Columbus, 1882–1982* (New York: Harper and Row, 1982), 190–227.

32. Davis, *History of Black Catholics in the United States*, 215–17 (quotations on p. 217), 313 n. 76; Ochs, *Desegregating the Altar*, 228.

33. Davis, *History of Black Catholics in the United States*, 231; Ochs, *Desegregating the Altar*, 179–81, 229, 246–54, 256–57.

34. Ochs, *Desegregating the Altar*, 257–58, 266, 272–74; Davis, *History of Black Catholics in the United States*, 240–42; Foley, *God's Men of Color*, 105–11. In 1929, the Handmaids of Mary joined with the Franciscan Third Order to form the Franciscan Handmaids of the Most Pure Heart of Mary. Sharps, "Black Catholics in the United States," 128.

35. Harry Sylvester, "Negro Seminary," *Commonweal* 33 (April 11, 1940): 615–16; "Sketch of St. Augustine's History," *St. Augustine's Messenger* 33 (March 1956): 72; Ochs, *Desegregating the Altar*, 266–73, 277; Sharps, "Black Catholics in the United States," 128–29.

36. Ochs, *Desegregating the Altar*, 289; Labbé, *Jim Crow Comes to Church*, 84–85; "Sisters of the Blessed Sacrament (1915) Foundress Directed Zeal to Black Catholics in La.," *Clarion Herald*, April 22, 1998; Lynch, *Sharing the Bread in Service*, vol. 1, 222–25.

37. Nickels, "Thomas Wyatt Turner and the Federated Colored Catholics," 225–32; Nickels, *Black Catholic Protest and the Federated Colored Catholics*, 305, 308; Thomas J. Harte, *Catholic Organizations Promoting Negro-White Race Relations in the United States* (Washington, DC: Catholic University of America Press, 1947), 2–5.

38. Nickels, "Journey of a Black Catholic," 6–8; Nickels, *Black Catholic Protest and the Federated Colored Catholics*, 16–18, 96–136, 286–312; Reynolds, *Jesuits for the Negro*, 194–95; Harte, *Catholic Organizations Promoting Negro-White Race Relations in the United States*, 6–8; George K. Hunton, *All of Which I Saw, Part of Which I Was: The Autobiography of George K. Hunton as Told to Gary MacEoin*, with an Introduction by Roy Wilkins (Garden City, NY: Doubleday, 1967), 58–59; W. E. B. Du Bois, "The Negro and the Catholic Church," *Crisis* 40 (March 1933): 68–69; John T. McGreevy, *Parish Boundaries: The Catholic Encounter with Race in the Twentieth-Century Urban North* (Chicago: University of Chicago Press, 1996), 45–47; Cyprian Davis, O.S.B., "Black Catholics in the Civil Rights Movement in the Southern United States: A. P. Tureaud, Thomas Wyatt Turner, and Earl Johnson," *U.S. Catholic Historian* 24 (Fall 2006): 77–78; Davis, *History of Black Catholics in the United States*, 252–53.

39. Nickels, "Thomas Wyatt Turner and the Federated Catholics," 230; "Congratulations and Prayers," *Colored Harvest* 71 (May 1959): 4–5; Ochs, *Desegregating the Altar*, 6, 321–43, 345; Foley, *God's Men of Color*, 124–62; Thaddeus C. Boucree, "Negro Priests, American Apostolate," *Our*

Colored Missions 39 (May 1953): 70; Mary Alice Fontenot and Kathleen Toups, *The Gentle Shepherd: A Memoir of Bishop Jules B. Jeanmard* (Rayne, LA: Hebert, 1998), xvii–xviii, 10, 41, 228.

40. *New York Times*, February 6, 2000; Lamanna and Coakley, "The Catholic Church and the Negro," 153–54; Osborne, *Segregated Covenant*, 33–34; McGreevy, *Parish Boundaries*, 31–32, 34–37; Patrick W. Carey, *Catholics in America: A History* (Westport, CT: Praeger, 2004), 106.

41. Thomas F. Doyle, "The Interracial Review: A Story of Ten Years," *Interracial Review* 17 (October 1944): 150; Harte, *Catholic Organizations Promoting Negro-White Race Relations in the United States*, 6–7, 9–61; Hunton, *All of Which I Saw, Part of Which I Was*, 57, 64–75, 88, 146–50; Frater Roy M. Gasnick, O.F.M., "A Short History of the Catholic Interracial Council," 7–9, folder 7, box 84, Louis J. Twomey Papers, Special Collections and Archives, Loyola University Library, Loyola University New Orleans (hereinafter cited as Twomey Papers); Nickels, *Black Catholic Protest and the Federated Colored Catholics*, 18; Ochs, *Desegregating the Altar*, 345–47; Martin A. Zielinski, "Working for Interracial Justice: The Catholic Interracial Council of New York, 1934–1964," *U.S. Catholic Historian* 7 (Spring–Summer 1988): 233–47.

42. Ochs, *Desegregating the Altar*, 349–50, 352–54; "Archbishop Rummel's Impact on Church Outstanding," *Clarion Herald*, November 12, 1964.

43. Hunton, *All of Which I Saw, Part of Which I Was*, 20; Nuesse, "Segregation and Desegregation at the Catholic University of America," 60, 63–66; Foley, "Catholic University Story," 134–35; Ochs, *Desegregating the Altar*, 355; Philip Gleason, *Contending with Modernity: Catholic Higher Education in the Twentieth Century* (New York: Oxford University Press, 1995), 155–56, 236, 367 n. 59; Harte, *Catholic Organizations Promoting Negro-White Race Relations in the United States*, 118–19, 123; Richard J. Roche, *Catholic Colleges and the Negro Student* (Washington, DC: Catholic University of America Press, 1948), 33–228. The Catholic University of America did not allow African American students to live in dormitories until 1949. Foley, "The Catholic University Story," 135.

44. "The Bishop's Teaching Authority," *American Ecclesiastical Review* 134 (April 1956): 274 (first quotation); Sr. Frances Jerome Woods, C.D.P., "The Popes on Minority Rights," 7–8 (second quotation on p. 8), folder 11, box 20, Twomey Papers; *The Church and Racism: Towards a More Fraternal Society* (Vatican City: Pontifical Commission "Justitia et Pax," 1988), 14–15; Roger-Henri Guerrand, "The Catholic Church's Struggle against Racialism," in *The Church and Racism*, ed. Gregory Baum and John Coleman (Edinburgh: T. C. Clark; New York: Seabury Press, 1982), 33; John LaFarge, S.J., *The Catholic Viewpoint on Race Relations* (Garden City, NY: Hanover House, 1956), 82–83; McGreevy, *Parish Boundaries*, 50–51; John LaFarge, "Summary of the Encyclical," *Catholic Mind* 37 (November 22, 1939): 921 (third quotation); Pius XII, "Progress and Problems of the American Church (*Serum Laetitiae*)," *Catholic Mind* 37 (November 22, 1939): 927 (fourth and fifth quotations).

45. Paul D. Williams, 2 page cv, August 2, 1977, Paul D. Williams, "How the Catholic Committee of the South Started," August 5, 1977, Paul D. Williams, "How I Became Interested in the South," August 5, 1977, folder "Catholic Committee of the South (Paul D. Williams), box 2, Paul D. Williams to Gerald P. O'Hara, May 3, 1939, Gerald P. O'Hara to Paul D. Williams May 6, 1939, folder 1, box 1, Paul D. Williams to Gerald P. O'Hara, January 20, 1941, 1, folder 6, box 1, Catholic Committee of the South Collection, Amistad Research Center, New Orleans, Louisiana (hereinafter cited as CCSC); *The Catholic Committee of the South, Report of the Proceedings and Addresses of the Second Annual Meeting, Birmingham, Alabama, April 20, 21 and 22, 1941*, 6–7, folder 2, box 34, Catholic Interracial Council of New York Collection, American Catholic

History Research Center and University Archives, Catholic University of America, Washington, DC (hereinafter cited as CICNYC); Vincent J. O'Connell, *Ten Years of the Catholic Committee of the South* (New Orleans: Catholic Committee of the South, 1949), 3–4, folder 1, box 4, series 20, National Catholic Conference for Interracial Justice Records, Marquette University, Milwaukee, Wisconsin; Wilfrid Parsons, "The Congress at Cleveland," *Columbia* 19 (August 1939): 2.

46. *The Catholic Committee of the South, Report of the Proceedings and Addresses of the Second Annual Meeting, Birmingham, Alabama, April 20, 21 and 22, 1941*, 5–7; Paul D. Williams to Gerald P. O'Hara, May 3, 1939, Gerald P. O'Hara to Paul D. Williams, May 6, 1939, folder 1, box 1, Gerald P. O'Hara to Fulton J. Sheen, March 20, 1940, folder 2, box 1, Paul D. Williams to Gerald P. O'Hara, January 20, 1941, 1–2, folder 6, box 1, "Minutes of the Meeting of the Bishops," January 29, 1941, folder 17, box 2, untitled biographical details of Gerald P. O'Hara, n.d., "A Brief Sketch of the Life of Rt. Rev. Msgr. T. James McNamara," n.d., Paul D. Williams, "How the Catholic Committee of the South Started," August 5, 1977, folder "Catholic Commitee of the South (Paul D. Williams)," box 2, CCSC; "Bishop Ireton's Death Ends Longest Period of Service in 138-Year History of Diocese," *Catholic Virginian*, May 2, 1958; Parsons, "The Congress at Cleveland," 2, 22; M. F. Everett, "Dawn over Dixie," *Interracial Review* 28 (January 1955): 11–12; Thomas E. O'Connell, "A New Chorus for Dixie," *Catholic Mind* 41 (January 1943): 36–37; Wilfrid Parsons, "Dawn over Dixie," *Columbia* 19 (June 1940): 5, 18; Harte, *Catholic Organizations Promoting Negro-White Race Relations in the United States*, 146.

47. Wilfrid Parsons, "Life and Death in Dixie," *Columbia* 20 (June 1941): 24; Gerald P. O'Hara to Peter L. Ireton, June 12, 1940, folder 3, box 1, Paul D. Williams to Richard O. Gerow, December 29, 1941, folder 10, box 1, Paul D. Williams to John X. Wegmann, June 8, 1942, folder 14, box 1, Gerald P. O'Hara to Jules B. Jeanmard, July 9, 1942, folder 16, box 1, Joseph F. Rummel to Gerald P. O'Hara, July 17, 1942, John X. Wegmann to Paul D. Williams, July 17, 1942, folder 17, box 1, John X. Wegmann to Paul D. Williams, October 8, 1942, folder 1, box 2, Paul D. Williams, "Some Qualifications," August 24, 1977, Paul D. Williams, "Mixed Meetings at CCS Conventions," August 27, 1977, 1, folder "Catholic Committee of the South (Paul D. Williams)," box 2, CCSC; Paul D. Williams to Peter L. Ireton, February 10, 1942, folder "Ireton, Bishop Peter L. Jan. 1939–Dec. 1942," no box, "Minutes of the Executive Board Meeting of the Catholic Committee of the South—Atlanta, Georgia, October 27, 1942," folder "Catholic Committee of the South," no box, Bishop Peter L. Ireton Papers, Archives of the Diocese of Richmond, Richmond, Virginia; Wilfrid Parsons, "No Lavender, No Old Lace," *Columbia* 22 (July 1943): 17; Edward J. Cleary, "Catholic Leaven at Work in Dixie," *Columbia* 23 (August 1944): 3, 15; Everett, "Dawn over Dixie," 11–13; Harte, *Catholic Organizations Promoting Negro-White Race Relations in the United States*, 148, 153.

48. "Victory and Peace. Statement Issued by the Archbishops and Bishops of the United States, November 14, 1942," 4–5 (quotations on p. 5), 7, folder 31, box 64, National Catholic Welfare Conference Collection, The American Catholic History Research Center and University Archives, Catholic University of America.

49. "Toward a Good Peace," *Catholic Virginian* 18 (December 1943): 46 (quotations); McGreevy, *Parish Boundaries*, 55.

50. Woods, "The Popes on Minority Rights," 11; Pope Pius XII, "Mystici Corporis Christi," *Catholic Mind* 41 (November 1943): 1–44. "For as the body is one and has many members, and all the members of the body, many as they are, form one body, so also it is with Christ. For in one Spirit we were all baptized into one body, whether Jews or Gentiles, whether slaves or free; and we were all given to drink of one Spirit." 1 Corinthians 12:12–13.

51. *The Catholic Committee of the South, Report of the Proceedings and Addresses of the Third Annual Meeting, Richmond, Virginia, April 26, 27 and 28,* 1942, 104 (first quotation), 112 (second quotation), folder 3, box 34, CICNYC; Williams to O'Hara, January 20, 1941, 1–2.

52. George K. Hunton, "The Richmond Conference," *Interracial Review* 17 (January 1944): 4–5; "Catholic Study Labor Relations," *Christian Century* 61 (February 9, 1944); Martensen, "Region, Religion and Social Action," 39, 41–42, 44–45 (quotation on p. 45); Harte, *Catholic Organizations Promoting Negro-White Race Relations in the United States*, 151–52; *New York Times*, April 13, 1943; "Southern Leaders Plan Solution of Racial Problems," *Bulletin of the Catholic Laymen's Association of Georgia*, April 24, 1943.

Chapter One

1. *The Official Catholic Directory Anno Domini 1964* (New York: P. J. Kenedy and Sons, 1964), General Summary, 2; Philip S. Ogilvie, "Quarterly Report (January 1, 1951 thru March 31, 1951)," 5, folder 20, box 2, Catholic Committee of the South Collection, Amistad Research Center, New Orleans, Louisiana (hereinafter cited as CCSC); "Bishop England High School, Charleston, S.C. 1964 Adult Lenten Series 'Religion and Race,'" folder 707.1/1, Archives of the Diocese of Charleston, Charleston, South Carolina (hereinafter cited as ADC); *New York Times*, October 3, 1954. Joseph T. Leonard, S.S.J., *Theology and Race Relations*, with a Foreword by Most Rev. Patrick A. O'Boyle (Milwaukee: Bruce, 1963), 248–49.

2. Numan V. Bartley, *The Rise of Massive Resistance: Race and Politics in the South during the 1950s* (Baton Rouge: Louisiana State University Press, 1969), 13–14; "The White-Negro Problem," *Catholic Digest* 20 (June 1956): 4. The 1956 poll of southern whites included Kentucky and Oklahoma, as well as the eleven former Confederate states.

3. Harold L. Cooper, S.J., "Priests, Prejudice and Race," *Catholic Mind* 57 (November–December 1959): 499–501; "Southern Field Service Report to the Directors of the National Catholic Conference for Interracial Justice August 1962," 8–10, folder 4, box 8, series 33, National Catholic Conference for Interracial Justice Records, Marquette University, Milwaukee, Wisconsin (hereinafter cited as NCCIJR); "Interpretation of Interviews Conducted with Selected Catholic Priests," n.d., 1–3, folder 10, box 1, Catholic Council on Human Relations Papers, Amistad Research Center (hereinafter cited as CCHRP); Joseph H. Fichter to Joseph F. Rummel, April 12, 19, 1956, folder 5, box 46, Joseph H. Fichter Papers, Special Collections and Archives, Loyola University Library, Loyola University New Orleans (hereinafter cited as Fichter Papers); *New York Herald Tribune*, April 8, 1962.

4. "Interpretation of Interviews Conducted with Selected Catholic Priests," 3–4; "Southern Field Service Report to the Directors of the National Catholic Conference for Interracial Justice August 1962," 8–9; Henry Cabirac to Francis J. Kichak, September 5, 1963, folder 11, box 9, series 33, NCCIJR; Joseph H. Fichter, *One-Man Research: Reminiscences of a Catholic Sociologist* (New York: John Wiley, 1973), 11, 47, 61, 76–111.

5. "Vatican City Daily Praises Archbishop's Action in Condemning Racial Prejudice," *Catholic Action of the South*, October 23, 1955; M. F. Everett, "No Race, Color Bar in Church," *Catholic Action of the South*, May 14, 1961; *Pacem in Terris: Encyclical Letter of Pope John XXIII, April 11, 1963* (Washington, DC: National Catholic Welfare Conference, 1963); *Arkansas Gazette*, October 25, 1963; Robert E. Tracy, *American Bishop at the Vatican Council: Recollections and Reflections*, 129–38, in "The Record of the Diocese of Baton Rouge in Work for the Negro in the

Community 1961–1968," Historical Vertical File, Archives of the Diocese of Baton Rouge, Baton Rouge, Louisiana (hereinafter cited as ADBR); R. Bentley Anderson, *Black, White, and Catholic: New Orleans Interracialism, 1947-1956* (Nashville: Vanderbilt University Press, 2005), xvi.

6. James J. Walsh to Henry Cabirac Jr., February 8, 1962, folder 8, box 1, CCHRP; John B. Hayes to Archbishop John T. Toolen, March 31, 1965, folder "Letters fav. to Toolen," box "Selma Demonstrations March 1965," Archbishop Thomas J. Toolen Papers, Archives of the Archdiocese of Mobile, Mobile, Alabama.

7. Mrs. J. C. Campbell, "Why Is an Integrated School Better Than a Segregated School?" n.d., folder 13, box 46, Charlotte Hays, "Visits with 2 Famous Segs," press clipping, no date, folder 11, box 52, Fichter Papers.

8. Vincent S. Waters, pastoral letter August 17, 1956, bound volume "Pastoral Letters V. S. Waters 1953–1956," Archives of the Diocese of Raleigh, Raleigh, North Carolina (hereinafter cited as ADR); Charles P. Greco, "Pastoral on Race Relations," August 4, 1963, folder 2, box 3, series 11, NCCIJR.

9. Donald A. Erickson and John D. Donovan, *The Three R's of NonPublic Education in Louisiana: Race, Religion, and Region* (Washington, DC: President's Commission on School Finance, 1972), 38, 69, 78–80, 97–98, 109–28, 132–35, 143–49, 187, 195, 198–201.

10. Stephen J. Ochs, *Desegregating the Altar: The Josephites and the Struggle for Black Priests, 1871-1960* (Baton Rouge: Louisiana State University Press, 1990, 399; *New Catholic Encyclopedia*, 2d ed., vol. 12 (Detroit: Gale, 2003), s.v. "Rummel, Joseph Francis," by H. C. Bezou; "Archbishop Rummel's Impact on Church Outstanding," *Clarion Herald*, November 12, 1964; Peter Finney Jr., "Abp. Rummel: Tireless Fighter for Desegregation," *Clarion Herald*, April 22, 1993 (quotation); *New York Times*, November 9, 1964; John B. Alberts, "Black Catholic Schools: The Josephite Parishes of New Orleans during the Jim Crow Era," *U.S. Catholic Historian* 12 (Winter 1994): 96–97.

11. Joseph F. Rummel to Richard O. Gerow, February 4, 1946, folder 4, box 7, Archbishop Joseph F. Rummel Papers, Archives of the Archdiocese of New Orleans (hereinafter cited as Rummel Papers, AANO); Ochs, *Desegregating the Altar*, 388, 399–400.

12. Rummel to Gerow, February 4, 1946 (first quotation), Gerald P. O'Hara to Joseph F. Rummel, February 8, 1946, Charles P. Greco to Joseph F. Rummel, February 9, 1946 (second quotation), J. A. Floersh to Joseph F. Rummel, February 14, 1946, William L. Adrian to Joseph F. Rummel, March 10, 1946, folder 4, box 7, Rummel Papers, AANO.

13. Thomas J. Toolen to Joseph F. Rummel, February 7, 1946 (quotation), Emmet M. Walsh to Joseph F. Rummel, February 16, 1946, John B. Morris to Joseph F. Rummel, February 19, 1946, folder 4, box 7, Rummel Papers, AANO; "Archbishop Thomas J. Toolen," *Catholic Week*, November 23, 1979.

14. Jules B. Jeanmard to Joseph F. Rummel, February 12, 1946, folder 4, box 7, Rummel Papers, AANO.

15. Richard O. Gerow to Joseph F. Rummel, February 12, 1946, folder 4, box 7, Rummel Papers, AANO.

16. Joseph F. Rummel to Francis B. Cotton, August 27, 1946, folder "Catholic Committee of the South—1946 7b I-c-16," "Catholic Committee of the South 78–014 box 1 52-03-06," AANO; Ochs, *Desegregating the Altar*, 403–4; "Minutes of Meeting of Southern Bishops," November 14, 1946, 1, folder "Catholic Committee of the South," Bishop Peter L. Ireton Papers, Archives of the Diocese of Richmond, Richmond, Virginia (hereinafter cited as Ireton Papers).

17. "Minutes of Meeting of Southern Bishops," November 14, 1946, 1–2 (quotations on p. 2); Ochs, *Desegregating the Altar*, 404.

18. "Commission Notes," *Christian Impact* 3 [The volume should be given as 4 (June 1953)]: 1, folder 1, box 4, series 20, NCCIJR; John E. Rousseau, "Negro Priest Ordained at St. Louis Cathedral," *Our Colored Missions* 39 (September 1953): 141 and *Claverite* 32 (July–August 1953): 15; "The Church and Desegregation," September 23, 1955, 7, folder "Catholic School Integration—Dept. of Health, Education + Welfare (1954–1972), 03-038 box 2, AANO; Ochs, *Desegregating the Altar*, 404.

19. Thaddeus C. Boucree, "Negro Priests, American Apostolate," *Our Colored Missions* 39 (May 1953): 70; Ochs, *Desegregating the Altar*, 404–5.

20. [Raleigh] *News and Observer*, March 20, May 16, 1945; Charles B. McLaughlin, "Much Progress Has Been Made . . . There Is Still Work to Be Done," *North Carolina Catholic*, February 9, 1964; Monsignor Thomas P. Hadden, interview by author, August 2, 2006; "Father Hadden Ordained in Rome," *Interracial Review* 32 (April 1959): 77; "Fr. Howze, First Negro Priest, Ordained by Bishop for Diocese," *North Carolina Catholic*, May 17, 1959.

21. Ochs, *Desegregating the Altar*, 405–6; Albert S. Foley, S.J., *God's Men of Color: The Colored Catholic Priests of the United States, 1854–1954* (New York: Farrar, Straus, 1955), 187–92.

22. John T. McGreevy, *Parish Boundaries: The Catholic Encounter with Race in the Twentieth-Century Urban North* (Chicago: University of Chicago Press, 1996), 71.

23. *The Official Catholic Directory Anno Domini 1964* (New York: P. J. Kenedy and Sons, 1964), General Summary, 2; Philip S. Ogilvie, "Quarterly Report (January 1, 1951 thru March 31, 1951)," 5, folder 20, box 2, Catholic Committee of the South Collection, Amistad Research Center, New Orleans, Louisiana (hereinafter cited as CCSC), February 16, 1964; "Racial Prejudice and a Southern Bishop," *St. Augustine's Messenger* 32 (September 1955): 268; William F. Powers, *Tar Heel Catholics: A History of Catholicism in North Carolina* (Lanham, MD: University Press of America, 2003), 6–11.

24. John Strange, "Bishop Waters, Third Bishop of Raleigh, Firmly Establishes Catholic Community," *North Carolina Catholic*, November 14, 1999; Gerald P. Fogarty, S.J., *Commonwealth Catholicism: A History of the Catholic Church in Virginia* (Notre Dame, IN: University of Notre Dame Press, 2001), 504–5; *Our Negro and Indian Missions: Annual Report of the Secretary of the Commission for the Catholic Missions Among the Colored People and the Indians*, January 1944, 13–14, Archives of the Society of St. Joseph of the Sacred Heart, Baltimore, Maryland (hereinafter cited as ASSJ); "Inter-Racial Labor Series Comes to End," *Catholic Virginian*, March 12, 1948.

25. McLaughlin, "Much Progress Has Been Made" (quotations); "Carolina Negroes Praise the Church," *Interracial Review* 21 (June 1948): 97; John Strange, "The Truth Is Still There," *North Carolina Catholic*, March 26, 1995.

26. *Our Negro and Indian Missions*, January 1949, 9–13 (first quotation), January 1950, 7–11, 19–21 (second and third quotations), ASSJ.

27. Vincent S. Waters, pastoral letter, January 29, 1951, scrapbook "Ban on Segregation 1953 volume III," ADR.

28. Vincent S. Waters, pastoral letter, February 9, 1953, bound volume "Pastoral Letters V. S. Waters 1953–1956," ADR; Galatians 3:28.

29. Vincent S. Waters, pastoral letter, June 12, 1953, bound volume "Pastoral Letters V. S. Waters 1953–1956" (first, second, and third quotations), ADR; [Raleigh] *News and Observer*, June 22, 1953 (fourth quotation); [Greensboro, North Carolina] *Greensboro Daily News*, June 22, 1953.

30. "The Catholic Clergy Say: Segregation Is Forbidden in Catholic Churches," folder 19, box 52, Fichter Papers.

31. "Minutes of the Monthly Meeting of the Commission on Human Rights of the Catholic Committee of the South," May 22, 1949, 3, folder 16, box 47, "Minutes of the Regular Monthly Meeting of the Commission on Human Rights of the Catholic Committee of the South," September 25, 1949, 1–2, "Minutes of the Special Meeting of September 29, 1949, Commission on Human Rights, Catholic Committee of the South," 1–2, "Minutes of the Meeting of Sunday, October 23, 1949 of the Commission on Human Rights of the Catholic Committee of the South," 2, folder 17, box 47, Lucien J. Caillouet, "Statement," September 27, 1949, Josephite Fathers, Vincentian Fathers, and Holy Ghost Fathers to Joseph F. Rummel, September 29, 1949, folder 14, box 52, Fichter Papers; Philip S. Ogilvie to Mari Sabusawa, October 24, 1949, folder 15, box 29, John LaFarge Papers, Georgetown University Library, Special Collections, Division, Washington, DC; "No Negroes in Holy Hour Procession, Park Rules," *Catholic Action of the South*, September 22, 1949; "Decision on Holy Hour March Waits Archbishop," *Catholic Action of the South*, September 29, 1949; [New Orleans] *Times-Picayune*, October 2, 1949 (first quotation); *New York Times*, October 15, 1955; [New Orleans] *Louisiana Weekly*, October 15, 1949 (second quotation); "Archbishop Cancels Program Because of Segregation," *Interracial Review* 22 (October 1949): 146; "Race Bigotry Cancels a Holy Hour," *Interracial Review* 22 (October 1949): 149; "Preaching and Practicing," *Ave Maria* 70 (October 29, 1949): 546–47; Adam Fairclough, *Race and Democracy: The Civil Rights Struggle in Louisiana, 1915–1972* (Athens: University of Georgia Press, 1995), 171; Ochs, *Desegregating in the Altar*, 368. The stadium in City Park that hosted the event had segregated seating. Anderson, *Black, White, and Catholic*, 57–59.

32. Joseph H. Fichter to Charles J. Plauche, May 9, 1950 (quotation), folder 15, box 52, "Extract of Diocesan Synod Archdiocese of New Orleans, 1950. Title IX *On Bringing about the Salvation of the Negro*," folder 5, box 48, Fichter Papers. In November 1950, Fichter reported that "discriminatory signs had disappeared from New Orleans' churches" but did not comment on whether ushers in some churches were still enforcing segregation. "Minutes of the meeting of the Advisory Board of the Commission on Human Rights," November 27, 1950, 1, folder 13, box 47, Fichter Papers.

33. L. J. Twomey to Vincent A. McCormick, September 18, 1951, 3, folder 8, box 19, L. J. Twomey to William J. Dunne, April 18, 1960, folder 4, box 21, L. J. Twomey to Charles Vatterott, December 6, 1963, folder 15, box 21, Louis J. Twomey Papers, Special Collections and Archives, Loyola University Library, Loyola University New Orleans (hereinafter cited as Twomey Papers); C. J. McNaspy, S.J., *At Face Value*, with a Foreword by Walker Percy and an Afterword by David A. Boileau (New Orleans: Institute of Human Relations, Loyola University of the South, 1978), 21, 73–74; Fichter, *One-Man Research*, 76–77, 113 n. 3; Joseph H. Fichter, "First Black Students at Loyola University: A Strategy to Obtain Teacher Certification," *Journal of Negro Education* 56 (Autumn 1987): 548–49; Joseph H. Fichter, *The Sociology of Good Works: Research in Catholic America*, with a Foreword by Paul M. Roman (Chicago: Loyola University Press, 1993), 95; Anderson, *Black, White, and Catholic*, 63–65, 79–80, 236 n. 27; Stephen P. Ryan, "Racial Attitudes in the South Today," *America* 84 (November 11, 1950): 158; Fairclough, *Race and Democracy*, 173–74. Fichter misdates the admission of the Sisters of the Holy Family to Loyola University of the South to 1951.

34. "Minutes of the Provincial Meeting on Interracial Relations, Grand Coteau, Louisiana, August 28, 29, 1952," 1–56 (first quotation on p. 2; second and third quotations on p. 6), Archives of the New Orleans Province of the Society of Jesus, Special Collections and Archives, Loyola University Library, Loyola University New Orleans; "An Epochal Pronouncement," *Blueprint* 7 (September 1954): 1, A. W. Crandell to "Reverend Fathers and dear Brothers in Christ," September 9, 1954, *Blueprint* (Special Service Edition, September 30, 1954): 1, Special Collections and Archives, Loyola University Library, Loyola University New Orleans; Twomey to Dunne, April

18, 1960, folder 4, box 21, Twomey Papers; Anderson, *Black, White, and Catholic*, 100–102; Fairclough, *Race and Democracy*, 174. The New Orleans Province comprised Alabama, Arkansas, Florida, Georgia, Louisiana, Mississippi, South Carolina, Tennessee, Texas, and New Mexico. The recommendations made at Grand Coteau became the basis of an official policy proclaimed in September 1954. R. Bentley Anderson, "Black, White, and Catholic: Southern Jesuits Confront the Race Question, 1952," *Catholic Historical Review* 91 (July 2005): 484–505. In 1949, Spring Hill College desegregated its summer school, and, in 1952, it admitted African Americans to evening classes taught at a Catholic high school. Charles Stephen Padgett, "Schooled in Invisibility: The Desegregation of Spring Hill College, Mobile, Alabama, 1948–1963" (PhD diss., University of Georgia, 2000), 46, 49–50; Charles S. Padgett, "'Without Hysteria or Unnecessary Disturbance': Desegregation at Spring Hill College, Mobile, Alabama, 1948–1954," *History of Education Quarterly* 41 (Summer 2001): 180, 182–83.

35. Joseph F. Rummel, "To the Clergy, Religious and Laity, Archdiocese of New Orleans," *Catholic Action of the South*, February 8, 1951.

36. "2 Archdiocesan HN Units Will Merge," *Catholic Action of the South*, November 6, 1952; "New Orleans Holy Name Union Votes Negro Units as Members," *Interracial Review* 25 (November 1952): 186.

37. "Pastoral Message of Archbishop Rummel: 'Let There Be No Segregation,'" folder 4, box 8, series 33, NCCIJR.

38. Fichter, *One-Man Research*, 105 (quotation); Commission on Human Rights to Joseph Francis Rummel, October 24, 1953, folder 16, box 45, Fichter Papers.

39. Saul E. Bronder, *Social Justice and Church Authority: The Public Life of Archbishop Robert E. Lucey* (Philadelphia: Temple University Press, 1982), 3–41, 45, 53–60, 63–67.

40. "Inter-racial Committee Is Headed by Brother Schnepp," *Alamo Register*, October 29, 1943; *Interracial Justice* (San Antonio: San Antonio Archdiocesan Committee on Interracial Relations, 1945), Georgetown University Library, Special Collections Division, Washington, DC; Daniel M. Cantwell, *Catholics Speak on Race Relations* (Chicago: Fides, 1952), 22, 30; "Racial Discrimination Always Works Injustice," *Interracial Review* 20 (December 1947): 193; Robert E. Lucey, "Who Is My Neighbor?" October 19, 1947, 3–9 (first quotation on p. 7; second quotation on p. 3), folder "Lucey Social Problems Folder 1," Robert E. Lucey to "Reverend and dear Father," February 28, 1948 (third quotation), folder "Organizations and Societies Catholic Interracial Council (1945–1969)," Archives of the Archdiocese of San Antonio, San Antonio, Texas (hereinafter cited as AASA); "Human Rights Transcend States' Rights," *Interracial Justice* 21 (November 1948): 162; "Texas Catholic Council Approves FEPC Report," *Interracial Review* 21 (May 1948): 80.

41. J. L. Manning to Henry Cabirac Jr., May 10, 1961 (quotation), folder 6, box 17, series 33, NCCIJR; J. L. Manning to Henry Cabirac Jr., June 14, 1961, February 7, 1962, folder 8, box 1, CCHRP; Solomon J. Karan to Vince Brangan, October 16, 1957, folder "[Texas] State Council State Officers State Deputy N.A. Quintanilla Corres: Racial Discrimination Incidents," Catholic Archives of Texas, Austin, Texas (hereinafter cited as CAT).

42. Manning to Cabirac, May 10, 1961; Henry Ringkamp Sr. to "Father [Peter] Resch, Feast of Holy Rosary 1951," October 7, 1951, Robert E. Lucey to Henry Ringkamp, July 31, 1953 (second quotation), Marianist Archives, San Antonio, Texas; "Civil Rights Survey," May 16, 1952, 4, folder 7, box 85, National Catholic Welfare Conference Collection, American Catholic History Research Center and University Archives, Catholic University of America, Washington, DC (hereinafter cited as NCWCC); Robert E. Lucey to Reverend Mother M. Angelique, Reverend

Mother M. Laserian, Reverend Mother M. Rose Kallus, Reverend Mother M. Paz, June 12, 1953 (first quotation), folder "Lucey, Robert E. [Archbishop] Social Problems: Race Relations Folder # 2 (1951–1965)," AASA.

43. Memorandum, J. M. Boyle to "The Archbishop," January 5, 1954, attached to Robert E. Lucey to "Our Reverend Pastors, Brothers and Sisters," February 10, 1954, Marianist Archives; Lucey to Angelique, Laserian, Kallus, Paz, June 12, 1953 (first quotation); untitled memorandum by Raymond P. O'Brien, September 5, 1949, J. Nicholas to R. E. Lucey, September 10, 1949 and attached untitled memorandum by Paul Decker, September 13, 1949, folder "Lucey Social Problems Folder 1," AASA; Robert E. Lucey to "Dear Sister Superior," April 5, 1954 (second quotation), Robert E. Lucey to "Reverend and dear Father," April 5, 1954, folder "Lucey, Robert E. (Archbishop) Social Problems: Race Relations Folder # 2 (1951–1965)," AASA; "The Catholic Church and the Negro," *Ebony* 13 (December 1957): 26; "Color, Race, Poverty Cannot Bar Children from School," *Alamo Register*, April 9, 1954.

44. Bartley, *Rise of Massive Resistance*, 14; Bronder, *Social Justice and Church Authority*, 69 (quotation).

45. *Basilica of St. Mary of the Immaculate Conception Catholic Church 200th Anniversary, 1791–1991* (Virginia Beach, VA: Hill's Printing, 1991), 37; Liz Schevtchuk, "Catholics Old Target of Klan Hatred," *Tennessee Register*, April 20, 1987; "Klan Placards on Selma Church," *Alumni News* 2 (March 22, 1950), folder "Selma-St. Elizabeth's," Local Administration, box 25, Society of Saint Edmund Archives, St. Michael's College, Colchester, Vermont; "Persons, Places and Things," [Davenport, Iowa] *Catholic Messenger*, October 29, 1964; James J. Thompson Jr., *The Church, the South and the Future* (Westminster, MD: Christian Classics, 1988), 47–68.

46. "The Catholic Committee of the South," January 24, 1951, 1–2, 6–7 (quotation on p. 7), folder 1, box 4, series 20, NCCIJR; "CCS Starts Drive for Social Action," *Catholic Action of the South*, February 1, 1951; Katherine Ann Martensen, "Region, Religion and Social Action: The Catholic Committee of the South, 1939–1956" (Master's thesis, University of New Orleans, 1978), 58–59. Among the eleven southern states, only the dioceses in Texas and the dioceses of Little Rock and Nashville, which covered Arkansas and Tennessee respectively, were not represented at the convention by their ordinaries. "The Catholic Committee of the South," January 24, 1951, 1, folder 1, box 4, series 20, NCCIJR.

47. John J. McCann, "The Catholic Committee of the South Department of Race Relations Convention Workshop Report," 1951, 1–7 (quotation on p. 6), folder 20, box 2, CCSC; Martensen, "Region, Religion and Social Action," 60–61.

48. Mary Dominic to George D. Hunton, May 18, 1950, folder 9, box 10, John LaFarge Papers, Georgetown University Library, Special Collections Division, Washington, DC; Patricia McGerr, "Alabama's Interracial Monastery," *Interracial Review* 23 (August 1950): 118–19; "Interracial Convent," *Ebony* 6 (March 1951): 102–4, 106; "Archbishop Thomas J. Toolen," *Catholic Week*, November 23, 1979; Gretta Palmer, "Southern Catholics Fight Race Hatred," *Look* 14 (March 28, 1950): 98–100, 103 (quotation on pp. 99–100); Mother Mary of the Child Jesus, O.B. to "Dearest Friend," n.d. and attached press clipping, "Ever Feel Like Throwing a Few Bricks? Here's a Nun Who Would Like to Be on the Receiving End If You Do," July 1954, folder 19, box 45, Fichter Papers; Daniel A. Lord, "Race Relations in Practice," *Our Colored Missions* 32 (December 1946): 189.

49. *Nashville Tennessean*, February 14, 1972, vertical file Adrian, Tennessee State Library and Archives, Nashville, Tennessee; Thomas Stritch, *The Catholic Church in Tennessee: The Sesquicentennial Story* (Nashville: The Catholic Center, 1987), 319–21, 333–34, 353.

50. "Bishop Richard O. Gerow," *Mississippi Methodist Advocate*, October 14, 1964; Ochs, *Desegregating the Altar*, 423 (first quotation), 429–32 (second quotation on pp. 429–30).

51. Jules B. Jeanmard to "The Clergy, Religious and Laity, Diocese of Lafayette," November 28, 1951 (quotation), folder 15, box 52, Fichter Papers.

52. "Status of Integration in Catholic Education," *North Carolina Catholic*, June 18, 1954; "A Moral, Religious Problem," *Catholic Virginian*, May 21, 1954.

53. Stritch, *Catholic Church in Tennessee*, 334 (first quotation); M. F. Everett, "The Great Taboo," *Catholic Action of the South*, May 27, 1954; "N.O. School Board Okays Court Segregation Ban," *Catholic Action of the South*, June 3, 1954; "A Moral, Religious Problem"; [New Orleans] *Times-Picayune*, July 9, 1954 (second quotation).

54. Ochs, *Desegregating the Altar*, 426–27 (first quotation on p. 426); "Society Policy and Integration," July 1954 (second and third quotations), folder 9, box 51, Twomey Papers; Sister M. Agatha to Mother M. Anselm, October 30, 1952, folder 3, box 3 "Louisiana Corporation Minute Books," Xavier University Archives, New Orleans, Louisiana; "Xavier University Marks 30th Year," *Interracial Review* 28 (November 1955): 193; Sr. Patricia Lynch, S.B.S., *Sharing the Bread in Service: Sisters of the Blessed Sacrament, 1891–1991*, vol. 2 (Bensalem, PA: Sisters of the Blessed Sacrament, 2001 [1998]), 83; Crandell to "Reverend Fathers and dear Brothers in Christ," September 9, 1954, 1–6 (fourth quotation on p. 3); "President of Xavier University Addresses Educational Unit," *Interracial Review* 18 (March 1945): 34. In the early 1950s, Xavier University had admitted whites to Christian Doctrine classes and some whites to summer classes, as well as permitting white faculty to take its own courses. On May 26, 1954, nine days after the *Brown* decision, the university graduated its first white student, Sister Paul Mary, S.B.S., who received a degree in Pharmacy. The action suggests that the charter's alteration recognized a de facto reality. Agatha to Anselm, October 30, 1952; "Xavier University and Integration," *Christian Impact* 3 (May 1954), n.p., folder 2, box 47, Fichter Papers.

55. "Status of Integration in Catholic Education"; "Schools in Texas Admit Negroes," *Catholic Action of the South*, September 9, 1954; M. F. Everett, "Church Leads Way," *Catholic Action of the South*, September 16, 1954; Reed Sarratt, *The Ordeal of Desegregation: The First Decade* (New York: Harper and Row, 1966), 278–81, 352–54.

56. Earl Heffner, "High Schools and Hospitals Open Doors to All Catholics," *North Carolina Catholic*, September 10, 1954; Bishop Albert L. Fletcher to "The Clergy, Religious and Laity," August 3, 1954, *Guardian*, August 13, 1954; "Status of Integration in Catholic Education"; Everett, "Church Leads Way"; "Schools in Texas Admit Negroes"; "Catholics Out Front as Schools Put End to Race Segregation," *Tennessee Register*, September 19, 1954; Padgett, "Schooled in Invisibility," 24, 29, 49–52, 54; Padgett, "Without Hysteria or Unnecessary Disturbance," 167, 184–86; Milton Lomask, "Father Maurice Challenges the South," *Sign* 36 (November 1956): 17, 19–20; Sarratt, *Ordeal of Desegregation*, 278–79; John J. Russell to Paul F. Tanner, July 14, 1958, folder 13, box 89, NCWCC; Joseph Francis Rummel, "Integration in Catholic Schools," July 31, 1956, 1–3, folder 5, box 20, Twomey Papers; "The Archbishop's Way," *Newsweek* 67 (March 5, 1956): 80; "Integration in Schools Is Postponed," *Catholic Action of the South*, August 12, 1956; Joseph H. Fichter to David E. Freeman, March 17, 1956, folder 4, box 46, "A Report on School Desegregation for 1960–61," August 19, 1960, 9, folder 23, box 52, Fichter Papers; Fichter, *One-Man Research*, 88–106, 109, 111; *New York Times*, July 8, 1959.

57. John F. Cronin, "Religion and Race," *America* 150 (June 30, 1984): 472; memorandum, George G. Higgins to Monsignor Carroll, November 4, 1957, "Suggested Draft on Race

Question," November 1957, "mjb" note to "Thel," November 15, 1957 (quotation), John F. Cronin to Edward Mooney, September 4, 1958, folder 13, box 89, NCWCC; John T. Donovan, *Crusader in the Cold War: A Biography of Fr. John F. Cronin, S.S. (1908-1994)* (New York: Peter Lang, 2005), 5-7, 97-98. According to Cronin, Cardinal Edward F. Mooney of Detroit, the NCWC's head, told him that there was insufficient time to make the statement ready for consideration. Cronin, "Religion and Race," 472.

58. Paul F. Tanner to Archbishop Thomas J. Toolen, Bishop Vincent S. Waters, Bishop John J. Russell, and Bishop Albert L. Fletcher, July 8, 1958, George E. Lynch to Paul F. Tanner, August 19, 1958 (first quotation), Philip Cullen to Paul F. Tanner, July 10, 1958 (second quotation), folder 13, box 89, NCWCC.

59. Albert L. Fletcher to Paul Tanner, July 11, 1958, folder 13, box 89, NCWCC.

60. Cronin, "Religion and Race," 472 (first quotation); John F. Cronin to Edward Mooney, September 4, 1958, John F. Cronin to Patrick A. O'Boyle, September 4, 1958 (second and third quotations), Joseph E. Ritter to John F. Cronin, September 12, 1958 (sixth quotation), folder 13, box 89, NCWCC; Gerald J. Schnepp, "Integration in Catholic Schools," *St. Augustine's Messenger* 31 (September 1954): 226, 232-33, 248-49; Donovan, *Crusader in the Cold War*, 102 (fourth quotation), 102-3 (fifth quotation).

61. Thomas K. Gorman to John F. Cronin, September 12, 1958 (first and second quotations), John J. Russell to John F. Cronin, October 25, 1958, 2 (third quotation), folder 13, box 89, NCWCC.

62. Russell to Cronin, October 25, 1958, 1-2 (quotations on p. 1).

63. Donovan, *Crusader in the Cold War*, 103 (first quotation); Cronin, "Religion and Race," 472 (second quotation).

64. Cronin, "Religion and Race," 472; "Minutes of the Annual Meeting of the Bishops of the United States," November 12, 1958, 3-5, 7 (quotations), American Catholic History Research Center and University Archives; "Communications Coverage of Two 1958 Statements of U.S. Catholic Bishops: Discrimination and the Christian Conscience," February 23, 1959, 1-8, folder 10, box 65, NCWCC; *New York Times*, November 14, 16, 1958; *Washington Post*, November 14, 1958; "Text of U.S. Bishops on 'Enforced Segregation,'" *Guardian*, November 21, 1958; "Bishops See Race Question as Mainly Moral, Religious" and "Discrimination and the Christian Conscience," *Catholic Virginian*, November 21, 1958; "Hatred Must Not Divide Nation," *North Carolina Catholic*, November 23, 1958. In November 1958, the NCWC Administrative Board comprised twelve prelates, including some from areas that bordered the South, but none from the region itself. "Statement of the Bishops of the United States—1958," in "A Syllabus on Racial Justice Grades 7-12 [Diocese of Baton Rouge]," n.d., 25, folder 11, box 6, series 33, NCCIJR.

65. "Discrimination and the Christian Conscience" (quotations).

66. "Discrimination and the Christian Conscience" (quotations); *New York Times*, November 14, 1958; L. J. Twomey to Geno Baroni, January 8, 1959, Martin H. Work to L. J. Twomey, February 9, 1958 [1959], folder 14, box 20, Twomey Papers; "Archbishop Speaks Again on Integration," *Guardian*, August 26, 1960; "Council on Human Relations Is Seen as 'Holy Crusade,'" *Catholic Action of the South*, April 2, 1961; pastoral letter, February 19, 1961, folder 49, box 036/6, Archives of the Archdiocese of Atlanta, Georgia (hereinafter cited as AAA); "In . . . Black and . . . White," folder 720.1, ADC; Robert E. Tracy, "Bishop Tracy's Notebook," *Catholic Commentator*, June 14, 1963; John J. Russell, "Work for Racial Justice in Spirit of Christian Charity, Bishop Urges," *Catholic Virginian*, July 12, 1963.

67. *New York Times*, July 8, 1959 (quotation), April 17, August 30, 1962; Fairclough, *Race and Democracy*, 234–51, 254–60; [New Orleans] *Times-Picayune*, April 18, 1962; Newell Schindler, "Studies First Year of N.O. Integration," *Catholic Commentator*, June 7, 1963; "New Orleans Schools Open Peacefully," *Catholic Virginian*, September 11, 1963.

68. Pastoral letter, February 19, 1961, folder 49, box 036/6, AAA; W. J. Nold to the "Reverend Pastors of Galveston and Harris Counties," April 3, 1961, RG 2.1.9. Chancery files, Bishops' files, Nold Wendelin J., folder 14, box 3, Archives of the Archdiocese of Galveston-Houston, Houston, Texas (hereinafter cited as AAGH); John P. Sisson to Walter B. Clancy, March 4, 1966, folder 6, box 2, series 33, "Desegregation of Southern Parochial Schools," August 19, 1963, folder 3, box 13, series 34, NCCIJR; "Deep South Dioceses Integrate Parochial Schools" [Boston] *Pilot*, June 29, 1963; *New York Times*, August 23, 1960, September 17, 1961, April 1, 1963, April 27, 1964, August 22, 1965; "Charleston Area Parochial Schools Admit 15 Negro Students," *Catholic Banner*, September 8, 1963; "Former Negro School Enrolls 12 White Pupils" and "'Calm Dignity' Seen Marking Integration," *Catholic Virginian*, September 11, 1963; Bonnie W. Heflin, "Bishop Tracy Details Plan to Open 'Schools to All' by 1967," *Catholic Commentator*, June 11, 1965; Sarratt, *Ordeal of Desegregation*, 278–79; Monsignor Mortimer Danaher, telephone interview by author, August 12, 2006.

69. Everett, "No Race, Color Bar in Church" (quotation); "Archbishop Vagnozzi Is the Seventh Apostolic Delegate to the U.S.," *Catholic Banner*, April 24, 1960.

70. "Southern Field Service," *National Catholic Conference for Interracial Justice Newsletter* December 1961, 2, folder 1, box 1, series 8, Henry A. Cabirac Jr. to Charles P. Greco, February 5, 1963, folder 9, box 6, Henry A. Cabirac Jr. to R. F. Horn Jr., May 4, 1964, folder 12, box 9, series 33, NCCIJR; John P. Sisson, "For Racial Justice," *Our Sunday Visitor*, November 10, 1968; G. J. Tarleton Jr., interview by author, July 21, 2005; Robert Craighead, interview by author, July 19, 2005; William L. Adrian to G. J. Tarleton Jr. et al., April 30, 1962, William L. Adrian to "Dear Sirs and Ladies," July 19, 1962 (quotation), in possession of G. J. Tarleton Jr.; "Meeting in Nashville," September 25, 1963, folder 12, box 14, series 33, NCCIJR.

71. *Pacem in Terris*, 12 (first quotation), 22; "Interfaith Committee Is Formed to Fight Race Bias on Moral Plane," "Bishop Durick Attends Civil Rights Meet," and "Catholic Archbishop Says Race Crisis Now Raised to Proper Level" (second quotation) *Catholic Week*, June 21, 1963. The representatives of southern dioceses at the White House meeting were Archbishop John P. Cody, Administrator of New Orleans, Archbishop Paul J. Hallinan of Atlanta, and Bishops Coleman F. Carroll of Miami, Joseph A. Durick Auxiliary of Mobile-Birmingham, Albert L. Fletcher of Little Rock, Richard O. Gerow of Natchez-Jackson, Thomas J. McDonough of Savannah, Francis F. Reh of Charleston, John J. Russell of Richmond, and Vincent S. Waters of Raleigh. "Interfaith Committee Is Formed to Fight Race Bias on Moral Plane."

72. Approval slips for "pastoral letter on racial harmony," folder 16, box 89, General Secretary [Paul F. Tanner] to J. Arthur Newcomb, September 20, 1963, folder 17, box 89, NCWCC; "On Racial Harmony Joint Pastoral Letter of the Bishops of the United States—1963" (quotations), folder 5, box 17, series 33, NCCIJR; "Text of Race Pastoral" and Russell Shaw, "Hierarchy Repeats 1958 Query on Racial Justice," *Southern Cross*, August 22, 1963; "Bishops Ask Personal Involvement in Quest for Racial Harmony" and "Richmond, Northern Virginia Councils Prepare for 'March,'" *Catholic Virginian*, August 23, 1963; "Text of U.S. Bishops' Statement on Racial Harmony," *Catholic Commentator*, August 23, 1963; "Get Personally Involved in Promoting Race Harmony," *North Carolina Catholic*, August 25, 1963; "Prayer for Divine Guidance Climaxes Huge Rights March," *Guardian*, August 30, 1963; "Archbishop O'Boyle Prays for Guidance at

Rights March," *Catholic Virginian*, August 30, 1963; Russell Shaw, "August 28—It Was a Day to Be Remembered," *Alamo Messenger*, September 6, 1963.

73. "News of Interest to Our S.B.S. Family," May 7, 1965, S.B.S. Original Annals, vol. 48 (January 1965): 110, Mother M. David to "My dear daughters in the Blessed Sacrament," August 25, 1965, S.B.S. Original Annals, vol. 48 (May 1965–): 152, H40 A1, Archives of the Sisters of the Blessed Sacrament Archives, Bensalem, Pennsylvania; Lynch, *Sharing the Bread in Service*, vol. 2, 109, 116.

74. John J. Russell, "Work for Racial Justice in Spirit of Christian Charity, Bishop Urges," *Catholic Virginian*, July 12, 1963; "Russell Shaw, "Bishops' 1958 Query on Race Still Stands," *Catholic Virginian*, August 23, 1963; John J. Russell to Joseph G. LeFrois, August 30, 1963, folder "Interracial Correspondence," box H, Bishop John J. Russell Papers, Archives of the Diocese of Richmond, Richmond, Virginia (hereinafter cited as Russell Papers); untitled National Catholic Welfare Conference Bureau of Information press release, September 20, 1963, folder 1, box 1, series 11, NCCIJR; "Bishop Calls for Positive Approach to Integration," *Catholic Banner*, September 8, 1963; "Interfaith Clergy, Laity Will Seek Racial Amity," September 21, 1963, press clipping, "Houston Conference on Religion and Race," October 15, 1963, folder 4, box 7, Bishop John E. McCarthy Papers, CAT.

75. *Shreveport Times*, October 25, 1963; *Arkansas Gazette*, October 25, 1963; "Religion and Race," *Commitment*, January 1965, 1, folder 1, box 1, series 8, NCCIJR; *New York Times*, November 17, 1963 (quotations); "A Disappointing Statement," *Commonweal* 79 (November 29, 1963): 267–68.

76. "Statement on 'Rights,'" *Texas Catholic Herald* [Houston edition], June 4, 1964; "Bishop Fletcher Urges Full Compliance with Rights Law," *Guardian*, July 10, 1964; "La. Prelates Urge Lawful Compliance," *Catholic Commentator*, July 10, 1964 (quotation); "Prelates Hail Rights Law," *Tennessee Register*, July 10, 1964; "Religious Leaders Hail Signing of Rights Bill" and "41 Area Priests Sign Compliance Document," *Catholic Virginian*, July 10, 1964; "Massive Church Support Tipped Civil Rights Scale," *Alamo Messenger*, July 10, 1964; "Texas CSL Backs Civil Rights Act," *Alamo Messenger*, August 14, 1964; "Bishops Speak on the Civil Rights Law," *Josephite Harvest* 76 (July–August 1964): 1.

77. "Colored Catholics Admitted to KC in N. Carolina," *St. Augustine's Messenger*, 7 (September 1954): 251; L. E. H. [Luke E. Hart], "Memo for E. and F. Committee Meeting," December 13, 1955, SC-1-10-2036, Charles J. Morgan to R. G. Peters, May 11, 1962, SC-1-10-2037, "Knights of Columbus Supreme Council Proceedings, Eighty-Second Annual Meeting, New Orleans, Louisiana, August 18–19–20, 1964," 128–31, KC-17-2-1964, Knights of Columbus Supreme Council Archives, New Haven, Connecticut; "Urge Acceptance of Negroes in KC," *North Carolina Catholic*, July 28, 1963; "Moral Education, By-Laws Change May Be Solutions to KC Problem," *Alamo Messenger*, September 13, 1963; "K. of C.'s and Race," *America*, November 30, 1963; John J. Russell to Luke E. Hart, January 7, 1964, John J. Russell to William Morlino, July 7, 1966, William Morlino to John J. Russell, July 16, 1966, John J. Russell to Chaplains, August 29, 1966, John F. Barrett to John J. Russell, June 29, 1967, Clarence R. Carrico to John J. Russell, July 2, 1967, John J. Russell to John F. Barrett, July 5, 1967, folder "Knights of Columbus—State, 1960–1971," box H, Russell Papers; "K. of C. 'Blackballing,'" *America*, August 8, 1964; "Love Held Key to Racism," *Guardian*, October 16, 1964; "Membership Rules Change by K. of C.," *Texas Catholic Herald* [Houston], August 27, 1964; William J. Whalen, "The Knights of Columbus: Are They Obsolete?" *U.S. Catholic*, December 1964, 6–7; "Bishop Russell Chides Knights on Race," *Catholic Virginian*, June 24, 1966; "Quit, Biased KCs Are Told," *Alamo Messenger*, July 15,

1966; "Texas Knights Battle against Racial Bias," *Lone Star Register*, August 24, 1967, Nicholas Scheiders et al., to the *Catholic Week*, March 29, 1968; Vincent M. Harris, "Texas Knights Are Charged by State Chaplain," *Texas Knight* 1 (February 1969): 3, folder 2, box 222, CAT; Christopher J. Kauffman, *Faith and Fraternalism: The History of the Knights of Columbus, 1882–1982* (New York: Harper and Row, 1982), 396–97, 400–401.

78. "Meditation on the Race Problem," *America* 99 (May 24, 1958): 253–54; "The History of the Catholic Daughters of the Americas" (quotation), accessed September 1, 2008, at http://www.catholicdaughters.org/history.shtml; McLaughlin, "Much Progress Has Been Made"; "The Record of the Diocese of Baton Rouge in Undertaking Special Work on Behalf of the Negroes of the Community," Historical Vertical File, ADBR; "Report of Highlights of Citizens Council Meeting held May 8th, 1962," folder 24, box 2, series 34, Kathleen Woods, minutes of Catholic Interracial Council of Greater Little Rock board of directors meeting held September 14, 1966, September 16, 1966, attached to Kathleen Woods to James J. McGuire, September 14, 1966, folder 6, box 2, series 33, NCCIJR. Founded in Utica, New York, as the national order of Daughters of Isabella, the organization became the Catholic Daughters of America in 1921 and, reflecting its growing international membership, the Catholic Daughters of the Americas in 1954, although its former title remained widely used in the South through the 1960s and so is used here. Berard L. Marthaler, O.F.M.Conv., and Carol Dorr Clement, *Catholic Daughters of the Americas: A Century in Review* (New York: Catholic Daughters of the Americas and Mercury Publishing Services, 2003), 9–10, 46, 105; "The History of the Catholic Daughters of the Americas."

79. "Archbishop Hallinan Cites Church in Human Relations," *Georgia Bulletin*, August 5, 1965, press clipping, folder 6, box 3, series 11, NCCIJR; *New York Times*, March 21, 1965; "Nuns 'Inspire' Selma Marchers," *Texas Catholic Herald* [Houston edition], March 18, 1965; "Selma Marchers' Dedication Praised," *Texas Catholic Herald* [Houston edition], March 25, 1965; M. F. Everett, "Would Christ March in Selma?" *Clarion Herald*, March 25, 1965; "Klan Head Says Only Imposters, No Priests, Nuns in Selma March," *Texas Catholic Herald* [Houston edition], September 24, 1965; Charles R. Gallagher, "The Catholic Church, Martin Luther King Jr., and the March in St. Augustine," *Florida Historical Quarterly* 83 (Fall 2004): 158.

80. "NAACP Bias Charges Are Denied by Hospital," *Southwest Louisiana Register*, April 22, 1965; William A. Osborne, *The Segregated Covenant: Race Relations and American Catholics* (New York: Herder and Herder, 1967), 56–58.

81. "Funds Cutoff for Diocesan School Children," *NC News Service*, January 24, 1967, folder 707.2, ADC; "State Catholic School Desegregation Cleared by U.S. Office of Education," *Southwest Louisiana Register*, July 20, 1967.

82. *Our Negro and Indian Missions*, 1965, 9, ASSJ; *Washington Post*, April 25, 1968; Mother Laurence Edward Ferguson, OP to Thomas S. Donnelan, October 22, 1968, Mother M. Bridget, M.S.C., to Thomas S. Donnelan, December 16, 1968, folder 4, box 014/6, AAA; *New York Times*, February 9, 1970; John M. Swomley Jr., "Who Wants Catholic Schools?" *Nation* 211 (December 14, 1970): 627.

83. "Detroit Convention," *National Catholic Conference for Interracial Justice Newsletter*, December 1961, 2, Sisson, "For Racial Justice"; "Purchasing Power Project," *Commitment*, September 1964, 2, folder 1, box 1, series 8, NCCIJR; Susan Youngblood Ashmore, *Carry It On: The War on Poverty and the Civil Rights Movement in Alabama, 1964–1972* (Athens: University of Georgia Press, 2008), 57, 108–9, 117, 120; Donovan, *Crusader in the Cold War*, 156–57; "Poverty and Racial Relations Statement," *Southern Cross*, December 1, 1966 (quotations); Michael Warner, *Changing Witness: Catholic Bishops and Public Policy, 1917–1994*, with a Foreword by George Weigel (Grand Rapids, MI: Williams B. Eerdmans, 1995), 85.

84. "Religious Leaders Mourn Dr. Martin Luther King," *Catholic Week*, April 12, 1968; *New York Times*, April 26, 1968; *Washington Post*, April 25, 1968; "Negro Priests' Caucus Takes 'Wait-See' Stand," and John R. Sullivan, "Bishops Reveal Report on Program for Social Action," *Southern Cross*, May 2, 1968; "On National Race Crisis," *Voice*, May 3, 1968 (quotations); "Bishops on Race: Too Little This Late," *National Catholic Reporter*, May 8, 1968; "Racial Agenda for Catholics," *Christianity Today* 12 (May 24, 1968): 39. In November 1966, the American Catholic hierarchy agreed to a restructuring process in which "The National Catholic Welfare Conference became the National Conference of Catholic Bishops (NCCB), an entity under canon law." Warner, *Changing Witness*, 76–77 (quotation on p. 76).

85. Kim Larsen, "Catholic Schools Spurn Segregationists," *Voice*, April 17, 1970; Lynch, *Sharing the Bread in Service*, vol. 2, 120.

Chapter Two

1. Samuel S. Hill Jr., *Southern Churches in Crisis* (New York: Holt, Rinehart and Winston, 1967); James R. Wood, "Authority and Controversial Policy: The Churches and Civil Rights," *American Sociological Review* 35 (December 1970): 1057–69; James R. Wood, "Personal Commitment and Organizational Constraint: Church Officials and Racial Integration," *Sociological Analysis* 33 (1972): 142–51; Charles Y. Glock and Rodney Stark, *Religion and Society in Tension* (Chicago: Rand McNally, 1965), 227–28, 239; Meredith B. McGuire, *Religion: The Social Context*, 3d ed. (Belmont, CA: Wadsworth, 1992), 97, 233–37, 264.

2. Wood, "Personal Commitment and Organizational Constraint," 150 (first quotation); McGuire, *Religion*, 237 (second quotation).

3. R. Bentley Anderson, *Black, White, and Catholic: New Orleans Interracialism, 1947–1956* (Nashville: Vanderbilt University Press, 2005), xvi (first quotation); "Archbishop Vagnozzi Is the Seventh Apostolic Delegate to the U.S.," *Catholic Banner*, April 24, 1960 (second and third quotations); *New York Times*, April 28, 1968; McGuire, *Religion*, 97 (fourth quotation); M. F. Everett, "No Race, Color Bar in Church," *Catholic Action of the South*, May 14, 1961 (fifth quotation); Richard J. Roche, *Catholic Colleges and the Negro Student* (Washington, DC: Catholic University of America Press, 1948), 14–15; "Rome and New Orleans," *Interracial Review* 30 (August 1957): 130; "Southern Bishops Issue Appeal for Racial Justice & Religious Harmony," *North Carolina Catholic*, June 6, 1965.

4. Roche, *Catholic Colleges and the Negro Student*, 15–16; Raymond O'Brien, untitled memorandum, September 5, 1949, "Lucy Social Problems folder 1," Archives of the Archdiocese of San Antonio, San Antonio, Texas (hereinafter cited as AASA); Harold L. Cooper, "Sermon in Holy Name Church," February 5, 1956, folder 13, box 53, Joseph H. Fichter Papers, Special Collections and Archives, Loyola University Library, Loyola University New Orleans, New Orleans, Louisiana (hereinafter cited as Fichter Papers); Oona Sullivan, "Selma Aftermath," *Jubilee* 13 (August 1965): 16; "Commission on Parochial and Institutional Life," *Interracial Review* 31 (February 1959): 34; Andrew S. Moore, *The South's Tolerable Alien: Roman Catholics in Alabama and Georgia, 1945–1970* (Baton Rouge: Louisiana State University Press, 2007), 71, 79, 142.

5. Charles P. Greco, *"With God's Help": Memoirs of Bishop Charles P. Greco* (New Haven, CT: Knights of Columbus, 1989), 162; *The Church of Christ Decree Enacted by the First Synod of Archdiocese of Atlanta, 1966*, 21, folder 10, box 006/6, Archives of the Archdiocese of Atlanta, Atlanta, Georgia (hereinafter cited as AAA); John A. O'Brien, "Priests' Councils Promote

Unity," *Mississippi Register*, September 26, 1969; "Galveston-Houston Priests Elect Fr. Fiorenza Chairman," *Texas Catholic Herald* [Houston edition], April 28, 1967, press clipping, folder 7, box 16, series 33, National Catholic Conference for Interracial Justice Records, Marquette University, Milwaukee, Wisconsin (hereinafter cited as NCCIJR); William F. Powers, *Tar Heel Catholics: A History of Catholicism in North Carolina* (Lanham, MD: University Press of America, 2003), 67–69.

6. Henry Bezou, "Desegregation and the Catholic School System," September 23, 1955, 3, folder 21, box 44, Fichter Papers; "Catholic School Integration Stand Explained in Superintendent's Statement," *Southwest Louisiana Register*, August 28, 1969; "Rights of the Catholic Negro," *American Ecclesiatical Review* 114 (June 1946): 459–62; Dolores Egger Labbé, *Jim Crow Comes to Church: The Establishment of Segregated Parishes in South Louisiana*, 2d ed. (New York: Arno Press, 1978 [Lafayette: University of Southwestern Louisiana, 1971]), 6; Anderson, *Black, White, and Catholic*, 8–9; Roche, *Catholic Colleges and the Negro Student*, 8–14; Robert E. Lucey address to the "Southwest Regional Conference of the National Council of Catholic Women," October 4, 1949, 27–28, "Lucey Social Problems folder 1," AASA; John J. Russell, "Official Catholic Education, August 27, 1954," *Catholic Banner*, September 5, 1954 (quotations); Anthony McDevitt to Mrs. Fagan Canzoneria, September 15, 1961, folder "Schools—1961–62," T. J. Toolen to George E. Lackey, May 9, 1962, folder "Schools 1962–1963," Archbishop Thomas J. Toolen Papers, Archives of the Archdiocese of Mobile, Mobile, Alabama (hereinafter cited as Toolen Papers); "Bishop Stresses Value of Catholic Education," *North-Central Louisiana Register*, September 3, 1965; "Integration in Diocese Catholic Schools Enrollment 'Based on Freedom of Choice,'" August 24, 1969, press clipping, H40 B2, folder 3, box 4, Archives of the Sisters of the Blessed Sacrament, Bensalem, Pennsylvania; Clement Bastnagel, "Is a Parish for Colored People a 'National' Parish?" *Ecclesiastical Review* 108 (May 1943): 382–84; "Rights of a Catholic Negro," *American Ecclesiastical Review* 114 (June 1946): 459–62; Walter B. Clancy, "Membership in a Non-Territorial Negro Parish," *Jurist* 24 (October 1964): 462–63; Charles B. McLaughlin, "Much Progress Has Been Made . . . There Is Still Work to Be Done," *North Carolina Catholic*, February 9, 1964; Eugene P. McManus, "'National' Parishes," *Social Digest* 8 (July–September 1965): 232–33.

7. "Justice: God's Vision, Our Discipleship, Pastoral letter to the People of the Diocese of Memphis, Bishop Carroll T. Dozier, D.D., Christmas 1972," 20 n. 2, in author's possession; Bezou, "Desegregation and the Catholic School System," 3 (quotation); Harold L. Cooper to Emile A. Wagner, February 28, 1956, 6–8, folder 13, box 1, series 21, NCCIJR.

8. "Teaching Authority of the Church," *America* 91 (July 10, 1954): 375; Harold L. Cooper to Emile A. Wagner, February 28, 1956, 4 (first quotation), folder 13, box 1, "Catholics in America Asked to Help End Racial Discrimination," *Catholic Telegraph-Register*, July 24, 1959, press clipping, folder 15, box 1, series 21, NCCIJR; Charles Plauche, "Thinking with the Church," May 27, 1955, folder 21, box 44, Fichter Papers; Robert D. Cross, *The Emergence of Liberal Catholicism in America* (Cambridge, MA: Harvard University Press, 1958), 79 (second, third, and fourth quotations); "Vatican City Daily Praises Archbishop's Action in Condemning Racial Prejudice," *Catholic Action of the South*, October 23, 1955 (fifth quotation); "Vatican Radio Lauds Catholic Role in March," *Catholic Virginian*, September 6, 1963; *Arkansas Gazette*, October 25, 1963.

9. William W. Scott to "Dear Editor," February 9, 1964, Francis R. Moeslein to Louis J. Twomey, February 13, 1964, folder 16, box 21, Louis J. Twomey Papers, Special Collections and Archives, Loyola University Library, Loyola University New Orleans (hereinafter cited as Twomey Papers); Gerard E. Sherry, "The Ace among Us," *Josephite Harvest* 77 (September–December 1965): 2.

10. "Normae of the National Catholic Welfare Conference," 1–4, 6, folder "Bishops—USCC 1958–1965," box H, Bishop John J. Russell Papers, Archives of the Diocese of Richmond, Richmond, Virginia (hereinafter cited as Russell Papers); John Edward McCarthy, "Texas Catholic Conference: Its First Ten Years" (Master's thesis, University of Saint Thomas [Houston], 1979), 11; "Toward a Good Peace," *Catholic Virginian*, December 1943; "Statement of the Bishops of the United States—1958," in "A Syllabus on Racial Justice Grades 7–12 [Diocese of Baton Rouge]," n.d., 23–25, folder 11, box 6, series 33, NCCIJR.

11. Glock and Stark, *Religion and Social Change*, 239 (quotation). Although Glock and Stark were referring to the Protestant Episcopal Church, their analysis also had validity for the Catholic Church in the United States.

12. Joseph T. Leonard, S.S.J., *Theology and Race Relations*, with a Foreword by Most Rev. Patrick A. O'Boyle (Milwaukee: Bruce, 1963), 278–79; "A Syllabus on Racial Justice Grades 7–12," 1 (first quotation); Cooper to Wagner, February 28, 1956, 3–4; "Monsignor Plauche, Forum, Ursuline Gymnasium, Sunday, Jan. 22 [1956]," folder 13, box 53, Fichter Papers; "The Bishop's Teaching Authority," *American Ecclesiastical Review* 134 (April 1956): 273–74 (second quotation on p. 273); Dick Meskill, "In the Shadow of San Fernando," *Alamo Messenger*, June 19, 1964 (third quotation); *New York Times*, March 21, 1965 (fourth quotation); C. Ellis Henican, "Catholic Loyalty," 10–13, in author's possession.

13. "Excerpts from the Code of Canon Law," attached to Emile A. Wagner Jr. to "Dear Member," April 30, 1956, folder 4, box 20, Twomey Papers; Paul J. Hallinan letter, August 18, 1961, folder 707.1, Archives of the Diocese of Charleston, Charleston, South Carolina (hereinafter cited as ADC); "Action against Negroes Declared Reserved Sin," *Southwest Louisiana Register*, October 16, 1959; "Penalties Disclosed on Disobeying Church," *Southwest Louisiana Register*, August 6, 1964 (first quotation); Gilbert Roxburgh, "Excommunication Seen as Spiritual Curative," *Catholic Action of the South*, April 15, 1962; "Rebel D.C. Priest, Followers Excommunicated," *San Antonio Light*, February 6, 1990, press clipping, folder "Black Catholics," AASA; Archdiocese of New Orleans Bureau of Information, "Excommunication" (quotation), folder "School Integration Incoming/Outgoing Correspondence Newspaper Clippings June 1960, March–December 1962," box "School Integration Files, 1956–1965" AR/00166, Archives of the Archdiocese of New Orleans, New Orleans, Louisiana (hereinafter cited as AANO).

14. Glock and Stark, *Religion and Society in Tension*, 227 (quotation); [Lafayette, Louisiana] *Daily Advertiser*, November 30, 1955; Labbé, *Jim Crow Comes to Church*, 2–4, 27–85; Anderson, *Black, White, and Catholic*, 42, 202; "Bishop Opens Schools, Hospitals to All Races," *Bulletin of the Catholic Laymen's Association of Georgia*, September 18, 1954; Sister M. Agatha to Mother M. Anselm, October 30, 1952, folder 3, box 3, Xavier University Archives, New Orleans, Louisiana; McLaughlin, "Much Progress Has Been Made." State segregation laws in Florida, Georgia, and Tennessee also applied to private, and hence Catholic, schools. Leonard, *Theology and Race Relations*, 248–49.

15. Cooper to Wagner, February 28, 1956, 9; Sherry, "The Ace among Us," 4; Leonard, *Theology and Race Relations*, 282; Albert L. Fletcher, "Official Announcement August 3, 1954," *Guardian*, August 13, 1954; *Our Negro and Indians Missions: Annual Report of the Secretary of the Commission for the Catholic Missions Among the Colored People and the Indians*, 1965, 7–8, Archives of the Society of St. Joseph of the Sacred Heart, Baltimore, Maryland (hereinafter cited as ASSJ); Charles Carruth, "South Not All Fire-Hoses and Police Dogs 'Story Has Been Heroic,' Says Atlanta Prelate," [New York] *Catholic News*, n.d., folder 51, box 2–3, Archbishop Paul J. Hallinan Papers, AAA; "Atlanta Archbishop Attacks K.K.K. as 'Desperate, Disarrayed'

Band," *Southern Cross*, April 29, 1965; Charles P. Greco, "Pastoral on Race Relations," August 4, 1963 (first and second quotations), folder 2, box 3, series 11, NCCIJR; "Bishop England High School, Charleston, S.C., 1964 Adult Lenten Series 'Religion and Race'" (third quotation), Joseph L. Bernardin to William J. Croghan, March 3, 1964, Joseph L. Bernardin, "Memorandum," March 12, 1964, folder 707.1/1, ADC.

16. *Our Negro and Indian Missions*, January 1949, 5–6, January 1953, 5–6, January 1954, 5–6, ASSJ; "Catholics a Minority in Arkansas," *Interracial Review* 30 (September 1957): 161.

17. Glock and Stark, *Religion and Society in Tension*, 227–28 (first quotation); "Bishop England High School, Charleston, S.C., 1964 Adult Lenten Series 'Religion and Race'" (second quotation).

18. Labbé, *Jim Crow Comes to Church*, 4; Anderson, *Black, White, and Catholic*, 6–7; James B. Bennett, *Religion and the Rise of Jim Crow in New Orleans* (Princeton, NJ: Princeton University Press, 2005), 232–33; John Francis, "The Church Moves Quietly but Surely," *Sign* 35 (July 1956): 70 (first quotation); "The White-Negro Problem," *Catholic Digest* 20 (June 1956): 2, 4; Brian Healy, "Negro Support Is Still Lacking in America, Says Bishop Perry," *Clarion Herald*, November 14, 1968 (second quotation).

19. Leonard, *Theology and Race Relations*, 281–82; Charles P. Greco, "Pastoral on Race Relations," August 4, 1963 (quotation).

20. Hill, *Southern Churches in Crisis*, xiii (first quotation), xiv (second and third quotations), 5 (fourth quotation), 73, 76–78, 82–83, 114, 137. Challenges and modifications to Hill include Wayne Flynt, "Dissent in Zion: Alabama Baptists and Social Issues, 1900–1914," *Journal of Southern History* 35 (Winter 1969): 523–42, and Keith Harper, *The Quality of Mercy: Southern Baptists and Social Christianity, 1890–1920* (Tuscaloosa: University of Alabama Press, 1996).

21. Edward K. Braxton, "Severe Cultural Divide Splits Church," *National Catholic Reporter* 34 (March 13, 1998): 7. Pope Leo XIII, "*Rerum Novarum*" (1891), and Pope Pius XI, "*Quadragesimo Anno*" (1931), cited in "Justice," 20 n. 2; Sister Frances Jerome Woods, C.D.P., "The Popes on Minority Rights," 7–8, folder 11, box 20, Twomey Papers; Roger-Henri Guerrand, "The Catholic Church's Struggle against Racialism," in *The Church and Racism*, ed. Gregory Baum and John Coleman (Edinburgh: T. C. Clark; New York: Seabury Press, 1982), 33–34; Pope Pius XII, "Progress and Problems of the American Church (*Sertum Laetitiae*)," *Catholic Mind* 37 (November 22, 1939): 927; "The Bishop's Teaching Authority," 274; Charles P. Greco, "Pastoral on Race Relations," August 4, 1963 (quotation), folder 2, box 3, series 11, NCCIJR; "Says Most Catholics Don't 'Lift Finger to Win a Convert,'" *North Carolina Catholic*, May 29, 1953.

22. William Osborne, "The Church and the Negro: A Crisis in Leadership," *Cross Currents* 15 (Spring 1965): 133–37 (first quotation on p. 133; second quotation on p. 137).

23. McGuire, *Religion*, 233–37, 264 (first quotation); J. B. Gremillion, *The Journal of a Southern Pastor* (Chicago: Fides, 1957), 19 (second quotation); "Discrimination and the Christian Conscience (II)," *Blueprint* 11 (February 1959): 2 (third quotation), Special Collections and Archives, Loyola University Library, Loyola University New Orleans.

24. Undisclosed to Jules B. Jeanmard, November 28, 1955 (first quotation), folder "Lourdes OL, Erath—Racial Incident 1955," Archives of the Diocese of Lafayette, Lafayette, Louisiana (hereinafter cited as ADL); Peter L. Berger, *The Sacred Canopy: Elements of a Sociological Theory of Religion* (Garden City, NY: Anchor Books, 1969 [1967]), 147 (second quotation); "How U.S. Catholics View Their Church," *Newsweek* 69 (March 20, 1967): 69 (third quotation); "Uninvolvement of Churches Favored," *Alamo Messenger*, April 19, 1968 (fourth quotation).

25. "Race Problem Solution Is Urged at Southern Meeting of Catholic Committee of the South," *Guardian*, February 2, 1951 (first quotation); Gremillion, *Journal*, 20 (second quotation);

Joseph B. Gremillion, "Louisiana Knights Tackle Secularism," *America* 87 (September 13, 1952): 566; Robert E. Lucey to Henry Cabirac Jr., April 22, 1963 (third quotation), folder 8, box 17, series 33, NCCIJR; "The Pulpit and the Status Quo," *Catholic Virginian*, December 2, 1966 (fourth quotation). Mulloy had grown up in North Dakota. Report of the Rural Life Committee of the Catholic Committee of the South, c. 1952, 3, folder 20, box 2, Catholic Committee of the South Collection, Amistad Research Center, New Orleans, Louisiana.

26. Gremillion, *Journal*, 68 (first quotation); Douglas J. Roche, "Two Southerners Speak Their Minds," *Sign* 41 (October 1961): 31, 75 (second quotation on pp. 31, 75); L. J. Twomey to Fabius Dunn, March 14, 1958, folder 10, box 20, L. Twomey to William J. Dunne, April 18, 1960 (third and fourth quotations), folder 4, box 21, Twomey Papers; "Discrimination and the Christian Conscience," *Blueprint* 11 (January 1959): 1–2, Special Collections and Archives, Loyola University Library, Loyola University New Orleans; Stephen F. Ryan, "After Jesuit Bend," *Interracial Review* 29 (February 1956): 31; "Social Justice Attitudes of Catholics Different?" *Southern Cross*, February 29, 1968.

27. Berger, *Sacred Canopy*, 140–41 (first quotation on p. 140; second quotation on p. 141); Osborne, "Church and the Negro," 149 (third quotation).

28. Edward R. F. Sheehan, "Not Peace, but the Sword: The New Anguish of American Catholicism," *Saturday Evening Post* 237 (November 28, 1964): 34 (first quotation); Osborne, "Church and the Negro," 140 (second quotation).

29. Cooper to Wagner, February 28, 1956, 6; Bezou, "Desegregation and the Catholic School System," September 23, 1955, 3; August Thompson to John F. Dearden, September 1, 1967, 5, attached to August Thompson to Louis Twomey, September 1, 1967, folder 15, box 22, Twomey Papers.

30. "Transcript of meeting with representatives of the Civil Rights Commission, Department of Health, Education and Welfare, Bishop Ernest L. Unterkoefler, Father John Bond and Father Francis Miller, May 24, 1971," 5 (first quotation), folder 728.40, ADC; [Charleston, South Carolina] *News and Courier*, May 17, 1969 (second quotation).

31. Memorandum, Tom Gibbons to Jack Sisson, "Bishop Drury's Turndown of Project Equality," February 14, 1967, folder 7, box 16, series 33, NCCIJR.

32. *Nashville Tennessean*, July 1, 1954; "Memphis Catholic Schools to Integrate," *Social Action Notes for Priests*, May 1963, 5, folder 7, box 14, series 33, NCCIJR; Andy Telli, "Breaking Barriers: 50th Anniversary of Integration of Catholic Schools," *Tennessee Register*, September 24, 2004; Thomas Stritch, *The Catholic Church in Tennessee: The Sesquicentennial Story* (Nashville: The Catholic Center, 1987), 334–37.

33. W. J. Nold to the "Reverend Pastors of Galveston and Harris Counties," April 3, 1961, RG 2.1.9 Chancery files, Bishops' files, Nold, Wendelin J., folder 14, box 3, Archives of the Archdiocese of Galveston-Houston, Houston, Texas (hereinafter cited as AAGH).

34. Louis J. Roempke, "Roman Catholic Schools Plan Integration by 1964," [Charleston, South Carolina] *News and Courier*, June 25, 1963, folder 707.1, ADC.

35. "Report on Private Consultation on Race Question at Jackson May 6 & 7" (quotation), attached to Thomas D. Timlin to Ernest L. Unterkoefler, May 9, 1966, folder 719.78, ADC.

36. Henry [Cabirac Jr.] to J. D. De Blieux, October 3, 1962, folder 12, box 6, series 33, NCCIJR; *New York Times*, October 7, 1962; Osborne, "Church and the Negro," 137; "Good-By, Leander," *Ave Maria* 96 (September 22, 1962): 16 (quotation); "Early Figures Confirm Big School Enrollment," *Catholic Action of the South*, April 29, 1962; L. J. Twomey to Paul W. Schott, April 16, 1962, folder 12, box 21, Twomey Papers; William A. Osborne, *The Segregated Covenant: Race Relations and American Catholics* (New York: Herder and Herder, 1967), 79–89. On

segregationist acceptance of Catholic desegregation instructions, see also Labbé, *Jim Crow Comes to Church*, 91.

37. Philip R. Viviani to Bishop Thomas J. McDonough, June 24, 1963, folder 2, box 25, Archives of the Diocese of Savannah, Savannah, Georgia; Joseph L. Bernardin, memorandum, March 12, 1964 (quotation), folder 707.1/1, ADC.

38. Paul J. Hallinan letter, August 18, 1961 (quotations), folder 707.1, ADC; Henry Cabirac Jr. to C. Ellis Henican, December 12, 1961, folder 20, box 3, Catholic Council on Human Relations Papers, Amistad Research Center (hereinafter cited as CCHRP); Thomas J. Shelley, *Paul J. Hallinan: First Archbishop of Atlanta* (Wilmington, DE: Michael Glazier, 1989), 127–28.

39. Petition to Bishop Vincent S. Waters, n.d., scrapbook "Ban on Segregation 1953 volume II," Vincent S. Waters, letter, May 23, 1953 (quotation), bound volume "Pastoral Letters V. S. Waters 1953–1956," Archives of the Diocese of Raleigh, Raleigh, North Carolina (hereinafter cited as ADR); [Raleigh] *News and Observer*, May 21, 27, 1953; *New York Times*, May 22, 1953; John Strange, "Bishop Waters' Integration Pastoral Made U.S. Church History 50 Years Ago," *North Carolina Catholic*, May 18, 2003.

40. [Raleigh] *News and Observer*, June 1, 1953; [Greensboro, North Carolina] *Greensboro Daily News*, June 1, 1953; [Raleigh] *Carolinian*, June 6, 1953; Vincent S. Waters, "Pastoral Letter of His Excellency," June 12, 1953, bound volume "Pastoral Letters V. S. Waters 1953–1956," ADR; Strange, "Bishop Waters' Integration Pastoral Made U.S. Church History 50 Years Ago"; Monsignor Thomas P. Hadden, interview by author, August 2, 2006.

41. "Attitude in Jesuit Bend Not Seen in Other Places," *Catholic Action of the South*, November 6, 1955; "Church Services Are Suspended for Irreverence to Priest," *Catholic Action of the South*, October 16, 1955 (first quotation); "Vatican City Daily Praises Archbishop's Action in Condemning Racial Prejudice"; "Complete Text of 'Touches of Color,'" *Catholic Action of the South*, November 6, 1955 (second quotation); "Action at Jesuit Bend Misinterpreted by Group," *Catholic Action of the South*, November 20, 1955; "Full Text of Archbishop's and Pastor's Messages Refutes False Statements," *Catholic Action of the South*, December 18, 1955; *New York Times*, October 15, 1955, August 25, 1957; Ryan, "After Jesuit Bend," 29; "An Historic Document," *Interracial Review* 28 (December 1955): 202–3; "Archbishop Rummel's Impact on Church Outstanding," *Clarion Herald*, November 12, 1964; Anderson, *Black, White, and Catholic*, 145–48; Stephen J. Ochs, *Desegregating the Altar: The Josephites and the Struggle for Black Priests, 1871–1960* (Baton Rouge: Louisiana State University Press, 1990), 434–40; Justin D. Poché, "Religion, Race, and Rights in Catholic Louisiana, 1938–1970" (PhD diss., University of Notre Dame, 2007), 161; Joseph H. Fichter, *One-Man Research: Reminiscences of a Catholic Sociologist* (New York: John Wiley, 1973), 107–8.

42. [Lafayette, Louisiana] *Daily Advertiser*, November 28, 29, December 1, 1955; "Excommunication in Erath," *Time* 66 (December 12, 1955): 88.

43. Jules B. Jeanmard, "A Decree" (first, second, third, and fourth quotations), attached to Jules B. Jeanmard to the "Parishioners of Our Lady of Lourdes Church," November 26, 1955, A. G. Cicognani to Jules B. Jeanmard, December 29, 1955 (fifth quotation), folder "Lourdes OL, Erath—Racial Incident 1955," ADL; "Excommunication in Erath," 66; [Lafayette, Louisiana] *Daily Advertiser*, November 30, December 1, 1955.

44. [Lafayette, Louisiana] *Daily Advertiser*, December 2, 4, 1955; "Erath Incident Result of Un-Christian Play on Hate and Emotions," *Southwest Louisiana Register*, December 9, 1955; "Lafayette Priest Blasts 'Southern Gentlemen' Acts," *Catholic Action of the South*, December 18, 1955.

45. Joseph F. Rummel to Emile A. Wagner, March 28, 1956, no box, folder "AF/2012/10976 Association of Catholic Laymen, 1956," AANO; [New Orleans] *Times-Picayune*, March 18, 28, May 5, 6 (quotation), 18, 25, 1956; *New York Times*, March 19, May 6, 1956, August 10, 1957; "In the Matter of an Appeal to His Holiness, Pope Pius XII by the Association of Catholic Laymen," July 1957, folder 10, box 83, Twomey Papers; "Rome and New Orleans," *America* 97 (August 24, 1957): 518. The pope made no formal response to the association's appeal because, under Church rules, it should have been addressed to the Sacred Congregation of the Council. The appeal also broke ecclesiastical discipline by being made public. *New York Times*, August 19, 1957, April 2, 1962.

46. "Excommunication Warning," [New Orleans] *States Item*, April 6, 1962, press clipping, folder 9, box 83, Twomey Papers; [New Orleans] *Times-Picayune*, April 17, 18, 1962, March 20, 25, 26, 1969, February 11, 2001; *New York Times*, April 7, 17, November 5, 1962, March 20, 21, 26, 1969; *Citizens' Report* 4 (March 1962): 1–2; Glen Jeansonne, *Leander Perez: Boss of the Delta* (Baton Rouge: Louisiana State University Press, 1977), 264–65; Justin D. Poché, "The Catholic Citizens' Council: Religion and White Resistance in Post-War Louisiana," *U.S. Catholic Historian* 24 (Fall 2006): 66–68; Charlotte Hays, "Visits with 2 Famous Segs," *Figaro*, December 17, 1975, folder 11, box 52, Fichter Papers; Robert B. Denhardt and Jerome J. Salomone, "Race, Inauthenticity, and Religious Cynicism," *Phylon* 33 (second quarter, 1972): 120–31; Anderson, *Black, White, and Catholic*, 256–57 n. 21; "Southern Field Service Report to the Directors of the National Catholic Conference for Interracial Justice August 1962," 9–10, folder 4, box 8, series 33, NCCIJR; Edward Hoag, "New Orleans: Looking Forward," *Ave Maria* 95 (June 2, 1962): 13.

47. [New Orleans] *Times-Picayune*, May 6, 1956.

48. J. D. De Blieux to Henry Cabirac Jr., May 1, 1961 (first quotation), folder 11, box 6, series 33, NCCIJR; T. J. Toolen to Simon William Boyd, May 30, 1962 (second quotation), folder "Schools 1962–1963," #2, Toolen Papers.

49. [New Orleans] *Times-Picayune*, August 31, September 2, 1962; "Archbishop Asks Opposition to 'Hate' Influence at Buras," *Clarion Herald*, August 29, 1963; "Bombed School Ordered Closed to Protect Pupils," *Guardian*, September 6, 1963; "Desegregation of Southern Parochial Schools," August 19, 1963, folder 3, box 13, series 34, NCCIJR.

50. Henry A. Cabirac Jr. to R. F. Horn Jr., May 4, 1964 (quotation), folder 12, box 9, "Minutes of Catholic Interracial Council of Greater Little Rock," March 28, 1965, 1, folder 6, box 2, series 33, NCCIJR.

51. Memorandum, Jack Sisson to Tom Gibbons and Matt Ahmann, "Project Equality in Tennessee," March 13, 1967 (first quotation), Joseph A. Durick to Mathew Ahmann, May 15, 1967 (second and third quotations), folder 3, box 15, series 33, NCCIJR.

52. M. F. Everett, "Despotic Police State Seen as Result of School Control Acts," *Catholic Action of the South*, July 1, 1954; M. F. Everett, "Errors in Statement by Trio Are Pointed Out," *Catholic Action in the South*, March 4, 1956; Commission on Human Rights to Joseph F. Rummel, n.d., 2, folder 10, box 46, Fichter Papers; "Anti-Integration Tax Bill Dies in Mississippi," *Interracial Review* 29 (June 1956): 106; Charles Harbutt, "The Church and Integration," *Jubilee* 6 (February 1959): 13; Wilson Minor, "In Mississippi: Rigid Segregation," *Sign* 35 (July 1956): 17; Maurice "Moon" Landrieu, interview by author, July 12, 2007; "Meeting of the Sub-Committee of the Research Committee," November 25, 1961, Henry C. Bezou, "Memorandum—Conference held with His Excellency, the Most Reverend Archbishop [Joseph F. Rummel] in his residence, Nov. 29, 1961," November 29, 1961, folder "Integration, School Board Meetings, Minutes + Notes (1954–1962)," 03-038 box 1, AANO; "Southern Field Service Report to the Directors of the

National Catholic Conference for Interracial Justice August 1962," 1-3; untitled "report of the activities of the New Orleans Council on Human Relations, n.d., folder 3, box 1, CCHRP.

53. Joseph Francis Rummel, "The Morality of Racial Segregation," February 15, 1956 (first quotation), attached to "The Morality of Segregation," February 11, 1956 (second quotation), folder 4, box 8, series 33, NCCIJR; Philip H. Des Merais et. al to Joseph F. Rummel, March 25, 1957, folder "School Integration File, 1953–1960 Outgoing/Incoming Correspondence," box "School Integration Files and Labor Issues, 1944–1963" AR/00173, AANO; "Reply of Emile A. Wagner, Jr., to an article appearing in the February, 1959 issue of 'Jubilee' entitled 'The Church and Integration,'" 6, folder 10, box 83, Twomey Papers; Robert L. Crain and Morton Inger, *School Desegregation in New Orleans: A Comparative Study of the Failure of Social Control* (Chicago: National Opinion Research Center, University of Chicago, 1966), 31; Donald A. Erickson and John D. Donovan, *The Three R's of Nonpublic Education in Louisiana: Race, Religion, and Region* (Washington, DC: President's Commission on School Finance, 1972), 83; "Constant Reader" to *America* 100 (December 8, 1958): 302.

54. Albert J. Gelpi, "The Shepherd and His Flock: The Church and Integration in New Orleans," *Current*, December 1961, 178, folder "Racial—Charleston + Atlanta," box 4528303 Subject Files Hallinan, AAA; Clarence A. Laws to Joseph F. Rummel, February 23, 1956 (quotations), folder 2, box 20, Twomey Papers; Anderson, *Black, White, and Catholic*, 76.

55. L. J. Twomey to Donald Zewe, January 11, 1960 (quotation), folder 3, box 21, Twomey Papers; C. Ellis Henican to John P. Cody, December 15, 1962, 2, folder 15, box 1, CCHRP; memorandum, Jack [John P. Sisson] to Matt [Mathew Ahmann], "Visit with Bishop Schexnayder, Lafayette, November 30, 1964," December 4, 1964, 2, memorandum, Jack Sisson to Matt Ahmann, "Lafayette diocese Catholic Council on Human Relations," December 4, 1964, folder 7, box 7, series 33, NCCIJR; Bishop Maurice Schexnayder "To the Clergy, Religious and Laity, Diocese of Lafayette," August 12, 1970, bound volume "Integration of Schools Diocese of Lafayette 1965–1973 The Auzenne Case Correspondence and Data 1970–1973," ADL.

56. Clark Porteous, "Tennessee: More Integration Ahead," *Sign* 35 (July 1956): 15.

57. Charles P. Sweeney, "Bigotry Turns to Murder," *Nation* 113 (August 31, 1921): 232–33; "Suspected of Preaching Catholic Doctrine, Negro Minister Beaten," *Bulletin of the Catholic Laymen's Association of Georgia*, March 25, 1922; Felicitas Powers, R.S.M., "Prejudice, Journalism, and the Catholic Laymen's Association of Georgia," *U.S. Catholic Historian* 8 (Fall 1989): 201–12; "Persons, Places and Things," [Davenport, Iowa] *Catholic Messenger*, October 29, 1964; *Josephites: A Century of Evangelization in the African American Community* (Baltimore: St. Joseph's Society of the Sacred Heart, 1993), 52; Glen Feldman, *Politics, Society, and the Klan in Alabama, 1915–1949* (Tuscaloosa: University of Alabama Press, 1999), 5, 29, 58–60, 64, 66–67, 72, 172–75, 204–5; Minor, "In Mississippi," 17 (first and second quotations); Albert S. Foley, S.J., *God's Men of Color: The Colored Catholic Priests of the United States, 1854–1954* (New York: Farrar, Straus, 1955), 193–95; Tara Little, "Catholic Leaders Closely Watched Racial Segregation Issues of 50 Years Ago," *Arkansas Catholic*, September 20, 2007, accessed February 3, 2009 at http://catholic.org/printer_friendly.php?id=25433&section=Cathcom.

58. *Our Negro and Indian Missions*, January 1958, 7–11 (first quotation), ASSJ; Bishop Joseph A. Durick, interview by Sister Rose Sevenich, O.S.F., 13 (second quotation), interview number 2, RG 10.02-17, Archives of the Diocese of Birmingham, Birmingham, Alabama (hereinafter cited as ADB).

59. Moore, *South's Tolerable Alien*, 11 (first quotation), 35–36; Harbutt, "Church and Integration," 13 (second quotation).

60. J. J. McCarthy to Louis J. Twomey, October 3, November 4, 1961, Ethel Daniell to Louis J. Twomey, October 28, December 15, 1961, folder 10, box 21, Mrs. J. R. Daniell, "The Boycott of the Red Ball Battery and Oxygen Company," folder 4, box 84, Twomey Papers; [New Orleans] *Times-Picayune*, May 18, 19, 1956; *Mobile Press*, January 23, 1957; "Subpoena the Klan," *America* 96 (February 9, 1957): 520; "Night Riders Visit Hill," *Springhillian* 32 (February 15, 1957): 3; Jim McDermott, "A Professor, a President and the Klan: The Integration of Spring Hill College," *America* 196 (April 16–23, 2007): 16; "Bigots Smear Cleric, Hire Secret Police," *Southern Patriot* 14 (June 1956): 1, "Mobile, Ala.," *Southern Patriot* 14 (June 1956): 4, folder 19, box 52, Fichter Papers.

61. "Assault Charge Filed by Priest," [New Orleans] *Times-Picayune*, April 29, 1963, press clipping, folder 10, box 1, CCHRP; "Drops Assault Charge in Race Case," *Guardian*, July 5, 1963; Peter Finney Jr., "Abp. Rummel: Tireless Fighter for Desegregation," *Clarion Herald*, April 22, 1993; "Archbishop Asks Opposition to 'Hate' Influence at Buras" (quotations); "Archbishop Closes Buras School," *Catholic Commentator*, September 6, 1963; "Arson-blasted Buras School to Open; Archbishop Confident of Peace There," *Clarion Herald*, September 26, 1963; "There Are Now Two Empty Buildings in Buras," *Tennessee Register*, September 10, 1965; William Pierce, "CORE Eyes Selma-Type Assault on Perez Realm," *National Catholic Reporter* 1 (August 4, 1965): 1; "Bomb Outside Church Could Not Stop Mass," *Clarion Herald*, March 25, 1965; Father Paul Donnelly, interview by Sister Rose Sevenich, O.S.F., 31–32, RG 11.02–08, ADB.

62. Francis E. Hyland to L. J. Twomey, April 3, 1961 (first quotation), folder 8, box 21, Twomey Papers; Francis E. Hyland to "My dear Peoples," April 10, 1961 (second quotation), Francis E. Hyland to Paul J. Hallinan, April 10, 1961, Francis E. Hyland to Thomas J. McDonough, April 13, 1961, Francis E. Hyland to Michael McKeever, April 13, 1961, folder 49, box 036/6, AAA.

63. *Savannah Morning News*, February 20, 1961; "3 Southern Sees Told to Prepare for Integration," *Guardian*, February 24, 1961; pastoral letter, February 19, 1961 (first quotation), folder 49, box 036/6, AAA; memorandum, Benjamin Muse, "The 1961 Desegregation Initiative of the Catholic Bishops of Charleston, Savannah and Atlanta," March 2, 1962, 4 (second quotation), folder 4, box 4, series 11, NCCIJR; Hyland to Twomey, April 3, 1961 (third quotation); "Bishop Francis Edward Hyland," accessed December 15, 2007, at http://www.catholic-hierarchy.org/bishop/bhyland.html.

64. Henry Cabirac to Marvin Bordelon, June 21, 1963 (first quotation), folder 13, box 9, memorandum, Henry Cabirac to Matt Ahmann, "January 23, 1964 Visit to Jackson, Mississippi," no date (second quotation), folder 11, box 11, series 33, NCCIJR; *Shreveport Times*, August 4, 1963.

65. Paul J. Hallinan to Vincent P. Brennan, May 15, 1962, folder 11, box 015/2, AAA; *New York Times*, October 17, November 11, December 27, 1969; Joseph Sweat, "Memphians Choosing Sides in St. Joseph Dispute," *Tennessee Register*, October 10, 1969 (quotation); Joseph Sweat, "'Union vs. Hospital,' A Production by the Original Sin Player," *Tennessee Register*, October 31, 1969; Joseph Sweat, "Bishop Durick Emerges as Racial Peacemaker," *Catholic Week*, January 2, 1970; Joan Turner Beifuss, "How Black Union Lost in Memphis," *National Catholic Reporter*, January 21, 1970; "Schools, Nuns' Hospital Are Targets of Protests," *Southwest Louisiana Register*, November 20, 1969; Joseph Sweat, "Catholics and Civil Rights: 'A Circle Closed,'" *Tennessee Register*, May 11, 1987; Joseph Sweat, "On the Bus to Visit Friends in High Places," *Tennessee Register*, July 4, 1994; "Hospital Workers Vote to End Strike," *Catholic Week*, January 2, 1970.

66. Thomas Delaney, "Priest Tells Why 'Discrimination Immoral,'" *Mississippi Register*, June 12, 1964; Twomey to Zewe, January 11, 1960 (quotation).

67. Sheehan, "Not Peace, but the Sword," 34; Archbishop Oscar H. Lipscomb, interview by author, July 24, 2007; "Individual Right of Priests, Religious to Public Protest Backed by

Archbishop," *Catholic Week*, May 24, 1968; "Archbishop Toolen Criticizes Presence of Priests, Sisters in Demonstrations," *Catholic Week*, March 19, 1965; "Selma Negroes Beaten and Gassed as Police Break Up Civil Rights March," *Clarion Herald*, March 11, 1965; S.J. Iverson, "Personal and Confidential: Demonstrations," *Clergy Bulletin* 1 (April 15, 1964): 2, folder 4, box 8, series 33, NCCIJR.

68. "Archbishop Toolen Criticizes Presence of Priests, Sisters in Demonstrations"; "Hundreds of Priests, Ministers, Rabbis Turned Back as Selma March Halted," *Texas Catholic Herald* [Houston edition], March 11, 1965; "Opposes Nuns in Selma March," *Witness*, March 25, 1965; Paul J. Hallinan, "Archbishop's Notebook," *Georgia Bulletin*, March 18, 1965; M. F. Everett, "Would Christ March in Selma?" *Clarion Herald*, March 25, 1965; memorandum, Jack [Sisson] to Matt [Mathew Ahmann], "Selma, Alabama—Archbishop Hallinan," March 11, 1965, folder 5, box 4, series 33, NCCIJR.

69. "Friendship House Opens New Shreveport Center," *Interracial Review* 27 (March 1954): 52; Bob Senser, "Southern Hospitality Wears Out," *Work*, September 1955, press clipping, folder "Friendship House," box CGRM 1/01, J. B. Gremillion to J. Earl Downs, February 7, 1955, "Local Chapter 'Friendship House' to Close Sunday, July 31," *Shreveport Sun*, July 30, 1955, press clipping, folder "Friendship House," box CGRM 5/01, Joseph Gremillion Papers, University of Notre Dame Archives, Notre Dame, Indiana; Gremillion, *Journal*, 34, 44–48, 196–97, 266–68.

70. Margaret Smith to Mathew Ahmann, November 4, 1963, memorandum, Matt [Ahmann] to Jack [Sisson], July 10, 1964, memorandum, Jack Sisson to Mathew Ahmann, "Little Rock Arkansas visit, September 9–11," September 15, 1964, 1–2, Kathleen Woods to Jim [McGuire]," May 20, 1966, folder 6, box 2, series 33, NCCIJR; "A Catholic Priest" to *Look* 28 (October 20, 1964): 10 (quotation).

71. Ouellet, "Testimony of a Selma Pastor," 23.

72. Osborne, *Segregated Covenant*, 76 (quotation); M. F. Everett, "Leander Perez: A Long-Awaited Showdown in Plaquemines Parish," *National Catholic Reporter*, September 7, 1966; R. O. Gerow to Canisius J. Hinde, June 18, 1964, folder 11, box 11, series 33, NCCIJR; Bob Beech, "Hattiesburg Ministers' Project June 13–23, 1964," in author's possession; William Jacobs and Malcolm Boyd, "Christian Witness to Christian Failure," *Ave Maria* 101 (January 16, 1965): 4.

73. Gremillion, *Journal*, 70.

74. Osborne, "The Church and the Negro," 145 (first quotation); Harold L. Cooper, "Priests, Prejudice and Race," *Catholic Mind* 57 (November–December 1959): 501 (second quotation); Rudolph Ehrensing, "New Orleans: Catholic City?" *Scholastic*, February 24, 1961, 22 (third quotation); Leo Farragher, "Integration: An Urgent Matter," *Priest* 20 (February 1964): 142 (fourth quotation); Benjamin B. Ringer and Charles Y. Glock, "The Political Role of the Church as Defined by Its Parishioners," *Public Opinion Quarterly* 18 (Winter 1954–1955): 337–47; petition to Bishop Vincent S. Waters, n.d.

75. Ehrensing, "New Orleans," 20.

76. Ibid.

77. "Statement of the Bishops of the United States—1958," in "A Syllabus on Racial Justice Grades 7–12," 25 (quotation).

Chapter Three

1. Andrew S. Moore, *The South's Tolerable Alien: Roman Catholics in Alabama and Georgia, 1945–1970* (Baton Rouge: Louisiana State University Press, 2007), 2, 9, 130, 137; Arthur G. Bradley to the *Catholic Week*, October 4, 1963; N. C. Brunson to the *Catholic Week*, October 11, 1963;

"Interpretation of Interviews Conducted with Selected Catholic Priests," n.d., 1–3, folder 10, box 1, Catholic Council on Human Relations Papers, Amistad Research Center, New Orleans; Joseph H. Fichter to Joseph F. Rummel, April 12, 1956, 1, folder 5, box 46, Joseph H. Fichter Papers, Special Collections and Archives, Loyola University Library, Loyola University New Orleans, New Orleans, Louisiana (hereinafter cited as Fichter Papers).

2. *New York Times*, April 7, 17, 18, 1962; [New Orleans] *Times-Picayune*, August 29, 1960 (quotation). Gaillot refused to reveal Save Our Nation, Inc.'s membership size, but, according to the *New York Times*, the group had "no substantial support." *New York Times*, April 14, 1962; transcript of WYES-TV New Orleans interview with Mrs. B. J. Gaillot Jr., broadcast February 7, 1961, 4, folder 12, box 83, Louis J. Twomey Papers, Special Collections and Archives, Loyola University Library, Loyola University New Orleans (hereinafter cited as Twomey Papers).

3. Mrs. B. J. Gaillot Jr., "God Gave the Law of Segregation to Moses on Mount Sinai" (N.p., 2d ed., 1960), 1–19 (first quotation on pp. 1–2; second quotation on p. 2), folder 50, box 036/6, Archives of the Archdiocese of Atlanta (hereinafter cited as AAA); transcript of WYES-TV New Orleans interview with Mrs. B. J. Gaillot Jr., broadcast February 7, 1961, 2, 4–5, 9–11 (third quotation on p. 10); [New Orleans] *Times-Picayune*, August 29, December 30, 1960.

4. Transcript of WYES-TV New Orleans interview with Mrs. B. J. Gaillot Jr., broadcast February 7, 1961, 10–11; Walter M. Abbott, "The Bible Abused," *Interracial Review* 36 (February 1963): 27.

5. Patrick Warren Mernagh and Deane Settoon Mernagh, *The Pope on Segregation* (N.p., 1955), 26, folder 8, box 84, Twomey Papers.

6. Jack Ricau, *Integration: Threat to Freedom and How to Defeat It* (New Orleans, privately printed, 1957), 2, 12–13, folder "Church and Segregation," 03–038 box 2 "Desegregation," Archives of the Archdiocese of New Orleans, New Orleans, Louisiana (hereinafter cited as AANO).

7. Herman P. Folse, "Why I Think Integrated Schools Would Be Better," n.d. (first quotation), folder 13, box 46, "Herman P. Folse to the Commission on Human Rights," February 28, 1956 (second quotation), folder 2, box 46, Fichter Papers; Urban E. Mathieu, "To whom it may concern of the 'worthy brothers,'" January 27, 1964, (third quotation) folder "SC-1-10-2550," Knights of Columbus, Supreme Council Archives, New Haven, Connecticut; Joyce Carmouche to Joseph F. Rummel, April 5, 1962, folder "School Integration File Incoming Correspondence 1961–1962," box "School Integration Files, 1953–1965" AR/00165, AANO.

8. G. T. Gillespie, "A Christian View on Segregation," November 4, 1954 (Winona, MS: Association of Citizens' Councils, n.d.), 8–13, folder 2, box 53, Deane Settoon Mernagh to Joseph Fichter, March 2, 1959, folder 16, box 52, Fichter Papers; Mark Newman, *Getting Right with God: Southern Baptists and Desegregation, 1945–1995* (Tuscaloosa: University of Alabama Press, 2001), 48–54; David L. Chappell, "Religious Ideas of the Segregationists," *Journal of American Studies* 32 (August 1998): 237–62; undisclosed to Jules E. [*sic*] Jeanmard, January 9, 1956, folder "Lourdes OL, Erath—Racial Incident 1955," Archives of the Diocese of Lafayette, Lafayette, Louisiana (hereinafter cited as ADL).

9. Deane Settoon Mernagh to *Shreveport Journal*, May 26, 1962, folder 2, box 3, series 11, National Catholic Conference for Interracial Justice Records, Marquette University, Milwaukee, Wisconsin (hereinafter cited as NCCIJR); "A Mother" to "Dear Sisters," c. March 1949 (first quotation), folder 4, box 49, Donald J. Plaisance to the "Commission of Human Rights [*sic*]," July 9, 1956, folder 8, box 46, Mrs. E. R. Morris to the Commission on Human Rights, February 16, 1956, folder 2, box 46, Fichter Papers; Esma Champagne to Thomas J. Toolen, March 30, 1965, folder "Letters fav. to Toolen," box "Selma Demonstrations March 1965," Archbishop Thomas J.

Toolen Papers, Archives of the Archdiocese of Mobile, Mobile, Alabama (hereinafter cited as Toolen Papers); Alfred J. Kronlage to Louis J. Twomey, December 7, 1955 (second quotation), folder 17, box 19, Twomey Papers.

10. Undisclosed to Emery Labbe, December 5, 1955, folder "Lourdes OL, Erath—Racial Incident 1955," ADL.

11. *New York Herald Tribune*, April 8, 1962; Emile A. Wagner Jr., "Religious Morality of Segregation," to Edmund B. Bunn, November 10, 1955, folder 3, box 84, Twomey Papers; Robert E. Lucey to John LaFarge, January 22, 1958, folder "Organizations and Societies Catholic Interracial Council (1945–1969)," Archives of the Archdiocese of San Antonio, San Antonio, Texas (hereinafter cited as AASA); H. G. Odenthal to John J. Russell, March 22, 1965 (quotation), folder "Interracial Correspondence," box H, Bishop John J. Russell Papers, Archives of the Diocese of Richmond, Virginia (hereinafter cited as Russell Papers).

12. Joseph F. Rummel, "The Morality of Racial Segregation," February 11, 1956, and Emile A. Wagner Jr. to Joseph F. Rummel, May 28, 1956, 11–12 (quotation on p. 11), in Emile A. Wagner Jr., "An Analysis by Emile A. Wagner, Jr. Catholic Layman of Archbishop Joseph Francis Rummel's Pastoral Letter entitled 'Morality of Racial Segregation,'" folder 2, box 85, Twomey Papers.

13. Lucey to LaFarge, January 22, 1958. Although the apostolic delegation to the United States confirmed to Lucey in 1942 that the Vatican had "constantly urged the opening of new churches an[d] schools" for African Americans, establishment of special parishes for blacks did not require permission from the Holy See, unlike the erection of national parishes for non-Americans. Joseph McShea to Robert E. Lucey, March 11, 1942 (quotation), Leo Binz to Robert E. Lucey, April 4, 1942, folder "SA Saint Catherine Misc. Folder No. 1 (1942–1958)," AASA.

14. Mernagh and Mernagh, *Pope on Segregation*, 1–22; "Questions on Faith," *Leaves* 19 (September–October 1953): 20–21 (quotations on p. 21).

15. Mernagh and Mernagh, *Pope on Segregation*, 27.

16. Wagner, "Religious Morality of Segregation," to Bunn, November 10, 1955 (first quotation); Wagner to Rummel, May 28, 1956, 11 (second quotation), in Wagner "An Analysis by Emile A. Wagner, Jr. Catholic Layman of Archbishop Joseph Francis Rummel's Pastoral Letter entitled 'Morality of Racial Segregation'"; *New York Herald Tribune*, April 8, 1962; Harold L. Cooper to Emile A. Wagner, February 28, 1956, 6, folder 13, box 1, series 21, NCCIJR; *New York Times*, August 10, 1957; Henry C. Bezou, "Desegregation and the Catholic School System," September 23, 1955, 3, folder 21, box 44, Fichter Papers.

17. Emile A. Wagner Jr. to Pope Pius XII, July 24, 1957, 1 (first and second quotations) and Emile A. Wagner Jr. and James Everett Brown, "In the Matter of an Appeal to His Holiness, Pope Pius XII by the Association of Catholic Laymen," 1–12 (third quotation on p. 11) in "In the Matter of an Appeal to His Holiness, Pope Pius XII by the Association of Catholic Laymen July 1957," folder 10, box 83, Twomey Papers.

18. *New York Times*, August 10, 1957; "The Morals of Integration," *Time* 70 (August 19, 1957): 54 (first quotation); "Rome and New Orleans," *America* 97 (August 24, 1957): 518 (second and third quotations); "The New Orleans School Crisis," December 18, 1960, transcript, Channel 13 WNTA Television, 40, folder 67, box 56, John LaFarge Papers, Georgetown University Library, Special Collections, Division, Washington, DC (hereinafter cited as LaFarge Papers); Joseph F. Rummel to Amleto G. Cicognani, September 21, 1957, folder "AF/2012/10973 Association of Catholic Laymen; Emile A. Wagner 1956–1957," no box, AANO; Louis J. Twomey to Peter Canisius Van Lierde, December 21, 1957 (quotation), folder 9, box 20, Louis J. Twomey to Peter Canisius Van Lierde, April 23, 1958, folder 10, box 20, Twomey Papers. An unnamed "high

Vatican source said 'the Church is unalterably opposed to all forms of discrimination—in New Orleans as much as in South Africa.'" *New York Times*, September 27, 1959.

19. "Reply of Emile A. Wagner, Jr., to an article appearing in the February, 1959 issue of 'Jubilee' entitled 'The Church and Integration,'" March 4, 1959, 3 (first quotation), 5 (second quotation), folder 10, box 83, Twomey Papers; George H. Robinson to Joseph F. Rummel, August 26, 1960, folder "School Integration File 1950–1962 Letters Issued to Pastors/Correspondence," box "School Integration Files and Labor Issues, 1944–1963" AR/00173, AANO; Viola Johnson to Thomas J. Toolen, April 30, 1964 (third quotation), folder "Integration Letters 1964," Toolen Papers.

20. Herman P. Folse to Louis Twomey, December 8, 1955, 1–3 (first quotation on p. 3; second and third quotations on p. 2), folder 17, box 19, Twomey Papers; Dr. Frank J. O'Connor to *America* 91 (April 17, 1954): 849 (fourth quotation).

21. Ricau, *Integration*, 19 (first quotation); J. M. Boggan (second quotation) to the *Catholic Week*, September 27, 1963.

22. A. N. Manucy to Thomas J. Toolen, March 20, 1965 (first quotation), folder "Letters fav. to Toolen," box "Selma Demonstrations March 1965," Toolen Papers; Champagne to Toolen, March 30, 1965 (second quotation).

23. Frank Gawrych to Vincent S. Waters, June 23, 1953 (first quotation), scrapbook "Ban on Segregation 1953 volume II," Archives of the Diocese of Raleigh, Raleigh, North Carolina (hereinafter cited as ADR); Sidney L. Villeré to Louis J. Twomey, July 7, 1958 (second quotation), folder 12, box 20, Twomey Papers.

24. Francis O. Leach to Cardinal Francis Spellman, March 29, 1965 (first quotation), Arthur Leman to John J. Russell, April 6, 1965 (second quotation), folder "Interracial Correspondence," box H, Russell Papers.

25. Ella DeMattie to the *Catholic Week*, September 27, 1963 (first quotation); John Francis to the *Catholic Week*, March 18, 1966; James M. Ober to the *Catholic Virginian*, March 29, 1968; Philip R. Viviani to the *Southern Cross*, June 17, 1965 (second and third quotations).

26. "Jesuit Priest Scores Supreme Court Decree," *Citizens' Report* 1 (August 1959): 1–2 (quotation on p. 2), folder 3, box 84, Twomey Papers; John P. Sisson to Joseph C. Allen, January 8, 1964, folder 5, box 1, series 33, NCCIJR.

27. John Will, "Archbishop Calls for Recognition of Human Rights," *Mobile Register*, press clipping, no date (first quotation), folder 11, box 1, series 33, NCCIJR; T. J. Toolen to Cardinal Lawrence Shehan, April 22, 1965 (second quotation), folder "Letters of relig leaders fav. to Toolen," box "Selma Demonstrations March 1965," Toolen Papers.

28. Mrs. Leo Tart to Vincent S. Waters, May 25, 1953 (first quotation), scrapbook "Ban on Segregation 1953 volume II," ADR; Mernagh to Fichter, March 2, 1959 (second quotation).

29. Kathleen B. Marston to the "Most Reverend Reh," August 2, 1963 (first quotation), folder 720.10, Archives of the Diocese of Charleston, Charleston, South Carolina (hereinafter cited as ADC); "A Committee for Catholic Truth" to "My Dear Fellow Catholic," May 9, 1958 (second quotation), folder "Race," box CGRM 1/03, Joseph Gremillion Papers, University of Notre Dame Archives, Notre Dame, Indiana (hereinafter cited as Gremillion Papers); undisclosed to Rummel, c. 1955 (third quotation), folder "Lourdes OL, Erath—Racial Incident 1955," ADL.

30. Wagner to Rummel, May 28, 1956, 13 (first quotation), in Wagner Jr., "An Analysis by Emile A. Wagner, Jr. Catholic Layman of Archbishop Joseph Francis Rummel's Pastoral Letter entitled 'Morality of Racial Segregation'"; Mathieu, "To whom it may concern of the 'worthy brothers,'" January 27, 1964 (second quotation).

31. "The New Orleans School Crisis," December 18, 1960, transcript, Channel 13 WNTA Television, 2–3, 5, 25, 40; Parents and Friends of Catholic Children, "Specious Garb of Marxism," n.d., folder 24, box 2, series 34, NCCIJR; "Father Drolet, Member of Red Group Is Out as Kenner Pastor" and "'Prominent' Negro Catholic Honored by Red Front," *Citizens' Report*, February 1963, 1–2, folder 2, box 53, Fichter Papers; "Fr. Fichter's 'Survey' Unit Flavored with Integrationists—Part II," *Citizens' Report* Special (April 1964), folder 4, box 84, Twomey Papers; Deane Settoon Mernagh to the *Shreveport Journal*, May 26, 1962.

32. "The New Orleans School Crisis," December 18, 1960, transcript, Channel 13 WNTA Television, 2–3, 5, 25, 40; "Jesuit Priest Scores Supreme Court Decree," 1–2; "Cardinal Cushing Becomes Life Member of Communist-Controlled NAACP," *Citizens' Report* 3 (November 1961): 1–2, folder 9, box 83, Twomey Papers; "Father Drolet, Member of Red Group Is Out as Kenner Pastor" and "'Prominent' Negro Catholic Honored by Red Front," 1–2.

33. Mrs. Richard to Joseph H. Fichter, postmarked December 21, 1958 (quotation), folder 16, box 52, Fichter Papers; Folse, "Why I Think Integrated Schools Would Be Better."

34. Catherine M. West to Thomas J. Toolen, April 26, 1964 (quotation), folder "Integration Letters 1964," Toolen Papers.

35. Tart to Waters, May 25, 1953.

36. "Reply of Emile A. Wagner, Jr., to an article appearing in the February, 1959 issue of 'Jubilee' entitled 'The Church and Integration,'" March 4, 1959, 10–15 (quotation on pp. 10–11), folder 10, box 83, Twomey Papers.

37. Wagner, "Religious Morality of Segregation," to Bunn, November 10, 1955 (quotation).

38. G. C. Boucvalt to Thomas J. Toolen, March 19, 1965 (first quotation), folder "Letters fav. to Toolen," box "Selma Demonstrations March 1965," Toolen Papers; Folse to Twomey, December 8, 1955, 2 (second, third, and fourth quotations).

39. Folse to Twomey, December 8, 1955, 1 (first quotation on p. 2; second quotation on p. 1); Wagner to Rummel, May 28, 1956, 3–4 (third and fourth quotations on p. 3), in Wagner Jr., "An Analysis by Emile A. Wagner, Jr. Catholic Layman of Archbishop Joseph Francis Rummel's Pastoral Letter entitled 'Morality of Racial Segregation'"; "Reply of Emile A. Wagner, Jr., to an article appearing in the February, 1959 issue of 'Jubilee' entitled 'The Church and Integration,'" March 4, 1959, 16 (fifth quotation); Kronlage to Twomey, December 7, 1955; Betty Tecklenburg Long to Francis E. Hyland, March 15, 1961 (sixth quotation on pp. 3, 4), folder 49, box 036/6, AAA.

40. "Guardian to Publish Analysis of Racial Problem in America," *Guardian*, July 24, 1959 (quotations); "W. W. O'Donnell in Overall Charge of Guardian Operation," *Guardian*, December 12, 1958; "Little Rock Ordinary a Man of Many Distinctions," *Guardian*, April 30, 1965.

41. William W. O'Donnell, "America's Race Problem," *Guardian*, July 31, 1959; William W. O'Donnell, "America's Race Problem," *Guardian*, August 7, 1959 (quotations); William W. O'Donnell, "America's Race Problem," *Guardian*, August 14, 1959.

42. William W. O'Donnell, "America's Race Problem," *Guardian*, September 4, 1959.

43. O'Donnell, "America's Race Problem," July 31, 1959 (first and second quotations); William W. O'Donnell, "America's Race Problem," *Guardian*, August 28, 1959 (third quotation); "Guardian Launches Two-Fold Follow-Up to 'Race' Editorials," *Guardian*, September 25, 1959; William W. O'Donnell, *America's Race Problem: A Catholic Editor's Analysis* (Little Rock: Guardian Press, 1959).

44. Folse, "Why I Think Integrated Schools Would Be Better" (quotation).

45. "Reply of Emile A. Wagner, Jr., to an article appearing in the February, 1959 issue of 'Jubilee' entitled 'The Church and Integration,'" March 4, 1959, 4 (third quotation), 11–12 (first quotation on p. 11; second quotation on pp. 11–12).

46. Undisclosed to Jeanmard, January 9, 1956.

47. Plaisance to the "Commission of Human Rights [sic]," July 9, 1956 (first quotation); Jackson G. Ricau and Joseph E. Viguerie to "Dear Holy Name High School Parents," December 2, 1959, 4 (second quotation), folder 3, box 21, Twomey Papers; "Joseph E. Viguerie Elected President of New South La. Council," *Councilor*, November 1958, 7, attached to Jack Ricau to Joseph H. Fichter, May 30, 1959, folder 16, box 52, Fichter Papers. The Subcommittee of the United States House of Representatives on the District of Columbia that made the report in December 1956 included segregationists. However, in 1960, Carl F. Hansen, superintendent of District of Columbia public schools, reported that their educational level had improved and delinquency in them declined during the period since their desegregation. *Congressional Report on What Happened When Schools Were Integrated in Washington, D.C.* (Greenwood, MS: Educational Fund of the Citizens' Councils, n.d.), folder 3, box 85, Twomey Papers; "Integration and Capital's Schools," *Interracial Review* 33 (June 1960): 165. Historian Jane Dailey has argued for the importance of miscegenationist fears among southern white Protestant segregationists. Jane Dailey, "Sex, Segregation, and the Sacred after *Brown*," *Journal of American History* 91 (June 2004): 119–44, esp. 125, 135.

48. M. Basilico to L. J. Twomey, March 9, 1960 (first quotation), De La Salle High School Parents to Louis J. Twomey, c. February 1960 (second quotation), folder 4, box 21, Twomey Papers; Joan B. Thyson of Sawyerville, Alabama, to Mother Superior, Mary Knoll Sisters, March 17, 1965 (third quotation), folder "Letters fav. to Toolen," box "Selma Demonstrations March 1965," Toolen Papers.

49. Parents and Friends of Catholic Children, "You Should Learn and Know the Truth about the Future of Your Children," vol. 1, 4–5 (first, second, and third quotations on p. 4; fourth and fifth quotations on p. 5), folder 2, box 83, Twomey Papers.

50. "Leander Perez, Mr. Jackson Ricau and Mrs. Gaillot Had the right to express their opinion—Should not have been treated like children," folder 3, box 84, Twomey Papers.

51. Kronlage to Twomey, December 7, 1955 (quotation).

52. Unidentified layman to Vincent S. Waters, June 20, 1953 (first quotation), scrapbook "Ban on Segregation 1953 volume III," ADR; undisclosed to Labbe, December 5, 1955 (second quotation).

53. Mernagh to Fichter, March 2, 1959.

54. "Reply of Emile A. Wagner, Jr., to an article appearing in the February, 1959 issue of 'Jubilee' entitled 'The Church and Integration,'" March 4, 1959, 16; Adam Fairclough, *Race and Democracy: The Civil Rights Struggle in Louisiana, 1915–1972* (Athens: University of Georgia Press, 1995), 237–39; Justin D. Poché, "Religion, Race, and Rights in Catholic Louisiana, 1938–1970" (PhD diss., University of Notre Dame, 2007), 261.

55. "Excommunication Warning," [New Orleans] *States Item*, April 6, 1962, press clipping, folder 9, box 83, Jackson G. Ricau, "The Revealing Story of My Excommunication—An Act of Desperation by the Race Mixers!" *Citizen* 6 (April 1962): 4–8, folder 9, box 84, Twomey Papers; [New Orleans] *Times-Picayune*, April 17 (quotations), 18, 1962, March 25, 26, 1969, February 11, 2001; *New York Times*, April 7, 17, November 5, 1962, March 26, 1969; Joseph F. Rummel to Jackson G. Ricau, March 31, 1962, *Citizens' Report* 4 (March 1962): 1–2; Glen Jeansonne, *Leander Perez: Boss of the Delta* (Baton Rouge: Louisiana State University Press, 1977), 264–69; Justin D. Poché, "The Catholic Citizens' Council: Religion and White Resistance in Post-War Louisiana," *U.S.*

Catholic Historian 24 (Fall 2006): 66–68; Charlotte Hays, "Visits with 2 Famous Segs," *Figaro*, December 17, 1975, folder 11, box 52, Fichter Papers; Fairclough, *Race and Democracy*, 261.

56. "Remarks by Leander Perez at Citizens Council Meeting, March 30, 1962" (first quotation), folder 4, box 84, Jackson Ricau, "The Tragic Truth about the Catholic Race-Mixing Program in New Orleans," July 25, 1962, 1–2 (fifth quotation on p. 1), folder 2, box 85, Twomey Papers; Ricau, "Revealing Story of My Excommunication," 7–8 (second quotation on p. 8; third and fourth quotations on p. 7); Hays, "Visits with 2 Famous Segs."

57. Peter J. Samkovitch to the *Voice*, July 12, 1968.

58. Dolores Egger Labbé, *Jim Crow Comes to Church: The Establishment of Segregated Parishes in South Louisiana*, 2d ed. (New York: Arno Press, 1978 [Lafayette: University of Southwestern Louisiana, 1971]), 86, 90–91 (quotations on p. 91), 94–95.

59. Labbé, *Jim Crow Comes to Church*, 91 (quotation).

60. Father T. R. Sehlinger, O.P., to the *Texas Catholic* [Dallas], April 6, 1968 (first quotation); Oscar B. Hofstetter Jr. to the *Tennessee Register*, May 11, 1987 (second quotation).

61. John Shelton Reed and Merle Black, "Jim Crow, R.I.P.," in John Shelton Reed, *Surveying the South: Studies in Regional Sociology* (Columbia: University of Missouri Press, 1993), 98; "David *Greenhouse* et al., Plaintiffs-Appellants, v. Most Reverend Charles Pascal *Greco* et al., Defendants-Appellees. No. 78–1802 United States Court of Appeals, Fifth Court 617 F.2d 408; 1980 U.S. App. Lexis 17433 May 19, 1980," accessed June 11, 2007, at http://web.lexis-nexis.com.ezproxy.loyno.edu/universe; Fairclough, *Race and Democracy*, 453.

Chapter Four

1. Vincent S. Waters, "Conferring the James J. Hoey Awards," *Interracial Review* 18 (November 1945): 168–69; M. F. Everett, "Errors in Statement by Trio Are Pointed Out," *Catholic Action of the South*, March 4, 1956; Josiah G. Chatham, "Religion and Race in the South: Catholic Perspectives Keynote Address" (quotations), March 19, 1965, folder 12, box 11, series 33, National Catholic Conference for Interracial Justice Records, Marquette University, Milwaukee, Wisconsin (hereinafter cited as NCCIJR); *New York Times*, March 20, 1965. Progressives sometimes cited Galatians 3:28: "There is neither Jew nor Greek; there is neither slave nor freeman; there is neither male nor female. For you are all one in Christ Jesus." Vincent S. Waters, pastoral letter dated February 9, 1953, *North Carolina Catholic*, February 20, 1953.

2. "Southern Collegians Resist Racism," *Catholic World* 172 (December 1950): 180 (quotation), 185. SERINCO underwent several name changes before adopting the name under which it is best known in February 1950. Fichter, *One-Man Research*, 79–80; R. Bentley Anderson, *Black, White, and Catholic: New Orleans Interracialism, 1947–1956* (Nashville: Vanderbilt University Press, 2005), xiv, 24, 85, 113, 185–86.

3. "Mississippi Bishop Urges Racial Justice," *Texas Catholic Herald* [Houston edition], August 13, 1964 (quotation); "Bishop Joseph Bernard Brunini," accessed September 18, 2014, at http://www.catholic-hierarchy.org/bishop/bbrunini.html; Vincent S. Waters to "My dear Brethren," May 18, 1953, scrapbook "Ban on Segregation 1953 volume III," Archives of the Diocese of Raleigh, Raleigh, North Carolina (hereinafter cited as ADR).

4. Genesis 1:27 (first quotation); "Pastoral Message of Archbishop Rummel: 'Let There Be No Segregation'" (second quotation), folder 4, box 8, series 33, NCCIJR; "Bishop to Integrate Savannah Schools on Sept. 1," *Voice*, June 28, 1963. "And he said: Let us make man to our image

and likeness.... And God created man in his own image: to the image of God he created him: male and female he created them." Genesis 1:26–27.

5. Robert E. Lucey address to the "Southwest Regional Conference of the National Council of Catholic Women, San Antonio, Texas, Tuesday, October 4, 1949," 11 (quotation), "Lucey Social Problems Folder 1," Archives of the Archdiocese of San Antonio, San Antonio, Texas (hereinafter cited as AASA); "Archbishop Robert Emmet Lucey," accessed September 18, 2014, at http://www.catholic-hierarchy.org/bishop/blucey.html; Vincent S. Waters, "The Mass and Interracial Justice," in John LaFarge, comp., *Sermons on Interracial Justice* (New York: Catholic Interracial Council of New York, 1957), 109, folder 12, box 53, Joseph H. Fichter Papers, Special Collections and Archives, Loyola University Library, Loyola University New Orleans, New Orleans, Louisiana (hereinafter cited as Fichter Papers).

6. Hugh A. Dolan, "Catholics and Race Relations," in LaFarge, comp., *Sermons on Interracial Justice*, 20 (quotation); Joseph H. Hodges, "The Kingdom of Christ," in LaFarge, comp., *Sermons on Interracial Justice*, 2–3; Alexander O. Sigur, "The Catholic Laity and the Mission Apostolate," in LaFarge, comp., *Sermons on Interracial Justice*, 46.

7. Albert L. Fletcher, *An Elementary Catholic Catechism on the Morality of Segregation and Racial Discrimination* (N.p., n.d.), 8–9, folder 3, box 1, series 11, NCCIJR; Vincent S. Waters to "Reverend and dear father and my dear Brethren," June 12, 1953, bound volume "Pastoral Letters of V. S. Waters 1953–1956," ADR; "Appeals for Unity, Harmony at Christian Family Meeting," *Catholic Action of the South*, August 26, 1956; National Catholic Welfare Conference Bureau of Information, "Pastoral letter, issued separately by the Most Rev. Thomas J. McDonough, Bishop of Savannah, Ga., the Most Rev. Francis E. Hyland, Bishop of Atlanta, Ga., and the Most Rev. Paul J. Hallinan, Bishop of Charleston, S.C.," February 19, 1961, folder 49, box 036/6, Archives of the Archdiocese of Atlanta, Atlanta, Georgia (hereinafter cited as AAA); "Pastoral Letter of Archbishop Joseph F. Rummel," August 14, 1960, *Interracial Review* 33 (October 1960): 242. On the nature of charity, see 1 Corinthians 13:4–7, 13.

8. Joseph B. Gremillion, "Opening Address, Annual Teachers' Institute, Diocese of Lafayette," September 30, 1955, 8 (quotation), folder "Articles and Talks," box CGRM 3/05, Joseph Gremillion Papers, University of Notre Dame Archives, Notre Dame, Indiana (hereinafter cited as Gremillion Papers); J. B. Gremillion, *The Journal of a Southern Pastor* (Chicago: Fides, 1957), 269–82.

9. Joseph Kiwanuka, "Christ in Africa," *White Fathers Missions* 8 (September 1950), n.p., folder 20, box 52, Fichter Papers.

10. Richard H. Brown to Louis J. Twomey, February 11, 1964, L. J. Twomey to Richard H. Brown, February 25, 1964 (first quotation), folder 16, box 21, Louis J. Twomey Papers, Special Collections and Archives, Loyola University Library, Loyola University New Orleans (hereinafter cited as Twomey Papers); "Discrimination and the Christian Conscience," *Blueprint* 11 (January 1959): 2, Special Collections and Archives, Loyola University Library, Loyola University New Orleans; Louis Twomey, "Catholic Prejudice," in LaFarge, comp., *Sermons on Interracial Justice*, 77; Sigur, "The Catholic Laity and the Mission Apostolate," 45, 47 (second quotation).

11. *Josephite News Views* (third quarter 1980), 5, Archives of the Society of St. Joseph of the Sacred Heart, Baltimore, Maryland (hereinafter cited as ASSJ); Stephen J. Ochs, *Desegregating the Altar: The Josephites and the Struggle for Black Priests, 1871–1960* (Baton Rouge: Louisiana State University Press, 1990), 426–27; Sr. Patricia Lynch, S.B.S., *Sharing the Bread in Service: Sisters of the Blessed Sacrament, 1891–1991*, vol. 2 (Bensalem, PA: Sisters of the Blessed Sacrament, 2001 [1998]), 83, 114, 120–22.

12. "A Syllabus on Racial Justice Grades 7–12," n.d., 15 (quotation), folder 11, box 6, series 33, NCCIJR.

13. Charles Harbutt, "The Church and Integration," *Jubilee* 6 (February 1959): 14 (quotation).

14. Bernardin J. Patterson, "Reflections of a Negro Priest," *Catholic World* 200 (February 1965): 269–70, 272 (first quotation); Ochs, *Desegregating the Altar*, 458; Gary Wray McDonogh, *Black and Catholic in Savannah, Georgia* (Knoxville: University of Tennessee Press, 1993), 188, 209; "Steve" [Albert S.] Foley to "Dear Hooty," January 8, 1948 (second quotation), folder 8, box 1, Albert Sidney "Steve" Foley Jr., S.J. Papers, Spring Hill College Archives, Mobile, Alabama (hereinafter cited as Foley Papers); Ken Foskett, *Judging Thomas: The Life and Times of Clarence Thomas* (New York: William Morrow, 2004), 65.

15. "Convention Raps Efforts to Circumvent Supreme Court Non-Segregation Ruling," *Guardian*, August 13, 1954; "Justice for Negroes," *Catholic Banner*, October 3, 1954 (first quotation); "A Syllabus on Racial Justice Grades 7–12," 15 (second quotation).

16. Robert E. Lucey to "Reverend and dear Father," April 5, 1954, "Lucey, Robert E. (Archbishop) Social Problems: Race Relations Folder # 2 (1951–1965)," AASA; Joseph Francis Rummel, "The Morality of Racial Segregation," February 11, 1956, 1–4 (quotations on p. 2), attached to Joseph Francis Rummel, "The Morality of Racial Segregation," February 15, 1956, folder 4, box 8, series 33, NCCIJR; Vincent S. Waters to "My dear Brethren," January 29, 1951 (first quotation), scrapbook "Ban on Segregation 1953 volume III," ADR; Waters to "Reverend and dear father and my dear Brethren," June 12, 1953 (second quotation); [Raleigh] *News and Observer*, March 20, 1945.

17. "Discrimination and the Christian Conscience (II)," *Blueprint* 11 (February 1959): 3, Special Collections and Archives, Loyola University Library, Loyola University New Orleans; L. J. Twomey to Henry S. Torres, November 2, 1961, folder 10, box 21, Twomey Papers; Joseph A. Fiorenza, interview by author, October 30, 2006.

18. Michael V. Namorato, *The Catholic Church in Mississippi, 1911–1984: A History* (Westport, CT: Greenwood Press, 1998), 101, 132.

19. Bishop John E. McCarthy, interview by author, October 25, 2006 (first and second quotations); Archbishop Joseph A. Fiorenza, interview by author, October 30, 2006 (third and fourth quotations); "Houston Priest Assigned to Spanish-speaking Post," undated *Texas Catholic Herald* clipping, folder 15, box 2, Bishop John E. McCarthy Papers, Catholic Archives of Texas, Austin, Texas; "Community Relations Unit Set Up," *Texas Catholic Herald* [Houston edition], May 14, 1964; "Human Relations Unit Sets Petition on Hospital District," *Texas Catholic Herald* [Houston edition], November 19, 1964; *New York Times*, November 18, 1998.

20. "Biographical data: Father J. B. Gremillion," n.d., folder 5, box CGRM 21, Gremillion Papers; Gremillion, *Journal of a Southern Pastor*, 44 (quotation).

21. M. F. Everett, "The Great Taboo," *Catholic Action of the South*, May 27, 1954 (first quotation); Emile Comar, "Seminary Doctorate to Honor Clarion Editor," *Clarion-Herald*, April 23, 1964; Mrs. N. C. Brunson to the *Catholic Week*, October 11, 1963 (second quotation). Everett was born in Glenwood Springs, Colorado, in 1903. "Hoey Awards," *St. Augustine's Messenger* 32 (December 1955): 354.

22. Undisclosed to Jules B. Jeanmard, December 3, 1955, folder "Lourdes, OL, Erath—Racial Incident 1955," Archives of the Diocese of Lafayette, Lafayette, Louisiana (hereinafter cited as ADL); Norman C. Francis, interview by author, July 6, 2007.

23. "Profile on John P. Nelson, Jr.," folder 5, box 84, Twomey Papers; Douglas J. Roche, "Two Southerners Speak Their Minds," *Sign* 41 (October 1961): 29 (quotation); John Robert

Payne, "A Jesuit Search for Social Justice: The Public Career of Louis J. Twomey, S.J., 1947–1969" (PhD, diss., University of Texas at Austin, 1976), 190; John P. "Jack" Nelson, interview by Jack Bass, November 16, 1979, 6, 12, 29, "Bass, Jack—Series I: Interviews: Nelson, John P. 'Jack'—11/16/79, 5/F6," Jack Bass Oral History Collection, Law Library, Tulane University, New Orleans, Louisiana; Kim Lacy Rogers, *Righteous Lives: Narratives of the New Orleans Civil Rights Movement* (New York: New York University Press, 1993), 56–57. Nelson was also deeply affected by the experience of seeing two African American girls stand longingly with their father in front of a park carousel, restricted to white use, while Nelson and his two young daughters got on. Nelson recalled, "That was an important moment in my life: It made me say, 'There's something wrong. This isn't right.'" "Jack Nelson Eulogy 3.15.06," 1–2 (quotation on p. 2) in author's possession.

24. "Data on the Rev. Louis J. Twomey, S.J.," folder 1, box 3, series 30, NCCIJR; C. J. McNaspy, S.J., *At Face Value*, with a Preface by Walker Percy and an Afterword by David A. Boileau (New Orleans: Institute of Human Relations, Loyola University of the South, 1978), 4 (first quotation), 21–38, 72–73; "Discrimination and the Christian Conscience (II)," 2–3; Roche, "Two Southerners Speak Their Minds," 29–30 (second quotation on p. 30; third quotation on p. 29); L. J. Twomey to Jonathan E. Perkins, July 14, 1948, folder 3, box 19, Louis J. Twomey, "Autobiographical Reflections on the Race Problem," March 25, 1963, 1–3 (fourth quotation on p. 1), folder 2, box 52, Louis J. Twomey, "The Race Problem: Basis of World Conflict," June 1, 1958, 1, 3, folder 11, box 51, Twomey Papers; Payne, "A Jesuit Search for Social Justice," 182–86.

25. Albert S. Foley, "Shadow of the White Camellia: Reminiscences of a Tangle with Terrorists," 26–29 (first and second quotations on p. 27; third and fourth quotations on p. 28), in author's possession; *Mobile Register*, December 4, 1990; Carol Ellis, "Guide to the Papers of Albert Sidney 'Steve' Foley Jr., S.J.," September 2002 (fifth quotation), Spring Hill College Archives, Mobile, Alabama.

26. Father Gerald M. LeFebvre, interview by author, November 10, 2006; McNaspy, *At Face Value*, 35; Katherine Ann Martensen, "Region, Religion and Social Action: The Catholic Committee of the South, 1939–1956" (Master's thesis, University of New Orleans, 1978), 53, 56; Fiorenza interview. Seminarians' Catholic Action Study of the South also held annual conferences that included race relations. Thomas Potts, "Seminarians Discuss Leadership," *St. Augustine's Catholic Messenger* 36 (October 1959): 246–47, 251; "Race Segregation 'Cries Out for Condemnation,' Seminarians Meeting Says," [Catholic Interracial Council of New York] *News Service*, September 3 [1960], folder 1, box 2, series 21, NCCIJR.

27. Janet and Harlan Hall to Vincent S. Waters, June 2, 1953 (first quotation), Louise Schaiell to Vincent S. Waters, June 23, 1953 (second, third, and fourth quotations), scrapbook "Ban on Segregation 1953 volume II," ADR.

28. Patty Edmonds, "Boston's Archbishop 'Personal, Progressive and Orthodox in Faith,'" *National Catholic Reporter* 27 (February 3, 1984): 1; "Bernard Law's Early Years—Much Travel, a Close-knit Family," *Boston Globe*, January 26, 1984 (first and second quotations), accessed April 20, 2005, at http://www.boston.com/globe/spotlight/abuse/archives/012684_early_years.htm.

29. "Racial Discrimination Always Works Injustice," *Interracial Review* 20 (December 1947): 193 (first quotation); John L. Morkovsky, "The Christian Solution," in *Interracial Justice* (San Antonio: San Antonio Archdiocesan Committee on Interracial Relations, 1945), 37 (second quotation), Georgetown University Library, Special Collections Division, Washington, DC; Robert E. Lucey, "Rainbow over Dixie," 5–6 (third quotation on p. 6), "Lucey Social Problems Folder 1," AASA; Martensen, "Region, Religion and Social Action," 44, 47–49, 52.

30. "Paul D. Williams," folder "Catholic Committee of the South—1950 8c I-c-16," "Catholic Committee of the South 78-014 box 1 52-03-06," Archives of the Archdiocese of New Orleans, New Orleans, Louisiana (hereinafter cited as AANO); Waters, "Conferring The James J. Hoey Awards," 169; "The Catholic Committee of the South," *Interracial Review* 18 (November 1945): 162 (quotation); "Williams Elected President of Southern Regional Council," *Interracial Review* 18 (November 1945): 162; "Lay Leader Re-elected Southern Council Head," *Interracial Review* 20 (January 1947): 14; "Council Reelects Catholic Layman," *Interracial Review* 20 (December 1947): 192; Paul D. Williams, "The Southern Regional Council and Civil Rights," *Interracial Review* 22 (January 1949): 10–12; Gerald P. O'Hara to Peter L. Ireton, June 12, 1940, folder 3, box 1, Catholic Committee of the South Collection, Amistad Research Center, New Orleans, Louisiana (hereinafter cited as CCSC); Martensen, "Region, Religion and Social Action," 51. The SRC lost many white members following its board of directors' endorsement of desegregation in 1949. *Encyclopedia of African-American Civil Rights: From Emancipation to the Present*, ed. Charles D. Lowery and John F. Marszalek, with a Foreword by David J. Garrow (Westport, CT: Greenwood Press, 1992), s.v. "Southern Regional Council," by Randall L. Patton.

31. Mark Newman, *The Civil Rights Movement* (Edinburgh: Edinburgh University Press, 2004), 45–46; H. J. C. [Monsignor Howard J. Carroll] to Cardinal Francis Spellman of New York, December 31, 1948, folder 11, box 89, National Catholic Welfare Conference Collection, The American Catholic History Research Center and University Archives, Catholic University of America, Washington, DC (hereinafter cited as NCWCC).

32. Frederick A. Koch, "Civil Wrongs," *North Carolina Catholic*, April 23, 1948.

33. Newman, *Civil Rights Movement*, 46–47; Numan V. Bartley, *The Rise of Massive Resistance: Race and Politics in the South during the 1950s* (Baton Rouge: Louisiana State University Press, 1969), 33.

34. "Catholic Committee of the South," *Interracial Review* 21 (September 1948): 131–32 (quotations on p. 131).

35. Untitled Catholic Committee of the South, press release, n.d. (first and third quotations), folder 22, box 2, "'Dixiecrat' Move Termed 'Immoral,'" no date, press clipping (second quotation), folder 24, box 2, CCSC; Martensen, "Region, Religion and Social Action," 52, 61; Bartley, *Rise of Massive Resistance*, 34–36.

36. *Christian Conscience* 6 (Summer 1948), folder 2, box 84, Twomey Papers; Jules A. Guste, "New Orleans Racial Progress in Catholic Spheres," *Notre Damean* 21 (May 1954), folder 10, box 48, Fichter Papers; Joseph H. Fichter, *One-Man Research: Reminiscences of a Catholic Sociologist* (New York: John Wiley, 1973), 47, 77; Anderson, *Black, White, and Catholic*, 21, 24–25, 27–30.

37. Thomas J. Shields to Joseph A. Fichter, September 9, 1948, Archives of the New Orleans Province of the Society of Jesus, Special Collections and Archives, Loyola University Library, Loyola University New Orleans (hereinafter cited as ANOPSJ); Daniel G. Quinn, "Report of Meetings and Activities," November 1948, folder 5, box 49, Joseph F. Rummel to Daniel G. Quinn, January 12, 1949, folder 3, box 49, Guste, "New Orleans Racial Progress in Catholic Spheres," box 48, folder 10, Fichter Papers; "Ursuline Slates Interracial Day," *Catholic Action of the South*, January 20, 1949; "Negro Priest to Address Students on Interracial Day," *Catholic Action of the South*, February 17, 1949; "Xavier Students Win in Interracial Day Contest," *Catholic Action of the South*, March 17, 1949; "Report for 1949, Minute Book No. 6," 112, folder 8, box 2, Xavier University Archives, New Orleans, Louisiana; Clare McGowan, "Interracial Justice Week," *Interracial*

Review 22 (May 1949): 71–72; "Slate Second Interracial Day," *Catholic Action of the South*, January 26, 1950; Anderson, *Black, White, and Catholic*, xiv–xv, 24–25, 33–36, 38–46, 51–55, 60, 62, 70–71, 73–79, 82–91, 94, 96–97, 112–13, 116–22, 133–34, 140, 153–57, 183–87, 192, 229 n. 75, 238 n. 59.

38. Janet Riley, "Minutes of a Meeting Sponsored by the Sub-committee on Race Relations on the Archdiocesan Committee of the Catholic Committee of the South," February 21, 1949, 1–2, "Minutes of a Meeting Sponsored by the Sub-committee on Race Relations of the Archdiocesan Committee of the Catholic Committee of the South," March 6, 1949, folder 16, box 47, Mrs. Stephen P. Ryan, "Catholic Action in Action," January 23, 1951, 1, 3–4, folder 4, box 48, *Commission on Human Rights of the Catholic Committee of the South: Its Principles, Objectives and Achievements* (New Orleans, n.p., n.d.) not paginated (quotations), folder 26, box 46, "Five Years of the Commission on Human Rights," *Christian Impact* 3 (February 1954), folder 2, box 47, Fichter Papers; Fichter, *One-Man Research*, 47, 78–79. This issue of the *Christian Impact* should have been numbered volume 4. Fichter served as the CHR's chaplain or moderator. Joseph H. Fichter to "Mr. Fairley," January 11, 1956, folder 24, box 45, Fichter Papers.

39. Janet Riley, "Minutes of a Meeting Sponsored by the Sub-committee of Race Relations on the Archdiocesan Committee of the Catholic Committee of the South," March 27, 1949, 1–2; Ryan, "Catholic Action in Action," 2; *Commission on Human Rights of the Catholic Committee of the South*; Stephen P. Ryan to Lawrence Walsh, December 19, 1949, box 45, "Active Membership Catholic Committee of the South, January 11, 1951," folder 6, box 47, Nora Wallbillich, "Commission on Human Rights of the Catholic Committee of the South, Minutes of Executive Board Meeting," September 24, 1952, 4, folder 14, box 47, Fichter Papers. In 1950, ten Xavier University professors were commission members and three of them held office in the organization. "CHR statement 1950," 2, folder 4, box 48, Fichter Papers. In March 1951, the Commission on Human Rights had 112 members: 44 African Americans and 68 whites. "Report of Commission's Activity—January 1–March 31, 1951," folder 17, box 46, Fichter Papers.

40. Ryan, "Catholic Action in Action," 2–3; "Meeting of the Commission on Human Rights, C.C.S.," December 18, 1949, 1–2, folder 17, box 47, Gladys [Williams], "Annual Report of the Executive Secretary of the Commission of Human Rights of the Catholic Committee of the South March, 1954–March, 1955," 1, folder 17, box 46, Fichter Papers; "Five Years of the Commission on Human Rights"; Stephen P. Ryan, "Catholic Activity in New Orleans," *Interracial Review* 23 (January 1950): 8; Fichter, *One-Man Research*, 80–81 (first quotation on p. 80; second quotation on p. 81); Anderson, *Black, White, and Catholic*, xiv. In 1951, a donation enabled the CHR to publish twenty-five hundred copies of the *Christian Impact*. "Minutes of the Meeting of the Commission on Human Rights," June 24, 1951, folder 20, box 47, Fichter Papers.

41. "The Catholic Committee of the South," January 24, 1951, 1–3, 6–7 (quotation on p. 7), folder 1, box 4, series 20, NCCIJR; "Southern Catholics Plan for the Future: The Race Relations Workshop," *Interracial Review* 24 (February 1951): 19–20; Vincent S. Waters, pastoral letter January 29, 1951, scrapbook "Ban on Segregation 1953 volume III," ADR; Ochs, *Desegregating the Altar*, 423; Joseph F. Rummel, "To the Clergy, Religious and Laity, Archdiocese of New Orleans," *Catholic Action of the South*, February 8, 1951; *New York Times*, November 9, 1964.

42. Francis interview; Fichter, *One-Man Research*, 76–77; L. J. Twomey to William Patrick Donnelly, June 1, 1952, folder 10, box 19, Twomey Papers; "Minutes of the Provincial Meeting on Interracial Relations, Grand Coteau, Louisiana, August 28, 29, 1952," 1–56, ANOPSJ; "An Epochal Pronouncement," *Blueprint* 7 (September 1954): 1; A. W. Crandell to "Reverend Fathers and dear Brothers in Christ," September 9, 1954, *Blueprint* (Special Service Edition, September 30, 1954):

1; Payne, "A Jesuit Search for Social Justice," 195–96; McNapsy, *At Face Value*, 73–74; Anderson, *Black, White, and Catholic*, 62–65, 70, 91–95, 99–102, 104, 113.

43. "Civil Wrongs"; "Commission Notes," *Christian Impact* 2 (March 1952): 2, folder 1, box 4, series 20, NCCIJR; "The Church and Race Relations in the South A Progress Report—1954," folder 25, box 46, Fichter Papers; "Names in the News," *Christian Impact* 3 [this volume should have been numbered volume 4] (January 1954): 1, folder 2, box 47, Fichter Papers; Thomas F. Jordan, "The CLC's Two Decades," *Colored Harvest* 67 (October 1955): 3; Kitty Beverly, "Texas Negro Honored," *Colored Harvest* 66 (December 1954): 9; "Catholic Interracial Councils," *Interracial Review* 28 (October 1954): 176; "Underscorings," *America* 90 (January 2, 1954): 352.

44. Ryan, "Catholic Action in Action," January 23, 1951, 2 (first quotation); attendance notebook, July 30, 1950–January 10, 1954, folder 11, box 47, "Meeting of the *Commission of Human Rights, Catholic Committee of the South*," September 24, 1950, 1 (second quotation), folder 19, box 47, "Minutes of the Meeting of the Advisory Board, Commission on Human Rights, CCS," July 15, 1951, Edna Cordier, "Minutes of the Executive Board Meeting of the Commission on Human Rights of the Catholic Committee of the South," July 23, 1952, 1–2, folder 14, box 47, Fichter Papers; Fichter, *One-Man Research*, 82 (third quotation). In January 1951, the CHR's records listed thirty-two active members. "Active Membership Catholic Committee of the South, January 11, 1951."

45. Gerald P. O'Hara to Peter L. Ireton, June 30, 1951 (quotation), folder "Catholic Committee of the South," Bishop Peter L. Ireton Papers, Archives of the Diocese of Richmond, Richmond, Virginia; "The Catholic Committee of the South," January 24, 1951, 1–3; Maurice V. Shean, "A Catholic Program in the South," *Interracial Review* 25 (December 1952): 195–96; Martensen, "Region, Religion and Social Action," 64–65.

46. J. B. Gremillion, "What Some Priests and Laymen Have and Are Doing," Catholic Committee of the South Convention, Richmond, Virginia, April 22, 1953, folder "CCS etc," box CGRM 2, Gremillion Papers; "Report of Inter-racial Workshop to Convention of Catholic Committee of the South—Richmond, Virginia, April 24, 1953," 1–2 (first quotation on p. 2), folder 20, box 48, Fichter Papers; "Message of the Bishops to the Convention of the Catholic Committee of the South," April 27, 1953, 1–2 (second quotation on p. 2), box 2, folder 14, CCSC; "Help Bring Christ into All Spheres of Life, Bishops Urge," *Catholic Virginian*, May 1, 1953. The six bishops from the South, including three auxiliary bishops, represented the dioceses of Charleston, Lafayette, New Orleans, Raleigh, and Richmond. "Help Bring Christ into All Spheres of Life."

47. Milton Lomask, "Father Maurice Challenges the South," *Sign* 36 (November 1956): 17–20, 74–75; Maurice V. Shean to Joseph F. Rummel, April 14, 1954, 1–3 (quotation on p. 3), folder "Catholic Committee of the South—1954 4a I-c-17," "Catholic Committee of the South 78–014 box 2 52-03-07," AANO; "Report of Meeting Held May 12th & 13th, 1954," 1–4, folder "Racial—Charleston + Atlanta," box 4528303 Subject Files Hallinan, AAA; "CCS Statement on Court Ruling," *Catholic Week*, May 22, 1954; "Segregation Verdict Seen Affecting Pupils in Public, Nonpublic Schools," *Bulletin of the Catholic Laymen's Association of Georgia*, May 29, 1954; Charles Keenan, "Church Leaders on School Segregation," *America* 91 (July 10, 1954): 379. Bishops or representatives from the dioceses of Alexandria, Charleston, Covington (Kentucky), Lafayette, Little Rock, Mobile, and Savannah-Atlanta attended the meeting. "Report of Meeting Held May 12th & 13th, 1954," 1, folder "Racial—Charleston + Atlanta," box 4528303 Subject Files Hallinan, AAA.

48. Catholic Committee of the South, "Segregation and the Catholic Schools: A Study," folder 12, box 48, Fichter Papers. Archbishop Joseph F. Rummel sent the study to all of his pastors. "Steps toward Desegregation in the Schools," *Christian Impact* 5 (September 1954): 1, folder 2, box 47, Fichter Papers.

49. John J. Russell to Paul F. Tanner, July 14, 1958 (quotations), folder 13, box 89, NWCCC; "C.C.S. Activity Report (1951–1952)," 4, folder "Catholic Committee of the South—1952 2b I-c-17," "Catholic Committee of the South 78–014 box 1 52–03–07," AANO; Martensen, "Region, Religion and Social Action," 73–76. According to Father Albert S. Foley, Bishop Thomas J. Toolen of Mobile was "the main mover in the scuttling of the Catholic Committee of the South" and "urged the other bishops to vote for" its "termination." Father Albert Foley to Oliver Adams, November 23, 1977, 8–9 (first quotation on p. 8; second and third quotations on p. 9), folder 18, box 9, Foley Papers.

50. Everett, "The Great Taboo" (quotations); L. J. Twomey to Charles O'Neil, March 25, 1955, folder 15, box 19, Twomey Papers.

51. Joseph H. Fichter to "the Members of the Commission on Human Rights," April 1, 1955, 1–3, folder 22, box 45, Commission on Human Rights attendance notebook, January 27–March 27, 1954, folder 12, box 47, Joseph H. Fichter to David F. Freeman, December 31, 1955, folder 23, box 45, Joseph H. Fichter to David F. Freeman, January 2, 1955 [1956], Joseph Francis Rummel to David Freeman, January 3, 1956, David F. Freeman to Joseph H. Fichter, January 16, 20, 1956, folder 24, box 45, "Evaluation of an Interracial Program," 1–8 (quotations on p. 1), folder 13, box 48, Fichter Papers; Fichter, *One-Man Research*, 79, 83–85; "Summary of Work Done Committee to Study De-Segregation of Catholic Schools of Archdiocese of New Orleans," n.d., Maria Hornung, "Committee to Study Desegregation in the Catholic Schools of the Archdiocese, Minutes of Meeting held July 29, 1955, at Notre Dame Seminary," folder "Desegregation Institute (1955–1967)," 03–038 box 2, Joseph F. Rummel, "De-segregation in Schools," August 19, 1955, folder "Desegregation—Archbishop Rummel," no box, AANO.

52. [New Orleans] *Times-Picayune*, January 21, 1956; "Evaluation of an Interracial Program," 2–3 (quotations on p. 3); Fichter, *One-Man Research*, 86–90. To ease their concerns and fears and prepare them for parochial school desegregation, James Hoflich, at Rummel's invitation, gave two talks to Catholic pastors in New Orleans about the process in St. Louis, where he was head of Catholic elementary schools. Joseph H. Fichter to David E. Freeman, March 17, 1956, folder 4, box 46, Fichter Papers.

53. Fichter to Freeman, March 17, 1956; Joseph H. Fichter to Arthur S. Miller, March 19, 1956, folder 4, box 46, Joseph H. Fichter to Joseph F. Rummel, April 12, 1956, folder 5, box 46, 1, Fichter Papers; "Evaluation of an Interracial Program," 4–5 (first, second, third, and fourth quotations on p. 4; fifth quotation on p. 5); Fichter, *One-Man Research*, 90–92 (sixth quotation on p. 92). In his memoirs, Fichter wrote that the CHR "arranged for two meetings at Xavier University, one each at St. Mary's Dominican College, Ursuline College, Loyola University, and the downtown Jesuit parish that had no elementary school, and two in high schools run by religious orders, St. Joseph's Academy and Cor Jesu High School." Fichter, *One-Man Research*, 91.

54. "Manhattan's Borough President," *Colored Harvest* 66 (March 1954): 13; "Tar Heel Laymen to Hear Huland Jack in Charlotte," *North Carolina Catholic*, June 3, 1955; "Hulan E. Jack Guest Speaker at Interracial Meet," *Catholic Action of the South*, February 26, 1956; [New Orleans] *Times-Picayune*, February 27, 28, 29, 1956; Fichter to Freeman, March 17, 1956; "Coming to Loyola University—Eighth Annual Catholic Interracial Sunday February 26, 1956," folder 23, box 46, untitled remarks by Archbishop Joseph F. Rummel at eighth Interracial Sunday, folder 15, box 48, Ernest A. Nichols, "To Whom It May Concern," March 7, 1956, folder 3, box 46, Fichter Papers; Fichter, *One-Man Research*, 11, 87, 94–96, 115 n. 22; *New York Times*, February 27, 1956; "Observe Catholic Interracial Sunday," *Catholic Action of the South*, March 4, 1956; "Evaluation of an Interracial Program," 4. Jack denied membership in any of the organizations and claimed they had used his name without his approval. [New Orleans] *Times-Picayune*,

February 28, 29, 1956; press clippings in folders 6 and 9, box 13, Hulan E. Jack Papers, Schomburg Center for Research in Black Culture, New York, New York.

55. Joseph F. Rummel to Joseph H. Fichter, March 26, 1956 (quotation), folder 4, box 46, Fichter Papers.

56. Joseph H. Fichter to Joseph Rummel, March 19, 1956, folder 4, box 46, Joseph H. Fichter to Albert J. Reiss Jr., April 5, 1956 (first quotation), folder 5, box 46, untitled memorandum, Commission on Human Rights, March 15, 1956, "Why Is an Integrated School Better Than a Segregated School? Four Winning Essays," folder 12, box 46, Herman P. Folse, "Why I Think Integrated Schools Would Be Better," n.d., folder 3, box 46, *Southern Catholic Parents Speak Up for Integrated Schools* (New Orleans: Catholic Committee of the South Commission on Human Rights, n.d. [1956])," folder 27, box 46, Fichter Papers; "Evaluation of an Interracial Program," 6; Fichter, *One-Man Research*, 85, 90–91, 97 (second quotation), 102–3; *Handbook on Catholic School Integration* (New Orleans: Catholic Committee of the South Commission on Human Rights, 1956), *Southern Catholic Teachers Favor Integrated Schools* (New Orleans: Catholic Committee of the South Commission on Human Rights, n.d. [1956]), folder 1, box 4, series 20, NCCIJR; Fichter to Freeman, March 17, 1956; Fichter to Rummel, March 19, 1956; "Evaluation of an Interracial Program," 5–6; "Catholic Parents," *Catholic Action of the South*, February 12, 1956.

57. Nichols, "To Whom It May Concern," March 7, 1956; John Cummins to "Dear Madam," June 17, 1956, folder 7, box 46, Donald J. Plaisance to Commission of Human Rights [sic], July 9, 1956, folder 8, box 46, Commission on Human Relations, untitled press release, dated May 21, 1956 (quotation), folder 6, box 48, Fichter Papers; L. J. Twomey to John J. Wright, May 18, 1956, folder 5, box 20, Twomey Papers; [New Orleans] *Times-Picayune*, May 21, June 11, 1956; Fichter, *One-Man Research*, 97–99.

58. Adam Fairclough, *Race and Democracy: The Civil Rights Struggle in Louisiana, 1915–1972* (Athens: University of Georgia Press, 1995), 205; Commission on Human Rights to Joseph H. Fichter, June 1956, folder 7, box 46, Gladys B. Williams, minutes "C.H.R. Executive Committee Meeting," June 20, 1956, folder 5, box 47, Gladys [B. Williams], "A Summary of the General Meeting of G.H.R. [sic]," June 24, 1956, folder 3, box 48, Joseph H. Fichter to Joseph F. Rummel, July 26, 1956, Clare Andrews to Henry R. Montecino, July 27, 1956 and attached Clare Andrews to Executive Board, Commission on Human Rights, July 27, 1956, folder 8, box 46, "Louisiana Passes Bills to Curb Teachers in Interracial Work," *Catholic Standard and Times*, July 20, 1956, press clipping, folder 11, box 52, Fichter Papers.

59. Williams, minutes "C.H.R. Executive Committee Meeting," June 20, 1956; Commission on Human Rights to Fichter, June 1956; Fichter to Rummel, July 26, 1956; Joseph H. Fichter to David F. Freeman, June 14, 29, 1956, Joseph H. Fichter to Gladys [B. Williams], June 30, 1956, folder 7, box 46, Joseph F. Rummel to Joseph H. Fichter, July 23, 1956, Joseph H. Fichter to "Dear Monte [Father Henry R. Montecino]," July 26, 1956, Henry R. Montecino to Joseph Francis Rummel, September 30, 1956, unsigned letter to David F. Freeman, August 16, 1956, Joseph H. Fichter to Joseph F. Rummel, February 28, 1957, Henry R. Montecino to Joseph H. Fichter, October 11, 1956, Joseph H. Fichter to Abel Caillouet, March 8, 1957, folder 8, box 46, Joseph H. Fichter to Joseph Francis Rummel, January 7, 1959, folder 9, box 46, Joseph H. Fichter form letter, April 8, 1959, folder 9, box 52, Fichter Papers; Joseph Francis Rummel, "Integration of Catholic Schools," July 31, 1956, folder 5, box 20, Twomey Papers; Fichter, *One-Man Research*, 99–101, 103–4. Fearing an adverse reaction from segregationists, the CHR had not publicized its Fund for the Republic grant. Joseph H. Fichter to David F. Freeman, January 20, 1956, folder 24, box 45; Fichter to Freeman, March 17, 1956.

60. Fichter, *One-Man Research*, 104–5.

61. Fichter to Rummel, July 26, 1956; Fichter to Caillouet, March 8, 1957 (quotation); *Is the Negro Ready for Desegregation?* (Rock Hill, SC: Catholic Committee of the South, n.d.), *The Desegregation Decision* (Rock Hill, SC: Catholic Committee of the South, n.d.), *Progress Report* (Rock Hill, SC: Catholic Committee of the South, n.d.), *What Do Negroes Want?* (Rock Hill, SC: Catholic Committee of the South, n.d.), *What Does Integration Mean?* (Rock Hill, SC: Catholic Committee of the South, n.d.), folder 3, box 85, *Is Interposition the Answer?* (Rock Hill, SC: Catholic Committee of the South, n.d.), folder 9, box 85, Twomey Papers; Fichter, *One-Man Research*, 104; "Catholics & Negroes," *Time* 72 (September 15, 1958): 53–54; "In Telephone Conversation with Rev. H. Montecino, S.J., November 23, 1956," folder "Catholic Committee of the South—1956 6 I-c-17," "Catholic Committee of the South 78-014 box 1 52-03-07," AANO.

62. L. J. Twomey to Maurice W. [sic] Shean, September 18, 1956, folder 1, box 4, series 20, NCCIJR.

63. "Interracial Justice Convention," *Colored Harvest* 70 (November 1958): 2–3 (first quotation on p. 2); "Memorandum on the National Catholic Conference for Interracial Justice," October 15, 1959, folder 13, box 89, NCWCC; Robert E. Lucey to Daniel M. Cantwell, July 24, 1958, folder "Organizations and Societies Catholic Interracial Council (1945–1969)," AASA; "U.S. Bishops' Condemnation of Racial Segregation Major Milestone in Series on Theme," *New World*, November 21, 1958, press clipping, folder 14, box 1, series 21, NCCIJR; "Resolutions Adopted at First National Catholic Conference on Interracial Justice," *Interracial Review* 31 (September 1958): 158–60 (second quotation on p. 159); *New York Times*, August 31, September 1, 1958; Ed Marciniak, "Interracial Councils in Chicago," *America* 99 (September 20, 1958): 640–42; David W. Southern, *John LaFarge and the Limits of Catholic Interracialism, 1911–1963* (Baton Rouge: Louisiana State University Press, 1996), 329–35. Thirteen of the thirty-six Catholic interracial councils represented were "located south of the Mason-Dixon line." Marciniak, "Interracial Councils in Chicago," 642.

64. John J. O'Connor, "Catholic Interracial Movement," *Social Order* 10 (September 1960): 291–95; memorandum, Francis T. Hurley to Paul F. Tanner, November 24, 1959, folder 13, box 89, NCWCC; National Catholic Conference for Interracial Justice, "A proposal to the Commission for the Catholic Missions Among the Colored People and the Indians," 1–2 (quotation on p. 1), folder 719.78, "Fact Sheet on the National Catholic Conference for Interracial Justice," folder 720.10, Archives of the Diocese of Charleston, Charleston, South Carolina (hereinafter cited as ADC); "National Catholic Conference for Interracial Justice, Program Highlights: 1960–1968 under the administration of Mathew H. Ahmann," 1, folder "Social Problems Project Equality Natl. Cath. Conf. for Interracial Justice (1961–1969)," AASA; *New York Times*, March 20, 21, 1965; John P. Sisson, "For Racial Justice," *Our Sunday Visitor*, November 10, 1968; Southern, *John LaFarge and the Limits of Catholic Interracialism*, 335–38. Some sources and historian David W. Southern date the NCCIJ's founding to the second meeting of the interim committee in St. Louis in June 1959, while the conference itself gave its founding date as August 1960 when its first national convention met in St. Louis. According to Matt Ahmann, "The Conference was incorporated in mid-1960. The decision to form the Conference was ratified August of 1960. The Conference opened its office doors in January of 1961." Mathew Ahmann to Benjamin Muse, February 10, 1965 (quotation), folder 2, box 3, series 4.1, NCCIJR; Southern, *John LaFarge and the Limits of Catholic Interracialism*, 336–37.

65. "Resolutions and Reports," *Interracial Review* 33 (November 1960): 280; *New York Times*, August 26, 29, 1960; Southern, *John LaFarge and the Limits of Catholic Interracialism*, 338, 341; "Sit-Down Education," *North Carolina Catholic*, February 21, 1960 (quotation); William H.

Chafe, *Civilities and Civil Rights: Greensboro, North Carolina, and the Black Struggle for Freedom* (Oxford: Oxford University Press, 1981 [1980]), 79–101.

66. National Catholic Conference for Interracial Justice, "Proposal for a Southern Field Service," n.d., 2–3, folder 7, box 4, series 30, "C.I.C. Launching Membership Drive," *Guardian*, September 25, 1964, press clipping, folder 6, box 2, "Southern Field Service Report to the Directors of the National Catholic Conference for Interracial Justice August 1962," 1, folder 4, box 8, series 33, National Catholic Conference for Interracial Justice, "Summary Proposal for Maintaining Southern Field Service Project," September 1962, 1–2, folder 7, box 4, series 30, NCCIJR; Mathew Ahmann, "Catholics and Race," *Commonweal* 73 (December 2, 1960): 248; "Council on Human Relations Is Seen as 'Holy Crusade,'" *Catholic Action of the South*, April 2, 1961; Peter Finney Jr., "Lay Persons Launched 1961 Desegregation Drive," *Clarion Herald*, January 18, 2001.

67. "Membership Drive," *Catholic Council on Human Relations Newsletter* 1 (July 1961): 2, folder 7, box 1, Henry Cabirac Jr. to Albert S. Foley, May 29, 1961, folder 8, box 1, "Minutes of a Combination Meeting of the Membership and Program Planning Committee Held September 6," folder 1, box 2, "Minutes of Directors' Meeting," July 11, 1962, 1, folder 2, box 2, Catholic Council on Human Relations Papers, Amistad Research Center (hereinafter cited as CCHRP); L. J. Twomey to Mathew Ahmann, July 26, 1961, folder 9, box 21, L. J. Twomey to Mathew Ahmann, October 25, 1961, folder 10, box 21, Twomey Papers.

68. "Biographical Sketch—Henry A. Cabirac, Jr.," folder 7, box 3, CCHRP; National Catholic Conference for Interracial Justice, "Summary Proposal for Maintaining Southern Field Service Project," September 1962, 1–2; "Southern Field Service," *National Catholic Conference for Interracial Justice Newsletter*, December 1961, 2, folder 1, box 1, series 8, Henry Cabirac Jr. to N. C. McGowen, May 23, 1962, folder 13, box 9, series 33, Henry Cabirac Jr. to Clarence Laws, November 29, 1961, folder 14, box 2, series 4.1, NCCIJR; L. J. Twomey to Mathew Ahmann, February 22, 1961, folder 7, box 21, Twomey Papers.

69. "Jack Nelson Eulogy 3.15.06," 3–4; L. J. Twomey to George G. Higgins, April 13, 1961, L. J. Twomey to Ruby Hurley, May 23, 1961, folder 8, box 21, [New Orleans] *Times-Picayune*, May 25, 1961 (quotation), press clipping, folder 13, box 83, "Kick Off Rally," poster, May 24, 1961, folder 9, box 83, Twomey Papers; *Alabama: 1961 Report to the Commission on Civil Rights from the State Advisory Committee*, folder 1, box 3, "Rights Group Urges Probing of Police Power in Alabama," *Mobile Press-Register*, September 10, 1961, press clipping, folder 4, box 3, Foley Papers; Foley to Adams, November 23, 1977, 12–14.

70. J. Michael Parker, "Fighter for Civil Rights," *San Antonio Express-News*, January 17, 2004, press clipping, folder "Bio: cv and Misc.," Sherrill Smith Papers, AASA; "Priest Protests South Injustices," *Alamo Messenger*, April 2, 1965. According to historian Saul E. Bronder, Smith planned, initiated, and organized the stand-ins in 1960, acting with Lucey's approval. However, Smith's interviews suggest that the protest began in 1961 and that he was a participant rather than its leader. Sherrill Smith, interview by Marilyn Kuehler, May 3 [1973], part II, 47–49, folder "Sherrill Smith," AASA; Parker, "Fighter for Civil Rights"; Saul E. Bronder, *Social Justice and Church Authority: The Public Life of Archbishop Robert E. Lucey* (Philadelphia: Temple University Press, 1982), 100–101.

71. Robert E. Lucey to Sherrill Smith, March 26, 1962 (first and second quotations), folder "Lucey, Robert E. (Archbishop) Social Problems: Race Relations Folder #2 (1951–1965)," AASA; Gerard E. Sherry to Mathew Ahmann, March 10, 1964, folder 3, box 5, series 33, NCCIJR; L. J. Twomey to John Ciekst, April 13, 1965 (third quotations), folder 6, box 22, Twomey Papers.

72. "Southern Field Service Report to the Directors of the National Catholic Conference for Interracial Justice August 1962," 1; National Catholic Conference for Interracial Justice, "Summary Proposal for Maintaining Southern Field Service Project," September 1962, 1–2; memorandum, Jack Sisson to Mathew Ahmann, "Trip to Birmingham, August 29–31, 1964," September 4, 1964, folder 2, box 6, series 33, "Southern Field Service Diocesan Profiles," n.d., 1–28, folder 2, box 5, series 30, NCCIJR; "Minutes of the Meeting of the Board of Directors of the Catholic Council on Human Relations," September 8, 1961, folder 2, box 2, CCHRP; "Most Reverend Paul J. Hallinan, Bishop of Charleston," folder 2, box 1, Archbishop Paul J. Hallinan Papers, AAA (hereinafter cited as Hallinan Papers).

73. "Group Urges Participation in D.C. Civil Rights March" and "Northern Va. Council Backs March in D.C.," *Catholic Virginian*, August 9, 1963; Russell Shaw, "Strong Religious Undercurrent Seen Marking D.C. March," *Catholic Virginian*, September 6, 1963; replies to questionnaire from the NCCIJ dated September 5, 1963, folder 2, box 18, series 33, NCCIJR; Southern, *John LaFarge and the Limits of Catholic Interracialism*, 351–52.

74. Memorandum, Henry Cabirac to Mathew Ahmann, "Visit to Richmond, March 17, 1964," folder 3, box 18, series 33, NCCIJR; John J. Russell to Joseph S. Wholey, March 26, 1964, folder "Interracial Correspondence," box H, Bishop John J. Russell Papers, Archives of the Diocese of Richmond, Richmond, Virginia (hereinafter cited as Russell Papers); Monsignor Thomas P. Hadden interview by author, August 2, 2005; National Catholic Conference for Interracial Justice to "Council Presidents and Chaplains," September 5, 1963, folder 5, box 13, series 33, NCCIJR; Ed Foster, "Priests Plan Return to Selma," *San Antonio Light*, March 12, 1965, press clipping, "Lucey Scrapbook #8," AASA; "Four Local Priests Take Part in March," *Alamo Messenger*, September 12, 1963, press clipping, Robert E. Lucey to Sherrill Smith, May 27, 1964, folder "Lucey Social Problems Folder #2," AASA.

75. Mathew Ahmann to Henry Cabirac, April 20, 1964, John P. Sisson Papers, Tallahassee, Florida (hereinafter cited as Sisson Papers); "President Hailed for Voting Rights Message," *North Carolina Catholic*, March 28, 1965; "Local Priests John Marchers in Alabama Rights Protest," *Alamo Messenger*, March 12, 1965; "Nuns 'Inspire' Selma Marchers," *Texas Catholic Herald* [Houston edition], March 18, 1965; Robert E. Lucey, "Murder in Alabama" and "Localities Respond to Call of Race Trouble in Selma," *Alamo Messenger*, March 19, 1965; Robert E. Lucey to Sherrill Smith, March 29, 1965, folder "Lucey Social Problems Folder #2," AASA; "A Message to 'Outsiders,'" *Ave Maria* 101 (April 17, 1965): 16; "Cleric Defends Dinner for Dr. King," *Oklahoma Courier*, January 8, 1965, press clipping, folder 5, box 4, series 33, "Remarks of Archbishop Paul J. Hallinan at Civic Dinner honoring Dr. Martin Luther King, Jr., Atlanta, January 27, 1965," folder 6, box 3, series 11, Jack [Sisson] to Matt [Ahmann], March 15, 1965, folder 3, box 18, series 33, NCCIJR; Gary M. Pomerantz, *Where Peachtree Meets Sweet Auburn: The Saga of Two Families and the Making of Atlanta* (New York: Scribner, 1996), 334–40; Paul J. Hallinan, "Archbishop's Notebook Selma (II) Another Commentary," *Georgia Bulletin*, March 18, 1965; Gerald P. Fogarty, S.J., *Commonwealth Catholicism: A History of the Catholic Church in Virginia* (Notre Dame, IN: University of Note Dame Press, 2001), 536, 619–20 n. 84; "Selma Marchers' Dedication Praised," *Texas Catholic Herald*, March 25, 1965; "Klan Head Says Only Imposters, No Priests, Nuns in Selma March," *Texas Catholic Herald*, September 24, 1965; "Bishop John Louis Morkovsky," accessed October 13, 2007, at http://www.catholic-hierarchy.org/bishop/bmork.html.

76. "South's Catholics Meet on Race," *National Catholic Reporter* 1 (March 24, 1965): 1; "Religion and Race in the South," *Social Digest* (July–September 1965): 182–279; "National Catholic

Conference for Interracial Justice, Report of the Director of the Southern Field Service August, 1965," 1, folder 1, box 5, series 33, NCCIJR; "Catholic Interracial Councils and Chapters," *Social Digest* 8 (July–September 1965): 267–77; "Southern Field Service Diocesan Profiles," n.d., 1–28.

77. John P. Sisson to John J. Russell, July 3, 1965, folder 3, box 1, NCCIJ Southern Field Service press release, July 3, 1965, folder 4, box 1, series 30, NCCIJR; "Social Change and Christian Response Program," *Georgia Bulletin*, July 29, 1965 (quotation). The four visiting prelates were Bishop Coleman F. Carroll of Miami, Bishop John J. Russell of Richmond, Bishop Victor J. Reed of Oklahoma City, and Bishop Charles P. Greco of Alexandria. "Southern Catholics' Meet Set on Human Relations Today," *Georgia Bulletin*, July 29, 1965,

78. "New Orleans, La.," *Josephite Harvest* 77 (January–February 1965): 21; "Fr. Richard Swift, Josephite, Dies," *Catholic Review*, June 7, 1974, press clipping, folder "B/Swift, Richard 3 +4 mag, newspaper + junque," George Brown, "2 Deep South Priests Say Church Must Lead," *Denver Post*, June 30, 1965, press clipping, folder "Morrissey, William J. 4 Junque," "He Lived the Gospel," *Josephite Harvest*, August 1984, clipping, folder "Morrissey, William J. Archives Biog. M-," ASSJ; William J. Jacobs, "Mississippi Report 6: I Was a White Man for the NAACP," *Ave Maria* 101 (February 20, 1965): 6–7; Danny Duncan Collum, *Black and Catholic in the Jim Crow South: The Stuff That Makes Community* (New York: Paulist Press, 2006), 1, 6–7, 14, 109, 129, 132–35, 137; Paul T. Murray, "Father Nathaniel and the Greenwood Movement," *Journal of Mississippi History* 72 (Fall 2010): 277–311; "Southern Field Service Diocesan Profiles," n.d., 10. According to Danny Duncan Collum's study of Holy Family Church, Morrissey was the NAACP's first white officer in Mississippi, serving as vice president of the Adams County chapter and president of the Natchez NAACP. Collum, *Black and Catholic in the Jim Crow South*, 1, 6–7, 132–33.

79. Catherine L. Wanslow, "Catholic Interracial Council of Fort Smith," October 18, 1964, 1, January 17, 1965, 1, "Civil Rights Work Brings Citation," *Guardian*, September 9, 1966, press clipping, "Fort Smith C.I.C. Names Officers, Board Members," *Guardian*, January 27, 1967, press clipping, Sister Anne Michele, "The Catholic Interracial Council of Fort Smith," March 19, 1967, folder 5, box 2, "Sister Is Named to Civil Rights Job," *Arizona Register*, May 12, 1967, press clipping, folder 19, box 3, series 33, NCCIJR; "'Dig Out' Racial Injustice, Fort Smith C.I.C. Told," *Guardian*, March 5, 1965; "Prayer for Divine Guidance Climaxes Huge Rights March," *Guardian*, August 30, 1963; *Arkansas Gazette*, February 1, 1964; "Southern Field Service Diocesan Profiles," n.d., 6; National Catholic Conference for Interracial Justice, untitled press release, July 10, 1963, folder 2, box 84, Twomey Papers; John McCarthy to John L. Morkovsky, April 20, 1964, "Record Department Boards and Committees," RG 2.1 "Catholic Council on Community Relations (CCCR)," Archives of the Archdiocese of Galveston-Houston, Houston, Texas; "Seeking Justice for All," *Texas Catholic Herald* [Houston edition], May 14, 1964; "Community Relations Unit Set Up."

80. "Bishop Coleman F. Carroll Named First Archbishop," *Voice*, May 10, 1968; Michael J. McNally, *Catholicism in South Florida, 1868–1968* (Gainesville: University of Florida Press, 1982), 102–12, 193; "New Metro Board to Deal with Race Problems Here," *Voice*, June 14, 1963; "Form Race Commission Here" and "Community Relations Board Appointed in Dade County," *Voice*, June 21, 1963; John J. Ward, "Good Race Relations Promoted," *Voice*, November 4, 1966; Coleman F. Carroll, "Diocesan and Religious Involvement in Human Relations," July 1965, 4–5, folder 4, box 2, series 30, NCCIJR; "Public Officials Called On to Ban All Discrimination" (quotation) and Edward A. McCarthy, "Relations Council Aims to Improve Lot of Many," *Voice*, April 24, 1964; "Racial Equality a Moral Issue, Bishop Declares," *Voice*, May 22, 1964; "Panel Discusses Better Negro Housing Here," *Voice*, June 12, 1964; "Challenge of Human Rights Topic

of Conference Sunday," *Voice*, July 24, 1964; "It's Up to Individual to Make Civil Rights Work, Panel Says," *Voice*, July 31, 1964; Frater John Bryne, "Miami Meeting," *Josephite Harvest* 76 (July–August 1964): 20–21; "Sessions on Negro Housing, Unemployment Saturday," *Voice*, March 26, 1965; "Negro Education Stressed," *Voice*, April 2, 1965.

81. "John Downey Toomey, Record of Priests, Diocese of Savannah," folder "Msgr. John D. Toomey," box "Deceased Priests," Archives of the Diocese of Savannah, Savannah, Georgia; "Racial Peace Is Everybody's Job," *Southern Cross*, July 18, 1963; *New York Times*, August 4, 1963; John D. Toomey, "An Open Letter to Dr. Martin Luther King," *Southern Cross*, August 19, 1965; "Southern Field Service Diocesan Profiles," n.d., 9, 11; "Data Sheet—Gerard E. Sherry," n.d., folder 3, box 5,"Review of the Year 1964 Georgia Council on Human Relations," 12, folder 6, box 4, series 33, NCCIJR; Gerard E. Sherry, "Report St. Martin's Human Relations Council 1963–1964 and 1964–1965," June 6, 1965, 1, folder 1, box 023/2, AAA. Sherry became a US citizen in 1955. "Data Sheet—Gerard E. Sherry."

82. Namorato, *Catholic Church in Mississippi*, 135; Donald Cunnigen, "Men and Women of Goodwill: Mississippi's White Liberals" (PhD diss., Harvard University, 1988), 113–14, 299 n. 12; Bernard L. Law, "Legal Segregation Is Dying," *Mississippi Register*, March 13, 1964 (quotations).

83. "Organization Meeting La. Human Relations Council," February 16, 1964, "Louisiana Council on Human Relations Constituent Assembly," July 11, 1964, "Board Elects," *Southwest Louisiana Register*, March 18, 1965, press clipping, "Board of Directors Hears of Unsolved Murders," *Louisiana Council on Human Relations Newsletter*, vol. 1, no. 1 (n.d.), 1–2, James R. Oliver, "Human Relations—What Can Be Done?" *Southwest Louisiana Register*, press clipping dated May 27, 1965, "Board of Advisors," *Louisiana Council on Human Relations* 1, no. 3 (n.d.), 2, "Title VI Meeting," *Louisiana Council on Human Relations Newsletter*, vol. 1, no. 4 (n.d.), 3, folder 8, box 6, "Dr. James Oliver Named Leading Faculty Member," *Southwest Louisiana Register*, August 21, 1965, press clipping, folder 6, box 7, series 33, memorandum Jack Sisson to Matt Ahmann, "Visit to Baton Rouge, May 30, 1964," June 1, 1964, folder 10, box 3, series 11, NCCIJR; James R. Oliver to Edward J. O'Donnell, February 22, 1995, folder "Racism," ADL; Alexander O. Sigur to Louis Twomey, April 2, 1964, folder 1, box 22, "Louisiana 1961 Report to the Commission on Civil Rights from the State Advisory Committee," folder 7, box 84, Paul Hilsdale to Andrew Maginnis, June 25, 1965, folder 8, box 22, Twomey Papers; James R. Oliver, "Social Revolution: How It Affects You," *Clarion Herald*, June 10, 1965; John P. Sisson, interview by author, July 30, 2007; John P. Sisson, résumé, January 1988, Sisson Papers. In 1964, the Institute of Industrial Relations became the Institute of Human Relations. "Loyola of the South and the Social Apostolate," *Blueprint* 17 (September 1964): 4.

84. "Bishop Carroll 'Man of the Year' in Dade," *Voice*, April 30, 1965; "Data on the Rev. Louis J. Twomey, S.J.," folder 1, box 3, series 30, NCCIJR; L. J. Twomey to Edwin E. Willis, June 9, 1965, folder 8, box 22, L. J. Twomey to Sister Mary Frances, July 26, 1965, folder 9, box 22, Twomey Papers; "Fighting for Equal Rights a Moral Act, not Political," *Voice*, May 8, 1964; "We Should Agree Rights Legislation Was Needed," *Voice*, June 26, 1964; "Reverently Obey Civil Rights Law, Bishop Urges," *Voice*, July 10, 1964; "Vote Rights Law Adoption Will Be Answer to Selma," *Voice*, March 19, 1965; "New Era in Human Relations," *Texas Catholic Herald* [Houston edition], July 2, 1964; "Rights Law Necessary to Compel Respect for Negro Rights," *Alamo Messenger*, July 10, 1964; "Off-target Criticism," *Texas Catholic Herald* [Houston edition], July 23, 1964; Declan Thompson to the *Texas Catholic Herald* [Houston edition], April 8, 1965; "Presidential Backing," *Georgia Bulletin*, March 18, 1965; John Catullus to the *Texas Catholic Herald* [Houston edition], March 25, 1965 (quotation).

85. Thomas H. Gibbons Jr., "Project Equality," *Collegium* 1 (July 1966), n.p., folder 18, box 1, Edmundite Missions Records, Amistad Research Center; "The White House Conference 'To Fulfill These Rights,'" June 1–2, 1966, 37–38, box 4528303 Subject Files Hallinan, AAA; Mathew Ahmann, "Project Equality," *Christianity and Crisis* 27 (May 29, 1967): 118–21; Richard M. McKeon, "Project Equality," *American Ecclesiastical Review* 158 (May 1968): 319–24.

86. "Detroit and St. Louis Use Vast Church Funds to Insure Fair Hiring," *National Catholic Reporter*, 1 (May 19, 1965): 1; Dick Meskill, "Archbishop Marshals Buying Power to Promote Employment Equality," *Alamo Messenger*, August 13, 1965; "Project Equality Growing," *America* 113 (September 5, 1965): 233; Archdiocese of San Antonio untitled press release, dated October 7 [1965], folder 4, box 2, series 8, memorandum, John P. Sisson to "Staff," "SFS Report to Staff, September 14–October 11, 1968," October 11, 1968, 2, folder 5, box 5, series 30, NCCIJR; Thomas H. Gibbons Jr. to Robert E. Lucey, February 27, 1967, folder "Social Problems Project Equality Natl. Cath. Conf. for Interracial Justice (1961–1969)," Sylvia Springer, "Rev. Sherrill Smith Receives Kennedy Freedom Award," press clipping, no date, folder "Bio: Honors/Awards Recognition," Sherrill Smith, interview by Lyle C. Brown, August 17, 1972, Oral History Memoir, Baylor University Program for Oral History, 21–25, folder "Oral History—Selma March," Sherrill Smith Papers, AASA; Bronder, *Social Justice and Church Authority*, 104, 118, 123.

87. Sisson to "Staff," "SFS Report to Staff, September 14–October 11, 1968," October 11, 1968, 2–3; Thomas H. Gibbons Jr. to John J. McMahon, May 24, 1966, folder "Interracial Correspondence," box H, Russell Papers; Albert L. Fletcher to Robert E. Lucey, July 10, 1968, folder "Social Problems Project Equality Miscellaneous (1968–1969)," AASA; memorandum, Jack Sisson to Matt Ahmann and Tom Gibbons, "Project Equality and other matters in the Diocese of Miami," February 23, 1967, folder 31, box 5, series 11, memorandum, Jack Sisson to Tom Gibbons and Matt Ahmann, "Project Equality in Tennessee," March 13, 1967, folder 3, box 15, series 33, memorandum, John P. Sisson to "Staff," "SFS Report to Staff, October 12–November 21, 1968," November 21, 1968, 1–2, memorandum, John P. Sisson to "Staff," "SFS Report to Staff, April 4–May 20, 1969," May 20, 1969, 1, folder 5, box 5, series 30, NCCIJR; "Bishop Joseph Durick Is Named Coadjutor," *Tennessee Register*, December 13, 1963; "Project Equality Announcement Draws High Praise, Support from across U.S.," *Tennessee Register*, March 10, 1967; "Project Equality, Inc., Opens 3rd Job Center," *Tennessee Register*, June 28, 1968; Doug Williams, "Project Equality Success Depends on Commitments," *Texas Catholic Herald* [Beaumont edition], November 29, 1968.

88. John P. Sisson, "Report of the Director of the Southern Field Service, August 1966," August 3, 1966, 2–7, 11–12 (quotation on p. 12), folder 2, box 5, series 30, memorandum, Jim McGuire to Matt [Ahmann], "Southern Field Service and the Meredith Freedom March," June 29, 1966, memorandum, Jack [Sisson] to Matt [Ahmann], "Meredith Mississippi Freedom March, June 6–26, 1966 (Jim sent a separate report of his activities from June 22 to June 28)," June 30, 1966, memorandum, Matt Ahmann to NCCIJ Board of Directors, "Conference Involvement in Meredith Mississippi March," June 30, 1966, folder 11, box 8, series 34, Mathew Ahmann to Edwin J. Wallin, July 1, 1966, Joseph B. Brunini to Mathew Ahmann, March 27, 1967, folder 11, box 14, Kathleen Woods to James J. McGuire, December 5, 1966, 4, folder 6, box 2, series 33, NCCIJR; "Mississippi Riot Averted," folder "Oral History-Selma March," Sherrill Smith Papers, AASA; John Dittmer, *Local People: The Struggle for Civil Rights in Mississippi* (Urbana and Chicago: University of Illinois Press, 1994), 389, 392–402; Amy L. Koehlinger, *The New Nuns: Racial Justice and Religious Reform in the 1960s* (Cambridge, MA: Harvard University Press, 2007), 80–81.

89. "Bishop Cody, New Orleans Coadjutor," *Voice*, August 18, 1961; "John Patrick Cardinal Cody," accessed October 1, 2014, at http://www.catholic-hierarchy.org/bishop/bcody.html; C. Ellis Henican to Mathew Ahmann, March 12, 1963, February 6, 1964, folder 10, box 3, CCHRP; Charles J. Plauche to Philip M. Hannan, February 9, 1967, folder 6, box 6, series 11, memorandum, Jack Sisson to Matt Ahmann et al., "Southern Field Service Program Report," February 18, 1966, 2, folder 3, box 5, memorandum, John P. Sisson to "Staff," "SFS Report to Staff, March 12–31, 1967," March 31, 1967, 4–5, folder 4, box 5, series 30, memorandum, Jim McGuire to Matt [Ahmann], "CIC of Northern Virginia—Trip Report," August 3, 1966, folder 2, box 18, series 18, NCCIJR; "Southern Field Service Diocesan Profiles," n.d., 16, 22.

90. Memorandum, John P. Sisson to "Staff," "SFS Report to Staff, March 12–31, 1967," March 31, 1967, 4 (first quotation); John P. Sisson to "Staff," "SFS Report to Staff, January 1–February 11, 1969," February 11, 1969, 2 (second quotation), folder 5, box 5, series 30, NCCIJR. In addition to the eleven southern states the Southern Field Service had responsibility for Arizona, Kentucky, New Mexico, Oklahoma, and West Virginia. "Southern Field Service Diocesan Profiles," n.d., 1–29.

91. Memorandum, Jack [John P. Sisson] to Matt [Ahmann], "Little Rock, Arkansas," October 23, 1968, folder 8, box 2, minutes, Catholic Interracial Council of Fort Smith, December 1, 1968, 1, folder 5, box 2, series 33, memorandum, John P. Sisson to "Staff," "SFS Report to Staff, July 16–September 30, 1969," September 30, 1969, 1 (quotation), folder 5, box 5, series 30, NCCIJR.

92. "Catholics Play Major Part in March for King" and Joseph Sweat, "Bishop Marches to Honor Martin Luther King," *Tennessee Register*, April 11, 1969.

93. "Bishop Ernest Leo Unterkoefler," accessed June 11, 2008, at http://www.catholic-hierarchy.org/bishop/bunte.html; Leland J. White, "A Bishop's Place," *Commonweal* 88 (June 14, 1968): 391; *New York Times*, May 14, 1968; "N. Va. Parishes Helping Poor People's Campaign," *Catholic Virginian*, June 14, 1968; Walter F. Sullivan to John P. Sisson, May 27, 1968, folder 4, box 18, series 33, NCCIJR; Leland J. White, "A Bishop's Place," *Commonweal* 88 (June 14, 1968): 391; *Encyclopedia of African-American Civil Rights: From Emancipation to the Present*, ed. Lowery and Marszalek, s.v., "Poor People's March on Washington," by Betty L. Plummer.

94. Mrs. J. C. Campbell, "Why Is an Integrated School Better Than a Segregated School?" n.d. [1956], folder 13, box 46, Fichter Papers.

95. Woods to McGuire, December 5, 1966, 2–3; William Barnaby Faherty, S.J., *Rebels or Reformers?: Dissenting Priests in American Life* (Chicago: Loyola University Press, 1987), 82–83 (quotation on p. 83).

Chapter Five

1. *New York Times*, August 10, 1957; John J. Russell, "Official Catholic Education, August 27, 1954," *Catholic Banner*, September 5, 1954; Anthony McDevitt to Fagan Canzoneria, September 15, 1961, folder "Schools—1961–62," no box, Archbishop Thomas J. Toolen Papers, Archives of the Archdiocese of Mobile, Mobile, Alabama; "Bishop Stresses Value of Catholic Education," *North-Central Louisiana Register*, September 3, 1965; M. F. Everett, "Errors in Statement by Trio Are Pointed Out," *Catholic Action of the South*, March 4, 1956.

2. Catholic Committee of the South, "Segregation and the Catholic Schools: A Study," 2–5, 46–51, folder 12, box 48, Joseph H. Fichter Papers, Special Collections and Archives, Loyola University Library, Loyola University New Orleans, New Orleans, Louisiana (hereinafter cited

as Fichter Papers); "Inter-Racial Committee on Education Is Proposed," *Catholic Virginian*, September 7, 1956.

3. Numan V. Bartley, *The Rise of Massive Resistance: Race and Politics in the South during the 1950s* (Baton Rouge: Louisiana State University Press, 1969), 67–74; Mark Newman, *The Civil Rights Movement* (Edinburgh: Edinburgh University Press, 2004), 51.

4. "A Moral, Religious Problem," *Catholic Virginian*, May 21, 1954 (first quotation); "Msgr. J. Flaherty Named Richmond Auxiliary Bishop," *Catholic Week*, August 19, 1966; *Mobile Press*, May 25, 1954 (second and third quotations); Jim McDermott, "A Quiet Change of Course," *America* 196 (April 9, 2007): 13, 15; "Segregation Banned in Public Schools," *Catholic Action of the South*, May 20, 1954 (fourth quotation); [New Orleans] *Times-Picayune*, May 28, 1954; Henry C. Bezou, "Address to the Council of Catholic School Cooperative Clubs," St. Leo the Great School, New Orleans, June 7, 1954, 1–3, 03–038 box 2, "Desegregation, Office of Catholic Schools, Corres. + Reports (1954–1976)," Archives of the Archdiocese of New Orleans, New Orleans, Louisiana (hereinafter cited as AANO).

5. Thomas Stritch, *The Catholic Church in Tennessee: The Sesquicentennial Story* (Nashville: The Catholic Center, 1987), 334; "Another Forthright Voice in the South," *Interracial Review* 28 (January 1955): 5 (quotation); Adam Fairclough, *Race and Democracy: The Struggle for Civil Rights in Louisiana, 1915–1972* (Athens: University of Georgia Press, 1995), 169–70; Bartley, *Rise of Massive Resistance*, 74–75; Douglas J. Roche, "Two Southerners Speak Their Minds," *Sign* 41 (October 1961): 30; Edward Hoag, "New Orleans Looking Forward," *Ave Maria* 95 (June 2, 1962): 13.

6. M. F. Everett, "Despotic Police State Seen as Result of School Control Acts," *Catholic Action of the South*, July 1, 1954.

7. Everett, "Despotic Police State Seen as Result of School Control Acts" (first quotation); Joseph F. Rummel to Robert F. Kennon, July 1, 1954 (second quotation), folder 38, box 2, Archbishop Joseph F. Rummel Papers, Joseph F. Rummel to "Reverend dear Father," July 16, 1954, no folder, no box, AANO; Fairclough, *Race and Democracy*, 171–72. According to historian Adam Fairclough, "a bill authorizing school boards to give financial assistance to children in private [segregated] schools never came to a vote." Fairclough, *Race and Democracy*, 171.

8. M. F. Everett, "To Obey Law or Not: Clear Issue Is Joined as School Bills Pass," *Catholic Action of the South*, July 8, 1954 (first and second quotations); "Parochial Schools Exempted from School Segregation Law; Archbishop's Opposition Stands," *N.C.W.C. News Service*, July 12, 1954, folder 7, box 84, Louis J. Twomey Papers, Special Collections and Archives, Loyola University Library, Loyola University New Orleans (hereinafter cited as Twomey Papers); Charles Keenan, "Louisiana Says 'No,'" *America* 91 (July 31, 1954): 439–40.

9. Fairclough, *Race and Democracy*, 169–70 (quotation on p. 169); M. F. Everett, "Prejudice Is Exposed as Mental Blindness," *Catholic Action of the South*, September 9, 1954; M. F. Everett, "Color Is Accidental, Not Basic Quality," *Catholic Action of the South*, September 16, 1954; M. F. Everett, "Segregation Exacts Heavy Cost in U.S.," *Catholic Action of the South*, September 23, 1954; M. F. Everett, "Law of Love Must Extend to All Men," *Catholic Action of the South*, September 30, 1954; M. F. Everett, "True Equality Ideal Basic to Democracy," *Catholic Action of the South*, October 7, 1954; M. F. Everett, "Non-Catholics Vote for Racial Justice," *Catholic Action of the South*, October 14, 1954; M. F. Everett, "School Segregation Is Unconstitutional," *Catholic Action of the South*, October 21, 1954; M. F. Everett, "What Price Justice?" *Catholic Action of the South*, October 28, 1954.

10. Fairclough, *Race and Democracy*, 170, 215–16.

11. Bartley, *Rise of Massive Resistance*, 59–60 (quotation on p. 60), 82–103.

12. Ibid., 90–91; "A Troubling Matter," *Southwest Louisiana Register*, July 15, 1955 (quotation).

13. A. J. Vincent to the[Lafayette, Louisiana] *Daily Advertiser*, December 4, 1955 (quotations); "Lafayette Priest Blasts 'Southern Gentlemen' Acts," *Catholic Action of the South*, December 18, 1955; Fairclough, *Race and Democracy*, 191–93.

14. "Archbishop Rummel," 3–4 (first, second, and third quotations on p. 3), folder 15, box 48, Fichter Papers; *New York Times*, February 27, 1956.

15. "Statement of Friendship to Colored People," February 19, 1956, folder 8, box 20, Twomey Papers.

16. James W. Ely Jr., *The Crisis of Conservative Virginia: The Byrd Organization and the Politics of Massive Resistance* (Knoxville: University of Tennessee Press, 1976), 39–42; "Inter-Racial Committee on Education Is Proposed" (quotation).

17. "Inter-Racial Committee on Education Is Proposed" (quotations); Ely, *Crisis of Conservative Virginia*, 44–46.

18. *New York Times*, September 2, 1956; Numan V. Bartley, *The New South, 1945–1980* (Baton Rouge: Louisiana State University Press, 1995), 195 (quotation), 218–19. The figures for Catholic enrollment in public and parochial schools refer to 1955. "Scores State Official on Segregation Issue," *Interracial Review* 28 (May 1955): 87.

19. Vincent S. Waters to "My dear Brethren," August 17, 1956, 1–4 (quotations on p. 2), bound volume "Pastoral Letters V. S. Waters 1953–1956," Archives of the Diocese of Raleigh, Raleigh, North Carolina.

20. Waters to "My dear Brethren," August 17, 1956, 3–4 (quotation on p. 3); William Bagwell, *School Desegregation in the Carolinas: Two Cases Studies* (Columbia: University of South Carolina Press, 1972), 96. Token public school desegregation began in September 1957 with the admission of eleven black students to schools in Charlotte, Greensboro, and Winston-Salem. Reed Sarratt, *The Ordeal of Desegregation: The First Decade* (New York: Harper and Row, 1966), 353.

21. "We Defend the NAACP," *Alamo Register*, October 19, 1956 (quotations); Bartley, *Rise of Massive Resistance*, 98, 146–47, 216. Although Shepperd obtained a temporary injunction against the NAACP, ten months later a state judge allowed the association to operate but with some restrictions. Bartley, *Rise of Massive Resistance*, 216.

22. *San Antonio Light*, March 25, 1957; Bartley, *Rise of Massive Resistance*, 141; "Excerpts from a Sermon by Archbishop Robert E. Lucey Delivered to a City-Wide Meeting of the Legion of Mary at Little Flower Parish, Sunday Afternoon, March 24, 1957" (quotations), folder "Interracial (Current)," box CGRM 5/03, Joseph Gremillion Papers, University of Notre Dame Archives, Notre Dame, Indiana.

23. "Press vs. Integration," *Guardian*, September 20, 1957 (quotations); Bartley, *New South*, 228–29.

24. Bartley, *New South*, 229–30.

25. Robert R. Brown, *Bigger Than Little Rock* (London: S.P.C.K., 1958), 92–98; *New York Times*, October 13, 1957. The Right Reverend Monsignor James E. O'Connell, rector of Little Rock's St. John's Home Missions Seminary, represented Bishop Fletcher at planning meetings. "Integration Problem Rites Set," *Guardian*, October 11, 1957.

26. "Integration Problem Rites Set."

27. Ernest Q. Campbell and Thomas F. Pettigrew, *Christians in Racial Crisis: A Study of Little Rock's Ministry* (Washington, DC: Public Affairs Press, 1959), 34 (quotation); "Services Held Seeking God's Aid in L.R. Crisis," *Guardian*, October 18, 1957. Sociologists Ernest Q. Campbell and Thomas F. Pettigrew estimated turnout at 6,000. They wrote that although eighty-five churches had issued an invitation to prayer, only fifty-three had "announced their intent to

participate," fifteen of them black churches. The *New York Times* estimated turnout at between 6,000 and 7,000, while Bishop Roger R. Brown claimed at least eighty-six churches and between 8,000 and 10,000 people had participated in the services. Campbell and Pettigrew, *Christians in Racial Crisis*, 31 (quotation), 34; *New York Times*, October 13, 1957; Brown, *Bigger Than Little Rock*, 104.

28. David L. Chappell, *Inside Agitators: White Southerners in the Civil Rights Movement*, with a Foreword by Clayborne Carson (Baltimore: Johns Hopkins University Press, 1994), 116; Lawrence M. Fridel, "High Enrollment in High School," *Our Colored Missions* 46 (March 1960): 43. In August 1959, Little Rock's public high schools reopened, and a white mob tried unsuccessfully to prevent desegregation at Central High School. Chappell, *Inside Agitators*, 118.

29. William W. O'Donnell, "America's Race Problem," *Guardian*, August 21, 1959 (first, second, and third quotations); C. J. Westerer to the *Guardian*, October 9, 1959 (fourth quotation); Jemore D. Stocking to the *Guardian*, October 9, 1959; Donald J. Thorman to the *Guardian*, October 23, 1959.

30. "Georgia Urged by Bishop not to Close Its Public Schools," *Guardian*, December 18, 1959 (quotations); "Public Education in Atlanta," *Commonweal* 71 (December 25, 1959): 360.

31. "The Image of Georgia," *Bulletin of the Catholic Laymen's Association of Georgia*, January 21, 1962 (quotation); Bartley, *Rise of Massive Resistance*, 333, 335.

32. Gladys Gunning to Francis E. Hyland, May 10, 1961, Norman Shands to Francis E. Hyland, May 19, 1961, Francis E. Hyland to Norman Shands, May 22, 1961, Harold J. Rainey to Henry De Give, July 31, 1961, Gladys Gunning to Francis E. Hyland, August 1, 1961, Francis E. Hyland to Mrs. George J. Gunning, August 7, 1961, Gladys Gunning to Francis E. Hyland, August 15, 1961 and attached report of the final meeting of the Religious Section of OASIS, August 14, 1961, folder 49, box 036/6, Archives of the Archdiocese of Atlanta, Atlanta, Georgia (hereinafter cited as AAA); *New York Times*, August 28, 1961 (quotations).

33. Hyland to Gunning, August 7, 1961 (first quotation); *New York Times*, August 28, 1961 (second and fourth quotations); *Atlanta Constitution*, February 1, 1968 (third quotation); Bartley, *Rise of Massive Resistance*, 335.

34. "Save Our Schools, Inc." n.d. (quotations), folder 7, box 1, Save Our Schools Collection, Amistad Research Center, New Orleans, Louisiana (hereinafter cited as SOSC); *New York Times*, May 1, 1960, January 28, 1961; Fairclough, *Race and Democracy*, 236; Kim Lacy Rogers, *Righteous Lives: Narratives of the New Orleans Civil Rights Movement* (New York: New York University Press, 1993), 50, 58, 66–67, 208, 209.

35. Fairclough, *Race and Democracy*, 236–37.

36. Joseph Francis Rummel to Lloyd J. Rittiner, June 20, 1960, folder "School Integration File Pastoral Letter of Archbishop Joseph Rummel, 1953–1960," box "School Integration Files, 1953–1965" AR/00165, AANO; L. J. Twomey to J. Skelly Wright, February 21, 1956, folder 2, box 20, Twomey Papers; Edwin Hoag, "Behind the New Orleans School Crisis," *Ave Maria* 92 (December 31, 1960): 27; *New York Times*, August 14, 1960.

37. Joseph F. Rummel to James H. Davis, June 22, 1960 (first quotation), folder "School Integration File, 1956–1962 South La. Citizens Council," box "School Integration Files and Labor Issues, 1944–1963" AR/00173, AANO; Fairclough, *Race and Democracy*, 235; "Pastoral Letter of Archbishop Joseph F. Rummel, New Orleans, La., August 14, 1960," *Interracial Review* 33 (October 1960): 242–43 (second, third, fourth, and fifth quotations on p. 242; sixth and seventh quotations on p. 243); *New York Times*, August 21, 22, 1960.

38. "To Read Is to Weep," *Blueprint* 13 (December 1960): 4–5, Special Collections and Archives, Loyola University Library, Loyola University New Orleans; Maurice "Moon" Landrieu, interview by author, July 12, 2007; Rogers, *Righteous Lives*, 59–60, 65; Fairclough, *Race and Democracy*, 238–45; Henry C. Bezou to the "Right Reverend, Very Reverend, and Reverend Pastors; to the Principals of Catholic Elementary Schools of New Orleans," November 14, 1960, 1 (quotation), folder "Integration, School Board Meetings, Minutes + Notes (1954–1962)," 03-038 box 1, AANO.

39. *New York Times*, November 16, 29, December 4, 1960, January 1, 1961 (quotation); "Father Drolet, Member of Red Group, Is Out as Kenner Pastor," *Citizens' Report*, special edition, February 1963, folder 2, box 53, Fichter Papers; Justin D. Poché, "Religion, Race, and Rights in Catholic Louisiana, 1938–1970" (PhD diss., University of Notre Dame, 2007), 83; Fairclough, *Race and Democracy*, 244, 247–48. This account relies primarily on the *New York Times*'s report of Drolet's action. According to the South Louisiana Citizens' Council, Foreman had been taking "his child into the school." "Father Drolet, Member of Red Group, Is Out as Kenner Pastor."

40. Hoag, "Behind the New Orleans School Crisis," 26, 28–29; "Save Our Schools Inc.," n.d. 5–6, box 1, folder 7, SOSC; *New York Times*, November 29, 1960, January 1, 1961 (quotation); Fairclough, *Race and Democracy*, 249–50.

41. "Sit-Down Education," *North Carolina Catholic*, February 21, 1960; "New Director Appointed for Southern Field Service Project of National Catholic Conference for Interracial Justice," n.d., folder 3, box 25, Archives of the Diocese of Savannah, Savannah, Georgia (hereinafter cited as ADS); John P. Sisson, interview by author, July 30, 2007; John P. Sisson, résumé, January 1988, John P. Sisson Papers, Tallahassee, Florida; John P. Sisson, résumé, n.d., folder 26, box 3, series 33, National Catholic Conference for Interracial Justice Records, Marquette University, Milwaukee, Wisconsin (hereinafter cited as NCCIJR); John P. Sisson, "A Southern City Changes Gracefully," *Interracial Review* 36 (May 1963): 98–100; Henry Libersat, "A Southerner Works for His South," *Southwest Louisiana Register*, December 10, 1964.

42. "Opinion Worth Noting," *America* 103 (May 21, 1960): 285. Kilpatrick was a native Oklahoman. George Lewis, *Massive Resistance: The White Response to the Civil Rights Movement* (London: Hodder Arnold, 2006), 111. See also William P. Hustwit, *James J. Kilpatrick: Salesman for Segregation* (Chapel Hill: University of North Carolina Press, 2013).

43. Robert L. Wilken, "Gadfly Freedom Riders," *North Carolina Catholic*, June 11, 1961. On the Freedom Rides, see Raymond Arsenault, *Freedom Riders: 1961 and the Struggle for Racial Justice* (New York: Oxford University Press, 2006).

44. "May God Not Give Us What We Deserve," *Catholic Week*, May 26, 1961.

45. Mrs. Frank Dominick to the *Catholic Week*, May 26, 1961 (first quotation); "Race Violence in Alabama Hit by Catholic Spokesmen," *Voice*, June 2, 1961 (second, third, and fourth quotations).

46. "Alabama Religious Leaders Say Defiance Not Solution," *Catholic Week*, January 25, 1963 (first, third, and fourth quotations); S. Jonathan Bass, *Blessed Are the Peacemakers: Martin Luther King Jr., Eight White Religious Leaders, and the "Letter from Birmingham Jail"* (Baton Rouge: Louisiana State University Press, 2001), 233–34 (second quotation on p. 233); Ed Clark, "Clark's Comments," *Catholic Week*, January 25, 1963 (fifth quotation). Besides Durick, the signatories were J. T. Beale, secretary-director, Christian Churches of Alabama; Rabbi Eugene Blackschleger, Temple Beth-Or, Montgomery; Episcopal Bishop C.C.J. Carpenter of Alabama; Reverend Soterios D. Gouvellis, priest, Holy Trinity-Holy Cross Greek Orthodox Church,

Birmingham; Rabbi Milton L. Grafman, Temple Emanu-El, Birmingham; Bishop Paul Hardin of the Alabama-West Florida Conference of the Methodist Church; Bishop Nolan B. Harmon of the North Alabama Conference of the Methodist Church; Episcopal Coadjutor Bishop George M. Murray of Alabama; Edward V. Ramage, moderator, Synod of the Alabama Presbyterian Church in the United States; and Earl Stallings, pastor, First Baptist Church, Birmingham. "Alabama Religious Leaders Say Defiance Not Solution."

47. "Negro Citizenry Urged to Withdraw Support from Racial Demonstrators," *Catholic Week*, April 19, 1963 (first through seventh quotations); Martin Luther King Jr., *Why We Can't Wait* (New York: Harper and Row, 1964), 76–95 (eighth quotation on p. 76). Beale, Blackschleger, and Gouvellis did not sign the April statement. For a detailed study of the January and April ministers' statements and King's response, see Bass, *Blessed Are the Peacemakers*.

48. "Priest in Civil Rights Post Clarifies Position Regarding 'Differences' with Rev. King," *Catholic Week*, May 10, 1963. Albert S. Foley Jr., "Report on a Talk with Martin Luther King: Monday, April 8, 1963," Albert S. Foley Jr., "Telephone Conversation between Fr. Foley & Martin Luther King Monday, April 8, 1963," Albert S. Foley Jr., "Report on Talk with Martin Luther King, Saturday, May 4, 1963," folder 39, box 4, Albert S. Foley to Reese Cleghorn, April 12, 1963, Wyatt T. Walker to Albert Foley, May 7, 1963, Albert S. Foley to Wyatt Tee Walker, Martin Luther King, Ralph Abernathy, Fred Shuttlesworth, and SCLC Board, May 8, 1963, Albert S. Foley to Matt Ahmann, June 18, 1963, folder 40, box 4, Albert Sidney "Steve" Foley Jr., S.J., Papers, Spring Hill College Archives, Mobile, Alabama (hereinafter cited as Foley Papers); "King Accused of Breaking Up Race Progress," *Birmingham News*, April 5, 1963, press clipping, folder 2, box 1, series 33, Albert S. Foley to Mathew Ahmann, April 18, 1963, folder 18, box 1, series 4.1, NCCIJR.

49. Joseph A. Durick, "Bishop Durick's Statement on Racial Tensions," *Catholic Week*, May 10, 1963 (first quotation); Albert S. Foley Jr., statement dated May 7, 1963 (second quotation), folder 39, box 4, Foley Papers; "Priest in Civil Rights Post Clarifies Position Regarding 'Differences' with Rev. King"; Newman, *Civil Rights Movement*, 87.

50. "Negroes Reminded That Obligations Accompany Rights," *Catholic Week*, May 17, 1963.

51. "Religious Leaders Score Racism," *Voice*, June 7, 1963.

52. "Bishop Gerow Appeals for Positive Steps toward Meeting Negro Grievances," *Catholic Week*, June 21, 1963 (quotations); William A. Osborne, *The Segregated Covenant: Race Relations and American Catholics* (New York: Herder and Herder, 1967), 89–90; Michael V. Namorato, *The Catholic Church in Mississippi, 1911–1984: A History* (Westport, CT: Greenwood Press, 1998), 51, 53, 90.

53. "Murder in Miss. Again," *Clarion Herald*, June 20, 1963; Clayborne Carson et al. (eds.), *The Eyes on the Prize Civil Rights Reader* (New York: Penguin, 1991), 160–62; A. J. Frederic Jr. to the *Catholic Commentator*, June 28, 1963 (quotation).

54. "Interfaith Committee Is Formed to Fight Race Bias on Moral Plane," *Catholic Week*, June 21, 1963; John J. Russell, "Work for Racial Justice in Spirit of Christian Charity, Bishop Urges," *Catholic Virginian*, July 12, 1963 (quotation).

55. *Savannah Evening Press*, July 13, 1963 (quotations); "Racial Peace Is Everybody's Job" and "In Search of Peace," *Southern Cross*, July 18, 1963; *New York Times*, August 4, September 2, 1963; Stephen Tuck, "A City Too Dignified to Hate: Civic Pride, Civil Rights, and Savannah in Comparative Perspective," *Georgia Historical Quarterly* 79 (Fall 1995): 539–59.

56. Charles P. Greco, "Pastoral on Race Relations," August 4, 1963 (quotations), folder 2, box 3, series 11, NCCIJR; *Shreveport Times*, August 4, 1963.

57. "Bishop Asks Cooperation in Desegregation," *Guardian*, September 6, 1963.

58. "Officials Receive Praise for Leadership at Charleston; U.S.C," *Catholic Banner*, September 22, 1963.

59. "Religious Leaders Issue Statement in Wake of Bombings, School Integration," *Catholic Week*, September 13, 1963; "Terror and Grief," *Catholic Virginian*, September 20, 1963; Bass, *Blessed Are the Peacemakers*, 179–80.

60. "Religious Leaders Issue Statement in Wake of Bombings, School Integration" (quotations); William James, "Priest Eye-Witness to Aftermath of Bombing," and Edward L. Foster, "Priest Reflects on Meeting a Mother Seeking Her Children," *Catholic Week*, September 20, 1963; Bass, *Blessed Are the Peacemakers*, 180–81. The signatories were the same as those who issued the April 1963 statement, except for Edward V. Ramage's replacement by John M. Crowell, his successor as moderator of the Synod of Alabama of the Presbyterian Church, U.S. "Religious Leaders Issue Statement in Wake of Bombings, School Integration."

61. "Love Thy Neighbor as Thyself Seems to be a Forgotten Law in Alabama" (first, second, third, and fourth quotations); "Bishop Extends Condolences to Grieving Families" (fifth and sixth quotations), "Vatican City Daily Calls Birmingham Church Bombing 'True Slaughter of the Innocents' by 'Racist Insanity'" (seventh and eighth quotations), "Priests Attend Funeral for Slain Children," *Catholic Week*, September 20, 1963. Durick and five other clergymen from Birmingham later flew to Washington at President Kennedy's request to discuss the racial situation in the city with him. The other clergymen were the Reverend Joseph C. Allen, administrator of St. Francis Xavier Parish, Bishop George M. Murray, Rabbi Milton L. Grafman, Bishop Nolan B. Harmon, and the Reverend Earl Stallings. "Bp. Durick Confers with President," *Catholic Week*, September 27, 1963.

62. Ed Clark, "It Is Time for Strong Men to Speak Up," *Catholic Week*, September 20, 1963.

63. Vincent S. Waters to "My dear Brethren," January 30, 1964, read at all masses February 9, 1964, folder 7, box 13, series 33, NCCIJR.

64. M. Carlotta to John J. Russell, March 9, 1964, folder "Sisters of Mercy," box K, John J. Russell to M. Carlotta, March 10, 1964 (first and second quotations), folder "Sisters of Mercy," box H, John J. Russell to Joseph S. Wholey, March 26, 1964, folder "Interracial Correspondence," box H, Bishop John J. Russell Papers, Archives of the Diocese of Richmond, Richmond, Virginia (hereinafter cited as Russell Papers); Henry Cabirac to Mathew Ahmann, March 17, 1964 (third quotation), folder 3, box 18, series 33, NCCIJR.

65. John J. Russell to Joseph S. Wholey, March 26, 1964, John J. Russell to Heslip M. Lee, April 27, folder "Interracial Correspondence," box H, Russell Papers; "Interracial Council to Gather for Communion Breakfast," *Catholic Virginian*, April 10, 1964; "The Pulpit and the Status Quo," *Catholic Virginian*, December 2, 1966; CICNV newsletter, May 1964, folder 2, box 18, series 33, NCCIJR; "Asks Faiths to 'Awaken Conscience' of Nation," *Southern Cross*, May 7, 1964.

66. "Interfaith Convocation on Civil Rights," Austin, Texas, April 28, 1964, folder 12, box 6, Texas Catholic Conference Records, Catholic Archives of Texas, Austin, Texas (hereinafter cited as CAT); "Archbishop Endorses Civil Rights Proposal," *Alamo Messenger*, May 22, 1964 (first quotation); "Archbishop Lucey Urges Support of Rights Bill," *Texas Catholic*, May 30, 1964, press clipping, "Lucey Scrapbook #8," AASA; Dick Meskill, "In the Shadow of San Fernando," *Alamo Messenger*, June 19, 1964 (second, third, and fourth quotations).

67. John L. Morkovsky to John Tower, May 26, 1964 (first quotation), John L. Morkovsky to Ralph Yarborough, May 26, 1964, John G. Tower to John L. Morkovsky, June 9, 1964, Ralph Yarborough to "Dear Friend," no date, folder DIO: Civil Rights, AGHA; "Statement on 'rights,'" *Texas*

Catholic Herald [Houston edition], June 4, 1964 (second quotation); "Bishop Wendelin Joseph Nold," accessed October 10, 2014, at http://www.catholic-hierarchy.org/bishop/bnold.html.

68. "Racial Bias in All Sections," *Voice*, April 17, 1964; "A Few Wild Leaders Hurt Whole Civil Rights Cause," *Voice*, April 24, 1964 (first quotation); "Fighting for Equal Rights a Moral Act, Not Political," *Voice*, May 8, 1964; "Civil Rightists Encouraged," *Voice*, May 22, 1964; "New Human Relations Council," *Voice*, April 3, 1964; "Public Officials Called On to Ban All Discrimination," *Voice*, April 24, 1964 (second quotation); Charles R. Gallagher, "The Catholic Church, Martin Luther King Jr., and the March in St. Augustine," *Florida Historical Quarterly* 83 (Fall 2004): 149–72 (third quotation on p. 165).

69. "Civil Rights and the Great Commandment," *Southern Cross*, May 28, 1964 (first quotation); Andrew S. Moore, *The South's Tolerable Alien: Roman Catholics in Alabama and Georgia, 1945–1970* (Baton Rouge: Louisiana State University Press, 2007), 100–104 (second quotation on p. 102); Gerard E. Sherry, "Moral Leadership," *Georgia Bulletin*, April 2, 1964; Paul H. Hallett, "After the Civil Rights Bill," *Southwest Louisiana Register*, June 18, 1964 (third quotation).

70. "We Should Agree Rights Legislation Was Needed," *Voice*, June 26, 1964; "Off-target Criticism," *Texas Catholic Herald* [Houston edition], July 23, 1964; "Education Vital in Poverty Fight," *Clarion Herald*, July 30, 1964; "After the Civil Rights Bill—What?" *North Carolina Catholic*, August 2, 1964; "Bishops Speak on the Civil Rights Law," *Josephite Harvest* 76 (July–August 1964): 1; "Bishop Fletcher Urges Full Compliance with Rights Law," *Guardian*, July 10, 1964 (first and second quotations); "41 Area Priests Sign Compliance Document," *Catholic Virginian*, July 10, 1964; "Civil Rights Statement of the North Carolina Council on Religion and Race," *North Carolina Catholic*, July 12, 1964 (third quotation); "Interracial Group Hails Passage of Rights Bill," *Alamo Messenger*, July 10, 1964 (fourth quotation); "Religious Leaders Hail Signing of Rights Bill," *Catholic Virginian*, July 10, 1964; "Civil Rights Law a Challenge To U.S.—Bishop Reh," *Catholic Banner*, July 19, 1964); "The Civil Rights Law," *Catholic Banner*, July 12, 1964; *Savannah Evening News*, July 8, 1964; untitled note, no date, and attached "A Plea to the Citizens of Savannah and Chatham County," folder 3, box 25, ADS; "Bishop Gerow's Statement," *Mississippi Register*, July 10, 1964; "La. Prelates Urge Lawful Compliance," *Catholic Commentator*, July 10, 1964.

71. M. C. Deason, "Editor's Desk," *Lone Star Register*, July 9, 1964.

72. "Texas CSL Backs Civil Rights Act," *Alamo Messenger*, August 14, 1964; "ACCM Asks Implementation of the Civil Rights Law," *Alamo Messenger*, August 28, 1964; "CFM Meeting in Lubbock Endorses Civil Rights," *Alamo Messenger*, August 21, 1964.

73. Letters from "San Antonio Lay Reader," Mrs. H. R. Kelly, and Mrs. Edmund L. Etlinger to the *Alamo Messenger*, May 29, 1964; letters from Howard B. Shachock, Francis Kendall, and Mrs. Edmund L. Etlinger to the *Alamo Messenger*, July 31, 1964; Richard B. Moran to Robert E. Lucey, May 23, 1964 (first quotation), "Lucey, Robert E. (Archbishop) Social Problems: Race Relations folder #3," AASA; Robert Wilson to the *Alamo Messenger*, August 21, 1964 (second quotation); Henry L. Stille to the *Alamo Messenger*, July 31, 1964 (third quotation).

74. "Bishop Opens Drive against Housing Bias," January 21, 1965 (first quotation), press clipping, folder 19, box 7, series 11, NCCIJR; Noah Golinkin to Stewart Udall, February 1, 1965, John J. Russell to "Reverend and Dear Father," February 9, 1965 (second quotation), CICNV newsletter, February 1965, March 1965, folder "Interracial Correspondence," box H, Russell Papers; "15,000 Sign Fair Housing Statement," *Catholic Virginian*, March 5, 1965; "Fair Housing Drive Called Success; More Work Needed" and "A Time to Stop Running," *Catholic Virginian*, August 6, 1965; Gerald P. Fogarty, S.J., *Commonwealth Catholicism: A History of the Catholic Church in Virginia* (Notre Dame, IN: University of Note Dame Press, 2001), 541–42.

75. Thomas J. Toolen, "Archbishop's Statement on Selma Racial Tension," *Catholic Week*, March 12, 1965 (quotations); *Encyclopedia of African-American Civil Rights: From Emancipation to the Present*, ed. Charles D. Lowery and John F. Marszalek, with a Foreword by David J. Garrow (New York: Greenwood Press, 1992), s.v. "Selma to Montgomery March," by Lorenzo Crowell.

76. "Archbishop Toolen Criticizes Presence of Priests, Sisters in Demonstrations," *Catholic Week*, March 19, 1965 (first, second, and fifth quotations); *Mobile Register*, March 18, 1965 (third and fourth quotations); *New York Times*, March 21, 1965; Gallagher, "The Catholic Church, Martin Luther King Jr., and the March in St. Augustine," 158.

77. "Archbishop Toolen Criticizes Presence of Priests, Sisters in Demonstrations" (first, second, and third quotations); "Vote Rights Bill Faces House Speed, Senate Stall," *Voice*, March 26, 1965; "Selma to Montgomery March"; "Senate Joint Resolution 30," March 22, 1965 (fourth quotation), folder "Letters of relig leaders fav. to Toolen," box "Selma Demonstrations March 1965," Archbishop Thomas J. Toolen Papers, Archives of the Archdiocese of Mobile, Mobile, Alabama (hereinafter cited as Toolen Papers); "Solons Laud Alabama Archbishop for Criticizing Sisters, Priests," *Alamo Messenger*, April 2, 1965.

78. "Selma Troubles Laid to Police Officials," March 12, 1965 (first quotation), press clipping, folder 13, box 25, series 20, NCCIJR; M. F. Everett, "Would Christ March in Selma?" *Clarion Herald*, March 25, 1965 (second quotation). In April 1965, a meeting of Hallinan's consultors found that "58 priests expressed their approval of the policy adopted, 6 juxta modum, 5 unfavorable, and 3 were undecided." "Agenda Consultors' Meeting, April 7, 1965," folder 3, box 008/1, AAA.

79. Robert E. Lucey, "Murder in Alabama," *Alamo Messenger*, March 19, 1965.

80. Caroline Krackenberger to Thomas J. Toolen, March 22, 1965 (first quotation), Mrs. Charles J. Van Trier to Thomas J. Toolen, March 19, 1965 (second quotation), Pearl A. Mason to Thomas J. Toolen, March 19, 1965, Mrs J. J. Nicholson to Thomas J. Toolen, March 20, 1965, A. N. Manucy to Thomas J. Toolen, March 20, 1965, Esma Champagne to Thomas J. Toolen, March 30, 1965, folder "Letters fav. to Toolen," box "Selma Demonstrations March 1965," Toolen Papers; the Reverend H. A. Lipscomb to the *Catholic Week*, March 19, 1965; letters from D. B. Moore and Charlena H. Kelly to the *Catholic Week*, March 26, 1965; Mr. and Mrs. Edward McCleary to the *Catholic Week*, April 2, 1965. See also other letters in this folder and in folder "Letters that were unfavorable to Archbishop Toolen's comments regarding the Selma demonstrations" in the same box. In April 1965, Toolen wrote that "I received about two thousand letters [regarding his comments on the Selma demonstrations], and four out of five from out of the state were in favor of my position. This kind of surprised me. I felt the people of Alabama would feel as I do, but was surprised that so many outside feel the same way." T. J. Toolen to Harold W. Seever, April 2, 1965 (quotation), folder "Letters of relig leaders fav. to Toolen," box "Selma Demonstrations March 1965," Toolen Papers. Bucking the trend seen in Toolen's and other southern dioceses, Archbishop Hallinan reported that letters to his chancery had been "better than 2 to 1" in favor of his permitting priests and laity to participate in the Selma demonstrations. "Letters Vote 2–1 in Support of Religious Activity at Selma," *Religious News Service*, March 31, 1965, folder "Civil Rights, 1965," box CCPF 2/15, University of Notre Dame Archives.

81. Ann M. Lloyd to Pope Paul VI, March 11, 1965, folder "Letters fav. to Toolen," box "Selma Demonstrations March 1965," Toolen Papers.

82. James R. Jackson to Thomas J. Toolen, March 23, 1965 (first quotation), Mrs. Albert E. Taylor to Thomas J. Toolen, March 23, 1965, Eileen B. James to Thomas J. Toolen, March 25, 1965 (second quotation), folder "Letters that were unfavorable to Archbishop Toolen's comments regarding the Selma demonstrations," box "Selma Demonstrations March 1965," Toolen Papers.

83. *Encyclopedia of African-American Civil Rights*, ed. Lowery and Marszalek, s.v. "Voting Rights Act of 1965," by Charles W. Eagles; "The Law of the Land," *Catholic Week*, August 13, 1965 (quotations).

84. T. J. Toolen to Lawrence Shehan, April 22, 1965, folder "Letters of religious leaders fav. to Toolen," box "Selma Demonstrations March 1965," Toolen Papers; John P. Sisson to Francis Wade, November 14, 1967, folder 11, box 1, series 33, NCCIJR; *New York Times*, February 17, 1967; *Richmond News Leader*, February 17, 1967; *Encyclopedia of African-American Civil Rights*, ed. Lowery and Marszalek, s.v. "*Loving v. Virginia*," by Peter Wallenstein; John J. Russell to "Your Excellency," November 28, 1966, John J. Russell to William M. Lewers, December 9, 13, 1966, John J. Russell to William P. Harrison, February 21, 1967, box K, folder "Miscegenation," Russell Papers. The signatories to the amicus curiae brief from the South were: Bishop John J. Russell of Richmond, Archbishop Paul A. Hallinan of Atlanta, Archbishop Philip M. Hannan of New Orleans, Archbishop Robert E. Lucey of San Antonio, Auxiliary Bishop Joseph B. Brunini, Apostolic Administrator of Natchez-Jackson, Bishop Lawrence M. DeFalco of Amarillo, Bishop Coadjutor Joseph A. Durick, Apostolic Administrator of Nashville, Bishop Thomas K. Gorman of Dallas-Fort-Worth, Coadjutor Bishop John L. Morkovsky, Apostolic Administrator of Galveston-Houston, Bishop L. J. Reicher of Austin, Bishop Thomas Tschoepe of San Angelo, Bishop Ernest L. Unterkoefler of Charleston, and Bishop Vincent S. Waters of Raleigh; and from the border states Cardinal Lawrence J. Shehan of Baltimore, Bishop Joseph H. Hodges of Wheeling, West Virginia, and Bishop Victor J. Reed of Oklahoma City and Tulsa. As Russell had written to the ordinaries of every diocese in states that prohibited interracial marriage, it seems that Louisiana bishops Charles P. Greco of Alexandria, Maurice Schexnayder of Lafayette, and Robert E. Tracy of Baton Rouge, like Toolen, declined to join the brief. Russell to Lewers, December 9, 13, 1966, William M. Lewers to John J. Russell, January 18, 1967, folder "Miscegenation," box K, Russell Papers; *New York Times*, February 17, 1967.

85. *New York Times*, January 18, 1968; "24 Bishops Support Fair Housing Ruling," *Georgia Bulletin*, January 25, 1968; *Atlanta Constitution*, March 8, 1968 (first and second quotations); "Va. House Unit Spurns Fair Housing," *Catholic Virginian*, March 1, 1968 (third quotation); St. Matthew 22:39; "Halfway There," *Catholic Virginian*, March 15, 1968 (fourth quotation); "Right to a Reply," and James M. Ober (fifth quotation) to the *Catholic Virginian*, March 29, 1968. The southern signatories of the amicus curiae brief were Bishop Coadjutor Joseph A. Durick, Apostolic Administrator of Nashville, Archbishop Paul A. Hallinan of Atlanta, Archbishop Robert E. Lucey of San Antonio, Coadjutor Bishop John L. Morkovsky of Galveston-Houston, Bishop John J. Russell of Richmond, and Bishop Ernest L. Unterkoefler of Charleston. "About This Brief," n.d., folder 719.82, Archives of the Diocese of Charleston, Charleston, South Carolina.

86. "Religious Leaders Mourn Dr. Martin Luther King," "Rev. Dr. Martin Luther King," T. J. Toolen, "Message from Archbishop" (quotation), *Catholic Week*, April 12, 1968; "State Memorial Services Honor Slain Dr. King," *Catholic Virginian*, April 12, 1968; "Martin Luther King," *Texas Catholic Herald* [Austin edition], April 12, 1968; "New Orleans Mourns Loss of Negro Rights Champion" and "Make His Dream Come True!" *Clarion Herald*, April 11, 1968; "Day of Prayer April 7," *Southwest Louisiana Register*, April 11, 1968; "Bp. Frey Offers Memorial Mass," *Southern Cross*, April 11, 1968; "What Price Equality?" *Texas Concho Register*, April 12, 1968; "Local Rites Honor Slain Rights Leader," and "Martin Luther King," *Texas Catholic*, April 13, 1968.

87. *Encyclopedia of African-American Civil Rights*, ed. Lowery and Marszalek, s.v. "Civil Rights Act of 1968," by Charles D. Lowery; *Encyclopedia of African-American Civil Rights*, ed. Lowery and Marszalek, s.v. "*Jones v. Alfred H. Mayer Co.*," by James Borchert; Hugh Davis

Graham, *The Civil Rights Era: Origins and Development of National Policy* (New York: Oxford University Press, 1990), 270–72, 375–76; Louis J. Reicher to "Dearly Beloved People of the Austin Diocese," May 17, 1968 (quotations), folder 1, box 44, Diocese of Austin Collection, CAT.

88. "Open Housing Is Morally Right," *Catholic Virginian*, June 14, 1968, press clipping, "CCM Plans Further 'Housing' Sundays," *Catholic Virginian*, August 2, 1968 (quotation), press clipping, folder 4, box 18, series 33, NCCIJR.

89. "Mississippi Churchmen Back Integration Order," *Catholic Banner*, January 8, 1970; Kim Larsen, "Catholic Schools Spurn Segregationists," *Voice*, April 17, 1970; "Let's Hope Ruling on Desegregation Ends School Bias," *Voice*, January 16, 1970; "Louisiana Bishops Ask Public School Support," *Clarion Herald*, January 22, 1970; "Diocese Acts to Prevent Segregationists' Move," *Southern Cross*, January 29, 1970; "Church Officials Back Chatham Desegregation," *Southern Cross*, June 3, 1971; Fairclough, *Race and Democracy*, 443; Carroll Joseph Dugas, "The Dismantling of De Jure Segregation in Louisiana, 1954–1974" (PhD diss., Louisiana State University, 1989), 253.

90. "Closes Catholic School Enrollment to Aid Integration Change-Over," *N C News Service*, January 13, 1970, folder 18, box 3, Archbishop Thomas E. Donnellan Papers, AAA; Larsen, "Catholic Schools Spurn Segregationists"; "Church Officials Back Chatham Desegregation"; William F. McKeever to "Reverend and dear Father," December 31, 1969, folder 1–8, box 1, Community Relations Board, Barry University Archives, Miami Shores, Florida; "Let's Hope Ruling on Desegregation Ends School Bias"; John L. May, "For the Record," *Catholic Week*, August 7, 1970 (quotation); "Diocesan School Board Establishes Committees to Assure Racial Justice," *Southwest Louisiana Register*, January 29, 1970.

91. Larsen, "Catholic Schools Spurn Segregationists" (first quotation); "Bishop Tracy Announces Guidelines for School Admittance in Diocese," *Catholic Commentator*, February 27, 1970 (second, third, fourth, and fifth quotations); Father Gerald M. LeFebvre, interview by author, November 10, 2006.

92. "State Religious Leaders Speak on Public Schools," *Church News*, January 1970, 12 (quotation); Jo-Ann Price, "Mississippi Churchmen Back Integration Order," *Southern Cross*, January 8, 1970; Donald Cunnigen, "Men and Women of Goodwill: Mississippi's White Liberals" (PhD diss., Harvard University, 1988), 362 n. 157.

93. "Miss. Parochial Schools Will Not Offer 'Refuge from Integration,'" *Religious Herald*, January 22, 1970 (first quotation); *Delta Democrat-Times*, January 5, 1970 (second, third, and fourth quotations).

94. "Diocesan School Supt. Resigns in Mississippi," *Southern Cross*, January 29, 1970; *Delta Democrat-Times*, January 25 (third quotation), February 25 (first and second quotations), 1970; Namorato, *Catholic Church in Mississippi*, 140–42.

95. *Delta-Democrat-Times*, February 25, 1970.

96. "Will Schools Meet Crisis?" *Southern Cross*, January 22, 1970.

Chapter Six

1. Albert J. Raboteau, "Black Catholics and Afro-American Religious History: Autobiographic Reflections," *U.S. Catholic Historian* 5 (1986): 123–24; James B. Bennett, *Religion and the Rise of Jim Crow in New Orleans* (Princeton, NJ: Princeton University Press, 2005), 228; John L. Morkovsky, "The Christian Solution," in *Interracial Justice* (San Antonio: San Antonio Archdiocesan Committee on Interracial Relations, 1945), 40–41, Georgetown University Library, Special

Collections Division, Washington, DC; Andrew S. Moore, *The South's Tolerable Alien: Roman Catholics in Alabama and Georgia, 1945–1970* (Baton Rouge: Louisiana State University Press, 2007), 116; Gary Wray McDonogh, *Black and Catholic in Savannah, Georgia* (Knoxville: University of Tennessee Press, 1993), 5; James M. Woods, *Mission and Memory: A History of the Catholic Church in Arkansas* (Little Rock: Diocese of Little Rock, 1993), 239; Charles B. McLaughlin, "Much Progress Has Been Made . . . There Is Still Work to Be Done," *North Carolina Catholic*, February 9, 1964; Monsignor Thomas P. Hadden, interview by author, August 2, 2006.

2. "The Catholic Clergy Say: Segregation Is Forbidden in Catholic Churches," folder 19, box 52, Joseph H. Fichter to Charles J. Plauche, May 9, 1950, folder 15, box 52, "Extract of Diocesan Synod Archdiocese of New Orleans, 1950. Title IX *On Bringing about the Salvation of the Negro*," folder 5, box 48, "Minutes of the Advisory Board—Commission on Human Rights, C.C.S.," July 6, 1950, 2, folder 13, box 47, Commission on Human Rights to Joseph Francis Rummel, October 24, 1953, folder 16, box 45, Joseph H. Fichter Papers, Special Collections and Archives, Loyola University Library, Loyola University New Orleans, New Orleans, Louisiana (hereinafter cited as Fichter Papers); Joseph F. Rummel, "Collection Indian and Negro Missions," January 29, 1951, 2, folder 5, box 19, Louis J. Twomey Papers, Special Collections and Archives, Loyola University Library, Loyola University New Orleans (hereinafter cited as Twomey Papers); Joseph F. Rummel, "Blessed are the Peacemakers," March 15, 1953, folder 4, box 8, series 33, National Catholic Conference for Interracial Justice Records, Marquette University, Milwaukee, Wisconsin (hereinafter cited as NCCIJR); *New York Times*, November 9, 1964; Vincent S. Waters, pastoral letter, January 29, 1951, scrapbook "Ban on Segregation 1953 volume III," Vincent S. Waters, pastoral letter, February 9, 1953, bound volume "Pastoral Letters V. S. Waters 1953–1956," Archives of the Diocese of Raleigh, Raleigh, North Carolina (hereinafter cited as ADR); Hadden interview.

3. W. J. Nold to "the Reverend Pastors," August 29, 1953 (quotations), F4 "Circular Letters 1953," box 3, RG 2.1.9 Chancery files, Bishops' files, Nold, Wendelin J., folder 4, box 3, Archives of the Archdiocese of Galveston-Houston, Houston, Texas (hereinafter cited as AAGH); Bishop Vincent M. Rizzotto, interview by author, November 1, 2006.

4. "Keep Your Cool," *Southwest Louisiana Register*, August 21, 1969, press clipping, folder 7, box 7, series 33, NCCIJR; Herbert J. May Jr., "The Official Policy of the Roman Catholic Church of the Diocese of Lafayette in Relation to Black Catholics, 1940 to 1978" (Master's thesis, University of Southwestern Louisiana, 1981), 66; Joseph L. Bernardin to Henry Cabirac Jr., May 16, 1961 (quotation), folder 720.9, Archives of the Diocese of Charleston, South Carolina, Charleston, South Carolina (hereinafter cited as ADC).

5. *Our Negro and Indian Missions: Annual Report of the Secretary of the Commission for the Catholic Missions Among the Colored People and the Indians*, January 1949, 5–6, 9–13, January 1951, 7–10, 22–23, January 1957, 12–14, January 1962, 7–12, Archives of the Society of St. Joseph of the Sacred Heart, Baltimore, Maryland (hereinafter cited as ASSJ); "Black Church Parishes in the Diocese of Lafayette," folder "Racism/Integration (Various)," Archives of the Diocese of Lafayette, Lafayette, Louisiana (hereinafter cited as ADL); "Father Tennelly's Report," *Colored Harvest* 66 (May 1954): 6–7; "Church in Charlotte," *Colored Harvest* 70 (February 1958): 1; J. B. Tennelly, "The Negro Missions," *Colored Harvest* 69 (October 1957): 2–3; Bob Giles, "Josephite Fathers 'Goodbye God, I'm Going to Texas,'" *Texas Catholic Herald* [Beaumont edition], March 14, 1980.

6. Charles Robert Gallagher, "Patriot Bishop: The Diplomatic and Episcopal Career of Archbishop Joseph P. Hurley, 1937–1967" (PhD diss., Marquette University, 1998), 463; "Negro Priests in the United States," *Interracial Review* 18 (September 1945): 130; Austin Chachere, "Negro Priests in

the United States," *Interracial Review* 19 (February 1946): 22–24; "America's Negro Priests," *Colored Harvest* 69 (September 1957): 5; Stephen J. Ochs, *Desegregating the Altar: The Josephites and the Struggle for Black Priests, 1871–1960* (Baton Rouge: Louisiana State University Press, 1990), 415, 419, 440–42, 444, 456–59; John E. Rousseau, "Negro Priest Ordained at St. Louis Cathedral," *Our Colored Missions* 39 (September 1953): 141; "1st Josephite Priest from New Orleans," *Catholic Action of the South*, May 29, 1955; [New Orleans] *Times-Picayune*, January 14, 1969; "Curriculum Vitae Most Reverend Moses B. Anderson, S.S.E., Auxiliary Bishop Archdiocese of Detroit," n.d., untitled curriculum vitae of James P. Robinson, "The Monsignor James P. Robinson, SSE—Story," 1, in "Monsignor James P. Robinson, SSE, 40th Anniversary Celebration Ordination to the Priesthood," c. 1997, folder "G13-1-3 File 4," Community Archives, Sisters of St. Joseph, Rochester, New York; "U.S. Negro Priests Now Number 82," *Interracial Review* 31 (June 1958): 106.

7. James A. Richardson, "Sisters in the Diocese," *Catholic Banner*, December 4, 1960; *Our Negro and Indian Missions*, January 1945, 11–12, January 1954, 7–12, January 1968, 7–11, ASSJ; Daniel A. Lord, "Race Relations in Practice," *Our Colored Missions* 32 (December 1946): 189; Patrica McGerr, "Alabama's Interracial Monastery," *Interracial Review* 23 (August 1950): 118–19; Mother Mary Dominic, O.P., to George D. Hunton, May 18, 1950, folder 9, box 10, John LaFarge Papers, Georgetown University Library, Special Collections Division, Washington, DC (hereinafter cited as LaFarge Papers); "Interracial Convent," *Ebony* 6 (March 1951): 102–4, 106; "Archbishop Thomas J. Toolen," *Catholic Week*, November 23, 1979; Gretta Palmer, "Southern Catholics Fight Race Hatred," *Look* 14 (March 28, 1950): 98–100, 103; Mother Mary of the Child Jesus, O.P. to "Dearest Friend," July 1954, and attached press clipping, "Ever Feel Like Throwing a Few Bricks? Here's a Nun Who Would Like to Be on the Receiving End if You Do," n.d., folder 19, box 45, Fichter Papers; "Nuns Who Staff Negro Missions," *Claverite* 42 (November–December 1963): 8–11; Raymond Bernard, "Jim Crow Vocations?" *Interracial Review* 22 (June 1949): 90–93; Raymond Bernard, "Integration in the Convent," *America* (April 21, 1956): 83–84; Raymond Bernard, "Sisterhoods and the Negro," *Interracial Review* 28 (March 1955): 42–45.

8. *Our Negro and Indian Missions*, January 1946, 7–8, 14–16, January 1947, 11–13, January 1948, 13–14 (quotation), January 1949, 5–6, 9–13, January 1950, 7–13, January 1951, 7–10, January 1953, 5–6, January 1954, 5–6, ASSJ; "Atlanta Catholic Colored Clinic Completes Two Years of Service," *Interracial Review* 20 (May 1947): 80; "Barriers Being Broken," *Colored Harvest* 65 (November 1953): 6; Sister M. Julian Griffin, V.S.C., in cooperation with Gillian Brown, *Tomorrow Comes the Song: The Story of Catholicism among the Black Population of South Georgia, 1850–1978* (Savannah: Diocese of Savannah, 1979), 7; Joseph L. Bernardin, "The Church and the Negro," and Bernard E. Ferrara, "Catholic Hospitals," *Catholic Banner*, December 4, 1960; Christopher J. Kauffman, *Ministry and Meaning: A Religious History of Health Care in the United States*, with a Foreword by Martin E. Marty (New York: Crossroad, 1995), 260–62.

9. "Over the Years," *North Carolina Catholic*, December 8, 1974; McLaughlin, "Much Progress Has Been Made . . . There Is Still Work to Be Done"; "Priest Describes Segregation as 'Un-Christian,'" *Catholic Virginian*, March 5, 1948; J. L. Manning to Henry Cabirac Jr., May 10, 1961, folder 8, box 1, Catholic Council on Human Relations Papers, Amistad Research Center, New Orleans, Louisiana (hereinafter cited as CCHRP); Robert E. Lucey to "Reverend and dear Father," February 28, 1948, folder "Organizations and Societies Catholic Interracial Council (1945–1969)," Archives of the Archdiocese of San Antonio, San Antonio, Texas (hereinafter cited as AASA); "2 Archdiocesan HN Units Will Merge," *Catholic Action of the South*, November 6, 1952; Joseph L. Bernardin to Henry Cabirac Jr., May 16, 1961 (quotation), folder 720.9, "The Negro Apostolate in South Carolina. Meeting of Priests in Colored Work. Oct. 5, 1960.

Columbia, S.C.," 9, folder 720.3, ADC; "Hoey Award Winners," *Colored Harvest* 68 (December 1956): 1. The Confraternity of Christian Doctrine was a lay catechetical organization.

10. Robert E. Lucey to Reverend Mother M. Angelique, Reverend Mother M. Laserian, Reverend Mother M. Rose Kallus, Reverend Mother M. Paz, June 12, 1953, folder "Lucey, Robert E. [Archbishop] Social Problems: Race Relations Folder # 2 (1951–1965)," AASA; James F. Vanderholt, "Assumption Seminary," Handbook of Texas Online, accessed October 16, 2014, http://www.tshaonline.org/handbook/online/articles/iwa04; Ochs, *Desegregating the Altar*, 404; Charles Stephen Padgett, "Schooled in Invisibility: The Desegregation of Spring Hill College, Mobile, Alabama" (PhD diss., University of Georgia, 2000), 46, 49–50; L. J. Twomey to Vincent A. McCormick, September 18, 1951, 3, folder 8, box 19, L. J. Twomey to Charles Vatterott, December 6, 1963, folder 15, box 21, Twomey Papers; Lou Twomey to John LaFarge, September 23, 1950, folder 15, box 29, LaFarge Papers; John McCann, "The Catholic Committee of the South Department of Race Relations Six Months Progress Report," 1950, 2, folder "Catholic Committee of the South—1950 8c I-c-16," "Catholic Committee of the South 78–014 box 1 52-03-06," Archives of the Archdiocese of New Orleans, New Orleans, Louisiana (hereinafter cited as AANO); Stephen P. Ryan, "Racial Attitudes in the South Today," *America* 84 (November 11, 1950): 158.

11. "Minutes of Province Meeting on Interracial Relations," Grand Coteau, August 28–29, 1952, 11, Archives of the New Orleans Province of the Society of Jesus, Special Collections and Archives, Loyola University Library, Loyola University New Orleans; Lucey to Angelique, June 12, 1953; "Underscorings," *America* 90 (October 17, 1953): 61; "College of Sacred Heart to Close in June '56," *Southwest Louisiana Register*, February 3, 1956 (quotation); R. Bentley Anderson, *Black, White, and Catholic: New Orleans Interracialism, 1947–1956* (Nashville: Vanderbilt University Press, 2005), xiv, 109–10, 186, 192. In 1956, the College of the Sacred Heart closed because of long-standing financial problems caused by insufficient enrollment and rising costs. [Lafayette, Louisiana] *Daily Advertiser*, January 25, 1956; "College of Sacred Heart to Close in June '56"; "Decision to Close Sacred Heart College Final, Superior Tells," *Southwest Louisiana Register*, February 17, 1956; "Last Commencement Is Held at College of Sacred Heart," *Southwest Louisiana Register*, June 1, 1956.

12. Memorandum, J. M. Boyle to Robert E. Lucey, "Interracial Committee," January 5, 1954, folder "Lucey, Robert E. (Archbishop) Social Problems: Race Relations Folder #2 (1951–1965)," AASA; "San Antonio Catholic Schools No Longer Segregated," *Christian Impact* 3 (April 1954): 1, folder 2, box 47, Fichter Papers. This volume of *Christian Impact* was in fact the fourth volume.

13. Henry Ringkamp Sr. to "Father [Peter] Resch, Feast of Holy Rosary 1951," October 7, 1951 (quotations), Henry Ringkamp, "Ringkamp—Marianist or Seventy Is the Sum of Our Years . . . Psalm 90," March 1981, 1, Central Catholic High School Yearbook 1951, Marianist Archives, San Antonio, Texas; "The Catholic Church and the Negro," *Ebony* 13 (December 1957): 26. In 1951, "A Negro student applied for admission to Central Catholic High School in San Antonio and was admitted by the school but refused to enroll because of course changes he would have to make." A year later, the school taught its first African American student, Bobby Peppermartin Smith. "Civil Rights Survey," May 16, 1952, 4 (quotation), folder 7, box 85, National Catholic Welfare Conference Collection, The American Catholic History Research Center and University Archives, Catholic University of America, Washington, DC. Brother Martin McMurtrey, interview by author, August 23, 2006; Brother Herbert Janson, interview by author, August 23, 2006.

14. *Our Negro and Indian Missions*, January 1962, 7–12, ASSJ; "Desegregation of Southern Parochial Schools," August 19, 1963, 1, folder 3, box 13, series 34, NCCIJR; A. Stephen Stephan

and Charles A. Hicks, "Integration and Segregation in Arkansas—One Year Afterward," *Journal of Negro Education* 24 (Summer 1955): 180; Woods, *Mission and Memory*, 215, 266.

15. Manning to Cabirac, May 10, 1961; Robert E. Lucey to Henry Ringkamp, July 31, 1953, Marianist Archives; Lucey to Angelique, Laserian, Kallus, and Paz, June 12, 1953; memorandum, Boyle to Lucey, "Interracial Committee," January 5, 1954; Robert E. Lucey to "Dear Sister Superior," April 5, 1954, Robert E. Lucey to "Reverend and dear Father," April 5, 1954 (quotation), "Lucey, Robert E. (Archbishop) Social Problems: Race Relations Folder #2 (1951–1965)," AASA; "Color, Race, Poverty Cannot Bar Children from School," *Alamo Register*, April 9, 1954.

16. *San Antonio News*, April 13, 1954; J. L. Manning to Henry Cabirac Jr., June 14, 1961 (quotation), box 1, folder 8, CCHRP; *Our Negro and Indian Missions*, January 1955, 12–13, 22–23, ASSJ; *The Official Catholic Directory Anno Domini 1954* (New York: P. J. Kenedy and Sons, 1954), 2. The statistics on African American Catholics in every American diocese and archdiocese gathered annually by the Commission for the Catholic Missions Among the Colored People and the Indians and reported in *Our Negro and Indian Missions* were those submitted by ordinaries, or, occasionally, by pastors responsible for African American missions. The figures counted black Catholics in special parishes and African American missions but not those who attended predominantly white churches.

17. Manning to Cabirac, May 10, 1961 (quotation), June 14, 1961; "Education," *National Catholic Conference for Interracial Justice Newsletter*, December 1961, 3, box 1, folder 1, series 8, NCCIJR; *Our Negro and Indian Missions*, January 1962, 7–12, ASSJ; Tara Little, "Catholic Leaders Closely Watched Racial Segregation Issues of 50 Years Ago," *Arkansas Catholic*, September 20, 2007, accessed February 3, 2009, at http://catholic.org/printer_friendly.php?id=25433&section=Cathcom. On segregationists fears of miscegenation, see Jane Dailey, "Sex, Segregation, and the Sacred after *Brown*," *Journal of American History* 91 (June 2004): 119–44; Phoebe Godfrey, "Bayonets, Brainwashing, and Bathrooms: The Discourse of Race, Gender, and Sexuality in the Desegregation of Little Rock's Central High," *Arkansas Historical Quarterly* 62 (Spring 2003): 42–67.

18. *Richmond News Leader*, May 13 (first quotation), May 14, 1954; *Richmond Times-Dispatch*, May 14, 1954; "A Moral, Religious Problem" and "Colored Sure to Enroll in High Schools" (second quotation), *Catholic Virginian*, May 21, 1954.

19. *Richmond News Leader*, May 13, 1954; *Richmond Times-Dispatch*, May 14, 1954; "Colored Sure to Enroll in High Schools."

20. "Freshmen Include 11 Colored Pupils," *Catholic Virginian*, September 10, 1954; "Proposal Would Abolish State's Public Schools," *Alamo Register*, July 23, 1954; "Racial Integration for More Virginia Parochial Schools," *Bulletin of the Catholic Laymen's Association of Georgia*, July 31, 1954; "Here and There," *Our Colored Missions* 40 (October 1954): 150; Benjamin Muse, *Virginia's Massive Resistance* (Bloomington: Indiana University Press, 1961), 3; *New York Times*, September 8, 1954; *Our Indian and Negro Missions*, January 1955, 12–13, January 1956, 11–12, January 1957, 12–14, ASSJ; James W. Ely Jr., *The Crisis of Conservative Virginia: The Byrd Organization and the Politics of Massive Resistance* (Knoxville: University of Tennessee Press, 1976), 30; "14 Va. Schools End First Year of Integration; Reaction 'Good,'" *Catholic Virginian*, June 24, 1955.

21. "Status of Integration in Catholic Education," *North Carolina Catholic*, June 18, 1954; M. F. Everett, "Church Leads Way," *Catholic Action of the South*, September 16, 1954; Francis A. Smyer (quotation), reply typed over Henry Cabirac Jr. to Francis A. Smyer, June 7, 1962, folder 15, box 1, CCHRP; *Our Negro and Indian Missions*, January 1955, 22–23, January 1956, 11–12, January 1957, 12–14, ASSJ; *Official Catholic Directory Anno Domini 1954*, 2.

22. *Our Negro and Indian Missions*, January 1955, 22–23, ASSJ; *Official Catholic Directory Anno Domini 1954*, 2; *Nashville Tennessean*, July 1, 1954; Reavis L. Mitchell, "The Black Man and the Catholic Church in Nashville" (Master's thesis, Middle Tennessee State University, 1971), 17; Andy Telli, "Breaking Barriers: 50th Anniversary of Integration of Catholic Schools," *Tennessee Register*, September 24, 2004; Monsignor James Hitchcock, interview by author, July 21, 2005; Thomas Stritch, *The Catholic Church in Tennessee: The Sesquicentennial Story* (Nashville: The Catholic Center, 1987), 334, 337; Hugh Davis Graham, *Crisis in Print: Desegregation and the Press in Tennessee* (Nashville: Vanderbilt University Press, 1967), 22; Neal R. Peirce, *The Border South States: People, Politics, and Power in the Five Border South States* (New York: Norton, 1975), 321, 341. Tennessee's school segregation laws, like those of Florida and Georgia, also applied to private, and hence, Catholic schools. "Bishop England High School, Charleston, S.C., 1964 Adult Lenten Series 'Religion and Race,'" folder 707.1/1, ADC.

23. Owen F. Campion, "Desegregation: To Be or Not to Be," *Tennessee Register*, February 23, 1987 (first quotation); Owen Francis Campion, "A History of the Diocese of Nashville" (Senior Honors thesis, Saint Bernard College, 1962), 83, 92; *Nashville Tennessean*, June 30, July 1, 1954 (second quotation); Charles M. Williams to Henry Cabirac Jr., August 11, 1961, folder 1, box 15, series 33, NCCIJR; Telli, "Breaking Barriers."

24. Campion, "A History of the Diocese of Nashville," 109; Mitchell, "The Black Man and the Catholic Church in Nashville," 16; Joel William McGraw, F.S.C., "Catholic Schools in West Tennessee 1849–1996," in Joel William McGraw, F.S.C., Milton J. Guthrie, and Josephine King, *Between the Rivers: The Catholic Heritage of West Tennessee* (Memphis: Catholic Diocese of Memphis, 1996), 325–26.

25. Mitchell, "The Black Man and the Catholic Church in Nashville," 15; Graham, *Crisis in Print*, 171–72, 176–77; Richard A. Pride and J. David Woodard, *The Burden of Busing: The Politics of Desegregation in Nashville, Tennessee* (Knoxville: University of Tennessee Press, 1985), 55–57; Reed Sarratt, *The Ordeal of Desegregation: The First Decade* (New York: Harper and Row, 1966), 90–92, 160–61, 214.

26. Campion, "Desegregation" (first and third quotations); Telli, "Breaking Barriers" (second quotation).

27. Telli, "Breaking Barriers"; *New York Times*, September 22, 1957; Hitchcock interview; King Hollands, interview by author, July 22, 2005; A. J. Spence, "Father Abram J. Ryan, Civil War Priest," *Tennessee Register*, May 4, 1987.

28. Mitchell, "The Black Man and the Catholic Church in Nashville," 17–19; Henry Cabirac to Rogue and Virginia Fajardo, April 23, 1964, folder 12, box 14, series 33, NCCIJR; Stritch, *Catholic Church in Tennessee*, 336.

29. Earl Heffner, "High Schools and Hospitals Open Doors to All Catholics," *North Carolina Catholic*, September 10, 1954.

30. Vincent S. Waters to pastors and high school principals, August 22, 1954 (first quotation), Vincent S. Waters to "all Pastors and Principals of Schools," August 24, 1955, bound volume "Pastoral Letters V. S. Waters 1953–1956," ADR; *African American Ministry and Evangelization* (Raleigh: Diocese of Raleigh, 2002), 9, in author's possession; Heffner, "High Schools and Hospitals Open Doors to All Catholics"; *Our Negro and Indian Missions*, January 1955, 7–11, January 1956, 11–12, ASSJ; "Integration in Action," *Sign* 38 (November 1958): 14; George E. Lynch to Henry Cabirac Jr., February 15, 1962 (second quotation), folder "Negroes, Catholic Parishes For," ADR; William F. Powers, *Tar Heel Catholics: A History of Catholicism in North Carolina* (Lanham, MD: University Press of America, 2003), 26.

31. Powers, *Tar Heel Catholics*, 26.

32. *Our Negro and Indian Missions*, January 1955, 22–23, ASSJ; *Official Catholic Directory Anno Domini 1954*, 2; Albert L. Fletcher, "Official Announcement, August 3, 1954," *Guardian*, August 13, 1954 (quotations).

33. Fletcher, "Official Announcement, August 3, 1954."

34. Stephan and Hicks, "Integration and Segregation in Arkansas," 180; *Our Negro and Indian Missions*, January 1955, 7–11 (quotation), ASSJ.

35. "Status of Integration in Catholic Education"; Charles Gallagher, *Cross and Crozier: The History of the Diocese of St. Augustine* (Jacksonville: Diocese of St. Augustine, 1999), 76; *New York Times*, October 31, 1967; Gallagher, "Patriot Bishop," 456, 461–62; Charles R. Gallagher, "The Catholic Church, Martin Luther King Jr., and the March in St. Augustine," *Florida Historical Quarterly* 83 (Fall 2004): 156–57; David R. Colburn, *Racial Change and Community Crisis: St. Augustine, Florida, 1877–1980* (New York: Columbia University Press, 1985), 160; Sarratt, *Ordeal of Desegregation*, 278–79, 352–54.

36. *Our Negro and Indian Missions*, January 1955, 22–23, ASSJ; W. J. Nold to the "Reverend Pastors of Galveston and Harris counties," April 3, 1961, box 3, folder "F14 Circular Letters Jan–May 1961," RG 2.1.9. Chancery files, Bishops' files, Nold, Wendelin J., AAGH.

37. *Official Catholic Directory Anno Domini 1954*, 2; Ed Holmes, "In Louisiana: Signs of Progress," *Sign* 35 (July 1956): 14–15; Wilson Minor, "In Mississippi: Rigid Segregation," *Sign* 35 (July 1956): 17; Moore, *South's Tolerable Alien*, 1–2, 11–13, 17–37, 117–18, 136–37; *The Encyclopedia of American Catholic History*, ed. Michael Glazier and Thomas J. Shelley (Collegeville, MN: Liturgical Press, 1997), s.v. "Hallinan, Paul J. (1911–68)," by Shelley, Thomas J.

38. "S.C. School Integration," *St. Augustine's Messenger* 31 (November 1954): 312; Milton Lomask, "Father Maurice Challenges the South," *Sign* 36 (November 1956): 17, 19–20.

39. *Mobile Register*, September 18, 1954; Padgett, "Schooled in Invisibility," 24, 29, 49–52, 54; Padgett, "Without Hysteria or Unnecessary Disturbance," 167, 184–86; Anderson, *Black, White, and Catholic*, 192; M. F. Everett, "Church Leads Way," *Catholic Action of the South*, September 16, 1954; "A Current List: Schools of Higher Learning Lower the Color Bar," *New South* 10 (February 1955): 8. According to Father Albert S. Foley, S.J., "In the fall of 1954, a dozen Negro students applied to the [Spring Hill] college, of whom nine were admitted and seven survived through the year." Albert S. Foley, "The Negro and Catholic Higher Education," *Interracial Review* 30 (October 1957): 172.

40. Joseph Francis Rummel, "De-Segregation in Schools," August 19, 1955, folder "Desegregation—Archbishop Rummel," AANO; "Integration Is Deferred for This School Year," *Catholic Action of the South*, August 28, 1955.

41. "Jesuit High Admits Two Negro Boys," *Texas Catholic*, September 10, 1955.

42. "Norfolk Catholic High School Open to Negro Pupils," *Catholic Virginian*, April 8, 1955 (quotations); *Our Indian and Negro Missions*, January 1957, 12–14, ASSJ.

43. Vincent S. Waters to "all Pastors and Principals of Schools," August 24, 1955.

44. *Our Negro and Indian Missions*, January 1957, 7–11 (quotation), ASSJ; McLaughlin, "Much Progress Has Been Made"; Powers, *Tar Heel Catholics*, 384–85.

45. Joseph Francis Rummel, "Integration in Catholic Schools," July 31, 1956, folder 5, box 20, Twomey Papers; "An Epochal Pronouncement," *Blueprint* 7 (September 1954): 1–2, A. W. Crandell to "Reverend Fathers and dear Brothers in Christ," September 9, 1954, *Blueprint* (Special Service Edition, September 30, 1954): 1–6, Special Collections and Archives, Loyola University Library, Loyola University New Orleans; Anderson, *Black, White, and Catholic*, 192, 193; Holmes, "In Louisiana," 14 (quotation).

46. *New York Times*, August 25, 1957, July 8, 1959; "Proceedings of the Consultors Meeting," October 23, 1957, 3 (quotation), folder 1, box 008/1, Archives of the Archdiocese of Atlanta, Atlanta, Georgia (hereinafter cited as AAA).

47. McLaughlin, "Much Progress Has Been Made"; Vincent S. Waters, "Religion and Integration," *North Carolina Catholic*, June 21, 1959 (first and second quotations); Henry Cabirac Jr. to Robert C. Ford, March 12, 1962, folder 5, box 13, Henry Cabirac Jr. to Robert C. Ford, March 7, 1963, "Ending Church Segregation," *Community*, January 1962, 5, folder 7, box 13, series 33, NCCIJR.

48. Bernardin, "The Church and the Negro" (first and second quotations); "Consolidation 1950–1960," *Catholic Banner*, December 4, 1960; "The Negro Apostolate in South Carolina. Meeting of Priests in Colored Work. Oct. 5, 1960. Columbia, S.C.," 1 (third quotation).

49. Michael J. McNally, *Catholic Parish Life on Florida's West Coast, 1860–1968* (St. Petersburg, FL: Catholic Media Ministries, 1996), 390 (first quotation); Michael J. McNally, *Catholicism in South Florida, 1868–1968* (Gainesville: University of Florida Press, 1982), 192; George H. Monohan, "Story of the Diocese of Miami," *Voice*, March 20, 1959; "Bishop Carroll 'Man of Year' in Dade," *Voice*, April 30, 1965 (second quotation); Coleman F. Carroll, "Diocesan and Religious Involvement in Human Relations," July 30, 1965, 5, folder 19, box 3, series 33, NCCIJR; "High Schools in Diocese Begin Integration," *Voice*, August 26, 1960; James J. Walsh to Henry Cabirac Jr., June 22, 1961 (third quotation), February 8, 1962, folder 8, box 1, CCHRP; *New York Times*, August 23, 1960; Sarratt, *Ordeal of Desegregation*, 99, 279.

50. D. C. McLeaish to Henry Cabirac Jr., June 18, 1962 (quotation), folder 15, box 1, CCHRP; Charles M. Williams to Henry Cabirac Jr., August 11, 1961, folder 1, box 15, series 33, NCCIJR; Sarratt, *Ordeal of Desegregation*, 218.

51. Albert L. Fletcher, *An Elementary Catholic Catechism on the Morality of Segregation and Racial Discrimination* (N.p., n.d.), preface, 3 (first quotation), 8–9, 11–16 (first quotation on p. 12; second quotation on p. 16), folder 3, box 1, series 11, NCCIJR; *Arkansas Gazette*, April 13, 1960. The National Catholic Welfare Conference also distributed the catechism nationally. "Catechism on Race from Little Rock Diocese," *Interracial Review* 33 (October 1960): 250.

52. *Our Negro and Indian Missions*, 1961, 7–12, ASSJ.

53. Vincent M. Harris to Henry Cabirac Jr., May 22, 1961 (first and second quotations), folder 6, box 5, series 11, Vincent M. Harris to "Dearly Beloved," April 3, 1961, Vincent M. Harris to Henry Cabirac Jr., June 8, October 17, 1961, folder 7, box 16, series 33, NCCIJR.

54. Memorandum, Benjamin Muse, "The 1961 Desegregation Initiative of the Catholic Bishops of Charleston, Savannah and Atlanta," March 2, 1962, 2, folder 4, box 4, series 11, NCCIJR; *Our Negro and Indian Missions*, January 1958, 7–11, ASSJ. There was one other instance of Catholic school desegregation in the Deep South when a black school enrolled three white children in Greenville, South Carolina, in the school year 1959–1960. Two white students remained enrolled the following year until the family moved away, leaving the school entirely African American. Memorandum, Muse, "The 1961 Desegregation Initiative of the Catholic Bishops of Charleston, Savannah and Atlanta," March 2, 1962, 2.

55. *New York Times*, July 8, 1959, September 2, 1960; Mrs. Bernard P. Wolfe, "Minutes of the Archdiocesan School Board Meeting," August 30, 1960, folder "Integration, School Board Meetings, Minutes + Notes (1954–1962)," 03-038 box 1, AANO; Adam Fairclough, *Race and Democracy: The Struggle for Civil Rights in Louisiana, 1915–1972* (Athens: University of Georgia Press, 1995), 234–39.

56. "Notes for Conference with Most Reverend Archbishop—Our Lady of Lake Hospital, October 14, 1960, 1-2, Minutes of Archdiocesan School Board Meeting," November 30, 1960, 1, folder "Integration, School Board Meetings, Minutes + Notes (1954–1962)," 03-038 box 1, AANO; "1960 Brings Unique Jubilee, Heavy Trial for Archbishop: Recovering from Ordeal Due to Fall," *Catholic Action of the South*, November 20, 1960.

57. "Telegram—Day Letter—November 12, 1960," folder "School Integration File 1950–1962 Letters Issued to Pastors/Correspondence," box "School Integration Files and Labor Issues, 1944–1963" AR/00173, AANO.

58. *New York Times*, November 16, 1960; Henry C Bezou to the "Right Reverend, Very Reverend, and Reverend Pastors; to the Principals of Catholic Elementary Schools of New Orleans," November 14, 1960, 1-2 (quotation on p. 2), folder "Integration, School Board Meetings, Minutes + Notes (1954–1962)," 03-038 box 1, AANO; "Minutes of Archdiocesan School Board Meeting," November 30, 1960, 1-4; Fairclough, *Race and Democracy*, 243–44.

59. "Minutes of Archdiocesan School Board Meeting," November 30, 1960, 1-4 (quotation on p. 3).

60. Ibid., 4.

61. *New York Times*, November 9, 1964; Henry Cabirac Jr. to Alexander O. Sigur, March 26, 1962, folder 8, box 7, series 33, NCCIJR; untitled article, *Catholic Action of the South*, November 27, 1960.

62. Thomas J. Shelley, *Paul J. Hallinan: First Archbishop of Atlanta* (Wilmington, DE: Michael Glazier, 1989), 118, 121–22; "Catholic Negro Co-ed Walks Tight Rope in Integration of Georgia University," *Alamo Messenger*, January 20, 1961, press clipping, folder "Black Catholics," AASA; "Suggested Statement on the Admission Policy of Catholic Schools," January 4, 1961, folder 11, box 015/2, AAA; Paul J. Hallinan to Paul Tanner, February 13, 1961, folder 1, box 89, National Catholic Welfare Conference Collection, The American Catholic History Research Center and University Archives, Catholic University of America, Washington, DC; Paul J. Hallinan to John J. McCarthy, January 4, 10, 1961, Paul J. Hallinan to Charles J. Baum, January 10, 1961, Paul J. Hallinan to John E. Kelly, February 15, 1961, folder 720.3, ADC; *Savannah Morning News*, February 20, 1961.

63. Paul J. Hallinan to Francis E. Hyland, January 18, February 7, 1961, Paul J. Hallinan to Thomas J. McDonough, January 18 February 7, 1961, Paul J. Hallinan to Martin C. Murphy, February 7, 1961, Paul J. Hallinan to "Dear Bill," February 8, 1961, Paul J. Hallinan to "Dear Joe," February 8, 1961, folder 720.3, ADC; Francis E. Hyland to Thomas J. McDonough, January 25, 1961, Francis E. Hyland to Paul J. Hallinan, January 25, February 10, 1961, folder 49, box 036/6, AAA; Francis E. Hyland to "Reverend and dear Father," February 14, 1961 and attached Francis E. Hyland to "My dear people," February 14, 1961 (quotations), folder 7, box 21, Twomey Papers.

64. Paul J. Hallinan, "Pastoral Letter Lent 1961," "Church Moves Steadily to Solve Race Problem" and "Bishop Calls for Christian Charity in Racial Problems," *Catholic Banner*, February 26, 1961; "Text of Bishop's Statement on Desegregation of Schools," *Savannah Morning News*, February 20, 1961 (first and second quotations); *New York Times*, February 20, 1961; Kathleen M. Hardy to Thomas J. McDonough, February 20, 1961, Dr. and Mrs. Carl R. Jordan to Thomas J. McDonough, February 20, 1961, Mrs. Francis Percival McIntire to Thomas J. McDonough, February 20, 1961, Mary Bennett to Thomas J. McDonough, February 20, 1961, Thomas J. McDonough to Mrs. Francis Percival McIntire, February 21, 1961 (third quotation), folder 10, box 24, Archives of the Diocese of Savannah, Savannah, Georgia (hereinafter cited as ADS);

Muse, "The 1961 Desegregation Initiative of the Catholic Bishops of Charleston, Savannah and Atlanta," March 2, 1962, 3–4.

65. Paul J. Hallinan to "Dear Father," March 14, 1961 (quotation), folder 707.1, ADC; "Pastoral Letter Gains Loyal Support in Diocese," *Catholic Banner*, March 19, 1961; Muse, "The 1961 Desegregation Initiative of the Catholic Bishops of Charleston, Savannah and Atlanta," 2.

66. David Murphy to Francis E. Hyland, February 19, 1961, Mary Bennett to Francis E. Hyland, February 20, 1961, Ferdinand Buckley to Francis E. Hyland, February 20, 1961, Henry L. De Give to Francis E. Hyland, February 20, 1961, unsigned to "Sir," February 21, 1961, "Disgusted Catholic" to "Dear Bishops," February 21, 1961, Rosemary Carey to Francis E. Hyland, February 22, 1961, Hughes Spalding to Francis E. Hyland, February 22, 1961, Gladys Gunning to Francis E. Hyland, February 23, 1961, unsigned to Francis E. Hyland, n.d., Francis E. Hyland to Hughes Spalding, March 2, 1961 (quotation), unsigned to "Whom It May Concern," March 10, 1961, Betty Tecklenburg Long to Francis E. Hyland, March 15, 1961, folder 49, box 036/6, AAA; Muse, "The 1961 Desegregation Initiative of the Catholic Bishops of Charleston, Savannah and Atlanta," 4; "Bishop Francis Edward Hyland," accessed December 15, 2007, at http://www.catholic-hierarchy.org/bishop/bhyland.html.

67. Fairclough, *Race and Democracy*, 254–56.

68. *A Syllabus on Racial Justice for Use in the Catholic Schools Grades 7–12 under the Direction of the Most Reverend Paul J. Hallinan, D.D., Bishop of Charleston*, 1–viii (quotation on p. vii), 1–59, folder 1, box 14, series 33, NCCIJR; Joseph L. Bernardin to Henry Cabirac Jr., September 21, 1961, folder 8, box 1, CCHRP; "Department of Education Prepares New Syllabus," *Catholic Banner*, October 22, 1961.

69. *A Syllabus on Racial Justice for Use in the Catholic Schools Grades 7–12*, 20–21, 23–24 (second quotation on p. 24; fourth quotation on p. 23), 30–33 (first quotation on p. 30; third quotation on p. 33; fifth, sixth, and seventh quotations on p. 31; eighth quotation on p. 32), 49–55.

70. W. J. Nold to "Dearly Beloved," April 3, 1961 (quotation) and Vincent M. Harris to Henry Cabirac Jr., May 22, 1961, folder 8, box 1, CCHRP.

71. Nold to "Dearly Beloved," April 3, 1961 (first quotation); Harris to Cabirac, May 22, 1961 (second quotation); Vincent M. Harris to Henry Cabirac Jr., October 17, 1961 (third quotation), folder 8, box 1, CCHRP. Elsewhere in Texas, the Diocese of Dallas-Fort Worth, which had begun parochial school desegregation in 1954, announced in June 1961 that several of its African American churches would be "integrated with the local territorial parishes." "Simple, Isn't It?" *Josephite Harvest* 73 (July–August 1961): n.p.

72. *New York Times*, September 17, 1961; [Sister Thomas Joseph McGoldrick, S.S.J.], "Integration of Catholic Schools in Northeast Florida," July 3, 2001, Archives of the Sisters of St. Joseph of St. Augustine, St. Augustine, Florida; "Desegregation of Southern Parochial Schools," August 19, 1963, 2; Monsignor Mortimer Danaher, telephone interview by author, August 12, 2006; *St. Augustine Record*, August 24, 1964; Sister Josephine Marie Melican, S.S.J., telephone interview by author, August 15, 2006; Colburn, *Racial Change and Community Crisis*, 174; McNally, *Catholic Parish Life*, 365, 366; Dennis Michael McCarron, "Catholic Schools in Florida, 1866–1992" (PhD diss., Florida State University, 1993), 180; Sister Mary Arnold, O.P., interview by author, August 14, 2006.

73. "Bishop Cody, New Orleans Coadjutor," *Voice*, August 18, 1961; John P. Cody to Mathew Ahmann, November 27, 1962 (quotation), folder "School Integration Incoming/Outgoing

Correspondence Newspaper Clippings June 1960, March–December 1962," box "School Integration Files, 1956–1965" AR/00166, AANO; Donald A. Erickson and John D. Donovan, *The Three R's of NonPublic Education in Louisiana: Race, Religion, and Region* (Washington, DC: President's Commission on School Finance, 1972), 87; Fairclough, *Race and Democracy*, 258–59.

74. "School Rolls Are Open to All Catholics," *Catholic Action of the South*, April 1, 1962; "Southern Field Service Report to the Directors of the National Catholic Conference for Interracial Justice August 1962," 1–3, folder 4, box 8, Henry [Cabirac Jr.] to J. D. De Blieux, October 3, 1962, folder 12, box 6, series 33, NCCIJR; untitled "report of the activities of the New Orleans [Catholic] Council on Human Relations," n.d., folder 3, box 1, CCHRP; "Early Figures Confirm Big School Enrollment," *Catholic Action of the South*, April 29, 1962; *New York Times*, April 14, 17, 21, August 30, September 1, 5, 9, October 7, 1962; [New Orleans] *Times-Picayune*, April 17, 18, August 31, September 2, 1962; Henry C. Bezou, "Report on Conference Held in Archbishop's Office," September 19, 1962, untitled page with three numbered points, folder "Catholic School Integration—Dept of Health, Education + Welfare (1954–1972)," 03–038 box 2, AANO; Edward Hoag, "New Orleans Looking Forward," *Ave Maria* 95 (June 2, 1962): 14; Newell Schindler, "Studies First Year of N.O. Integration," *Catholic Commentator*, June 7, 1963; "New Orleans Schools Open Peacefully," *Catholic Virginian*, September 11, 1963; "Desegregation of Southern Parochial Schools," August 19, 1963, 2; Anderson, *Black, White, and Catholic*, 192–93. Reed Sarratt's claim that "Approximately 12,000 white students withdrew from the parochial schools during the first year of desegregation," greatly overestimated the outflow. Sarratt, *Ordeal of Desegregation*, 280–81 (quotation on p. 81).

75. Henry Cabirac to C. Ellis Henican, August 17, 1962, folder 23, box 3, CCHRP; John Beecher, "Magnolia Jungle," *Ramparts* 3 (December 1964): 45; Erickson and Donovan, *Three R's of NonPublic Education in Louisiana*, 88–90, 188.

76. "'Church Can't Tolerate' Blemish of Prejudice," *Catholic Action of the South*, April 8, 1962; *New York Times*, June 11 (first quotation), September 6, 1962; Paul J. Hallinan to "My dear Catholic people," June 10, 1962, folder 50, *A Syllabus on Racial Justice for Use in the Catholic Schools Grades 7–12 of the Archdiocese of Atlanta*, folder 51, box 036/6, Paul J. Hallinan to "Dear Father," July 2, 1962 (second and third quotations), Paul J. Hallinan, untitled press release, September 4, 1962, Conald Foust to Harold J. Rainey, September 12, 1962, folder 11, box 015/2, AAA; Kevin M. Kruse, *White Flight: Atlanta and the Making of Modern Conservatism* (Princeton, NJ: Princeton University Press, 2005), 173. Marist College and D'Youville Academy, both operated by religious orders in Atlanta, were among the schools that desegregated. Harold J. Rainey to "The Editor, The *Atlanta Constitution*," June 13, 1962, Vincent P. Brennan to Paul J. Hallinan, July 25, 1962, folder 11, box 015/2, AAA.

77. "Archbishop Orders Catholic Hospitals in Atlanta See on Racial Integrated Policy," March 25, 1963, folder 52, box 6, Archbishop Paul J. Hallinan Papers, memorandum, "Sister Mary Melanie, R.S.M., Administrator" to "Chief Admission Officer and All Employees in the Department of Admissions," "Bed Placement Policy," July 27, 1965, Robert M. Nash to Sister Mary Melanie, June 21, 1966, Robert M. Nash to Sister Mary Jacob Engelhartd, n.d., unsigned to John W. Gardner, June 21, 1966, folder 1, box 065/2, AAA; Paul J. Hallinan, "Admission Policy, Local Catholic Hospitals," *Georgia Bulletin*, March 27, 1963; Gerard E. Sherry, *Archbishop Paul J. Hallinan* (Notre Dame, IN: University of Notre Dame Press, 1965), 22–23; *Atlanta Inquirer*, July 13, 1963; Gerard E. Sherry, "Georgia Race Progress Shows Great Contrast in Urban and Rural Areas," *Clarion Herald*, September 9, 1965; Mathew Ahmann to Gerard Sherry, October

28, 1964, folder 3, box 5, memorandum, Jack [Sisson] to Matt [Ahmann], "St. Joseph's Infirmary, Atlanta," June 8, 1965 (quotations), folder 5, box 4, series 33, NCCIJR.

78. "Meeting in Nashville," September 25, 1963, folder 12, Sister Mary Laura to Henry A. Cabirac Jr., March 12, 1964, memorandum, Jack Sisson to Matt Ahmann, "Visit to Knoxville, Tennessee Wednesday, October 28/29, 1964," November 2, 1964, folder 9, box 14, series 33, NCCIJR; Steve Landregan, interview by author, October 22, 2006.

79. Henry Cabirac to Wendelin J. Nold, March 22, 1963 and accompanying note from Cabirac to Matt [Ahmann], Henry Cabirac to John L. Morkovsky, August 28, 1963, Vincent M. Harris to Henry Cabirac, October 2, 1963, folder 7, box 16, Charles W. Ternes to Henry Cabirac, April 7, 1964, folder 9, box 15, series 33, NCCIJR; Frank H. Ross and Lisa May, *Recall, Rejoice, Renew: Diocese of Galveston-Houston 1847–1997* (Dallas: Taylor, 1997), 53; "Bishop John Louis Morkovsky," accessed October 13, 2007, at http://www.catholic-hierarchy.org/bishop/bmork.html; Harris to Cabirac, October 17, 1961; *Our Negro and Indian Missions*, January 1964, 7–20, 1965, ASSJ. Although Beaumont officially desegregated the first grade of public schools in September 1963, no African Americans applied for admission to white schools. In April 1964, a federal district court approved Beaumont's twelve-year desegregation plan. John D. Worrell, "Twenty Years in Beaumont," attached to Charles W. Ternes to J. Oscar Lee, June 5, 1964, folder 9, box 15, series 33, NCCIJR.

80. Hadden interview; *Our Negro and Indian Missions*, January 1964, 7–20, 1965, 12 (quotation), 1966, 11, ASSJ.

81. Eddie L. English to T. J. Toolen, September 23, 1963, (first quotation), T. J. Toolen to Thomas Lorigan, September 24, 1963, (second quotation), T. J. Toolen to Eddie L. English, September 24, 1963, folder "E 1963," Archbishop Thomas J. Toolen Papers, Archives of the Archdiocese of Mobile, Mobile, Alabama (hereinafter cited as Toolen Papers); Moore, *South's Tolerable Alien*, 116–17.

82. Calvin Valcour to Thomas J. Toolen, June 29, 1962, folder "Schools 1962–1963," Toolen Papers; Henry Cabirac to Jane Duffin, April 9, 1963, box 5, folder 15, series 34, Wilhelmina Valcour to Henry Cabirac Jr., September 10, 1963, folder 26, box 3, series 33, NCCIJR; John P. Sisson, "A Southern City Changes Gracefully," *Interracial Review* 36 (May 1963): 98; "Archbishop Orders Alabama High, Grade Schools to Integrate," *Southern Cross*, April 30, 1964.

83. "Memphis Area Schools to Be Integrated," *Tennessee Register*, April 12, 1963; *New York Times*, April 1, 1963; Roger Biles, "A Bittersweet Victory: Public School Desegregation in Memphis," *Journal of Negro Education* 55 (Autumn 1986): 474–75; Joel William McGraw, F.S.C., "The Catholic School System of West Tennessee and the African American Catholics," in McGraw, Guthrie, and King, *Between the Rivers*, 378–86; "Report on August 30 [1963] Trip," folder 3, box 6, series 11, press release, National Catholic Welfare Conference Bureau of Information, April 8, 1963, folder 11, box 14, series 33, NCCIJR.

84. "Diocesan Schools Adopt Open Admission Policy," *Southern Cross*, June 29, 1963; Thomas J. McDonough to "Reverend and dear Father," June 21, 1963, folder 2, "St. Vincent's Will Accept Negro Students," *Savannah Morning News*, June 25, 1963, press clipping, George Landry, "Catholic Schools in Diocese to Desegregate Next Fall," *Macon Telegraph*, July 24, 1963, press clipping, Bishop Thomas J. McDonough to Paul J. Hallinan, September 5, 1963 (quotations), folder 1, box 25, ADS; *Savannah Morning News*, June 24, August 31, 1963; *New York Times*, June 24, September 1, 2, 1963; "Alabama, Georgia Schools Integrate," *Alamo Messenger*, September 13, 1963; Stephen Tuck, "A City Too Dignified to Hate: Civic Pride, Civil Rights, and Savannah in Comparative Perspective," *Georgia Historical Quarterly* 79 (Fall 1995): 539.

85. "Diocese of Charleston, S.C. to Integrate Schools in '64," *Voice*, July 5, 1963; Linda Myers, "Catholic Schools to Be Integrated," *Charleston Evening Post*, June 24, 1963, press clipping, folder 707.1, Francis F. Reh to Albert L. Fletcher, March 30, 1964, folder 707.2/1, ADC; "Statement of the Diocese of Charleston Concerning the Admission of Parochial and Diocesan Schools in South Carolina," *Catholic Banner*, September 1, 1963; "Charleston Area Parochial Schools Admit 15 Negro Students," *Catholic Banner*, September 8, 1963; "Enrollment Sets New Record in Parochial Schools," *Catholic Banner*, September 13, 1964.

86. "'64 School Mix Set in Diocese," press clipping, dated July 29, 1963, folder 11, box 6, series 33, NCCIJR; Robert E. Tracy, "High Schools in East Baton Rouge Parish," *Catholic Commentator*, August 2, 1963.

87. Sarratt, *Ordeal of Desegregation*, 168; "Former Negro School Enrolls 12 White Pupils," *Catholic Virginian*, September 11, 1963.

88. *New York Times*, April 27, 1964 (first, second, and third quotations); "Archbishop Orders Alabama High, Grade Schools to Integrate"; Sid Goldstein, "Four Negroes Enrolled at John Carroll High," *Birmingham Post Herald*, September 3, 1964, press clipping, folder 23, box 1, series 33, NCCIJR.

89. T. J. Toolen to John S. Homlish, May 20, 1964 (quotation), folder "Integration letters 1964," Toolen Papers; Goldstein, "Four Negroes Enrolled at John Carroll High"; memorandum, Jack Sisson to Mathew Ahmann, "Trip to Birmingham, August 29–31, 1964," September 4, 1964, folder 1, box 6, "Enrollment Record High in Diocese," *Catholic Week*, September 11, 1964, press clipping, folder 2, box 1, series 33, NCCIJR.

90. Neil R. McMillen, "Development of Civil Rights, 1956–1970," in *A History of Mississippi*, ed. Richard Aubrey McLemore (Hattiesburg: University and College Press of Mississippi, 1973), vol. 2, 162–63; *New York Times*, August 10, September 5, 1964; "No Incidents as Students Registered," August 19, 1964, press clipping, vertical file "Race Relations, July–Dec. 1964," McCain Library and Archives, University of Southern Mississippi, Hattiesburg, Mississippi; Michael V. Namorato, *The Catholic Church in Mississippi, 1911–1984: A History* (Westport, CT: Greenwood Press, 1998), 136–37; Donald Cunnigen, "Men and Women of Goodwill: Mississippi's White Liberals" (PhD diss, Harvard University, 1988), 359–60 n. 150; R. O. Gerow to Mother David [Virginia Young], December 10, 1964, H40 A1 S.B.S. Original Annals 47 (January 1964): 125 (first quotation), Archives of the Sisters of the Blessed Sacrament, Bensalem, Pennsylvania (hereinafter cited as ASBS); United States Commission on Civil Rights, *Hearings before the United States Commission on Civil Rights, Volume II Administration of Justice Hearings held in Jackson, Miss., February 16–20, 1965* (Washington, DC: United States Commission on Civil Rights, 1965; repr., New York: Arno Press, 1971), 411 (second quotation).

91. *New York Times*, August 22, 1965 (first and second quotations); "Diary of Bishop Gerow," vol. 6: 1960–1966, 1735 (third quotation), Archives of the Diocese of Jackson, Jackson, Mississippi. Parochial school enrollment slipped from 16,705 in the school year 1964–1965 to 14,282 by 1968–1969 because of desegregation and rising tuition fees. Namorato, *Catholic Church in Mississippi*, 91, 137.

92. Bennie W. Heflin, "Bishop Tracy Details Plan to Open 'Schools to All' by 1967," and Robert E. Tracy, "School Plan," *Catholic Commentator*, June 11, 1965 (quotation); Father Gerald M. LeFebvre, interview by author, November 10, 2006.

93. Maurice Schexnayder to the "Right Reverend, Very Reverend and Reverend Pastors, Diocese of Lafayette," May 25, 1965 (quotation), Ignatius A. Martin to George A. Bodin, May 25,

1965, bound volume "Integration of Schools Diocese of Lafayette 1965–1973 Correspondence, Directives, Reports 1965–1971," ADL; "Lafayette Diocese Will 'Open Schools to All,'" *Catholic Commentator*, June 4, 1965; William A. Osborne, *The Segregated Covenant: Race Relations and American Catholics* (New York: Herder and Herder, 1967), 52; Ignatius A. Martin to Herbert C. Kane, June 27, 1966, folder "(Title II HESA) Kane, Herbert C., HEW-441c, Corres. re: Integration (1966–1967)," 03–038 box 1, AANO.

94. "To Desegregate Schools in Alexandria Diocese," *Clarion Herald*, June 17, 1965.

95. "Bishop Stresses Value of Catholic Education," *North-Central Louisiana Register*, September 3, 1965 (quotation); "Alexandria 'Confused' over School Aid Cutoff," *Clarion Herald*, February 2, 1967, press clipping, folder 9, box 6, series 33, NCCIJR; "Schools Comply with Civil Rights Act," *North-Central Louisiana Register*, July 14, 1967.

96. Sister Lover Marie, Our Mother of Mercy School, Church Point, n.d., Sister Karum, Academy of the Sacred Heart, Grand Coteau, n.d., bound volume "Integration of Schools Diocese of Lafayette 1965–1973 Correspondence, Directives, Reports 1965–1971," ADL; "Warn Schools on Segregation," *Southwest Louisiana Register*, August 21, 1969; "Catholic School Integration Stand Explained in Superintendent's Statement," *Southwest Louisiana Register*, August 28, 1969; Sister M. Francis Anthony to Mother Mary Elizabeth Fitzpatrick, December 20, 1970, folder "Correspondence," H40 B2, box 13 "LA: Eunice," "St. Edward, New Iberia, Evaluation of 'Paired' SBS Schools in the Diocese of Lafayette," November 10, 1972, folder 3, H40 B2, box 4, ASBS; Erickson and Donovan, *Three R's of NonPublic Education in Louisiana*, 97, 111–12, 135, 143–44, 149, 198, 284.

97. Sister Lover Marie, Our Mother of Mercy School, Church Point, n.d.; Sister Karum, Academy of the Sacred Heart, Grand Coteau, n.d.; Erickson and Donovan, *Three R's of Non-Public Education in Louisiana*, 135, 144, 149, 197, 284.

98. William J. Jacobs, "Mississippi Report 2: Notebook on Our Own Congo," *Ave Maria* 101 (January 23, 1965): 5; memorandum, Jack [Sisson] to Matt [Ahmann], "Bogalusa Visit, May 14 and 15," May 24, 1965, folder 1, box 7, series 33, NCCIJR; *New York Times*, November 9, 1964, May 10, 1965; "Grave Problems Cited at Second Conference," *Clarion Herald*, May 9, 1968.

99. Appendix 5: "Clergy Bulletin," volume 2, number 15, p. 3 (quotation), Appendix 6: "Clergy Bulletin," volume 2, number 35 (July 1, 1966), Appendix 8: memorandum, John Kennedy to Robert E. Tracy, "Policies of the Diocese Relative to the Employment of Negroes," n.d., "The Record of the Diocese of Baton Rouge in Work for the Negro in the Community 1961–1968," Historical Vertical File, Archives of the Diocese of Baton Rouge, Baton Rouge, Louisiana; John J. Russell to "Dearly Beloved," August 31, 1965, folder "Interracial Correspondence," box H, Bishop John J. Russell Papers, Archives of the Diocese of Richmond, Richmond, Virginia (hereinafter cited as Russell Papers); Philip M. Hannan to "Derar Principal," June 28, 1966, folder "(Title II HESA) Kane, Herbert C., HEW-441c, Corres. re: Integration (1966–1967)," 03–038 box 1, AANO; "Project Equality Announcement Draws High Praise, Support from Across U.S.," *Tennessee Register*, March 10, 1967; Mathew Ahmann, "Project Equality," *Christianity and Crisis* 27 (May 29, 1967): 118–21; memorandum, John P. Sisson, to "Staff," "SFS Report to Staff, April 13-May 14, 1968," May 14, 1968, 1, folder 5, "Report of the Director of the Southern Field Service (SFS), September 1967," 7, folder 4, box 5, series 30, Thomas M. Nunan to John P. Sisson, April 30, 1968, folder 2, box 2, series 33, NCCIJ; Doug Williams, "Project Equality Success Depends on Commitments," *Texas Catholic Herald* [Beaumont edition], November 29, 1968.

100. Robert M. Nash to Sister Mary Melanie, June 21, 1966, Robert M. Nash to Sister Mary Jacob Engelhardt, n.d., unsigned to John W. Gardner, June 21, 1966, Sister M. Jacob to Sister M.

Geraldine and Marjorie Ray, June 23, 1966, untitled press release from St. Joseph's Infirmary, Atlanta, Georgia, n.d., untitled press release, June 24, 1966, untitled report by Sister Mary Jacob, n.d., "U.S. Okay Given to 7 Hospitals," *Atlanta Constitution*, June 25, 1966, press clipping, Marjory Rutherford, "All Hospitals Here Expect Approval," *Atlanta Constitution*, June 29, 1966, press clipping, folder 1, box 065/2, AAA; "Two Hospitals in Archdiocese Denied Funds for Medicare," *Georgia Bulletin*, June 16, 1966; *New York Times*, August 13, 1966; Osborne, *Segregated Covenant*, 57–58.

101. "A Catholic Hospital Segregates, Loses Funds," *National Catholic Reporter*, December 14, 1966 (quotation), press clipping, folder 9, box 6, memorandum, Jack Sisson to Sister Maureen, "Catholic Hospitals," June 24, 1966, Mathew Ahmann to Marie Finbarr, January 26, 1968, Mathew Ahmann to Marie Agatha, February 14, 1968, Claire Teeling to Charles P. Greco, May 27, 1968, folder 1, box 8, series 33, Charles P. Greco to Claire Teeling, July 6, 1968, box 1, series 26, NCCIJR; "The Franciscan Missionaries of Our Lady: The Sisters Who Served in the North American Province," 9, 11, accessed February 1, 2009, at http://www.fmolsisters.com/OurHistory.cfm?page=history; "The Franciscan Missionaries of Our Lady Health System: A Brief History," 5, 7, 9–10, 20, 21, accessed February 1, 2009, at http://www.fmolsisters.com/OurHistory.cfm?page=history.

102. *Our Negro and Indian Missions*, January 1966, 12–14, January 1967, 7–11, January 1968, 12–14, ASSJ; memorandum, Jack Sisson to Sister Mary Peter, "Teaching Sisters in Alexandria Diocese," August 4, 1967, folder 9, box 6, series 33, NCCIJR; *Washington Post*, April 25, 1968; *New York Times*, February 8, 1970; John M. Swomley Jr., "Who Wants Catholic Schools?" *Nation* 211 (December 14, 1970): 627; Amy L. Koehlinger, *The New Nuns: Racial Justice and Religious Reform in the 1960s* (Cambridge, MA: Harvard University Press, 2007), 128–29, 132–35, 142–43; Mother Laurence Edward Ferguson, O.P., to Thomas S. Donnelan, October 22, 1968, Mother M. Bridget, M.S.C., to Thomas S. Donnelan, December 16, 1968, folder 4, box 014/6, AAA; "Request for Sisters [August 2, 1965]," 144, H40 A1 Sisters of the Blessed Sacrament Original Annals, vol. 48 (May 1965–), Mother M. David to Robert G. Hoyt, January 27, 1967, H40 A1 S.B.S Original Annals, vol. 50 (1967): 12, ASBS.

103. *Our Negro and Indian Missions*, January 1967, 7–11 (first, second, and third quotations), ASSJ; "The Record of the Diocese of Baton Rouge in Undertaking Special Work on Behalf of the Negroes of the Community," in "The Record of the Diocese of Baton Rouge in Work for the Negro in the Community 1961–1968"; [Press Department, US Catholic Conference], "Louisiana Schools," *Documentary Service*, February 9, 1967 (fourth quotation), folder 707.2, ADC; Harold Howe II to Robert E. Tracy, June 9, 1967, folder 11, box 6, series 33, NCCIJR; "State Catholic School Desegregation Cleared by U.S. Office of Education," *Southwest Louisiana Register*, July 20, 1967.

104. NC News Service, "Funds Cutoff for Diocesan School Children," January 24, 1967, folder 707.2, ADC; "Alexandria 'confused' over school aid cutoff" (quotation); *Our Negro and Indian Missions*, January 1967, 7–11, ASSJ.

105. Harold Howe II to Ignatius A. Martin, May 24, 1967, folder "Integration of Schools," Richard von Phul Mouton to "Dear Principal," March 14, 1967, Richard von Phul Mouton to "Pastors, Principals and Lay Board Chairmen," May 26, 1967, bound volume "Integration of Schools Diocese of Lafayette 1965–1973 Correspondence, Directives, Reports 1965–1971," ADL; "State Catholic School Desegregation Cleared by U.S. Office of Education"; Wayne O. Reed to John J. Wakeman, June 30, 1967, memorandum, Jack [Sisson] to Matt [Ahmann], "Father Murray Clayton, *new* Chancellor, Alexandria, La.," July 19, 1967, folder 9, box 6, series 33, NCCIJR; "Schools Comply with Civil Rights Act."

106. "Vanishing of National Parishes Welcomed in Pluralistic American Society," *Alamo Messenger*, April 17, 1964; *Our Negro and Indian Missions*, January 1965, 11, January 1968, 12–14, January 1969, 7–10, ASSJ; "Protest New Parish Boundaries," *National Catholic Reporter*, n.d., press clipping, folder 11, box 14, Alexander O. Sigur to John P. Sisson, June 18, 1969, folder 8, box 7, series 33, NCCIJR; Sister Elise, "SBS Serves in Fayette," *Mission Fields at Home* 26 (November–December 1969): 4–5; Mitchell, "The Black Man and the Catholic Church in Nashville," 6–7; Dr. G. J. Tarleton Jr., interview by author, July 21, 2005; Dolores Egger Labbé, *Jim Crow Comes to Church: The Establishment of Segregated Catholic Parishes in South Louisiana*, 2d ed. (New York: Arno Press, 1978 [Lafayette: University of Southwestern Louisiana, 1971]), 87; *The Church of Christ: Decree Enacted by the First Synod of Archdiocese of Atlanta, 1966*, 29 (first quotation), 56, folder 10, box 006/6, AAA; Ernest L. Unterkoefler to the United States Commissioner of Education, April 1, 1967, 2, 4, folder 707.2, ADC.

107. *Our Negro and Indian Missions*, January 1967, 7–11, January 1969, 7–10, January 1970, 11–13, January 1976, 7–11, ASSJ; Reverend Peter Blom, "Position Paper: Committee on Separate Parish—CADL," September 14, 1968 (first quotation), folder 8, box 7, series 33, NCCIJR; "Absurdity Marches On," *Southwest Louisiana Register*, July 4, 1968; Rhonda J. Evans, Craig J. Forsyth, and Stephanie Bernard, "One Church or Two? Contemporary and Historical Views of Race Relations in One Catholic Diocese," *Sociological Spectrum* 22 (2002): 226–27; John J. Russell to Joseph F. Oberle, August 23, 1968, folder St. Augustine (Fulton), Parish Files, Richmond, John J. Russell to Stephen Ford, April 12, 1969, Thomas J. Quinlan to John J. Russell, April 16, 1969, John J. Russell to Thomas J. Quinlan, August 19, 1970, Frederick A. Heckel to John J. Russell, July 17, 1971 (second quotation), folder St. Vincent DePaul's, Newport News, 1959–1973, Parish Files, Archives of the Diocese of Richmond; Nessa Theresa Baskerville Johnson, *A Special Pilgrimage: A History of Black Catholics in Richmond* (Richmond, VA: Diocese of Richmond, 1978), 54–56, 61.

108. "All Must Join Hands to Solve School Desegregation Problems," *Southwest Louisiana Register*, July 24, 1969; "Warn Schools on Segregation"; "Bishops Support Public Schools," *Southwest Louisiana Register*, January 22, 1970; "Diocesan School Board Establishes Committees to Assure Racial Justice," *Southwest Louisiana Register*, January 29, 1970; Kim Larsen, "Catholic Schools Spurn Segregationists," *Voice*, April 17, 1970; *New York Times*, January 25, July 26, 1970; *Atlanta Journal-Constitution*, September 26, 1982; John M. Bond to Robert Keane, March 30, 1972, folder 728.41, ADC; Richard von Phul Mouton to "Pastors with Schools," June 4, 1969, Richard von Phul Mouton to Edward R. D'Alessio, January 13, 1970, bound volume "Integration of Schools Diocese of Lafayette 1965–1973 Correspondence, Directives, Reports 1965–1971," ADL; Theodore M. Hesburgh to John Dearden, January 27, 1971, Mel Buechele, "Let's Demand Justice," attached to Emile Comar to Richard Mouton, March 7, 1972, untitled document, June 10, 1971, Office of Civil Rights, "Catholic Schools of the Roman Catholic Diocese of Lafayette, Louisiana," attached to Lloyd R. Henderson to Richard von Phul Mouton, February 20, 1973, bound volume "Integration of Schools Diocese of Lafayette 1965–1973 The Auzenne Case Correspondence and Data 1970–1973," ADL; Mother M. David to Dear Sisters, February 16, 1970 (quotation), S.B.S. Original Annals Jan–Mar 1970: 139, ASBS; LeFebvre interview; Erickson and Donovan, *Three R's of NonPublic Education in Louisiana*, 105–9, 129–31, 144–49, 194, 196–97, 202, 274–75; "Transcript of meeting with representatives of the Civil Rights Commission, Department of Health, Education and Welfare, Bishop Ernest L. Unterkoefler, Father John Bond and Father Francis Miller," May 24, 1971, 2, folder 728.40, ADC.

Chapter Seven

1. *Our Negro and Indian Missions: Annual Report of the Secretary of the Commission for the Catholic Missions Among the Colored People and the Indians*, January 1946, 17–18, Archives of the Society of St. Joseph of the Sacred Heart, Baltimore, Maryland (hereinafter cited as ASSJ).

2. Ormonde Lewis, interview by author, August 17, 2005; "Integration in Diocese Catholic Schools Enrollment 'Based on Freedom of Choice,'" August 24, 1969, press clipping, H40 B2, folder 3, box 4, Archives of the Sisters of the Blessed Sacrament, Bensalem, Pennsylvania (hereinafter cited as ASBS); "Negroes Constitute One-Eighth of Mississippi's Catholics," *Interracial Review* 18 (January 1945): 32; *Our Negro and Indian Missions*, January 1948, 13–14, January 1953, 5–6, January 1954, 5–6, January 1961, 7–12, January 1962, 7–12, January 1969, 5–6, ASSJ; Arthur Butler to *Our Colored Missions* 46 (March 1960): 43–44 (quotation); Gary Wray McDonogh, *Black and Catholic in Savannah, Georgia* (Knoxville: University of Tennessee Press, 1993), 97, 111, 116–18.

3. Michael J. McNally, "A Peculiar Institution: A History of Catholic Parish Life in the Southeast (1850–1980)," in *The American Catholic Parish: A History from 1850 to the Present*, vol. 1, ed. Jay P. Dolan (Mahwah, NY: Paulist Press, 1987), 183.

4. Lewis interview; Barbara Vickers, interview by author, August 11, 2006; *New York Times*, July 7, 1991; *Austin American Statesman*, July 9, 1991; *St. Petersburg Times*, October 16, 1991; Ken Foskett, *Judging Thomas: The Life and Times of Clarence Thomas* (New York: William Morrow, 2004), 54–56, 64–66 (first quotation on p. 65; second quotation on pp. 65–66); Andrew Peyton Thomas, *Clarence Thomas: A Biography* (San Francisco: Encounter Books, 2001), 69–70; Monsignor Thomas P. Hadden, interview by author, August 2, 2006.

5. McDonogh, *Black and Catholic in Savannah, Georgia*, 188, 200 (quotation).

6. "Thirty-Fifth Negro Priest," *Interracial Review* 23 (October 1950): 149; "Bishop Francis Ordained," *Josephite Harvest* 78 (Summer 1976): 2; Sr. Caroline Hemesath, O.S.F., *Our Black Shepherds: Biographies of the Ten Black Bishops of the United States* (Washington, DC: Josephite Pastoral Center, 1987), 71, 73–74 (quotation on p. 74); *New York Times*, September 5, 1997. Headquartered in New Orleans, the Sisters of the Holy Family operated in a few southern states during the civil rights era. In January 1955, the *Interracial Review* reported that "The Sisterhood . . . has 301 professed Sisters, 17 novices and four postulants. In the two homes for the aged, two orphanages, 34 parochial and private schools, one academy, five combination junior high-elementary schools, 21 elementary schools and six other State-accredited schools, the Sisters care for a total of 11,177 persons. Members of the Sisterhood now serve in Louisiana, Texas, Florida, Alabama, Oklahoma and British Honduras." "Negro Sisterhood Opens New Motherhouse," *Interracial Review* 28 (January 1955): 16.

7. "Black and Catholic—1 Bishop Joseph A. Francis," *America* 142 (March 29, 1980): 256; Millard F. Everett, "Bishop-elect Perry Leader for Racial Justice," *Clarion Herald*, October 7, 1965; Hemesath, *Our Black Shepherds*, 27, 29–30.

8. *We've Come This Far by Faith: A Centennial History of Saint Nicholas Catholic Church Houston's Historic Black Parish 1887–1987* (Houston: American Photocopy and Print Co., 1987), 48, Archives of the Archdiocese of Galveston-Houston, Houston, Texas (hereinafter cited as AAGH).

9. "Chronicle of St. Elizabeth's Convent [Selma, Alabama], September 26, 1940" (quotation), box 13, Local Administration, Society of Saint Edmund Archives, St. Michael's College,

Colchester, Vermont (hereinafter cited as SSEA); Mary Linda Hronek, "A Catholic High School Integrates," *Interracial Review* 36 (December 1963): 243; [Albert Foley], "The Diocese of Mobile-Birmingham," 6, folder 40, box 8, Albert Sidney "Steve" Foley Jr., S.J., Papers, Spring Hill College Archives, Mobile, Alabama (hereinafter cited as Foley Papers); Adam Fairclough, *Race and Democracy: The Struggle for Civil Rights in Louisiana, 1915–1972* (Athens: University of Georgia Press, 1995), 14.

10. Madeline E. Johnson, interview by author, October 31, 2006.

11. McDonogh, *Black and Catholic in Savannah, Georgia*, 1 (quotation); Foskett, *Judging Thomas*, 54, 70; Thomas, *Clarence Thomas*, 69, 74–75.

12. Etienne Barrois, "King of the River People?" *Commonweal* 76 (July 6, 1962): 365–66 (quotation on p. 366).

13. *Our Negro and Indian Missions*, January 1953, 13–17, ASSJ; *New York Times*, September 1, 1962 (quotation).

14. Hubert Singleton, "50 Year History of the Knights and Ladies of Peter Claver," *St. Augustine's Messenger* 36 (October 1959): 232–36, 238–41; *New Catholic Encyclopedia*, 2d ed., vol. 8 (Detroit: Thomson Gale, 2003), s.v. "Knights of Peter Claver," by E. B. Perry and editors; Clarence J. Howard, "The K.P.C. Convenes in Galveston," *St. Augustine's Messenger* 19 (October 1941): 198–200, box 11, folder "Josephite Archives—St. Augustine's Messenger—(1941–49)," Catholic Archives of Texas, Austin, Texas (hereinafter cited as CAT).

15. Edward LaSalle, "A New Approach," *Claverite* 22 (December 1942) quoted in Justin D. Poché, "Religion, Race, and Rights in Catholic Louisiana, 1938–1970" (PhD diss., University of Notre Dame, 2007), 52. In 1948, the KPC national convention decided to reduce the *Claverite* to a quarterly magazine for financial reasons. "The Los Angeles Convention," *Claverite* 28 (September 1948): 2.

16. A. P. Tureaud, "Thanks," *Claverite* 28 (September 1948): 8; "Kneeling before the Altar and Standing before the Bench: Life Sketch of an Outstanding Catholic Negro Layman Alexander Pierre Tureaud, Sr.," *St. Augustine's Messenger* 38 (April 1961); 109–10; A. T. LeCesne, "A Tribute to a Noble Knight," *Claverite* 51 (March–April 1972): 5, 7; O. C. W. Taylor, "Historical News," *Claverite* 54 (April–June 1975): 57–58; Poché, "Religion, Race, and Rights in Catholic Louisiana," 53–54, 83–84; Fairclough, *Race and Democracy*, 56–58, 65–68, 73, 106–8.

17. Poché, "Religion, Race, and Rights in Catholic Louisiana," 53–54; Fairclough, *Race and Democracy*, 69, 72–73 (quotation on p. 72), 112; Vernon J. Parenton and Roland J. Pellegrin, "Social Structure and the Leadership Factor in a Negro Community in South Louisiana," *Phylon* 17 (1st qtr., 1956): 74–78; "Bertrandville Happening," *Josephite Harvest* 79 (November–December 1967): 14, 16.

18. "The Dignity of Man," *Claverite* 26 (January 1947): 2; Peter Wellington Clarke, "Je Parle," *Claverite* 26 (January 1947): 4; "Color and Racial Prejudice," *Claverite* 26 (February 1947): 2; Peter Wellington Clarke, "Je Parle," *Claverite* 26 (February 1947): 8 (quotation); "All Mixed Up Now," *Claverite* 26 (March 1947): 2.

19. Janet Riley, "Minutes of a Meeting Sponsored by the Sub-Committee on Race Relations of the Archdiocesan Committee of the Catholic Committee of the South," February 21, March 27, 1949, "Minutes of the Monthly Meeting of the Commission on Human Rights of the Catholic Committee of the South," May 22, 1949, folder 16, box 47, "Commission on Human Rights of C.C.S. Membership List," n.d., folder 7, box 47, unsigned to "Father Jeffords," n.d., folder 10, box 46, Oscar A. Bouise to the "Essay Contest Committee," October 27, 1954, folder 14, box 46, "Meeting of the Commission on Human Rights, Catholic Committee of the South," September

24, 1950, 1, folder 19, box 47, Joseph H. Fichter Papers, Special Collections and Archives, Loyola University Library, Loyola University New Orleans, New Orleans, Louisiana (hereinafter cited as Fichter Papers); Albert Foley, "The House That Caritas Built," *Integrity* 6 (February 1952): 31; "Interracial Law School Cited at Tureaud Dinner," *Catholic Action of the South*, May 29, 1955; Fairclough, *Race and Democracy*, 58. In March 1951, the CHR had forty-four African American and sixty-eight white members. Patricia Ryan, "Report of Commission's Activity—January 1–March 31, 1951," folder 17, box 46, Fichter Papers.

20. "Minutes of the Monthly Meeting of the Commission on Human Rights of the Catholic Committee of the South," May 22, 1949; "Minutes of the Regular Monthly Meeting of the Commission on Human Rights of the Catholic Committee of the South," September 25, 1949, "Minutes of the Special Meeting of September 29, 1949, Commission on Human Rights, Catholic Committee of the South," folder 17, box 47, Lucien J. Caillouet, "Statement," September 27, 1949, folder 14, box 52, Fichter Papers; "No Negroes in Holy Hour Procession, Park Rules," *Catholic Action of the South*, September 22, 1949; "Decision on Holy Hour March Waits Archbishop," *Catholic Action of the South*, September 29, 1949; *New York Times*, October 15, 1955; Fairclough, *Race and Democracy*, 171; R. Bentley Anderson, *Black, White, and Catholic: New Orleans Interracialism, 1947–1956* (Nashville: Vanderbilt University Press, 2005), 57–59. According to historian R. Bentley Anderson, "In early 1950, Tureaud, representing the National Association for the Advancement of Colored People, filed suit to desegregate City Park. Blacks gained access to the park golf course in 1952, and the park itself was desegregated in 1958." Anderson, *Black, White, and Catholic*, 232 n. 30.

21. Poché, "Religion, Race, and Rights in Catholic Louisiana," 137–38 (quotations on p. 138); "Negro Priest to Address Students on Interracial Day," *Catholic Action of the South*, February 17, 1949. Clarence J. Howard was born in Rocky Mount, North Carolina, in 1907 but raised in Norfolk, Virginia. Albert S. Foley, S.J., "U.S. Colored Priests: Hundred-Year Survey," *America* 89 (June 13, 1953): 295; Albert S. Foley, S.J., *God's Men of Color: The Colored Catholic Priests of the United States, 1854–1954* (New York: Farrar, Straus, 1955), 196–97.

22. "Meeting of the Commission on Human Rights, Catholic Committee of the South," September 24, 1950, 1; "Commission Notes," *Christian Impact* 2 (April 1952) 1, folder 1, box 47, Fichter Papers; Katherine Ann Martensen, "Region, Religion and Social Action: The Catholic Committee of the South, 1939–1956" (Master's thesis, University of New Orleans, 1978), 65–66; Fairclough, *Race and Democracy*, 144.

23. Hemesath, *Our Black Shepherds*, 149, 151–52.

24. "2 Archdiocesan HN Units Will Merge," *Catholic Action of the South*, November 6, 1952.

25. Gladys D. [indecipherable] to Vincent Waters, June 16, 1953 (first and second quotations), scrapbook "Ban on Segregation 1953 volume II," Doris B. Rice, "A Personal Opinion," June 24, 1953 (third and fourth quotations), scrapbook "Ban on Segregation 1953 volume I," Archives of the Diocese of Raleigh, Raleigh, North Carolina; John Francis, "The Church Moves Quietly but Surely," *Sign* 35 (July 1956): 72; "Catholic Interracial Councils," *Interracial Review* 28 (October 1954): 176; Thomas F. Jordan, "The CLC's Two Decades," *Colored Harvest* 67 (October 1955): 3; Kitty Beverly, "Texas Negro Honored," *Colored Harvest* 66 (December 1954): 9; "Council of the Month: CIC of San Antonio, Texas," *Interracial Review* 34 (March 1961): 84.

26. "Use Patience, Charity in School Integration Problem, 1,500 at Claverite Convention Are Advised," *Guardian*, August 6, 1954; "Convention Raps Efforts to Circumvent Supreme Court Non-Segregation Ruling," *Guardian*, August 13, 1954; "Report of the Special Committee on Integration," *Claverite* 34 (September–October 1955): 16–17 (quotation on p. 16).

27. Andy Telli, "Breaking Barriers: 50th Anniversary of Integration of Catholic Schools," *Tennessee Register*, September 24, 2004 (quotation).

28. Telli, "Breaking Barriers" (first quotation); King Hollands, interview by author, July 22, 2005 (second quotation).

29. Monsignor James Hitchcock, interview by author, July 21, 2005; Hollands interview; Reavis L. Mitchell, "The Black Man and the Catholic Church in Nashville" (Master's thesis, Middle Tennessee State University, 1971), 20–22; Telli, "Breaking Barriers"; Owen F. Campion, "Desegregation: To Be or Not to Be," *Tennessee Register*, February 23, 1987; Thomas Stritch, *The Catholic Church in Tennessee: The Sesquicentennial Story* (Nashville: The Catholic Center, 1987), 335.

30. Telli, "Breaking barriers" (quotation); Hollands interview; Campion, "Desegregation"; Mitchell, "The Black Man and the Catholic Church in Nashville," 20–21, 23–24.

31. Clark Porteous, "Tennessee: More Integration Ahead," *Sign* 35 (July 1956): 16.

32. Charles Stephen Padgett, "Schooled in Invisibility: The Desegregation of Spring Hill College, Mobile, Alabama, 1948–1963" (PhD diss., University of Georgia, 2000), 54, 57, 66–67, 70–71, 77, 86, 97; Charles Stephen Padgett, "Hidden from History, Shielded from Harm: Desegregation at Spring Hill College, 1954–1957," *Alabama Review* 56 (October 2003): 278–310.

33. Albert S. Foley, S.J., "Stages in the Desegregation Process at Spring Hill College, Mobile, Ala.," 1–5 (first quotation on p. 1), 6–7 (second, third, and fourth quotations on p. 6), folder 40, box 8, Foley Papers; Jim McDermott, "A Quiet Change of Course," *America* 196 (April 9, 2007): 16–17.

34. "Priest Airs Sin of Segregation," [New Orleans] *States Item*, May 21, 1956, press clipping, attached to the *Christian Impact*, n.d., folder 3, box 47, Fichter Papers; Foley, *God's Men of Color*, 200–201; "Au Revoir Father Howard," *Claverite* 30 (October 1951): 2.

35. "Interracial Seminary," *Sign* 35 (September 1955): 47–49; Ochs, *Desegregating the Altar*, 421–22, 429–40. In 1957, Father Albert S. Foley, S.J., wrote that "St. Augustine's Seminary began four years ago to enroll white seminarians, which indeed it had done during the period 1932–1936. As a result of its integration policy, the seminary has been obliged to forfeit its state tax exemption, in accordance with the law passed by the Mississippi legislature more than a year ago." Albert S. Foley, "The Negro and Catholic Higher Education," *Interracial Review* 30 (October 1957): 171. In 1955, the faculty of St. Augustine's Seminary comprised six African American and thirteen white clergy, who taught five white and forty-five black minor seminarians and fourteen black and thirteen white major seminarians. Stephen J. Ochs, *Desegregating the Altar: The Josephites and the Struggle for Black Priests, 1871–1960* (Baton Rouge: Louisiana State University Press, 1990), 422.

36. "Biographical Sketch—Clarence A. Laws, Regional Secretary, NAACP," n.d., folder 1, box 7, series 34, National Catholic Conference for Interracial Justice Records, Marquette University, Milwaukee, Wisconsin (hereinafter cited as NCCIJR); Poché, "Religion, Race, and Rights in Catholic Louisiana," 210 (quotations).

37. Daniel C. Thompson, *The Negro Leadership Class* (Englewood Cliffs, NJ: Prentice-Hall, 1963), 31–32 (first, second, third, and fourth quotations on p. 31; fifth quotation on p. 32); Kim Lacy Rogers, *Righteous Lives: Narratives of the New Orleans Civil Rights Movement* (New York: New York University Press, 1993), 82.

38. Fairclough, *Race and Democracy*, 49–50, 61; Carl L. Bankston III and Stephen J. Caldas, *A Troubled Dream: The Promise of Failure of School Desegregation in Louisiana* (Nashville: Vanderbilt University Press, 2002), 107.

39. Carlos A. Lewis, "Directory of U.S. Negro Priests," *Interracial Review* 30 (July 1957): 119–21.

40. "Guardian to Publish Analysis of Racial Problem in America," *Guardian*, July 24, 1959; William W. O'Donnell, "America's Race Problem," *Guardian*, July 31, August 7, 14, 21, 28, September 4, 1959; Hubert D. Singleton to the *Guardian*, October 2, 1959.

41. Anonymous letter to the *Guardian* (quotations), and "Guardian Launches Two-Fold Follow-Up to 'Race' Editorials," *Guardian*, September 25, 1959.

42. "1st Josephite Priest from New Orleans," *Catholic Action of the South*, May 29, 1955; *The Josephites: A Century of Evangelization in the African American Community* (Baltimore: St. Joseph's Society of the Sacred Heart, 1993), 51; "Here and There," *Our Colored Missions* 27 (August 1941): 116; Ochs, *Desegregating the Altar*, 3, 319, 361–62, 440–43.

43. Ora M. Lewis Martin, "The Dilemma of Reverence Versus Respect," *Claverite* 38 (November–December 1959): 7–9 (first and second quotations on p. 7; third quotation on p. 8); Poché, "Religion, Race, and Rights in Catholic Louisiana," 225. KPC membership totalled 12,318 in 1955 and 12,767 in 1960. "Membership Statistics," *Claverite* 44 (January–February 1965): 15.

44. Mrs. B. Hubbard to "Your Excellency," May 19, 1959, folder "St. Vincent de Paul's 1959–1973, Newport News," ADRV.

45. Marc Crawford, "Brave Teens Supply Leadership Parents Heed Their Counsel," *Jet* 15 (March 5, 1959): 24–28; *New York Times*, July 8, 1959 (quotation); Poché, "Religion, Race, and Rights in Catholic Louisiana," 199–202.

46. Richard J. Swift to *America* 103 (April 16, 1960): 69; Lewis interview; Foskett, *Judging Thomas*, 43–44, 55, 67–68; McDonogh, *Black and Catholic in Savannah, Georgia*, 56–57; Gary W. McDonogh, "Black and Catholic in Savannah," in *Sea and Land: Cultural and Biological Adaptations in the Southern Coastal Plain*, ed. James L. Peacock and James C. Sabella (Athens: University of Georgia Press, 1988), 64; [Henry A. Cabirac Jr.] untitled note "May 20 [1963], Savannah, Georgia," folder 4, box 5, series 33, NCCIJR; Thomas, *Clarence Thomas*, 79; "Father Foley's Talk on the Freedom Riders," n.d., 15, folder 22, box 4, Foley Papers; Norman C. Francis, interview by author, July 6, 2007.

47. L. G. Allain, Horace Bohannon, Charles Goosby, Thomas W. Hines, John Thomas, Evarie S. Thompson, and Johnnie Yancey to Francis E. Hyland, December 11, 1960, 1–3 (quotation on p. 2), folder 49, box 036/6, Archives of the Archdiocese of Atlanta, Atlanta, Georgia (hereinafter cited as AAA); "3 Southern Sees Told to Prepare for Integration," *Guardian*, February 24, 1961.

48. James Sulton, "So I Became a Catholic," *Interracial Review* 29 (September 1956): 150–52; Thomas J. Shelley, *Paul J. Hallinan: First Archbishop of Atlanta* (Wilmington, DE: Michael Glazier, 1989), 126 (quotations); Numan V. Bartley, *The Rise of Massive Resistance: Race and Politics in the South during the 1950s* (Baton Rouge: Louisiana State University Press, 1969), 334–38; "Catholic Negro Co-Ed Walks Tight Rope in Integration of Georgia University," *Alamo Messenger*, January 20, 1961, press clipping, folder "Black Catholics," Archives of the Archdiocese of San Antonio, San Antonio, Texas (hereinafter cited as AASA).

49. Clarence J. Biggers to Paul J. Hallinan, August 23, 1962 (quotation), Paul J. Hallinan, September 4, 1962, untitled press release, folder 11, box 015/2, AAA.

50. Joel William McGraw, F.S.C., "The Catholic School System of West Tennessee and the African American Catholics," in Joel William McGraw, F.S.C., Milton J. Guthrie, and Josephine King, *Between the Rivers: The Catholic Heritage of West Tennessee* (Memphis: Catholic Diocese of Memphis, 1996), 378–79, 381–83.

51. "Memphis Area Schools to Be Integrated," *Tennessee Register*, April 12, 1963; McGraw, "The Catholic School System of West Tennessee and the African American Catholics," 378–79.

52. McGraw, "The Catholic School System of West Tennessee and the African American Catholics," 379–80, 383–86.

53. *Our Negro and Indian Missions*, January 1956, 7–10, January 1960, 7–12, 1961, 7–14, January 1962, 7–12, January 1963, 7–10, ASSJ.

54. *Our Negro and Indian Missions*, January 1963, 7–10 (quotation), ASSJ.

55. Michael J. McNally, *Catholicism in South Florida, 1868–1968* (Gainesville: University of Florida Press, 1984), 192; *Our Negro and Indian Missions*, 1963, 11–14, ASSJ.

56. G. J. Tarleton Jr., interview by author, July 21, 2005; Mary Craighead, interview by author, July 19, 2005; Hollands interview.

57. Noella Mitchell et al. to Sister Mary Bonaventure, March 5, 1962, and William L. Adrian to "Dear Sirs and Ladies," March 11, 1962 (quotations), in possession of G. J. Tarleton Jr.

58. Tarleton interview; Robert Craighead, interview by author, July 19, 2005; William L. Adrian to G. J. Tarleton Jr. et al., April 30, 1962 (quotations), in possession of G. J. Tarleton Jr.

59. Tarleton interview; Robert Craighead interview; William L. Adrian to "Dear Sirs and Ladies," July 19, 1962 (quotations), in possession of G. J. Tarleton Jr.; "Archbishop Vagnozzi Is the Seventh Apostolic Delegate to the U.S.," *Catholic Banner*, April 24, 1960.

60. "The Big A Is Twenty-Five Years Old," *Josephite Harvest* 77 (Winter 1975–76): 11, 12, 15; Fairclough, *Race and Democracy*, 283–84.

61. "Josephite Camera," *Josephite Harvest* 77 (January–February 1965): 21; William H. Barnes, "NBC," *Josephite Harvest* 76 (January–February 1964): 20–21; Fairclough, *Race and Democracy*, 277–78, 284.

62. "Richmond," *Josephite Harvest* 76 (September–October 1964): 12.

63. Mathew Ahmann, "Catholic Initiatives for Interracial Justice: Summer, 1963), press release, July 27, 1963, folder 1, box 84, Louis J. Twomey Papers, Special Collections and Archives, Loyola University Library, Loyola University New Orleans (hereinafter cited as Twomey Papers); "Council on Human Relations Is Seen as 'Holy Crusade,'" *Catholic Action of the South*, April 2, 1961; "Council on Human Relations Lauds Tulane Policy Change," *Catholic Action of the South*, May 14, 1961; Peter Finney Jr., "Lay Persons Launched 1961 Desegregation Drive," *Clarion Herald*, January 18, 2001; "Biographical Sketch—Clarence A. Laws, Regional Secretary, NAACP"; minutes, Board of Directors of the National Catholic Conference for Interracial Justice, February 23, 1963, folder 20, box 3, Amistad Research Center, New Orleans, Louisiana; memorandum, Jack [John P. Sisson] to Matt [Mathew Ahmann], "Selma, Alabama," November 25, 1964, folder 3, box 3, series 34, NCCIJR; Millard Everett, "Changer of Hearts," *Today*, October 1963: 3, 5.

64. "Statement by Clarence A. Laws Southwest Regional Secretary of the National Association for the Advancement of Colored People before the 47th Annual Convention of the Knights of Peter Claver, Municipal Auditorium, Lafayette, Louisiana, August 6, 1962," 1–6 (quotations on p. 3), folder 1, box 7, series 34, NCCIJR; "Biographical Sketch—Clarence A. Laws, Regional Secretary, NAACP."

65. Wilhelmina Valcour to Thomas J. Toolen, May 15, 1962, Philip Cullen to Mrs. Calvin Valcour, May 17, 1962, S. W. Boyd to T. J. Toolen, May 18, 1962, T. J. Toolen to Simon William Boyd, May 30, 1962, Calvin Valcour to Thomas J. Toolen, June 29, 1962, folder "Schools 1962–1963," Mr. and Mrs. Cecil T. Hunter to Thomas J. Toolen, June 3, 1963, T. J. Toolen to Mr. and Mrs. Cecil T.

Hunter, June 11, 1963, folder "School Letters 1963," Toolen Papers; Henry Cabirac Jr. to Clarence Laws, May 4, 1962, folder 14, box 2, series 4.1, Henry Cabirac to Jane Duffin, April 9, 1963, folder 15, box 5, series 34, Henry Cabirac to J. O. Tate, July 23, 1963, folder 2, box 12, memorandum, Jack Sisson to Mathew Ahmann, "Trip to Birmingham, August 29–31, 1964," folder 1, box 6, series 33, "Interim Report of the Southern Field Service's—1963 Activities," 2–3, August 2, 1963, folder 7, "Southern Field Service Report for November 1963 through September, 1964—A Survey of Activities; and General Observations," 12, folder 8, box 4, series 30, NCCIJR; "Archbishop Orders Alabama High, Grade Schools to Integrate," *Southern Cross*, April 30, 1964.

66. J. E. Taylor Jr. to John F. Quinn, April 19, 1962 (quotation), J. E. Taylor Jr. and William E. Jones, "The Negro and the Catholic Church—Archdiocese of San Antonio 1962," folder "Organizations and Societies Catholic Interracial Council (1945–1969)," AASA; "Vanishing of National Parishes Welcomed in Pluralistic American Society," *Alamo Messenger*, April 17, 1964.

67. Henry Cabirac Jr. to John I. Reddix, February 9, 21, 1962, February 14, March 4 (quotations), 1963, folder 1, box 8, series 33, NCCIJR; Fairclough, *Race and Democracy*, 198–99, 220–22, 313.

68. "Statement of Interracial Justice Adopted by 46th Annual Convention National Council Knights and Ladies of Peter Claver," August 9, 1961, folder 1, box 7, series 34, NCCIJR; "Statement of Interracial Justice Adopted by 47th Annual Convention National Council Knights and Ladies of Peter Claver," 1–4 (quotations on p. 2), folder 2, box 25, Archives of the Diocese of Savannah, Savannah, Georgia (hereinafter cited as ADS).

69. "Statement of Interracial Justice Adopted by 47th Annual Convention National Council Knights and Ladies of Peter Claver," 1–4 (first quotation on p. 3; second quotation on p. 1); "Southern Field Service Report to the Directors of the National Catholic Conference for Interracial Justice August 1962," 19, folder 4, box 8, series 33, NCCIJR.

70. Thomas R. Lee Jr., "Annual Report of Executive Secretary," *Claverite* 41 (May–June 1962): 18, 25 (quotation); Eugene B. Perry, "The Negro's Fight for Equality," *Claverite* 42 (November–December 1963): 6–7; Wallace L. Young Jr., "Report of the Executive Secretary," *Claverite* 46 (May–June 1967): 32; "Joseph H. Jacques," *Claverite* 47 (November–December 1968): 6; "Report of Southern Field Service, November 1963–July 1964," 4, folder 8, box 4, series 30, NCCIJR; Francis interview.

71. James B. Johnson to Thomas J. Toolen, May 17, 1963, James B. Johnson and Charles S. Smoot, untitled resolution, Gulf Coast Conference of the Knights of Peter Claver, May 5, 1963 (first five quotations), T. J. Toolen to James B. Johnson, May 24, 1963 (sixth quotation), folder "Knights of St. Peter Claver," no box, Toolen Papers.

72. H. H. Dusuau, "Annual Report of the Executive Secretary," *Claverite* 42 (May–June 1963): 13; "Catholic Role in D.C. March Large, Varied," *Catholic Virginian*, August 30, 1963; Perry, "The Negro's Fight for Equality," 6 (quotation); Russell Shaw, "Strong Religious Undercurrent Seen Marking D.C. March," *Catholic Virginian*, September 6, 1963.

73. Hemesath, *Our Black Shepherds*, 38; "Father Hadden Ordained in Rome," *Interracial Review* 32 (April 1959): 77; Hadden interview; Eymard Galligan to "Dear Father General [Jeremiah T. Purtill]," October 22, 1963, Folder "Correspondence—Local Admin/South-Selma," Superior General Correspondence with South, SSEA; Moses B. Anderson, S.S.E., Curriculum Vitae, G 13-1-3 File 4, Community Archives, Sisters of St. Joseph, Rochester, New York (hereinafter cited as Community Archives); "Current African-American Bishops' Bios," accessed April 28, 2005, at http://www.usccb.org/saac/bshbio2.htm; *New York Times*, March 9, 1977.

74. "Dialogue: Father August Thompson [and] John Howard Griffin," *Ramparts* 2 (Christmas 1963): 24–33 (quotation on. p. 29); Ochs, *Desegregating the Altar*, 405, 459; August Thompson to Louis Twomey, September 1, 1967, folder 15, box 22, Twomey Papers.

75. "Dialogue," 24–33 (first quotation on p. 29; second quotation on p. 31); "Bishop Raps Article on Church Segregation," n.d., press clipping, folder 9, box 6, series 33, NCCIJR.

76. Thomas P. Martin, Joseph D. English, and H. Harleston Fleming to Francis Reh, December 12, 1963 (quotation), folder 711.33/2, ADC.

77. The Committee for True Catholicism in Race Relations to Richard O. Gerow, February 13, 1964, folder 11, box 11, series 33, NCCIJR.

78. Fairclough, *Race and Democracy*, 298–99, 320; Peter Johnson, interview by author, October 19, 2006; [New Orleans] *Times-Picayune*, October 1, 1963; John Beecher, "Magnolia Ghetto," *Ramparts* 3 (December 1964): 46; Arthur J. Chapital Sr. to John P. Cody, October 17, 1963 and attached "Petition to the Greater New Orleans Community," folder "School Integration File June 1962–October 1963 Incoming/Outgoing Correspondence/Newspaper Clippings," box "School Integration Files, 1956–1965," AR/00166, AANO.

79. Vickers interview; *St. Augustine Record*, June 15, 1964; "St. Augustine Pastor Seeks End to Strife," *Florida Catholic*, June 19, 1964 (quotation); Charles R. Gallagher, "The Catholic Church, Martin Luther King Jr., and the March on St. Augustine," *Florida Historical Quarterly* 83 (Fall 2004): 149–72; David R. Colburn, *Racial Change and Community Crisis: St. Augustine, Florida, 1877–1980* (New York: Columbia University Press, 1985), 157–60, 162, 172–73, 214.

80. Robert G. McDole to Richard Oliver Gerow, June 4, 1964, folder 11, box 13, series 33, NCCIJR; Brother Cyprian Davis, O.S.B., interview by author, July 10, 2007; John Dittmer, *Local People: The Struggle for Civil Rights in Mississippi* (Urbana and Chicago: University of Illinois Press, 1994), 246–47.

81. Agnes Godwin and Frances Perres to Thomas J. Toolen, May 20, 1964, folder "Integration Letters 1964," no box, Toolen Papers; "Claver Knights Urge Orderly Rights Action," *Texas Catholic Herald* [Houston edition], August 13, 1964 (quotations).

82. Moses B. Anderson, S.S.E., Curriculum Vitae, James P. Robinson, S.S.E., Curriculum Vitae, G 13-1-3 File 4, Community Archives; Jim Robinson to "Dear Father General [Eymard P. Galligan]," February 25, 1965 (quotations), Folder "Correspondence—Local Admin/South—Elizabeth City, NC," Superior General Correspondence with South, SSEA.

83. *Selma Times-Journal*, January 17, 1983; *New Catholic Encyclopedia*, 2d ed., vol. 2., s.v. "Bowman, Thea," by C. Davis; Cornelia F. Sexauer, "A Well-Behaved Woman Who Made History: Sister Mary Antona's Journey to Selma," *American Catholic Studies* 115 (Winter 2004): 37–57; Christopher J. Kauffman, *Ministry and Meaning: A Religious History of Catholic Health Care in the United States*, with a Foreword by Martin E. Marty (New York: Crossroad, 1995), 263–64.

84. Letter from members of St. Jude and St. John the Baptist churches, Montgomery, Alabama, to Thomas T. Toolen, March 21, 1965 (quotations), folder "Letters unfav. to Toolen," box "Selma Demonstrations March 1965," Toolen Papers; Pressley Bickerstaff to the *Catholic Week*, April 2, 1965.

85. Sister Mary Christopher to Sister Mary John, "March 1, 1965 (cont. March 20)," folder 14, box G 13-1-2, RG 831.102, Community Archives.

86. "Selma Negroes Beaten and Gassed as Police Break Up Civil Rights March," *Clarion Herald*, March 11, 1965; "Selma Pastor Ousted," *National Catholic Reporter* 1 (June 30, 1965): 1; Kate Trainor to Matt [Ahmann], June 30, 1965, Mathew Ahmann to Kate Trainor, June 30, 1965 and attached Charles Maxey et al., telegram to Thomas J. Toolen, June 26, 1965 (first quotation),

parishioners of St. Elizabeth Parish, Selma, Alabama, to Pope Paul VI, n.d. (second quotation), folder 22, box 26, series 20, NCCIJR; *Chicago Sun-Times*, July 4, 1965; Oona Sullivan, "Selma Aftermath," *Jubilee* 13 (August 1965): 16. There is disagreement about the numbers involved. According to the *National Catholic Reporter*, thirteen hundred people from St. Elizabeth Church and six other African American churches in Selma wrote to Toolen calling for Ouellet's retention. On Ouellet see Paul T. Murray "'The Most Righteous White Man in Selma': Father Maurice Ouellet and the Fight for Voting Rights," *Alabama Review* 68 (January 2015): 31-73.

87. "Ask Claver Knights Push Freedom Plan," *Clarion Herald*, August 12, 1965 (quotations).

88. Rollins E. Lambert, "Negro Priests Speak Their Minds," *Sign* 44 (November 1964): 11, 13; Jerome LeDoux to *Sign*, November 6, 1964 (quotation), folder 8, box 4, series 21, NCCIJR. The statistics for black priests are from Lambert's article. LeDoux estimated that there were approximately 147 African American Catholic priests in the United States in 1964. Perry claimed there were 164 black priests in 1965, 62 of them Divine Word missionaries like himself. LeDoux to the *Sign*, November 6, 1964; "American Negro Bishop Will Work for Christian Dignity," *Catholic Reporter*, October 8, 1965, press clipping, folder 12, box 3, series 4.1, NCCIJR. Although Archbishop Paul J. Hallinan ordained the Archdiocese of Atlanta's first black diocesan priest, William E. Calhoun of Carrollton, Georgia, in May 1963, ordination of blacks as diocesan priests in the South remained extremely rare. Five years later, Father Aloysius Clarke was the archdiocese's only African American priest. "Negro Convert Becomes Priest," *Catholic Week*, May 31, 1963; Noel C. Burtenshaw to Thomas A. Donellan, June 26, 1968, box 1, folder 8, Archbishop Thomas A. Donnellan Papers, AAA; *New York Times*, October 4, 1970.

89. Clarence A. Laws, "The Negro Apostolate 'Several Viewpoints,'" July 30, 1965, 1 (second, third, and fourth quotations), 3 (first quotation), folder 5, box 84, Twomey Papers.

90. "Ordinations Go South," *Josephite Harvest* 77 (January–February 1965): 1. The four African Americans were Thomas F. Honore, Vernon P. Moore, U. Michael Nicholas, and William L. Norvel. "Josephites to Be Ordained," *Josephite Harvest* 77 (January–February 1965): 12-13.

91. Memorandum, Jack [Sisson] to Matt [Ahmann], "Cardinal Sheehan and Archbishop Toolen statements at the investiture of the pallium, March 23 in New Orleans," March 29, 1965, folder 13, box 25, series 20, NCCIJR; "Archbishop Cody Gets Pallium in Historic Rite," *Mississippi Register*, April 2, 1965; Dennis Bonnette, "Race: The Failure of the Church," *Ave Maria* 102 (October 23, 1965): 5-7; Catholic Students of Xavier University to John P. Cody, March 30, 1965 (quotations), folder "School Integration File Incoming/Outgoing Correspondence 1965," box "School Integration Files, 1953–1965" AR/00165, AANO.

92. "Negro Layman Now Heads Xavier U.," *Clarion Herald*, June 27, 1968; Edward J. Ray, "Xavier University of Louisiana Holds Inaugural Ceremonies for President," *Claverite* 48 (March–April 1969): 6-8; S.B.S. Original Annals, vol, 51 (1968): 117, ASBS; "Outstanding Leader," *Josephite Harvest* 76 (Spring 1974): 22-23.

93. "They Will Accept Me as a Bishop," *Alamo Messenger*, October 8, 1965; "Bishop Perry States Position," [New Orleans] *Times-Picayune*, December 29, 1965 (first and second quotations), press clipping, folder 9, box 11, series 34, NCCIJR; Newell Schindler, "First Negro Bishop in U.S. This Century Is Consecrated," [Davenport, Iowa] *Catholic Messenger*, January 13, 1966; Era Bell Thompson, "Bishop Perry of New Orleans," *Catholic Digest* May 1966, 18 (quotation).

94. "Equality, Not 'Power,' Key to Negro Struggle," *Clarion Herald*, August 11, 1966 (quotation), press clipping, folder 9, box 11, series 34, NCCIJR; "Bishop Perry Cites Negro Equality Goal," *Texas Catholic Herald* [Houston edition], August 5, 1966; "Average Negro Not Interested in 'Black Power,' Bishop Says," *Guardian*, August 12, 1966.

95. *Our Negro and Indian Missions*, January 1966, 12–14, January 1967, 7–11, ASSJ; Ernest L. Unterkoefler to the United States Commissioner of Education, April 1, 1967, folder 707.2, ADC; "Drexel Pupils to Be Transferred When School Closes in June," *Georgia Bulletin*, March 23, 1967, press clipping, folder 5, box 4, series 33, NCCIJR; Lucien Salvant, "The Parting Pangs of Progress," *Josephite Harvest* 80 (February 1968): 9; Hadden interview.

96. "Catholic School Integration Stand Explained in Superintendent's Statement," *Southwest Louisiana Register*, August 28, 1969; Kathleen Woods to James J. McGuire, December 5, 1968, 2, folder 6, box 2, series 33, NCCIJR; "Integration in Diocese Catholic Schools Enrollment 'Based on Freedom of Choice'"; "School Personnel Urge Race Action," *Southwest Louisiana Register*, January 22, 1970; Francis M. Hammond, "Overview," *Interracial Review* 40 (Fall 1970): 3–4; Donald A. Erickson and John D. Donovan, *The Three R's of NonPublic Education in Louisiana: Race, Religion, and Region* (Washington, DC: President's Commission on School Finance, 1972), 38, 69, 78–80, 135, 187, 198; Hadden interview.

97. James M. Woods, *Mission and Memory: A History of the Catholic Church in Arkansas* (Little Rock: Diocese of Little Rock, 1993), 246–47; Walter B. Clancy to John P. Sisson, November 8, 1968, folder 7, box 2, series 33, NCCIJR; *Arkansas Gazette*, March 20, 1969; *Our Negro and Indian Missions*, January 1967, 7–11 (quotation), January 1970, 11–13, ASSJ.

98. Salvant, "Parting Pangs of Progress," 9–10 (quotations on p. 10).

99. Ibid., 9–10 (first quotation on p. 9; second, third, and fourth quotations on p. 10). After reconsideration, the church remained open.

100. August Thompson to John F. Dearden, September 1, 1967, 1–7 (quotations on p. 5), attached to August Thompson to Louis Twomey, September 1, 1967, folder 15, box 22, Twomey Papers.

101. "Statement of Black Catholic Clergy Caucus," April 18, 1968 (quotations), folder 8, box 2, series 34, the Reverend Rollins Lambert et al. to Ramsey Clark, April 16, 1968, Peggy Roach to Dick Lamanna, May 20, 1968, folder 9, box 5, series 16, NCCIJR; John R. Sullivan, "Negro Priests Think Church White, Racist," *Southern Cross*, April 25, 1968; Brother Joseph M. Davis, "Reflections on a Central Office for Black Catholicism," *Homiletic and Pastoral Review* 69 (July 1969): 771–73; Richard Rashke, "Trust for Black Catholics?" *Commonweal* 92 (March 20, 1970): 35; Neil O'Connell, "Oral History Interview with Brother Joseph Davis, S.M., January 21, 1972, Washington, D.C.," 1, 19–22, Joseph M. Davis Papers, University of Notre Dame Archives, Notre Dame, Indiana; Joseph M. Davis, S.M., and Cyprian Rowe, F.M.S., "The Development of the National Office for Black Catholics," *U.S. Catholic Historian* 7 (Spring–Summer 1988): 268–69. In October 1963, the Second Vatican Council approved the idea of restoring a permanent diaconate. In answer to a recommendation from the NCCB, in June 1967 Pope Paul VI approved reinstallation of a permanent diaconate in the United States, open to married men over thirty-five years old. In October 1968, after a petition from the NCCB, the Vatican gave formal authorization for a permanent diaconate in America. Deacons underwent a two-year training period, after which they could perform most of the functions of a priest except offer Mass or hear confessions. The Black Catholic Clergy Caucus envisaged that a permanent black diaconate would help offset the lack of black priests in African American communities. "Council Approves Deacon Larger Role for Bishops," *Catholic Commentator*, November 8, 1963; *Washington Post*, April 25, 1968; Elmer Von Feldt, "Permanent Deacons: Vehicles of Grace," *Columbia* 48 (December 1968): 4; George F. O'Dea to John J. Russell, October 13, 1967 and attached George F. O'Dea to John F. Dearden, October 12, 1967, folder "Josephite Fathers," box F, Bishop John J. Russell Papers, Diocese of Richmond Archives, Richmond, Virginia (hereinafter cited as Russell

Papers); "Josephites and the Permanent Deaconate," *Josephite Harvest* 79 (Summer 1977): 2–4; Ochs, *Desegregating the Altar*, 448–49. Michael Warner explains that the NCCB becomes "the United States Catholic Conference (USCC) when commenting on public policy or acting as an entity incorporated under civil law." Michael Warner, *Changing Witness: Catholic Bishops and Public Policy, 1917–1994*, with a Foreword by George Weigel (Grand Rapids, MI: Williams B. Eerdmans, 1995), 76.

102. Sullivan, "Negro Priests Think Church White, Racist" (first, second, and third quotations); Cyprian Davis interview (fourth quotation).

103. Davis, "Reflections on a Central Office for Black Catholicism," 774–76; Lawrence E. Lucas, "The Black Voice," *Tennessee Register*, December 13, 1969, press clipping, "American Bishops Discuss Black Catholicism Proposal," *Texas Catholic Herald*, February 14, 1969, press clipping, "3 Bishops Will Study Black Need," *West Virginia Register*, press clipping, dated March 7, 1969, "Bishops, Black Priests, Cite Fruitful Meeting," *Southern Cross*, March 20, 1969, press clipping, "Black Clergy Office Plans Are Advancing," *Clarion Herald*, May 1, 1969, press clipping, folder 8, box 2, series 34, NCCIJR; O'Connell, "Oral History Interview with Brother Joseph Davis, S.M.," 21–24; Davis and Rowe, "Development of the National Office for Black Catholics," 269, 271; "Negro Nuns Meeting to Discuss Racism," *Voice*, July 5, 1968; S.B.S. Original Archives, vol. 51 (1968): 149, ASBS; Pat Kiely, "A Cry for Black Nun Power," *Commonweal* 88 (September 27, 1968): 650; Mary Lou Burger, "Reaction Mostly Favors Black Nuns' Conference," *Southern Cross*, June 5, 1969; John C. Haughey, "Black Sisters Become Soul Sisters," *America* 121 (August 2, 1969): 67; *New York Times*, August 24, 1970; Ronald L. Sharps, "Black Catholics in the United States: A Historical Chronology," *U.S. Catholic Historian* 12 (Winter 1994): 134–35; M. Shawn Copeland, "A Cadre of Women Religious Committed to Black Liberation: The National Black Sisters' Conference," *U.S. Catholic Historian* 14 (Winter 1996): 128–34; Ochs, *Desegregating the Altar*, 447.

104. Ernest L. Unterkoefler to Charles J. Buam, May 30, 1968, folder 707.9, ADC. In January 1968, Unterkoefler wrote that "Due to Federal regulations, it has become necessary for us to hasten our program to eliminate dual school systems." *Our Negro and Indian Missions*, January 1968, 7–11, ASSJ.

105. Claude S. and Nettie M. Jones to "Bishop Koeffler [sic]," June 2, 1968 (first and second quotations), Mr. B. F. and Mrs. Martha Richardson to Ernest L. Unterkoefler, June 2, 1968 (third quotation), Mr. and Mrs. Charles Harris to Unterkoefler, June 2, 1968, Laura Brownlee to Ernest L. Unterkoefler, June 2, 1968, Mr. and Mrs. James Rosemond to Ernest L. Unterkoefler, June 2, 1968, folder 707.9, ADC.

106. Mr. and Mrs. Thomas A. Mosley Sr. to Ernest L. Unterkoefler, June 2, 1968 (quotation), J. P. and Thelma C. Williams to Ernest L. Unterkoefler, June 2, 1968, folder 707.9, ADC.

107. Reverend William V. Coleman, "A Survey of Student Background and Attitudes at St. Pius X High School, Savannah, Georgia," folder 7, box 19, ADS. The source does not provide the survey's date.

108. John J. Russell to George F. O'Dea, September 16, 1969, box F, folder "Josephite Fathers," Russell Papers; Thomas J. Quinlan to John J. Russell, April 16, 1969, no box, folder "St. Vincent de Paul's, Newport News, 1959–1973," Parish Files, ADRV; *New York Times*, January 14, 1969 (quotations).

109. *New York Times*, March 12, 1969; "3 Bishops Will Study Black Need"; John C. Haughey, "Black Catholicism," *America* 120 (March 22, 1969): 325–27; Davis, "Reflections on a Central Office for Black Catholicism," 774; O'Connell, "Oral History Interview with Brother Joseph Davis, S.M.," 28–30; Davis and Rowe, "The Development of the National Office for Black

Catholics," 271–72; Roland Freeman, "National Black Office Not Separatist," *Clarion Herald*, February 19, 1970 (quotations); Rashke, "Trust for Black Catholics?" 35–37; "Bishops Open Office for Black Catholics," *Catholic Week*, July 10, 1970.

110. Andrew S. Moore, *The South's Tolerable Alien: Roman Catholics in Alabama and Georgia, 1945–1970* (Baton Rouge: Louisiana State University Press, 2007), 156.

111. "Diocese Speeds Up School Desegregation," *Southwest Louisiana Register*, August 20, 1970; "Diocese Answers School Critics," *Southwest Louisiana Register*, June 17, 1971; "Charges Levied against Diocesan Schools," *Religious New Service*, June 7, 1971, bound volume "Integration of Schools Diocese of Lafayette 1965–1973 The Auzenne Case Correspondence and Data 1970–1973," Archives of the Diocese of Lafayette, Lafayette, Louisiana (hereinafter cited as ADL).

112. "Diocese Answers School Critics"; Maurice Schexnayder, untitled statement, August 3, 1970 (quotation), untitled press release by Diocese of Lafayette Bureau of Information, n.d., Bishop Maurice Schexnayder to the "Clergy, Religious and Laity Diocese of Lafayette," August 12, 1970, "Relevant Considerations in Opposing the Application for Preliminary Injunction and in Moving to Stay the Proceedings," August 26, 1970, Maurice Schexnayder to Luigi Raimondi, September 22, November 2, 1970, Theodore M. Hesburgh to Cardinal John Dearden, January 27, 1971, Cardinal John Dearden to Theodore M. Hesburgh, March 19, 1971, Maurice Schexnayder to Cardinal John Dearden, April 2, 1971, "Catholic Schools of the Roman Catholic Diocese of Lafayette, Louisiana" attached to Lloyd R. Henderson to Richard von Phul Mouton, February 20, 1973, bound volume "Integration of Schools Diocese of Lafayette 1965–1973 The Auzenne Case Correspondence and Data 1970–1973," ADL; "Catholic School Integration Suit," *America* 123 (August 8, 1970): 50; *New York Times*, July 26, 1970; "Bishop Announces Speedup In School Integration," *Southwest Louisiana Register*, August 20, 1970; Erickson and Donovan, *Three R's of NonPublic Education in Louisiana*, 273–83, 285–89.

113. Salvador L. Diesi to Camille F. Gravel Jr., December 22, 1971 (quotation), bound volume "Integration of Schools Diocese of Lafayette 1965–1973 The Auzenne Case Correspondence and Data 1970–1973," ADL. In April 1973, the court ruled the *Auzenne* case moot. "Minutes of the Diocesan Board of Directors' Meeting 15 May 1973," 3, bound volume "Integration of Schools Diocese of Lafayette 1965–1973 The Auzenne Case Correspondence and Data 1970–1973," ADL; Erickson and Donovan, *Three R's of NonPublic Education in Louisiana*, 284.

Chapter Eight

1. George Schuster and Robert M. Kearns, *Statistical Profile of Black Catholics*, with a Foreword by Bernard Quinn (Washington, DC: Josephite Pastoral Center, 1976), 34–35; *The Official Catholic Directory Anno Domini 1941* (New York: P. J. Kenedy and Sons, 1941), general summary. The 197,481 figure comprised African Americans in the eleven southern states, Delaware, Maryland, the District of Columbia, West Virginia, Kentucky, and Oklahoma. Schuster and Kearns, *Statistical Profile of Black Catholics*, 35.

2. Mark Newman, *Getting Right with God: Southern Baptists and Desegregation, 1945–1995* (Tuscaloosa: University of Alabama Press, 2001), 20; Frank S. Loescher, *The Protestant Church and the Negro* (Philadelphia: University of Pennsylvania Press, 1948), 19, 52, 58; Clive Webb, *Fight against Fear: Southern Jews and Black Civil Rights* (Athens: University of Georgia Press, 2001), 43. In 1958, the PCUSA and the United Presbyterian Church of North America merged

to form the United Presbyterian Church in the United States of America. Winfred E. Garrison, "The Year in Religion," *Biblical Recorder* [Baptist State Convention of North Carolina], January 11, 1958; Randall Balmer and John R. Fitzmier, *The Presbyterians*, with a Foreword by Henry Warner Bowden (Westport, CT: Praeger, 1994), 102.

3. James R. Wood, "Authority and Controversial Policy: The Churches and Civil Rights," *American Sociological Review* 35 (December 1970): 1060; Peter C. Murray, *Methodists and the Crucible of Race, 1930-1975* (Columbia: University of Missouri Press, 2004), xv-xvi; Joel L. Alvis Jr., *Religion and Race: Southern Presbyterians, 1946-1983* (Tuscaloosa: University of Alabama Press, 1994), 2-3.

4. T. B. Maston, "Southern Baptists and the Negro (Part 1)," *Home Missions* 37 (July 1966): 19; Ernest Q. Campbell and Thomas F. Pettigrew, *Christians in Racial Crisis: A Study of Little Rock's Ministry* (Washington, DC: Public Affairs Press, 1959), 90-92; William A. Osborne, *The Segregated Covenant: Race Relations and American Catholics* (New York: Herder and Herder, 1967), 241.

5. James J. Thompson Jr., *The Church, the South and the Future* (Westminster, MD: Christian Classics, 1988), 47-64; Jackson Toby, "Bombing in Nashville: A Jewish Center and the Desegregation Struggle," *Commentary* 25 (May 1958); 385-89; Webb, *Fight against Fear*, xv-xvi, 41-46, 50, 52, 55-56, 142-43, 218-19.

6. Mary Bennett to Thomas J. McDonough, February 20, 1961 (quotation), box 24, folder 10, Archives of the Diocese of Savannah, Savannah, Georgia (hereinafter cited as ADS).

7. Webb, *Fight against Fear*, xvi-xvii, 114-16, 218-19.

8. Ibid., 114, 116 (quotation); "The White-Negro Problem," *Catholic Digest* 20 (June 1956): 2, 4. The survey included the District of Columbia and the border states of Kentucky, Maryland, Oklahoma, and West Virginia in its definition of the South.

9. Murray, *Methodists and the Crucible of Race*, xiv, 3 (quotation), 5, 16-17, 43-45; David M. Reimers, *White Protestantism and the Negro* (New York: Oxford University Press, 1965), 146-53; Kenneth K. Bailey, *Southern White Protestantism in the Twentieth Century* (New York: Harper and Row, 1964), 127-29, 128-29 n. 66; Loescher, *Protestant Church and the Negro*, 53, 55.

10. Alvis Jr., *Religion and Race*, 3-4, 6, 14-15, 22; Reimers, *White Protestantism and the Negro*, 123, 137-39; Loescher, *Protestant Church and the Negro*, 53-54.

11. Gardiner H. Shattuck Jr., *Episcopalians and Race: Civil War to Civil Rights* (Lexington: University Press of Kentucky, 2000), 26, 42-43, 51, 54-55; Loescher, *Protestant Church and the Negro*, 53-54, 54-55 n. 6; Reimers, *White Protestantism and the Negro*, 123-26.

12. *New York Times*, February 6, 2000; John T. McGreevy, *Parish Boundaries: The Catholic Encounter with Race in the Twentieth-Century Urban North* (Chicago: University of Chicago Press, 1996), 20, 29-36, 55-57, 59, 61-62, 70, 71, 98-109, 250; Osborne, *Segregated Covenant*, 33, 160-61, 204-5; Thomas J. Sugrue, *The Origins of the Urban Crisis: Race and Inequality in Postwar Detroit* (Princeton, NJ: Princeton University Press, 1996), 192; Nancy M. Davis, "Finding Voice: Revisiting Race and American Catholicism in Detroit," *American Catholic Studies* 114 (2003): 39-46; Donald J. Kemper, "Catholic Integration in St. Louis, 1935-1947," *Missouri Historical Review* 73 (October 1978): 5.

13. Ellen Madden Lancaster, "Catholic Education in St. Louis Today," *Interracial Review* 21 (July 1948): 106-8; Robert McClory, "Black Catholics: Souls on Ice?" *U.S. Catholic* 46 (April 1981): 25; *New York Times*, February 6, 2000; McGreevy, *Parish Boundaries*, 34, 36, 62; Osborne, *Segregated Covenant*, 95, 98, 100-106, 112-13, 130, 135, 161, 205; Kemper, "Catholic Integration in St. Louis," 1-22.

14. Reimers, *White Protestantism and the Negro*, 109–12; W. Edward Orser, "Racial Attitudes in Wartime: The Protestant Churches during the Second World War," *Church History* 41 (September 1972): 337–53.

15. Reimers, *White Protestantism and the Negro*, 112–13 (first quotation on p. 112), 136, 141; Loescher, *Protestant Church and the Negro*, 17, 42–44, 132–33; Grover C. Bagby, "Race Relations and Our Concern," *Methodist Story*, January 1965: 3 (second, third, and fourth quotations).

16. Orser, "Racial Attitudes in Wartime," 343–44; Bailey, *Southern White Protestantism*, 135.

17. *Annual of the Southern Baptist Convention* (hereinafter cited as *Annual, SBC*), 1946, 120, 124–25, 127; 1947, 35, 47–48, 340–43; Loescher, *Protestant Church and the Negro*, 136–37.

18. *Annual, SBC*, 1948, 337 (first quotation); Ernest Trice Thompson, *Presbyterians in the South*, vol. 3: 1890–1972 (Richmond, VA: John Knox Press, 1973), 532; Davis C. Hill, "Southern Baptist Thought and Action in Race Relations, 1940–1950" (ThD diss., Southern Baptist Theological Seminary, 1952), 24 (second quotation).

19. Shattuck, *Episcopalians and Race*, 41–43.

20. "Toward a Good Peace," *Catholic Virginian*, December 1943.

21. Osborne, *Segregated Covenant*, 161–63; *Buffalo Star*, July 12, 1946; *Louisiana Weekly*, October 15, 1949; *Our Negro and Indian Missions: Annual Report of the Secretary of the Commission for the Catholic Missions Among the Colored People and the Indians*, January 1947, 5–6, Archives of the Society of St. Joseph of the Sacred Heart, Baltimore, Maryland (hereinafter cited as ASSJ); "A Survey of U.S. Bishops' Statements on Racial Bigotry," [Davenport, Iowa], *Catholic Messenger*, November 20, 1958 (quotation); Clarence J. Howard to John McCann, September 9, 1950, folder "Catholic Committee of the South—1950 8c I-c-16," "Catholic Committee of the South 78–014 box 1 52–03–06," Archives of the Archdiocese of New Orleans, New Orleans, Louisiana.

22. Alice Renard, "A Negro Looks at the Church," *Commonweal* 46 (June 13, 1947): 209–12; D. J. Corrigan, "Plight of Negro Catholics," *Homiletic and Pastoral Review* 48 (October 1947): 45–47; McClory, "Black Catholics," 25 (first quotation); Stephen J. Ochs, *Desegregating the Altar: The Josephites and the Struggle for Black Priests, 1871–1960* (Baton Rouge: Louisiana State University Press, 1990), 459; McGreevy, *Parish Boundaries*, 101; Timothy B. Neary, "Crossing Parochial Boundaries: Interracialism in Chicago's Catholic Youth Organization, 1930–1954," *American Catholic Studies* 114 (2003): 24 (second quotation).

23. Patrick J. Molloy to Henry Cabirac Jr., May 13, 1961, folder 8, box 1, Catholic Council on Human Relations Papers, Amistad Research Center, New Orleans, Louisiana (hereinafter cited as CCHRP); *New York Times*, September 28, 1947; Joseph R. Ritter "To the Reverend Clergy and Beloved Laity of the Archdiocese of St. Louis," September 20, 1947, in untitled press clipping, dated February 3, 1961, box 4528303, folder "Racial—Charleston + Atlanta," Subject Files Hallinan, Archives of the Archdiocese of Atlanta, Atlanta, Georgia (hereinafter cited as AAA); "Archbishop Joseph E. Ritter," *Interracial Review* 20 (October 1947): 147; Gerald J. Schnepp, "Integration in St. Louis Schools," *Catholic Mind* 51 (October 1953); 613–17; Gerald J. Schnepp, "Integration in Catholic Schools," *St. Augustine's Messenger* 31 (September 1954): 226, 232–33, 248–49; James Rorty, "How St. Louis Broke the Race Barrier," *Ave Maria* 101 (April 20, 1957), reprint, folder 13, box 83, "Peaceful School Integration," *Christian Impact*, n.d., folder 3, box 84, Louis J. Twomey Papers, Special Collections and Archives, Loyola University Library, Loyola University New Orleans, New Orleans, Louisiana (hereinafter cited as Twomey Papers); "The Catholic Church and the Negro," *Ebony* 13 (December 1957): 21; Kemper, "Catholic Integration in St. Louis," 1–22; Osborne, *Segregated Covenant*, 112–13. Public

schools did not desegregate in St. Louis until 1955. "Educator Tells of Integration," [New Orleans] *Times-Picayune*, January 21, 1956.

24. M. F. Everett, "Church Leads Way," *Catholic Action of the South*, September 16, 1954; Albert S. Foley, "Catholic Desegregation in the Nation's Capital," folder 60a, Albert S. Foley, "Washington's Mild Revolution," folder 82, box 2a, Albert Sidney "Steve" Foley Jr., S.J. Papers, Spring Hill College Archives, Mobile, Alabama (hereinafter cited as Foley Papers); *Washington Post*, August 11, 12, 1987; Osborne, *Segregated Covenant*, 100–101; "New Notes," *Christian Impact* 2 (February 1952), folder 1, box 47, Joseph H. Fichter Papers, Special Collections and Archives, Loyola University Library, Loyola University New Orleans (hereinafter cited as Fichter Papers); Charles Harbutt, "The Church and Integration," *Jubilee* 6 (February 1959): 10. Taken from the Archdiocese of Baltimore in 1947, the Archdiocese of Washington comprised the Maryland counties of Montgomery, Prince George's, Charles, Calvert, and St. Mary's, as well as the District of Columbia. *Washington Post*, August 11, 1987. In 1956, O'Boyle ordered parochial school desegregation in Calvert, Charles, and St. Mary's Counties. *New York Times*, June 10, 1956.

25. Joseph F. Rummel, "Blessed are the Peacemakers," March 15, 1953, folder 4, box 8, series 33, National Catholic Conference for Interracial Justice Records, Marquette University, Milwaukee, Wisconsin (hereinafter cited as NCCIJR); Harbutt, "Church and Integration," 8; Ochs, *Desegregating the Altar*, 404.

26. *Annual, SBC*, 1948, 337; "Seminary Asked to Admit Negroes," *Christian Index*, June 1, 1950; "SBC Seminaries to Enrol Negroes," *Baptist Courier*, April 5, 1951; Henlee Barnette, "Negro Students in Southern Baptist Seminaries," *Review and Expositor* 53 (April 1956): 207–9; Reimers, *White Protestantism and the Negro*, 119, 127–32; Alvis, *Religion and Race*, 90; David E. Sumner, *The Episcopal Church's History: 1945–1985* (Wilton, CT: Morehouse-Barlow, 1987), 34; Shattuck, *Episcopalians and Race*, 39–40; Murray, *Methodists and the Crucible of Race*, 67.

27. Alvis, *Religion and Race*, 22–25; Reimers, *White Protestantism and the Negro*, 142; Bagby, "Race Relations and Our Concern," 3 (quotation); Murray, *Methodists and the Crucible of Race*, 61–64, 67.

28. Sumner, *Episcopal Church's History*, 31, 35–36, 179, 193 (quotation); Shattuck, *Episcopalians and Race*, 42–43, 45–49, 51–52, 54–55, 233 n. 42.

29. Katherine Ann Martensen, "Region, Religion and Social Action: The Catholic Committee of the South, 1939–1956" (Master's thesis, University of New Orleans, 1978), 30–31, 60 (quotation), 69, 72–73, 75–76; W. J. Nold to "the Reverend Pastors," August 29, 1953, F4 "Circular Letters 1953," box 3, RG 2.1.9 Chancery files, Bishops' files, Nold, Wendelin J., folder 4, box 3, Archives of the Archdiocese of Galveston-Houston, Houston, Texas; Herbert J. May Jr., "The Official Policy of the Roman Catholic Church of the Diocese of Lafayette in Relation to Black Catholics, 1940 to 1978" (Master's thesis, University of Southwestern Louisiana, 1981), 66; Vincent S. Waters, pastoral letter, January 29, 1951, scrapbook "Ban on Segregation 1953 volume III," Vincent S. Waters, pastoral letter, February 9, 1953, bound volume "Pastoral Letters V. S. Waters 1953–1956," Archives of the Diocese of Raleigh, Raleigh, North Carolina; Rummel, "Blessed are the Peacemakers"; Monsignor Thomas P. Hadden, interview by author, August 2, 2006.

30. "Race Segregation Rejected in Catholic Student Poll," [Cleveland, Ohio] *Catholic Universe Bulletin*, October 9, 1953, press clipping, folder 10, box 52, Fichter Papers.

31. "Minutes of Province Meeting on Interracial Relations," Grand Coteau, August 28–29, 1952, 11, Archives of the New Orleans Province of the Society of Jesus, Special Collections and Archives, Loyola University Library, Loyola University New Orleans; Robert E. Lucey to

Reverend Mother M. Angelique, June 12, 1953, folder "Lucey, Robert E. (Archbishop) Social Problems: Race Relations Folder #2 (1951–1965)," Archives of the Archdiocese of San Antonio, San Antonio, Texas (hereinafter cited as AASA); "College of Sacred Heart to Close," *Southwest Louisiana Register*, February 3, 1956; Harbutt, "Church and Integration," 10; John LaFarge, S.J., *The Catholic Viewpoint on Race Relations* (Garden City, NY: Hanover House, 1956), 98–99.

32. Campbell and Pettigrew, *Christians in Racial Crisis*, 157–61 (quotations on p. 160); Alvis, *Religion and Race*, 57; *Annual, SBC*, 1954, 56; "Ruling on Segregation Endorsed," *Christian Index*, June 10, 1954; Charles Keenan, "Church Leaders on School Segregation," *America* 91 (July 10, 1954): 379.

33. Murray, *Methodists and the Crucible of Race*, 70–72 (quotations on p. 71); Campbell and Pettigrew, *Christian in Racial Crisis*, 154.

34. *Statements Adopted by Religious Groups Re Segregation in the Public Schools* (New York: Department of Racial and Cultural Relations, National Council of Churches of Christ in the U.S.A., 1954): 4–5 (first quotation on p. 5); "Protestantism Speaks on Justice and Integration," *Christian Century* 75 (February 5, 1958): 164–65 (second quotation on p. 165); Sumner, *Episcopal Church's History*, 37 (third and fourth quotations); Shattuck, *Episcopalians and Race*, 68; Campbell and Pettigrew, *Christians in Racial Crisis*, 149.

35. "The Churches Speak," *New South* 9 (August 1954): 1; Keenan, "Church Leaders on School Segregation," 379; Thompson, *Presbyterians in the South*, vol. 3, 540–41; Bailey, *Southern White Protestantism in the Twentieth Century*, 143–44; Reimers, *White Protestantism and the Negro*, 116; Shattuck, *Episcopalians and Race*, 68; S. Jonathan Bass, "Not Time Yet: Alabama's Episcopal Bishop and the End of Segregation in the Deep South," *Anglican and Episcopal History* 63 (June 1994): 238 (quotation); Murray, *Methodists and the Crucible of Race*, 72; Hodding Carter III, *The South Strikes Back* (Garden City, NY: Doubleday, 1959), 165.

36. Keenan, "Church Leaders on School Segregation," 378 (quotation); Thomas Stritch, *The Catholic Church in Tennessee: The Sesquicentennial Story* (Nashville: The Catholic Center, 1987), 334.

37. "White-Negro Problem," 4; Robert R. Taylor, untitled note, November 7, 1941, folder 7, box 104, National Catholic Welfare Conference Collection, The American Catholic History Research Center and University Archives, Catholic University of America, Washington, DC (hereinafter cited as NCWCC); Daniel M. Cantwell, "Riot Spirit in Chicago," *Commonweal* 54 (July 27, 1951): 375–76; Davis, "Finding Voice," 44; McGreevy, *Parish Boundaries*, 72–78, 88, 93, 98–103, 105–7 (first quotation on p. 107), 109 (second quotation), 120–21; Sugrue, *Origins of the Urban Crisis*, 192, 213–14, 250–51; Dorothy Ann Blatnica, "'In Those Days': African-American Catholics in Cleveland, 1922–1961," *U.S. Catholic Historian* 12 (Winter 1994): 115–16.

38. "Race Prejudice Is Costly," *Our Colored Missions* 39 (November 1953): 166 (quotation); McGreevy, *Parish Boundaries*, 103–6; Blatnica, "In Those Days," 116.

39. Bob Senser, "A View of the Catholic Interracial Councils," *Interracial Review* 28 (January 1955): 7; Sr. Margaret Ellen Traxler, "American Catholics and Negroes," *Phylon* 30 (4th qtr., 1969): 357; McGreevy, *Parish Boundaries*, 73–76, 98–100, 120–21; Sugrue, *Origins of the Urban Crisis*, 214, 235–41; *New York Times*, January 29, 1961. On Trumbull Park, see Arnold R. Hirsch, "Massive Resistance in the Urban North: Trumbull Park, Chicago, 1953–1966," *Journal of American History* 82 (September 1995): 522–50.

40. "Negroes in the K. of C.," *Interracial Review* 18 (January 1945): 20–21; "Knights and Negroes," *America* 90 (March 13, 1954): 618; "Bishop Flays KC Discrimination," *St. Augustine's Messenger* 31 (May 1954): 154, 166 (second and third quotations), 169 (first quotation); "Knightly Chivalry," *St. Augustine's Messenger* 31 (December 1954): 333; Francis J. Heazel to Z. L. Begin,

March 15, 1954 (fourth quotation), SC-1-10-2033, Knights of Columbus Supreme Council Archives, New Haven, Connecticut (hereinafter cited as KCSCA).

41. "Knights and Negroes," 618 (first and second quotations); "Three Negroes in San Antonio First to Join Knights of Columbus," *Interracial Review* 24 (July 1951): 110; "Negroes Contend Race Bias Alive in Texas K of C," *Texas Catholic Herald* [Houston edition], press clipping, n.d., folder "Tx State Council Subject Files Blacks in K.C. 1963–1969," Catholic Archives of Texas, Austin, Texas; Emanuel A. Romero to *America* 91 (May 8, 1954): 176; "Interracial K. of C.—Case History," *America* 91 (June 19, 1954): 309; Julian J. Reiss to Daniel G. Marshall, October 13, 1945, SC-5-6-269, Reynaldo G. Garza to Alfred J. Hoedebeck, March 9, 1954, SC-1-10-2033, Luke E. Hart to Paul N. Casserly, April 22, 1954, SC-1-10-2035, KCSCA; Joseph J. Greblunas, "Integration in the K. of C," *Interracial Review* 28 (May 1954): 83–84; "Integration Aids K. of C." *Colored Harvest* 66 (June 1954): 13; George K. Hunton with Gary MacEoin, *All of Which I Saw, Part of Which I Was: The Autobiography of George K. Hunton*, with an Introduction by Roy Wilkins (Garden City, NY: Doubleday, 1967), 136–37, 236; "Official Notice Needed," *Colored Harvest* 66 (June 1954): 6–7; Osborne, *Segregated Covenant*, 168. In 1954, Dayton Council no. 500 in Ohio admitted six African Americans. "Six Negroes made K. of C. Members," *Catholic Banner*, June 13, 1954.

42. William J. Gaffney to Supreme Knight, March 12, 1954 (first quotation), Maurice J. McAuliffe to Luke E. Hart, March 9, 1954 (second quotation), SC-1-10-2033, KCSCA.

43. Everett, "Church Leads Way"; "Segregation in Okla. Catholic Schools End," *Tennessee Register*, September 5, 1954; "Survey Reveals Catholic Schools of South Lead Entire Region in Putting Supreme Court's Ban on Segregation into Effect," *Guardian*, September 17, 1954; "Catholics Out Front as Schools Put End to Race Segregation," *Tennessee Register*, September 19, 1954; "S.C. School Integration," *St. Augustine's Messenger* 31 (November 1954): 312; Milton Lomask, "Father Maurice Challenges the South," *Sign* 36 (November 1956): 17, 19–20; McGreevy, *Parish Boundaries*, 122; Osborne, *Segregated Covenant*, 171.

44. "End Hospital Discrimination," *Colored Harvest* 67 (September 1955): 6 (quotation); Osborne, *Segregated Covenant*, 56, 103–6, 135, 216; Murray, *Methodists and the Crucible of Race*, 103.

45. "Negro Priest's First Mass," *Interracial Review* 22 (June 1949): 93; Edward K. Braxton, "The Black Catholic Experience in America," *Origins* 10 (January 22, 1981): 499; Osborne, *Segregated Covenant*, 174, 215–16; Ochs, *Desegregating the Altar*, 404–5, 457–59.

46. *Annual, SBC*, 1955, 56; 1956, 45, 332; 1957, 59; 1958, 53; 1959, 81; 1960, 72, 273; 1961, 85; Campbell and Pettigrew, *Christians in Racial Crisis*, 140–41, 146–47, 149–51, 154–55, 162–63; W. D. Weatherford, *American Churches and the Negro: An Historical Study from Early Slave Days to the Present* (Boston: Christopher Publishing House, 1957), 255–56; Murray, *Methodists and the Crucible of Race*, 80–90 (quotation on p. 84).

47. "Southern Presbyterians Issue Sharp Condemnation of Racial Discrimination," *Religious News Service*, May 1, 1957; Campbell and Pettigrew, *Christians in Racial Crisis*, 140–41 (quotations on p. 141).

48. Joseph Francis Rummel, "The Morality of Racial Segregation," February 11, 1956, 1–4, attached to Joseph Francis Rummel, "The Morality of Racial Segregation," February 15, 1956, folder 4, box 8, series 33, "U.S. Bishops' Condemnation of Racial Segregation Major Milestone in Series on Theme," [Chicago] *Catholic New World*, November 21, 1958 (quotation), press clipping, folder 14, box 1, series 21, NCCIJR; Osborne, *Segregated Covenant*, 144.

49. John F. Cronin, "Religion and Race," *America* 150 (June 30, 1984): 472; John T. Donovan, *Crusader in the Cold War: A Biography of Fr. John F. Cronin, S.S. (1908–1994)* (New York: Peter

Lang, 2005), 103; McGreevy, *Parish Boundaries*, 90–91; "Discrimination and the Christian Conscience," *Interracial Review* 31 (December 1958): 217–19.

50. *Annual of the Alabama Baptist State Convention*, 1957, 31, 129–30; *Annual of the Louisiana Baptist Convention*, 1957, 72–73; [Florence, South Carolina] *Florence Morning News*, April 19, 1956 (quotation).

51. Roy V. Sims to L. U. Amason, November 14, 1958, folder 8, box 2, Brooks Hays Papers, Southern Baptist Historical Library and Archives, Nashville, Tennessee (hereinafter cited as SBHLA); Numan V. Bartley, *The Rise of Massive Resistance: Race and Politics in the South during the 1950s* (Baton Rouge: Louisiana State University Press, 1969), 300–301; Murray, *Methodists and the Crucible of Race*, 73, 105.

52. Murray, *Methodists and the Crucible of Race*, 80–90, 107; Reimers, *White Protestantism and the Negro*, 123, 142, 156, 175–77 (quotation on p. 176); J. Oscar Lee, "Reporting on Race Relations in Some Churches," *Royal Service* 51 (May 1957): 23.

53. Bailey, *Southern White Protestantism in the Twentieth Century*, 147. According to a 1959 survey, forty-eight of eighty-two Methodist-related colleges and universities in the United States had African American students. Murray, *Methodists and the Crucible of Race*, 103.

54. Vincent S. Waters, pastoral letter August 17, 1956, bound volume "Pastoral Letters V. S. Waters 1953–1956," Archives of the Diocese of Raleigh, Raleigh, North Carolina; "Excerpts from a Sermon by Archbishop Robert E. Lucey Delivered to a City-Wide Meeting of the Legion of Mary at Little Flower Parish, Sunday Afternoon, March 24, 1957," folder "Interracial (Current)," box CGRM 5/03, Joseph Gremillion Papers, University of Notre Dame Archives, Notre Dame, Indiana; *San Antonio Light*, March 25, 1957; Bartley, *Rise of Massive Resistance*, 140–43; Saul E. Bronder, *Social Justice and Church Authority: The Public Life of Archbishop Robert E. Lucey* (Philadelphia: Temple University Press, 1982), 70; Joseph Francis Rummel, "De-Segregation in Schools," August 19, 1955, folder "Desegregation—Archbishop Rummel," Archives of the Archdiocese of New Orleans, New Orleans, Louisiana; "Integration Is Deferred for This School Year," *Catholic Action of the South*, August 28, 1955; "A Report on School Desegregation for 1960–1961," August 19, 1960, 9, folder 23, box 52, Fichter Papers; Osborne, *Segregated Covenant*, 47.

55. James Graham Cook, *The Segregationists* (New York: Appleton-Century-Crofts, 1962), 194–202, 242–43; Neil R. McMillen, *The Citizens' Council: Organized Resistance to the Second Reconstruction, 1954–64* (Urbana: University of Illinois Press, 1971), 59–72, 80, 114, 171–79, 293–96; Howard Dorgan, "Response of the Main-line Southern White Protestant Pulpit to *Brown v. Board of Education*, 1954–1965," in *A New Diversity in Contemporary Southern Rhetoric*, ed. Calvin M. Logue and Howard Dorgan (Baton Rouge: Louisiana State University Press, 1987), 46 (quotation).

56. Michael B. Friedland, *Lift Up Your Voice Like a Trumpet: White Clergy and the Civil Rights and Antiwar Movements, 1954–1973* (Chapel Hill: University of North Carolina Press, 1998), 27–28, 30.

57. G. Jackson Stafford, "It Happened in a Baptist Church," in "Supreme Court's Decision on Segregation [Folder 1]," January 1, 1956, Executive Committee Records, SBHLA; Ralph McGill, "The Agony of the Southern Minister," *New York Times Magazine*, September 27, 1959; Alvis, *Religion and Race*, 65–66; Friedland, *Lift Up Your Voice Like a Trumpet*, 44–45.

58. Paul W. Turner, "The Role of Church Leadership in Communities Facing School Desegregation," in *Christianity and Race Relations: Messages from the Sixth Annual Christian Life Workshop* (Dallas: Christian Life Commission of the Baptist General Convention of Texas, 1962), 56–58; Margaret Anderson, *The Children of the South* (New York: Farrar, Straus and

Giroux, 1966); Mary L. Cleveland, "A Baptist Pastor and Social Justice in Clinton, Tennessee," *Baptist History and Heritage* 14 (April 1979): 20–23; Friedland, *Lift Up Your Voice Like a Trumpet*, 33; David L. Chappell, *Inside Agitators: White Southerners in the Civil Rights Movement*, with a Foreword by Clayborne Carson (Baltimore: Johns Hopkins University Press, 1994), 107–8, 119–20; "Father Drolet, Member of Red Group, Is Out as Kenner Pastor," *Citizens' Report*, special edition, February 1963, folder 2, box 53, Fichter Papers.

59. *Wall Street Journal*, February 14, 1958; *New York Times*, 23 August 1958 (first quotation); "Atlanta Pulpits Appeal for Interracial Talks," *Interracial Review* 34 (March 1961): 82 (second quotation).

60. Thomas F. Pettigrew, "Our Caste-Ridden Protestant Campuses," *Christianity and Crisis* 21 (May 29, 1961): 88–91; Bailey, *Southern White Protestantism in the Twentieth Century*, 147–48; Osborne, *Segregated Covenant*, 47–48; Archbishop Lawrence J. Shehan, *On Racial Justice: Pastoral Letter of March 1, 1963* (Washington, DC: National Catholic Welfare Conference, 1963), 7–8, folder 2, box 85, Twomey Papers; Thomas A. Spalding, *The Premier See: A History of the Archdiocese of Baltimore, 1789–1994* (Baltimore: Johns Hopkins University Press, 1995), 433–34.

61. McGreevy, *Parish Boundaries*, 122 (first quotation), 134; Mathew Ahmann, "How 'Deliberate' Is School Integration?" *Lamp* 60 (February 1962): 29 (second quotation).

62. "The Catholic Church and the Negro in the Archdiocese of Chicago Clergy Conference September 20–21, 1960," 23 (quotation), folder 14, box 83, Twomey Papers; McGreevy, *Parish Boundaries*, 136–39.

63. "Backs Negro Right to Protest Injustice," *Our Sunday Visitor*, March 27, 1960, Archives of the Diocese of Charleston, Charleston, South Carolina (hereinafter cited as ADC); "Anti-Discrimination Demonstrations Win Support of Catholics," *Guardian*, March 25, 1960; "Statements on Direct Action by National Catholic Conference for Interracial Justice," folder 1, box 2, series 8, NCCIJR; "Opinion Worth Noting," *America* 103 (May 21, 1960): 285; "When Laymen Fail," *Ave Maria* 93 (April 1, 1961): 16 (quotation); J. Michael Parker, "Fighter for Civil Rights," *San Antonio Express-News*, January 17, 2004, press clipping, folder "Bio: cv and Misc.," Sherrill Smith Papers, AASA.

64. *Annual, SBC,* 1961, 84 (first and second quotations); *Resolutions adopted by the American Baptist Convention: Portland, Oregon, June 17, 1961* (Valley Forge, PA: Division of Christian Social Concern, American Baptist Convention, 1961), 5 (third quotation), folder 426, box 4, MS360, Wendell Randolph Grigg Papers, Z. Smith Reynolds Library Special Collections and Archives, Wake Forest University, Winston-Salem, North Carolina.

65. "Phone to Pal from Fr. Philip Berrigan, S.S.J.," August 21, 1961, Frank A. Hall to Paul Tanner, August 22, 1961, folder 14, box 89, NCWCC; *New York Times*, March 21, 1965; Philip Berrigan, "The Challenge of Segregation," *Interracial Review* 34 (February 1961): 30–31, 53; Gregory Nelson Hite, "The Hottest Places in Hell: The Catholic Church and Civil Rights in Selma, Alabama, 1937–1965" (PhD. diss., University of Virginia, 2002), 61–62; McGreevy, *Parish Boundaries*, 151; Friedland, *Lift Up Your Voice Like a Trumpet*, 52–62.

66. Terry Sullivan, "What Is It Like to Be a Freedom Rider?" *Interracial Review* 35 (June 1962): 143–45; Diane Nash, "Inside the Sit-Ins and Freedom Rides: Testimony of a Southern Student," in *The New Negro*, ed. Mathew H. Ahmann (Notre Dame, IN: Fides, 1961), 43–60; Hite, "Hottest Places in Hell," 65–66; Friedland, *Lift Up Your Voice Like a Trumpet*, 63–65; "Why We Went to Albany: A Report by the Catholic Members of the Chicago Interreligious Delegation to Albany, Georgia, September 1962," "Albany Report," September 6, 1962, folder 2, box 4, series 33, NCCIJR; Roland Sibrie, "An Outside Agitator in Albany," *Claverite* 41 (November–December 1962): 10–12.

67. Anna Holden, "A Call to Catholics," *Interracial Review* 35 (June 1962): 141.

68. John LaFarge, "Religion and Race Meeting," *America* 108 (February 2, 1963): 159; Stephen C. Rose, "Special Report: Religion and Race," *Christianity and Crisis* 23 (February 4, 1963); 10–11; David Beal, "Matt Ahmann and Interracial Justice," *Today* 18 (November 1964): 3–4; John F. Cronin, "Report on Interreligious Activity for Racial Justice January–June 1963," 1, folder 2, box 25, Archives of the Diocese of Savannah, Savannah, Georgia (hereinafter cited as ADS); John Cogley, "The Church Heeds a New Call," *New York Times Magazine*, May 2, 1965, 50; Martin Luther King, "A Challenge to the Churches and Synagogues," in *Race: Challenge to Religion*, ed. Mathew Ahmann (Chicago: Henry Regnery, 1963), 155–69 (first quotation on p. 157); "An Appeal to the Conscience of the American People," in *Race*, ed. Ahmann, 171–73 (second and third quotations on p. 171); John P. Sisson, "For Racial Justice," *Our Sunday Visitor*, November 10, 1968; Osborne, *Segregated Covenant*, 222–23. The ten NCRR conferences were located in Atlanta, New Orleans, and San Antonio in the South, and in Chicago, Detroit, Oakland, Pittsburgh, St. Louis, San Francisco, and Seattle. However, according to Gerard E. Sherry, editor of archdiocesan newspaper the *Georgia Bulletin*, the Atlanta conference "came to nought" because of "The indifferentism and the fears of others." Osborne, *Segregated Covenant*, 41; Gerard E. Sherry, "Hallinan Profile," 23 (quotations), folder 53, box 6, AAA. By April 1964, there were local conferences on religion and race in fifty-six cities. In May, the NCRR closed its central office in New York City for financial reasons and allocated its work on a rotational annual basis among its three sponsoring agencies. In 1966, a third National Conference on Religion and Race met in Indianapolis. "Racial Problem Going into Deep Crisis Phase, Priest Says in Report on Meeting," *Southern Cross*, June 1, 1963; "Committee to Fight Racial Prejudice," *Southern Cross*, June 15, 1963; "Religion-Race Office Closing Seen No Cutback," *Southern Cross*, April 23, 1964; *New York Times*, April 16, 1964; "Churchmen on Civil Rights," July 20, 1963, 2, folder 2, Mario William Shaw to Thomas J. McDonough, March 3, 1966, "1966 National Conference on Religion and Race," folder 4, box 25, ADS; Osborne, *Segregated Covenant*, 223.

69. "Interracial Storm Is Brewing over Catholic Women's Club," *Catholic Commentator*, July 12, 1963; *New York Times*, July 3, March 21, 1965; McGreevy, *Parish Boundaries*, 143–45 (quotation on p. 144); Osborne, *Segregated Covenant*, 221; "Racial Bars Dropped by Illinois Club," *Catholic Virginian*, July 19, 1963; "Priests and Seminarians Lead Integration March," *Catholic Commentator*, July 12, 1963; untitled article, *Commitment*, July 1963, 1, folder 1, box 1, series 8, NCCIJR.

70. "March on Gywnn Oak Park," *Time* 82 (July 12, 1963): 17–18; "Baltimore Prelate Restricts Priests in Racial Protest," *Voice*, July 19, 1963; Trueblood Mattingly, "Gywnn Oak," *America* 109 (August 10, 1963): 136–37; Robert H. Heinze, "Eugene Carson Blake among 283 Arrested in Baltimore," *Presbyterian Life* 16 (August 1, 1963): 24–27; John J. Tyne, "Welcome to Gwynn Oak," *Josephite Harvest* 75 (November–December 1963): 17; Spalding, *Premier See*, 434–35; R. Douglas Brackenridge, *Eugene Carson Blake: Prophet with Portfolio* (New York: Seabury Press, 1978), 92–101.

71. Kyle Haselden, "Baptists in Travail," *Christian Century* 80 (May 22, 1963): 674; Arthur Lichtenberger, "Statement by the Presiding Bishop of the Episcopal Church, May 26, 1963," *The Episcopal Society for Cultural and Racial Unity Newsletter*, August 6, 1963 (first quotation), folder 3, box 36, Episcopal Society for Cultural and Racial Unity Records, Martin Luther King, Jr. Center for Nonviolent Social Change, Atlanta, Georgia (hereinafter cited as King Center); *Minutes of the General Assembly of the United Presbyterian Church in the United States of America*, 1963, 141–42; "American Baptist Convention May 1963" (second quotation), folder 9, box

49, RG6, National Council of Churches Archives, Presbyterian Historical Society, Philadelphia, Pennsylvania (hereinafter cited as NCCA); "End All Racial Barriers, Assembly Urges Southern Presbyterian Units," *Religious News Service*, April 30, 1963 (third quotation).

72. "Interfaith Committee Is Formed to Fight Race Bias on Moral Plane," *Catholic Week*, June 21, 1963; "JFK's Civil Rights Program Endorsed by Head of NCCW," *Catholic Commentator*, July 19, 1963 (quotation). The National Council of Catholic Women had seventeen representatives at the White House Conference in July 1963, including three based in the South, Mrs. Robert T. Lawrence, first vice president, from the Diocese of Nashville; Mrs. Norman I. Boatwright, Diocese of Savannah; and Miss Margaret Edmunds, Diocese of Richmond. Mrs. Joseph McCarthy to "Dear President," July 15, 1963, folder 15, box 89, NCWCC.

73. "Testimony on Civil Rights Legislation Presented to Committee on Judiciary House of Representatives by National Catholic Welfare Conference, Synagogue Council of America, National Council of Churches in the United States of America, July 24, 1963," folder 1, box 84, Twomey Papers; Russell Shaw, "Are We Involved in the Problem?" *North Carolina Catholic*, August 25, 1963; "Church in U.S. Has Almost Total Integration Pattern," *Southern Cross*, August 1, 1963; Donovan, *Crusader in the Cold War*, 146–48.

74. "On Racial Harmony Joint Pastoral Letter of the Bishops of the United States—1963" (first quotation), folder 5, box 17, series 33, NCCIJR; Patrick A. O'Boyle to "Your Excellency," August 9 (second quotation), August 16, 1963, folder 16, box 89, NCWCC; Donovan, *Crusader in the Cold War*, 149.

75. Patrick O'Boyle to "Your Excellency," September 4, 1963 and attached "Text of Speech originally planned to be delivered at Lincoln Memorial. Altered before actual delivery," no box, folder 720.10, ADC; Sherrill Smith to *Alamo Messenger*, August 23, 1963; "Archbishop O'Boyle Prays for Guidance at Rights March," *Catholic Virginian*, August 30, 1963; Russell Shaw, "August 28—It Was a Day to Be Remembered," *Alamo Messenger*, September 6, 1963; *New York Times*, September 23, 1968; Shattuck, *Episcopalians and Race*, 132; McGreevy, *Parish Boundaries*, 149, 197; Friedland, *Lift Up Your Voice Like a Trumpet*, 86–89. The Catholics on the guest's platform at the March on Washington comprised Archbishop Patrick A. O'Boyle of Washington, DC, Archbishop Lawrence J. Shehan of Baltimore; Bishops John J. Russell of Richmond and Michael W. Hyle of Wilmington, Delaware; Auxiliary Bishops Philip M. Hannan of Washington, T. Austin Murphy of Baltimore, and Ernest Unterkoefler of Richmond; Monsignor Daniel Cantwell of the Chicago Catholic Interracial Council and NCCIJ, Father Harold R. Perry of St. Augustine's Seminary, Father John LaFarge, and Raymond Hilliard and John P. Nelson of the NCCIJ. Shaw, "August 28—It Was a Day to Be Remembered."

76. "Cardinal Spellman Calls Racial Discrimination an 'Outrage,'" *Catholic Commentator*, July 19, 1963; Russell Shaw, "Bishops' 1958 Query on Race Still Stands," *Catholic Virginian*, August 23, 1963; "Cardinal Urges Enactment of Civil Rights Bill Now!" folder 13, box 83, Twomey Papers; *New York Times*, April 7, 1964; "All Dioceses in Michigan Pledge Aid to Civil Rights," *Voice*, April 10, 1964; "Archbishop Endorses Civil Rights Proposal," *Alamo Messenger*, May 22, 1964; "Statement on 'Rights,'" *Texas Catholic Herald* [Houston edition], June 4, 1964; "N.M. Prelates Ask Faithful to Back Rights," *Alamo Messenger*, June 5, 1964; "Bishops Urge Civil Rights Legislation," *Lone Star Register*, June 18, 1964, press clipping, folder 12, box 6, Texas Catholic Conference Records, Catholic Archives of Texas, Austin, Texas; J. D. Conway, "No Moral Issue Involved in Civil Rights?" *Voice*, June 26, 1964; "Massive Church Support Tipped Civil Rights Scale," *Alamo Messenger*, July 10, 1964; Osborne, *Segregated Covenant*, 179.

77. Henry Cabirac to John L. Morkovsky, August 28, 1963, Vincent M. Harris to Henry Cabirac, October 2, 1963, folder 7, box 16, series 33, NCCIJ; Osborne, *Segregated Covenant*, 56–58, 71, 87, 103–6, 135, 216–18; Reed Sarratt, *The Ordeal of Desegregation: The First Decade* (New York: Harper and Row, 1966), 279.

78. "Urges Acceptance of Negroes in KC," *North Carolina Catholic*, July 28, 1963; "Lay Leaders Rebuke Chicago KCs for Not Admitting Negro Members," *Alamo Messenger*, August 9, 1963; "Chicago KC Crisis Evokes Examination of Procedure," *Alamo Messenger*, November 22, 1963; "For Whites Only?" *Criterion*, August 2, 1963 (quotation), press clipping, "Knights Welcome in K. of C.—Hart," *Milwaukee Sentinel*, press clipping, dated August 19, 1963, "K. of C. Claims No Color Barrier; Reports 10,000 Negro Members," *Milwaukee Journal*, August 19, 1963, press clipping, "K. of C. Here Rejects Negro; 6 Top Officials Resign," *Chicago Sun Times*, November 12, 1963, press clipping, Jo-ann Price, "Catholics in Rift on Civil Rights," *New York Herald Tribune*, November 18, 1963, press clipping, "KC's Hart Favors Review of Admission Procedures," *Criterion*, November 22, 1963, press clipping, SC-1-16-2043, Eugene R. Liner to Albert Meyer, November 10, 1963, "K. of C.'s and Race," *America*, November 30, 1963, press clipping, SC-1-10-2029, KCSCA; "Hart Claims KCs Welcome Negroes," *Alamo Messenger*, September 6, 1963; "Moral Education, By-Laws Change May Be Solutions to KC Problem," *Alamo Messenger*, September 13, 1963; Osborne, *Segregated Covenant*, 168.

79. *New York Times*, November 4, 1963; Thompson, *Presbyterians in the South*, vol. 3, 549.

80. *New York Times*, April 26, 29, May 2, 1964; "Massive Church Support Tipped Civil Rights Scale"; Donovan, *Crusader in the Cold War*, 150–52; Friedland, *Lift Up Your Voice Like a Trumpet*, 100–101 (quotation on p. 100); James F. Findlay Jr., *Church People in the Struggle: The National Council of Churches and the Black Freedom Movement, 1950–1970* (New York: Oxford University Press, 1993), 48–75; *Annual, SBC*, 1964, 73–74, 229; K. Owen White to Mr. and Mrs. E. H. Harrell, April 1, 1964, folder 7, box 1, K. O. White Collection, SBHLA; "This Statement on Race Was Turned Down," *Biblical Recorder*, May 30, 1964; "And This One Passed by Close Margin," *Biblical Recorder*, May 30, 1964; "Southern Presbyterians Tackle Race Issue at General Assembly," *Religious News Service*, April 27, 1964.

81. "Southern Presbyterians Act to Speed Up Integration," *Religious News Service*, April 28, 1964 (first quotation); "Southern Presbyterians Tackle Race Issue at General Assembly" (second quotation).

82. Murray, *Methodists and the Crucible of Race*, 154–59, 165, 173, 175–76 (quotation on p. 175); Reimers, *White Protestantism and the Negro*, 156–57.

83. "United Presbyterians Elect Negro Leader as President," *Religious News Service*, May 22, 1964; "United Presbyterian Timetable Asks End of Segregated Synods," *Religious News Service*, May 28, 1964; "Resolutions adopted by the American Baptist Convention, Atlantic City, New Jersey, May 22, 1964," folder 9, box 49, RG6, NCCA (quotation).

84. *New York Times*, April 27, August 10, 1964; "Churchmen Hail Rights Law, Urge Cooperation," *Southern Cross*, July 9, 1964; "Prelates Hail Rights Law," *Tennessee Register*, July 10, 1964; "Cardinal McIntyre Declines to Take Fair Housing Stand," *Alamo Messenger*, July 31, 1964; Osborne, *Segregated Covenant*, 227–28; *Knights of Columbus Supreme Council Proceedings, Eighty-Second Annual Meeting, New Orleans, Louisiana, August 18–19–20, 1964*, 31, 44–45, 128–31, 179–81, 193–97.

85. McGreevy, *Parish Boundaries*, 175–84 (first quotation on p. 180; second quotation on pp. 180–81); Gerard E. Sherry, "The Ace among Us," *Josephite Harvest* 77 (September–December 1965): 2–3; Andrew M. Greeley and Paul B. Sheatsley, "Attitudes toward Racial Integration,"

Scientific American 225 (December 1971): 16–19; Osborne, *Segregated Covenant*, 178–79; *New York Times*, March 19, 29, April 5, 9, 27, 1964; "Some Sad Instances," *Blueprint* 16 (April 1964): 2, Special Collections and Archives, Loyola University Library, Loyola University New Orleans. In Maryland's Democratic primary, Wallace was supported by 55.5 percent of Catholic voters compared to 41.7 percent of Protestants and 8.1 percent of Jews. "Says Majority of Maryland Catholics Supported Alabama's Wallace," *Alamo Messenger*, May 29, 1964.

86. Michael J. Harmon to Louis J. Twomey, September 19, 1964, folder 3, box 22, Twomey Papers; Jane [Duffin] to Henry Cabirac, October 23, 1963, and attached "Lafayette, La. Voter Registration Project," folder 9, box 5, series 21, Jane Duffin to Wiley A. Branton, July 10, 1964, and attached "Voter-Education Project, Lafayette, La., June 8–29 [1964]," folder 15, box 5, series 34, NCCIJR; McGreevy, *Parish Boundaries*, 151–52; Helen M. Ciernick, "Catholic College Students in the San Francisco Bay Area and the Civil Rights Movement," *U.S. Catholic Historian* 24 (Spring 2006): 131–41; Hite, "Hottest Places in Hell," 79–84. On the Grail movement, see Alden V. Brown, *The Grail Movement and American Catholicism, 1940–1975* (Notre Dame, IN: University of Notre Dame Press, 1989).

87. John Dittmer, *Local People: The Struggle for Civil Rights in Mississippi* (Urbana and Chicago: University of Illinois Press, 1994), 242–71; James W. Silver, *Mississippi: The Closed Society*, new and enlarged ed. (New York: Harcourt, Brace and World, 1966), 282; Findlay, *Church People in the Struggle*, 106 n. 54; Robert G. McDole to Richard Oliver Gerow, June 4, 1964, folder 11, box 13, series 33, NCCIJR; "Priests Are Halted in Voting Drive," *Alamo Messenger*, June 19, 1964; Margaret Rozga, "March on Milwaukee," *Wisconsin Magazine of History* 90 (Summer 2007): 38; Patrick Jones, "'Not a Color, but an Attitude': Father James Groppi and Black Power Politics in Milwaukee," in *Groundwork: Local Black Freedom Movements in America*, ed. Jeanne Theoharis and Komozi Woodard, with a Foreword by Charles Payne (New York: New York University Press, 2005), 263–64; "Davenport Girl Serves in Mississippi Project," [Davenport, Iowa] *Catholic Messenger*, July 2, 1964; "Rights Worker Says Progress Made," [Davenport, Iowa] *Catholic Messenger*, August 20, 1964; "Ministers, Adult Laymen Recruited by National Council of Churches for Work in Mississippi Summer Project—June 15 to Sept. 1, 1964 Listed by Denominations," 8, folder 38, box 2, Delta Ministry Papers, King Center (hereinafter cited as DM Papers).

88. "Southern Presbyterians Tackle Race Issue at General Assembly"; "Orderly Rights Demonstrations Endorsed by Methodists," *Religious News Service*, May 5, 1964; Sumner, *Episcopal Church's History*, 41–42 (quotation on p. 42); Shattuck, *Episcopalians and Race*, 145–46; "American Baptists Favor Equality, Unity Moves," *Christian Index*, June 4, 1964; "Resolutions adopted by the American Baptist Convention, Atlantic City, New Jersey, May 22, 1964."

89. "Nuns 'Inspire' Selma Marchers," *Texas Catholic Herald* [Houston edition], March 18, 1965; Maurice Ouellet, "The Testimony of a Selma Pastor," *Jubilee* 13 (August 1965): 22; Charles E. Fager, *Selma, 1965: The March That Changed America*, 2d ed. (Boston: Beacon Press, 1985), 97–98, 100, 104; Sumner, *Episcopal Church's History*, 42–43; Shattuck, *Episcopalians and Race*, 146, 154; Alvis, *Religion and Race*, 111–13; *Minutes of the One-Hundred-Fifth General Assembly of the Presbyterian Church in the United States*, 1965, 83, 158–60.

90. Lawrence M. O'Rourke, *Geno: The Life and Mission of Geno Baroni* (New York: Paulist Press, 1991), 44–50; Warren Hinckle and David Welsh, "Five Battles of Selma," *Ramparts* 4 (June 1965): 37 (quotation); Mike McManus, "Is He One of the Few Relevant White Men in This City?" *Washington Post Magazine*, June 1, 1969, 16; "Selma, Civil Rights, and the Church Militant," *Newsweek* 65 (March 29, 1965): 75; "Catholic Prelates Deplore Tragedy of Selma," *Voice*, March 19, 1965; "Priests in Racial March Defended," *Guardian*, April 2, 1965; *New York*

Times, March 9, 20, 21, April 5, 1965; Maurice Ouellet, "The Testimony of a Selma Pastor," *Jubilee* 13 (August 1965): 22; Brother Cyprian Davis, O.S.B., interview by author, July 10, 2007; John T. McGreevy, "Racial Justice and the People of God: The Second Vatican Council, the Civil Rights Movement, and American Catholics," *Religion and American Culture* 4 (Summer 1994): 221; Amy L. Koehlinger, *The New Nuns: Racial Justice and Religious Reform in the 1960s* (Cambridge, MA: Harvard University Press, 2007), 53; Osborne, *Segregated Covenant*, 243–44; Hite, "Hottest Places in Hell," 280–92. Catholic dioceses that sent clergy included Atlanta, Galveston-Houston, and San Antonio in the South; Baltimore, St. Louis, Oklahoma City and Tulsa, Washington, and Wilmington in border south areas; and Brooklyn, Boston, Chicago, New York, and Pittsburgh in the North. *New York Times*, March 21, 1965; "Selma Marchers' Dedication Praised," *Texas Catholic Herald* [Houston edition], March 25, 1965.

91. "Testimony on Voting Rights Legislation Presented to Committee on Judiciary, House of Representatives by Commission on Religion and Race, National Council of Churches of Christ in the United States of America, Social Action Department, National Catholic Welfare Conference, Social Action Commission, Synagogue Council of America," March 25, 1965, folder 10, box 85, NCWCC; "Lawmakers Told Votes Rights Legislation Imperative Now," *Catholic Virginian*, April 2, 1965 (quotation).

92. [New Orleans] *Times-Picayune*, March 24, 1965; Cogley, "Clergy Heeds a New Call," 48. "Nuns Appear in Selma Protests," NCWC News Service, March 11, 1965, folder 21, box 26, series 20, NCCIJR; "Nuns 'Inspire' Selma Marchers"; John L. Wright Jr., "Clergy and Sisters Are in the Front in Selma," [Dubuque, Iowa] *Witness*, March 25, 1965; Joseph Fiorenza, "Nuns in Selma: A New Role for Sisters," *Texas Catholic Herald* [Houston edition], March 25, 1965; *New York Times*, March 21, 28, August 21, 1965, April 5, 1968; Sr. Thomas Marguerite, "Nuns at Selma," *America* 112 (April 3, 1965): 454–56; Edward J. O'Donnell to Luke Robertson, September 26, 1996, 2, folder "Racism/Integration (Various)," Archives of the Diocese of Lafayette, Lafayette, Louisiana; "Mass Held for Rights Martyr," *Voice*, April 2, 1965; "LBJ Calls for Legislation to Control Ku Klux Klan," *Voice*, April 2, 1965; "Road from Selma: Hope—and Death," *Newsweek* 65 (April 5, 1965): 23, 26–27; McGreevy, *Parish Boundaries*, 156; Jonathan Daniels, "Singing the Song of Selma," *Catholic Digest* 30 (July 1966): 14–18; Charles W. Eagles, *Outside Agitator: Jon Daniels and the Civil Rights Movement in Alabama* (Chapel Hill: University of North Carolina Press, 1993), 2, 166–80.

93. *New York Times*, March 15, 17, 22, October 21, 1965; Osborne, *Segregated Covenant*, 125, 199, 201–2; "Nuns 'Inspire' Selma Marchers"; "Invoke Mary for Racial Peace, Paul VI Pleads," *Guardian*, March 19, 1965; "Bishop Leads Interfaith March for Rights," *Catholic Reporter*, March 26, 1965, folder 1, box 27, series 20, NCCIJR; McGreevy, *Parish Boundaries*, 156, 164, 166–69, 197–201, 209–10; Don Patrinos, "Priest Leader of Civil Rights Drive Gets Praise of Milwaukee Ordinary," *National Catholic Reporter* 2 (December 15, 1965): 1, 10; Frank A. Aukofer, "What Makes Fr. Groppi March?" c. 1967, press clipping, folder 720.8, ADC; "Case Histories," *Ave Maria* 103 (January 8, 1966): 4–5. On Groppi, see Jones, "Not a Color, but an Attitude," 260–81.

94. *Annual, SBC*, 1965, 90–92 (first quotation on p. 91; second and third quotations on p. 92).

95. *New York Times*, May 14, 1965; "Project Equality—Practicing What Is Preached," *Josephite Harvest* 77 (November–December 1965): 14; Thomas H. Gibbons Jr., "Project Equality," *Collegium* 1 (July 1966), folder 719.78, ADC; Dick Meskill, "Archbishop Marshals Buying Power to Promote Employment Equality," *Alamo Messenger*, August 13, 1965; Osborne, *Segregated Covenant*, 200. By 1967, Project Equality had eighty-four religious judicatories participating across America: eighteen Catholic, forty-seven Protestant, three Unitarian-Universalist, fourteen

Jewish, and two Eastern Orthodox and claimed that 15,000 businesses ranging from small shops to large corporations had agreed to cooperate. Nevertheless, doubts persisted about the project's effectiveness in some areas, which alongside concerns about its significant administrative costs deterred some religious bodies, including some Catholic dioceses, from participating. Mathew Ahmann, "Project Equality," *Christianity and Crisis* 27 (May 29, 1967): 118–19; Michael Stone, "Project Equality Today: A Case Study of the Church in the Social Order," *Project Equality News* 3 (February 1970), folder 5, box 84, Twomey Papers.

96. "Service Groups of Three Faiths Join in Effort to Combat Poverty," *Texas Catholic Herald* [Houston edition], January 21, 1966.

97. "Lafayette Diocese Will 'Open Schools to All,'" *Catholic Commentator*, June 4, 1965; Robert E. Tracy, "School Plan," *Catholic Commentator*, June 11, 1965; "To Desegregate Schools in Alexandria Diocese," *Clarion Ledger*, June 17, 1965; Osborne, *Segregated Covenant*, 57–58; McGreevy, *Parish Boundaries*, 210; "Negroes in Catholic Colleges," *Josephite Harvest* 78 (March–April 1966): 10.

98. "Most Schools Sign U.S. Compliance," *Baptist Record*, April 15, 1965; Thompson, *Presbyterians in the South*, vol. 3, 546; "Mississippi College Votes to Integrate Grad School," *Baptist and Reflector*, June 19, 1969; [Memphis] *Commercial Appeal*, October 30, November 13, 1969; W. T. Moore, *His Heart Is Black* (Atlanta: Home Mission Board of the Southern Baptist Convention, 1978), 80.

99. *Our Negro and Indian Missions*, January 1968, 5–6, 12–14, January 1969, 5–10, January 1970, 5–6, 11–13, January 1972, 7–20, ASSJ; *New York Times*, October 9, 1971; Hadden interview.

100. Alvis, *Religion and Race*, 93–98; Thompson, *Presbyterians in the South*, vol. 3, 547; Murray, *Methodists and the Crucible of Race*, 184; "The Disciples in Dallas," *Christianity Today* 11 (October 14, 1966): 52; "Racial Turmoil Batters the Church," *Christianity Today* 9 (June 4, 1965): 45; Shattuck, *Episcopalians and Race*, 153–54.

101. Mark Newman, *The Civil Rights Movement* (Edinburgh: Edinburgh University Press, 2004), 110, 123–27; "American Baptists in Midstream," *Christianity Today* 10 (June 10, 1966): 47; "Resolution on 'Power and Justice' Passed by the General Council of the American Baptist Convention, November 3, 1966 [first and second quotations]," file BT 734.2.B2 A3 "Baptists and Race Problems—American Baptist Convention, 1966–," Baptist Joint Committee, Washington, DC; *Minutes of the One-Hundred-Sixth General Assembly of the Presbyterian Church in the United States*, 1966, 90–91 (third quotation on p. 91).

102. "Presbyterian Leaders Are Authorized to Press School Desegregation Suit," *Religious News Service*, May 20, 1966; "Two Divisions of Board of Missions Allocate $130,000 to Delta Ministry," News from the Board of Missions of the Methodist Church, October 4, 1966, folder 2, box 19, DM Papers; Findlay, *Church People in the Struggle*, 111–68; Mark Newman, *Divine Agitators: The Delta Ministry and Civil Rights in Mississippi* (Athens: University of Georgia Press, 2004); Shattuck, *Episcopalians and Race*, 148–53, 176–81; Sumner, *Episcopal Church's History*, 43–44, 46–49.

103. "Poverty and Racial Relations Statement," *Southern Cross*, December 1, 1966; Donovan, *Crusader in the Cold War*, 156; *Our Negro and Indian Missions*, January, 1966, 7, 10, January 1967, 7–18, January 1969, 7–10, January 1971, 7–20, ASSJ; "Project Equality Announcement Draws High Praise, Support from across U.S.," *Tennessee Register*, March 10, 1967; "Project Adopted in Ohio," *Tennessee Register*, March 10, 1967; "Operation 'STAR,'" May, 1965, folder 7, box 12, series 33, NCCIJR; "Project Star," *Josephite Harvest* 78 (March–April 1966): 2–3; Osborne, *Segregated Covenant*, 180, 199.

104. "Race Problems, Northern Ghettos Linked," *Voice*, November 18, 1966; Osborne, *Segregated Covenant*, 187, 198; McGreevy, *Parish Boundaries*, 184–91; Traxler, "American Catholics and Negroes," 357–58; *New York Times*, July 11, 1966; February 12, 14, April 12, August 14, 1968.

105. *New York Times*, January 14, 18, 24, 1966, June 25, 1967, July 28, 1968; "Cardinal Defies Phone Threat, Makes Plea for Fair Housing," *Texas Catholic Herald* [Houston edition], January 21, 1966 (quotation); Thomas J. Smith, "Milwaukee Protests: What Do They Mean?" 1967, press clipping, folder 720.8, ADC; "Fr. Groppi Arrested," *Alamo Messenger*, August 10, 1967; "Father Groppi," *National Catholic Reporter* 3 (August 23, 1967): 4; "Groppi Found Guilty," *National Catholic Reporter* 3 (August 30, 1967): 3; "Support for Ajax," *Time* 90 (September 22, 1967): 84; Paul J. Weber, "Groppi's War on Milwaukee," *America* 117 (September 30, 1967): 342–43.

106. *New York Times*, November 7, 1967.

107. Joseph M. Cronin, "Negroes in Catholic Schools," *Commonweal* 85 (October 7, 1966): 13–16; McGreevy, *Parish Boundaries*, 240–41 (first quotation on p. 241); "New York Priest Defends Schools against Charges of Segregation," [Davenport, Iowa] *Catholic Messenger*, August 25, 1966 (second quotation).

108. Osborne, *Segregated Covenant*, 192; Berkeley Rice, "Boston: 'I Am a Symbol of Resistance'—Hicks," *New York Times Magazine*, November 5, 1967, 31, 33, 122.

109. McGreevy, *Parish Boundaries*, 209–14; Spalding, *Premier See*, 436–38, 445; "Project Cabrini," *Commitment*, October 1965, 2, folder 1, box 1, series 8, NCCIJR; Koehlinger, *New Nuns*, 105–7, 176–97.

110. *Annual, SBC*, 1968, 66–69 (quotation on p. 68), 73; Newman, *Civil Rights Movement*, 129–30; "Mission Agency Discontinues National Crisis Committee," *Baptist and Reflector*, August 19, 1971; Edward E. Plowman, "Southern Presbyterian, Reformed Churches Vote to Merge," *Christianity Today* 12 (July 5, 1968): 38; *Minutes of the One-Hundred-Eighth General Assembly of the Presbyterian Church in the United States*, 1968, 101; Alvis, *Religion and Race*, 123–25, 128–29.

111. Culbert G. Rutenber, "American Baptists Respond to Black Power Challenge," *Christian Century* 85 (July 3, 1968): 878–80; Edward E. Plowman, "Cleavages in A.B.C.," *Christianity Today* 12 (June 21, 1968): 40 (quotation).

112. "Churches Confront Urban Crises," *Christianity Today* 12 (June 21, 1968): 46; Willmar L. Thorkelson, "United Presbyterian General Assembly," *Christian Century* 85 (June 19, 1968): 823; Arthur H. Matthews, "United Presbyterians Confront Change," *Christianity Today* 12 (June 7, 1968): 39 (quotation).

113. "Churches Confront Urban Crises," *Christianity Today* 12 (June 21, 1968): 46; *Christianity Today* 15 (June 4, 1971): 37 (quotation); Murray, *Methodists and the Crucible of Race*, 201–2, 207–8. In April 1968, the merger of the Methodist Church and the Evangelical United Brethren Church created the United Methodist. Adon Taft, "Racial Birth Pangs for United Methodists," *Christianity Today* 12 (May 10, 1968): 34.

114. "On National Race Crisis," *Voice*, May 3, 1968 (first quotation); "Bishops on Race: Too Little This Late," *National Catholic Reporter* 4 (May 8, 1968): 3, 7; "Racial Agenda for Catholics," *Christianity Today* 12 (May 24, 1968): 39 (second quotation); Michael Warner, *Changing Witness: Catholic Bishops and Public Policy, 1917–1994*, with a Foreword by George Weigel (Grand Rapids, MI: Williams B. Eerdmans, 1995), 76–77; Koehlinger, *New Nuns*, 110–12; McGreevy, *Parish Boundaries*, 212–14, 227–29.

115. McGreevy, *Parish Boundaries*, 227 (quotation), 238–39; *New York Times*, October 14, 1974, December 15, 1975, September 2, 1976, September 10, 1982; Robert Reinhold, "More Segregated Than Ever," *New York Times Magazine*, September 30, 1973, 40; Edward P. Jones, "Seattle

Catholics Aid Integration," *Impact* 7 (June–July 1977): 4; *Boston Globe*, September 18, 1980; Richard Gribble, "Cardinal Humberto Medeiros and the Desegregation of Boston's Public Schools, 1974–1976," *Journal of Church and State* 48 (Spring 2006): 327–53.

116. *New York Times*, November 4, 1963; "Southern Baptists Survey Negro-White Cooperation," *Baptist Press*, October 18, 1968; Alvis, *Religion and Race*, 93–98; Thompson, *Presbyterians in the South*, vol. 3, 547; *United Methodist Information*, June 27, 1972, file BT 734.2.M5 "Methodists and Race Problems, 1969–," Baptist Joint Committee; Frederick A. Norwood, *The Story of American Methodism: A History of the United Methodists and Their Relations* (Nashville: Abingdon Press, 1974), 432; Murray, *Methodists and the Crucible of Race*, 194–95, 198–99, 222–25. The merger of Methodist annual conferences in Mississippi was not finally resolved until 1975. Murray, *Methodists and the Crucible of Race*, 228–30.

117. Robert W. Prichard, *A History of the Episcopal Church* (Harrisburg, PA: Morehouse, 1991), 243; Shattuck, *Episcopalians and Race*, 166–69, 182–85; "Statement of Black Catholic Clergy Caucus," April 18, 1968, folder 8, box 2, series 34, NCCIJR; John R. Sullivan, "Negro Priests Think Church White, Racist," *Southern Cross*, April 25, 1968; [New Orleans] *Times-Picayune*, January 14, 1969; *New York Times*, November 12, 1969; Roland Freeman, "Black Catholics Seek Self-Determination," *Catholic Banner*, February 19, 1970.

118. George H. Gallup, *The Gallup Poll: Public Opinion 1935–1971*, vol. 3, 1959–1971 (New York: Random House, 1972), 2200; "Black Manifesto's Birthday: Frosting on the Cake?" *Christianity Today* 14 (May 22, 1970): 37; Findlay, *Church People in the Struggle*, 199–225; Shattuck, *Episcopalians and Race*, 187–90, 193–95.

119. Sumner, *Episcopal Church's History*, 50–58; Shattuck, *Episcopalians and Race*, 199–204, 210–11.

120. *New York Times*, May 22, 1969, November 21, 1970; Jerry Filteau, "Church Anti-poverty Drive Gears Up for November Effort," *Southern Cross*, November 9, 1972; "Human Development," *Southern Cross*, November 16, 1972 (quotation); "Campaign for Human Development Helps the Poor," *Southern Cross*, November 1, 1973; Geno Baroni, "The Ethnic Factor/Ministry in Cities," *Origins* 5 (December 18, 1975): 407; Linda B. Major, "Church Enters Housing Crisis," *Southern Cross*, January 21, 1971.

121. *New York Times*, November 21, 1970, May 16, August 21, 1971.

122. "ABC Elects First Negro President," *Baptist Standard*, May 21, 1969; Sumner, *Episcopal Church's History*, 39; "Baptists Elect Negro Pastor to Convention Executive Board," *American Baptist News Service*, December 23, 1969, folder 22, box 1, DM Papers.

123. Jo-Ann Price, "Mississippi Churchmen Back Integration Order," *Southern Cross*, January 8, 1970; "Bishops Support Public Schools," *Southwest Louisiana Register*, January 22, 1970; "Diocesan School Board Establishes Committees to Assure Racial Justice," *Southwest Louisiana Register*, January 29, 1970; Kim Larsen, "Catholic Schools Spurn Segregationists," *Voice*, April 17, 1970; *Annual, SBC*, 1970, 78–79; 1971, 78–79; [Greenville, Mississippi] *Delta Democrat-Times*, January 5, February 1, 2, 3, 4, 25, 1970; "Mississippi Adopts School Statement," *Baptist Message*, January 29, 1970; "South Carolina Christian Response Urged," *Baptist Message*, January 29, 1970; "16 Baptist Churches in Mississippi Push Segregation," *Religious Herald*, January 29, 1970; James F. Cole, "Advocates of the Public School System," *Baptist Message*, February 5, 1970; "Religious Leaders Support Public Education System," *Alabama Baptist*, February 5, 1970.

124. *Our Negro and Indian Missions*, January 1969, 5–6, 18–19, ASSJ; Murray, *Methodists and the Crucible of Race*, 234; C. Albert Koob, "Where Is the Catholic School System Heading?" *America* 123 (September 19, 1970): 169–70; John M. Swomley Jr., "Who Wants Catholic

Schools?" *Nation* 211 (December 14, 1970): 627–28; "Bishops Meet on Problems of U.S. Catholic Schools," *Southern Cross*, January 7, 1971; *New York Times*, April 7, August 15, 21, September 10, 1971, January 10, 1972; McGreevy, *Parish Boundaries*, 236; Spalding, *Premier See*, 459–61.

125. *New York Times*, August 15, 21, September 10, 1971, January 10, 1972, July 27, 1975, November 14, 1976, April 25, 1982, May 22, 1988; Robert McClory, "Church Losing Ground," *National Catholic Reporter* 13 (February 4, 1977): 1, 4; Davis, "Finding Voice," 54–55; McGreevy, *Parish Boundaries*, 242; "Catholic Parish Agree to Recruit Blacks after Two Were Rejected," *Jet* 40 (September 9, 1971): 20–21.

126. Robert McClory, "Baroni Named HUD Assistant Secretary," *National Catholic Reporter* 13 (March 11, 1977): 1; O'Rourke, *Geno*, 43–53, 71–99; Geno Baroni, "March to Montgomery," *Catholic Virginian*, April 2, 1965; "The U.S. Bishops and Catholic Social Teaching: Introduction," in *Catholic Social Thought: The Documentary Heritage*, ed. David J. O'Brien and Thomas A. Shannon (Maryknoll, NY: Orbis, 1992), 489–91.

127. Robert L. Johnston, "Church on Racism? 'Disinterest Deafening,'" *National Catholic Reporter* 11 (September 26, 1975): 1, 4; Sumner, *Episcopal Church's History*, 3, 58.

Chapter Nine

1. *Our Negro and Indian Missions: Annual Report of the Secretary of the Commission for the Catholic Missions Among the Colored People and the Indians*, January 1972, 5–6 (quotation), 7–20, Archives of the Society of St. Joseph of the Sacred Heart, Baltimore, Maryland (hereinafter cited as ASSJ); Elbert J. Lalande, "Two Mobile Churches Unite," *Catholic Week*, February 5, 1971; "Bishops Meet on Problems of U.S. Catholic Schools," *Southern Cross*, January 7, 1971; "Diocesan School Board Acts to Remove Dual Schools," *Southwest Louisiana Register*, January 21, 1971; "Focus: Catholic Education and the Black Community," *Impact* 1 (May–June 1971): 2.

2. "A Conversation with the Pastor of an Integrated Parish," *Morning Star*, August 10, 1972; Brad Collins, "Black and Catholic in America," *Extension* 81 (March–April 1987): 8–9; minutes, Social Justice Commission Meeting, December 12, 1970, attached to John L. May to Sister Mary Joan Serda, January 11, 1971, folder "Social Justice Commission—Mobile," Bishop John L. May Papers, Archives of the Archdiocese of Mobile, Mobile, Alabama (hereinafter cited as May Papers); Andrew S. Moore, *The South's Tolerable Alien: Roman Catholics in Alabama and Georgia, 1945–1970* (Baton Rouge: Louisiana State University Press, 2007), 156–57; Richard M. Myhalyk, S.S.E., "The Establishment of Queen of Peace Parish in Selma, Alabama in 1971: A Primary Source Presentation," 1–6, unpublished paper in author's possession; John L. May to Charles F. Aucoin, January 12, 1971, Charles F. Aucoin to John L. May, February 19, 1971, John L. May to Eymard Galligan, February 24, 1971, Eymard Galligan to John L. May, March 1, 1971, John L. May to "Dear Catholic People of Selma," April 2, 1971, folder "Three Folders on Amalgamation," box 10, Local Administration, Society of Saint Edmund Archives, St. Michael's College, Colchester, Vermont (hereinafter cited as SSEA).

3. Paul Morin to Eymard Galligan, April 23, 1971 (quotations), Eymard Galligan to John L. May, May 10, 1971, John L. May to John Crear, May 11, 1971, Paul Morin to John L. May, May 14, 1971, John L. May to Nelson Ziter, May 28, 1971, folder "Three Folders on Amalgamation," box 10, Local Administration, SSEA; "New Faces and Old Friends," *Your Edmundite Missions News*

Letter 28 (October 1971): 12, Community Archives, Sisters of St. Joseph, Rochester, New York (hereinafter cited as Community Archives).

4. Myhalyk, "Establishment of Queen of Peace Parish in Selma, Alabama in 1971," 6; Alston Fitts III, *Selma: Queen City of the Black Belt* (Selma, AL: Clairmont Press, 1989), 158; untitled recollection by Joan Marshall, n.d., folder 3, box G 13-1-4, RG 832, "Spotlight on Selma, Alabama," December 1971, folder 8, box G 13-1-1, "Developments in Selma—1969–1975," "Queen of Peace School Ready to Close Doors," *Selma News Record*, April 27, 1976, press clipping, "New Direction for Sisters of St. Joseph," *Selma News Record*, June 10, 1976, press clipping, folder 8A, box G 13-1-1, RG 831.102, Alston Fitts III, "A Sign of Hope in Selma," *St. Anthony Messenger*, August 1985, 30 (quotation), folder 3, box G 13-1-4, RG 832.12.1, Community Archives.

5. *Our Negro and Indian Missions*, January 1971, 7–20, January 1972, 7–20 (quotation), ASSJ; Dolores Egger Labbé, *Jim Crow Comes to Church: The Establishment of Segregated Catholic Parishes in South Louisiana*, 2d ed. (New York: Arno Press, 1978 [Lafayette: University of Southwestern Louisiana, 1971]), 87.

6. *Our Negro and Indian Missions*, January 1972, 7–20 (quotation), ASSJ.

7. Ibid.

8. John L. May, "For the Record," *Catholic Week*, April 30, 1971 (first, second, and third quotations); "Bishop May Praises Supreme Court Ruling" (fourth quotation), *Catholic Week*, April 30, 1971.

9. John L. May to "My dear Friends," July 18, 1971, no box, folder "Bishop May—letters," May Papers; *New York Times*, September 6, 9, 1971. On busing in Mobile, see Richard A. Pride, *The Political Use of Racial Narratives: School Desegregation in Mobile, Alabama, 1954–1997* (Urbana: University of Illinois Press, 2002).

10. H. J. Ladue to Ernest L. Unterkoefler, March 2, 1971, Ernest L. Unterkoefler to J. Fleming McManus, March 8, 1971, George Lewis Smith to Ernest L. Unterkoefler, March 17, 1971, John M. Bond to Lloyd Henderson, March 29, 1971, folder 728.39/1, "Statement by Rev. John M. Bond, Superintendent of Catholic Schools," n.d., 1–3 (quotation on p. 3), "Transcript of meeting with representatives of the Civil Rights Commission, Department of Health, Education and Welfare, Bishop Ernest L. Unterkoefler, Father John Bond and Father Francis Miller," May 24, 1971, 1–3, John M. Bond to J. V. Nichols, May 31, 1971, folder 728.40, Archives of the Diocese of Charleston, Charleston, South Carolina (hereinafter cited as ADC).

11. "Transcript of meeting with representatives of the Civil Rights Commission, Department of Health, Education and Welfare, Bishop Ernest L. Unterkoefler, Father John Bond and Father Francis Miller," May 24, 1971, 3–4 (quotation on p. 3); D. H. Twens to Ernest L. Unterkoefler, March 17, 1972, folder 728.41, ADC.

12. John M. Bond to "Dear Parents and Parishioners," April 17, 1971, Robert P. Stockton, "Catholic Schools to Be Restructured," April 22, 1971, press clipping, folder 728.39/1, "Focus: Catholic Education and the Black Community," *Impact* 1 (May–June 1971): 1, "The Fate of Immaculate Conception School Children Unknown," [Charleston] *New and Courier*, May 19, 1971 (quotation), press clipping, folder 728.40, ADC.

13. John L. Manning to John M. Bond, June 15, August 14, 1971, Malcolm M. Brennan to John M. Bond, June 21, 1971, John E. Ferrara to John M. Bond, August 10, 1971 (first quotation), John M. Bond to John L. Manning, August 25, 1971, John M. Bond to Ernest L. Unterkoefler, August 26, September 20, 1971 (second quotation), folder 728.40/1, ADC.

14. "Report of Peninsula Committee, School Board of Diocese of Charleston," February 1973, Ernest L. Unterkoefler to Joseph P. Moroney, April 3, 1973, John M. Bond to Frederick J. Hopgood, April 5, 1973, Robert P. Stockton, "Peninsula Catholic Schools Set for Reorganization," [Charleston] *News and Courier*, April 10, 1973, press clipping, Joanne E. Loman to Ernest L. Unterkoefler, April 18, 1973, John M. Bond to Orion P. D. Canant, June 6, 1973, John M. Bond to Ernest L. Unterkoefler, June 7, 15, 1973, Ernest L. Unterkoefler to John M. Bond, June 13, 1973, folder 728.42, minutes of Cathedral School Board, May 28, 1974, Sister M. Bridget to Ernest L. Unterkoefler, May 31, 1974, folder 728.43, ADC.

15. Thomas R. Duffy to Ernest L. Unterkoefler, August 24, 1971, Edward L. Nutter to John W. McDevitt, August 24, 1971, folder "Duffy—K of C," ADC; T. W. Kappe to John L. Morkovsky, June 17, 1971 (first quotation) and attached T. W. Kappe to "Dear Sirs," June 1, 1971, Mrs. Raymond L. Haak to John L. Morkovsky, June 11, 1971 (second quotation) and attached "Mrs. Hoak [sic] Hits KC's Policies," *Galveston Daily News*, June 1, 1971, John L. Morkovsky to Lino Perez Jr., June 15, 1971 (third quotation), Lino Perez Jr. to John L. Morkovsky, July 1, 1971 (fourth quotation), folder "Knights of Columbus Correspondence, 1971," RG 2.1.9., Records Department Association, Archives of the Archdiocese of Galveston-Houston, Houston, Texas.

16. *Knights of Columbus Supreme Council Proceedings, Ninetieth Annual Meeting, Toronto, Ontario, August 15–16–17, 1972*, 36, 54–56 (first quotation on p. 55; second and third quotations on p. 54); Christopher J. Kauffman, *Faith and Fraternalism: The History of the Knights of Columbus, 1882–1982* (New York: Harper and Row, 1982), 400.

17. Barbara Babin Lacour, *Called to Action: The Knights of Columbus in Louisiana, 1962–1992* [N.p.: Jostens Publishing Company, 1994), 153 (first quotation); William H. Dunn, *Knights of Columbus in Texas, 1902–1977* (Austin: Texas State Council, Knights of Columbus, 1978), 181 (second and third quotations).

18. Memorandum, John E. McCarthy to John L. Morkovsky, "Houston Council on Human Relations," September 28, 1972, memorandum, John L. Morkovsky to "All Pastors, Diocese of Galveston-Houston," "Houston Council on Human Relations," n.d., folder 18, box 2, John E. McCarthy Papers, Texas Catholic Conference Records, Catholic Archives of Texas, Austin, Texas (hereinafter cited as CAT); "25th Jubilee," *Josephite Harvest* 83 (July–August 1971): 2, transcription, folder "Morrissey, William J. Archives Biog. M-," ASSJ; *New York Times*, September 5, 1971.

19. *New York Times*, March 16, 1988; "A First for Black Catholics," *Time* 131 (March 28, 1988): 71; *The Josephites: A Century of Evangelization in the African American Community* (Baltimore: St. Joseph's Society of the Sacred Heart, 1993), 73–74; Stephen J. Ochs, *Desegregating the Altar: The Josephites and the Struggle for Black Priests, 1871–1960* (Baton Rouge: Louisiana State University Press, 1990), 448–50 (quotations on p. 448).

20. Ochs, *Desegregating the Altar*, 449–50 (quotation on p. 449).

21. "David *Greenhouse* et al., Plaintiffs-Appellants, v. Most Reverend Charles Pascal *Greco* et al., Defendants-Appellees No. 78–1802 United States Court of Appeals, Fifth Circuit 617 F.2d 408; 1980 U.S. App. Lexis 17433, May 19, 1980," accessed June 11, 2007, at http://web.lexis-nexis.com.ezproxy.loyno.edu/universe; "Parents Sue Alexandria Diocese over Race," *Morning Star*, April 13, 1972 (quotations); "Black Families Sue Louisiana Diocese to Desegregate Schools," *Catholic Virginian*, April 14, 1972; L. Marie Guillory, "The Impact of the Constitution on Segregation in Church Schools," in *Catholic Schools and Racial Integration: Perspectives, Directions, Models* (Washington, DC: National Catholic Conference for Interracial Justice, 1977), 12–13, 14–15, folder 10, box 1, series 8, National Catholic Conference for Interracial Justice Records, Marquette University, Milwaukee, Wisconsin.

22. "Parents Sue Alexandria Diocese over Race."

23. "David *Greenhouse* et al., Plaintiffs-Appellants, v. Most Reverend Charles Pascal *Greco* et al., Defendants-Appellees No. 78-1802 United States Court of Appeals, Fifth Circuit 617 F.2d 408; 1980 U.S. App. Lexis 17433, May 19, 1980"; "David *Greenhouse* et al., Plaintiffs-Appellants, v. Most Reverend Charles Pascal *Greco* et al., Defendants-Appellees No. 75-2050 United States Court of Appeals for the Fifth Circuit 544 F.2d 1302; 1977 U.S. App. Lexis 10608, January 10, 1977," accessed June 11, 2007, at http://web.lexis-nexis.com.ezproxy.loyno.edu/universe; "David *Greenhouse* et al. v. Most Reverend Charles Pascal *Greco* et al., Civ. A. No. 17741 United States District Court for the Western District of Louisiana, Alexandria Division 368 F. Supp. 736; 1973 U.S. Dist. Lexis 10527, December 20, 1973," accessed June 11, 2007, at http://web.lexis-nexis.com.ezproxy.loyno.edu/universe.

24. *Our Negro and Indian Missions*, January 1971, 7-20, ASSJ; Donald A. Erickson and John D. Donovan, *The Three R's of NonPublic Education in Louisiana: Race, Religion, and Region* (Washington, DC: President's Commission on School Finance, 1972), 111.

25. Justin D. Poché, "Religion, Race, and Rights in Catholic Louisiana, 1938–1970" (PhD diss., University of Notre Dame, 2007), 292–93; Erickson and Donovan, *Three R's of NonPublic Education in Louisiana*, 112–27 (quotation on p. 125).

26. *Our Negro and Indian Missions*, 1973, 7–11 (quotation), ASSJ"; Erickson and Donovan, *Three R's of NonPublic Education in Louisiana*, 127.

27. "Mississippi Black Catholic Caucus Formed," *Impact* 1 (May–June 1971), folder 728.40, ADC; Nessa Theresa Baskerville Johnson, *A Special Pilgrimage: A History of Black Catholics in Richmond* (Richmond, VA: Diocese of Richmond, 1978), 60–63 (first quotation on pp. 62–63); *New York Times*, August 21, 23 (second quotation), 1971.

28. Johnson, *A Special Pilgrimage*, 63 (quotation); Walter F. Sullivan to Gladys J. Archer, March 11, 1974, folder "Black Caucus," box 42, Bishop Walter F. Sullivan Papers, Archives of the Diocese of Richmond, Richmond, Virginia (hereinafter cited as Sullivan Papers); *New York Times*, August 21, 1971; "Apostolic Administrator Runs Diocese as Pope's Deputy," *Catholic Virginian*, May 4, 1973.

29. "Focus: Catholic Education and the Black Community," 2; Sr. Patricia Lynch, S.B.S., *Sharing the Bread in Service: Sisters of the Blessed Sacrament, 1891–1991*, vol. 2 (Bensalem, PA: Sisters of the Blessed Sacrament, 2001 [1998]), 186; *Josephites*, 75; Erickson and Donovan, *Three R's of NonPublic Education in Louisiana*, 6 (first quotation), 111–12; Herbert J. May Jr., "The Official Policy of the Roman Catholic Church of the Diocese of Lafayette in Relation to Black Catholics, 1940 to 1978" (Master's thesis, University of Southwestern Louisiana, 1981), 84–85 (second quotation on p. 84).

30. *Our Negro and Indian Missions*, 1973, 7–11 (quotations), 12–13, ASSJ; May, "The Official Policy of the Roman Catholic Church of the Diocese of Lafayette in Relation to Black Catholics," 88. Bishop Michael J. Begley of Charlotte, a diocese erected by the Vatican in 1971, was seemingly an exception, writing in 1974 that "We are doing away entirely with black parishes and are assigning parish lines to former black parishes." However, in African American population centers, territorial parishes amounted to de facto black parishes. *Our Negro and Indian Missions*, 1974, 18–20, ASSJ.

31. *Our Negro and Indian Missions*, 1973, 7–13, 1974, 7–11 (quotation), January 1975, 7–11, ASSJ; *Arkansas Gazette*, March 25, 1973.

32. *New York Times*, August 6, 1972; Albert J. Raboteau, "Black Catholics and Afro-American Religious History: Autobiographic Reflections," *U.S. Catholic Historian* 5 (1986): 126 (first

quotation); Lawrence E. Mick, "Diversity within the Roman Rite's Fundamental Unity," *North Carolina Catholic*, July 29, 2001 (second quotation); Gary Wray McDonogh, *Black and Catholic in Savannah, Georgia* (Knoxville: University of Tennessee Press, 1993), 295, 305–7.

33. *New York Times*, August 6, 1972; Bill Kenkelen, "Blacks 'Find Context for Catholicism,'" *National Catholic Reporter* 16 (March 7, 1980): 6; Robert McClory, "Black Catholics: Souls on Ice?" *U.S. Catholic* 46 (April 1981): 27; "Pioneer in African-American Liturgy, Liturgical Music Dies," *Texas Catholic*, December 3, 2004. On the development of black liturgy and Rivers's place within it, see Clarence Joseph Rivers, "Thank God We Ain't What We Was: The State of the Liturgy in the Black Catholic Community," *U.S. Catholic Historian* 5 (1986): 81–89; Ronald L. Sharps, "Black Catholic Gifts of Faith," *U.S. Catholic Historian* 15 (Fall 1997): 48–49, 51–52.

34. Maurice Ouellet, "The Testimony of a Selma Pastor," *Jubilee* 13 (August 1965): 23 (first quotation); [New Orleans] *Times-Picayune*, August 18, 1991 (second quotation).

35. *New York Times*, August 6, 1972 (quotation); [New Orleans] *Times-Picayune*, August 18, 1991; *Savannah News-Press*, supplement, February 20, 1995; J. Michael Parker, "Black Catholics Feel at Home," August 5, 1995, press clipping, folder "Black Catholics," Archives of the Archdiocese of San Antonio, San Antonio, Texas (hereinafter cited as AASA); McDonogh, *Black and Catholic in Savannah, Georgia*, 6, 306–8, 343 n. 1. St. Benedict's Church in Savannah, Georgia, for example, created a gospel choir in 1973. McDonogh, *Black and Catholic in Savannah, Georgia*, 6.

36. *New York Times*, August 6, 1972; Raboteau, "Black Catholics and Afro-American Religious History," 126 (first quotation); "Blacks Said to Hinder Afro Music in Church," *National Catholic Reporter* 10 (May 31, 1974): 2 (second quotation); McDonogh, *Black and Catholic in Savannah, Georgia*, 343 n. 1.

37. *New York Times*, August 6, 1972.

38. *New York Times*, August 23, October 2, 1971; Gary MacEoin, "Blacks in Rome: 'To Tell Things the Way They Are,'" *National Catholic Reporter* 7 (October 22, 1971): 10–11 (quotation on p. 10); Joseph Davis, "Black Catholics in Rome: Stating the Case in Person," *National Catholic Reporter* 8 (November 26, 1971): 9.

39. Dawn Gibeau, "Black Named Bishop; Third in U.S. History," *National Catholic Reporter* 9 (November 24, 1972): 1, 17.

40. "Josephite Convert—Now Bishop," *Josephite Harvest* 85 (March–April 1973): 1; Gibeau, "Black Named Bishop," 17 (quotations).

41. "Josephite Convert—Now Bishop," 1 (first quotation)"; Black Bishop Says U.S. Catholic Attitudes 'Too White,'" *Catholic Virginian*, May 4, 1973 (second and third quotations).

42. Johnson, *A Special Pilgrimage*, 66 (first quotation), 115; "Black Catholics Issue Liturgy Guide," *National Catholic Reporter* 10 (March 22, 1974): 8 (second quotation); McClory, "Black Catholics," 27.

43. *Our Negro and Indian Missions*, 1973, 7–11, 1974, 7–11 (quotation), ASSJ.

44. Barbara Lenox, "Father Figaro Gives Voice for Black Catholics," *Morning Star*, October 7, 1976 (first quotation); *Our Negro and Indian Missions*, January 1975, 7–11 (second and third quotations), ASSJ; Ochs, *Desegregating the Altar*, 406; James S. Tinney, "Black Catholics: Is There a Future?" *Christianity Today* 18 (September 27, 1974): 44; Anne Healey, "Black Catholics Gaining Prominence," [Washington, DC] *Catholic Standard*, September 19, 1974. Sullivan's statement implied an ordination in the spring of 1975. He was probably referring to Walter Barrett, ordained a deacon in March 1974 and a priest in 1975. "Richmond Chapter National Black Lay Catholic Caucus March 1974," folder "Black Caucus," box 42, Sullivan Papers.

45. "Josephite Named Bishop," *Josephite Harvest* 76 (Summer 1974): 16; "Eugene A. Marino, Auxiliary Bishop Archdiocese of Washington, D.C.," *Impact* 4 (December 1974): 1, 6; Tinney, "Black Catholics," 44–45; *New York Times*, May 31, 1974; Healey, "Black Catholics Gaining Prominence"; "Elected to NCCL Board," *Claverite* 53 (January–March 1974): 11.

46. Joseph M. Davis to "Dear Father," June 30, 1974, folder "National Office for Black Catholics 1973–1974," box 7, Texas Catholic Herald Records, CAT; Bob Giles, "Josephite Visits Houston for Work with 'Harvest,'" *Texas Catholic Herald* [Houston edition], February 22, 1974 (first quotation); Tinney, "Black Catholics," 44 (second quotation). Father F. Michael Perko, S.J., provides different figures on the number of African American departures but confirms the trend. He states that "From 1970 to 1975, 125 of the nation's 900 black sisters left their ministries, as did 25 of America's 190 black priests." F. Michael Perko, S.J., *Catholic and American: A Popular History* (Huntington, IN: Our Sunday Visitor Publishing Division, 1989), 308.

47. *New York Times*, May 31, 1974; "Blacks Polled on Seminaries," *National Catholic Reporter* 9 (September 28, 1973): 20 (quotations).

48. *Our Negro and Indian Missions*, January 1976, 7–11 (quotations), ASSJ.

49. *Our Negro and Indian Missions*, 1974, 7–11, 18–20, January 1975, 7–11, January 1976, 7–11 (quotations), 18–20, ASSJ.

50. "Black Perspectives on Evangelization," *Origins* 4 (January 16, 1975): 472–79 (first quotation on p. 472; second quotation on p. 476; third quotation on p. 475; fourth and fifth quotations on p. 478; sixth quotation on p. 477; seventh quotation on p. 474). Representatives from the National Black Catholic Clergy Caucus, the NBSC, the National Black Lay Catholic Caucus and the Knights and Ladies of Peter Claver prepared the document for the NOBC.

51. Walter F. Sullivan to Otis Ogden, January 23, 1974, Walter F. Sullivan to Gladys J. Archer, March 11, 1974, folder "Black Caucus," box 42, Sullivan Papers; "Bishop Walter F. Sullivan," *Catholic Virginian*, July 19, 1974 (quotation); Johnson, *A Special Pilgrimage*, 69, 75; *Our Negro and Indian Missions*, 1973, 7–11, January 1975, 18–20, January 1976, 7–11, 18–20, ASSJ.

52. Johnson, *A Special Pilgrimage*, 69 (quotation).

53. *Louisiana Weekly*, April 19, 1975 (quotations); "Colored Priest for the Holy Ghost Fathers," n.d., folder 26, box 9, Albert Sidney Foley. Jr., Papers, Spring Hill College Archives, Mobile, Alabama.

54. "Black Catholicism," *Origins* 5 (November 27, 1975): 368 (quotations), also published as "Black Catholics in the United States Archbishop Jean Jadot," *Catholic Mind* 74 (March 1976): 7–9.

55. "A Call to Action," *Josephite Harvest* 78 (Fall 1976): 1–2; "A.D. 1977," 1–3 (first quotation on p. 1), folder 3, box 4, Reverend Joseph H. Biltz Papers, Butler Center for Arkansas Studies, Main Library, Little Rock, Arkansas (hereinafter cited as Biltz Papers); "Black Catholics & the Bicentennial," *Origins* 5 (December 18, 1975): 411–17 (second and third quotations on p. 416).

56. Jean McCann, "'Church Looks Past Blacks' Ignores Black Experience, Priest Says," *National Catholic Reporter* 12 (January 23, 1976): 17.

57. Robert L. Johnston, "Church on Racism? 'Disinterest Deafening,'" *National Catholic Reporter* 11 (September 26, 1975): 1, 4; McClory, "Black Catholics," 26; John McCarthy to James Sheehan, March 11, 1974, folder 6, box 43, Texas Catholic Conference Records, CAT; Gerard E. Sherry, "Ending Racism No Part-Time Thing, Says NCCIJ Leader," *Southern Cross*, October 2, 1975 (first quotation); minutes, Racial Attitudes Committee, Social Ministry Commission, Catholic Diocese of Richmond, December 29, 1975, 2 (second quotation), minutes, Social

Ministry Commission, April 10, 1976, 3, June 12, 1976, 2, September 19, 1976, 2, May 21, 1977, 1, folder "Social Ministry Commission Minutes," box 42, Sullivan Papers; Social Justice Commission Minutes, December 8, 1975, October 4, 1976, February 14, May 9, October 10, 1977, November 12, 1978, folder "Social Justice Commission," May Papers.

58. "Proposal: The Establishment of an Archdiocesan Office for Black Catholic Concerns," iii, attached to untitled, undated memorandum by Pam Crayton, c. 1981, folder 1, box 013/5, Archives of the Archdiocese of Atlanta, Atlanta, Georgia (hereinafter cited as AAA); Roger Yockey, "Black Action in Church Necessary," *National Catholic Reporter* 12 (July 17, 1976): 20; Carl Fisher, "Black Leadership—Urgent Need," *Josephite Harvest* 78 (Spring 1976): 18–19 (quotation on p. 19); "Josephite History," accessed February 5, 2015 at http://www.josephitepastoralcenter.org/resources/black-history-month/; "U.S. Gets Fourth Black Auxiliary," *National Catholic Reporter* 12 (May 14, 1976): 2; *New York Times*, September 5, 1997.

59. "A.D. 1977," 1–4 (first quotation on p. 1; second quotation on p. 3); "Bicentennial Social Action Being Shaped," *Guardian*, March 19, 1976; Andrew J. McDonald, "Bishop's Office, Diocese of Little Rock," *Guardian*, September 24, 1976, press clipping, folder 4, box 3, Biltz Papers.

60. "A.D. 1977," 7–9 (first quotation on p. 7; second quotation on p. 8; third, fourth, fifth, sixth, and seventh quotations on p. 9).

61. "A.D. 1977," 4–5; Richard P. McBrien, "'Call to Action' Response," June 17, 1977, press clipping, folder 3, box 4, Biltz Papers; Robert McClory, "Seeking Black Leadership," *National Catholic Reporter* 13 (February 18, 1977): 4 (quotations); *New York Times*, January 16, 1977, March 9, 1977, February 28, 1990.

62. McClory, "Seeking Black Leadership," 4 (first, second, and third quotations); *New York Times*, March 9, 1977 (fourth quotation); "Black Named Ordinary of New Diocese," *National Catholic Reporter* 13 (March 18, 1977): 1–2; "Bishop Howze Made Head of New Diocese," *Josephite Harvest* 79 (Spring 1977): 10. The new Diocese of Biloxi comprised seventeen counties in southeast Mississippi taken from the Diocese of Natchez-Jackson, which became the Diocese of Jackson. *New York Times*, March 9, 1977.

63. "Meeting in Texas," *Josephite Harvest* 79 (Spring 1977): 1; Elbert F. Harris, "Issues Concerning the Development of the Catholic Church in the Black Community," 1–8 (quotation on p. 2), folder 3, box 45, Texas Catholic Conference Records, CAT; "Touring Josephite Missions: Natchez-Holy Family," *Josephite Harvest* 78 (March–April 1966): 17.

64. "Conference of Black Catholics State of Texas April 11–14, 1977 Houston, Texas," folder 2, box 58, Lawrence J. Payne to Timothy J. Murphy, November 11, 1977, "Black Apostolate III: Implementation of Resolutions Received from the First Texas Black Catholic Conference," Houston, April 11–14, 1977 (first and second quotations), memorandum, John McCarthy to "Delegates to the 1977 General Assembly," "A. Final Disposition of 1977 Resolutions B. Miscellaneous Items Regarding the 1977 General Assembly," December 2, 1977, 3–4, folder 16, box 70, Lawrence J. Payne, "Resolutions and Documentation from the First Texas Black Catholic Conference," May 1, 1977, folder 18, box 70, Larry J. Payne general letter, January 3, 1977, Matthew J. O'Rourke to "Dear Fellow Josephite," March 8, 1977, Larry J. Payne to Richard Daly, May 11, 1977, folder 3, box 45, Tom R. Byrd to Richard Daly, October 16, 1981 (third quotation), Richard Daly to Tom R. Byrd, October 26, 1981, folder 1, box 99, Texas Catholic Conference Records, CAT.

65. Johnson, *A Special Pilgrimage*, 76–77 (quotation on p. 77). According to Johnson, the Diocese of Richmond gained its first African American priest, Father Walter Barrett, in 1977. However, Bishop Walter F. Sullivan noted that the diocese ordained its first black priest in 1975. Johnson, *A Special Pilgrimage*, 60, 75; *Our Negro and Indian Missions*, January 1976, 7–11, ASSJ.

66. Charles E. Mahon, "Racism a Fact of Life in Southern Virginia," *Impact!* 9 (May 1979): 6, National Office for Black Catholics Collection, Archives and Special Collections, St. Thomas University, Miami Gardens, Florida.

67. Lawrence S. Earley, "Black Catholics Discuss Need for Ministry," *North Carolina Catholic*, July 1, 1979.

68. Earley, "Black Catholics Discuss Need for Ministry" (quotation); Earley, "More Black Priests, Nuns Are Needed."

69. "Brothers and Sisters to Us: U.S. Catholic Bishops Pastoral Letter on Racism, 1979" (quotations), accessed August 7, 2004, at http://www.usccb.org/saac/bishopspastoral.htm; *New York Times*, September 5, 1997.

70. "Brothers and Sisters to Us."

71. Ibid.

72. Bill Kenkelen, "Must Racism Remain 'A Fact of Seminary Life'?" *National Catholic Reporter* 16 (March 7, 1980): 6; Kenkelen, "Blacks 'Find Context for Catholicism'"; McClory, "Black Catholics," 26; Vernon C. Polite, "Getting the Job Done Well: African American Students and Catholic Schools," *Journal of Negro Education* 61 (Spring 1992): 215.

73. Untitled article, *Josephite News Views*, 3d quarter, 1980, 6, folder "Morrissey, William J. Archives Biog. M-," ASSJ; *New Catholic Encyclopedia*, vol. 2, 2d ed. (Detroit: Gale, 2003), s.v. "Bowman, Thea"; M. Shawn Copeland, O.P., "African American Catholics and Black Theology: An Interpretation," in *Black Theology: A Documentary History*, vol. 2: 1980–1992, ed. James H. Cone and Gayraud S. Wilmore (Maryknoll, NY: Orbis, 1993), 109 (quotation).

74. Tori Stuart, "Frustration Still Felt," *Voice*, July 11, 1980 (quotation).

75. Cyprian Davis, O.S.B., "The Catholic Church in the Black Community Today: A General Overview," *City of God* 2 (Summer 1980): 34–35, 37–38 (quotation). Some estimates suggested a figure of between 250 and 300 African priests. Tori Stuart, "Black Justice—The National View," *Voice*, July 25, 1980; McClory, "Black Catholics," 24; "Commission for Black Catholic Concerns Archdiocese of Atlanta," attached to Pamela G. Crayton, August 18, 1981, folder 1, box 013/5, AAA.

76. McClory, "Black Catholics," 23, 25 (first quotation); Stuart, "Black Justice—The National View" (second quotation).

77. Edward K. Braxton, "The Black Catholic Experience in America," *Origins* 10 (January 22, 1981): 500 (quotation); "Resolution," n.d., folder 1, box 013/5, AAA.

78. "National Black Lay Catholic Caucus, Southeastern Lay Conference, February 20–21, 1982, Baton Rouge, La." (quotations), Karen M. Clemons, March 2, 1982, "Lay Ministry—A Necessary Necessity," folder 2, box 013/5, AAA.

79. Arthur Jones, "Church Misses Suburban Challenge," *National Catholic Reporter* 18 (March 19, 1982): 2 (first quotation); "Racism Pastoral Called 'Best Kept Secret,'" *Morning Star*, December 26, 1984 (second quotation), press clipping, box D 38 R10000 "Racism (Copied Publications, Etc.)," Archives of the Diocese of Lafayette, Lafayette, Louisiana (hereinafter cited as ADL).

80. "What We Have Seen and Heard, Black Bishops' Pastoral Letter on Evangelization, September 9, 1984," in *Documents of American Catholic History Volume 3: 1966 to 1986*, ed. John Tracy Ellis (Wilmington, DE: Michael Glazier, 1987), 895–927 (first and second quotations on p. 913; third quotation on p. 912; fourth quotation on pp. 912–13; fifth quotation on p. 923). The letter's signatories were Bishop Joseph L. Howze of Biloxi, Auxiliary Bishop Harold R. Perry of New Orleans, Auxiliary Bishop Eugene A. Marino of Washington, Auxiliary Bishop Joseph A. Francis

of Newark, Auxiliary Bishop James P. Lyke of Cleveland, Auxiliary Bishop Emerson J. Moore of New York, Auxiliary Bishop Moses B. Anderson of Detroit, Auxiliary Bishop Wilton D. Gregory of Chicago, Auxiliary Bishop J. Terry Steib of St. Louis, and Auxiliary Bishop John H. Ricard of Baltimore. "Racism Major Obstacle to Evangelism, Black Bishops Say," *Morning Star*, October 3, 1984.

81. "What We Have Seen and Heard," 898, 900–904 (first, second, third, and fourth quotations on p. 902; fifth quotation on p. 901), 913 (sixth quotation).

82. *New York Times*, September 10, 1985 (quotations); *Wall Street Journal*, November 5, 1985.

83. *New York Times*, November 14, 1985 (quotation); "1st Black Archbishop in U.S. Sees Hope," n.d., press clipping, box "Ethnic Black," CAT.

84. *New York Times*, November 14, 1985; "Economic Justice for All (U.S. Catholic Bishops, 1986)," in *Catholic Social Thought: The Documentary Heritage*, ed. David J. O'Brien and Thomas A. Shannon (Maryknoll, NY: Orbis, 1992), 572–680 (quotation on p. 620).

85. Untitled article, *Josephite News Views*, 3d qtr. (1980): 6; "An Evaluation of the Edmundite Presence in Gadsden and Anniston, Alabama," July 17, 1985, 13 (first quotation), folder "Closing of All Saints and St. Martin Deporres," box 17, Local Administration, SSEA; *Wall Street Journal*, November 5, 1985; Thea Bowman, "Let the Church Say 'Amen!'" *Extension* 81 (March–April 1987): 10–11 (second quotation on p. 11); Diane Batts Morrow, "'In the Larger Black Community': Catholicism in *Black Women in America*," *U.S. Catholic Historian* 18 (Spring 2000): 73; Clarence Williams, "Black Catholics Reach Out," *Extension* 81 (March–April 1987): 13.

86. "An Evaluation of the Edmundite Presence in Gadsden and Anniston, Alabama," 13–14 (first quotation on p. 13); Rob Levin, "Priest's Lonely Dream in 1911 Came True for Atlanta's Blacks," *Atlanta Journal and Constitution*, October 12, 1986 (second and third quotations), press clipping, folder 9, box 044/5, AAA.

87. Father Timothy Gollob, interview by author, October 19, 2006; Carol Luker, "Black Liturgy: Cultural Expressions Central to Blacks' Identity as Catholics," *Texas Catholic*, July 10, 1987; Rita McInerney, "Day of Reflection Planned for Black Catholics," *Georgia Bulletin*, August 21, 1986.

88. McInerney, "Day of Reflection Planned for Black Catholics"; "National Black Catholic Congress, May 21–24, 1987, The Catholic University of America, Washington, D.C.," box D38 R100 00 Racism (Copied Publications, Etc.), ADL. Continuing tensions between the NOBC and other black Catholic organizations meant that the NOBC "was not chosen as one of the bodies officially convoking the Congress." Edward K. Braxton, "The National Black Catholic Congress: An Event of the Century," *U.S. Catholic Historian* 7 (Spring–Summer 1988): 305.

89. *New York Times*, May 24, 1987; Albert J. Raboteau, "Introductory Reflections," *U.S. Catholic Historians* 7 (Spring–Summer 1988): 299; Braxton, "The National Black Catholic Congress," 301–2. According to Braxton, there were almost "1,500 delegates and observers . . . from 108 of the 175 dioceses in the United States." Braxton, "The National Black Catholic Congress," 301. Cathy Green and Monique Irvin reported that over 1,500 black Catholics attended the congress from over 110 dioceses. Cathy Green and Monique Irvin, "The National Black Catholic Congress," *Word* 5 (July–August 1987): 2.

90. "The Pastoral Plan," *Word* 5 (July–August 1987): 3–11; "Resolutions Passed by General Assembly," *Word* 5 (July–August 1987): 12 (quotation).

91. Braxton, "National Black Catholic Congress," 302 (first and second quotations), 305 (third quotation); Sr. Thea Bowman, F.P.S.A., "Black History and Culture," *U.S. Catholic Historian* 7 (Spring–Summer 1988): 309 (fourth quotation); Morrow, "In the Larger Black Community," 73.

92. Wilton D. Gregory, D.S.L., "Black Catholic Liturgy: What Do You Say It Is?" *U.S. Catholic Historian* 7 (Spring–Summer 1988): 319.

93. Ibid., 318.

94. *New York Times*, September 12, 13 (quotations), 1987.

95. Ibid., September 13, 1987.

96. Ibid., September 9, 13, 1987. According to the *New York Times*, there were 250 African American permanent deacons. Ibid., September 13, 1987.

97. Collins, "Black and Catholic in America," 8 (quotation); "Unity of God's People," *Extension* 81 (March–April 1987): 16; Gollob interview; James F. Geraghty to Steve Ochs, January 13, 1988, folder "Racism," ADL.

98. Susan Hansen, "Catholic Group for Racial Justice Seeks Comeback," November 6, 1987, press clipping, John P. Sisson Papers, Tallahassee, Florida.

99. Ibid.

100. "Black Auxiliary Bishop Appointed to Diocese," *National Catholic Mentor* 2 (January–February 1988): 1; *New York Times*, March 16, 1988; *The Church and Racism: Toward a More Fraternal Society* (Vatican City: Pontifical Commission "Justitia et Pax," 1988), 1–45 (first quotation on p. 44); "U.S. Bishops on Racism," insert in *Commitment*, summer 1991, 1–4 (second quotation on p. 2), folder 4, box 1, series 8, National Catholic Conference for Interracial Justice Records, Marquette University, Milwaukee, Wisconsin; *Josephites*, 71.

101. "Three to Be Ordained Saturday, May 28," *Arkansas Catholic*, May 20, 1988; McDonogh, *Black and Catholic in Savannah, Georgia*, 5, 185–86; Ochs, *Desegregating the Altar*, 453.

102. *New York Times*, June 25, July 3, 5, 15 (quotations), 1989, October 26, 2004; "Black Priest Wants Separate Rite," July 7, 1989, press clipping, folder "Black Catholics," AASA; "Stallings Suspended," *Christian Century* 106 (July 19–26, 1989): 680–81; J. Deotis Roberts, "The Status of Black Catholics," *Journal of Religious Thought* 48 (Summer–Fall 1991): 74–75.

103. *New York Times*, July 13, 1989.

104. J. Michael Parker, "Black Priest's New Church Called Sign of Frustration," September 3, 1989, press clipping, "Catholic Meet Delegates Are Urged to Remain Neutral on Rebel Priest," July 17, 1989 (quotation), press clipping, folder "Black Catholics," AASA; Joe Michael Feist, "Black and Catholic," *Texas Catholic*, July 28, 1989.

105. *New York Times*, August 6, 1989.

106. "Racism Taints Church, Catholics Say," September 3, 1989, press clipping, folder "Black Catholics," AASA.

107. *Durham Morning Herald*, July 7, 1989. On African American Catholic responses to Stallings outside the South, see *New York Times*, July 10, 1989.

108. Parker, "Black Priest's New Church Called Sign of Frustration" (quotation); "Racism Taints Church, Catholics Say."

109. "Priest Is Fired for Plan to Join Black Sect," *San Antonio Light*, July 3, 1989, press clipping, folder "Black Catholics," AASA; *New York Times*, August 4, 1989 (quotation), February 11, 1990; McDonogh, *Black and Catholic in Savannah, Georgia*, 2, 328.

110. *New York Times*, February 5, 6, 11, June 15, 1990; "Rebel D.C. Priest, Followers Excommunicated," *San Antonio Light*, February 6, 1990 (quotation), folder "Black Catholics," AASA; "Stallings Excommunicated," *Christian Century* 107 (February 21, 1990): 176.

111. *New York Times*, February 11, 1990, September 9, 1991; [New Orleans] *Times-Picayune*, December 30, 1990, August 18, 1991; "Stallings Ordains Women," *Christian Century* 108 (September 18–25, 1991): 841; "Rifts in Stallings' Ranks," *Christian Century* 108 (November 6, 1991): 1023; Paul Elie, "Hangin' with the Romeboys," *New Republic* 206 (May 11, 1992): 20, 22. The AACC had grown to only forty-two hundred members by 1994. "Stallings Dedicates a

Cathedral," *Christian Century* 111 (September 7–14, 1994): 809; Archbishop Richard W. Bridges of the Independent Catholic Old Church, a California-based group with links to Old Catholic churches founded in nineteenth-century Europe by bishops who rejected papal authority, consecrated Stallings a bishop in May 1990 and an archbishop in September 1991. *New York Times*, September 9, 1991; "Stallings Ordains Women," 841; "Rifts in Stallings' Ranks," 1023.

112. Elie, "Hangin' with the Romeboys," 22.

113. Ibid.

114. Ibid. (first and second quotations); *San Antonio Express-News*, July 14, 1990 (third quotation).

115. *New York Times*, October 5, 1988; undisclosed to Harry J. Flynn, n.d. [1990], folder "Racism," ADL; Parker, "Black Priest's New Church Called Sign of Frustration"; [New Orleans] *Times-Picayune*, August 18, 1991 (quotation).

116. *Washington Post*, April 27, 1990; [New Orleans] *Times-Picayune*, August 18, 1991; *New York Times*, August 8, 1991; McDonogh, *Black and Catholic in Savannah, Georgia*, 8 (quotation), 307–8, 318, 328; Carl L. Bankston III and Stephen J. Caldas, *A Troubled Dream: The Promise and Failure of School Desegregation in Louisiana* (Nashville: Vanderbilt University Press, 2002), 107, 214–15; Erickson and Donovan, *Three R's of NonPublic Education in Louisiana*, 67.

Conclusion

1. Charles A. Mahon, "Bishop John Joyce Russell Fifty Years a Priest on July 8, 1973," *Catholic Virginian*, June 22, 1973.

SELECTED BIBLIOGRAPHY

I. Primary Sources

A. Annuals and Proceedings

Annual of the Alabama Baptist State Convention, 1957.
Annual of the Louisiana Baptist Convention, 1957.
Annual of the Southern Baptist Convention, 1946–1961, 1964, 1965, 1968, 1970, 1971.
The Catholic Committee of the South, Report of the Proceedings and Addresses of the Second Annual Meeting, Birmingham, Alabama, April 20, 21 and 22, 1941.
The Catholic Committee of the South, Report of the Proceedings and Addresses of the Third Annual Meeting, Richmond, Virginia, April 26, 27 and 28, 1942.
Knights of Columbus Supreme Council Proceedings, Eighty-Second Annual Meeting, New Orleans, Louisiana, August 18–19–20, 1964.
Knights of Columbus Supreme Council Proceedings, Ninetieth Annual Meeting, Toronto, Ontario, August 15–16–17, 1972.
Minutes of the General Assembly of the United Presbyterian Church in the United States of America, 1963.
Minutes of the One-Hundred-Fifth General Assembly of the Presbyterian Church in the United States, 1965.
Minutes of the One-Hundred-Sixth General Assembly of the Presbyterian Church in the United States, 1966.
Minutes of the One-Hundred-Eighth General Assembly of the Presbyterian Church in the United States, 1968.

B. Archival Collections

Amistad Research Center, New Orleans, Louisiana.
Catholic Committee of the South Collection.
Catholic Council on Human Relations Papers.
Edmundite Mission Records.

Archives and Special Collections, St. Thomas University, Miami Gardens, Florida.
National Office for Black Catholics Collection.

Archives of the Archdiocese of Atlanta, Atlanta, Georgia.
Archbishop Thomas E. Donnellan Papers.
Archbishop Paul J. Hallinan Papers.
Miscellaneous Folders.

Subject Files Hallinan.
Archives of the Archdiocese of Galveston-Houston, Houston, Texas.
Miscellaneous Folders.
Nicholas Gallagher Collection.

Archives of the Archdiocese of Mobile, Mobile, Alabama.
Bishop John L. May Papers.
Archbishop Thomas J. Toolen Papers.

Archives of the Archdiocese of New Orleans, New Orleans, Louisiana.
Archbishop Joseph F. Rummel Papers.
Miscellaneous Folders.

Archives of the Archdiocese of San Antonio, San Antonio, Texas.
Miscellaneous Folders.

Archives of the Diocese of Baton Rouge, Baton Rouge, Louisiana.
Historical Vertical File.

Archives of the Diocese of Charleston, Charleston, South Carolina.
Miscellaneous Folders.

Archives of the Diocese of Jackson, Jackson, Mississippi.
"Diary of Bishop Gerow," vol. 6: 1960–1966.

Archives of the Diocese of Lafayette, Lafayette, Louisiana.
Bound volume "Integration of Schools Diocese of Lafayette 1965–1973 Correspondence, Directives, Reports 1965–1971."
Bound volume "Integration of Schools Diocese of Lafayette 1965–1973 The Auzenne Case Correspondence and Data 1970–1973."
Miscellaneous Folders.

Archives of the Diocese of Raleigh, Raleigh, North Carolina.
Bound volume "Pastoral Letters V. S. Waters 1953–1956."
Scrapbook "Ban on Segregation 1953 volume II."
Scrapbook "Ban on Segregation 1953 volume III."

Archives of the Diocese of Richmond, Richmond, Virginia.
Peter L. Ireton Papers.
Parish Files.
Bishop John J. Russell Papers.
Bishop Walter F. Sullivan Papers.

Archives of the Diocese of Savannah, Savannah, Georgia.
Miscellaneous Folders.

Selected Bibliography

Archives of the New Orleans Province of the Society of Jesus, Special Collections and Archives, Loyola University Library, Loyola University New Orleans, New Orleans, Louisiana.
Miscellaneous Correspondence.

Archives of the Sisters of St. Joseph of St. Augustine, St. Augustine, Florida.
Miscellaneous Folders.

Archives of the Sisters of the Blessed Sacrament, Bensalem, Pennsylvania.
Miscellaneous Folders.

Archives of the Society of St. Joseph of the Sacred Heart, Baltimore, Maryland.
Miscellaneous Folders.

Baptist Joint Committee, Washington, DC.
Office Files.

Barry University Archives, Miami Shores, Florida.
Community Relations Board.

Butler Center for Arkansas Studies, Main Library, Little Rock, Arkansas.
Reverend Joseph H. Biltz Papers.

Catholic Archives of Texas, Austin, Texas.
Bishop John E. McCarthy Papers.
Diocese of Austin Collection.
Texas Catholic Conference Records.
Texas Catholic Herald Records.

Community Archives, Sisters of St. Joseph, Rochester, New York.
Miscellaneous Folders.

Georgetown University Library, Special Collections, Division, Washington, DC.
John LaFarge Papers.

Knights of Columbus Supreme Council Archives, New Haven, Connecticut.
Miscellaneous Folders.

Marianist Archives, San Antonio, Texas.
Miscellaneous Folders.

Marquette University, Milwaukee, Wisconsin.
National Catholic Conference for Interracial Justice Records.

Martin Luther King, Jr. Center for Nonviolent Social Change, Atlanta, Georgia.
Delta Ministry Papers.

Episcopal Society for Cultural and Racial Unity Records.
McCain Library and Archives, University of Southern Mississippi, Hattiesburg, Mississippi.
Vertical file "Race Relations, July–Dec. 1964."

National Council of Churches Archives, Presbyterian Historical Society, Philadelphia, Pennsylvania.
Miscellaneous Folders.

Schomburg Center for Research in Black Culture, New York, New York.
Hulan E. Jack Papers.

Society of Saint Edmund Archives, St. Michael's College, Colchester, Vermont.
Miscellaneous Folders.

Southern Baptist Historical Library and Archives, Nashville, Tennessee.
Brooks Hays Papers.
Executive Committee Records.
K. O. White Collection.

Special Collections and Archives, Loyola University Library, Loyola University New Orleans, New Orleans, Louisiana.
Joseph H. Fichter Papers.
Louis J. Twomey Papers.

Spring Hill College Archives, Mobile, Alabama.
Albert Sidney "Steve" Foley Jr., S.J. Papers.

Tennessee State Library and Archives, Nashville, Tennessee.
Vertical file "Adrian."

The American Catholic History Research Center and University Archives, Catholic University of America, Washington, DC.
Catholic Interracial Council of New York Collection.
National Catholic Welfare Conference Collection.

University of Notre Dame Archives, Notre Dame, Indiana.
John J. Egan Papers.
Joseph Gremillion Papers.

Xavier University Archives, New Orleans, Louisiana.
Miscellaneous Folders.

Z. Smith Reynolds Library Special Collections and Archives, Wake Forest University, Winston-Salem, North Carolina.
Wendell Randolph Grigg Papers.

Selected Bibliography 407

C. Oral Histories and Interviews

Oral Histories

Archives of the Diocese of Birmingham, Birmingham, Alabama.
Father Paul Donnelly, interview by Sister Rose Sevenich, O.S.F., RG 11.02–08.
Bishop Joseph A. Durick, interview by Sister Rose Sevenich, O.S.F., interview number 2, RG 10.02–17.

Law Library, Tulane University, New Orleans, Louisiana.
John P. "Jack" Nelson, interview by Jack Bass, November 16, 1979, "Bass, Jack—Series I: Interviews: Nelson, John P. 'Jack'—11/16/79, 5/F6," Jack Bass Oral History Collection.

University of Notre Dame Archives, Notre Dame, Indiana.
Neil O'Connell, "Oral History Interview with Brother Joseph Davis, S.M., January 21, 1972, Washington, D.C.," Joseph M. Davis Papers.

Interviews

Sister Mary Arnold, O.P., by author, August 14, 2006.
Mary Craighead, by author, July 19, 2005.
Robert Craighead, by author, July 19, 2005.
Monsignor Mortimer Danaher, telephone interview by author, August 12, 2006.
Brother Cyprian Davis, O.S.B., by author, July 10, 2007.
Archbishop Joseph A. Fiorenza, by author, October 30, 2006.
Norman C. Francis, by author, July 6, 2007.
Father Timothy Gollob, by author, October 19, 2006.
Monsignor Thomas P. Hadden, by author, August 2, 2006.
Monsignor James Hitchcock, by author, July 21, 2005.
King Hollands, by author, July 22, 2005.
Brother Herbert Janson, by author, August 23, 2006.
Madeline E. Johnson, by author, October 31, 2006.
Peter Johnson, by author, October 19, 2006.
Steve Landregan, by author, October 22, 2006.
Father Gerald M. LeFebvre, by author, November 10, 2006.
Maurice "Moon" Landrieu, by author, July 12, 2007.
Ormonde Lewis, by author, August 17, 2005.
Bishop John E. McCarthy, by author, October 25, 2006.
Brother Martin McMurtrey, by author, August 23, 2006.
Sister Josephine Marie Melican, S.S.J., telephone interview by author, August 15, 2006.
Bishop Vincent M. Rizzotto, by author, November 1, 2006.
John P. Sisson, by author, July 30, 2007.
G. J. Tarleton Jr., by author, July 21, 2005.
Barbara Vickers, by author, August 11, 2006.

D. Pamphlets

The Church and Racism: Towards a More Fraternal Society. Vatican City: Pontifical Commission "Justitia et Pax," 1988.*Commission on Human Rights of the Catholic Committee of the South: Its Principles, Objectives and Achievements.* New Orleans, n.p., n.d.

Congressional Report on What Happened When Schools Were Integrated in Washington, D.C. Greenwood, MS: Educational Fund of the Citizens' Councils, n.d.

The Desegregation Decision. Rock Hill, SC: Catholic Committee of the South, n.d.

Fletcher, Albert L. *An Elementary Catholic Catechism on the Morality of Segregation and Racial Discrimination.* N.p., n.d.

Handbook on Catholic School Integration. New Orleans: Catholic Committee of the South Commission on Human Rights, 1956.

Is Interposition the Answer? Rock Hill, SC: Catholic Committee of the South, n.d.

Is the Negro Ready for Desegregation? Rock Hill, SC: Catholic Committee of the South, n.d.

McNaspy, S.J., C. J. *Let's Talk Sense about the Negro.* New York: America Press, 1961.

Mernagh, Patrick Warren, and Deane Settoon Mernagh. *The Pope on Segregation.* N.p., 1955.

O'Donnell, William W. *America's Race Problem: A Catholic Editor's Analysis.* Little Rock: Guardian Press, 1959.

Pacem in Terris: Encyclical Letter of Pope John XXIII, April 11, 1963. Washington, DC: National Catholic Welfare Conference, 1963.

Progress Report. Rock Hill, SC: Catholic Committee of the South, n.d.

Resolutions adopted by the American Baptist Convention: Portland, Oregon, June 17, 1961. Valley Forge, PA: Division of Christian Social Concern, American Baptist Convention, 1961.

Ricau, Jack. *Integration: Threat to Freedom and How to Defeat It.* New Orleans, privately printed, 1957.

Shehan, Archbishop Lawrence J. *On Racial Justice: Pastoral Letter of March 1, 1963.* Washington, DC: National Catholic Welfare Conference, 1963.

Southern Catholic Parents Speak Up for Integrated Schools. New Orleans: Catholic Committee of the South Commission on Human Rights, n.d. [1956].

Southern Catholic Teachers Favor Integrated Schools. New Orleans: Catholic Committee of the South Commission on Human Rights, n.d. [1956].

Statements Adopted by Religious Groups Re Segregation in the Public Schools. New York: Department of Racial and Cultural Relations, National Council of Churches of Christ in the U.S.A., 1954.

These Men They Call Knights. N.p., 2001.

What Do Negroes Want? Rock Hill, SC: Catholic Committee of the South, n.d.

What Does Integration Mean? Rock Hill, SC: Catholic Committee of the South, n.d.

E. Catholic Newsletters, Newspapers, and Periodicals

Alamo Messenger, 1960–1969.
Alamo Register, 1943–1956.
America, 1924–2007.
American Ecclesiastical Review, 1946–1968.
Arkansas Catholic, May 20, 1988, September 20, 2007.
Ave Maria, 1949–1965.

Blueprint, 1952–1964.
Bulletin of the Catholic Laymen's Association of Georgia, 1922–1962.
Catholic Action of the South, 1949–1962.
Catholic Banner, 1954–1970.
Catholic Commentator, 1963–1970.
Catholic Council on Human Relations Newsletter, July 1961.
Catholic Digest, June 1956, May, July 1966.
Catholic Messenger, November 20, 1958, July 2, August 20, 1964, October 29, 1964, January 13, August 25, 1966.
Catholic Mind, 1939–1976.
Catholic Reporter, March 26, 1965.
Catholic Standard, September 19, 1974.
Catholic Virginian, 1943–1974.
Catholic Week, 1954–1979.
Catholic World, 1950–1965.
Christian Conscience, Summer 1948, July 1952.
Christian Impact, 1952–1955.
Clarion Herald, 1963–2001.
Claverite, 1935–1975.
Colleqium, July 1966.
Colored Harvest, 1953–1959.
Columbia, 1939–1983.
Commitment, 1963–1965, Summer 1991.
Commonweal, 1940–1970.
Community, January 1962.
[Press Department, US Catholic Conference] *Documentary Service,* February 9, 1967.
Ecclesiastical Review, May 1943.
Extension, March–April 1987.
Georgia Bulletin, 1963–1966, August 21, 1986.
Guardian, 1951–1976.
Homiletic and Pastoral Review, October 1947, July 1969.
Impact, May–June 1971, December 1974, June–July 1977, May 1979.
Integrity, 1950–1952.
Interracial Review, 1944–1970.
Josephite Harvest, 1961–1978.
Jubilee, February 1959, August 1965.
Jurist, October 1964.
Lamp, February 1962.
Leaves, September–October 1953.
Lone Star Register, July 9, 1964, August 24, 1967.
Lumen Vitae, October–December 1953.
Mission Fields at Home, November–December 1969.
Mississippi Register, 1964–1969.
Morning Star, August 10, 1972, 1976–1978, 1984.
National Catholic Conference for Interracial Justice Newsletter, December 1961.
National Catholic Mentor, January–February 1988.

National Catholic Reporter, 1965–1998.
N C News Service, January 13, 1970.
N.C.W.C. News Service, July 12, 1954.
North Carolina Catholic, 1948–2003.
North-Central Louisiana Register, September 3, 1965, July 14, 1967.
Notre Damean, January 1948, May 1954.
Nuns Newsletter, March 1965.
Oklahoma Courier, August 13, 1965.
Origins, January 16, November 27, December 18, 1975, January 22, 1981.
Our Colored Missions, 1941–1960.
Our Sunday Visitor, March 27, 1960, November 10, 1968.
Pilot, June 29, 1963.
Priest, February 1964.
Project Equality News, February 1970.
Ramparts, 1963–1965.
Sign, 1955–1964.
Social Digest, July–September 1965.
Southern Cross, 1963–1975.
Southwest Louisiana Register, 1955–1971.
Springhillian, February 15, 1957.
St. Anthony Messenger, August 1985.
St. Augustine's Messenger, 1941–1961.
Tablet, November 16, 1957.
Tennessee Register, 1954–2004.
Texas Catholic, September 10, 1955, June 4, 1964, April 6, 13, 1968, July 10, 1987, July 28, 1989, December 3, 2004.
Texas Catholic Herald [Austin edition], April 12, 1968.
Texas Catholic Herald [Beaumont edition], November 29, 1968, March 14, 1980.
Texas Catholic Herald [Houston edition], 1964–1967, 1974.
Texas Concho Register, April 12, 1968.
Texas Knight, 1969.
Today, October 1963, November 1964.
U.S. Catholic, February, December 1964, April 1981.
Voice, 1959–1970.
White Fathers Missions, September 1950.
Witness, March 25, 1965.
Word, July–August 1987.
Your News Letter, June 1965.
Your Edmundite Missions News Letter, October 1971.

F. US Government Documents and Court Records

Erickson, Donald A., and John D. Donovan. *The Three R's of NonPublic Education in Louisiana: Race, Religion, and Region*. Washington, DC: President's Commission on School Finance, 1972.

"David *Greenhouse* et al. v. Most Reverend Charles Pascal *Greco* et al., Civ. A. No. 17741 United States District Court for the Western District of Louisiana, Alexandria Division 368 F. Supp. 736; 1973 U.S. Dist. Lexis 10527, December 20, 1973," accessed June 11, 2007, at http://web.lexis-nexis.com.ezproxy.loyno.edu/universe.

"David *Greenhouse* et al., Plaintiffs-Appellants, v. Most Reverend Charles Pascal *Greco* et al., Defendants-Appellees No. 75–2050 United States Court of Appeals for the Fifth Circuit 544 F.2d 1302; 1977 U.S. App. Lexis 10608, January 10, 1977," accessed June 11, 2007, at http://web.lexis-nexis.com.ezproxy.loyno.edu/universe.

"David *Greenhouse* et al., Plaintiffs-Appellants, v. Most Reverend Charles Pascal *Greco* et al., Defendants-Appellees. No. 78–1802 United States Court of Appeals, Fifth Court 617 F.2d 408; 1980 U.S. App. Lexis 17433 May 19, 1980," accessed June 11, 2007, at http://web.lexis-nexis.com.ezproxy.loyno.edu.

United States Commission on Civil Rights. *Hearings before the United States Commission on Civil Rights, Volume II Administration of Justice Hearings Held in Jackson, Miss., February 16–20, 1965*. Washington, DC: United States Commission on Civil Rights, 1965; repr., New York: Arno Press, 1971.

G. Miscellaneous

African American Ministry and Evangelization. Raleigh, NC: Diocese of Raleigh, 2002.

"Brothers and Sisters to Us: U.S. Catholic Bishops Pastoral Letter on Racism, 1979," accessed August 7, 2004, at http://www.usccb.org/saac/bishopspastoral.htm.

Catholic Schools and Racial Integration: Perspectives, Directions, Models. Washington, DC: National Catholic Conference for Interracial Justice, 1977.

Christianity and Race Relations: Messages from the Sixth Annual Christian Life Workshop. Dallas: Christian Life Commission of the Baptist General Convention of Texas, 1962.

"Current African-American Bishops' Bios," accessed April 28, 2005, at http://www.usccb.org/saac/bshbio2.htm.

Foley, Albert S. "Shadow of the White Camellia: Reminiscences of a Tangle with Terrorists." Unpublished manuscript in possession of the author.

"The Franciscan Missionaries of Our Lady Health System: A Brief History," 5, 7, 9–10, 20, 21, accessed February 1, 2009, at http://www.fmolsisters.com/OurHistory.cfm?page=history.

"The Franciscan Missionaries of Our Lady: The Sisters Who Served in the North American Province," accessed February 1, 2009, at http://www.fmolsisters.com/OurHistory.cfm?page=history.

LaFarge, John, comp. *Sermons on Interracial Justice*. New York: Catholic Interracial Council of New York, 1957.

"The History of the Catholic Daughters of the Americas," accessed September 1, 2008, at http://www.catholicdaughters.org/history.shtml.

Interracial Justice. San Antonio: San Antonio Archdiocesan Committee on Interracial Relations, 1945.

"Josephite History," accessed February 5, 2015, at http://www.josephitepastoralcenter.org/resources/black-history-month/.

Myhalyk, S.S.E., Richard M. "The Establishment of Queen of Peace Parish in Selma, Alabama in 1971: A Primary Source Presentation." Unpublished paper in author's possession.

Our Negro and Indian Missions: Annual Report of the Secretary of the Commission for the Catholic Missions Among the Colored People and the Indians, January 1944–January 1976.
John P. Sisson Papers, in possession of Sisson, Tallahassee, Florida.

H. Magazines, Newsletters, Newspapers

Advocate, June 6, 1953.
Alabama Baptist [Alabama Baptist State Convention], February 5, 1970.
American Baptist News Service, December 23, 1969.
Atlanta Constitution, February 1, 1968.
Atlanta Inquirer, July 13, 1963.
Atlanta Journal-Constitution, September 26, 1982.
Arkansas Gazette, April 13, 1960, October 25, 1963, February 1, 1964, March 20, 1969, March 25, 1973, March 19, 1976.
Baptist and Reflector [Tennessee Baptist Convention], June 19, 1969, August 19, 1971.
Baptist Courier [Baptist State Convention of South Carolina], April 5, 1951.
Baptist Message [Louisiana Baptist Convention], January 29, February 5, 1970.
Baptist Press, October 18, 1968.
Baptist Record [Mississippi Baptist Convention], April 15, 1965.
Baptist Standard [Baptist General Convention of Texas], May 21, 1969.
Biblical Recorder [Baptist State Convention of North Carolina], January 11, 1958, May 30, 1964.
Boston Globe, September 18, 1980, January 26, 1984.
Buffalo Star, July 12, 1946.
[Raleigh] *Carolinian*, June 6, 1953.
Chicago American, June 27, 1965.
Chicago Sun-Times, May 25, 1956, July 4, 1965.
Christian Century, 1944–1995.
Christian Index [Georgia Baptist Convention], June 1, 1950, June 10, 1954, June 4, 1964.
Christianity and Crisis, May 29, 1961, February 4, 1963, May 29, 1967.
Christianity Today, 1965–1974.
Church News [Episcopalian Diocese of Mississippi], January 1970.
Citizens' Report, 1959–1964.
Clarion Ledger, June 17, 1965.
[Memphis] *Commercial Appeal*, October 30, November 13, 1969.
Councilor, November 1958.
[Lafayette, Louisiana] *Daily Advertiser*, November 28, 29, 30, December 1, 2, 4, 1955, January 25, 1956.
[Greenville, Mississippi] *Delta Democrat-Times*, January 5, 25, February 1, 2, 3, 4, 25, 1970.
Durham Morning Herald, July 7, 1989.
Ebony, March 1951, December 1957, May 1968.
The Episcopal Society for Cultural and Racial Unity Newsletter, August 6, 1963.
[Florence, South Carolina] *Florence Morning News*, April 19, 1956.
[Greensboro, North Carolina] *Greensboro Daily News*, June 1, 2, 8, 22, 1953.
Jet, March 5, 1969, September 9, 1971.
Look, March 28, 1950, October 20, 1964.
[New Orleans] *Louisiana Weekly*, October 15, 1949, April 19, 1975.

Mississippi Methodist Advocate, October 14, 1964.
Mobile Press, May 25, 1954.
Mobile Register, September 18, 1954, March 18, 1965, December 4, 1990.
Nashville Tennessean, June 30, July 1, 1954.
Nation, August 31, 1921, December 14, 1970.
New Republic, May 11, 1992.
New York Herald Tribune, April 8, 1962.
New York Times, 1927–2000.
[Charleston, South Carolina] *News and Courier*, May 17, 1969.
[Raleigh] *News and Observer*, March 20, May 16, 1945, May 21, 27, June 1, 22, 1953, February 16, 1964.
Newsweek, March 5, 1956, March 29, April 5, 1965, March 20, 1967.
Presbyterian Life, August 1, 1963,
Religious Herald [Baptist General Association of Virginia], January 22, 29, 1970.
Religious News Service, 1957, 1963–1966.
Richmond News Leader, May 13, 14, 1954, November 20, 1963, February 17, 1967.
Richmond Times-Dispatch, May 14, 1954, November 20, 1963.
San Antonio Express, January 13, 2001.
San Antonio Light, March 25, 1957.
San Antonio News, April 13, 1954.
Saturday Evening Post, November 28, 1964.
Savannah Evening Press, July 13, 1963, July 8, 1964.
Savannah Morning News, February 20, 1961, June 24, August 31, 1963, February 13, 1970.
Savannah News-Press, February 20, 1995.
Selma Times-Journal, January 17, 1983.
Shreveport Times, August 4, October 25, 1963.
St. Augustine Record, June 15, August 24, 1964.
St. Petersburg Times, October 16, 1991.
Time, December 12, 1955, March 5, 1956, July 12, 1963, September 15, 1958, September 22, 1967.
[New Orleans] *Times-Picayune*, 1949–2001.
United Methodist Information, June 27, 1972.
Wall Street Journal, February 14, 1958, November 5, 1985.
Washington Post, November 14, 1958, April 25, 1968, June 1, 1969, August 11, 12, 1987, April 27, 1990.

I. Books

Anderson, Margaret. *The Children of the South*. New York: Farrar, Straus and Giroux, 1966.
Basilica of St. Mary of the Immaculate Conception Catholic Church 200th Anniversary, 1791–1991. Virginia Beach, VA: Hill's Printing, 1991.
Brown, Robert R. *Bigger Than Little Rock*. Greenwich, CT: Seabury Press, 1958.
Cantwell, Daniel M. *Catholics Speak on Race Relations*. Chicago: Fides, 1952.
Carson, Clayborne, et al., eds. *The Eyes on the Prize Civil Rights Reader*. New York: Penguin, 1991.
Carter III, Hodding. *The South Strikes Back*. Garden City, NY: Doubleday, 1959.
Century Book. Bensalem, PA: Sisters of the Blessed Sacrament, 1991.
Cook, James Graham. *The Segregationists*. New York: Appleton-Century-Crofts, 1962.

Escott, Paul D., David R. Goldfield, Sally G. McMillen, and Elizabeth Hayes Turner. *Major Problems in the History of the American South, Volume II: The New South.* 2d ed. Boston: Houghton Mifflin, 1999.

Fager, Charles E. *Selma, 1965: The March That Changed America.* 2d ed. Boston: Beacon Press, 1985.

Fichter, Joseph H. *One-Man Research: Reminiscences of a Catholic Sociologist.* New York: John Wiley, 1973.

Gallup, George H. *The Gallup Poll: Public Opinion 1935–1971*, vol. 3: *1959–1971*. New York: Random House, 1972.

Gillard, John T. *The Catholic Church and the American Negro.* Baltimore: St. Joseph Society's Press, 1929.

———. *Colored Catholics in the United States.* Baltimore: Josephite Press, 1941.

Greco, Charles P. *"With God's Help": Memoirs of Bishop Charles P. Greco.* New Haven, CT: Knights of Columbus, 1989.

Gremillion, J. B. *The Journal of a Southern Pastor.* Chicago: Fides, 1957.

Hunton, George K. *All of Which I Saw, Part of Which I Was: The Autobiography of George K. Hunton as Told to Gary MacEoin.* With an Introduction by Roy Wilkins. Garden City, NY: Doubleday, 1967.

The Josephites: A Century of Evangelization in the African American Community. Baltimore: St. Joseph's Society of the Sacred Heart, 1993.

King, Jr., Martin Luther. *Why We Can't Wait.* New York: Harper and Row, 1964.

LaFarge, S.J., John. *The Catholic Viewpoint on Race Relations.* Garden City, NY: Hanover House, 1956.

Leonard, S.S.J., Joseph T. *Theology and Race Relations.* With a Foreword by Most Rev. Patrick O'Boyle. Milwaukee, WI: Bruce, 1963.

Odum, Howard W. *Southern Regions of the United States.* Chapel Hill: University of North Carolina Press, 1936.

The Official Catholic Directory Anno Domini 1941. New York: P. J. Kenedy and Sons, 1941.

The Official Catholic Directory Anno Domini 1945. New York: P. J. Kenedy and Sons, 1945.

The Official Catholic Directory Anno Domini 1954. New York: P. J. Kenedy and Sons, 1954.

The Official Catholic Directory Anno Domini 1964. New York: P. J. Kenedy and Sons, 1964.

The Official Catholic Directory Anno Domini 1980. New York: P. J. Kenedy and Sons, 1980.

Reynolds, S.J., Edward D. *Jesuits for the Negro.* New York: America Press, 1949.

Schuster, George, and Robert M. Kearns, *Statistical Profile of Black Catholics.* With a Foreword by Bernard Quinn. Washington, DC: Josephite Pastoral Center, 1976.

Silver, James W. *Mississippi: The Closed Society.* New and enlarged ed. New York: Harcourt, Brace and World, 1966.

Thompson, Daniel C. *The Negro Leadership Class.* Englewood Cliffs, NJ: Prentice-Hall, 1963.

The Word in the World: Divine Word Missionaries '76 Black Apostolate. N.p., n.d.

Zanca, Kenneth J., ed. *American Catholics and Slavery, 1789–1866: An Anthology of Primary Documents.* Lanham, MD: University Press of America, 1994.

J. Articles

"An Appeal to the Conscience of the American People." In *Race: Challenge to Religion*, edited by Mathew Ahmann, 171–73. Chicago: Henry Regnery, 1963.
Bagby, Grover C. "Race Relations and Our Concern." *Methodist Story*, January 1965: 3–5.
Barnette, Henlee. "Negro Students in Southern Baptist Seminaries." *Review and Expositor* 53 (April 1956): 207–10.
Bowman, F.P.S.A., Sr. Thea. "Black History and Culture." *U.S. Catholic Historian* 7 (Spring-Summer 1988): 307–10.
Braxton, Edward K. "The National Black Catholic Congress: An Event of the Century." *U.S. Catholic Historian* 7 (Spring–Summer 1988): 301–6.
"The Churches Speak." *New South* 9 (August 1954): 1–6.
"A Current List: Schools of Higher Learning Lower the Color Bar." *New South* 10 (February 1955): 7–9.
Davis, O.S.B., Cyprian. "The Catholic Church in the Black Community Today: A General Overview." *City of God* 2 (Summer 1980): 32–38.
Davis, S.M., Joseph M., and Cyprian Rowe, F.M.S. "The Development of the National Office for Black Catholics." *U.S. Catholic Historian* 7 (Spring–Summer 1988): 265–89.
Du Bois, W. E. B. "The Negro and the Catholic Church." *Crisis* 40 (March 1933): 68–69.
"Economic Justice for All (U.S. Catholic Bishops, 1986)." In *Catholic Social Thought: The Documentary Heritage*, edited by David J. O'Brien and Thomas A. Shannon, 572–680. Maryknoll, NY: Orbis, 1992.
Ehrensing, Rudolph. "New Orleans: Catholic City?" *Scholastic*, February 24, 1961, 20–22.
Foley, S.J., Albert S. "Adventures in Black Catholic History: Research and Writing." *U.S. Catholic Historian* 5 (1986): 103–18.
Gregory, D.S.L., Wilton D. "Black Catholic Liturgy: What Do You Say It Is?" *U.S. Catholic Historian* 7 (Spring–Summer 1988): 316–21.
King, Martin Luther. "A Challenge to the Churches and Synagogues." In *Race: Challenge to Religion*, edited by Mathew Ahmann, 155–69. Chicago: Henry Regnery, 1963.
Lee, J. Oscar. "Reporting on Race Relations in Some Churches." *Royal Service* 51 (May 1957): 23.
Maston, T. B. "Southern Baptists and the Negro (Part 1)." *Home Missions* 37 (July 1966): 18–19.
Nash, Diane. "Inside the Sit-Ins and Freedom Rides: Testimony of a Southern Student." In *The New Negro*, edited by Mathew H. Ahmann, 43–60. Notre Dame, IN: Fides, 1961.
"The National Black Catholic Congress of 1987." *U.S. Catholic Historian* 7 (Spring–Summer 1988): 299–356.
Raboteau, Albert J. "Black Catholics and Afro-American Religious History: Autobiographic Reflections." *U.S. Catholic Historian* 5 (1986): 119–27.
———. "Introductory Reflections." *U.S. Catholic Historian* 7 (Spring–Summer 1988): 299–300.
Rivers, Clarence Joseph. "Thank God We Ain't What We Was: The State of the Liturgy in the Black Catholic Community." *U.S. Catholic Historian* 5 (1986): 81–89.
Roberts, J. Deotis. "The Status of Black Catholics." *Journal of Religious Thought* 48 (Summer-Fall 1991): 73–78.
Stephan, A. Stephen, and Charles A. Hicks. "Integration and Segregation in Arkansas—One Year Afterward." *Journal of Negro Education* 24 (Summer 1955): 172–87.

"What We Have Seen and Heard, Black Bishops' Pastoral Letter on Evangelization, September 9, 1984." In *Documents of American Catholic History*, edited by John Tracy Ellis, vol. 3: 1966–1986: 895–927. Wilmington, DE: Michael Glazier, 1987.

II. Secondary Sources

A. Books

Alvis, Jr., Joel L. *Religion and Race: Southern Presbyterians, 1946–1983*. Tuscaloosa: University of Alabama Press, 1994.

Anderson, R. Bentley. *Black, White, and Catholic: New Orleans Interracialism, 1947–1956*. Nashville: Vanderbilt University, 2005.

Bailey, Kenneth K. *Southern White Protestantism in the Twentieth Century*. New York: Harper and Row, 1964.

Balmer, Randall, and John R. Fitzmier. *The Presbyterians*. With a Foreword by Henry Warner Bowden. Westport, CT: Praeger, 1994.

Bartley, Numan V. *The Rise of Massive Resistance: Race and Politics in the South during the 1950s*. Baton Rouge: Louisiana State University Press, 1969.

———. *The New South, 1945–1980*. Baton Rouge: Louisiana State University Press, 1995.

Bass, S. Jonathan. *Blessed Are the Peacemakers: Martin Luther King, Jr., Eight White Religious Leaders, and the "Letter from Birmingham Jail."* Baton Rouge: Louisiana State University Press, 2001.

Bennett, James B. *Religion and the Rise of Jim Crow in New Orleans*. Princeton, NJ: Princeton University Press, 2005.

Berger, Peter L. *The Sacred Canopy: Elements of a Sociological Theory of Religion*. Garden City, NY: Anchor Books, 1969 [1967].

Bronder, Saul E. *Social Justice and Church Authority: The Public Life of Archbishop Robert E. Lucey*. Philadelphia: Temple University Press, 1982.

Campbell, Ernest Q., and Thomas F. Pettigrew. *Christians in Racial Crisis: A Study of Little Rock's Ministry*. Washington, DC: Public Affairs Press, 1959.

Carey, Patrick W. *Catholics in America: A History*. Westport, CT: Praeger, 2004.

Collum, Danny Duncan. *Black and Catholic in the Jim Crow South: The Stuff That Makes Community*. New York: Paulist Press, 2006.

Crain, Robert L., and Morton Inger. *School Desegregation in New Orleans: A Comparative Study of the Failure of Social Control*. Chicago: National Opinion Research Center, University of Chicago, 1966.

Cross, Robert D. *The Emergence of Liberal Catholicism in America*. Cambridge, MA: Harvard University Press, 1958.

Davis, O.S.B., Cyprian. *The History of Black Catholics in the United States*. New York: Crossroad, 1990.

Donovan, John T. *Crusader in the Cold War: A Biography of Fr. John F. Cronin, S.S. (1908–1994)*. New York: Peter Lang, 2005.

Dunn, William H. *Knights of Columbus in Texas, 1902–1977*. Austin: Texas State Council, Knights of Columbus, 1978.

Faherty, S.J., William Barnaby. *Rebels or Reformers?: Dissenting Priests in American Life*. Chicago: Loyola University Press, 1987.

Fairclough, Adam. *Race and Democracy: The Civil Rights Struggle in the Louisiana, 1915–1972*. Athens: University of Georgia Press, 1995.

Fichter, Joseph H. *The Sociology of Good Works: Research in Catholic America*. With a Foreword by Paul M. Roman. Chicago: Loyola University Press, 1993.

Findlay, Jr., James F. *Church People in the Struggle: The National Council of Churches and the Black Freedom Movement, 1950–1970*. New York: Oxford University Press, 1993.

Fogarty, S.J., Gerald P. *Commonwealth Catholicism: A History of the Catholic Church in Virginia*. Notre Dame, IN: University of Notre Dame Press, 2001.

Foley, S.J., Albert S. *God's Men of Color: The Colored Catholic Priests of the United States, 1854–1954*. New York: Farrar, Straus, 1955.

Fontenot, Mary Alice, and Kathleen Toups. *The Gentle Shepherd: A Memoir of Bishop Jules B. Jeanmard*. Rayne, LA: Hebert, 1998.

Friedland, Michael B. *Lift Up Your Voice Like a Trumpet: White Clergy and the Civil Rights and Antiwar Movements, 1954–1973*. Chapel Hill: University of North Carolina Press, 1998.

Gallagher, Charles. *Cross and Crozier: The History of the Diocese of St. Augustine*. Jacksonville, FL: Diocese of St. Augustine, 1999.

Glazier, Michael, and Thomas J. Shelley, eds. *The Encyclopedia of American Catholic History*. Collegeville, MN: Liturgical Press, 1997.

Gleason, Philip. *Contending with Modernity: Catholic Higher Education in the Twentieth Century*. New York: Oxford University Press, 1995.

Glock, Charles Y., and Rodney Stark. *Religion and Society in Tension*. Chicago: Rand McNally, 1965.

Griffin, V.S.C., Sr. M. Julian, in cooperation with Gillian Brown. *Tomorrow Comes the Song: The Story of Catholicism among the Black Population of South Georgia, 1850–1978*. Savannah: Diocese of Savannah, 1979.

Harte, Thomas J. *Catholic Organizations Promoting Negro-White Race Relations in the United States*. Washington, DC: Catholic University of America Press, 1947.

Hemesath, O.S.F., Sr. Caroline. *Our Black Shepherds: Biographies of the Ten Black Bishops of the United States*. Washington, DC: Josephite Pastoral Center, 1987.

Hennesey, S.J., James. *American Catholics: A History of the Roman Catholic Community in the United States*. With a Foreword by John Tracy Ellis. New York: Oxford University Press, 1981.

Hill, Jr., Samuel S. *Southern Churches in Crisis*. New York: Holt, Rinehart and Winston, 1967.

Johnson, Nessa Theresa Baskerville. *A Special Pilgrimage: A History of Black Catholics in Richmond*. Richmond, VA: Diocese of Richmond, 1978.

Kauffman, Christopher J. *Faith and Fraternalism: The History of the Knights of Columbus, 1882–1982*. New York: Harper and Row, 1982.

———. *Ministry and Meaning: A Religious History of Health Care in the United States*. With a Foreword by Martin E. Marty. New York: Crossroad, 1995.

Koehlinger, Amy L. *The New Nuns: Racial Justice and Religious Reform in the 1960s*. Cambridge, MA: Harvard University Press, 2007.

Labbé, Dolores Egger. *Jim Crow Comes to Church: The Establishment of Segregated Catholic Parishes in South Louisiana*. 2d ed. New York: Arno Press, 1978 [Lafayette: University of Southwestern Louisiana, 1971].

Lacour, Barbara Babin. *Called to Action: The Knights of Columbus in Louisiana, 1962–1992*. N.p.: Jostens Publishing Company, 1994.

Loescher, Frank S. *The Protestant Church and the Negro*. Philadelphia: University of Pennsylvania Press, 1948.

Lynch, S.B.S., Sr. Patricia. *Sharing the Bread in Service: Sisters of the Blessed Sacrament, 1891–1991*. Vols. 1–2. Bensalem, PA: Sisters of the Blessed Sacrament, 2001 [1998].

Marthaler, O.F.M.Conv., Berard L., and Carol Dorr Clement. *Catholic Daughters of the Americas: A Century in Review*. New York: Catholic Daughters of the Americas and Mercury Publishing Services, 2003.

McDonogh, Gary Wray. *Black and Catholic in Savannah, Georgia*. Knoxville: University of Tennessee Press, 1993.

McGraw, Joel William, F.S.C., Milton J. Guthrie, and Josephine King. *Between the Rivers: The Catholic Heritage of West Tennessee*. Memphis: Catholic Diocese of Memphis, 1996.

McGreevy, John T. *Parish Boundaries: The Catholic Encounter with Race in the Twentieth-Century Urban North*. Chicago: University of Chicago Press, 1996.

———. *Catholicism and American Freedom: A History*. New York: W. W. Norton, 2003.

McGuire, Meredith B. *Religion: The Social Context*. 3d ed. Belmont, CA: Wadsworth, 1992.

McNally, Michael J. *Catholicism in South Florida, 1868–1968*. Gainesville: University of Florida Press, 1982.

———. *Catholic Parish Life on Florida's West Coast, 1860–1968*. St. Petersburg, FL: Catholic Media Ministries, 1996.

McNaspy, S.J., C. J. *At Face Value*. With a Foreword by Walker Percy and an Afterword by David A. Boileau. New Orleans: Institute of Human Relations, Loyola University of the South, 1978.

Moore, Andrew S. *The South's Tolerable Alien: Roman Catholics in Alabama and Georgia, 1945–1970*. Baton Rouge: Louisiana State University Press, 2007.

Moore, W. T. *His Heart Is Black*. Atlanta: Home Mission Board of the Southern Baptist Convention, 1978.

Murray, Peter C. *Methodists and the Crucible of Race, 1930–1975*. Columbia: University of Missouri Press, 2004.

Namorato, Michael V. *The Catholic Church in Mississippi, 1911–1984: A History*. Westport, CT: Greenwood Press, 1998.

New Catholic Encyclopedia, vol. 7. New York: McGraw-Hill, 1967.

New Catholic Encyclopedia. 2d ed., vols. 2, 8, 12. Detroit: Thomson Gale, 2003.

Newman, Mark. *Getting Right with God: Southern Baptists and Desegregation, 1945–1995*. Tuscaloosa: University of Alabama Press, 2001.

———. *Divine Agitators: The Delta Ministry and Civil Rights in Mississippi*. Athens: University of Georgia Press, 2004.

Nickels, Marilyn Wenzke. *Black Catholic Protest and the Federated Colored Catholics, 1917–1933*. New York: Garland, 1988.

Norwood, Frederick A. *The Story of American Methodism: A History of the United Methodists and Their Relations*. Nashville: Abingdon Press, 1974.

Ochs, Stephen J. *Desegregating the Altar: The Josephites and the Struggle for Black Priests, 1871–1960*. Baton Rouge: Louisiana State University Press, 1990.

O'Rourke, Lawrence M. *Geno: The Life and Mission of Geno Baroni*. New York: Paulist Press, 1991.

Osborne, William A. *The Segregated Covenant: Race Relations and American Catholics*. New York: Herder and Herder, 1967.

Powers, William F. *Tar Heel Catholics: A History of Catholicism in North Carolina.* Lanham, MD: University Press of America, 2003.

Raboteau, Albert J. *A Fire in the Bones: Reflections on African-American Religious History.* Boston: Beacon Press, 1995.

Reimers, David M. *White Protestantism and the Negro.* New York: Oxford University Press, 1965.

Rice, Madeleine Hooke. *American Catholic Opinion in the Slavery Controversy.* New York: Columbia University Press, 1944.

Roche, Richard J. *Catholic Colleges and the Negro Student.* Washington, DC: Catholic University of America Press, 1948.

Rogers, Kim Lacy. *Righteous Lives: Narratives of the New Orleans Civil Rights Movement.* New York: New York University Press, 1993.

Ross, Frank H., and Lisa May. *Recall, Rejoice, Renew: Diocese of Galveston-Houston 1847–1997.* Dallas: Taylor, 1997.

Shattuck, Jr., Gardiner H. *Episcopalians and Race: Civil War to Civil Rights.* Lexington: University Press of Kentucky, 2000.

Shelley, Thomas J. *Paul J. Hallinan: First Archbishop of Atlanta.* Wilmington, DE: Michael Glazier, 1989.

Sherry, Gerard E. *Archbishop Paul J. Hallinan.* Notre Dame, IN: University of Notre Dame Press, 1965.

Southern, David W. *John LaFarge and the Limits of Catholic Interracialism, 1911–1963.* Baton Rouge: Louisiana State University Press, 1996.

Spalding, Thomas W. *The Premier See: A History of the Archdiocese of Baltimore, 1789–1994.* Baltimore: Johns Hopkins University Press, 1989.

Stritch, Thomas, *The Catholic Church in Tennessee: The Sesquicentennial Story.* Nashville: The Catholic Center, 1987.

Sumner, David E. *The Episcopal Church's History: 1945–1985.* Wilton, CT: Morehouse-Barlow, 1987.

Warner, Michael. *Changing Witness: Catholic Bishops and Public Policy, 1917–1994.* With a Foreword by George Weigel. Grand Rapids, MI: Williams B. Eerdmans, 1995.

Webb, Clive. *Fight against Fear: Southern Jews and Black Civil Rights.* Athens: University of Georgia Press, 2001.

We've Come This Far by Faith: A Centennial History of Saint Nicholas Catholic Church Houston's Historic Black Parish 1887–1987. Houston: American Photocopy and Print Co., 1987.

Woods, James M. *Mission and Memory: A History of the Catholic Church in Arkansas.* Little Rock: Diocese of Little Rock, 1993.

B. Articles

Alberts, John B. "Black Catholic Schools: The Josephite Parishes of New Orleans during the Jim Crow Era." *U.S. Catholic Historian* 12 (Winter 1994): 77–98.

Anderson, R. Bentley. "Black, White, and Catholic: Southern Jesuits Confront the Race Question, 1952." *Catholic Historical Review* 91 (July 2005): 484–505.

Black, Merle. "The Modification of a Major Cultural Belief: Declining Support for 'Strict Segregation' among White Southerners, 1961–1972." *Journal of the North Carolina Political Science Association* 1 (Summer 1979): 4–21.

Copeland, O.P., M. Shawn. "African American Catholics and Black Theology: An Interpretation." In *Black Theology: A Documentary History*, edited by James H. Cone and Gayraud S. Wilmore, vol. 2: 1980–1992: 99–115. Maryknoll, NY: Orbis, 1993.

———. "A Cadre of Women Religious Committed to Black Liberation: The National Black Sisters' Conference." *U.S. Catholic Historian* 14 (Winter 1996): 123–44.

Curran, S.J., R. Emmett. "'Splendid Poverty': Jesuit Slaveholding in Maryland, 1805–1838." In *Catholics in the Old South: Essays on Church and Culture*, edited by Randall M. Miller and Jon L. Wakelyn, 125–46. Macon, GA: Mercer University Press, 1983.

Davis, O.S.B., Cyprian. "Black Catholics in Nineteenth-Century America." *U.S. Catholic Historian* 5 (1986): 1–17.

———. "The Holy See and American Black Catholics: A Forgotten Chapter in the History of the American Church." *U.S. Catholic Historian* 7 (Spring–Summer 1988): 157–81.

———. "Black Catholics in the Civil Rights Movement in the Southern United States: A. P. Tureaud, Thomas Wyatt Turner, and Earl Johnson." *U.S. Catholic Historian* 24 (Fall 2006): 69–81.

Evans, Rhonda D., Craig J. Forsyth, and Stephanie Bernard. "One Church or Two? Contemporary and Historical Views of Race Relations in One Catholic Diocese." *Sociological Spectrum* 22 (2002): 225–44.

Fessenden, Tracy. "The Sisters of the Holy Family and the Veil of Race." *Religion and American Culture* 10 (Summer 2000): 187–224.

Fichter, Joseph H. "First Black Students at Loyola University: A Strategy to Obtain Teacher Certification." *Journal of Negro Education* 56 (Autumn 1987): 535–49.

Gallagher, Charles R. "The Catholic Church, Martin Luther King Jr., and the March in St. Augustine." *Florida Historical Quarterly* 83 (Fall 2004): 149–72.

Greeley, Andrew M., and Paul B. Sheatsley. "Attitudes toward Racial Integration." *Scientific American* 225 (December 1971): 13–19.

Guerrand, Roger-Henri. "The Catholic Church's Struggle against Racialism." In *The Church and Racism*, edited by Gregory Baum and John Coleman, 31–34. Edinburgh: T. C. Clark; New York: Seabury Press, 1982.

Jones, Patrick. "'Not a Color, but an Attitude': Father James Groppi and Black Power Politics in Milwaukee." In *Groundwork: Local Black Freedom Movements in America*, edited by Jeanne Theoharis and Komozi Woodard, with a Foreword by Charles Payne, 259–81. New York: New York University Press, 2005.

Kemper, Donald J. "Catholic Integration in St. Louis, 1935–1947." *Missouri Historical Review* 73 (October 1978): 1–22.

Lamanna, Richard A., and Jay J. Coakley, "The Catholic Church and the Negro." In *Contemporary Catholicism in the United States*, edited by Philip Gleason, 147–93. Notre Dame, IN: University of Notre Dame Press, 1969.

McGreevy, John T. "Racial Justice and the People of God: The Second Vatican Council, the Civil Rights Movement, and American Catholics." *Religion and American Culture* 4 (Summer 1994): 221–54.

McNally, Michael J. "A Peculiar Institution: A History of Catholic Parish Life in the Southeast (1850–1980)." In *The American Catholic Parish: A History from 1850 to the Present*, edited by Jay P. Dolan, vol. 1: 117–234. Mahwah, NY: Paulist Press, 1987.

Miller, Randall M. "A Church in Cultural Captivity: Some Speculations on Catholic Identity in the Old South." In *Catholics in the Old South: Essays on Church and Culture*, edited by Randall M. Miller and Jon L. Wakelyn, 11–52. Macon, GA: Mercer University Press, 1983.

———. "The Failed Mission: The Catholic Church and Black Catholics in the Old South." In *Catholics in the Old South: Essays on Church and Culture*, edited by Randall M. Miller and Jon L. Wakelyn, 149–70. Macon, GA: Mercer University Press, 1983.

———. "Slaves and Southern Catholicism." In *Masters and Slaves in the House of the Lord: Race and Religion in the American South, 1740–1870*, edited by John B. Boles, 127–234. Lexington: University Press of Kentucky, 1988.

Murray, Paul T. "Father Nathaniel and the Greenwood Movement." *Journal of Mississippi History* 72 (Fall 2010): 277–311.

———. "'The Most Righteous White Man in Selma': Father Maurice Ouellet and the Fight for Voting Rights," *Alabama Review* 68 (January 2015): 31-73.

Nickels, Marilyn Wenzke. "Thomas Wyatt Turner and the Federated Colored Catholics." *U.S. Catholic Historian* 7 (Spring–Summer 1988): 215–32.

Nuesse, C. Joseph. "Segregation and Desegregation at the Catholic University of America." *Washington History* 9 (Spring–Summer 1997): 54–70.

Orser, W. Edward. "Racial Attitudes in Wartime: The Protestant Churches during the Second World War." *Church History* 41 (September 1972): 337–53.

Osborne, William. "The Church and the Negro: A Crisis in Leadership." *Cross Currents* 15 (Spring 1965): 129–50.

Padgett, Charles S. "'Without Hysteria or Unnecessary Disturbance': Desegregation at Spring Hill College, Mobile, Alabama, 1948–1954." *History of Education Quarterly* 41 (Summer 2001): 167–88.

———. "Hidden from History, Shielded from Harm: Desegregation at Spring Hill College, 1954–1957." *Alabama Review* 56 (October 2003): 278–310.

Piehl, Mel. "American Catholics and Social Reform, 1789–1989." In *Perspectives on the American Catholic Church, 1789–1989*, edited by Stephen J. Vicchio and Virginia Geiger, 317–39. Westminster, MD: Christian Classics, 1989.

Plaisance, O.S.B., Aloysius F. "The Catholic Church and the Confederacy." *American Benedictine Review* 15 (June 1964): 159–67.

Poché, Justin D. "The Catholic Citizens' Council: Religion and White Resistance in Post-War Louisiana." *U.S. Catholic Historian* 24 (Fall 2006): 47–68.

Polite, Vernon C. "Getting the Job Done Well: African American Students and Catholic Schools." *Journal of Negro Education* 61 (Spring 1992): 211–22.

Rector, Theresa A. "Black Nuns as Educators." *Journal of Negro Education* 51 (Summer 1982): 238–53.

Reed, John Shelton, and Merle Black. "How Southerners Gave Up Jim Crow." *New Perspectives* 17 (Fall 1985): 15–19.

Ringer, Benjamin B., and Charles Y. Glock. "The Political Role of the Church as Defined by Its Parishioners." *Public Opinion Quarterly* 18 (Winter 1954–1955): 337–47.

Rousey, Dennis C. "Catholics in the Old South: Their Population, Institutional Development, and Relations with Protestants." *U.S. Catholic Historian* 24 (Fall 2006): 1–21.

Rozga, Margaret. "March on Milwaukee." *Wisconsin Magazine of History* 90 (Summer 2007): 28–39.

Sharps, Ronald L. "Black Catholics in the United States: A Historical Chronology." *U.S. Catholic Historian* 12 (Winter 1994): 119–41.

———. "Black Catholic Gifts of Faith." *U.S. Catholic Historian* 15 (Fall 1997): 29–55.

Slonecker, Blake. "A Church Apart: Catholic Desegregation in Newton Grove, North Carolina." *North Carolina Historical Review* 63 (July 2006): 322–54.

Spalding, C.F.X., David. "The Negro Catholic Congresses, 1889–1894." *Catholic Historical Review* 55 (October 1969): 337–57.

"The U.S. Bishops and Catholic Social Teaching: Introduction." In *Catholic Social Thought: The Documentary Heritage*, edited by David J. O'Brien and Thomas A. Shannon, 489–91. Maryknoll, NY: Orbis, 1992.

Traxler, Sr. Margaret Ellen. "American Catholics and Negroes." *Phylon* 30 (4th qtr., 1969): 355–66.

Wood, James R. "Authority and Controversial Policy: The Churches and Civil Rights." *American Sociological Review* 35 (December 1970): 1057–69.

———. "Personal Commitment and Organizational Constraint: Church Officials and Racial Integration." *Sociological Analysis* 33 (1972): 142–51.

Woods, C.D.P., Sr. Frances Jerome. "Congregations of Religious Women in the Old South." In *Catholics in the Old South: Essays on Church and Culture*, edited by Randall M. Miller and Jon L. Wakelyn, 99–123. Macon, GA: Mercer University Press, 1983.

Zielinski, Martin A. "Working for Interracial Justice: The Catholic Interracial Council of New York, 1934–1964." *U.S. Catholic Historian* 7 (Spring–Summer 1988): 233–60.

C. Theses and Dissertations

Campion, Owen Francis. "A History of the Diocese of Nashville." Senior Honor's thesis, Saint Bernard College, 1962.

Cunnigen, Donald. "Men and Women of Goodwill: Mississippi's White Liberals." PhD diss., Harvard University, 1988.

Dugas, Carroll Joseph. "The Dismantling of De Jure Segregation in Louisiana, 1954–1974." PhD diss., Louisiana State University, 1989.

Gallagher, Charles Robert. "Patriot Bishop: The Diplomatic and Episcopal Career of Archbishop Joseph P. Hurley, 1937–1967." PhD diss., Marquette University, 1998.

Hill, Davis C. "Southern Baptist Thought and Action in Race Relations, 1940–1950." ThD diss., Southern Baptist Theological Seminary, 1952.

Hite, Gregory Nelson. "The Hottest Places in Hell: The Catholic Church and Civil Rights in Selma, Alabama, 1937–1965." PhD diss., University of Virginia, 2002.

Martensen, Katherine Ann. "Region, Religion and Social Action: The Catholic Committee of the South, 1939–1956." Master's thesis, University of New Orleans, 1978.

May, Jr., Herbert J. "The Official Policy of the Roman Catholic Church of the Diocese of Lafayette in Relation to Black Catholics, 1940 to 1978." Master's thesis, University of Southwestern Louisiana, 1981.

———. "A Canonical Investigation of Racial Parishes and Its Application to the Diocese of Lafayette, Louisiana, 1918–1978." Degree of Licentiate in Canon Law diss., Catholic University of America, 1983.

McCarron, Dennis Michael. "Catholic Schools in Florida, 1866–1992." PhD diss., Florida State University, 1993.

Mitchell, Reavis L. "The Black Man and the Catholic Church in Nashville." Master's thesis, Middle Tennessee State University, 1971.

Padgett, Charles Stephen. "Schooled in Invisibility: The Desegregation of Spring Hill College, Mobile, Alabama, 1948–1963." PhD diss., University of Georgia, 2000.

Payne, John Robert. "A Jesuit Search for Social Justice: The Public Career of Louis J. Twomey, S.J., 1947–1969." PhD diss., University of Texas at Austin, 1976.

Poché, Justin D. "Religion, Race, and Rights in Catholic Louisiana, 1938–1970." PhD diss., University of Notre Dame, 2007.

Richard, Ann Marie. "A Rhetorical Analysis of the June, 1958, Radio Speeches of Louis J. Twomey." Master's thesis, Louisiana State University, 1971.

INDEX

Abernathy, Geraldine, 170
Abernathy, Ralph B., 221
Adrian, William L., 22, 31, 32, 33, 53, 59, 112, 144–45, 160, 175, 182–83, 184–85, 211
African American Catholics, x, xi, xii, 169–200; *Auzenne v. School Board of the Roman Catholic Diocese of Lafayette*, 199–200; Black Catholic Eucharist Celebration, 256; "Black Perspectives on Evangelization," 251; and Black Power, 194, 196, 198–99, 244, 245, 247; "Brothers and Sisters to Us" (1979), 257–58, 259, 260, 261; "Call to Action, A," 253, 254, 255, 257; characterizations of, 178, 180, 186, 187, 192; and civil rights movement, 12, 94, 102, 172–73, 175, 178, 181, 183–84, 185, 186, 187, 188–89, 190–91, 192, 193–94, 219–20, 248, 273, 367n20, 385n75; deacons, 196, 233, 242, 247, 249, 250, 251, 254, 256, 257, 260, 262, 263, 266, 375n101, 401n96; diversity within, xi, 171–72, 178, 247, 252, 256, 259, 261, 262, 265, 266, 268; and liturgy, 245, 246–47, 248–49, 251, 252, 255, 256, 257, 259, 260, 261, 262, 265, 266, 267, 268, 273, 275, 396n33; and Knights of Columbus, 29, 194, 212–13, 222–23, 241; membership size in the South, 169, 289; membership size in the South and border states, 201, 376n1; membership size in the United States, 4, 201, 233, 250, 263; National Black Catholic Seminarians Association, 197; and National Council of Catholic Laity, 250; and NCCW, 250; nuns, number of, 250, 258, 263, 397n46; opinion polls, 176, 198, 250–51; prelates, number of, 248, 250, 260, 261, 263, 264, 265, 268, 400n80; press for Catholic desegregation, 159, 160, 174–75, 180–81, 182, 186–87, 189–90; priests, number of, 5, 7, 13, 37, 141, 192, 196, 250, 258, 263, 265, 267, 397n46, 399n75; response to closure of African American Catholic institutions, 21, 41, 194–95, 197, 198, 232, 234–35, 237–38, 244–45, 252, 255–56, 273; response to George A. Stallings Jr., 265–67; and Selma protests, 191; seminarians, 8, 11–12, 13, 24, 90, 141, 179, 197, 208, 214, 242–43, 249, 250–51, 252, 258, 368n35; Southern Regional Black Clergy Conference, 198; Texas Black Catholic Conference, 255–56; "What We Have Seen and Heard, Black Bishops' Pastoral Letter on Evangelization" (1984), 260, 263, 399n80. *See also individual names and organizations*
African-American Catholic Congregation (AACC), 267, 401n111. *See also* Stallings, George A., Jr.
Agostinelli, Floyd H., 226
Ahmann, Matt, 100, 102, 187, 218, 220, 226, 333n64
Aiken, SC, 240
Alabama Christian Movement for Human Rights, 123
Alabama State Advisory Committee to the United States Commission on Civil Rights, 101, 124
Alamo Messenger, 129, 130, 132. *See also* San Antonio, Archdiocese of
Alamo Register, 116. *See also* San Antonio, Archdiocese of
Albany, GA: civil rights protests in, 220; St. Theresa Grammar School, 160
Alexandria, LA, Diocese of, 22, 68, 150, 154, 277, 281, 282, 285, 330n47; African American priests in, 140, 189, 214; Catholic church segregation in, 163,

425

189; Catholic hospital desegregation in, 165; Catholic school desegregation in, 37, 163, 166, 227, 243, 275; and Civil Rights Act of 1964, 38–39; federal funds cut off to Catholic schools in, 166; federal funds restored to Catholic schools in, 166; Friendship House, Shreveport, 62; *Greenhouse v. Greco*, 243. *See also* Greco, Charles P.; Gremillion, Joseph B.; Ferriday, LA; Marksville, LA; Monroe, LA; *Ramparts*; Thompson, August L.

Allen, Joseph C., 345n61

Allin, John M., 229

Alter, Karl J., 222

Amarillo, Diocese of, 29, 277, 279, 280, 281, 282, 283, 285, 286; Catholic high school desegregation in, 32, 144; Catholic population size, 144. *See also* DeFalco, Lawrence M.

America, 212, 213

American Baptist Convention, 201, 216; African American churches in, 216; Black Churchmen of the American Baptist Convention, 231; calls for open churches, 210, 214, 221; elects African American president, 234; endorses *Brown v. Board of Education* (1954), 210; endorses open housing legislation and federal rent subsidies, 228; General Council supports Black Power, 228; opposes racial discrimination, 214, 224; praises the civil rights movement, 219, 221; presents award to Martin Luther King Jr., 225; supports civil rights demonstrations, 225. *See also* Northern Baptist Convention

American Catholic hierarchy, ix, xii, 4–5, 6, 7, 8, 9, 14, 15–16, 33–36, 37–38, 43, 44, 120, 142, 198, 199, 206–7, 211, 214, 215, 219, 221–22, 229, 230, 231–32, 232–33, 235, 248, 255, 260, 261, 263, 269, 270, 305n57, 309n84; annual statement (1919), 10–11; annual statement (1942), 15–16; annual statement (1943), 16, 36, 207; antipoverty funding by, 233; and Black Manifesto, 232–33; "Bonds of Union" (1963), 38; "Brothers and Sisters to Us" (1979), 257–58, 259, 260, 261; Campaign for Human Development, 233; "Economic Justice for All" (1986), 260–61; "National Race Crisis" (1968), 40–41, 231; "On Racial Harmony" (1963), 38, 221–22, 270; "Race Relations and Poverty" (1966), 40; "Racial Discrimination and the Christian Conscience" (1958), 35–36, 64, 70, 154, 215, 270; and urban problems, 231–32; "What We Have Seen and Heard, Black Bishops' Pastoral Letter on Evangelization" (1984), 260, 263, 399n80. *See also* National Catholic Welfare Conference (NCWC); National Conference of Catholic Bishops (NCCB); United States Catholic Conference (USCC)

American Ecclesiastical Review, 46

American Jewish Congress, 222. *See also* Jews

Anderson, Moses B., 141, 189, 191, 253, 400n80

Anderson, Myers, 181

Anderson, R. Bentley, xi, xii, 44, 367n20

Anniston, AL, 122; All Saints Church, 261

Anti-Catholicism, 11, 30–31, 48, 59–60, 65, 87, 88–89, 99, 148, 203, 270

Anti-Semitism, 203

Antona [Ebo, Betty], Sr. Mary, 191

"Appeal for Law and Order and Common Sense, An" (1963), 123

Area 11 Christian Family Movement, 130

Ariatti, Bernard Raynal "Ray," 105

Arizona, 339n90

Arkansas Council on Human Relations, 104

Arkansas State Advisory Committee to the United States Commission on Civil Rights, 104

Asheville, NC: St. Anthony's Church, 248; St. Lawrence Church, 248

Association of Catholic Laymen, 56, 57, 66, 69, 79, 215, 315n45

Association of Methodist Ministers and Laymen, 215. *See also* Laymen's Union

Assumption Seminary, San Antonio. *See* St. John's Seminary

Athens, GA, St. Mary's Hospital, 159

Atlanta, Archdiocese of, xii, 107, 181, 277, 281, 282, 285; African American churches in, 60, 140, 167, 261; African American priests in, 254, 373n88; Catholic hospital desegregation in, 159, 165, 222; Catholic school desegregation in, 37, 60–61, 150, 154–55, 155–56, 158–59, 182, 218, 359n76; cosponsors reception for Nobel Peace Prize winner Martin Luther King Jr., 103; Eugene A. Marino appointed archbishop, 264; Eugene A. Marino resigns as archbishop, 268; ordains first African American diocesan priest, 373n88; public school desegregation in, 118–19, 135, 155–56; and Selma protests, 62, 103, 388n90; St. Martin's Human Relations Council, 105, 107; *Syllabus on Racial Justice, A*, 159. *See also* Athens, GA; Atlanta, GA; Atlanta, Diocese of; *Georgia Bulletin*; Hallinan, Paul J.; Hyland, Frances E.; Marietta, GA; Sherry, Gerard E.

Atlanta, Diocese of, 60–61, 119, 150, 154–56, 277, 280

Atlanta, GA, 140, 218, 254, 384n68; African American Catholics in the civil rights movement, 181; African American churches in, 60; Colored Clinic, 159; D'Youville Academy, desegregation of, 379n76; Holy Family Hospital, 159, 165; Marist College, desegregation of, 359n76; Our Lady of Lourdes Church, 261; public school desegregation in, 37, 118–19, 155, 158–59; reception for Nobel Peace Prize winner Martin Luther King Jr. in, 103; Sacred Heart Church, 167; and Selma protests, 103; S.B.S. and civil rights march in, 38; St. Joseph Church, 167; St. Joseph's Infirmary, 159, 165; St. Paul of the Cross Church, 140. *See also* Atlanta, Archdiocese of; Atlanta, Diocese of

Aucoin, Charles F., 237

Aureli, Michael, 263–64

Austin, Diocese of, 277, 278, 280, 282, 283, 285, 286; Catholic school desegregation in, 151. *See also* Austin, TX; *Lone Star Register*; Reicher, Louis J.

Austin, TX, 103, 126. *See also* Austin, Diocese of

Auzenne v. School Board of the Roman Catholic Diocese of Lafayette, 199–200

Ball, Charles Chester L. E., 179

Baltimore, Archdiocese of, 205, 379n24, 385n75; Catholic school desegregation in, 218; and Gwynn Oak Amusement Park protest, 221; and Selma protests, 388n90. *See also* Baltimore, MD; Baltimore Black Catholic Caucus; Shehan, Lawrence J.

Baltimore, MD, 3, 5, 6, 230; African-American Catholic Congregation in, 267; Baltimore Black Catholic Caucus, 248; Baltimore Clergymen's Interfaith Committee on Human Rights, 221; Baltimore Hebrew Congregation, 221; Loyola College, desegregation of, 207; St. Mary's Seminary, 87. *See also* Baltimore, Archdiocese of; Shehan, Lawrence J.

Baltimore Black Catholic Caucus, 248

Baltimore Clergymen's Interfaith Committee on Human Rights, 221

Baltimore Hebrew Congregation, 221

Bane, Raymond, 126

Baptist Laymen of Alabama, 215

Baptist Laymen of Mississippi, 215

Barnes, William H., 185

Baroni, Geno, 235

Barrett, George, 104

Barrett, Walter, 396n44, 398n65

Barry College, Miami Shores, desegregation of, 157

Bartek, Mrs. George, 134

Basilico, M., 77

Bass, Harry, 217

Batesburg, SC, First Baptist Church, 217

Baton Rouge, Diocese of, 87, 154, 277, 282, 285; African American Catholic churches in, 238; African American Catholic schools in, 166, 244–45; Catholic Daughters of America in, 39; Catholic school desegregation in, 161, 162–63, 166, 227, 244–45; and Civil Rights Act (1964), 38–39; and fair employment, 164–65; gives African American churches territorial boundaries, 238; public school desegregation in, 126, 135–36, 161, 162, 163. *See also* Baton Rouge, LA; *Catholic Commentator*; East Baton Rouge Parish, LA (county); Tracy, Robert E.

Baton Rouge, LA: Our Lady of the Lake Hospital, 153; Southern University, 141, 198, 244; St. Agnes School, 244; St. Agnes-St. Francis Xavier School, 244–45; St. Francis Xavier Church, 244; St. Gerard Church, 57. *See also* Baton Rouge, Diocese of

Bay St. Louis, MS, St. Augustine's Seminary, 11–12, 13, 22, 24, 32, 90, 100, 177, 368n35

Beale, J. T., 343n46, 344n47

Beaumont, Diocese of, 278, 280, 281, 282, 285, 286; Project Equality, 106, 165. *See also* Galveston-Houston, Diocese of

Beaumont, TX, public school desegregation in, 159, 360n79

Begin, Floyd L., 212

Begley, Michael J., 281, 395n30

Belhaven College, Jackson, MS, desegregation of, 228

Belle Chasse, LA, 55; Our Lady of Perpetual Help Church, 60

Belmont, NC: Belmont Abbey College, desegregation of, 148; Sacred Heart Junior College, desegregation of, 48

Belmont Abbey College, Belmont NC, desegregation of, 148

Benedict XIV, Pope, 68

Benedict XV, Pope, 11

Benedictine Sisters, 104, 142

Bennett, James B., 6

Bennett, Mary, 203

Berger, Peter L., 50, 51

Bernardin, Joseph L., 54, 141, 151

Berrigan, Philip, 219

Bertrand, Joseph, 223

Bertrandville, LA, 173

Bezou, Henry C., 45, 58, 112, 113, 121, 152, 153

Biblical references: I Corinthians 7:20, 67; I Corinthians 12:12–13, 16, 297n50; I Corinthians 13: 4–7, 325n7; I Corinthians 13:13, 325n7; Galatians 3:28, 300n28, 324n1; Genesis 1:26–27, 84, 324n4; Genesis 9:21–27, 66; Genesis: 11:1–9, 66; Genesis 21:9–12, 67; Peter 2:17–19, 67; Peter 3:1–7, 67; I St. John 4:20, 85; St. John 13:34, 85, 154; St. John 13:35, 85; St. Luke 10:25–37, 85; St. Mark 12:31, 85; St. Matthew 22:39, 85; St. Matthew 25:40, 85; St. Matthew 28:19, 85; I Timothy 6:1–2, 67

Biggers, Clarence J., 182

Biloxi, Diocese of, 278, 279, 282, 285; African American churches in, 195, 263; erection of, 398n62; Joseph L. Howze installed as bishop, 255. *See also* Biloxi, MS; *Mississippi Register*; Natchez-Jackson, Diocese of

Biloxi, MS: Nativity Church, 195; Our Mother of Sorrows Church, 195; Our Mother of Sorrows School, 195; public school desegregation in, 162; St. Michael's Church, 195

Birmingham, AL, 343n46, 345n61; civil rights protests in, 122, 123–24; First Baptist Church, 344n46; Freedom Rides attacked in, 122; Holy Trinity-Holy Cross Greek Orthodox Church, 343n46; "Letter from a Birmingham Jail," 124; Our Lady Queen of the Universe, bomb planted outside, 60; public school desegregation in, 127, 161; riots in, 124, 127; Sixteenth Street Baptist Church, bombing of, 127; St. Francis Xavier Church, 345n61; Temple Emanu-El, 344n46

Birmingham, Diocese of, office for black Catholics, 261. See also *Catholic Week*; Gadsden, AL; Mobile-Birmingham, Diocese of

Birmingham News, 124

Black Catholic Clergy Caucus, 196, 198, 199, 232, 245, 374n101. *See also* National Black Catholic Clergy Caucus

Black Churchmen of the American Baptist Convention, 231

Black Economic Development Conference. *See* National Black Economic Development Conference (BEDC)

Black Manifesto, 232–33

Black Methodists for Church Renewal, 231

"Black Perspectives on Evangelization," 251

Black Power, 107, 194, 196, 198–99, 228, 244, 245, 247

Black Presbyterian Leadership Conference, 231

Blackschleger, Eugene, 343n46, 344n47

Blake, Eugene Carson, 221
Boatwright, Mrs. Norman I., 385n72
Bogalusa, LA, Annunciation Church, 164
Boggan, J. M., 70–71
Boileau, David A., 62, 104
Boland, Thomas A., 235
Bonaventure, Sr. Mary, 184
Bond, John M., 240, 241
"Bonds of Union" (1963), 38
Boney, F. N., 137
Bonzano, Giovanni, 10
Bossier Parish (county), LA, 163
Boston, Archdiocese of: Catholic schools in, 232; public school desegregation in, 232; and Selma protests, 388n90. *See also* Boston, Diocese of; Boston, MA
Boston, Diocese of, 5. *See also* Boston, Archdiocese of
Boston, MA, 5, 230, 232
Boucvalt, G. C., 74
Bouise, Oscar A., 173
Bourges, Anthony, 13
Boutwell, Albert, 124
Bowman, John W., 24
Bowman, Sr. Thea [Bertha], 191, 261, 262
Brady, Fern G., 185
Braxton, Edward K., 259, 262, 401n89
Brennan, Andrew J., 25, 281
Bridges, Richard W., 402n111
Bronder, Saul E., 30, 334n70
Brooklyn, Diocese of; 214; and Selma protests, 388n90. *See also* Brooklyn, NY
Brooklyn, NY: Columbus Council no. 126 (Knights of Columbus), 212–13; St. Columba Council no. 1119 (Knights of Columbus), 212. *See also* Brooklyn, Diocese of
"Brothers and Sisters to Us" (1979), 257–58, 259, 260, 261
Brown, John O., 104
Brown, Richard H., 85
Brown, Robert R., 117, 342n27
Brown II (1955), 113
Brown v. Board of Education (1954), 19, 20, 21, 30, 31, 32, 33, 36, 56, 72, 87, 91, 96, 97, 99, 111, 112, 113, 114, 115, 117, 118, 143, 144, 146, 147, 148, 149, 175, 187, 209, 210, 211, 214, 216, 218, 270, 271, 275, 304n54
Brunini, Joseph B., 281, 348n84; addresses Knights of Columbus annual convention (1964), 84; background of, 88; and Catholic schools, 136, 239; and Mississippi Council on Human Relations, 105; and Mississippi Religious Leadership Conference, 136
Brunson, Mrs. N. C., 89
Buffalo, Diocese of, 207. *See also* Buffalo, NY
Buffalo, NY, 211, 232. *See also* Buffalo, Diocese of
Bulletin of the Catholic Laymen's Association of Georgia, 119
Buras, LA: Our Lady of Good Harbor Church, 172; Our Lady of Good Harbor School, 57, 60, 158, 171–72. *See also* Perez, Leander
Burgess, John M., 234
Burke, John E., 9
Burns, John P., 190
Burns, Leonard L., 186, 190
Busing, 230, 232, 239, 393n9
Butler, Arthur, 169
Butler, Loretta, 164
Byrd, Tom R., 256

Cabirac, Henry A., Jr., 37, 57, 61, 101, 102, 103, 105, 128, 186, 187
Caddo Parish, LA (county), 163
Caillouet, Lucien J., 153
Calhoun, Malcolm, 225
Calhoun, Roy L., 241
Calhoun, William E., 373n88
"Call to Action, A," 253, 254, 255, 257
Callahan, P. H., 10
Campaign for Human Development, 233
Campbell, Ernest Q., 342n27
Campbell, Mrs. J. C., 108
Campbell, Will D., 217
Campion, Owen F., 144, 145
Canonici, Paul V., 136
Canon law, ix, 45, 46, 52, 69, 204, 309n84
Cansler, Mrs. O. J., 192
Canton, MS, 107, 190

Cantwell, Daniel, 385n75
Carmichael, Stokely, 228
Carmouche, Joyce, 67
Carpenter, C. C. J., 210, 217, 343n46
Carroll, Coleman F., 104, 105, 124, 151, 183, 281, 306n71, 336n77
Castle, Oretha, 190
Catholic Action of the South, 28, 88, 97, 112, 285. See also Everett, M. F.; New Orleans, Archdiocese of
Catholic Banner, 87, 285. See also Charleston, Diocese of
Catholic Board for Mission Work Among the Colored People, 9, 11
Catholic Church: bureaucracy and, 43, 51–52, 63, 83; "Call to Action, A" 253, 254, 255, 257; Campaign for Human Development, 233; Catholic Board for Mission Work Among the Colored People, 9, 11; Catholic Hospital Association, 213; Catholic Press Association, 105; Commission for the Catholic Missions Among the Colored People and the Indians, 6, 237, 353n16; compared to Jews, 202–3; foreign missions of, 85; as a hierarchical body, ix, x, 41, 43, 46–47, 52, 53–54, 61, 118, 186, 202, 269; higher education desegregation in the South, survey of, 216; liturgy of, ix, 245, 246–47, 249, 255, 256, 257, 259, 260, 261, 262, 265, 266, 267, 268, 273, 275, 396n33; membership size in the South, 19, 287; membership size in the United States, 4, 201, 233, 250, 263; nuns, number of, 250; opinion polls and surveys, 19, 50, 203, 209, 211, 226, 250–51; as a "perfect society," ix, 10; polity, 43–47, 52, 61, 62, 202, 216–17, 269, 270; priests, number of, 250, 263; Second Plenary Council of the Church in the United States, 4–5; slaveholding by, 3; and slavery, 3–4; Third Plenary Council of the Church in the United States, 6, 7; universality of, ix, 36, 84, 94, 156, 187, 188, 263. See also American Catholic hierarchy; National Catholic Welfare Conference (NCWC); National Conference of Catholic Bishops (NCCB); United States Catholic Conference (USCC)
Catholic Commentator, 125, 285. See also Baton Rouge, Diocese of
Catholic Committee of the South (CCS), 90, 92–93, 174, 303n46, 330n46, 330n47; convention (1942), 16; convention (1944), 16; convention (1946), 23, 92; convention (1951), 31, 51, 94, 95, 209, 270; convention (1953), 95–96, 270; decline of, 33, 96–97, 99, 209, 270, 331n49; founding of, 15; governance of, 15, 16; ineffectiveness of, 95, 96; response to *Brown v. Board of Education* (1954), 96
Catholic Committee on Urban Ministry (CCUM), 255
Catholic Conference of the South, 15. See also Catholic Committee of the South (CCS)
Catholic Council on Human Relations (CCHR), 100–101, 107, 185–86
Catholic Daughters of America, 39, 308n78
Catholic Daughters of the Americas, 308n78. See also Catholic Daughters of America
Catholic Digest, 203, 211, 298n2
Catholic Herald Citizen, 225. See also Milwaukee, Archdiocese of
Catholic higher education desegregation in the South, survey of, 216
Catholic Hospital Association, 213
Catholic Interracial Council of New York, 13, 14, 68
Catholic Press Association, 105
Catholic State League of Texas, 130
Catholic University of America, 295n30; excludes African Americans, 10, 14, 296n43; readmits African Americans, 14
Catholic Virginian, 51, 134, 285. See also Richmond, Diocese of
Catholic Week, 72, 89, 122–23, 127, 131, 132, 133, 191, 285. See also Clark, Ed; Mobile-Birmingham, Diocese of
Catholics and civil rights movement, 12, 20, 38, 71, 73, 94, 101–4, 106–7, 108, 116, 123–24, 125, 126, 127, 128, 129, 131–33, 134, 172–73, 175, 178, 181, 183–84, 185, 187,

188–89, 190–91, 192, 193–94, 219–21, 222, 225, 226, 227, 229, 230, 242, 248, 272, 273, 274, 336n78, 385n75
Cavallo, Joe, 261
Champagne, Esma, 71
Chaney, James, 190
Chaney, Robert Eugene, 265
Charleston, Diocese of, 22 140, 249, 278, 282, 283, 330n47; African American churches in, 246; Catholic church desegregation in, 151; Catholic interracial council, 107; Catholic school desegregation in, 53, 54, 60, 154–55, 161, 197–98, 240–41, 251, 357n54, 375n104; council no. 110 (Knights of Peter Claver), St. Peter's Parish, Charleston, 189; deacon training in, 249, 251; desegregation of diocesan organizations, 141; Diocesan Council of Catholic Men, 141; Knights of Columbus in, 241; and Poor People's March on Washington, 108; Project SAIL, 230; public school desegregation in, 127, 161; and Selma protests, 226; St. Francis Xavier Hospital, 189; *Syllabus on Racial Justice, A*, 156. *See also* Aiken, SC; *Catholic Banner*; Columbia, SC; Georgetown, SC; Hallinan, Paul J.; Orangeburg, SC; Reh, Francis F.; Rock Hill, SC; Unterkoefler, Ernest L.
Charleston, SC, 47, 53, 108, 127, 155, 161, 240–41; Cathedral School, 240, 241; Cathedral school desegregation in, 54; Catholic interracial council, 107; council no. 110 (Knights of Peter Claver), St. Peter's Parish, 189; hospital workers' strike in, 52; Immaculate Conception School, 240, 241; Knights of Columbus, racial discrimination in, 241; Organization of Catholic Parents, 54, 155; Project SAIL in, 230; public school desegregation in, 127, 161; Sacred Heart School, 240–41; St. Francis Xavier Hospital, 189. *See also* Charleston, Diocese of
Charlotte, Diocese of, 278, 280, 281, 285, 395n30
Charlotte, NC, 146, 150; Our Lady of Consolation Church, 140, 141; public school desegregation in, 340n20
Charlottesville, VA, St. Thomas Church, 103

Chatham, Josiah G., 84
Chicago, Archdiocese of, 218–19; African American churches in, 7, 13, 207; Catholic interracial council in, 100, 212, 220, 222, 230, 385n75; Catholic school desegregation in, 218; ordains black priests, 214; and Selma protests, 388n90. *See also* Chicago, IL; Clements, George H.; Cody, John P.; Gregory, Wilton D.; Meyer, Albert G.; Mundelein, George W.
Chicago, IL: Annunciata Elementary School, 235; Catholic desegregation in, 218; Catholic interracial council in, 100, 220, 222, 385n75; Catholic segregation in, 7, 13, 207, 212, 213, 222–23, 230; CCCO, 229; Chicago Catholic group marches in Albany, GA, 220; civil rights movement in, 229; Illinois Club for Catholic Women, 220; Knights of Columbus in, 222–23; Loyola University Chicago, 177, 220; NCRR in, 384n68; opposition to desegregation in, 211, 212, 235, 274; Project Cabrini in, 230; secular segregation in, 91; St. Monica Church, 7; Trumbull Park, 212, 381n59. *See also* Chicago, Archdiocese of
Christian Conscience, 93, 98. *See also* Southeastern Regional Interracial Commission (SERINCO)
Christopher, Sr. Mary, 191–92
Cicognani, Amleto Giovanni, 13, 14, 23, 31, 35, 56, 140, 207
Cincinnati, OH, CORE voter registration drive in, 225
Citizens Committee of Greater New Orleans, 190
Citizens' Council, 216
Citizens' Council of New Orleans, 56. *See also* Citizens' Councils; Greater New Orleans Citizens' Council; South Louisiana Citizens' Council
Citizens' Councils, 36, 55, 56, 57, 66, 73, 79, 98, 99, 113–14, 120, 121, 150, 153, 155, 187, 203, 214, 216. See also *Citizens' Council*; Citizens' Council of New Orleans; Defender of States' Rights; Greater New

Orleans Citizens' Council; South Carolina Association of Citizens' Councils; South Louisiana Citizens' Council; Southern Gentlemen's Organization of Louisiana

Civil Rights Act (1964), 21, 38–39, 70, 105, 129–30, 165, 166, 190, 224, 228, 240

Civil Rights Act (1968), 134, 230

Civil rights movement and Catholics, 12, 20, 38, 71, 73, 94, 101–4, 106–7, 108, 116, 123–24, 125, 126, 127, 128, 129, 131–33, 134, 172–73, 175, 178, 181, 183–84, 185, 187, 188–89, 190–91, 192, 193–94, 219–21, 222, 225, 226, 227, 229, 230, 242, 248, 272, 273, 274, 336n78, 385n75

Clancy, Walter B., 104

Clark, Adele, 115

Clark, Ed, 123, 127–28

Clarke, Aloysius, 373n88

Clarke, Peter Wellington, 173

Clarksdale, MS: public school desegregation, in, 162; St. Elizabeth School Board, 136

Claverite, 172, 173, 180, 366n15. *See also* Knights of Peter Claver (KPC)

Clayton, Murray, 166

Clements, George H., 207, 214

Cleveland, Diocese of, 218. *See also* Cleveland, OH

Cleveland, OH: African American church in, 5; Cleveland Council no. 733 (Knights of Columbus), 212, 213. *See also* Cleveland, Diocese of

Clinton, TN, First Baptist Church, 217

Cody, John P.: and the Archdiocese of Chicago, 229; and the Archdiocese of New Orleans, 39, 52, 60, 62, 107, 157, 158, 193, 220, 281, 306n71

Cold War, 34, 73, 85, 93, 111, 117, 211

Coleman, Jean Winchester, 176

College of the Sacred Heart, Grand Coteau, LA: closure of, 352n11; desegregation of, 142, 209

Collegeville, MN, St. John's Abbey Seminary, 24

Collum, Danny Duncan, 336n78

Columbia, SC, Catholic schools in, 240

Columbus, GA, First Presbyterian Church (PCUS), 217

Commission for the Catholic Missions Among the Colored People and the Indians, 6, 237, 353n16

Commission on Human Rights (CHR), 26, 94, 186, 329n40, 332n59; decline of, 99; founding of, 94, 173; and Joseph H. Fichter, 97, 99, 174, 329n38, 331n53; leadership of, 94, 95, 173, 174; membership of, 94, 95, 99, 101, 173, 329n39, 330n44, 367n19; opposition to, 99; program of, 97–99, 177

Committee for Catholic Truth, A, 73

Commonweal, 171

Confraternity of Christian Doctrine, 141, 352n9

Congregation of the Holy Ghost. *See* Holy Ghost Fathers

Congress of Industrial Organizations, 93, 172

Congress of Racial Equality (CORE), 101–2, 103, 104, 106, 185, 190, 219, 220, 221, 225

Connally, John, 103

Connolly, Joseph, 221

Connor, Eugene "Bull," 124

Cooper, Harold L., 63

Coordinating Committee of Greater New Orleans, 185

Corpus Christi, Diocese of, 278, 280, 281, 282, 286; Catholic school desegregation in, 144

Corrigan, Daniel, 221

Costello, M. J., 32

Council of Churches of Greater Washington, 130

Craighead, Robert, 184

Crandell, A. William, 33

Crear, John, 238

Creoles of color, 4, 6, 171–72, 178, 262, 268

Criterion, 222–23

Croghan, Leo, 47, 48

Cronin, John F., 33–35, 38, 40, 106, 226, 305n57

Cross, Richard D., 45

Crowell, John M., 345n60

Cuddy, John, 154, 155

Cullen, Philip, 34

Dade County (Metro) Community Relations Board, 104

Dailey, Jane, 323n47

Daily Advertiser (Lafayette, LA), 114
Dallas, TX: Holy Cross Church, 261; Jesuit High School, 149; Southern Methodist University, 208, 218; St. Paul Hospital, 159
Dallas-Fort Worth, Diocese of, 278, 280, 282; Catholic church desegregation in, 358n71; Catholic school desegregation in, 144, 358n71. *See also* Dallas, TX; *Texas Catholic*
Daniell, Joseph R., 59
Daniels, Jonathan, 227
Danville, VA, and Poor People's March on Washington, 108
Daphne, AL, Shrine of the Holy Cross, 199
Dauphin, Vernon, 24
David, Mary (Virginia Young), 38
Davidson College, Davidson, NC, desegregation of, 218
Davis, Mrs. Albert, 109
Davis, Cyprian, 5, 197, 258
Davis, Jimmie, 120
Davis, Joseph M., 249, 253, 255, 259
De La Salle Christian Brothers, 160, 182
Deacons, 196, 233, 242, 247, 249, 250, 251, 254, 256, 257, 260, 262, 263, 266, 374n101, 401n96
Dearden, John F., 195, 197, 219, 222, 230
Deason, M. C., 130
DeBlieux, J. D., 57, 105
Decline in vocations, 21, 40, 52, 165–66, 194, 195, 234, 237, 250, 252, 397n46
Dees, James P., 216
DeFalco, Lawrence M., 281, 348n84
Defender of States' Rights, 216
Dejoie, C. C., Jr., 27
Dell'Acqua, Angelo, 100
Delta Ministry, 229
DeMattie, Ella, 72
Detroit, Archdiocese of: Archbishop's Commission on Human Relations, 219; Archdiocesan Opportunity Program, 230; Project Commitment, 230; Project Equality, 106, 227; and public school desegregation in, 232; St. Martin De Porres High School, 234–35. *See also* Dearden John F.; Detroit, MI; *Michigan Catholic*; Mooney, Edward F.

Detroit, MI, 384n68; Catholic church segregation in, 211; public school desegregation in, 232; St. Martin De Porres High School, 234–35; white Catholic opposition to desegregation in, 211, 274. *See also* Detroit, Archdiocese of; Dearden, John F.
Diaconate. *See* Deacons
Dickinson, TX, Father Roach Council no. 3217 (Knights of Columbus), 241
Diesi, Salvador L., 200
Dirksen, Everett M., 128
Disciples of Christ, 201, 232; African American churches in, 204; African American membership size, 202; desegregation within, 216; endorses *Brown v. Board of Education* (1954), 210; National Christian Missionary Convention, 204; opposes racial discrimination, 214; opposes segregation, 205; overall membership size, 202; polity, 202; segregation within, 204, 216, 228; and urban problems, 231
Divine Word Missionaries. *See* Society of the Divine Word (S.V.D.)
Divini Redemptoris (1937), 68
Dolan, Hugh A., 84
Dominican College, New Orleans, 97, 331n53
Dominican Nuns of Perpetual Rosary and Adoration, 31, 141
Dominican Sisters, 145, 146
Dominick, Mrs. Frank, 123
Donnelly, Joseph F., 199
Donnelly, Patrick, 98
Donovan, John D., 244, 245
Dorgan, Howard, 216
Dorsey, John Henry, 7, 10
Drexel, Katherine, 8, 11
Driver, Z. Z., 217
Drolet, Jerome A., 121, 217, 343n39
Duke University, NC, desegregation of, 218
Dunn, Bernard, 24
Dunn, William H., 242
Durick, Joseph A., 59, 103, 127, 281, 306n71, 345n61, 348n84, 348n85; and civil rights protests in Birmingham, 123–24, 343n46; participates in Memphis civil rights

marches, 108; and Project Equality, 57–58, 106; and St. Joseph Hospital strike, 61
Dyer, Joseph, 249

East Baton Rouge Parish, LA (county), 126, 161, 162, 163
Eastland, James O., 111
Ebo, Betty (Sr. Mary Antona), 191
Ecimovich, Frank, 60
"Economic Justice for All" (1986), 260–61
Edmundites. *See* Society of Saint Edmund (S.S.E.)
Edmunds, Margaret, 385n72
Egan, Joe, 255
Ehrensing, Rudolph, 63, 64
Eisenhower, Dwight D., 33, 117; administration of, 121
Elizabeth City, NC, St. Catherine's Church, 189, 191
Elliott, John A., 183
Enette, Rawlin B., 141, 198
England, John, 3
English, Eddie L., 160
Epiphany Apostolic College, New Windsor, NY, 179
Erath, LA, Our Lady of Lourdes Church, 55–56, 67–68
Erickson, Donald A., 244, 245
Ernest, Jerome, 264
Escambia County Community Council, FL, 121
Everett, M. F., 97, 101, 112, 113; background of, 88, 326n21
Evers, Medgar, 125
Excommunication, 44, 47, 54, 145, 207; in Erath, LA, 55–56; in New Orleans, 56–57, 79

Fairclough, Adam, 172–73, 178, 340n7
Falconio, Diomede, 9
Farragher, Leo, 63
Faubus, Orval, 33, 117, 118
Fayette, MS, St. Anne's Church, 242
Fayetteville, NC, 150

Federal Council of Churches, 205. *See also* National Council of Churches
Federation of Colored Catholics (FCC), 10, 12–13
Feibelman, Julian B., 120
Ferriday, LA: St. Charles Church, 189
Fichter, Joseph H., 27, 28, 72, 78, 93, 94, 95, 97, 98, 99, 100, 120, 174, 301n32, 301n33, 329n38, 351n53
Figaro, Mark, 249
Finbarr, Mother Marie (Anne Marie Twohig), 165
Fiorenza, Joseph A., 88, 103, 281
Fisher, Carl A., 254
Flaherty, J. Louis, 112, 134, 143, 144
Fletcher, Albert L., 34, 62, 75, 108, 142, 151–52, 195, 239, 246, 281, 306n71, 341n25; and Catholic school desegregation, 33, 147, 213; Day of Prayer, 118; endorses Civil Rights Act of 1964, 129–30
Floersh, John A., 22
Florida State Advisory Committee to the United States Commission on Civil Rights, 104
Folcroft, PA, 224
Foley, Albert S., 96, 177, 331n49, 355n39, 368n35; background of, 90; and Birmingham civil rights protests, 124; chairs Alabama State Advisory Committee to the United States Commission on Civil Rights, 101, 124
Folse, Herman P., 67, 70, 74–75, 76
Foreman, Lloyd A., 121, 343n39
Forman, James, 232–33
Fort Myers, FL, St. Francis Xavier School, 157
Fort Smith, AR: Catholic Interracial Council of Fort Smith, 107–8; St. Anne's Academy, 152; St. Scholastica's Academy, 104, 142
Francis, Joseph A., 193, 254, 255, 257, 259, 399n80; background of, 170–71
Francis, Norman C., 94, 95, 121, 186, 190, 193
Franciscan Handmaids of the Most Pure Heart of Mary, 250, 295n34
Franciscan Sisters of Perpetual Adoration, 191
Frederic, A. J., Jr. 125

Freedom Rides, 122–23, 181, 219–20
Frey, Gerald L., 135, 249, 281
Friendship House, Shreveport, 62
Fund for the Republic of the Ford Foundation, 97, 98, 99, 333n59

Gadsden, AL, St. Martin de Porres Church, 261
Gaffney, William J., 213
Gaillot, Una M., 65–66, 67, 79, 121, 155, 319n2
Gallagher, Raymond J., 227
Galligan, Eymard P., 191, 237
Galveston, Diocese of, 277, 278, 281, 293; African American Catholic population size, 148, 169. *See also* Galveston-Houston, Diocese of
Galveston, TX: Catholic school desegregation in, 37, 53, 156–57; Galveston Council no. 787 (Knights of Columbus), 241; public school desegregation in, 37, 157, 159. *See also* Galveston, Diocese of; Galveston-Houston, Diocese of
Galveston County, TX, Catholic school desegregation in, 53, 156–57, 218. *See also* Galveston, Diocese of; Galveston-Houston, Diocese of; Galveston, TX
Galveston-Houston, Diocese of, 278, 280, 281, 283, 286; African American churches in, 171, 246; Catholic church desegregation in, 140, 209, 246; Catholic church segregation in, 140, 209; Catholic Council on Community Relations, 88, 104; Catholic hospital desegregation in, 159, 222; Catholic school desegregation in, 37, 53, 152, 156–57, 159, 218; Knights of Columbus, racial discrimination in, 241; ordains African American priest, 251; and Project Equality, 40, 53, 106, 165; and Selma protests, 103, 388n90; urges passage of civil rights bill, 38, 129. *See also* Dickinson, TX; Galveston, Diocese of; Galveston County, TX; Guillory, Curtis J.; Harris County, TX; Houston, TX; Houston Council on Human Relations; Morkovsky, John L.; Nold, Wendelin J.; *Texas Catholic Herald*

Gawrych, Frank, 71
Georgetown, SC, 251
Georgetown University, 5, 128, 223; desegregation of, 207
Georgia Bulletin, 105, 129, 132, 285. *See also* Atlanta, Archdiocese of
Georgia Council on Human Relations, 105
Georgia State Advisory Committee to the United States Commission on Civil Rights, 105
Gerety, Peter L. 199
Gerow, Richard O., 23, 24, 31–32, 94, 186, 219, 282, 306n71; and Catholic school desegregation, 162; caution of, 59, 61; condemns violence, 38, 125; and Meredith March, 107; and Mississippi Summer Project, 225
Gibbons, James, 10
Gibbons, Tom, 53
Gibson, Theodore R., 124
Gilbert, James D., 136
Glock, Charles Y., 46, 47, 48, 63, 311n11
Gollob, Timothy, 261
Goodman, Andrew, 190
Gorman, Thomas K., 35, 282, 348n84
Gossman, F. Joseph, 256–57, 282
Gouvellis, Soterios D., 343n46, 344n47
Grafman, Milton L., 344n46, 345n61
Grail, The, 225
Grand Coteau, LA: College of the Sacred Heart, closure of, 352n11; College of the Sacred Heart, desegregation of, 142, 209
Gray, Cassandra, 157
Gray Commission, 144
Greater Little Rock Interracial Ministerial Alliance, 217
Greater New Orleans Citizens' Council, 73, 79, 99. *See also* Citizens' Council of New Orleans; Citizens' Councils; South Louisiana Citizens' Council
Greco, Charles P., 22, 48, 49, 105, 150, 189, 282, 336n77, 348n84; and Catholic church segregation, 163; and Catholic hospital desegregation, 165; and Catholic school desegregation, 163; caution of, 61; and

Friendship House, Shreveport, 62; pastoral letter (August 1963), 47, 126; pastoral letter (June 1965), 163. *See also Greenhouse v. Greco*; *Ramparts*
Greenhouse v. Greco, 243
Greening, Bruce, 266–67
Greensboro, NC: Our Lady of the Miraculous Medal Church, 175; public school desegregation in, 341n20; St. Benedict Church, 84
Greenville, MS, Sacred Heart College, 11
Greenville, NC, 150
Greenville, SC: Catholic school desegregation in, 197–98, 240, 356n54: Our Lady of the Rosary School, 197; and Poor People's March on Washington, 108; St. Anthony's School, 197–98; St. Mary's School, 197
Greenwood, MS, 104
Gregory, Wilton D., 262, 400n80
Gregory XV, Pope, 68
Gregory XVI, Pope, 3
Gremillion, Joseph B., 50, 51, 62, 63, 85, 88
Grier, Dolores, 265
Griffin, John Howard, 189
Groppi, James, 225, 227, 230
Guardian, 75, 76, 117, 118, 179, 285, 286. *See also* Little Rock, Diocese of
Guillory, Curtis J., 264, 268
Gunn, John E., 12

Haak, Gladys, 241
Haas, Francis J., 92
Hadden, Thomas P., 24, 188–89, 256–57, 266
Hall, Harlan, 90–91
Hall, Janet, 90–91
Hall, Wilhelmina P., 250
Hallett, Paul H., 129
Hallinan, Paul J., 282, 306n71, 348n84, 348n85, 373n88; and Catholic church desegregation, 151; and Catholic hospital desegregation, 159; and Catholic school desegregation, 54, 60–61, 154–55, 158–59, 161, 181–82; and National Catholic Conference for Interracial Justice (NCCIJ), 102, 103; and National Conference on Religion and Race (NCRR), 220; and open housing, 134; and Selma protests, 62, 103, 132, 347n78, 347n80

Handmaids of Mary, 11, 295n34
Hannan, Philip M., 282, 348n84, 385n75
Hansen, Bill, 219
Harbutt, Charles, 59
Hardin, Paul, 344n46
Harlem, NY, 11, 227; Resurrection Church, 268
Harmon, Nolan B., 344n46, 345n61
Harris, Elbert F., 255–56
Harris, Vincent M., 39, 152, 157, 282
Harris County, TX, Catholic school desegregation in, 53, 156–57, 218
Hart, Luke E., 212, 223, 224
Harvey, Lois Warren, 265
Hatfield, Barbara Davis, 176
Hattiesburg, MS, Rosary Catholic Mission Hall, 63
Haynesville, AL, 227
Hays, Brooks, 117
Havey, Phil, 219
Hawkins, Edler G., 224
Head Start, 40
Health, Education and Welfare (HEW), Department of, 165, 166, 239, 244. *See also* Office of Civil Rights (OCR)
Healy, Alexander Sherwood, 5
Healy, Austin J., 221
Healy, James Augustine, 5, 7, 255
Healy, Patrick Francis, 5
Heazel, Francis J., 212
Hebert, Stanley P., 253
Hendersonville, NC: Our Lady of the Hills Camp, 149–50
Hickey, James A., 265
Hicks, Louise Day, 230
Highwood, NJ, St. Anthony's Mission House, 11
Hill, Samuel S., Jr., 48–49
Hilliard, Raymond, 385n75
Hines, John E., 206, 218, 225
Hinton, Frederick M., 259
Hodges, Joseph H., 348n84
Hoflich, James, 331n52
Hofstetter, Oscar B., Jr., 80
Holden, Anna, 220
Hollands, King, 176
Hollings, Ernest F., 154
Holy Ghost Fathers, 6, 9, 11, 140, 246

Honore, Thomas F., 373n90
Hot Springs, AR, St. Gabriel's Mission, 246
Houston, TX, 227; Catholic school desegregation, 37, 53, 152, 156–57, 218; Houston Council on Human Relations, 104, 242; Our Mother of Mercy Church, 171, 179; public school desegregation in, 37, 152, 157, 159; 227; St. Mary's Church, 152, 159; St. Mary's School, 152, 159; St. Nicholas Church, 171; St. Thomas Novena Church, 171; Texas Southern University, 152. *See also* Galveston-Houston, Diocese of
Houston Council on Human Relations, 104, 242
Howard, Clarence J., 174, 177, 367n21
Howze, Joseph L., 251, 255, 260, 262, 263, 282, 399n80; appointed auxiliary bishop of Natchez-Jackson, 248–49; appointed bishop of Biloxi, 255; ordination of, 24
Hubbard, Mrs. B., 180
Humphrey, Hubert, 223
Hunter, Charlayne, 182
Huntsville, AL: St. Joseph's Mission, 161; St. Joseph's School, 161
Hurley, Joseph P., 102, 129, 147, 151, 190, 271, 282
Hyland, Francis E., 60–61, 75, 119, 150, 154–55, 156–56, 181, 218, 282
Hyle, Michael, W., 385n75

Iakovos, Archbishop, 225
Illinois Club for Catholic Women, 220
Imani Temple, Washington, DC, 265, 266, 267
Incarnate Word College, San Antonio, desegregation of, 142, 209
Institute for Black Catholic Studies, Xavier University, New Orleans, LA, 258
Institute of Human Relations, Loyola University of the South, New Orleans, LA, 105, 334n67
Institute of Industrial Relations, Loyola University of the South, New Orleans, LA, 27, 101, 142, 334n67
Interracial Justice (1945), 29, 91–92
Inter-Religious Committee Against Poverty, 227

Interreligious Convocation on Civil Rights, 223
Ireland, John, 7, 9
Ireton, Peter L., 15, 32, 95, 96, 143, 144, 149, 232

Jack, Hulan E., 98, 99, 331n54
Jackson, Diocese of, 281, 282, 285; creation of, 279, 398n62; Office of Inter-Cultural Awareness, 261. *See also* Natchez-Jackson, Diocese of
Jackson, James R., 133
Jackson, MS: Belhaven College, desegregation of, 228; Christ the King Catholic School, 125; Congress of Racial Equality (CORE) protest in, 219; Freedom Rides in, 161; Meredith March in, 106, 107; Mississippi Council on Human Relations chapter, 105; public school desegregation in, 162; St. Richard Church, 84
Jacksonville, FL, Bishop Kenny High School, desegregation of, 157
Jadot, Jean, 253
James, Eileen B., 133
James, Irene, 234
Janssens, Francis, 8–9
Jeanmard, Jules B., 13, 23, 24, 50, 77, 282; and Erath, 55–56, 78; excommunications by, 56–57, 78; pastoral letter (November 1951), 32
Jesuit Bend, LA, 177; St. Cecilia's Chapel, 55
Jesuit High School, Dallas, TX, 149
Jesuit High School, New Orleans, LA, 158
Jet, 180
Jewish Community Council of Greater Washington, 131
Jews, 15, 26, 66, 67, 85, 103, 104, 119, 123, 201, 204, 217, 218, 224, 225, 234, 274, 297n50, 324n11, 344n46, 344n47, 387n85; American Jewish Congress, 222; attacks on southern synagogues, 203; compared to Catholics and Protestants in the South, 202–3, 274; and Gwynn Oak Amusement Park protest, 221; Jewish Community Council of Greater Washington, 131; and Little Rock public school desegregation crisis, 117–18; and March on Washington for Jobs and Freedom, 222; and Mississippi Summer

Project, 225; opinion polls of, 203, 226, 274; population size in South, 202; and Project Equality, 389n95; and Selma protests, 225, 274; Synagogue Council of America, 220, 221, 223, 226, 227; views on segregation of, 203
John, Joseph Alexander, 11
John XXIII, Pope, 35, 37, 132
John Paul II, Pope, 263
Johnson, Benjamin, 95
Johnson, Lester, 170
Johnson, Lyndon B., 105, 132, 133, 190, 226; administration of, 71
Johnson, Madeline E., 171
Johnson, Nessa, 245 249, 252, 256, 398n65
Johnson, Paul B., Jr., 105
Johnson, Viola, 70
Joliet, IL, 227
Jollivette, Cyrus, 258
Jones, Annabelle, 261
Jones, Claude S., 197
Jones, Girault M., 120, 210
Jones, Nettie M., 197
Jones v. Alfred H. Mayer Co. (1968), 135
Jordan, Carl, 181
Josephite Harvest, 195. *See also* Josephites
Josephites, xii, 8, 9–10, 11, 12, 22, 24, 31, 87, 104, 140, 171, 173, 183, 186, 195, 252; African American priests in, 7, 140–41, 179, 193, 243, 250, 254, 255–56, 265, 373n90; appoint Eugene A. Marino as Vicar General, 242; and civil rights movement, 185, 219, 242; conflicts within, 242–43; ordain African American deacons, 233; St. Joseph's Seminary, 242–43; welcome *Brown v. Board of Education* (1954), 32–33
Jubilee, 87
Junior Daughters, 10
Junior Knights, 10

Kammer, Michael P., 149
Kansas City, Diocese of, Catholic school desegregation in, 207
Kappe, T. W., 241
Karenga, Maulana, 256
Kelly, Eugene, 47, 48

Kelly, George A., 230
Kemp, Raymond, 267–68
Kennedy, John F., 37–38, 103, 125, 127, 161, 187, 221, 222, 345n61
Kenner, LA, Our Lady of Perpetual Help Church, 121, 217
Kennon, Robert F., 112
Kentucky, 339n90. *See also* Louisville, KY, Archdiocese of
Kieran, John F., 104
Kilgore, Thomas, Jr., 234
Kilpatrick, James Jackson, 122, 343n42
King, Martin Luther, Jr., 72, 103, 179, 193, 221, 225, 245, 263, 344n48; and Albany, GA, 220; and Birmingham, AL, 123–24; death of, 40, 108, 134, 230; and Meredith March, 106; and National Conference on Race and Religion (NCRR), 220; and Selma protests, 39, 132, 191; and St. Augustine, FL, 129
King, Martin Luther, Sr., 38
King, Paul, 184
King, Paul M., 141
Kinnard, Charles, 175–76
Klutke, Paul, 104
Knights of Columbus, 10, 194, 212–13; in Alabama, 123; annual convention (1964), 39, 84; blackball system of, 39, 212, 222, 223, 224; in Charleston, SC, 241; in Chicago, 222, 223; in Cleveland, OH, 212, 213; in Dayton, OH, 381n41; in Galveston, TX, 241; in Louisiana, 51, 242; and March on Washington for Jobs and Freedom, 73; in New York City, 212–13; reforms membership application rules, 39, 224, 241–42; in San Antonio, Archdiocese of, 29, 212; in St. Louis, 222; in Texas, 29, 212, 241, 242
Knights of Peter Claver (KPC), 12, 70, 178, 186–87, 189, 242, 261, 273, 397n50; convention (1948), 366n15; convention (1954), 175; convention (1955), 175; convention (1959), 180; convention (1961), 187; convention (1962), 186, 187–88; convention (1964), 190; convention (1965), 192; convention (1966), 194; founding of, 9–10; Gulf Coast Conference

(1963), 188; membership of, 172, 188, 369n43; and the National Association for the Advancement of Colored People (NAACP), 172–73, 174, 175, 186, 187. See also *Claverite*; Junior Daughters; Junior Knights; Ladies Auxiliary of Peter Claver
Knoxville, TN: Immaculate Conception School, 151; St. Mary's Memorial Hospital, 159
Koch, Frederick A., 92
Koehlinger, Amy L., xii
Krackenberger, Caroline, 132–33
Kronlage, Alfred J., 67, 78
Ku Klux Klan, 11, 30–31, 48, 59–60, 88, 90, 190, 202, 206, 214, 270
Kwanzaa, 256

Labbé, Dolores Egger, 80
Labbe, Emery, 67
Lacour, Barbara Babin, 242
Ladies Auxiliary of Peter Claver, 180, 190, 261, 397n50; convention (1954), 175; founding of, 10; membership of, 172; and the National Association for the Advancement of Colored People (NAACP), 175
LaFarge, John, 12, 13, 68, 222, 385n75
Lafayette, Diocese of, xii, 59, 68, 245, 279, 281, 282, 283, 285, 286, 330n46, 330n47; African American Catholic size, 13, 169; African American churches in, 13, 140, 246; African American priests in, 13, 24, 140, 173, 214, 249, 263; Annual Teachers' Institute (1955), 85; appoints Vicar for Black Catholics, 249; *Auzenne v. School Board of the Roman Catholic Diocese of Lafayette*, 199–200; Catholic church segregation in, 140, 167, 209; Catholic interracial council, 107; Catholic school desegregation in, 37, 154, 163, 166, 199–200, 227, 245, 275; and Civil Rights Act (1964), 38–39; and Erath, 55–56, 11; federal funds cut off to Catholic schools in, 166; federal funds restored to Catholic schools in, 166; and public school desegregation in, 167; voter registration in, 32, 173, 225. *See also* Belle Chasse, LA; College of the Sacred Heart, Grand Coteau, LA; Erath, LA; Frey, Gerald L.; Grail, The; Jeanmard, Jules B.; Lafayette, LA; Opelousas, LA; Schexnayder, Maurice; *Southwest Louisiana Register*
Lafayette, LA, 113; Grail, The, 225; Immaculate Heart of Mary Church, 13; Our Lady of Wisdom Catholic Center, 86
Laghi, Pio, 261
Lambert, Norman, 31
Lambert, Rollins, 196, 214
Landrieu, Maurice "Moon," 58, 121
Langan, Joseph, 101
LaSalle, Edward, 172
Laufer, Sr. Maria Theodosia, 174
Law, Bernard F., 91, 105, 261
Lawrence, Mrs. Robert T., 385n72
Laws, Clarence A., 58, 173, 174, 178, 186, 192
Laymen's Union, 215. *See also* Association of Methodist Ministers and Laymen
Leach, Francis O., 71
Leary, Timothy A., 238
Leaves, 68–69
LeDoux, Jerome, 192, 247, 268, 373n88
LeDoux, Louis V., 24
LeFebvre, Gerald M., 90
Legion of Mary, 25
Leman, Arthur, 71–72
Leo XIII, Pope, 29
Lessard, Raymond W., 264, 282
"Letter from a Birmingham Jail" (1963), 124
Lewis, Carlos, 32
Lewis, Gerald, 55
Lewis, John, 222
Lichtenberger, Arthur, 221
Lieberman, Morris, 221
Liner, Eugene R., 223
Lissner, Ignatius, 11
Little Rock, AR: Catholic Interracial Council of Little Rock, 62, 100, 104, 107–8, 109; Central Presbyterian Church (PCUS), 217; Greater Little Rock Interracial Ministerial Alliance, 217; Methodist conference in, 210; public school desegregation crisis in, 117–18,

341n37, 342n28; St. Bartholomew School, 118. *See also* North Little Rock, AR
Little Rock, Diocese of, 23, 154, 249, 279, 281, 282, 283, 285, 303n46, 330n47; African American churches in, 195, 246, 252, 263; African American schools in, 118, 195; Catholic Interracial Council of Fort Smith, 107–8; Catholic Interracial Council of Little Rock, 62, 100, 104, 107–8, 109; Catholic school desegregation in, 33, 142, 147, 152, 213, 239; and Little Rock public school desegregation crisis, 117–18, 341n25, 341n37; ordains first African American priest, 265. *See also* Boileau, David A.; Clancy, Walter B.; Fletcher, Albert R.; Fort Smith, AR; *Guardian*; Hot Springs, AR; Little Rock, AR; McDonald, Andrew J.; Morris, John B.; North Little Rock; O'Donnell, William W.; Paris, AR
Liturgy, ix, 245, 246–47, 248–49, 251, 252, 255, 256, 257, 259, 260, 261, 262, 265, 266, 267, 268, 273, 275, 396n33
Liuzzo, Viola, 226
Lloyd, Ann M., 133
Lombard, Rudolph, 103
Lombard, Thelma P., 250
Lone Star Register, 130, 285. *See also* Austin, Diocese of
Long, Betty Tecklenburg, 75
Lord, John Wesley, 225
Lorigan, Thomas, 160
Los Angeles, 29; African-American Catholic Congregation in, 267
L'Osservatore Romano, 20, 45, 55, 70, 127. *See also* Vatican
Louisiana Council on Human Relations (LCHR), 105
Louisiana State Advisory Committee to the United States Commission on Civil Rights, 101, 105
Louisville, KY, Archdiocese of, Catholic school desegregation in, 208. *See also* Kentucky
Loving v. Virginia (1967), 134
Loyola College, Baltimore, desegregation of, 207
Loyola University. *See* Loyola University of the South
Loyola University Chicago, 177, 220
Loyola University of the South, 46, 63, 67, 72, 85, 89, 93, 94, 97, 98, 99, 109, 114, 120, 174, 331n53; desegregation of, 27, 28, 95, 142, 148, 158; Institute of Human Relations, 105, 334n67; Institute of Industrial Relations, 27, 101, 142, 334n67
Lowndes County, AL, 226
Lucas, Lawrence E., 268
Lucey, Robert E., 68, 91–92, 95, 100, 103, 106, 187, 222, 227, 282, 320n13, 334n70, 348n84; background of, 29; condemns segregation, 29, 84, 87; condemns states' rights, 29; and desegregation, 29–30, 51, 142–43, 271, 348n85; endorses civil rights bill, 128–29; opposes massive resistance, 117, 216; and Selma protests, 132; view of civil rights organizations, 101–2
Lumas, Eva, 265
Lyke, James P., 282, 400n80
Lyman, Marian, 171
Lynch, George F., 34, 146

Machesky, Nathaniel, 104
Macon, GA, Mount de Sales High School, 160
Malcolm X, 245
Maloney, Harry J., 173
Malverne, NY, 230
Manning, J. L., 29–30, 143
Mansfield, TX, 116
Manucy, A. N., 71
March on Washington for Jobs and Freedom, 38, 71, 73, 102–3, 188, 222, 385n75
Marianists, 30, 142
Mariannhill Fathers, 68
Marietta, GA, St. Joseph School, 182
Marino, Eugene A., 251, 255, 282, 399n80; appointed archbishop of Atlanta, 264; appointed auxiliary bishop of Washington, 250; appointed Vicar General of the Society of St. Joseph of the Sacred Heart (Josephites), 242; elected secretary of the National Conference of Catholic Bishops

(NCCB), 260; resigns as archbishop of Atlanta, 268
Markoe, William M., 12, 13
Marksville, LA: Holy Ghost School, 243; Marksville Catholic School, 243; Presentation School, 243
Marrero, LA, St. Joseph the Worker Church, 180–81, 268
Marston, Kathleen B., 72
Martin, Ira, 234
Martin, Ora M. Lewis, 180
Mary, Sr. Paul, 304n54
Maryland, 3, 207–8, 230, 379n24; 1964 Democratic primary election in, 224, 387n85. *See also* Baltimore, MD
Mathieu, Urban E., 67, 73
Maximum Illud (1919), 11
May, John L., 135, 237, 238, 239, 249, 251, 265, 283
Mays, James L., 225
McAuliffe, Maurice J., 213
McCann, John, 174
McCarthy, John E., 88, 103, 242, 282
McCarthy, Mrs. Joseph, 221
McCarthy, Joseph R., 73
McCord, L. B., 216
McDevitt, John W., 224, 241–42
McDole, Robert, 219
McDonald, Andrew J., 126, 261
McDonogh, Gray Wray, 171, 268
McDonough, Thomas J., 60, 126, 154–55, 156, 160, 161, 181, 203, 282, 306n71
McGowan, Raymond, 15
McGreevy, John T., 211, 218, 220, 224, 230, 232
McGuire, Meredith B., 43, 50
McIntyre, Francis J., 35
McKnight, Albert J., 252
McLaughlin, Charles B., 238–39, 282
McLeaish, D. C., 151
McNally, Michael J., 151, 169
McNamara, T. James, 15, 16, 126
McNeil, Joseph, 181
McNeil, Robert, 217
Medicare Act (1965), 39, 165, 227
Memphis, TN: Bertrand High School, 145; Christian Brothers High School, 160, 182–83; St. Augustine School, 145, 176; St. Joseph Hospital, 61; St. Patrick Church, 107
Menard, Lota B., 55, 56
Meng, John J., 230
Meredith, James, 106–7
Meredith College, Raleigh, NC, desegregation of, 218
Meredith March, 106–7, 194
Mernagh, Deanne Setoon, 66, 67, 68, 69, 72, 73, 78
Mernagh, Patrick Warren, 66, 67, 68, 69
Meskill, Dick, 46, 129
Methodist Church, 4, 5, 201, 232, 344n46; African American membership size, 202; Black Methodists for Church Renewal, 231; Central Jurisdiction, 203–4, 208, 214, 216, 223–24, 228, 232; and Delta Ministry, 229; desegregation of Methodist colleges and universities, 218, 228, 382n53; Duke University, NC, desegregation of, 218; endorses *Brown v. Board of Education* (1954), 210; endorses civil rights bill, 223; endorses civil rights protests, 235; merger with Evangelical United Brethren Church, 390n113; North Central Jurisdiction, 224; Northeastern Jurisdiction, 224; opposes segregation, 205, 208, 214; opposes racial discrimination, 204, 205, 214; overall membership, 202; Perkins School of Theology at Southern Methodist University, desegregation of, 208; polity, 202; response of Methodist conferences and jurisdictions to *Brown v. Board of Education* (1954), 210; segregation within, 203, 208, 214, 216, 232; and Selma protests, 225; South Central Jurisdiction, 214, 228; Southeastern Jurisdiction, 210, 214, 228; support for segregation within, 210, 215. *See also* United Methodist Church
Meyer, Albert G., 218–19, 220
Miami, Archdiocese of, 135, 258, 277, 279, 280, 282, 286. *See also* Carroll, Coleman F.; Miami, Diocese of; *Voice*
Miami, Diocese of, 124, 183, 249, 277, 279, 280, 281; Catholic school desegregation in,

37, 151, 157; Diocesan Council on Human Relations, 104–5, 129. *See also* Carroll, Coleman F.; Dade County [Metro] Community Relations Board; *Voice*

Miami, FL, 37; Archbishop Curley High School, 151; Congress of Racial Equality (CORE) in, 104; Corpus Christi Church, 183; Dade County [Metro] Community Relations Board, 104; Holy Redeemer Church, 104–5, 183; Mercy Hospital, 151; National Association for the Advancement of Colored People (NAACP) in, 104, 124, 129; Notre Dame Academy, 151; Orchard Villa School, 151; public school desegregation in, 37, 135, 151; St. Rose of Lima, 258

Michigan Catholic, 211. *See also* Detroit, Archdiocese of

Mill Hill Fathers, 6, 7

Miller, Randall, M., 3–4

Milwaukee, Archdiocese of, 224–25. *See also* Groppi, James

Milwaukee, WI, 121; civil rights movement in, 227, 230

Minor, Wilson, 59

Mississippi Black Catholic Caucus, 245

Mississippi Council on Human Relations, 105

Mississippi Register, 91, 105, 285. *See also* Natchez-Jackson, Diocese of

Mississippi Religious Leadership Conference, 136

Mississippi Summer Project, 225

Mit brennender Sorge (1937), 14

Mitchell, George S., 96

Mitchell, John, 180

Mitchell, Noella, 184

Mitchell, Reavis L., 146

Mobile, AL: desegregates lunch counters, 101; McGill Institute, 141; Spring Hill College, 28, 33, 60, 90, 112, 141, 148, 176–77, 302n34, 355n39

Mobile, Diocese of, 23, 249, 254, 277, 279, 280, 283, 285; African American Catholic population of, 169; and busing in Mobile, 239, 393n9; and public school desegregation, 135; and Selma, 237–38. *See also Catholic Week*; May, John L.; Mobile-Birmingham, Diocese of

Mobile Register, 72

Mobile-Birmingham, Diocese of, 34, 68, 278, 279, 283, 285, 330n47; bars priests from demonstrating, 62; Catholic church segregation in, 160; Catholic school desegregation in, 57, 1154, 60, 161–62, 186, 190; and fair employment, 165; Knights of Columbus in, 123; and National Catholic Conference for Interracial Justice (NCCIJ), 102, 186; and public school desegregation in, 160. *See also* Anniston, AL; Birmingham, AL; *Catholic Week*; Daphne, AL; Huntsville, AL; Mobile, Diocese of; Selma, AL; Mon Louis Island, AL; Montgomery, AL; Orrville, AL; Society of Saint Edmund (S.S.E.); Toolen, Thomas J.

Moeslein, Francis R., 46

Mon Louis Island, AL, Mon Luis Mission, 171

Mon Luis Mission, Mon Louis Island, AL, 171

Monroe, LA, St. Francis Hospital, 165

Montgomery, AL: Church of the Ascension, 217; St. John the Baptist Church, 191; St. Jude Church, 191

Mooney, Edward F., 34, 35, 305n57

Moore, Andrew S., xii, 59

Moore, Emerson J., 400n80

Moore, Vernon P., 373n90

Moran, Richard B., 130

Morial, Ernest N., 190

Morin, Paul, 237–38

Morkovsky, John L., 246, 251, 283, 348n84, 348n85; appointed coadjutor bishop of Galveston-Houston, 159; desegregates Catholic hospitals, 159; desegregates Catholic schools, 159; and discrimination in the Knights of Columbus, 241; and Project Equality 53; and Selma protests, 103; supports civil rights bill, 129

Morris, John B., 22–23, 283

Morrisroe, Richard F., 227

Morrissey, William J., 104, 242, 336n78

Mosley, Thomas A., Sr., 198

Motley, Fannie, 177

Mound Bayou, MS, 24

Mulloy, William T., 51, 313n25
Mundelein, George W., 13
Murphy, Edward, 16
Murphy, T. Austin, 385n75
Murray, George M., 344n46, 345n61
Murray, Peter C., 203, 224
Murtagh, Lawrence, 103
Myrtle Grove, LA, 55
Mystical Body of Christ, x, 10, 16, 19, 20, 24, 25, 26, 28, 29, 30, 41, 50, 69, 83–84, 94, 142, 152, 156, 187, 194, 205, 269, 270

Nash, Diane, 220
Nashville, Diocese of, 279, 281, 283, 286, 303n46, 385n72; African American Catholic churches in, 144, 145, 167, 184; African American Catholic population size, 144; African American priest in, 251; Catholic hospital desegregation in, 159, 222; Catholic interracial council, 107; Catholic school desegregation in Knoxville, 151; Catholic school desegregation in Memphis, 160, 182–83; Catholic school desegregation in Nashville, 33, 53, 59, 144–46, 175–76, 213, 271; Memphis deanery of, 53, 144; Nashville deanery of, 53, 144; overall Catholic population size, 144; and Project Equality, 40, 57–58, 106, 165. *See also* Adrian, William L.; Durick, Joseph A.; Knoxillle, TN; Memphis, TN; Nashville, TN; Niedergeses, James D.
Nashville, TN, 31; Cathedral High School, 145–46, 175, 176, 184, 271; Catholics and civil rights movement in, 184; Father Ryan High School, 145–46, 175, 176; Holy Family Church, 144; Holy Family School, 144; Immaculate Mother Academy, 31, 144, 175–76; Nashville Interscholastic Athletic Association, 176; Overbrook School, 145; St. Cecilia Academy, 145; St. Thomas Hospital, 159; St. Vincent de Paul Church, 145, 184–85, 251
Nashville Interscholastic Athletic Association, 176
Natchez, MS, Holy Family Church, 104, 336n78

Natchez, Diocese of. *See* Mound Bayou, MS; Natchez-Jackson, Diocese of
Natchez-Jackson, Diocese of, 23, 59, 154, 189–90, 278, 279, 281, 282, 285, 398n62; African American Catholic membership size, 248; Catholic church desegregation in, 31–32, 94, 195; Catholic school desegregation in, 125, 136, 162, 239, 361n91; and housing, 233; Joseph L. Howze installed as auxiliary bishop, 248–49; and Meredith March, 107; and Mississippi Religious Leadership Conference, 136; ordains first African American diocesan priest, 24, 249; overall Catholic membership size, 248; and public school desegregation in, 136; segregation within, 189–90; Systematic Training and Redevelopment, Inc., 229. *See also* Biloxi, MS; Brunini, Joseph B.; Canton, MS; Clarksdale, MS; Fayette, MS; Gerow, Richard O.; Hattiesburg, MS; Howze, Joseph L.; Law, Bernard F.; Mississippi Black Catholic Caucus; *Mississippi Register*; Natchez, MS; Waveland, MS
Natchitoches, LA, 243
Natchitoches Parish, LA (county), 163. *See also* Natchitoches, LA
National Association of Black Catholic Administrators, 261
National Association for the Advancement of Colored People (NAACP); antilynching campaign of, 13; in Birmingham, AL, 127; and Catholics, 12, 13, 20, 72, 94, 101–2, 104, 116, 129, 136, 165, 172–73, 175, 178, 181, 185, 186, 187, 189, 190, 192, 220, 227, 230, 242, 248, 273, 336n78, 367n20; in Chicago, 220; in Florida, 165; founding of, 12–13; in Louisiana, 94, 101, 102, 104, 172, 173, 178, 185, 187, 190, 367n20; in Memphis, 182, 183; in Miami, 104, 124, 129; in Milwaukee, 227, 230; in Mississippi, 104, 125, 136, 242, 336n78; in Natchez, MS, 104, 242, 336n78; in New Bern, NC, 189; in New Orleans, 101, 172, 178, 183, 190, 367n20; in North Carolina, 165, 189; in Richmond, VA, 185; in Savannah, GA, 181; in St. Augustine, FL, 190; in Texas, 116, 341n21

National Black Catholic Clergy Caucus, 248, 253, 255, 259, 261, 266, 267, 397n50. *See also* Black Catholic Clergy Caucus

National Black Catholic Congress: National Black Pastoral Plan, 261–62, 26; in 1987, 261–62, 264, 400n88, 400n89; in the nineteenth century, 7–8, 12

National Black Catholic Seminarians Association, 197

National Black Economic Development Conference (BEDC), 233

National Black Lay Catholic Caucus, 197, 233, 242, 245, 248, 259, 397n50; Southeastern Lay Conference of, 259

National Black Sisters' Conference (NBSC), 197, 248, 259, 261, 397n50

National Catholic Conference for Interracial Justice (NCCIJ), 159, 165, 186, 188, 218, 270, 273; budgetary problems of, 108; consultation in Jackson, MS, 53; criticism of, 255; decline of, 253, 258, 259, 264; Department of Educational Services, 230; establishes Southern Field Service, 37, 100; founding of, 37, 100, 333n64; and Freedom Rides, 219; and *Loving v. Virginia* (1967), 134; and March on Washington for Jobs and Freedom, 38, 102, 222, 385n75; and Meredith March, 106–7; and open housing, 134; and Project Cabrini, 230; and Project Equality, 40, 106, 227, 258; and Project SAIL, 230; Religion and Race in the South Conference, 103; and Selma protests, 103, 226; and sit-ins, 100, 219; Social Change and Christian Response Conference, 103. *See also* Southern Field Service of the National Catholic Conference for Interracial Justice (NCCIJ)

National Catholic Interracial Federation, 13

National Catholic Reporter, 258, 259, 373n86

National Catholic War Council, 10

National Catholic Welfare Conference (NCWC), 38, 223, 227, 231, 305n57, 309n84, 356n51; Administrative Board, 15, 33–34, 35, 36, 46, 215, 222, 305n64; Social Action Department, 15, 33, 100, 106, 220, 221, 226

National Center for Urban Ethnic Affairs, 235

National Citizens Committee for Community Relations, 105

National Committee of Black Churchmen, 233

National Conference of Catholic Bishops (NCCB), 40–41, 195, 197, 199, 231, 235, 254, 260, 265, 309n84, 374n101; opens Secretariat for Black Catholics, 264

National Conference on Religion and Race (NCRR), 220, 221, 384n68

National Council of Catholic Laity, 250

National Council of Catholic Women (NCCW), 221, 385n72; African American office holders, 250; Southwest Regional Conference of, 84

National Council of Churches (NCC), 217, 220, 221, 222, 223, 225, 226, 227, 233; Delta Ministry, 229. *See also* Federal Council of Churches

National Office for Black Catholics (NOBC), 199, 232, 233, 242, 246, 247, 248, 249, 254, 255, 397n50, 400n88; conference (1980), 258–59

"National Race Crisis" (1968), 40–41, 231

National Urban League, 73; in New Orleans, 99, 173

Neary, Timothy B., 207

Negro Betterment Council (NBC), New Orleans, 185

Nelson, John P. "Jack," 101, 105, 120; influences upon, 89, 327n23; and March on Washington for Jobs and Freedom, 102, 385n75

Neshoba County, MS, 190

New Bern, NC, St. Joseph Church, 189

New Braunfels, TX, 30

New Mexico, 339n90

New Orleans, Archdiocese of, 6, 14, 22, 30, 52, 87, 94, 277, 278, 281, 282, 283, 285, 331n48, 331n52; African American membership size, 169; African American priests in, 24, 140, 214, 247, 249; Archdiocesan Union of Holy Name Societies, 28, 174, 175; Catholic church segregation in, 8, 12, 26, 27, 28, 90, 139, 158, 164, 167, 180, 208, 209, 301n32, 26;

Catholic Council on Human Relations (CCHR), 100–101, 107, 185–86; Catholic school desegregation in, 33, 36–37, 53–54, 56, 57, 58–59, 60, 97, 120, 148–49, 150, 152–54, 156, 157–58, 171–72, 177, 178, 218, 270, 271, 359n74; Catholic Schools Cooperative Club, desegregation of, 39; and Civil Rights Act (1964), 38–39; and civil rights movement, 185, 190; clergy opinion within, 61, 63; desegregates Archdiocesan Union of Holy Name Societies, 28; desegregates seminaries, 24; forbids priest from demonstrating, 62; Holy Name parade (1949), 26–27, 174, 301n31; installs Harold R. Perry as auxiliary bishop, 171, 193; Jesuit Bend, 55, 177; Notre Dame Seminary, 24, 59, 90, 141, 208, 252; and public school desegregation, 112–13, 120–21; response to *Brown v. Board of Education* (1954), 32, 112; Synod of the Archdiocese of New Orleans (1949), 26, 139, 180, 208; Synod of the Archdiocese of New Orleans (1950), 139, 208

New Orleans, LA, xii, 3, 4, 6, 58, 65, 66, 67, 79, 87, 89, 90, 170, 178, 321n18, 331n52, 384n68; African-American Catholic Congregation in, 267; Association of Catholic Laymen, 56, 57, 66, 69, 79, 215, 315n45; Catholic church segregation in, 8, 10, 12, 27, 28, 301n32; Catholic Council on Human Relations (CCHR), 100–101, 107, 185–86; Citizens Committee of Greater New Orleans, 190; Citizens' Council of New Orleans, 56; Coordinating Committee of Greater New Orleans, 185; Cor Jesu High School, 331n53; Dominican College, 97, 331n53; Greater New Orleans Citizens' Council, 73, 79, 99; Holy Name parade (1949), 26–27, 174, 301n31; Jesuit High School, 158; National Association for the Advancement of Colored People (NAACP) in, 101, 172, 178, 183, 190, 367n20; National Urban League in, 99, 173; Negro Betterment Council (NBC), 185; Parents and Friends of Catholic Children, 77, 79; public school desegregation, 36–37, 120–21, 152, 156, 182, 207, 217; Save Our Nation, Inc., 65, 319n2; Save Our Schools (SOS), 119–20, 121; South Louisiana Citizens' Council, 56, 73, 77, 79, 343n39; St. Augustine Church, 268; St. Augustine High School, 140–41, 179, 185, 219; St. Francis de Sales Church, 247; St. James Major Church, 58, 164; St. Joseph Academy, 331n53; St. Katherine Church, 8; St. Louis Cathedral, 24, 94; St. Mary's Dominican College, 331n53; St. Peter Claver Church, 104, 185; St. Peter Claver School, 185; St. Raphael Church, 94; St. Theresa (The Little Flower) of the Child Jesus Church, 193; visit of Pope John Paul II to, 263. *See also* Commission on Human Rights (CHR); Cody, John P.; Gaillot, Una M.; Laws, Clarence A.; Loyola University of the South; Nelson, John P. "Jack"; New Orleans, Archdiocese of; Fichter, Joseph H.; Rummel, Joseph F.; Tureaud, A. P.; Twomey, Louis J.; Xavier University

New Orleans Province of the Society of Jesus, 27–28, 33, 95, 149, 150, 302n34

New Windsor, NY: Epiphany Apostolic College, 179

New York, Archdiocese of, 207, 222, 230, 233, 262; and Selma protests, 388n90. *See also* Harlem, NY; O'Connor, John; Spellman, Francis

New York City, NY, 212–13, 215, 219, 384n68. *See also* Brooklyn, NY; Catholic Interracial Council of New York; Harlem, NY

New York Times, 162, 172, 199, 342n27

Newark, Archdiocese of, 11, 235, 254

Newark, NJ, St. Charles Borromeo School, 235. *See also* Newark, Archdiocese of

Newport News, VA: St. Alphonsus Church, 167; St. Vincent de Paul Church, 167

Newton Grove, NC, 54–55, 72, 78, 140, 146, 175

Nicholas, U. Michael, 373n90

Niedergeses, James D., 251, 283

Nold, Wendelin J., 53, 129, 140, 156–57, 159, 218, 222, 283

Norfolk, VA, 108, 143–44, 251, 266; African-American Catholic Congregation in,

267; Norfolk Catholic High School, 149; St. Joseph School, 144; St. Mary of the Immaculate Conception Church, 167; St. Mary's Academy, 266

North Carolina Catholic, 46, 92, 95, 100, 122, 285. *See also* Raleigh, Diocese of

North Carolina Catholic Laymen's Association, 25

North Carolina Council on Religion and Race, 130

North Little Rock, AR, St. Augustine Church, 263. *See also* Little Rock, AR

Northern Baptist Convention, 201; African American churches in, 204; African American membership size, 202; condemns segregation, 205; overall membership size, 202; renamed the American Baptist Convention, 210; welcomes Harry S. Truman's civil rights program, 206. *See also* American Baptist Convention

Norvel, William L., 373n90

Notre Dame Seminary, New Orleans, LA, 24, 59, 90, 141, 208, 252

Nuns, x, xii, 3, 4, 8, 9, 11, 12, 14, 23, 27, 31, 33, 44, 51, 61, 83, 86, 87, 90, 103, 128, 136, 141, 142, 145, 146, 160, 170, 174, 191, 230, 232, 244, 246, 249, 250, 251, 252, 254, 255, 256, 258, 261, 263, 265, 272–73, 295n34, 301n33, 365n6, 397n46; civil rights activity of, 38, 39, 62, 71, 91, 104, 107, 108, 131, 132, 133, 220, 226, 227, 229; decline in vocations, 165–66, 195, 237, 250, 397n46; slaveholding by, 3

Oakland, CA, 384n68
Ober, James M., 134
Oblate Sisters of Providence, 3, 14, 250
O'Boyle, Patrick A., 34, 35, 207, 214–15, 222, 223, 226, 248, 379n24; and March on Washington for Jobs and Freedom, 38, 385n75
Ochs, Stephen J., xii, 242–43
O'Connell, James E., 341n25
O'Connell, Vincent J., 90, 93, 94
O'Conner, Frank J., 70
O'Connor, John, 260
O'Connor, John J., 11
Octogesima Adveniens (1971), 253

O'Dea, George F., 219
Odenthal, H. G., 68
O'Donnell, William W., 75–76, 118, 179
Office of Civil Rights (OCR), 239–40, 241
Office of Economic Opportunity (OEO) 229, 230
Ogden, David, 217
Ogden, Dunbar H., 217
O'Hara, Gerald P., 15, 22, 95, 283
Oklahoma, 339n90. *See also* Oklahoma City and Tulsa, Diocese of
Oklahoma City and Tulsa, Diocese of, 213, 225; and Selma protests, 388n90. *See also* Oklahoma
Oliver, James R., 105
"On Racial Harmony" (1963), 38, 221–22, 270
Opelousas, LA: Academy of the Immaculate Conception (AIC), 199, 200; Belmont Academy, 200; Holy Ghost Church, 261; Holy Ghost School, 199, 200; NAACP in, 102; Opelousas Catholic High School, 200
Opinion polls and surveys, 19, 50, 81, 176, 198, 203, 209, 211, 223, 226, 233, 250–51
Orangeburg, SC, 251
Oratorian Fathers, 33, 148, 213
Oregon-Washington, Baptist State Convention of, elects African American office holder, 234
Organization of Catholic Parents, 54, 155
Organizations Assisting Schools in September (OASIS), 119
O'Rourke, Matthew J., 242
Orrville, AL, Chapel of the Immaculate Conception, 160
Ortemond, Lula B., 55
Osborn, Aubrey, 24
Osborne, William A., xi–xii, 49, 51, 52, 63
O'Sullivan, Timothy, 54
Ouellet, Maurice F., 62, 192, 247, 373n86
Our Lady of the Lake College, San Antonio, TX, desegregation of, 142, 209

Pacem in Terris (1963), 20, 37, 38, 132
Parents and Friends of Catholic Children, 77, 79
Paris, AR, 147

Passionist Fathers, 140
Patterson, Bernardin J., 87
Paul VI, Pope, 133, 192, 253, 375n101
Pensacola, FL, 37, 121, 160, 169, 186
Percy, Walker, 89
Perez, Leander, 79, 113, 121, 158, 174
Perez, Lino, Jr., 241
Perkins School of Theology, Southern Methodist University, Dallas, TX, desegregation of, 208
Perko, F. Michael, 397n46
Perry, Eugene B., 188
Perry, Harold R., 48, 57, 102, 171, 186, 188, 192, 193–94, 196, 199, 233, 248, 251, 260, 268, 373n88, 385n75, 399n80
Pettigrew, Thomas F., 342n27
Philadelphia, Archdiocese of, 204, 207, 214
Philadelphia, PA, 213; African-American Catholic Congregation in, 267. *See also* Philadelphia, Archdiocese of
Pierre, Carroll, 180
Pittsburgh, Diocese of, and Selma protests, 388n90. *See also* Pittsburgh, PA
Pittsburgh, PA, 5, 384n68. *See also* Pittsburgh, Diocese of
Pius X, Pope, 9
Pius XI, Pope, 11, 14, 16, 29, 68
Pius XII, Pope, 14, 16, 31, 35, 36, 46, 69, 94, 187
Plaisance, Donald J., 77
Plaquemines Parish, LA (county), 79, 113, 158, 174. *See also* Buras, LA
Plauche, Charles J., 22, 27, 101, 112, 190
Poché, Justin D., 172
Ponquinette, Julia, 177
Poor People's Campaign. *See* Poor People's March on Washington
Poor People's March on Washington, 108
Pope on Segregation, The (1955), 66
Portland in Oregon, Archdiocese of, 226
Powell, Elmer S., 100, 198
Presbyterian Church in the United States (PCUS), 201, 205; abolishes segregated presbyteries, 232; African American churches, 206, 208, 228; African American membership size, 202; Belhaven College, desegregation of, 228; Black Presbyterian Leadership Conference, 231; calls for desegregation of denominational institutions, 221, 223; college desegregation of, 218, 228; condemns the Ku Klux Klan, 206, 214; condemns segregation, 209; criticizes direct action, 225; Davidson College, desegregation of, 218; Department of Christian Relations, 206; endorses *Brown v. Board of Education* (1954), 209; endorses civil disobedience, 225–26, 228; endorses open housing, 231; evangelism among African Americans, 206; opposes racial discrimination, 206, 214; overall membership size, 202; Permanent Committee on Social and Moral Welfare, 206; polity, 202; response of synods to *Brown v. Board of Education* (1954) and desegregation, 210; segregation within, 204, 208; and Selma protests, 225; seminary desegregation, 208; Snedecor Memorial Synod, 204, 208; Snedecor Region, 208; and SCLC, 231; Southwest Georgia Presbytery, 217; Stillman College, 206; supports civil rights, 206; survey of church desegregation in, 223; Union Theological Seminary, 208. *See also* Columbus, GA; Little Rock, AR; Presbyterian Laymen for Sound Doctrine and Responsible Leadership
Presbyterian Church in the United States of America (PCUSA), 201, 208; African American membership size, 202; endorses *Brown v. Board of Education* (1954), 210; merger with the United Presbyterian Church of North America, 376n2; opposes racial discrimination, 214; opposes segregation, 205; orders desegregation of synods and presbyteries, 216; overall membership size, 202; polity, 202; segregation within, 204, 216, 228. *See also* United Presbyterian Church in the United States of America
Presbyterian Laymen for Sound Doctrine and Responsible Leadership, 215
President's Committee on Equal Employment Opportunity, 106

Prince Hall Masons, 173
Project Cabrini, 230
Project Equality, 40, 53, 57–58, 106, 165, 227, 229, 231, 258, 388n95
Protestant Episcopal Church, 201, 221, 311n11; African American membership size, 202; and Black Manifesto, 232–33; condemns racial discrimination, 208; condemns segregation, 205, 210; and Delta Ministry, 229; desegregation within, 206, 208–9; elects African American diocesan bishop, 234; endorses *Brown v. Board of Education* (1954), 210; General Convention Special Program (GCSP), 229, 233; and National Committee of Black Churchmen, 233; overall membership size, 202; polity, 202, 217; response of diocesan leaders to *Brown v. Board of Education* (1954), 210; School of Theology at the University of the South, desegregation of 208–9; segregation within, 204, 206, 216; and Selma protests, 225; seminary desegregation, 208–209; support for segregation within, 208, 215; supports civil rights struggle, 225; Union of Black Clergy and Laymen, 232; Virginia Theological Seminary, desegregation of, 208. *See also* Allin, John M.; Burgess, John M.; Carpenter, C. C. J.; Corrigan, Daniel; Lichtenberger, Arthur; Montgomery, AL; Savannah, GA; Statesville, NC
Providence, RI, 227
Province of New Orleans, 154, 193
Pung, Robert E., 32
Purcell, Clare, 210
Putnam, Joseph, 247

Quadragesimo Anno (1931), 29
Quinn, John F., 186, 187

Raboteau, Albert J., 246, 247
"Race Relations and Poverty" (1966), 40
Race Riddles, 29
"Racial Discrimination and the Christian Conscience" (1958), 35–36, 64, 70, 154, 215, 270

Rainach, William M., 113
Raleigh, Diocese of, 34, 149–50, 252, 278, 280, 282, 283, 285, 330n46, 385n72; African American Catholic opinion in, 175, 197–98, 256; African American liturgy, lack of, 257; African American priests in, 24, 140, 141, 214, 256–57; Catholic church desegregation in, 25–26, 54–55, 139–40, 159, 175, 209, 248; Catholic Daughters of America in, 39; Catholic interracial councils in, 95, 175; Catholic school desegregation in, 33, 146, 213; desegregation of Chancery personnel, 150; Legion of Mary, 25; Newton Grove, 54–55, 72, 78, 140, 146, 175; North Carolina Catholic Laymen's Association, 25; office for black Catholics, 258. *See also* Belmont, NC; Charlotte, NC; Elizabeth City, NC; Fayetteville, NC; Gossman, F. Joseph; Greensboro, NC; Greenville, NC; Hadden, Thomas P.; Hendersonville, NC; Howze, Joseph L.; New Bern, NC; *North Carolina Catholic*; Raleigh; Walsh, Emmet M.; Waters, Vincent S.
Raleigh, NC: Cathedral Latin Catholic High School, desegregation of, 146; Meredith College, desegregation of, 218
Ramage, Edward V., 344n46, 345n60
Ramparts, 158, 189
Rapides Parish, LA (county), 163
Ray, Sam Hill, Jr., 72
Reddix, John I., 187
Reed, Victor J., 219, 336n77, 348n84
Reedy, John, 54
Reh, Francis F., 53, 127, 161, 283, 306n71
Reicher, Louis J., 135, 151, 283, 348n84
Reimers, David M., 216
Religious of the Sacred Heart, 142
Rerum Ecclesiae (1926), 11
Rerum Novarum (1891), 29
Resch, Peter, 142
Ribn, Roy, 128
Ricard, John H., 400n80
Ricau, Jackson G., 66–67, 69, 70, 77, 79
Rice, Doris B., 175
Richard, Mrs., 74
Richardson, Martha, 197

Richmond, Diocese of, 277, 280, 281, 282, 283, 285, 330n46, 385n72, 399n65; African American Catholic churches in, 167, 183, 185; African American Catholics, differences among, 245, 252; African American deacon in, 249, 396n44; Black Catholic Eucharist Celebration, 256; Catholic high school desegregation in, 32, 96, 143–44, 149, 209; Catholic interracial councils in, 95, 102–3, 107, 128, 188; and civil rights bill, 38; and civil rights movement, 103, 108, 185; Diocesan Council of Catholic Men, 135; Diocesan Council of Catholic Women, 115, 134; Diocesan Holy Name Union, 141; "Ethnicity and Race" hearings, 256; and fair housing, 130–31, 134, 135; office for black Catholics, 258; ordains first African American priest, 251, 396n44, 398n65; Richmond Black Lay Catholic Caucus, 249; Social Ministry Commission, 253–54. *See also Catholic Virginian*; Charlottesville, VA; Danville, VA; Flaherty, J. Louis; Ireton, Peter L.; Newport News, VA; Norfolk, VA; Richmond, VA; Roanoke, VA; Russell, John J.; Sullivan, Walter F.

Richmond, VA, 15, 32, 95, 96, 102, 107, 108, 122, 128, 130, 143, 144, 188, 208, 245, 249, 251, 252; African-American Catholic Congregation in, 267; Cathedral High School, 185; Holy Rosary Church, 167, 183; St. Joseph Church, 185; Van de Vyver School, 143

Richmond Black Lay Catholic Caucus, 249
Richmond *News Leader*, 122
Ringer, Benjamin B., 63
Ringkamp, Henry C., 142
Riots, 10–11, 16, 40, 107, 119, 124, 127, 134, 154, 205, 228, 230, 258
Ritter, Joseph E., 34, 207, 211, 213, 215, 222
Rivers, Clarence J., 246, 247, 248, 249, 393n33
Rizzotto, Vincent M., 104, 407
Roanoke, VA: African American lay Catholic caucus in, 252; Catholic school desegregation in, 144; St. Gerard Church, 167
Robinson, James P., 141, 190–91
Rock Hill, SC, St. Anne School, 33, 148, 152, 213

Rockefeller Foundation, 34
Rodgers, William J., 214
Romero, Emanuel A., 212
Romero, Etta B., 55, 56
Rousseve, Maurice, 13
Rousseve, Numa, J., 173
Rousseve, Numa J., Jr., 150
Rousso, Anthony, 180–81
Rowe, Cyprian L., 259
Rummel, Joseph F., 14, 15, 22, 23, 24, 30, 59, 78, 85, 87, 93, 98, 99, 101, 108, 114, 140, 154, 175, 283, 330n48, 331n52; and Association of Catholic Laymen, 56, 69, 79; bars priests from participating in civil rights demonstrations, 62; and Catholic church desegregation, 28, 90, 94, 96, 139, 180; and Catholic school desegregation, 36–37, 53, 58, 58–59, 93, 97, 99, 101, 108, 120, 121, 140, 148–49, 150, 152–53, 157–58, 178, 186, 270; caution of, 29, 95, 150; death of, 107; and desegregation of Archdiocesan Union of Holy Name Societies, 28, 175; excommunications by, 56, 79, 158; and Holy Name parade (1949), 26–27, 174; and Jesuit Bend, 55, 56; and National Urban League in New Orleans, 73; pastoral letter (February 1951), 28; pastoral letter (March 1953), 28, 84, 96; pastoral letter (February 1956), 58, 68, 214 and public school desegregation, 32, 112–13, 120, 121; and seminary desegregation, 24, 141

Russell, John J., 35, 36, 39, 96, 102, 103, 125, 128, 130–31, 134, 135, 148, 183, 275, 283, 306n71, 336n77, 348n84, 348n85, 385n75
Ryan, Abram J., 146
Ryan, John A., 15
Ryan, Patricia, 95

Sacred Heart Junior College, Belmont, NC, desegregation of, 148
Samkovitch, Peter J., 80
San Antonio, Archdiocese of, 186–87, 271, 277, 280, 281, 282, 285, 286; Archdiocesan Committee on Interracial Relations, 29; Archdiocesan Council of Catholic Men, 114–15, 130; Catholic Interracial

Council [San Antonio], 14, 95, 100, 101, 130; Catholic school desegregation in, 30, 142–43, 209, 353n13; desegregates Catholic organizations and societies, 29–30; Knights of Columbus in, 29, 212; lacks African American staff, 268; Our Lady of the Lake College, San Antonio, desegregation of, 142, 209; and Project Equality, 40, 106, 165, 227; and Selma protests, 103, 388n90; St. John's Seminary, San Antonio, desegregation of, 141; St. Mary's University, San Antonio, desegregation of, 142, 209; supports civil rights bill, 38, 128. *See also Alamo Messenger*; *Alamo Register*; Lucey, Robert E.; New Braunfels, TX; San Antonio, TX; Smith, Sherrill

San Antonio, TX, 101, 141, 209, 212, 219, 254, 384n68; Central Catholic High School, desegregation of, 30, 142, 352n13; Holy Redeemer Church, 266; Incarnate Word College, desegregation of, 142, 209; Our Lady of the Holy Rosary Council no. 3345 (Knights of Columbus), 212; Our Lady of the Lake College, desegregation of, 142, 209; St. John's Seminary, desegregation of, 141; St. Joseph Church, 187; St. Mary's University, desegregation of, 142, 209; St. Peter Claver Church, 186, 187. *See also* San Antonio, Archdiocese of

San Francisco, CA, 384n68

Sarratt, Reed, 359n74

Savannah, Diocese of, 9, 11, 60, 135, 154–55, 160–61, 181, 203, 264, 280, 281, 282, 283, 285, 385n72; ordains first African American diocesan priest, 265. *See also* Albany, GA; *Bulletin of the Catholic Laymen's Association of Georgia*; Frey, Gerald L.; Macon, GA; McDonald, Andrew J.; McDonough, Thomas J.; Savannah, GA; Savannah Beach, GA; *Southern Cross*; Toomey, John D.

Savannah, GA, 126, 155, 160–61, 170, 268; St. Benedict the Moor Church, 181; St. Benedict the Moor School, 170, 171; St. James Church, 105; St. John's Episcopal Church, 228; St. Mary's Church, 181; St. Pius X High School, 181,198

Savannah Beach, GA, St. Michael's Church, 155

Savannah Morning News, 155

Savannah-Atlanta, Diocese of, 22, 277, 280, 285, 330n47. *See also* O'Hara, Gerald P.; Savannah, Diocese of

Save Our Nation, Inc., 65, 319n2

Save Our Schools (SOS), 119–20, 121

Schaiell, Louise, 91

Schexnayder, Maurice, 59, 154, 167, 186, 199, 200, 246, 283, 348n84

Schneider, Christopher, 171–72

Schutten, Carl M., 58

Schwerner, Michael, 190

Seattle, WA, 384n68

Second National Catholic Social Action Congress (1939), 15

Second Plenary Council of the Church in the United States, 4–5

Second Vatican Council, ix, 20, 38, 39, 44, 52, 107, 191, 193, 217, 220, 226, 227, 230, 241, 242, 247, 374n101; Constitution of the Sacred Liturgy, 246; Decree on the Apostolate of the Laity, 251

Sehlinger, T. R., 80

Selma, AL, 30–31, 141, 227, 237–38, 247; Assumption Church, 237, 238; Assumption School, 237, 238; Our Lady Queen of Peace Church, 238; protests in, 39, 62, 71, 103, 106, 131–33, 191–92, 225, 227, 235, 274, 347n80, 388n90; Queen of Peace School, 238; St. Elizabeth Church, 30–31, 191, 192, 237, 238, 373n86; St. Elizabeth School, 237, 238

Seminarians' Catholic Action Study of the South, 327n26

Sertum Laetitiae (1939), 14, 15

Shannon, James P., 226

Shean, Maurice V., 96, 99

Shehan, Lawrence J., 72, 221, 223, 230, 348n84, 385n75

Shepperd, John Ben, 116, 341n21

Sherry, Gerard E., 105, 129, 337n81, 384n68

Shields, Thomas J., 27, 93, 149

Shivers, Allan, 116
Shores, Arthur, 127
Shreveport, LA: Friendship House, 62; St. Joseph Church, 50
Sign, 150, 192
Sigur, Alexander O., 86, 105
Simpson, George A., 104, 129
Singleton, Hubert D., 179
Sisson, John P. "Jack", 37, 103, 105, 106–7, 121
Sister de la Croix, 104
Sisters of Mercy, 128, 160
Sisters of Mercy of the Holy Name Cross, 174
Sisters of Saint Francis of Perpetual Adoration, 61
Sisters of Saint Francis of Rochester, Minnesota, 230
Sisters of St. Joseph, Rochester, New York, 191
Sisters of St. Mary, 191
Sisters of the Blessed Sacrament (S.B.S.), 8, 9, 12, 33, 145, 167, 173, 185, 195, 304n54; civil rights activity of, 38
Sisters of the Holy Family, 4, 27, 142, 170, 244, 250, 273, 301n33, 365n6
Sit-ins, 100, 101, 122, 181, 184, 219, 235, 242
Smith, A. Frank, 218
Smith, Andrew C., 112
Smith, Bobby Peppermartin, 352n13
Smith, Sherrill, 101, 102, 103, 106, 107, 219, 334n70
Smith, Vincent, 13
Smyer, Francis A., 144
Snell, Sam V., 115
Society of African Missions (S.M.A.), 9, 11
Society of Mary. *See* Marianists
Society of Saint Edmund (S.S.E.), 31, 62, 141, 171, 189, 190–91, 192, 237–38, 247, 253, 261
Society of St. Joseph of the Sacred Heart. *See* Josephites
Society of the Divine Word (S.V.D.), 9, 11–12, 22, 23, 24, 31, 32, 55, 57, 60, 100, 140, 170, 171, 173, 174, 177, 179, 192, 249. *See also* *St. Augustine's Messenger*; St. Augustine's Seminary, Bay St. Louis, MS
Soleevila, Frank, 136
Soulfull Worship (1974), 249

South Carolina Association of Citizens' Councils, 216
South Louisiana Citizens' Council, 56, 73, 77, 79, 343n39. *See also* *Citizens' Councils*; Citizens' Council of New Orleans; Greater New Orleans Citizens' Council
Southeastern Regional Interracial Commission (SERINCO), 84, 93–95, 98, 99, 173, 174, 186, 324n2. *See also* *Christian Conscience*
Southern, David W., 333n64
Southern Baptist Convention (SBC), 117, 205, 214, 221, 222, 223, 228, 229, 253; African American leadership in state conventions, 234; Alabama and Louisiana Baptist state conventions support segregation, 215; Charter of Principles in Race Relations, 206; church loan fund, 231; college desegregation, 218, 228; Committee on Race Relations, 206; condemns violence, 219, 227; criticizes the civil rights movement, 219, 227; endorses *Brown v. Board of Education* (1954), 209–10; Home Mission Board, 232; overall membership size, 201; polity, 202; resolution against violence, 219; seminary desegregation, 208; Social Service Commission, 206; supports open churches, 231; supports public schools, 234; survey of church segregation in, 223, 232; urges compliance with civil rights legislation, 227. *See also* Baptist Laymen of Alabama; Baptist Laymen of Mississippi; Batesburg, SC; Clinton, TN; Hays, Brooks
Southern Christian Leadership Conference (SCLC), 103, 106, 108, 123–24, 178–79, 190, 231
Southern Cross, 126, 129, 285. *See also* Savannah, Diocese of
Southern Field Service of the National Catholic Conference for Interracial Justice (NCCIJ), 57, 188; closure of, 108; founding of, 37, 100; headquarters of, 101; and Meredith March, 107; Project Equality, 106; Religion and Race in the South Conference, 103; response of ordinaries to, 102, 128, 186;

responsibilities of, 37, 107, 339n90; and Selma, 103; Social Change and Christian Response Conference, 103. *See also* Cabirac, Henry A., Jr.; Sisson, John P. "Jack"
Southern Gentlemen's Organization of Louisiana, 56, 114
Southern Methodist University, Dallas, TX, 208, 218
Southern Pines, NC, St. Joseph of the Pines Hospital, 141
Southern Regional Black Clergy Conference, 198
Southern Regional Council (SRC), 16, 92, 119, 328n30
Southern University, Baton Rouge, LA, 141, 198, 244
Southwest Louisiana Register, 114, 129, 142, 286. *See also* Lafayette, Diocese of
Spalding, Martin J., 4–5
Spellman, Francis, 35, 71, 205, 207, 215, 222, 227
Spence, John S., 226
Spiritans. *See* Holy Ghost Fathers
Spring Hill College, Mobile, AL, 28, 33, 60, 90, 112, 141, 148, 176–77, 302n34, 355n39
St. Anthony's Mission House, Highwood, NJ, 11
St. Augustine, Diocese of; 129, 147, 151, 157. *See also* Fort Myers, FL; Hurley, Joseph P.; Jacksonville, FL; St. Augustine, FL; Tallahassee, FL
St. Augustine, FL, 157; civil rights movement protests in, 129, 190
St. Augustine's Messenger, 179. *See also* Society of the Divine Word (S.V.D.); St. Augustine's Seminary, Bay St. Louis, MS
St. Augustine's Seminary, Bay St. Louis, MS, 11–12, 13, 22, 24, 32, 90, 100, 177, 368n35. See also *St. Augustine's Messenger*
St. John's Abbey Seminary, Collegeville, MN, 24
St. John's Seminary, San Antonio, desegregation of, 141
St. Joseph, MO, Diocese of, Catholic school desegregation in, 207
St. Joseph's College (preparatory seminary), St. Benedict, LA, desegregation of, 24, 141

St. Joseph's Seminary, Washington, DC, 242–43
St. Louis, Archdiocese of, 205, 207, 222, 331n52; and Project Equality, 106, 227; and Selma protests, 388n90. *See also* Ritter, Joseph E.; Steib, J. Terry
St. Louis, MO, 222, 384n68; public school desegregation in, 379n23; St. Louis University, desegregation of, 207. *See also* Ritter, Joseph E.; St. Louis, Archdiocese of
St. Louis University, St. Louis, MO, desegregation of, 207
St. Mary's Dominican College, New Orleans, LA, 331n53
St. Mary's Seminary, Baltimore, MD, 87
St. Mary's University, San Antonio, TX, desegregation of, 142, 209
St. Paul, MN, St. Peter Claver, 9
St. Petersburg, FL: Bishop Barry High School, desegregation of, 157; public school desegregation in, 157
St. Petersburg, FL, Diocese of, 238–39, 279, 280, 281, 282
Stafford, G. Jackson, 217
Stallings, Earl, 344n46, 345n61, 402n107
Stallings, George A., Jr., xii, 265, 266, 267, 268, 275, 402n111
Stanley, Thomas B., 144
Stark, Rodney, 46, 47, 48, 311n11
Statesville, NC, Trinity Episcopal Church, 216
Steib, J. Terry, 174–75, 400n80
Stein, Norbert, 185
Sterling, Donald, 267
Stern Family Fund, 120
Stickle, William, 103
Stille, Henry L., 130
Stritch, Samuel A., 23
Student Nonviolent Coordinating Committee (SNCC), 102, 106, 220, 222
Sturbenz, Mark, 161
Sullivan, Terry, 219
Sullivan, Walter F., 245, 249, 251, 252, 266, 283, 396n44, 399n65
Sulton, James, 181–82
Summer School of Catholic Action, 90, 109
Summi Pontificatus (1939), 14, 94

Swift, Richard J., 104
Synagogue Council of America, 220, 221, 223, 226, 227. *See also* Jews
Syracuse, NY, 227

Tallahassee, FL, Blessed Sacrament Catholic Elementary School, 157
Tanner, Paul F., 35, 283
Tarleton, G. J., Jr., 184
Tart, Mrs. Leo, 72, 74
Taylor, James E., Jr., 186–87
Tennessee Secondary School Athletic Association, 176
Terence, I., 182–83
Texas Black Catholic Conference, 255–56
Texas Catholic, 149, 286. *See also* Dallas-Fort Worth, Diocese of
Texas Catholic Conference, 255–56
Texas Catholic Herald, 106, 286
Texas Southern University, Houston, TX, 152
Third Plenary Council of the Church in the United States, 6, 7
Thomas, Clarence, 171
Thompson, August L., 189, 195–96
Thompson, Daniel C., 178
Thompson, Eric Trice, 225
Thrasher, Thomas P., 217
Thyson, Joan B., 77
Tolton, Augustine, 7, 8
Toolen, Thomas J., 23, 24, 31, 34, 72, 123, 130, 188, 283, 348n84; and Catholic church segregation, 160; and Catholic school desegregation, 57, 59, 160, 161–62, 186, 190; condemns violence, 38, 124, 127, 131; forbids nuns from demonstrating, 131; forbids priests from demonstrating, 62, 131, 192; opposition to the Catholic Committee of the South, 331n49; praises Martin Luther King Jr., 134; rejects NCCIJ, 102; and Selma protests, 39, 62, 71, 131–33, 191, 192, 226, 347n80, 373n86
Toomey, John D., 105, 126
Tower, John G., 129
Tracy, Robert E., 164, 238, 283, 348n84; and Catholic school desegregation, 161, 162–63, 166, 244–45; pastoral letter (August 1963), 161; pastoral letter (September 1963), 126; and public school desegregation, 135; rejects NCCIJ, 102; and Second Vatican Council, 38
Traxler, Margaret Ellen (Sr. Mary Peter), 107
Traxler, Sr. Mary Peter (Margaret Ellen), 107
Trier, Mrs. Charles J. Van, 133
Troy, NY, 5
Truman, Harry S., 29, 92, 93, 206; administration of, 206
Trumbull Park, Chicago, 212, 381n59
Tschoepe, Thomas, 283, 348n84
Tureaud, A. P., 94, 172, 173, 174, 178, 367n20
Turner, Allegra W., 182
Turner, Jesse H., Jr., 182, 183
Turner, Jesse H., Sr., 182, 183
Turner, Paul, 217
Turner, Thomas Wyatt, 10, 12–13
Twohig, Anne Marie (Mother Marie Finbarr), 165
Twomey, Louis J., 27, 46, 50, 51, 58, 60, 61, 67, 70, 73, 74, 77, 85–86, 89–90, 95, 100, 101, 102, 105, 109

Uncles, Charles Randolph, 7, 8
Union of Black Clergy and Laymen, 232
United Methodist Church: antipoverty programs of, 231, 232; Black Methodists for Church Renewal, 231; endorses Project Equality, 231; formation of, 390n113; merger of Mississippi conferences, 391n116; racial conferences within, 232. *See also* Methodist Church
United Presbyterian Church in the United States of America, 232, 377; Commission on Religion and Race, 221; elects African American moderator, 224; financial policies to aid African Americans, 231; formation of, 376n2; and public school desegregation case in Wilcox County, AL, 229. *See also* Presbyterian Church in the United States of America (PCUSA)
United Presbyterian Church of North America, 376n2
United States Catholic Conference (USCC), 196, 235, 250, 375n101

United States Commission on Civil Rights: Alabama State Advisory Committee to, 101, 124; Arkansas State Advisory Committee to, 104; Florida State Advisory Committee to, 104; Georgia State Advisory Committee to, 105; Louisiana State Advisory Committee to, 101, 105
University of Georgia, 119, 154, 182
University of Notre Dame, 225
Unterkoefler, Ernest L., 52, 102, 108, 197, 240, 249, 251, 348n84, 348n85, 375n104, 385n75
Ursuline College, New Orleans, LA, 27, 93, 142, 331n53
Utah-Idaho Baptist Convention: elects African American office holder, 234

Vacherie, LA, Our Lady of Peace Church, 174–75
Vagnozzi, Egidio, 37, 44, 184, 192
Vatican, ix, x, xi, 4–5, 6, 7, 9, 10–11, 14, 19, 20, 23, 31, 35, 41, 44, 45, 46, 67, 68, 69–70, 157, 159, 192, 193, 205, 248, 255, 258, 267, 269, 315n45, 320n13, 320n18, 374n101, 395n30; *The Church and Racism: Towards a More Fraternal Society* (1988), 264. *See also* Second Vatican Council; *L'Osservatore Romano*
Verrett, Joseph C., 140–41, 179
Viguerie, Joseph E., 77
Villeré, Sidney L., 71
Vincent, A. J., 114
Virginia Commission on Interracial Cooperation, 25
Virginia Council on Human Relations, 185
Vivian, C. T., 103
Viviani, Philip R., 72
Voice, 80, 129, 258, 286. *See also* Miami, Archdiocese of; Miami, Diocese of
Voting Rights Act (1965), 21, 39, 105, 132, 133, 226

Wade, Francis, 13
Wagner, Emile A., Jr., 56, 57, 68, 69, 70, 73, 74, 75, 76, 79, 98, 120
Wagner, Richard, 219
Wake Forest College, Winston-Salem, NC, desegregation of, 218

Walker, Matthew, 176
Wallace, George C., 71, 123, 127, 161, 239; 1964 Democratic primary elections, Catholic support for, 224–25, 387n85
Wallin, Edwin J., 107
Walsh, Emmet M., 22–23, 141
Warner, Michael, 375n101
Washington, Archdiocese of, 96, 207–8, 248, 265, 267, 277, 379n24; Eugene A., Marino appointed auxiliary bishop, 250; and Selma protests, 388n90. *See also* Hickey, James A.; O'Boyle, Patrick A.; Stallings, George A., Jr.; Washington, DC
Washington, DC, 2, 4, 5, 122; African-American Catholic Congregation in, 267; Council of Churches of Greater Washington, 130; Holy Comforter-St. Cyprian Church, 267; Imani Temple, 265, 266, 267; Jewish Community Council of Greater Washington, 131; March on Washington for Jobs and Freedom, 38, 71, 73, 102–3, 188, 222, 385n75; public school desegregation in, 77, 323n47; St. Augustine Church, 10; St. Joseph's Seminary, 242–43. *See also* Catholic University of America; Georgetown University
Washington, NC: Mother of Mercy Church, 159; St. Agnes Church, 159
Waters, Vincent S., 24–25, 30, 33, 34, 44, 46, 87, 130, 149–50, 150–51, 283, 306n71, 348n84; bars clergy from civil rights demonstrations, 103, 189, 191; and Newton Grove, 54–55, 72, 140, 146, 175; opposes massive resistance, 115–16, 216; orders church desegregation, 25–26, 54–55, 71, 72, 94, 96, 139–40, 159, 175; orders hospital desegregation, 146; orders school desegregation, 33, 146, 149, 213; pastoral letter (January 1951), 25; pastoral letter (February 1953), 25–26; pastoral letter (June 1953), 26, 96; pastoral letter (January 1964), 128
Watson, Ted, 241
Waveland, MS, 177; St. Clare Church, 32
Webb, Clive, 203
Webster College, Webster Groves, MO, desegregation of, 207

Webster Groves, MO, Webster College, desegregation of, 207
West, Catherine M., 74
West Virginia, 339n90. *See also* Wheeling, Diocese of
Westerer, C. J., 118
Westwego, LA, 158
"What We Have Seen and Heard, Black Bishops' Pastoral Letter on Evangelization" (1984), 260, 263, 399n80
Wheeling, Diocese of, 209; Catholic school desegregation in, 209. *See also* West Virginia
White, Thomas St. Clair, 266
White Catholic migrants to the South, 20, 90–91, 274
Wichita, KS, 227
Wilcox County, AL, 229
Wilken, Robert L., 122
Williams, Charles M., 183
Williams, Elizabeth, 11
Williams, Paul D., 15, 92, 96
Williams, Joseph, 170
Wilmington, Diocese of, and Selma protests, 388n90. *See also* Hyle, Michael, W.
Wilson, R. A., 184
Wilson, Robert, 130
Winston-Salem, NC, public school desegregation in, 341n20
Wisconsin, 1964 Democratic primary election in, 224–25. *See also* Milwaukee, WI
Wood, James R., 43
Wright, J. Skelly, 120, 121, 152
Wyse, Gregory F., 127

Xavier University, New Orleans, LA, 12, 28, 33, 84, 94, 95, 97, 164, 173, 181, 193, 246, 262, 304n54, 329n39, 331n53; opens Institute for Black Catholic Studies, 258

Yancey, John T., 213
Yarborough, Ralph, 129
Young, Andrew J., 103
Young, Virginia (Mary David), 38

Ziter, Nelson B., 238

www.ingramcontent.com/pod-product-compliance
Lightning Source LLC
Chambersburg PA
CBHW030600230426
43661CB00053B/1783